Family Rights at Work: A Guide to
Employment Law

# Family Rights at Work: A Guide to Employment Law

Robin Allen QC, Head of Cloisters

Rachel Crasnow, Barrister at Cloisters

JORDANS

Published by
Jordan Publishing Limited
21 St Thomas Street
Bristol BS1 6JS

**British Library Cataloguing-in-Publication Data**

A catalogue record for this book is available from the British Library.

ISBN 978 1 84661 196 4

Typeset by Letterpart Ltd, Reigate, Surrey

Printed and bound in Great Britain by CPI Group (UK) Ltd, Croydon, CR0 4YY

# LIST OF CONTRIBUTORS

Robin Allen QC is head of Cloisters and specialises in employment, equality, discrimination and human rights, public law and local authority work. He has been dubbed by Chambers and Partners 'an unrivalled authority on employment law in Europe' and in a 2011 review of barristers' appearances in the Industrial Relations Law Reports (conducted by the Equal Opportunities Review) deemed the number one under 'All-Time Top 40 Advocates'. His clients vary from FTSE companies to Equality Commissions and he regularly appears in the European Court of Justice and the Supreme Court. Previous publications include (with Rachel Crasnow and Anna Beale) *Human Rights and Employment Law* (OUP 2007).

Anna Beale is an employment and discrimination specialist with a prolific appellate practice. She has particular expertise in the field of equal pay. Reported decisions include *BP plc v Elstone* [2010] ICR 879 and *Wong v Igen Ltd* [2005] 1CR 931. She has contributed to a number of publications including (with Robin Allen QC and Rachel Crasnow) *Human Rights and Employment Law* (OUP 2007).

Tom Brown specialises in employment, discrimination, public and human rights law and has experience spanning a range of clients and sectors of industry. He often provides advice for regulatory and public bodies including the Equality and Human Rights Commission. Tom has regularly appeared in the Employment Appeal Tribunal and the Court of Appeal and recently acted in *Buckland v Bournemouth University* [2010] ICR 908. In 2002–2003 Tom acted as judicial assistant to the late Lord Bingham of Cornhill, then Senior Law Lord.

Yvette Budé initially qualified as a solicitor before pursuing an employment and discrimination practice at the bar. She acts for both employers and employees. Yvette has appeared in numerous landmark decisions including *Fecitt and ors v NHS Manchester* [2011] EWCA Civ 1190 (which recalibrated the law on causation in cases of whistleblowing), serves as Junior Counsel to the Crown (C panel) and has been called to the New York Bar.

Sally Cowen has been practising in all areas of Employment since 1995, but has a particular interest in discrimination claims. She appears in the High Court, EAT, County Courts and ET. She also appears in the Scottish ET and EAT. Her crossover practice with personal injury gives her ease in the county court when dealing with discrimination claims and in the calculation of damages. Sally acts for employees and employers and she is regularly instructed by large service industry companies including major banks, NHS Trusts and charities.

Rachel Crasnow is a leading employment specialist with a reputation for combining European, employment and equality law skills. She is commended by Chambers and Partners for her expertise in discrimination law and represents both claimant and respondent clients in high-profile cases. Rachel has considerable appellate experience including most recently *O'Brien v DCA* which has been considered by both the Supreme Court and the European Court of Justice. As well as contributing to numerous publications including *Employment Law and Human Rights* (OUP 2007) and *Blackstone's Guide to the Equality Act* (OUP 2011), Rachel lectures to lawyers and jurists across Europe at the prestigious European Commission funded European Rights Academy on topics such as the burden of proof in domestic and European law.

Sarah Fraser Butlin is an experienced employment law practitioner with particular expertise in multi-ground discrimination claims and appellate work. In addition to her private practices Sarah teaches at the University of Cambridge and has contributed to numerous publications including the Industrial Law Journal and the *Discrimination Handbook* (LAG second edition).

David Massarella is recognised by Chambers and Partners as a leading junior in employment law with a thriving appellate practice including such landmark decisions as *Meikle v Nottinghamshire County Council* [2005] ICR 1 and *Hardy & Hansons v Lax* [2005] ICR 1565. He is co-author of the forthcoming guide to the Equality Act 2010 (Legal Action Group) and has contributed to leading publications including the Solicitor's Journal. David's experience of equality matters incorporates both employment matters and the provision of goods and services.

Chris Milsom is an employment law specialist who has acted for clients ranging from FTSE 250 companies, the Equality and Human Rights Commission, the Church of England, NHS Trusts and leading trade unions. Chris has accrued experience in a wide variety of industry sectors and in all major areas of discrimination law acting for both claimants and respondents. He has provided advocacy tuition to students at the College of Law and has contributed to the New Law Journal. Chris has regularly appeared before the Employment Appeal Tribunal and advises on employment matters in the civil courts such as stress at work claims and restrictive covenants.

Sally Robertson specialises in the full range of discrimination and employment law and has regularly appeared in the EAT and the Court of Appeal. She has particular expertise of local authority and non-for-profit sectors including advice and representation in highly complex TUPE situations. Her work in the area of disability discrimination is especially renowned, bolstered by her consistent contributions to the *Disability Rights Handbook* and her practice in cases involving mental health and social security concerns. She has co-authored 'Recent developments in Social Security law' for the Legal Action bulletin since 1994.

# FOREWORD

The ability of men and women to fulfill the demands of work and also to enjoy a family life reaps real benefits, not only for employers and workers but also for the general well-being of society. We know this to be true. Working parents who can spend quality time with their children tend to be happier, healthier people, who are therefore more productive when they are at work. A working life that relentlessly takes you out of the home at dawn and back into it after bedtime is bad for your health, your relationships, your children and your sanity. We know this to be true too.

Yet the case for enabling workers to achieve that elusive balance between work and family life has still to be made out. Making provision for such a balance is still regarded, in some quarters, as inconsistent with economic growth and with the doctrine that 'time is money'.

But the law has stepped in, at first hesitatingly and then in ever-increasing strides. The need for respect and protection for workers' family lives has become part of the zeitgeist of our age. The laws that govern workers' family rights are now many and various, yet the connections between them are not always apparent. The thinking behind them has also changed. The notion that a balance between work and family life is an issue only for women is now disappearing, as more men want to share family responsibilities, or realise that they should share them, and as more men understand just how much they stand to lose by not achieving that balance for themselves.

This is therefore an important book, written at an important point in time. Understanding all these laws and how to apply them correctly is essential for everyone concerned with the world of work. Workers and employers alike need to know what their rights and obligations are. The authors, all experts in the field, are therefore to be congratulated for providing, in one place and in a readily accessible and comprehensive format, a book that fully explains all the relevant legal principles and the connections between them. In both structure and content this book has successfully achieved its aim of providing both thoughtful analysis and practical guidance for all those who need to understand, to advise on or to apply laws which will govern working people's lives for many years to come. It deserves a place on everyone's bookshelf.

*Mrs Justice Laura Cox, January 2012*

# PREFACE

This book has been written for employment law practitioners (lawyers and human resource practitioners who engage with the law) who need to address the effect that family obligations have in the employment context. No employer can afford to treat their workers as simply economic units without a life outside the workplace. Even in straightened economic times the tensions between family and work life obligations will remain a real concern. Moreover the increasing realisation that men and women will want to, and we would say *should*, share family responsibilities, means that working out how to deal with this interface will be of ever greater importance. Trying to address the law in relation to this interface and to help employer and employee to get this right is what has made writing this book so interesting to us.

We believe that all of us whether employer or employee, judge or tribunal member, witness or party, legislator or employment law practitioner also have a personal stake in the adequate protection of the balance between work and home. We hope that in the chapters that follow we have been able to convey some of our enthusiasm for the protections that employment law provides to family life, for we believe that by protecting and respecting the forum of the family, the workplace will be respected by employees, careers can flourish and the economy will be best placed to grow.

Employment lawyers have long had to focus on diversity issues. They have had to grapple with equality in all its forms and to reconcile the expectations of employees concerning dignity at work with arguments from utility, economic necessity and of course sometimes pure prejudice. The extent to which they will have had to do this, and the extent to which they have seen the concept of Family Rights at Work in the round, may well differ. We hope this book will help to extend and enlarge such knowledge.

The aim of this book is, therefore, to try to assist the employment law practitioner to understand more deeply the relevant EU and domestic jurisprudence and to use it with some confidence in an employment law context. It does of course assume a certain amount of knowledge in relation to employment law. We have tried to consider how the key demands made by family life upon the workplace might affect the way in which employment law generally and employment disputes in particular might be seen and resolved in the future. We certainly hope that the book will provoke all those involved with employment law to reconsider their work from this fresh perspective.

The book has been a long time in gestation and there are many people who have contributed to the development of our thinking in this area, but our apologies must go first to those who have suffered when the book has had to take first place, especially our families. Our thanks go to Gay Moon and Matthew Dodd, and our families for their tolerance and encouragement, constructive criticism and more, over a long period. The same must be said of all the families of the dedicated co-authors, without whom this book would simply not have been written. They are Anna Beale, Sally Robertson, Sally Cowan, David Massarella, Christopher Milsom, Tom Brown, Sarah Fraser Butlin and Yvette Budé. Without naming any of them individually, we must also thank all our colleagues in Cloisters where the pursuit of a modern inclusive family-friendly approach to employment law is an aim shared by all.

There are too many others who have helped with thoughts and ideas, information and cases, to name them all individually. Our thanks (and apologies in advance for not identifying them) go to those who have not been so identified. Our thanks also go to all those at Jordan Publishing for their continued encouragement and support even when things were at their slowest.

There is never a good time to finish writing a book like this since there is always a new development on the way or a case which, seeming once to clarify an issue, is suddenly and unexpectedly overruled. Nevertheless we have tried to state the law as at August 2011. Some changes since then have been picked up in the process of proof reading and amendments to the text made accordingly.

We apologise in advance for the inevitable mistakes that will be spotted by those more eagled-eyed than we are. We would welcome any comments or suggestions for improvements were we ever to write another edition.

We believe that family rights at work are now better secured than ever before. Our task as employment law practitioners is to ensure that these gains are maintained and that our understanding of what is necessary next is based on informed equality principles. We hope that in a small way we have contributed to achieving that.

Robin Allen

Rachel Crasnow
*January 2012*

# CONTENTS

# TABLE OF CASES

References are to paragraph numbers.

# TABLE OF STATUTES

**References are to paragraph numbers.**

# TABLE OF STATUTORY INSTRUMENTS

**References are to paragraph numbers.**

# TABLE OF EC MATERIALS

**References are to paragraph numbers.**

# TABLE OF INTERNATIONAL MATERIALS

**References are to paragraph numbers.**

# Chapter 1

# AN INTRODUCTION TO FAMILY-FRIENDLY LAW

*Robin Allen QC*

## A CHANGING APPROACH TO FAMILY LIFE

### Introduction

**1.1**    Fifty years ago, most men and many women in the United Kingdom, would have thought it absurd to consider that an employee should have special rights at work because of his or her family status. Until the Equal Pay Act 1970 and the Sex Discrimination 1975 were passed, not only were women frequently paid less than men, but they were also expected to work less than men because they were seen as being principally responsible for the home. Caring responsibilities for young and old were universally expected to be carried out by women. It was not thought remotely unfair or wrong that in some employments women should be expected to cease work on becoming married.

**1.2**    There were other ways during the twentieth century in which it was appreciated that the margins between work and home were not rigidly drawn. Many employers exploited the fact that women did not wish to go out to work by providing opportunities to do 'homework'. This was usually very low paid and often operated under the fiction that the homeworker was self-employed.[1] Often such homework was done by family groups. Wages Council legislation frequently made special provision for such workers.[2] Over time it could not be ignored that many people worked at home and in some cases this gave rise to exploitation.[3] Now of course such workers are often specifically included in protective legislation.[4]

---

[1]    *Airfix Footwear Ltd v Cope* [1978] IRLR 396.

[2]    The need for international protection for such workers was widely recognised and in 1996 the International Labour Organisation adopted Home Work Recommendation 1996, and C177 Home Work Convention 1996.

[3]    See for instance Ewing K, 'Homeworking: A Framework for Reform', *Ind Law J*, (1982) 11(1): 94–110.

[4]    For instance, the National Minimum Wage Act 1998 defined a 'worker' in s 54(3) so as to extend to such homeworkers by removing the requirement that the work is executed 'personally' (see s 35(1)) and by stating that an individual who 'contracts with a person, for the purposes of that person's business, for the execution of work to be done in a place not under the control or management of that person' is also in scope (see section 35(2)).

**1.3**    The problems encountered by atypical families, where women had to work, or where there was no female presence, were more often ignored. Indeed often those home-based responsibilities, which women were supposed to undertake, were thought to provide a morally justifiable reason for not employing women at all.

**1.4**    It was inevitable that sooner or later this would be challenged for many reasons: the stereotype did not apply in all cases; it was stultifying for women to be channelled away from work and into home responsibilities; it was not fair; and inappropriate in an increasingly consumerist society which demanded a higher family income.

**1.5**    With the benefit of hindsight those two Acts can now be clearly seen to have been the start of a new period in which these old certainties came to be challenged by legal action usually commenced to reflect one or more of the reasons set out above. Such litigation gave rise to a snowball effect, one case leading to another and one campaign encouraging a further challenge to the irrelevance and ill-effects of such stereotypes. Challenges were brought to discrimination in the treatment of pregnant women,[5] to the less favourable treatment of part-time workers,[6] to the refusal to permit job-sharing,[7] as well as to the different treatment of women in relation to pay.

**1.6**    Although these Acts promised women the opportunity to challenge the confines within which they had previously lived their lives and the stereotypes that were applied to them, it was soon evident that these two Acts suffered from a major deficit when they were passed. Neither specifically addressed the difficulties women had when pregnant. Each left open the question whether they protected women from discrimination by reason of pregnancy or maternity. Yet it remains clear that the stimulus that these two Acts gave to both the legal and social arguments about the reality of family life and its interaction with work have led in many ways to the establishment of the present substantive rights that this book considers in detail. These two Acts were not the only initiatives though. At the same time new legislation in Europe increased the range and content of family rights relating to employment. The interaction of European and domestic legislation has been the main story over the period from these two Acts to their replacement by the Equality Act 2010. That interaction will continue for some time but at least now the fact of this interaction is acknowledged by lawmakers, litigants, courts and judges. Now no politician could possibly suggest that work does not impinge on family life and no sensible employer could ignore that inter-relationship. The fact of that inter-relationship is not the issue. Making the relationship work sensibly and practically so as both to recognise the reality of the caring responsibilities of workers and the competitive, economic and organisational pressures on employers, is now what matters.

---

[5]    See the discussion below.
[6]    See *R (ex part the EOC) v Secretary of State for Employment* [1994] ICR 317.
[7]    See *Clymo v London Borough of Wandsworth* [1989] ICR 250.

## EQUAL TREATMENT FOR PREGNANT WOMEN AND WOMEN IN THE MATERNITY PERIOD

**1.7** The first question that was actively debated was whether the Sex Discrimination Act 1975 provided protection to pregnant women who had to cease work by reason of their pregnancy even though they did not wish to give up their work altogether. Initially there was much discussion in the employment tribunals of the question whether the Sex Discrimination Act 1975 protected women who were pregnant or away from work because they were pregnant. The key question was whether it was necessary to compare an employer's treatment of such women with the treatment of men. But litigants and courts and tribunals asked, how could such a comparison be framed?

**1.8** Initially, it was thought that this meant that the 1975 Act did not apply because a comparison could not be made.[8] Later, it was held that the Act could apply because the correct approach was to ask whether the pregnancy was capable of being matched by analogous circumstances, for example by comparing the circumstances of a pregnant female employee with those of a sick male employee. But there was a central problem with this approach: men do not get pregnant and pregnancy is not an illness.

**1.9** Only once the European Court of Justice (ECJ) came to give judgment on a reference from the House of Lords in Case C-32/93 *Webb v Emo Air Cargo (UK) Ltd*[9] was this approach seen to be the ridiculous construct it was. In this case the ECJ were asked what European Community law required in such a context. It held that the dismissal of a female worker on account of her pregnancy constituted direct discrimination on grounds of sex and that there could be no question of comparing the situation of a pregnant woman with that of a man who was incapable for medical or other reasons.

**1.10** This case made a largely male judiciary realise that women had to be treated differently when they were undertaking roles which only women have in life and that to seek to treat them in the same way as men was itself discriminatory. When the case returned to the House of Lords,[10] that court, to its credit, accepted the ruling and disregarded the relatively clear language of the Sex Discrimination Act which suggested that a comparative exercise was always necessary.[11] It can truly be said that this ruling opened the door to a much more profound understanding by courts and tribunals of the mismatch between the reality of female life and rules that ignored this reality.

---

[8]   See *Hayes v Malleable Working Men's Club and Institute* [1985] ICR 703, and *Turley v Allders Department Stores Ltd* [1980] ICR 66.

[9]   [1994] ICR 770.

[10]   [1995] 1 WLR 1454, [1996] 2 CMLR 990, [1995] ICR 1021.

[11]   Although not expressed in this way, this was an example of the European Court of Justice realising that discrimination can occur when there is the same treatment of persons who are not similarly situated whereas normally discrimination occurs when there is different treatment of those who are similarly situated: see e g Case C-236/09 *Association Belge des Consommateurs Test-Achats ASBL v Conseil des Ministres* [2011] 2 CMLR 38.

**1.11**   The logic of the decision in *Webb* once made was compelling and lead on to much more discussion as to how the interface between family life and work should be treated. Jurists within the United Kingdom began to realise that the situation of mothers is special and different and demands to be addressed because the future of each successive generation depends on it. The logic of this realisation went further than merely maternity: children have to be cared for through a long life and not merely in a maternity period. Moreover, once the obligation to care for children was recognised it was but a short step to recognise that it also extended to other family members. If men and women were to have equal treatment in the workplace then it was natural they would also seek equality at home in the role of carer. How this was to happen and how it could be accommodated became the subject of intense debate and ultimately of new rights. It was acknowledged that the continuation of the gender pay gap was in large part caused by the failure to address this issue. Unless the role of the carer at home was recognised as imposing some limits on participation in work and unless some rights were given in that context, women would always be at a disadvantage. This book is concerned with discussing the rights and obligations which have evolved to meet this new social reality. Although it addresses the rights that have evolved in domestic law as a result of these social changes, it is also important to put those rights in their wider international context since there is no doubt that the domestic rights have evolved to give effect to these wider obligations. The dominant role has gone to the International Labour Organisation which foresaw the need to accommodate family obligations with an effective economy from a very early stage.

## THE ROLE OF THE INTERNATIONAL LABOUR ORGANISATION (ILO)

**1.12**   The ILO, which is a specialised United Nations agency, has had a major role in setting standards for the proper organisation of work, and in that capacity has set key norms that underpin many of the rights discussed in this book. All the member states of the European Union have ratified the relevant Conventions and they are taken into account by the Court of Justice of the European Union and the European Court of Human Rights as setting norms. It was the ILO Equal Remuneration Convention 1951 (No 100) that led the way for the Equal Pay Act 1970 and the adoption of the right to equal pay for work of equal value in the Treaty of Rome. However, the role of the ILO in relation to maternity rights goes much further back.

**1.13**   In its third-ever Convention, made in the year of its inception in 1919, the ILO first addressed the rights of women on maternity.[12] That Convention made initial proposals for the right of women to be away from work during a period post birth and for them to be protected from dismissal. It was revised in 1952[13] and replaced by a new consolidated Convention in 2000.[14]

---

[12]   See ILO Maternity Protection Convention 1919 (No 3).
[13]   See ILO Maternity Protection Convention (Revised) 1952 (No 103).
[14]   See ILO Maternity Protection Convention 2000 (No 183).

**1.14** The 2000 Convention provides that states should provide 14 weeks of maternity benefit to women. Women who are absent from work on maternity leave should be entitled to a cash benefit which ensures that they can maintain themselves and their child in proper conditions of health and with a suitable standard of living and which shall be no less than two-thirds of her previous earnings or a comparable amount. The convention also requires ratifying states to take measures to ensure that a pregnant woman or nursing mother is not obliged to perform work which has been determined to be harmful to her health or that of her child, and provides for protection from discrimination based on maternity. The Convention requires states to prohibit employers from terminating the employment of a woman during pregnancy or absence on maternity leave, or during a period following her return to work, except on grounds unrelated to pregnancy, childbirth and its consequences, or nursing. It requires that women returning to work should be returned to the same position or an equivalent position paid at the same rate, and that a woman must have the right to one or more daily breaks or a daily reduction of hours of work to breastfeed her child. This Convention is also supported by an ILO Recommendation that even further rights should be given.

**1.15** Soon after the Equal Remuneration Convention the ILO addressed discrimination at work on a wider basis in the ILO Discrimination (Employment and Occupation) Convention 1958 (No 111). Convention No 111 recognised in Article 5 that after suitable discussions it may be provided that:

> 'special measures designed to meet the particular requirements of persons who, for reasons such as sex, age, disablement, family responsibilities or social or cultural status, are generally recognised to require special protection or assistance, shall not be deemed to be discrimination.'

**1.16** Convention 111 was supported by an ILO Recommendation concerning the Employment (Women with Family Responsibilities) Recommendation (No 123).[15] That recommendation noted in its preamble how the changes in the relationship between family and work life were increasing. Thus from a very early stage it has been recognised that family responsibilities may need to be addressed by special measures.

**1.17** In 1985, the ILO brought its guidance further up to date in the Workers with Family Responsibilities Convention 1981 (No 156), and the Workers with Family Responsibilities Recommendation 1981 (No 165). The key aim of the Convention was set out in Article 3:

> 'With a view to creating effective equality of opportunity and treatment for men and women workers, each Member shall make it an aim of national policy to enable persons with family responsibilities who are engaged or wish to engage in

---

[15] It is intriguing to note that the recommendation did not address workers but women with family responsibilities. This changed in the later Convention 156 and Recommendation 165.

employment to exercise their right to do so without being subject to discrimination and, to the extent possible, without conflict between their employment and family responsibilities.'

**1.18**   Recommendation No 165 amplified the aims of the Convention across a broad range from terms and conditions of employment, training, social security, and help for those exercising family responsibilities, within the context of national policy.

**1.19**   In parallel with this work of the ILO setting standards for the world at large, the Council of Europe (the same body responsible for the European Convention on Human Rights) has set standards for Europe in particular.

## THE EUROPEAN SOCIAL CHARTER

**1.20**   The European Social Charter was made by the Council of Europe originally in 1961 but there is now a revised version which is gradually coming into force across Europe. The European Social Charter addressed family rights from the outset in Articles 8, 16 and 27 which now say:

'8. Employed women, in case of maternity, have the right to a special protection.

...

16. The family as a fundamental unit of society has the right to appropriate social, legal and economic protection to ensure its full development.

...

27. All persons with family responsibilities and who are engaged or wish to engage in employment have a right to do so without being subject to discrimination and as far as possible without conflict between their employment and family responsibilities.'

As is explained below this has played an important role in the development of the law of the European Union.[16]

## THE EUROPEAN UNION

**1.21**   When the Equal Treatment Directive[17] was passed in 1976 it stated that the principle of equal treatment required that there be no discrimination whatsoever on grounds of sex either directly or indirectly by reference in

---

[16]   The reference to the European Union encompasses the work of the European Communities before the European Union was formally adopted by the Lisbon Treaty.

[17]   Council Directive 76/207/EEC of 9 February 1976 on the implementation of the principle of equal treatment for men and women as regards access to employment, vocational training and promotion, and working conditions.

particular to marital *or family status.*[18] This reference to family status was a nod in the direction of the international obligations to which reference has already been made. The family status protection was, however, not much used. By about 1985 there was increasing concern,[19] expressed at all levels within the European Union about the social consequences of the creation of the Single European Market. There was a perceived need for the formulation and implementation of a comprehensive social dimension for the European Commission's 1992 programme. In 1988, a working party of the Commission proposed a body of minimum social provisions. Following a Resolution on Fundamental Rights of the European Parliament in March 1989, a first draft of a Community Charter of Fundamental Social Rights was published by the Commission in May 1989, a second draft was produced in October 1989 and the summit in Strasbourg on 9 December 1989 approved the final Charter.

**1.22**  As a result the Community Charter of the Fundamental Social Rights of Workers, was adopted on 9 December 1989 by a declaration of all member states, with the exception of the United Kingdom. This established the major principles on which the European labour law model is based and shaped the development of the European social model in the following decade and up to the present day.[20] The key provision of the Community Charter concerning family rights at work was Article 16 which said:

> '16. Equal treatment for men and women must be assured. Equal opportunities for men and women must be developed.
>
> To this end, action should be intensified wherever necessary to ensure the implementation of the principle of equality between men and women as regards in particular access to employment, remuneration, working conditions, social protection, education, vocational training and career development.
>
> Measures should also be developed enabling men and women to reconcile their occupational and family obligations.'

**1.23**  Of course the Community Charter left open what such measures were to be. First, the European Council agreed Council Directive 92/85/EEC on the introduction of measures to encourage improvements in the safety and health at work of pregnant workers and workers who have recently given birth or are breastfeeding. It was the Social Charter that then became the driving force for the first parental leave legislation in the European Union. Secondly, a framework agreement was reached between the 'social partners' (the European level trades unions and employers organisations) on 14 December 1995 on parental leave. The agreement was then made into law by being annexed to

---

18   Article 2.
19   For a summary of the discussion leading to the Social Charter see http://www.eurofound. europa.eu/areas/industrialrelations/dictionary/definitions/ communitycharterofthefundamentalsocialrightsofworkers.htm (visited 3 October 2011).
20   The fundamental social rights declared in the Community Charter are further developed in the Charter of Fundamental Rights of the European Union that became legally binding with the ratification of the Treaty of Lisbon on 1 December 2009.

Council Directive 96/34/EC of 3 June 1996 on the framework agreement on parental leave concluded by UNICE, CEEP and the ETUC.

**1.24** That latter Directive did not immediately apply to the United Kingdom because John Major had opted out of these social provisions in the European Treaties. However, in 1997 the incoming Labour administration extended their application to the United Kingdom.[21]

**1.25** As a result of these and other measures in Case C-243/95 *Hill and Stapleton v Revenue Commissioners and Another*[22] the European Court of Justice was able to say:

> '42. Community policy is to encourage and, if possible, adapt working conditions to family responsibilities. Protection of women within family life and in the course of their professional activities is, in the same way as for men, a principle which is widely regarded in the legal systems of the member states as being the natural corollary of the equality between men and women, and which is recognised by Community law.'

**1.26** There were other important directives made in consequence of the Community Charter. Perhaps the most important for this book was the protection given to part-time workers by Council Directive 97/81/EC of 15 December 1997 concerning the Framework Agreement on part-time working concluded by UNICE, CEEP and the ETUC. This made it much easier for workers who for family reasons worked part-time to secure equal treatment with those who were full-time participants in the labour market without having to go through extensive evidential steps to prove that they suffered indirect sex discrimination. It also ensured that part-time men were treated on the same basis as women. This was important particularly because men would not so easily be able to claim indirect sex discrimination as women.

**1.27** The discussion of the creation of a rights-based Europe did not end with the Community Charter. At the end of the 1990s there was much discussion about a European Charter of Fundamental Rights and this was finally agreed on 7 December 2000. Articles 23 and 33 address family life and work. While Article 23 address equality between men and women generally, Article 33 specifically states:

'Article 33

Family and professional life

1.    The family shall enjoy legal, economic and social protection.

---

[21]  See Council Directive 97/75/EC of 15 December 1997.
[22]  [1999] ICR 48.

2.     To reconcile family and professional life, everyone shall have the right to protection from dismissal for a reason connected with maternity and the right to paid maternity leave and to parental leave following the birth or adoption of a child.'

**1.28**    The importance of this statement is still being worked out. Its place as a founding principle of European law is, however, assured and hence it has an impact on everything that is written in this book. It is therefore important to understand what was intended by this provision. As to this the Explanatory Memorandum to the Charter explains that:

'Article 33(1) is based on Article 16 of the European Social Charter. The second paragraph draws on Council Directive 92/85/EEC on the introduction of measures to encourage improvements in the safety and health at work of pregnant workers and workers who have recently given birth or are breastfeeding and Directive 96/34/EC on the framework agreement on parental leave concluded by UNICE, CEEP and the ETUC. It is also based on Article 8 (protection of maternity) of the European Social Charter and draws on Article 27 (right of workers with family responsibilities to equal opportunities and equal treatment) of the revised Social Charter. "Maternity" covers the period from conception to weaning.'

**1.29**    Each year has brought more case-law showing that the European Charter of Fundamental Rights is of increasing importance to the Court of Justice of the European Union (CJEU). This gives rise to some important points. First, it has to be borne in mind that this Charter was made part of the Lisbon Treaty. Secondly, although the United Kingdom has expressed reservations as to the effect that the Charter is to have in relation to the domestic law of the UK, the extent to which this reservation is effective is still controversial. In any event, the CJEU has no difficulty in referring to this Charter[23] and as is explained below European legislation refers to it as a basis for specific measures.

**1.30**    The European Commission consulted the European social partners in 2006 and 2007 on ways of further improving the reconciliation of work, private and family life and, in particular, the existing Community legislation on maternity protection and parental leave, and on the possibility of introducing new types of family-related leave, such as paternity leave, adoption leave and leave to care for family members. As a result, Directive 96/34/EC has now been replaced by a fresh Directive also giving effect to an agreement between the social partners: Council Directive 2010/18/EU of 8 March 2010 implementing the revised Framework Agreement on parental leave concluded by BUSINESSEUROPE, UEAPME, CEEP and ETUC and repealing Directive 96/34/EC. This Directive is explicitly based on the provisions of Article 33 of the Charter of Fundamental Rights of the European Union.

**1.31**    It seems unlikely that this will be the last step in the European evolution of the rights and obligations necessary to accommodate the demands of family

---

[23]    See C-447/09, *Reinhard Prigge, Michael Fromm, Volker Lambach v Deutsche Lufthansa AG*, judgment 13 September 2011 at [38].

life with work. One particular aspect of European social policy that has yet to be fully worked out concerns the extent to which more women must be encouraged to work for longer periods to take account of the expected diminution in the size of the labour market as a result of the change in the age structure of Europe's population. In the next 20 years or so it is expected on current demographic trends that there will be a very marked decrease in the number of people of working age. Already that is being seen as a reason to make it easier for men and women to combine responsibilities connected to family life with that of work.[24]

## THE EUROPEAN COURT OF HUMAN RIGHTS

**1.32**   As can be seen, the ILO Conventions and Recommendations have provided a really important impetus to the development of the specific protections discussed in this book. So have the developments in Europe explained above. They have given rise to and reflected new social norms. Nowhere has this been more evident that in the case-law of the European Court of Human Rights, in particular in *Markin v Russia*.[25]

**1.33**   In that case a male Russian soldier who was the sole carer for his children complained that he was not given equal rights to those available for a woman and that this was a breach of the right not to suffer discrimination in Article 14 of the European Convention on Human Rights when taken with Article 8, the right to a private and family life.[26] The court was shown the ILO Conventions relating to family life at work and a report of the ILO. It commented at [26]–[27] on relevant parts of ILO Report 'Maternity at work: A review of national legislation' (2005):

> 'While maternity leave aims to protect working women during their pregnancy and recovery from childbirth, parental leave refers to a relatively long-term leave available to either parent, allowing them to take care of an infant or young child over a period of time usually following the maternity or paternity leave period.
>
> ...
>
> The Workers with Family Responsibilities Recommendation, 1965 (No 123) and the Maternity Protection Recommendation, 1952 (No 95) ... only included provisions on maternity leave and only women's need to reconcile work with family responsibilities were considered. One important change in the policy of the ILO with the adoption of the current Recommendations [and the Convention on

---

[24]   See the European Commission publication 'Confronting demographic change: a new solidarity between the generations', Brussels, 16.3.2005 COM(2005) 94 final.

[25]   [2010] ECHR 1435. This case is being appealed to the Grand Chamber though at the time of writing no judgment has been given.

[26]   The court noted at [45] that '... although Article 8 does not include a right to parental leave or impose any positive obligation on States to provide parental leave allowances, if a State does decide to create a parental leave scheme, it must do so in a manner which is compatible with Article 14 of the Convention...' It referred to *Petrovic v Austria* (2001) 33 EHRR 14, [1998] ECHR 21.

Workers with Family Responsibilities, 1981 (No 156)] was the recognition of fathers' involvement in family responsibilities in general and in this case especially with regard to parental leave. This was an important step towards the creation of effective equality of opportunity and treatment for men and women workers...

Contrary to the other regions, all the countries analysed in Europe provide a period of parental leave to take care of a newborn or young child, even if the length of the leave differs from country to country...

A major difference between maternity and parental leave is the scope of the provisions. While maternity leave is available only for women, parental leave provisions normally are also available for men. In some countries, it is a shared entitlement, where either the mother or the father has the right to take parental leave... In other countries, each parent has an individual right to parental leave, which cannot be transferred to the other parent ... As mentioned above, according to the EU Directive on parental leave, it should be available to both parents as an individual entitlement. To promote equal opportunities and equal treatment between men and women, parental leave should, in principle, be granted on a non-transferable basis...

The introduction of parental leave provisions available to both fathers and mothers can be an effective tool for promoting gender equality. It recognises the fact that fathers also have caring responsibilities. But even if parental leave by definition is available to both mothers and fathers, women are most often the ones who take parental leave, once maternity leave is finished. Generally, men's take-up rates are very low (ILO, 1997). For this reason, some countries have introduced a paternity quota that can only be taken by the father and is lost if he does not use it...'

**1.34**   A 2007 report was published in the United Kingdom as to how parental leave has been addressed internationally.[27]

---

[27]   The court noted at [28]–[30] '28. A report entitled "International Review of Leave Policies and Related Research" published in July 2007 by the United Kingdom Department for Business, Enterprise and Regulatory Reform describes leave entitlements for workers with dependent children in twenty-four countries (twenty-one European countries, Australia, Canada and the United States of America). According to that report the United States of America is the only country where there is no statutory right to parental leave. In contrast to maternity and paternity leave, which are by definition gender-related, parental leave can be taken by either parent in all countries under examination except one (in Hungary only the mother is entitled to take parental leave during the child's first year; during the child's second and third years, however, parental leave may be taken by either parent). 29. Parental leave is a family entitlement in ten countries, to be divided between parents as they choose (Australia, Austria, Canada, Denmark, Estonia, France, Germany, Hungary, Poland and Spain); an individual entitlement in another ten countries, with each parent entitled to a certain portion of parental leave (Belgium, the Czech Republic, Greece, Iceland, Ireland, Italy, Portugal, Slovenia, the Netherlands and the United Kingdom); and mixed (part family, part individual entitlement) in three countries (Iceland, Norway and Sweden). Various measures have been introduced to encourage fathers to take parental leave. Mostly these take the form of wholly or partly individualised entitlements, whereby fathers not using their 'quota' will lose it, since unused leave cannot be transferred to a partner. Another approach is to offer bonus leave days to fathers who take some parental leave (as, for example, in Italy, Finland and Germany). 30. Parental leave may be unpaid (as, for example, in Greece, Ireland, Italy, the Netherlands, Spain and the United Kingdom). A majority of countries (16), however, provide some element of

**1.35**   The judgment of the First Section of the court in *Malkin* was based on these ILO documents and emphasised just where the present consensus lies and its implications for the European Convention at [45]–[49]:

'45 The Court reiterates in this connection that, by enabling one of the parents to stay at home to look after the children, parental leave and related allowances promote family life and necessarily affect the way in which it is organised. Parental leave and parental allowances therefore come within the scope of Article 8 of the Convention. It follows that Article 14, taken together with Article 8, is applicable. Accordingly, although Article 8 does not include a right to parental leave or impose any positive obligation on States to provide parental leave allowances, if a State does decide to create a parental leave scheme, it must do so in a manner which is compatible with Article 14 of the Convention (see, *mutatis mutandis*, *Petrovic,* cited above, ss 26 to 29).

46. The Court observes that the applicant, being a serviceman, had no statutory right to parental leave. It is undisputed that civilians, both men and women, as well as servicewomen, are entitled to parental leave. The denial of parental leave to the applicant was accordingly based on a combination of two grounds: military status plus sex. The Court has to examine whether, in relation to parental leave, the difference in treatment between parents depending on their military or civilian status and on their sex is acceptable under Article 14.

47. The Court will first examine whether there is an objective and reasonable justification for the difference in treatment between men and women as regards entitlement to parental leave. It reiterates that the advancement of the equality of the sexes is today a major goal in the member states of the Council of Europe and very weighty reasons would have to be put forward before such a difference of treatment could be regarded as compatible with the Convention (see *Burghartz v Switzerland*, 22 February 1994, s 27, Series A, no 280-B, and *Schuler-Zgraggen v Switzerland*, 24 June 1993, s 67, Series A, no 263).

48. The Court is not convinced by the [Russian] Constitutional Court's argument that, as far as parental leave is concerned, the different treatment of male and female military personnel is justified by the special social role of mothers in the upbringing of children (see paragraph 19 above). It observes that in contrast to maternity leave and associated allowances, which are primarily intended to enable the mother to recover from the fatigue of childbirth and to breastfeed her baby if she so wishes, parental leave and the parental leave allowances relate to the subsequent period and are intended to enable the parent to stay at home to look after the infant personally. Whilst being aware of the differences which may exist between mother and father in their relationship with the child, the Court considers that, as far as the role of taking care of the child during this period is concerned, both parents are "similarly placed" (see *Petrovic*, cited above, s 36).

---

payment to the parent on leave. In seven cases (Austria, Belgium, the Czech Republic, Estonia, France, Italy and Poland) the payment is rather low, whether a flat rate or means-tested, or is paid for only part of the leave period, or a combination of these. Only nine countries pay an earnings-related benefit set at more than half of normal earnings. In some cases – notably the Czech Republic, France and Poland – parents on leave receive a general 'child-rearing' benefit that is paid to all parents with young children, not just those taking leave.'

49. The court notes that, in the *Petrovic v Austria* case, a distinction on the basis of sex with respect to parental leave allowances was found not to be in violation of Article 14. In that case a broad margin of appreciation was granted to the respondent state because of the great disparity in the 1980s between the legal systems of the contracting states in the sphere of parental benefits. The court held that at the material time there was no European consensus in this field, as the majority of contracting states did not provide for parental leave or related allowances for fathers (see *Petrovic*, cited above, ss 38 to 42). However, in the more recent case of *Weller v Hungary* the court took a step away from the approach adopted in the *Petrovic* case and found that the exclusion of natural fathers from the entitlement to receive parental allowances, when mothers, adoptive parents and guardians were entitled to them, amounted to discrimination on the ground of parental status (see *Weller,* cited above, ss 30 to 35). It is also significant that since the adoption of the judgment in the *Petrovic* case the legal situation as regards parental leave entitlements in the contracting states has evolved. In an absolute majority of European countries the legislation now provides that parental leave may be taken by both mothers and fathers (see paragraphs 26 to 30 above). In the court's opinion, this shows that society has moved towards a more equal sharing between men and women of responsibility for the upbringing of their children and that men's caring role has gained recognition. The court considers that it cannot overlook the widespread and consistently developing views and associated legal changes to the domestic laws of contracting states on this issue (see, *mutatis mutandis, Smith and Grady v the United Kingdom*, nos 33985/96 and 33986/96, s 104, ECHR 1999-VI). It follows that the respondent state can no longer rely on the absence of a common standard among the contracting states to justify the difference in treatment between men and women as regards parental leave. Nor can the reference to the traditional perception of women as primary child-carers provide sufficient justification for the exclusion of the father from the entitlement to take parental leave if he so wishes. Accordingly, the court concludes that no convincing or weighty reasons have been offered by the Government to justify the difference in treatment between men and women as regards entitlement to parental leave.'

## THE FUTURE OF FAMILY-FRIENDLY POLICY WITHIN THE UK

**1.36** Making work family-friendly has been good politics within the UK for some time now. Whatever the political hue of the party in power it cannot afford to neglect the interface between family and work life. Before the current coalition government the Secretary of State for the Department for Work and Pensions established in 2009 a Taskforce to explore the challenges around improving the availability and quality of family-friendly working practices – focusing on working hours and patterns – and provide recommendations for change. The Taskforce was made up of experts from business, organisations that represent businesses, employees and families, non-government bodies and government departments. It made many recommendations for cultural change which were largely accepted by the last government.[28] The Conservative manifesto for the 2010 Election promised 'We will make Britain the most family-friendly country in Europe. We will support families in the tax and benefits system, extend flexible working and improve parental leave.' The Coalition Agreement of the incoming government also committed itself to '... encourage[ing] shared parenting from the earliest stages of pregnancy – including the promotion of a system of flexible parental leave.'[29]

**1.37** To conclude, this book aims to bring together these rights so as to show the once bright line between work and home has dimmed and the realisation that as human beings with dependents and obligations to a life outside work we cannot be treated as mere work units when in the office or factory.

---

[28]   See 'Flexibility for the future: The Government's response to the recommendations of the Family Friendly Working Hours Taskforce', Department for Work and Pensions, 30 March 2010.
[29]   See 'The Coalition: our programme for government', Cabinet Office 2010 at [14] p 20.

# Chapter 2

# SEX DISCRIMINATION

*Anna Beale*

## BACKGROUND

**2.1** This chapter summarises the key principles of the law on sex discrimination, as it relates to family rights. It provides a general overview of the law, whereas its specific application in various situations is considered in the chapters which follow.

**2.2** The law on sex discrimination is now contained within the Equality Act 2010 ('EA 2010'). This Act consolidates and, in some cases, amends, the provisions previously contained in the Sex Discrimination Act 1975 ('SDA 1975'), and the Equal Pay Act 1970 ('EPA 1970'), which dealt with sex discrimination in pay and other contractual terms. As the EA 2010 came into force only in October 2010, much of the case-law referred to in this chapter was decided under the previous legislation. Generally speaking, this case-law is likely to remain binding under the EA 2010.

**2.3** The domestic legislation falls to be interpreted in accordance with Directive 2006/54/EC on the implementation of the principle of equal opportunities and equal treatment of men and women in matters of employment and occupation ('the Equal Treatment Directive') and Council Directive 92/85/EEC on the introduction of measures to encourage improvements in the safety and health of pregnant workers, and workers who have recently given birth or are breastfeeding ('the Pregnant Workers Directive'). The current Equal Treatment Directive is a re-cast version of the original Equal Treatment Directive, Directive 76/207/EEC. Other relevant pieces of European legislation are referred to in the text below.

## THE EQUALITY ACT 2010

**2.4** The EA 2010 prohibits the following types of discrimination connected with family rights:

(a) direct discrimination on the ground of pregnancy and maternity (sections 4 and 18 of the EA 2010);

(b) direct discrimination on the ground of sex (sections 4 and 13 of the EA 2010);

(c)     direct discrimination on the ground of marriage and civil partnership (sections 4 and 13 of the EA 2010);

(d)     indirect sex discrimination (sections 4 and 19 of the EA 2010);

(e)     indirect discrimination related to marriage and civil partnership (sections 4 and 19 of the EA 2010);

(f)     harassment related to sex, or of a sexual nature (section 26 of the EA 2010);

(g)     victimisation (section 27 of the EA 2010);

(h)     unequal pay and other contractual terms and conditions (sections 65 and 66 of the EA 2010), including, in some circumstances, unequal terms relating to calculation of pay whilst on maternity leave (sections 73 and 74 of the EA 2010).

**2.5**     These provisions are considered in more detail below, but it is first necessary to explain who is protected by the Act, and the areas of the employment relationship in which discrimination will be unlawful.

## Who is protected by the Equality Act?

**2.6**     Whilst only employees – ie individuals who work under a contract of service – are covered by certain family-related employment rights, such as unfair dismissal, the protection offered by the EA 2010 is far broader. Protection under Part 5 of the Act extends to individuals in relationships akin to, or linked to, employment, such as participants in vocational training, or members of a trade union.

**2.7**     The relationships of the following bodies and individuals are covered by Part 5 of the Act:

(a)     employees and applicants for employment;[1]

(b)     members of the armed forces;

(c)     contract workers and principals;[2]

(d)     police officers;[3]

(e)     partnerships and limited liability partnerships;[4]

---

[1]     EA 2010, s 39.
[2]     EA 2010, s 41.
[3]     EA 2010, s 42.
[4]     EA 2010, ss 44 and 45.

(f)    barristers, pupils and advocates;[5]

(g)    holders of personal and public office;[6]

(h)    qualifications bodies;[7]

(i)    employment service providers, including employment agencies and providers of vocational training;[8]

(j)    trade organisations;[9]

(k)    local authority members carrying out official business.[10]

**2.8**    The protection against discrimination and harassment extends to discrimination or harassment arising out of and closely connected to one of the above types of relationship, but occurring after the relationship has ended.[11]

**2.9**    Some of the more commonly-occurring types of relationship are considered briefly below.

## *Employees*

**2.10**    The employment relationship features most frequently in the case-law dealing with sex discrimination, and is presumed to be the setting throughout this chapter.

**2.11**    The definition of employment in the EA 2010 is broader than that in the Employment Rights Act 1996 (ERA 1996), and covers any employment under a contract of employment, a contract of apprenticeship, or a contract personally to do work, as well as Crown employment, and employment as a relevant member of the House of Commons or House of Lords staff.[12] There will be a contract 'personally to do work' if: (1) there is a contract; (2) under the contract, the claimant has undertaken personally to execute any work or labour

---

5    EA 2010, ss 47 and 48.
6    EA 2010, ss 49–51.
7    EA 2010, s 53.
8    EA 2010, s 55.
9    EA 2010, s 57.
10    EA 2010, s 58.
11    EA 2010, s 108. From the wording of s 108, it is not clear that post-relationship victimisation is so protected, although it was under the pre-EA 2010 statutes. The Equal Opportunities Review Diary (issue 211) reported that the GEO had confirmed that there was no intention to exclude post-employment victimisation from the EA 2010, and that claimants could rely on the pre-EA 2010 case-law, including *Coote v Granada Hospitality Ltd*, ECJ, Case C-185/97 [1998] IRLR 656, and *Rhys-Harper v Relaxion Group Plc* [2003] UKHL 33; [2003] ICR 867, in support of such claims.
12    EA 2010, s 83(2).

(rather than sub-contracting to others); and (3) the personal obligation to execute work or labour is the dominant purpose of the contract.[13]

## The armed forces

**2.12** Members of the armed forces are treated as employees under the EA 2010,[14] but they are subject to special procedural provisions. Prior to bringing a claim, they must submit an internal service complaint about the matter.[15] For this reason, the time limit for bringing the claim is extended to six months.[16]

## Contract workers

**2.13** Section 41 of the EA 2010 makes it unlawful for a principal, defined as a person who makes work available for an individual who is employed by another person, and supplied by that person in furtherance to a contract to which the principal is a party (a 'contract worker'), to discriminate against that contract worker.

**2.14** Employers frequently utilise the services of workers who are not their own employees, but are supplied by or through another entity. This is often an agency, which may employ the worker. Depending on the circumstances of the case, the worker could potentially sue both the agency (as employer, under section 39 of the EA 2010) and the end-user (as principal, under section 41 of the EA 2010). However, there are also situations where the principal alone might be liable; for example if a worker's engagement with a particular end-user is terminated owing to her pregnancy.

**2.15** Section 41 also covers other similar relationships. It has been held that a salesperson employed by a licensee who has a licence to sell goods in a department store can claim against the department store as principal.[17] As is now made explicit by section 41(5), the contract worker–principal relationship may also arise even where there is no direct contract between the principal and the worker's employer. This occurred in *MHC Consulting Services v Tansell*,[18] where the claimant was employed by his own computer consultancy company, through which he contracted with an employment agency to supply his services to the principal.

## Partnerships

**2.16** Sections 44 and 45 of the EA 2010 prohibit discrimination in general partnerships, limited partnerships, and limited liability partnerships. Thus if a

---

[13]  See *Mirror Group Newspapers v Gunning* [1986] 1 WLR 546; [1986] ICR 145.
[14]  EA 2010, s 83(3).
[15]  EA 2010, s 121(1).
[16]  EA 2010, s 123(2).
[17]  *Harrods Ltd v Remick*.
[18]  [2000] ICR 789.

solicitor were to be refused a partnership because she worked flexibly owing to childcare responsibilities, she could potentially bring an indirect discrimination claim.

## Holders of personal and public office

**2.17** Sections 49–52 of the EA 2010 cover discrimination against individuals who are, or wish to become, personal or public office holders. The 'personal office holder' provisions are likely to cover individuals such as company directors (if they are not employees). Public office holders will include members of public bodies such as statutory commissions and the BBC Trust,[19] members of the judiciary and statutory officials such as members of tribunals.

**2.18** Political offices and posts, such as ministerial offices held by Members of Parliament, or offices held by members of the Welsh Assembly, the Scottish Parliament and the London Assembly, are not covered by the EA 2010.[20]

## Qualifications bodies

**2.19** Section 53 of the EA 2010 prohibits discrimination by qualifications bodies, which are authorities or bodies which can confer qualifications needed for, or facilitating engagement in, a particular trade or profession.[21] The broad range of qualifications and bodies found to have been covered under the pre-Equality Act legislation includes the Common Professional Examination Board and the Council of Legal Education;[22] the Department of Education and Science when conferring qualified teacher status;[23] the GMC in awarding medical qualifications[24] and the Legal Services Commission when it grants a franchise for legal aid work.[25] The definition is not, however, broad enough to extend to the selection of candidates for the office of councillor by eg the Labour Party, because such selection does not confer a qualification in this sense.[26] Nor does it cover general school and university-level educational qualifications.[27]

**2.20** Further, no discrimination claim may be brought against a qualifications body where the act complained of is subject to a statutory appeal, or

---

[19] See the Employment Code of Practice, para 11.48.
[20] Para 2 of EA 2010, Sch 6.
[21] EA 2010, s 54.
[22] *Bohon-Mitchell v Common Professional Examination Board and Council of Legal Education* [1978] IRLR 525.
[23] *Hampson v Department of Education and Science* [1989] IRLR 69.
[24] *Tariquez-Zaman v The General Medical Council*, UKEAT/0292/06/DM; UKEAT/0517/06/DM.
[25] *Patterson v Legal Services Commission* [2004] IRLR 153.
[26] *Triesman v Ali* [2002] EWCA Civ 93; [2002] IRLR 489 and *Ahsan v Watt* [2007] UKHL 51; [2008] IRLR 243.
[27] EA 2010, s 54(4).

proceedings in the nature of an appeal.[28] This is particularly important in cases relating to the GMC, the decisions of which are subject to a variety of appeal and review processes.[29]

## *Employment service providers*

**2.21**  Under section 55 of the EA 2010, it is unlawful for organisations providing a service for finding employment for persons, or supplying employers with persons to do work (most obviously employment agencies) to discriminate. Thus an agency which refused to take on a client because she wanted to seek only part-time work, could potentially be liable for indirect discrimination under section 55.

**2.22**  Section 55 also prohibits discrimination by bodies providing vocational training and guidance, such as providing CV writing classes, English or Maths classes to help adults into work, training in IT skills, or work placements.[30]

## *Volunteers*

**2.23**  The legal position prior to the advent of the EA 2010 was that volunteers who did not receive valuable consideration from their 'employer' in exchange for a contractual obligation to render services or work personally for that 'employer' were not covered by the discrimination statutes.[31] It appears likely that this will remain the position under the EA 2010.

## **In which situations is discrimination prohibited?**

**2.24**  The areas in which discrimination is prohibited vary slightly according to the relationship between the claimant and the respondent. In the case of an employer and employee, the employer may not discriminate in relation to the following aspects of the relationship:

(a)   the arrangements made for deciding whom to offer employment to;[32]

(b)   the terms on which applicants are offered employment;[33]

(c)   in not offering employment to applicants;[34]

(d)   employees' terms of employment;[35]

---

28   EA 2010, s 120(7).
29   See *Khan v GMC* [1994] IRLR 646; *Chaudhary v Specialist Training Authority Appeal Panel and Others (No 2)* [2005] EWCA Civ 282; [2005] ICR 1086.
30   Explanatory Notes to the Equality Act 2010, para 190.
31   *X v Mid Sussex Citizens Advice Bureau* [2011] EWCA Civ 28; [2011] ICR 460.
32   EA 2010, s 39(1)(a).
33   EA 2010, s 39(1)(b).
34   EA 2010, s 39(1)(c).
35   EA 2010, s 39(2)(a).

(e)   the way in which access is afforded to opportunities for promotion, transfer or training or for receiving any other benefit, facility or service;[36]

(f)   dismissal, including constructive dismissal;[37]

(g)   any other detriment.

**2.25**  The concept of 'detriment' is broadly defined. It covers any treatment of such a kind that a reasonable worker would or might take the view that in all the circumstances it was to his or her detriment, or disadvantage.[38] Thus it could include treatment as diverse as a derogatory comment about pregnancy; a failure to keep in contact with an employee on maternity leave, or a refusal to allow an employee to work flexibly.

**2.26**  If the relationship of the claimant and respondent is not that of employer and employee, it is important to check the relevant section to see precisely which acts are prohibited. However, each of the sections set out at **2.7** above includes a clause prohibiting 'any other detriment'.

## Pregnancy and maternity discrimination

**2.27**  Until the Sex Discrimination Act 1975 was amended to include a specific prohibition of direct pregnancy and maternity discrimination on 1 October 2005, all such claims fell to be determined under the general provisions on direct sex discrimination. Both the pre-October 2005 provisions, and the subsequently introduced section 3A of the Sex Discrimination Act 1975 gave rise to protracted debate as to whether domestic law was compliant with European law. A recast specific prohibition of pregnancy and maternity discrimination now appears as section 18 of the EA 2010.

**2.28**  In the context of family rights, it makes sense to consider section 18 first. This is particularly so because section 18 excludes the operation of the direct discrimination provisions contained in section 13 of the EA 2010 where the treatment complained of falls within the ambit of section 18.[39] Women subjected to discrimination on the ground of their pregnancy and maternity leave may, however, still need to have recourse to a claim under section 13 in circumstances where the discrimination falls outside the relatively narrow 'protected period' defined in section 18. This is discussed further at **2.56–2.65** below.

**2.29**  Section 18 provides that a person (A) will discriminate against a woman (B) if:

---

[36]   EA 2010, s 39(2)(b).
[37]   EA 2010, s 39(2)(c).
[38]   *Shamoon v Chief Constable of the Royal Ulster Constabulary* [2003] UKHL 11; [2003] ICR 337, at para 35.
[39]   EA 2010, s 18(7).

(a)  During the protected period, in relation to a pregnancy of B's, A treats B
     unfavourably:

    (i)   because of the pregnancy;[40]
    (ii)  because of illness suffered by her as a result of it.[41]

(b)  A treats B unfavourably because she is on compulsory maternity leave.[42]

(c)  A treats B unfavourably because she is exercising or seeking to exercise, or
     has exercised or sought to exercise, the right to ordinary or additional
     maternity leave.[43]

## The protected period

**2.30**  The 'protected period' referred to in section 18(2) begins when the
woman's pregnancy begins, and ends:

(a)  if the woman has the right to ordinary and additional maternity leave, at
     the end of her additional maternity leave period or (if earlier) when she
     returns to work after the pregnancy;[44]

(b)  if she does not have that right, at the end of the period of two weeks
     beginning with the end of the pregnancy.[45]

**2.31**  This means that a woman who does not fall within the definition of an
'employee' under section 230 of the ERA 1996, and is therefore not entitled to
take ordinary or additional maternity leave, will only have the protection of
section 18 of the EA 2010 until two weeks after she has given birth. This will
apply to many of the women in the types of non-employment relationship
covered by Part 5 of the Equality Act 2010 (see **2.7** above).

**2.32**  In the recent case of *Danosa v LKB Lizings SIA*,[46] the Court of Justice of
the European Union (hereafter CJEU) held that a member of a capital
company's Board of Directors, who provided services to that company and was
an integral part of it, had to be regarded as having the status of worker under
Directive 92/85 (the Pregnant Workers Directive) if she carried out that activity,
for some time, under the direction or supervision of another body of that

---

[40]  EA 2010, s 18(2)(a).
[41]  EA 2010, s 18(2)(b).
[42]  EA 2010, s 18(3). Compulsory maternity leave is available to employees who are entitled to
      ordinary maternity leave, and is the period of two weeks commencing with the day on which
      childbirth occurs; see reg 8 of the Maternity and Parental Leave Regulations 1999.
[43]  EA 2010, s 18(4). Ordinary maternity leave lasts for 26 weeks from its commencement; reg 7(1)
      of the Maternity and Parental Leave Regulations 1999. Additional maternity leave lasts for 26
      weeks from *its* commencement; reg 7(4) of the Maternity and Parental Leave
      Regulations 1999. See further Chapter 4.
[44]  EA 2010, s 18(6)(a).
[45]  EA 2010, s 18(6)(b).
[46]  Case no. C-232/09, [2011] 2 CMLR 2.

company, and received remuneration for her services. Her dismissal, which was assumed to be on the ground of pregnancy for the purpose of the hearing, was therefore unlawful.

**2.33** The relevance of this decision is that a 'worker' within the meaning of the Pregnant Workers Directive is entitled to a number of benefits, including a continuous period of maternity leave of at least 14 weeks,[47] and special protection from dismissal during that period.[48] The claimant in *Danosa* itself would probably be classified, on the facts in the judgment, as an employee in UK law, and would thus qualify for these benefits in the UK. However, the general definition of 'worker' in EU law, which covers any person who performs services for and under the direction of another person, in return for which he or she receives remuneration, appears to be broader than the definition of 'employee' in UK law.

**2.34** It is therefore arguable that the limitation of entitlement to maternity leave to 'employees' as defined in the ERA 1996 is in breach of European law. If this is correct, the limitation of the protected period in respect of non-employees in section 18 of the EA 2010 may also contravene European law. A female worker in this situation may, however, be able to bring a claim in respect of pregnancy or maternity discrimination under the direct discrimination provisions of section 13 of the EA 2010 (in relation to which, see **2.56–2.67** below).

**2.35** It is important to note that an employer cannot avoid the prohibition on discrimination in section 18 of the EA 2010 by taking a decision to treat a woman unfavourably because of pregnancy or maternity leave during the protected period, but waiting until after the protected period to implement that decision. In such circumstances, the treatment will be regarded as occurring during the protected period.[49] This provision of the EA 2010 gives effect to the CJEU case-law.

*Case Example*

C, who worked for a firm of architects in Belgium, R, took maternity leave. She returned to work in December 1995. During C's pregnancy, R took the decision to dismiss her and also sought to recruit a new employee to her position. However, C was not in fact given notice of dismissal until February 1996. Belgian law did not prohibit a decision to dismiss made during pregnancy or maternity leave as long as the notification to the employee came more than one month after the end of maternity leave. The CJEU held that taking preparatory steps towards notifying a woman of her dismissal on the ground of pregnancy/birth of a child before the end of maternity leave contravened Article 10 of the Pregnant Workers Directive. It further held that taking a decision to dismiss on the grounds of pregnancy and/or birth of a child was contrary to Articles 2(1) and 5(1) of the Equal Treatment Directive, whenever it was notified.

---

[47]  Article 8 of the Directive.
[48]  Article 10 of the Directive.
[49]  EA 2010, s 18(5).

*Paquay v Societe D'architectes Hoet + Minne SPRL*[50]

## *'Unfavourably'*

**2.36** Pregnancy and maternity discrimination is different from most of the other forms of discrimination prohibited by EA 2010, because it does not require a comparison with another worker. As will be discussed further below, ordinary direct sex discrimination requires a woman to show that she has been treated less favourably than a man would have been treated in the same circumstances. Section 18 of the EA 2010 merely requires that a woman be 'unfavourably' treated because of her pregnancy, pregnancy-related illness or maternity leave.

**2.37** There is no definition of 'unfavourably' in the EA 2010. Nor is any guidance provided by the Explanatory Notes or the Code of Practice on Employment. It appears likely that the concept of 'unfavourable treatment' would cover the type of treatment sufficient to fit the definition of a 'detriment' (see **2.25** above). Thus, to take a simple example, a woman who is not consulted about a change affecting her because she is on maternity leave would be treated 'unfavourably', even if a man who was absent from work at the same time would have been treated in the same way.

**2.38** However, based on the pre-Equality Act case-law, the definition should also be capable of covering a failure to provide a pregnant woman, or a woman who is on maternity leave, with certain types of special protection which are not available to workers who are not pregnant. This would include the rights guaranteed under the Pregnant Workers Directive, such as the right to a risk assessment in certain types of employment, not to be exposed to hazardous agents or working conditions, to be exempted from night work, and to take time off for ante-natal examinations.[51]

**2.39** The fact that no comparison is required under the EA 2010 does not mean that comparative evidence cannot be relied upon by a claimant seeking to show pregnancy or maternity discrimination. For example, a woman who believes she has been dismissed because she is pregnant will often want to bolster her claim by showing that a comparable employee in similar circumstances has not been dismissed, even though such a comparison is not strictly necessary.

## *'Because of'*

**2.40** Under the provisions of the SDA 1975, the question to be asked by courts in determining the cause of particular treatment was whether it was 'on

---

[50]  Case C-460/06; [2008] 1 CMLR 12.
[51]  Articles 4, 6, 7 and 9 of the Pregnant Workers Directive.

the ground of' a protected characteristic. The wording has changed slightly under the EA 2010, and the question is now whether treatment is 'because of' eg pregnancy or maternity.

**2.41** Both the Explanatory Notes to the Equality Act[52] and the Code of Practice on Employment[53] state that the change in wording does not signify any change in the test, and that the pre-Equality Act case-law will continue to apply.

**2.42** The question of whether a particular action was taken because of a protected characteristic is an objective test of causal connection. If the reason, or part of the reason (in relation to which see **2.43** below) for the employee's unfavourable treatment is pregnancy or the fact that she has taken maternity leave, it does not matter whether or not the employer consciously adverted to that reason. Nor is motive relevant. If, for example, an employer were to prevent a pregnant woman from undertaking certain types of task on the assumption that this would make her day easier, that would amount to discrimination in just the same way as a similar act occasioned by a malicious motive (assuming that the removal of those tasks could be seen as a detriment).[54]

**2.43** It is also unnecessary that the protected characteristic be the only cause of the unfavourable treatment. It need not even be the principal cause of the treatment. As long as it is a significant influence on the outcome, that will be sufficient.[55]

*Case Example*

C, who was a teacher of religious education and personal relationships at a Roman Catholic School, was dismissed from the school after she became pregnant by a Roman Catholic priest. The school argued that the dismissal was not because C was pregnant per se, but because her pregnancy was a manifestation of a relationship between a religious education teacher and a Roman Catholic priest and that relationship and the pregnancy had become public knowledge. The Employment Tribunal accepted that argument, and found that there was no sex discrimination, but their decision was overturned on appeal. The EAT held that the matters relied upon by the school were all causally connected to C's pregnancy, and the dismissal was therefore on the ground of sex. The judgment also indicates that even if the decision had been taken partly on the basis of C's pregnancy, and partly because she had had a relationship with a Roman Catholic priest, it nevertheless would have amounted to sex discrimination arising out of C's pregnancy.

---

[52] At para 61.
[53] At para 3.11.
[54] See generally on these principles *Birmingham City Council v Equal Opportunities Commission* [1989] AC 1155.
[55] *Nagarajan v London Regional Transport* [2000] 1 AC 501 at p 513.

*O'Neill v Governors of St Thomas More Roman Catholic Voluntary Aided Upper School*[56]

**2.44**   The pre-EA 2010 case-law was clear that an employer had to know, or at least believe or suspect, that a woman was pregnant before it could subject her to discrimination on the ground of her pregnancy. This must remain so under the EA 2010, insofar as the alleged cause of the unfavourable treatment is the pregnancy itself.

**2.45**   However, matters are slightly complicated by the specific prohibition of unfavourable treatment because of pregnancy-related illness in section 18(2)(b) of the EA 2010. It is not immediately apparent from the wording of the section that the employer must be aware that the illness is pregnancy related before a discrimination claim can be made out. Such knowledge appears to have been necessary under the pre-EA 2010 law,[57] but under those provisions, the detrimental treatment had to be on the ground of pregnancy, so knowledge of the pregnancy would inevitably have been required. The Code of Practice on Employment maintains that knowledge of pregnancy remains necessary to make unfavourable treatment unlawful,[58] but in the authors' view the point requires either legislative or judicial clarification.

## Unfavourable treatment because of a woman's pregnancy

**2.46**   Unfavourable treatment of a woman because of her pregnancy, prohibited by section 18(2)(a) of the EA 2010, is perhaps the easiest type of unfavourable treatment to conceptualise. Clearly, it would cover dismissal of or failure to promote a woman owing to her pregnancy, as well as selecting her for redundancy on that ground, giving her less interesting tasks or failing to put her forward for training, and making derogatory or upsetting comments about her pregnancy.

**2.47**   Section 18(2)(a) also, as already discussed at **2.38** above, prohibits a failure to provide a pregnant woman with the special protection to which she is entitled under the Pregnant Workers Directive.[59] However, it is important to note that not all of these protections apply to every pregnant worker. For example, the requirement that a pregnant worker's tasks be risk-assessed applies only to work which involves particular types of risks, of the kind set out in Annexes I and II to the Pregnant Workers Directive.

*Case Example*

C was a primary school teacher employed by R. She complained that R's failure to produce an individual risk assessment after she had informed the headteacher of

---

[56]   [1997] ICR 33.
[57]   See by analogy *Del Monte Foods v Mundon* [1980] ICR 694.
[58]   See para 8.18.
[59]   There are also specific statutory provisions guaranteeing these rights contained in the Employment Rights Act 1996 and the Management of Health and Safety at Work Regulations 1999; see further in Chapter 3 below.

her pregnancy amounted to direct pregnancy discrimination. Her claim was dismissed by the ET and EAT, on the basis that the type of work she did did not involve a risk of harm or danger to her as a pregnant worker. The EAT held that a risk assessment will only be required if: (a) the employee has notified the employer of her pregnancy in writing; (b) the work is of a kind which could involve a risk of harm or danger to the health and safety of a new or expectant mother or to that of her baby; and (c) the risk arises from either processes or working conditions or physical, biological or chemical agents in the workplace at the time.

*O'Neill v Buckinghamshire County Council*[60]

**2.48** It should be noted that, on its face, section 18(2) covers only discrimination against a woman who is pregnant, because it prohibits only unfavourable treatment of a woman 'in relation to a pregnancy of hers'. This suggests that the section does not encompass unfavourable treatment because a woman is perceived to be pregnant, or unfavourable treatment of another person because of the woman's pregnancy (associative discrimination). It is possible, however, that a claim for perceived or associative pregnancy discrimination may be brought under section 13 of the EA 2010. These points are discussed further at **2.56–2.65** and in Chapter 9 below.

**2.49** The section also does not appear to cover women undergoing IVF treatment who are not yet pregnant. However, some such women may be able to bring a claim under section 13 of the EA 2010; see **2.68–2.69** below.

**2.50** It is important to remember that section 18(2)(a) only provides protection against pregnancy discrimination during the protected period. Women subjected to unfavourable treatment outside of the protected period because they have been pregnant will have to rely on such protection as is available under section 13 of the EA 2010 (see **2.56–2.69** below).

## Unfavourable treatment because of pregnancy-related illness

**2.51** Section 18(2)(b) makes explicit the prohibition of unfavourable treatment of women suffering pregnancy-related illness during pregnancy or maternity leave which was established by European case-law.

*Case Example*

C was employed by R as a driver. In August 1990, she informed R that she was pregnant, and as a result of a pregnancy-related illness, she did not work again until the middle of August 1991. R's contracts of employment contained a clause entitling R to dismiss employees after they had been absent owing to sickness for more than 26 weeks, and C was dismissed under this clause in February 1991. The CJEU held that her dismissal amounted to sex discrimination, even though a male worker absent for the same period would also have been

---

[60]  [2010] IRLR 384.

dismissed. Dismissal of a female worker during pregnancy for absence due to incapacity for work resulting from her pregnancy was to be regarded as essentially based on the fact of her pregnancy.

*Brown v Rentokil Ltd*[61]

**2.52**   As with section 18(2)(a), section 18(2)(b) provides protection against unfavourable treatment because of pregnancy-related illness only during the protected period. The CJEU has held that detrimental treatment on the ground of pregnancy-related illness occurring after the end of maternity leave will not automatically amount to sex discrimination merely because it relates to pregnancy. A woman who suffers detriment for this reason will have to show that she has been less favourably treated than a man would have been treated in similar circumstances in order to claim sex discrimination.[62]

## Unfavourable treatment because of maternity leave

**2.53**   Unfavourable treatment because a woman is on compulsory maternity leave, or because she is exercising, or seeks to exercise, or has exercised, or sought to exercise, her right to ordinary or additional maternity leave is prohibited by section 18(3) and (4) of the EA 2010.

**2.54**   Whilst the protection relating to compulsory maternity leave applies only whilst a woman is on that maternity leave, the protection relating to ordinary and additional maternity leave is not limited in time. Thus a woman may bring a complaint under section 18(4) if, for example, she is refused a promotion six months after returning to work, because she exercised her right to take maternity leave.

**2.55**   The most obvious examples of treatment made unlawful by section 18(3) and (4) are dismissal or selection for redundancy because a woman has taken maternity leave. Other examples of prohibited unfavourable treatment would include:

(a)   failing to consult a woman about a redundancy situation affecting her because she is on maternity leave;

(b)   failing to provide a woman with an appraisal because she is on maternity leave;

(c)   failing to inform a woman about a promotion opportunity because she is on maternity leave;

---

[61]   Case C-394/96; [1998] 2 CMLR 1049; [1998] IRLR 445.
[62]   *Handels-Og Kontorfunktionaerernes Forbund I Danmark v Dansk Arbejdsgiverforening* [1992] ICR 332.

(d) dismissing a woman who has taken maternity leave because the employer wishes to retain her temporary replacement on the basis that he/she is more efficient.[63]

## Pregnancy-related treatment outside the protected period

**2.56** As explained above, there are certain situations where unfavourable treatment related to pregnancy will not be covered by section 18 of the EA 2010. In particular, this will occur where the relevant treatment is decided upon and occurs outside of the 'protected period', for example where:

(a) a woman is treated unfavourably because her employer or potential employer believes her to be pregnant, even though she is not in fact pregnant;

(b) an employer or potential employer treats a woman unfavourably because she has been pregnant in the past.[64]

**2.57** The status of such claims under the EA 2010 is, unfortunately, not clear.

**2.58** Section 18(7) of the EA 2010 disapplies the direct discrimination provisions of section 13 insofar as they relate to sex discrimination, for claims of unfavourable treatment because of pregnancy or pregnancy-related illness arising during the protected period, and maternity leave.

**2.59** This disapplication is limited to claims of <u>sex discrimination</u> made under section 13 of the EA 2010 in respect of these matters. However, on its face, section 13 covers direct discrimination because of pregnancy and maternity as well as sex. It prohibits direct discrimination because of any of the protected characteristics listed in section 4 of the EA 2010, which include pregnancy and maternity. A straightforward reading of sections 18(7) and 13 therefore suggests that a claim may be brought under section 13 in respect of pregnancy or maternity discrimination both within and outside the protected period.

**2.60** However, this conclusion is cast into some doubt by section 25(5) of the EA 2010, which provides that pregnancy and maternity discrimination is discrimination within section 17 (which deals with non-work cases) and section 18. There is no reference to section 13, as there is in relation to all of the other protected characteristics. This suggests that section 13 is not intended to encompass the protected characteristic of pregnancy and maternity, and thus that any pregnancy-related claim that does not fall within section 18 must be brought as a claim of direct sex discrimination.

---

[63] *Rees v Apollo Watch Repairs Plc* [1996] ICR 466.
[64] In practice, this scenario is only likely to give rise to difficulties in circumstances where a woman has been pregnant, but has not taken maternity leave, e g if she suffers a miscarriage. Women treated unfavourably because they have exercised or sought to exercise their right to maternity leave can bring a claim under the EA 2010, s 18(3) or (4), as set out at **2.54** above.

**2.61**   Further, section 13 of the EA 2010 requires a comparative exercise: the claimant must have been treated less favourably than a person who does not have her protected characteristic. Under section 23 of the EA 2010, there must be no material difference between the circumstances of the claimant and her comparator. The Act therefore appears to reintroduce the requirement for a comparator in pregnancy discrimination cases (or cases of sex discrimination which arise out of pregnancy), where the treatment complained of falls outside section 18.[65]

**2.62**   The general assumption under the pre-Equality Act law, following clarification in *R (EOC) v Secretary of State for Trade and Industry*[66] was that treatment relating to pregnancy, whether or not occurring within the protected period, would amount to discrimination without the need to identify a comparator. Thus if a woman could show that she was dismissed because her employer incorrectly believed her to be pregnant, that would amount to sex discrimination, as would an employer's refusal to offer a woman a job because she had in the past been pregnant (but had not taken maternity leave, e g because she suffered a miscarriage).

**2.63**   There is no suggestion within the Explanatory Notes to the EA 2010 that the legislature intended to alter this position.

**2.64**   Further, there is a strong argument that to do so would amount to a breach of European law. The preamble to Directive 2006/54/EC provides, at recital (23) that:

> 'It is clear from the case-law of the Court of Justice that unfavourable treatment of a woman related to pregnancy or maternity constitutes direct discrimination on grounds of sex. Such treatment should therefore be expressly covered by this Directive.'

The recital does not place any limitations on the type of treatment 'related to' pregnancy or maternity which must be regarded as direct discrimination, although some have been identified in the case-law to which it refers.[67] Arguably, the EA 2010 should not impose exceptions additional to those identified by the CJEU.

**2.65**   At the time of writing, the question of whether a comparator is required in pregnancy-related claims falling outside section 18 of the EA 2010 remains unclear. Either clarificatory case-law or further legislation is likely to be required to resolve this quandary.

---

[65]   For further discussion of this point, see Sean Jones 'Equality Act 2010: The Pregnancy Discrimination Mystery' at http://www.employmentcasesupdate.co.uk/site.aspx?i=ed6083.

[66]   [2007] EWHC 438 (Admin); [2007] ICR 1234.

[67]   For example, treatment based on pregnancy-related illness arising outside the protected period is not pregnancy discrimination, and a claimant in such a situation must show that she has been less favourably treated than a male comparator in similar circumstances; see **2.64** above.

**2.66** There are two further situations not presently covered by section 18 which have been held by the CJEU to amount to, or to be akin to, pregnancy discrimination, and thus not to require a comparator.

**2.67** Firstly, a woman who falls within the EU law definition of a 'worker' is entitled to the benefit of a continuous period of maternity leave of at least 14 weeks,[68] and special protection against dismissal over that period, as well as the other benefits set out in the Pregnant Workers Directive.[69] Under the domestic legislation, ordinary and additional maternity leave, as well as special protection against dismissal over that period, are afforded only to employees. In order properly to give effect to EU law, section 13 of the EA 2010 should be interpreted such as to provide female workers who do not fall within this definition, and are not afforded these rights and protections, with the opportunity to bring a claim for direct pregnancy/sex discrimination.

**2.68** Secondly, the CJEU has held that dismissing a female worker who is undergoing IVF treatment, and is between the stage of follicular puncture and the immediate (first) transfer of the in vitro fertilised ova into the uterus, in circumstances where the reason for the dismissal is that she has undergone that treatment, is a breach of articles 2(1) and 5(1) of Directive 76/207[70] (now recast as Directive 2006/54). In order to give effect to EU law, a woman in this situation should have the right to claim direct pregnancy/sex discrimination under section 13 of the EA 2010, without the need to rely upon a comparator.

**2.69** However, special protection for women undergoing IVF is limited to the very short period considered in *Mayr* itself. The domestic courts have held that unfavourable treatment e g because a woman is undergoing hormone therapy preparatory to follicular puncture will not be treated as akin to pregnancy discrimination. In such circumstances, the woman will need to show that she has been treated less favourably than a man would be in similar circumstances.[71]

## Direct sex discrimination

**2.70** Direct sex discrimination occurs where a worker has been treated less favourably than a person of the opposite sex would have been treated, because of his or her sex. The concept therefore involves a comparison with the way in which a person of the opposite sex, but otherwise with the same relevant circumstances as the claimant, was or would have been treated by the employer.[72] This comparator can be a real person (an actual comparator), or – as is more usually the case – a constructed hypothetical comparator.

---

[68]   Article 8 of the Pregnant Workers Directive.
[69]   See *Danosa v LKB Lizings SIA* [2011] 2 CMLR 2 and **2.32**–**2.34** above.
[70]   *Mayr v Backerei und Konditorei Gerhard Flockner OHG*, Case C-506/06; [2008] 2 CMLR 27.
[71]   *Sahota v Home Office and another* [2010] ICR 772.
[72]   EA 2010, s 23.

**2.71** Much of the litigation relating to direct discrimination in the years leading up to the EA 2010 focused on the burden of proof in such claims. This trend looks set to continue under the new legislation.

**2.72** Section 136 of the EA 2010 provides:

(a)  that if there are facts from which a court could decide, in the absence of any other explanation, that person (A) contravened the provision relied upon by the claimant, the court must hold that the contravention occurred; but

(b)  this will not apply if A shows that A did not contravene the provision.

**2.73** Thus, in an employment case, the burden of proof will shift to the employer in the circumstances described at **2.72** above. Such circumstances have been referred to in the pre-EA 2010 case-law as a 'prima facie case' of discrimination.

**2.74** Guidance on the process that should be used by tribunals in considering a direct discrimination claim, taking into account the burden of proof provisions, was provided by the Court of Appeal in *Wong v Igen Ltd.*[73] A number of courts have considered the provision since; in particular, the Court of Appeal in *Madarassy v Nomura International Plc.*[74] In that case, the court held that something more than a mere difference in status (eg, in a sex discrimination case, the fact that the claimant is a woman and her comparator a man) and a difference in treatment is required to shift the burden of proof to the employer.

**2.75** In recent years, certain judges and courts have advocated moving away from the two-stage approach set out in section 136 and its predecessors (ie considering first whether there is a prima facie case of discrimination, and if so, whether the employer has proved that no discrimination took place), and instead moving straight to consideration of the 'reason why' a particular act was done. This line of cases follows on from the approach of Lord Nicholls in *Shamoon v Chief Constable of the Royal Ulster Constabulary.*[75] It recognises that, particularly in cases involving hypothetical comparators, the question of how such a comparator would have been treated is essentially the same as asking why the claimant was treated in the way she was. In a sex discrimination case, if a male hypothetical comparator would have been treated differently, the reason for the treatment is the claimant's sex. If a male hypothetical comparator would have been treated in the same way, the reason will not be the

---

[73]  [2005] EWCA Civ 142; [2005] ICR 931; see in particular the annex to the Court of Appeal's judgment.
[74]  [2007] EWCA Civ 33; [2007] ICR 867.
[75]  [2003] ICR 337 at paras 7–12.

claimant's sex. Determining why a claimant was treated in the way she was will generally require the tribunal to consider the inferences that can be drawn from primary facts.[76]

**2.76** In the context of family rights, the direct sex discrimination provisions are likely to play a relatively limited role, as most situations will be covered by the prohibition of direct discrimination because of pregnancy or maternity leave. There are important exceptions, however:

(a) Men cannot bring claims under section 18 of the EA 2010. If a man is treated less favourably than a woman would be, for example because he takes time off to look after his children, and his employer perceives this to be a 'female' role, he will need to bring a direct sex discrimination claim under section 13 of the EA 2010.

(b) It is possible that claims for associative pregnancy or sex discrimination may be available under section 13 of the EA 2010. This point is considered further in Chapter 9 below.

(c) As already discussed at **2.69** above, a woman subjected to less favourable treatment related to IVF, who does not fall within the very specific window set out in *Mayr v Backerei und Konditorei Gerhard Flockner OH,*[77] will have to rely upon a section 13 direct sex discrimination claim.

(d) Subject to resolution of the discussion at **2.56–2.65** above, it is possible that a woman subjected to less favourable treatment relating to pregnancy (whether perceived or actual) which is decided upon and occurs outside the protected period may have to bring a direct sex discrimination claim rather than a pregnancy discrimination claim.

**2.77** Under section 13(6)(b) of the EA 2010, where a man brings a direct sex discrimination claim, no account is to be taken of special treatment afforded to a woman in connection with pregnancy or childbirth. The equivalent provision in the SDA 1975 has, however, been interpreted by the EAT as meaning that this exception will only apply where the treatment is no more favourable than is reasonably necessary for this purpose (or, to put it another way, is a proportionate means of achieving a legitimate aim).

*Case Example*

C and his female comparator R were both associate solicitors working for E. Whilst R was on maternity leave, it was decided that one of C and R had to be made redundant. The selection criteria applied included a criterion called 'lock up' which measured the length of time between the undertaking of a piece of work and the receipt of payment from the client. C scored 0.5 out of a maximum of 2 on this criterion. As R was on maternity leave, meaning that 'lock up' could not be

---

[76] See for an explanation of the 'reason why' process *Amnesty International v Ahmed* [2009] ICR 1450, especially para 24.

[77] Case C-506/06; [2008] 2 CMLR 27.

measured for her at the date of the redundancy selection exercise, E awarded R the maximum score of 2. C was made redundant as his overall score was 27 compared with R's 27.5. C's claim of sex discrimination was upheld. The EAT took the view that awarding R the maximum score went beyond what was reasonably necessary to ensure R was not disadvantaged by being on maternity leave. There were other ways in which this might have been achieved, such as measuring R's performance on 'lock up' as at the last date on which R worked.

*Eversheds Legal Services Ltd v De Belin*[78]

**2.78**   This decision has attracted a certain amount of adverse commentary, on the basis that it appears to be contrary to the plain words of the statute.[79]

**2.79**   It has also been suggested the wording of the EA 2010 may give rise to further complications for employers in this type of situation. Assuming that a pregnancy/maternity discrimination claim may be brought under section 13, in relation to which see **2.56–2.65** above, a male claimant may be able to argue that he has been subjected to discrimination contrary to section 13 because he does <u>not</u> have the protected characteristic of pregnancy or maternity. This is because section 13(6)(b) of the EA 2010 only applies to permit special treatment in connection with pregnancy or childbirth where the protected characteristic relied upon by the male claimant is sex, not where it is pregnancy/maternity. Further, as pregnancy and maternity is now a protected characteristic independent of sex, a woman who does not have that protected characteristic could potentially bring a pregnancy/maternity discrimination claim under section 13 if she is treated less favourably than a pregnant female comparator.[80]

**2.80**   It seems likely that this provision will give rise to further litigation in the near future.

## Marriage and civil partnership discrimination

**2.81**   A person who is married or is a civil partner may bring a claim of direct discrimination on the basis that he/she has been treated less favourably than a person who is not married, or a civil partner, would have been.[81]

**2.82**   Marriage will cover any formal union of a man and woman which is legally recognised in the UK as a marriage. A civil partnership is a registered civil partnership under the Civil Partnership Act 2004 (which includes those registered outside the UK).[82]

---

[78]   [2011] IRLR 448.
[79]   See e g *Highlights: June 2011* [2011] IRLR 445.
[80]   See Gary Hodkinson *Redundancy Selection: between the devil and the deep sea*, ELA Briefing, Vol 18, No 6, July 2011.
[81]   EA 2010, ss 8 and 13.
[82]   Code of Practice on Employment, para 2.32.

**2.83** The provision does not operate in reverse, so a person who is not married or in a civil partnership may not complain that he/she has been treated less favourably than a married person, or a person in a civil partnership.[83]

**2.84** There are relatively few situations where a claim for direct marriage or civil partnership discrimination is likely to succeed where other claims would not. In most cases where a claim of marital status discrimination has been raised, the claimant has succeeded on other grounds; for example, *Horsey v Dyfed County Council*,[84] where the employer's assumption that a married woman would follow her husband's job was held to be direct sex discrimination. It is possible to envisage other cases of stereotyped assumptions which could result in a successful marriage/civil partnership discrimination case. For example, if an employer were to deny a married man time off to care for his children on the basis that, unlike an unmarried man, he would have a wife available to provide childcare, that would be likely to breach sections 8 and 13 of the EA 2010.

**2.85** Marriage and civil partnership are also protected characteristics for the purpose of indirect discrimination claims under section 19.[85]

## Indirect discrimination

**2.86** Indirect sex discrimination, which is prohibited by section 19 of the EA 2010, occurs when an employer applies a particular provision, criterion or practice (referred to hereafter as a 'PCP') which appears on its face to be neutral, but in fact places (for example) women at a particular disadvantage when compared with men. If a woman can show that she personally is placed at a particular disadvantage by the PCP, and if her employer is unable objectively to justify its application to her, she will be able to bring a claim of indirect sex discrimination.

**2.87** Perhaps the most obvious, and most frequently litigated, example of indirect discrimination is where an employer refuses to allow employees to work part-time. Although the make-up of the workforce is changing, there has in the past been general recognition that such a rule places women, who still tend disproportionately to have primary responsibility for childcare, at a particular disadvantage. Unless an employer has a real need to impose such a rule – arising, for example, from the particular nature of his/her business – its application to a woman who wishes to work part-time in order to care for her family may well be indirect sex discrimination.

**2.88** The factual circumstances in which indirect sex discrimination may arise in the context of family rights are discussed in detail in Chapter 7. This chapter provides a general overview of the structure of an indirect discrimination claim.

---

[83] EA 2010, s 13(4).
[84] [1982] ICR 755.
[85] EA 2010, s 19(3).

## Statutory provisions

**2.89**   Because indirect discrimination is a little more complicated than direct discrimination, it is useful to look first at the wording of the statutory prohibition contained in section 19 of the EA 2010:

> '(1)   A person (A) discriminates against another (B) if A applies to B a provision, criterion or practice which is discriminatory in relation to a relevant protected characteristic of B's.
>
> (2)   For the purpose of section (1), a provision, criterion or practice is discriminatory in relation to a relevant protected characteristic of B's if:
>
> > (a)   A applies, or would apply, it to persons with whom B does not share the characteristic;
> >
> > (b)   it puts, or would put, persons with whom B shares the characteristic at a particular disadvantage when compared with persons with whom B does not share it;
> >
> > (c)   it puts, or would put, B at that disadvantage, and
> >
> > (d)   A cannot show it to be a proportionate means of achieving a legitimate aim.'

**2.90**   Sex is one of the protected characteristics to which section 19 applies.[86] There can be no indirect pregnancy and maternity discrimination, because pregnancy and maternity are, of necessity, protected characteristics applying only to women.

**2.91**   Below, each element of the statutory concept of indirect discrimination is considered individually.

## Provision, criterion or practice

**2.92**   Neither the Equality Act 2010, nor the various discrimination statutes which preceded it, contains a definition of the term 'provision, criterion or practice'.

**2.93**   However, in most potential indirect discrimination cases, it will be obvious whether a PCP has been applied. Some examples of PCPs include:

(a)   a written term of a worker's contract (eg a requirement to work full-time);

(b)   a term of a collective agreement (eg a term in a collectively-agreed redundancy policy);

(c)   an internal rule contained in a company handbook;

(d)   a criterion (whether essential or desirable) for appointment or promotion to a post;

---

[86]   EA 2010, s 19(3).

(e)    a matrix to be used in determining whether a person should be selected for redundancy;

(f)    a criterion to be applied in considering whether to award a pay rise;

(g)    an unwritten practice that has been followed over a period of time.

**2.94**   Where the courts have been called upon to consider whether a PCP has been applied, they have adopted a broad interpretation of the phrase.

**2.95**   The requirement under section 19(2)(a) that the employer applies, or would apply, the PCP equally to those employees who do not share the complainant's protected characteristic does not mean that the PCP has to amount to a universal rule to be applied at all times. A discretionary one-off management decision may amount to a PCP, as long as it would have, at that time, been applied equally to a man.[87]

**2.96**   Further, it is not necessary that a PCP be an absolute barrier. It is likely to be sufficient that the rule or policy relied upon makes it much more difficult to do something, which in turn particularly disadvantages women, or men. Thus where the EAT found that a union had adopted a policy of providing only limited representational support for workers making a claim for back pay under the Equal Pay Act (a policy which particularly disadvantaged women), that amounted to a PCP, even though the women received some support for their claims.[88] A rule providing that part-time working would be permitted only in exceptional circumstances would probably also be capable of being a PCP.

**2.97**   A claimant may also rely on the combined effect of multiple PCPs.

*Case Example*

C was a technician in the army, and a single mother. Her home was in St Vincent and the Grenadines. She complained that she had been placed at a particular disadvantage by two PCPs, namely: (1) that she must be available for duty 24/7 (which she said gave rise to indirect sex discrimination); and (2) that she could not have her half-sister to stay with her in the Service Families Accommodation because the half-sister was a foreign national, and was only entitled to stay in the UK for a short period (which she said was indirect race discrimination). The EAT held that the tribunal had been entitled to consider the combined effect of the two PCPs, as the disadvantage suffered by C was a consequence of both. Neither PCP was justifiable in circumstances where the employer insisted on imposing the other PCP.

*MoD v DeBique*[89]

---

[87]   See *British Airways v Starmer* [2005] IRLR 862, discussed further in Chapter 7 below.

[88]   See *GMB v Allen* [2007] IRLR 752, at paras 58–62; not challenged in the appeal to the Court of Appeal.

[89]   [2010] IRLR 471, at paras 162–170 in particular.

### *'Particular disadvantage' when compared with persons without the protected characteristic*

**2.98**  As with a claim for direct discrimination, an indirect discrimination claim requires the tribunal to undertake a comparison. However, the comparative exercise under section 19 is of a very different nature from that under section 13, because it is between groups rather than between individuals.

**2.99**  If we take as an example an indirect sex discrimination claim brought by a woman, the tribunal has to determine whether the PCP relied upon by the claimant puts or would put women at a particular disadvantage when compared with men.

**2.100**  As the comparative exercise under section 19(2)(b) of the EA 2010 is a group one, however, it is not sufficient for a claimant to show that she personally suffers a particular disadvantage as a result of her sex. She must show that women more generally are placed at a particular disadvantage by the PCP when compared with men. This is not always a straightforward exercise. The most difficult question to arise in many indirect discrimination claims is: which group of women should be compared with which group of men?

**2.101**  Section 23 of the EA 2010 requires there to be 'no material difference' between the circumstances relating to each case in the comparison. This means that, in general, the comparison under section 19(2)(b) should be between groups of men and groups of women in the same material circumstances.

**2.102**  For many years, the test for indirect discrimination under the SDA 1975 required a claimant to show that a 'requirement or condition' was such that the proportion of women who could comply with it was considerably smaller than the proportion of men who could comply with it. The wording of this test required claimants to identify a 'pool' of people within which the requirement or condition would be applied, and then produce statistical evidence to show that the proportion of women within the pool who could comply with the requirement was considerably smaller than the proportion of men.

**2.103**  The wording of section 19(2)(b) of the EA 2010 is broader than the previous test under the SDA 1975, and does not necessarily require such a precise statistical comparison. However, because section 23 requires a comparison of groups in the same material circumstances, it will still be necessary to identify the appropriate pool within which the comparison must be made, save in the case of PCPs which obviously place one sex at a disadvantage when compared with the other (see the discussion of this point in connection with part-time working in Chapter 7 at **7.98–7.101**). Furthermore, the clearest way in which to demonstrate that a particular PCP places women, or men as the case may be, at a particular disadvantage, will often be by producing statistics which support that contention.

**2.104** Clear guidance on identifying the appropriate 'pool' in an indirect discrimination case has proved frustratingly difficult to come by over the years. The higher courts have not as yet set out any universal formula showing how to conduct this process. What follows is only the author's view on a potential way through the various, often apparently contradictory, decisions.

**2.105** The recent trend in the case-law on 'pools', decided under the various pre-EA 2010 statutes, but likely still to be considered binding under the new legislation, appears to stem from the speech of Baroness Hale of Richmond in *Rutherford v Secretary of State for Trade and Industry (No 2)*.[90] Rutherford was an unusual case, in which the claimants argued that the upper age limit for unfair dismissal claims (at the time 65 years of age) was indirectly discriminatory against men. Against that background, the majority of the House of Lords held that the correct pool to test the proposition was the workforce aged over 65. As the statutory bar applied to everyone over 65, there could be no disparate impact on men.

**2.106** In reaching this conclusion, Baroness Hale held that the pool in an indirect discrimination claim should consist only of people who want a particular benefit, or not to suffer a particular disadvantage, and will be differentially affected by a criterion applicable to that benefit or disadvantage. She went on to say that indirect discrimination cannot be shown by bringing into the equation people who have no interest in the advantage or disadvantage in question.

**2.107** This approach can work well in claims involving national provisions which apply to the whole country, or alternatively where there is a clearly defined existing workforce, all of whom are affected, or could potentially be affected, by a particular PCP. Two case examples can be used to illustrate this.

*Case Examples*

Where it was claimed that the requirement for employees to have more than two years' service at 16 hours or more per week in order to bring a claim for unfair dismissal was indirectly discriminatory on grounds of sex, the appropriate pool in which to consider the disparate impact of the rule was the entire workforce. As all employees have an interest in having a remedy available to them if they are unfairly dismissed, they should all be included in the pool.

*R v Secretary of State for Employment ex p. Seymour Smith and Perez (No. 2)*[91]

C, a female single parent who had childcare responsibilities, complained that a new rostering system, under which she was required to work longer hours during the day, indirectly discriminated against women. The Tribunal took the view that the pool for comparison consisted only of single parent train operators. The EAT disagreed. It held that the pool must comprise all who are affected by the PCP, not

---

[90] [2006] UKHL 19; [2006] ICR 785.
[91] [2000] 1 ICR 244.

an arbitrary sub-set of those employees. Thus the ET should have considered a pool containing all train operators who were subject to the new rostering agreements.

*London Underground v Edwards*[92]

**2.108**   However, the danger of Baroness Hale's guidance, if applied too rigidly in all situations, is that it can lead tribunals to define the pool by reference to the very characteristic which gives rise to the disadvantage.

**2.109**   This point can be illustrated by reference to two cases. In *British Medical Association v Chaudhary*,[93] the PCP relied upon was the BMA's refusal to support race discrimination claims against the various medical regulatory bodies. The claimant contended that this was indirectly discriminatory against BMA members of Asian origin. The Court of Appeal defined the pool as consisting of all BMA members who wanted the advice and support of the BMA for race discrimination claims against the specific medical regulatory bodies. No members of that pool could obtain the BMA's support for their claims, so there was no disparate impact on any social group.

**2.110**   Sedley LJ commented in *British Airways plc v Grundy*[94] that there was an argument that the proper pool in *Chaudhary* consisted of members seeking support for any kind of legal claim. Had that pool been used, it might have been concluded that failure to support race discrimination claims had a disparate impact on Asian members.[95] In the author's view, the pool advanced by Sedley LJ is more appropriate than that applied by the Court of Appeal. A pool consisting only of members who wish to bring race discrimination claims is defined by reference to the characteristic giving rise to the disadvantage. A pool consisting of those who want legal support for their claims covers only those who want a particular benefit, but is also sufficiently wide to test the discriminatory impact of the challenged PCP.

**2.111**   *Chaudhary* was an unusual and difficult case, but the problems that may be thrown up by too strict an adherence to Baroness Hale's guidance can also be seen in connection with the more common flexible working scenario that arose for decision in *Hacking & Paterson and Hacking & Paterson Management Services Ltd v Wilson*.[96] It was the employer's practice to refuse any request made by its property managers for flexible working. The claimant argued that this practice was indirectly discriminatory against women. Lady Smith, sitting alone in the Scottish EAT, held that she was bound by *Rutherford* to conclude that the appropriate pool to test the discriminatory impact of the employer's refusal was limited to those property managers who wanted the benefit of flexible working. She then went on to conclude that this did not mean that the claimant's claim should be struck out, because within that pool it was not

[92]   [1995] 1 ICR 574.
[93]   [2007] EWCA Civ 788; [2007] IRLR 800.
[94]   [2008] EWCA Civ 875; [2008] IRLR 815.
[95]   [2007 EWCA Civ 1020; [2008] IRLR 74 at para 30.
[96]   UKEATS/0054/09/BI, 27 May 2010.

necessarily the case that 'all would have suffered what can properly be characterised as a disadvantage, or that the disadvantage to them would necessarily have been the same'.

**2.112** This approach gives rise to a number of difficulties. How can a claimant establish which of the employer's employees 'want' the benefit of flexible working? How can the tribunal determine (without a great deal of complex factual enquiry) which persons within this difficult-to-ascertain group should or should not be considered to be suffering a 'disadvantage'? Further, the pool chosen is again defined by the characteristic the discriminatory impact of which it is intended to assess.

**2.113** The author suggests that the pool in *Hacking and Paterson* should have consisted of all the employer's property managers. This pool complies with Baroness Hale's guidance in two ways. First, it can be said that the benefit sought by the claimant, along with all other property managers, was to be able to work as a property manager, and the practice of refusing requests for flexible working disadvantaged her in doing so. Secondly, it would be wrong to test the discriminatory impact of a PCP using a pool which will necessarily only exist at one moment in time (ie those employees who want the benefit of flexible working at the time of the claim). In future, other employees may also want that benefit. The best way to test whether the PCP has a discriminatory impact is to consider the proportion of male and female property managers who work flexibly over a period of time.

**2.114** It is also important to note that Baroness Hale's approach works less well in cases where there are unlikely to be any statistics about the pool which has a direct interest in, or is directly affected by, the advantage or disadvantage in question. This is quite understandable, as Baroness Hale was not, in *Rutherford*, dealing with this kind of case. For example, where a job advertisement contains an age criterion, the ideal pool would be all persons who want, and are otherwise qualified for, the job – but it would be impossible to obtain statistics relating to such a group.

**2.115** In such circumstances, the case-law suggests that a looser approach may be taken in determining the appropriate pool.

*Case Example*

Greater Manchester Police had a policy under which they would not generally appoint individuals who were in receipt of an occupational pension. C argued that this was indirectly discriminatory on grounds of sex. He relied on statistics showing the proportion of men and women in receipt of an occupational pension in the economically active population. The employer argued that this pool was not appropriate because it included people who would not otherwise be qualified for the position C had applied for. The EAT held that the pool does not have to be a statistically perfect match of the group which would have been capable of and interested in doing the job. The employer could have provided evidence to show that the statistics relied upon by C distorted the picture which would have been produced using a 'true' pool, but it had not done so.

*Greater Manchester Police Authority v Lea*[97]

**2.116**  Ultimately, the most important point the tribunal has to bear in mind in determining the appropriate pool is that the pool is simply a tool to test whether a particular PCP has a disparate impact on people possessing a protected characteristic. As such, it must not be narrowed by qualifications or conditions which are not logically relevant to the statistical exercise in hand[98] – but nor must it be widened to such a degree that it no longer tests the discriminatory impact of the challenged PCP.

**2.117**  Once the purpose of defining a pool is clear, the pools adopted in most of the leading cases are easy to understand. To take a few examples:

(a)  In *University of Manchester v Jones*,[99] the claimant argued that an advertisement stating a preference for applicants aged 27–35 indirectly discriminated against women. She said that her case should be tested using a pool consisting only of graduates who had obtained their degrees as mature students. The Court of Appeal held that in fact the correct pool was all persons who satisfied the job criteria save for the age requirement. This is clearly correct. All such persons were required to comply with the age limit, not only mature students.

(b)  In *London Underground v Edwards*, referred to above, all of the employees were affected by the new shift pattern and therefore it was correct to test the discriminatory impact of that pattern by looking at a pool containing all employees.

(c)  In *Pike v Somerset County Council*,[100] the claimant complained about a rule under which part-time teaching service ceased to be pensionable where the teacher was already in receipt of a teacher's pension. This rule did not apply to full-time teachers. The Court of Appeal concluded that the logical pool in which to test the impact of this rule consisted of all retired teachers who had returned to teaching. It should not be broadened to include all teachers, as pre-retirement teachers did not have an interest in post-retirement rules.

**2.118**  Once the pool has been ascertained, the tribunal will need to determine whether it can be shown that, within that pool, persons with the protected characteristic are placed at a particular disadvantage.

**2.119**  Assuming these are available, the most straightforward way to do this will generally involve using statistics.

---

[97]  [1990] IRLR 372.
[98]  *Rutherford (No 2)* [2006] ICR 785 per Lord Walker of Gestingthorpe, para 66.
[99]  [1993] 1 ICR 474.
[100]  [2009] EWCA Civ 808; [2010] 1 ICR 46.

**2.120** To take a simple example, a woman brings a claim that a rule recently introduced by her employer to the effect that employees may no longer work part-time is indirectly discriminatory. She can show that, of the employer's 300 employees, 150 are male and 150 are female. 50 of the female employees work part-time. Only two of the male employees work part-time.

**2.121** The female employee could show a particular disadvantage to women in two ways. First, she could point to the fact that only two men are disadvantaged by the new rule, whereas 50 women are so disadvantaged. Secondly, she could express the figures as a percentage. 1.33% of men in the pool are disadvantaged by the criterion. By contrast, 33.33% of the women in the pool are disadvantaged. Alternatively, it can be said that 98.67% of men are able to comply with the employer's new requirement of full-time working, whereas only 66.67% of the female workforce can comply. It is easy to see from any of these analyses that the requirement puts women at a particular disadvantage.

**2.122** In cases where the figures are less obvious, and the gap in the proportions is smaller, there are various ways in which a claim of particular disadvantage might be supported:

(a) A claimant can produce figures showing that the disparate impact, whilst relatively small in percentage terms, has persisted over a long period of time.[101]

(b) Evidence could be obtained from a statistician as to the statistical significance of the gap in the proportions.

(c) In circumstances where the pool is too small to be statistically significant or reliable, claimants may produce national statistics, or rely on the 'common knowledge' of the Tribunal to bolster their position.[102]

**2.123** From the perspective of an employer, it is important not to take allegations of disparate impact at face value. Employers may be able to challenge the pool put forward by a claimant on the basis that it is too narrow (or alternatively too wide), or too small and therefore not representative of the workforce. Arguments based on assumptions about the make-up of the national workforce can be challenged using specific statistics relating to the employer's own enterprise.

*Case Example*

C, a woman who worked as a hospital steward was paid less than comparators who transferred over to her employer, Carillion, on more favourable terms and conditions. In C's hospital wing, there were four male and two female stewards

---

[101] See e g *R v Secretary of State for Employment ex parte Seymour-Smith and Perez (No 2)* [2000] 1 WLR 435.

[102] Contrast the results in *London Underground v Edwards No. 2)* [1999] 1 ICR 494 and *Nelson v Carillion Services Ltd* [2003] EWCA Civ 544; [2003] ICR 1256.

who had transferred over on the more favourable terms and conditions, and C and a male steward who were paid less. C argued that this was the appropriate pool for consideration, and that it demonstrated disparate impact because 80% of the men were on the transferred terms, as opposed to only 66.66% of the women. The Court of Appeal did not accept that C had shown disparate impact, because the pool she relied upon was artificial (in circumstances where 300 workers had transferred over from Carillion), and as the pool was so small, the gap in proportions could be merely fortuitous.

*Nelson v Carillion Services Ltd*[103]

## Does the PCP put, or would it put, the claimant at that particular disadvantage?

**2.124** Under section 19(2)(c) of the EA 2010, the claimant must show that the PCP which places (for example) women at a particular disadvantage also puts, or would put, her at that disadvantage.

**2.125** What will amount to a 'particular disadvantage' is not defined by the EA 2010. The Code of Practice on Employment provides the following guidance as to what might be covered:

'It could include denial of an opportunity or choice, deterrence, rejection or exclusion. The courts have found that "detriment", a similar concept, is something that a reasonable person would complain about – so an unjustified sense of grievance would not qualify. A disadvantage does not have to be quantifiable and the worker does not have to experience actual loss (economic or otherwise). It is enough that the worker can reasonably say that they would have preferred to be treated differently.'[104]

**2.126** The EAT in *Eweida v British Airways Plc*[105] expressed the view that, in order to be placed at a 'particular disadvantage' by a PCP, it is not necessary for a claimant to show that he/she is unable to comply with it. It may be that a claimant can show particular disadvantage even where he/she has complied with the PCP. The example given by the EAT was of a woman who wishes for childcare reasons to work part-time but feels compelled to work full-time, which is a job requirement, because her employer will not consider part-time work and she cannot afford to lose her job.[106]

**2.127** Section 19(2)(c) permits an employee to claim where the PCP puts <u>or</u> <u>would put</u> him/her at a particular disadvantage. This means that a claim may arise even where the claimant has not yet been placed at a particular disadvantage by the PCP complained of, but may be so affected in the future.

---

[103]   See fn 101 above for reference.
[104]   Para 4.9.
[105]   [2009] ICR 303.
[106]   *Eweida*, para 45.

One example might be a challenge to a redundancy policy which is less favourable to part-time than to full-time workers, brought before a redundancy situation arises.

## *Is the PCP a proportionate means of achieving a legitimate aim?*

**2.128**   Under section 19(2)(d) of the EA 2010, if a claimant can show that her employer has applied to her a PCP which he/she would apply equally to men, and which places women, and the claimant, at a particular disadvantage, the burden moves to the employer to show that the PCP is a proportionate means of achieving a legitimate aim.

**2.129**   The phrase 'legitimate aim' is not defined in the EA 2010. Some examples of what may be a legitimate aim in the context of direct age discrimination are provided in article 6 of Directive 2000/78/EC. These include legitimate employment policy, labour market and vocational training objectives. However, the aims accepted as legitimate in the context of sex discrimination in the European and domestic case-law go beyond those set out in article 6.

**2.130**   The Code of Practice on Employment gives the following guidance on the meaning of 'legitimate aim':

> 'The aim of the provision, criterion or practice should be legal, should not be discriminatory in itself, and must represent a real, objective consideration. The health, welfare and safety of individuals may qualify as legitimate aims, provided that risks are clearly specified and supported by evidence.'[107]

**2.131**   The Code goes on to say that reasonable business needs and economic efficiency may also be legitimate aims.[108]

**2.132**   A number of potentially legitimate aims are set out and discussed in Chapter 7 below at **7.110–7.115**.

**2.133**   It is, however, worth noting at this stage that, until recently, there was clear domestic authority to the effect that costs savings <u>alone</u> cannot be a legitimate aim justifying indirect discrimination. Costs savings could be taken into account, in conjunction with other matters, as justification, but could not be the sole aim relied upon by an employer.[109]

**2.134**   Whilst Cross has not explicitly been overruled, the EAT has suggested in two recent cases, *Woodcock v Cumbria Primary Care Trust*,[110] and *Cherfi v G4S Security Services Ltd*,[111] that costs alone should be capable of justifying

---

[107]   Employment Code of Practice, para 4.28.
[108]   Employment Code of Practice, para 4.29.
[109]   *Cross v British Airways Plc* [2005] IRLR 423 at para 72.
[110]   [2011] ICR 143.
[111]   UKEAT/0379/10/DM, 24 May 2011.

indirect discrimination. In both cases, the EAT was able to hold that the aim relied upon by the employers was not simply cost savings (so any further comments were obiter) but went on to say that there was no apparent reason why an employer should not be permitted to justify a PCP on the basis that the cost of avoiding the discriminatory impact occasioned by it would be disproportionately high. Critics suggest that this approach is contrary to the position developed in EU case-law such as *Hill v Revenue Commissioners*.[112] It seems likely that there will be further litigation on this point in the coming years.

**2.135** Identifying the legitimate aim relied upon by an employer is a very important aspect of any indirect discrimination claim. The employer can gain a possibly decisive advantage by defining the 'legitimate aim' on which he/she relies so narrowly that only the particular PCP applied will suffice to achieve it.

> *Case Example*
>
> C, a female police officer, complained that a policy under which other officers who worked a 24/7 rotating shift received a special priority payment was indirectly discriminatory. The employer's argument, accepted by the ET, was that its wish to reward night-time working was a legitimate aim. The Court of Appeal found that the various alternative approaches suggested by C (eg using a scoring matrix that did not single out 24/7 working, or giving priority payments to those who were not able to undertake 24/7 working for childcare reasons) would not achieve the aim relied upon by the employer. The employer was therefore able to justify any discriminatory impact caused by the policy.
>
> *Blackburn and another v Chief Constable of West Midlands Police*[113]

**2.136** There are various ways in which a claimant can challenge this approach, if it is utilised by employers.

(a)   The claimant can argue that the employer has not correctly defined its aim. For example, in *Blackburn*, the claimant could have sought to show that the employer's aim was not in fact rewarding 24/7 working, but providing effective 24/7 coverage. It is possible that the special priority payments would not have been considered a proportionate means of achieving this aim.

(b)   Alternatively, the claimant could argue that the only means of achieving the particular aim have so great a discriminatory impact, that the policy cannot be regarded as proportionate, even if the aim is legitimate.[114]

**2.137** Assuming, then, that the aim is legitimate, how is proportionality assessed?

---

[112]   Case C-243/95; [1995] ICR 48.
[113]   [2008] EWCA Civ 1208; [2009] IRLR 135.
[114]   *Allen v GMB* [2008] EWCA Civ 810; [2008] ICR 1407.

**2.138** The concept of proportionality is rooted in European law. In *Bilka-Kaufhaus GmbH v Weber von Hartz*,[115] the CJEU held that, in order to justify the exclusion of part-time workers from an occupational pension scheme, which was challenged under what was then article 119 of the Treaty of Rome, the employer had to show that the exclusion corresponded to a real need on the part of the undertaking, was appropriate with a view to achieving the objectives pursued, and was necessary to that end.

**2.139** The *Bilka* concept of proportionality has been watered down somewhat in the domestic case-law, such that it is generally accepted that the measure relied upon must be 'reasonably' rather than 'absolutely' necessary to achieve the desired aim.[116] However, it still requires the court to conduct an objective balancing exercise, weighing the justification relied upon against the discriminatory effect of the condition. As Sedley LJ commented in *Allonby v Accrington & Rossendale College and others*:[117]

'Once a finding of a condition having a disparate and adverse impact on women had been made, what was required was at the minimum a critical evaluation of whether the college's reasons demonstrated a real need to dismiss the applicant; if there was such a need, consideration of the seriousness of the disparate impact of the dismissal on women including the applicant; and an evaluation of whether the former were sufficient to outweigh the latter.'

**2.140** Further, it is generally accepted that, if the legitimate aim relied upon by the employer can be achieved through the application of a policy which is less discriminatory than the one in fact adopted, the adoption of the more discriminatory policy will not be proportionate.[118]

**2.141** The Code of Practice on Employment focuses on the latter point in its guidance on the meaning of proportionality:

'Although not defined by the Act, the term "proportionate" is taken from EU Directives and its meaning has been clarified by decisions of the CJEU (formerly the ECJ). EU law views treatment as proportionate if it is an "appropriate and necessary" means of achieving a legitimate aim. But "necessary" does not mean that the provision, criterion or practice is the only possible way of achieving the legitimate aim; it is sufficient that the same aim could not be achieved by less discriminatory means.'[119]

**2.142** Some recent decisions of the EAT demonstrate that employers cannot simply make generalisations about categories of employees or types of working in order to justify rules that have a discriminatory impact. Thus in *MoD v DeBique*,[120] the EAT upheld the tribunal's decision that the MoD, as a

---

[115] [1987] 1 ICR 110.
[116] See eg *Hardys & Hansons v Lax* [2005] EWCA Civ 846; [2005] ICR 1565.
[117] [2001] EWCA Civ 529; [2001] 1 ICR 1189.
[118] See eg *Seldon v Clarkson Wright & Jakes* [2009] IRLR 267 at para 62.
[119] Statutory Code of Practice on Employment, para 4.31.
[120] [2010] IRLR 471.

government department, should not simply have accepted the immigration policy which prevented the claimant's half sister from staying in the country to care for her child, but should have sought a relaxation of that policy or a concession. The EAT in *Pulham v London Borough of Barking and Dagenham*[121] commented that, in order properly to weigh the discriminatory impact of a PCP against the cost of eliminating that impact, the tribunal must be given sufficient information both about the discriminatory impact on the claimants, and about the costs relied upon, and the financial background against which the affordability of those costs falls to be judged.

**2.143** As the 'proportionate means of achieving a legitimate aim' test is objective, it is possible for an employer to argue that its requirements are fulfilled even if the 'legitimate aim' relied upon at trial was not in the employer's mind at the relevant time. However, it may well be more difficult for employers to justify a PCP relying on an aim which was not considered when the PCP was applied.[122] This is particularly so in view of the greater emphasis in the recent cases described above on the need for proper evidence from both sides with which to conduct the balancing exercise. Such evidence is less likely to be available if the employer has not previously considered the aim on which it relies at trial.

**2.144** The following case provides a good example of the 'balancing exercise' in practice.

*Case Example*

C was employed by R, a brewing company which ran a chain of public houses, as a Retail Recruitment Manager (RRM). She wished to return to work part-time after maternity leave. Whilst C was on maternity leave, there was a reorganisation, and the new post of Tenant Support Manager (TSM) was created. This included some parts of the role of RRM, but also provision of training for tenants and involvement in promotions. R refused to allow C to do the TSM job on a part-time basis, and C's employment ended. R raised a number of objections to C's suggestion that the job could have been shared between two employees; in particular that, when trying to allocate tenants to pubs, the TSM would have to interview each candidate, meet the outgoing tenant and remaining staff, and familiarise him/herself with the pub, which would not be possible in a jobshare. R also argued that there was no obvious way to split the workload, and that both jobsharers would have to attend particular meetings, which would involve a duplication of time and effort. The ET concluded that, whilst there were potential difficulties with a jobshare, R had not given proper consideration to the proposition, and the points it raised did not outweigh the serious impact of the refusal on C. The refusal was therefore found to be an act of indirect sex discrimination.

---

[121]  [2010] ICR 333 at para 46.

[122]  See *R (on the application of Elias) v Secretary of State for Defence* [2006] EWCA Civ 1293; [2006] 1 WLR 3213 at para 129 and *British Airways plc v Starmer* [2005] IRLR 862 at para 43.

*Hardys and Hansons v Lax*[123]

## Harassment

**2.145** Harassment is unlikely to be the primary cause of action in most cases involving family rights, but it does provide an additional string to a claimant's bow and, importantly, does not require a comparator in the same way as direct sex discrimination.

**2.146** The EA 2010 provisions as to harassment are contained in section 26, which provides as follows:

'(1) A person (A) harasses another (B) if –
    (a) A engages in unwanted conduct related to a relevant protected characteristic; and
    (b) the conduct has the purpose or effect of:
        (i) violating B's dignity; or
        (ii) creating an intimidating, hostile, degrading, humiliating or offensive environment for B.
(2) A also harasses B if –
    (a) A engages in conduct of a sexual nature, and
    (b) the conduct has the purpose or effect referred to in subsection (1)(b).
(3) A also harasses B if –
    (a) A or another person engages in unwanted conduct of a sexual nature or that is related to gender reassignment or sex,
    (b) the conduct has the purpose or effect referred to in subsection (1)(b), and
    (c) because of B's rejection of or submission to the conduct, A treats B less favourably than A would treat B if B had not rejected or submitted to the conduct.
(4) In deciding whether conduct has the effect referred to in subsection (1)(b), each of the following must be taken into account –
    (a) the perception of B;
    (b) the other circumstances of the case;
    (c) whether it is reasonable for the conduct to have that effect.
(5) The relevant protected characteristics are –
    (a) age;
    (b) disability;
    (c) gender reassignment;
    (d) race;
    (e) religion or belief;
    (f) sex;
    (g) sexual orientation.'

**2.147** The protected characteristic of pregnancy and maternity is omitted from section 26(5). Some commentators have suggested that this omission means that harassment related to pregnancy or maternity is not covered by

---

[123] [2005] EWCA Civ 846; [2005] ICR 1565; see in particular paras 16–17 for the balancing exercise.

section 26.[124] However, in the author's view, it is quite possible that the omission was not intended to lead to this result. The rationale behind the separate section 18 prohibition on pregnancy discrimination must have been that pregnancy and maternity discrimination does not require a comparator, and does not, therefore, fit easily into the direct discrimination provisions of section 13. This argument does not apply in relation to harassment, as section 26 requires only that the relevant conduct be 'related to' sex. This wording quite naturally covers harassment arising from pregnancy and maternity (as all such harassment must be 'related to' sex), and there is therefore no need for any separate prohibition of harassment 'related to' the protected characteristic of pregnancy or maternity.

**2.148** The wording of the Act is, however, ambiguous on this point, and the issue requires legislative or judicial clarification. As matters stand, claimants should plead any conduct that could amount to pregnancy, or maternity-related harassment as harassment under section 26 of the EA 2010, pregnancy discrimination under section 18 (if applicable) and direct pregnancy/maternity and sex discrimination under section 13.

**2.149** This is not the place for an exhaustive consideration of the harassment provisions in the EA 2010. However, the points made below should assist practitioners seeking to rely on section 26 in the context of family rights.

**2.150** Sex-related harassment under section 26 comes in three forms:

(1) unwanted conduct 'related to sex' which has the purpose or effect of violating a person's dignity or creating an intimidating, hostile, degrading, humiliating or offensive environment for them;

(2) unwanted conduct 'of a sexual nature' which has the above purpose or effect;

(3) less favourable treatment of person because they have rejected or submitted to unwanted conduct related to sex or of a sexual nature which had the above purpose or effect.

**2.151** Pre-EA 2010 case-law suggests that 'unwanted conduct' is not limited to conduct to which objection has been taken. Conduct which is obviously detrimental or disadvantageous – even if it only occurs on one occasion – will

---

[124] See Sean Jones 'Equality Act 2010: The Pregnancy Discrimination Mystery' at http://www.employmentcasesupdate.co.uk/site.aspx?i=ed6083. The argument continues that harassment on the grounds of pregnancy or maternity could be the subject of a direct discrimination claim under s 13, subject to the as-yet-unresolved question of whether s 13 covers direct pregnancy and maternity discrimination (in relation to which, see **2.56–2.65** above). Whilst EA 2010, s 212 defines detriment such as to exclude harassment, s 212(5) provides that, where the Act disapplies a prohibition on harassment in relation to a specified protected characteristic, conduct relating to that characteristic may nevertheless amount to a detriment within EA 2010, s 13.

be covered regardless of whether the claimant has objected to it.[125] Further, the fact that the claimant has 'put up with' the conduct, by remaining in the employment, or even accepting or initiating conversations of a sexual nature to try to head off the more unpleasant excesses of her employer does not necessarily mean that the conduct will not be regarded as 'unwanted'.[126] In the author's view, as long as the conduct is in fact unwanted by the claimant, the statutory wording suggests that it should be held to be 'unwanted conduct' within the meaning of section 26, although the authorities do not, at present, go so far.

**2.152** The Code of Practice on Employment gives as examples of unwanted conduct: spoken or written words or abuse, imagery, graffiti, physical gestures, facial expressions, mimicry, jokes, pranks, acts affecting a person's surroundings or other physical behaviour. In the author's view, 'unwanted conduct' is also broad enough to cover actions taken by an employer affecting a worker's conditions or status, such as a demotion, or a removal of certain tasks.[127]

**2.153** The unwanted conduct must have the purpose or effect set out in section 26(1)(b): it must violate the claimant's dignity, or create an intimidating, hostile, degrading, humiliating or offensive environment for him/her. If the conduct can be shown to have this purpose, no further inquiry is necessary. If the effect of the conduct is relied upon, the tribunal must take into account the matters set out at section 26(4) in determining whether the conduct should be regarded as having the relevant effect. These matters include both a subjective question (the perception of the worker) and objective issues (the other circumstances of the case, and whether it is reasonable for the conduct to have that effect). This enables tribunals to take the view that a hypersensitive claimant who takes offence unreasonably should not succeed, but also to take into consideration other circumstances which may explain and justify the hypersensitivity.

**2.154** Conduct 'related to sex' is broadly defined. The Code of Practice on Employment states that it will cover any conduct connected to a protected characteristic, whether or not the employee bringing the complaint has that characteristic. This means that a person who is subjected to unwanted conduct because he or she is associated with a person with a protected characteristic, or perceived to have a protected characteristic, or is in the vicinity of a person who is abused because they have a protected characteristic, can claim harassment.[128]

**2.155** Subject to the discussion at **2.147–2.148** above, unwanted conduct connected to:

---

[125]  See *Reed and Bull v Steadman* [1999] IRLR 299 and *Driskel v Peninsula Business Services Ltd* [2000] IRLR 151.

[126]  *Kamarzyn v Munchkins Restaurant Ltd*, (2010) UKEAT/0359/09/LA, 28 January 2010.

[127]  Para 7.7.

[128]  See the Code of Practice on Employment at paras 7.9–7.11.

(a)    a woman's pregnancy (whether meted out to the woman herself, or to her partner or any other person associated with her); or

(b)    the fact that a woman is undergoing IVF treatment;[129] or

(c)    the paternity of a woman's child,

could be covered by section 26 of the EA 2010.

> *Case Example*
>
> Following a party at work, at which C was widely understood to have had sexual intercourse with a male colleague who was not her partner, C's colleagues became aware that she was pregnant. There was office gossip about the paternity of C's child (the father was, in fact, C's partner). C was upset and embarrassed by the gossip. The ET rejected C's claim for harassment on the basis that the comments made might have been indiscreet in a minor way, but there was nothing in the conduct which could possibly be regarded as intimidating, hostile, degrading and humiliating. The EAT held that it had been wrong to do so. The gossip was connected with pregnancy, had caused C 'discomfort' and constituted a course of unwanted conduct, meeting the definition of harassment.
>
> *Nixon v Ross Coates Solicitors and another*[130]

**2.156** 'Conduct of a sexual nature' is said in the Code of Practice on Employment to cover verbal, non-verbal or physical conduct, including unwelcome sexual advances, touching, forms of sexual assault, sexual jokes, displaying pornographic photographs or drawings, or sending emails with materials of a sexual nature.[131]

**2.157** Unlike the other forms of harassment connected with sex, the prohibition under section 26(1)(c) of less favourable treatment caused arising from a worker's rejection of or submission to unwanted conduct of the type defined in section 26(1)(a) and (b) does require a comparator. However, the comparator will not be a person of a different sex, but the victim of the harassment him or herself, assuming, hypothetically, that he/she had not rejected or submitted to the harassment.

**2.158** Examples of the type of situation likely to be covered by this subsection given in the Code of Practice on Employment include that of a female worker who is turned down for promotion because she rejects her boss's unwanted sexual advances, whether by her boss himself, or by a more senior individual who is friendly with her boss.[132]

---

[129]    See *Sahota v Home Office and another* [2010] ICR 772, where the claim failed because the words used could not reasonably be considered to have the required effect; see para 20.

[130]    UKEAT/0108/10/ZT, 6 August 2010. It is arguable that in using the word 'discomfort' the EAT set the bar for the required purpose or effect of the conduct rather lower than it is set in the statute.

[131]    Code of Practice on Employment, para 7.13.

[132]    Code of Practice on Employment, paras 7.14 and 7.15.

**2.159**  In the family rights context, section 26(1)(c) may be apt to cover the situation arising when a relationship breaks down, and the unwilling former partner is subjected to a detriment because he or she does not wish to continue the relationship. Prior to the advent of the new harassment provisions in the SDA 1975, this factual scenario was difficult to fit into the discrimination law matrix; see *Emokpae v Chamberlin Solicitors and another*.[133]

## Victimisation

**2.160**  Section 27 of the EA 2010 makes it unlawful to subject a person to a detriment because he/she has done, or is believed to have done, a protected act. The following acts have protected status under section 27:

(a)  bringing proceedings under the EA 2010;

(b)  giving evidence of information in connection with proceedings under the EA 2010;

(c)  doing any other thing for the purposes of or in connection with the EA 2010;

(d)  making an allegation (whether or not express) that a person has contravened the EA 2010.

**2.161**  Regulation 8 of the Equality Act 2010 (Commencement No 4 etc.) Order 2010 provides that references in section 27 to actions done under or by reference to the EA 2010 also cover the same actions done under or by reference to the pre-existing discrimination statutes.

**2.162**  Section 27, unlike its predecessor in the SDA 1975, does not require the tribunal to undertake any comparative exercise. It simply has to consider the reason why the claimant was subjected to a detriment. If the reason, or part of the reason, is that he/she has done a protected act, section 27 will apply.

*Case Example*

C brought a claim of sex discrimination against her employer arising from a failure to inform or consult with her on developments and job opportunities in her department during her maternity leave. She claimed that her employer had subsequently victimised her by issuing a counter-claim seeking to recoup her maternity pay, in circumstances where other women who had left employment after maternity leave, without doing a protected act, had not been pursued for their maternity pay. Both the ET and the EAT upheld her claim for victimisation.

*Visa International Service Association v Paul*[134]

---

[133]  [2005] ICR 931.
[134]  [2004] IRLR 42.

## Equal pay

**2.163** The general provisions as to equal pay contained in the EA 2010 fall outside the scope of this book. However, the EA 2010 also provides a certain level of pay protection for women on maternity leave.

**2.164** Sections 73 and 74 of the EA 2010 provide that a maternity equality clause will apply to modify a woman's contract in the following situations.

(a)   Where, had the woman not been on maternity leave, she would have received a pay increase. In such circumstances, the maternity equality clause will ensure that any contractual maternity pay to which she is entitled reflects that pay increase.[135]

(b)   Where, had the woman not been on maternity leave, she would have received:

(i)    pay or bonus in respect of periods prior to her maternity leave; or
(ii)   bonus in respect of her period of compulsory maternity leave; or
(iii)  bonus in respect of times after the end of the protected period (ie, in most cases, after the end of ordinary or additional maternity leave).
In such circumstances, the maternity equality clause will ensure that the pay or bonus is received by the woman on the date on which it would have been received had she not been on maternity leave.[136]

(c)   Where, had the woman not taken maternity leave, she would have received a pay increase after the end of the protected period. In such circumstances, the maternity equality clause will ensure that the woman is entitled to the same pay increase as she would have received had she not taken maternity leave.[137]

**2.165** Unlike the situation in a normal equal pay claim, there is no requirement for an actual male comparator in order to succeed under these provisions.

**2.166** Section 75 of the EA 2010 provides that a maternity equality rule applies in order to protect the rights of members of occupational pension schemes who take maternity leave. In brief, the section ensures that women are not treated differently by the trustees of the pension scheme because they are or have been on maternity leave, save that there may be modifications to the amount a woman is required to contribute whilst on maternity leave.

**2.167** Section 76(2) of the EA 2010 provides that a woman may not make a complaint under the relevant pregnancy and maternity provision (ie section 18 and section 39(2) for an employee) in relation to any term of her work that

---

[135]  Section 74(1)–(5) EA 2010.
[136]  Sections 74(6) and (7).
[137]  Section 74(8).

relates to pay, but in relation to which a maternity equality clause or rule has no effect. This prevents women on maternity leave from attempting to claim equal pay with comparators who are not on maternity leave.

# Chapter 3

# PREGNANCY-RELATED RIGHTS

*Sally Robertson*

## HEALTH AND SAFETY AT WORK DURING PREGNANCY

### Introduction

**3.1**    Pregnancy is not an illness. It does, however, give rise to vulnerability, to both the woman and the child. As such, the health and safety and other needs of pregnant workers and workers who have recently given birth or who are breastfeeding are given special protection through the Pregnant Workers Directive, 92/85/EEC, and legislation made under that Directive. This Chapter looks at the specific safeguards under the Management of Health and Safety at Work Regulations 1999, SI 1999/3242 (MHSWR 1999) and the Employment Rights Act 1996 (ERA 1996), as well as more general healthcare benefits available to pregnant women and those who have given birth in the past 12 months.

**3.2**    The protected special status of pregnant workers starts from conception. For health and safety purposes, that protection continues for six months from the birth, or for as long as she is still breastfeeding.[1] If the baby was born alive at any stage of pregnancy, or was stillborn after 24 weeks of pregnancy, this protection also applies. For other purposes, the special protection ends at variable times, precisely when depending on the woman's particular circumstances.[2] Once outside that protected period, the standard protection against discrimination applies – see Chapter 2.

**3.3**    An employer's responsibilities are not restricted to employees, pregnant or otherwise. The presence of any woman of child-bearing age working in the undertaking is sufficient to trigger a risk assessment under the Management of Health and Safety at Work Regulations 1999, regs 3(1) and 16(1). An employer is responsible for taking appropriate preventative action to remove or reduce the risk. That duty applies irrespective of employment status: the key trigger is

---

[1]    Management of Health and Safety at Work Regulations 1999, SI 1999/3242, reg 1(2).

[2]    The protection under the Maternity and Parental Leave etc Regulations 1999, SI 1999/3312, regs 6 and 7, continues until the end of additional maternity leave. Depending on the timing of the end of ordinary maternity leave, additional maternity leave could end 52 weeks after the birth. MPLR, reg 2(1) gives a different definition of 'childbirth', suggesting that being born alive triggers the protection only if the live birth was after 24 weeks. The Equality Act 2010, s 18(6), limits the protected period in relation to a pregnancy to the woman's return to work if that is earlier than the end of her additional maternity leave.

that the risks to the health and safety of a new or expectant, or breastfeeding mother must arise out of or in connection with the conduct of the undertaking.[3] Additionally, from 1 October 2011, to put the position beyond doubt, amendments to the MHSWR provide specific protection for agency workers.[4] Additional duties, specific to the individual worker's needs arise once she has told her employer and, if she is an agency worker, the hirer and the agency.

## Healthcare benefits

**3.4**    Pregnant women, whether working or not, are entitled as of right to two NHS healthcare benefits: prescriptions and dental treatment.

**3.5**    NHS prescriptions are free during pregnancy and during the 12 months after the birth. The woman will need to apply for a maternity exemption certificate on Form FW8, which she can get from her doctor, midwife or health visitor. She completes part of the form; the healthcare professional then signs it to confirm that her information is correct. The completed form FW8 should be sent to

> NHS Help with Health Costs
> Maternity Exemption
> Newcastle upon Tyne
> NE2 1BF

**3.6**    She will also be entitled to free dental treatment for any course of treatment that starts when she is pregnant, as well as for courses of treatment that start during the year after the baby is born. She just needs to tell the dentist she qualifies. To show entitlement to free dental treatment, she can use her maternity exemption certificate.

**3.7**    Exemption certificates are valid during the month before the application is received. Until the exemption certificate arrives, she will need to apply for refunds: on the official NHS receipt form FP57 (for prescriptions) or FP64 (for dental treatment).

**3.8**    If the baby is born early, she will continue to be entitled to free prescriptions until the certificate expires. If the baby is born late, she will need to apply for an extension.

## Ante-natal care

**3.9**    Under the ERA 1996 pregnant employees are entitled to paid time off during working hours for ante-natal care.[5] The entitlement to paid time off covers the entire time of the appointment, including travel and waiting time. If

---

3    MHSWR, reg 3(1)(b).
4    MHSWR, regs 16A, 17A, 18A, 18AB.
5    Employment Rights Act 1996 (ERA 996), ss 55, 56.

she gives a time estimate, that is simply being helpful and is not conclusive. If the waiting or travel time take longer than expected, the employer should pay in full. There is no legal requirement to try and avoid appointments during working hours.

**3.10** From 1 October 2011, agency workers who have completed the qualifying period of doing some work in the same role for a hirer in each of 12 consecutive calendar weeks have the same rights.[6] Time spent by an agency worker working during an assignment before 1 October 2011 does not count towards the qualifying period, so agency workers in practice will not be legally entitled to paid time off for antenatal care until 24 December 2011.[7] The definition of 'qualifying period' is complex. Completing the qualifying period is a continuous requirement, with detailed rules linking separate spells in the same role, and for some purposes treating the requirement as satisfied. See **3.26–3.40** for more information.

**3.11** The right to paid time off for antenatal care is triggered by the advice of a registered doctor, midwife or nurse to seek an appointment in order to receive antenatal care.[8] Such advice will be specific to the needs of each individual: certain factors or health conditions may result in a need for additional care.[9]

**3.12** The worker does not have to produce any proof that she is pregnant, nor that an antenatal appointment has been made, in order to be entitled to time off to attend the first appointment during her pregnancy for which she asks to take time off.[10]

**3.13** It is only for her second and subsequent requests that an employer, agency or hirer can ask her to produce for inspection a certificate from a healthcare professional stating that she is pregnant and an appointment card or some other document to show the appointment has been made.

**3.14** Asking for such proof is optional, but once it has been requested, the worker will not be entitled to time off until she has complied with the request.[11] Although there is no requirement that the request be in writing, nor that a record be kept of the worker's compliance, it is sensible to do both.

---

[6]  ERA 1996, ss 57ZA to 57ZD, Agency Workers Regulations 2010, SI 2010/93, reg 7. Note that it makes no difference if the worker has been supplied by different agencies. What counts is that she has worked some hours in the same job for the same hirer for each of 12 consecutive calendar weeks.

[7]  Agency Workers Regulations 2010, reg 7(12).

[8]  ERA 1996, s 55(1), s 57ZA(1).

[9]  These are listed in the NICE guideline *Antenatal care CG62,* at Appendix C.

[10]  ERA 1996, s 55(3), s 57ZA(3).

[11]  ERA 1996, s 55(2), s 57ZA(2). Note that for the first two or three appointments (including the first booking appointment) the certificate is unlikely to be on a MATB1 form as that is not issued more than 20 weeks before the week the baby is expected, ie it is issued only around the 21st week of pregnancy. The Health and Safety Executive has suggested that a Med 3 certificate, now a 'fit note', may be used instead.

**3.15**   Antenatal care is not defined but anything within the scope of the NICE guidelines *Routine antenatal care for healthy pregnant women*[12] should be covered. That includes antenatal classes and also includes relaxation and parent craft classes where these have been recommended specifically and certainly where such appointments have been included on an appointment card or the recommendation has been confirmed in writing by a healthcare professional.

**3.16**   A man has no legal right to accompany a partner to antenatal appointments. However, the Government is keen to encourage employers to let expectant fathers take off time to attend antenatal appointments without losing pay. The recommendations are set out in *Fathers-to-be and antenatal appointments: a good practice guide.* This is available from the Department for Business Innovation and Skills.[13]

## *Payment*

**3.17**   A worker who is permitted to take time off for antenatal care is also entitled to be paid for the period of her absence from work at the appropriate hourly rate.[14]

**3.18**   Where the normal working hours are fixed, the hourly rate is one week's pay divided by the number of normal working hours.

**3.19**   However, if her normal working hours are variable, section 56(3) of the ERA 1996 sets out the steps to follow. The hourly rate for both employees and agency workers is worked out by dividing a week's pay by the average of the normal working hours over the past 12 weeks. Add up all the normal working hours during the 12 weeks before the week in which she takes time off and divide that sum by 12 to reach the average. This calculation is based on 'normal working hours', not on how many of those 'normal working hours' were actually worked. Time away from what would otherwise have been normal working hours should not affect the calculation.[15]

**3.20**   Where an employee has been employed for less than 12 weeks, section 56(4) gives the employer flexibility to calculate a sum that fairly represents what her average would be likely to be over a normal 12 week period at that time of year. There is no need for an equivalent provision for an agency worker as she is entitled to paid time off for antenatal care only once she has completed the 12 week qualifying period.

---

[12]   National Institute for Health and Clinical Excellence, clinical guideline 62, March 2008, revised June 2010, available from www.nice.org.uk/guidance.
[13]   Download the guide from http://www.bis.gov.uk/files/file20795.pdf.
[14]   ERA 1996, s 56, s 57ZB.
[15]   Thus if an agency worker has been away from her work assignment, for example on jury service, that should not reduce her normal working hours. Instead, base the calculation on what would have been her normal working pattern during the 12 weeks before the week in which she takes time off.

## Complaining to an employment tribunal

**3.21** An employee has the right to complain to an employment tribunal that her employer has 'unreasonably' refused to permit her to take time off, or has failed to pay all or any part of the payment to which she was entitled.[16]

**3.22** Once an employer has agreed to permit time off, entitlement to pay follows. If an employer wants to challenge the reasonableness of any particular antenatal appointment, the only feasible method is to refuse to permit that time off. For example, if a woman was offered a choice of appointments, some being outside working hours but had chosen to make appointments during her working hours, that would be a factor an employment tribunal would take into account. But it may not be conclusive. A tribunal should take account of all relevant factors, which will vary depending on an individual's circumstances. Other relevant factors could be the effect of travelling by public transport during peak times; having to pay for extra childcare, perhaps at overtime rates; and whether it is reasonable to have to take an older child, or children, to the particular appointment.

**3.23** An agency worker has the right to complain to an employment tribunal that either her temporary work agency or the hirer (or both) have unreasonably refused to permit her to take time off. A complaint of failure to pay can be made against a temporary work agency only.[17]

**3.24** The claim must reach the tribunal within three months of the date of the appointment concerned. For example, if the appointment was on 1 April, the claim should be with the tribunal no later than 30 June. If a claim is late, the tribunal may consider that complaint if satisfied that it was not reasonably practicable for the complaint to have been presented within the first three months and that it has been presented within a reasonable period thereafter.

**3.25** A tribunal is limited in the remedies it can give under the ERA 1996. It may make a declaration that a complaint is well-founded. If the employer or agency had unreasonably refused to permit time off, a tribunal can award the amount of pay the worker should have been paid and can apportion the sum between agency and hirer.[18] For cases of underpayment or non-payment, a tribunal can award the amount it finds due. However, employers should not be sanguine about their duties. Claims of direct pregnancy and maternity discrimination under section 18(2)(a) of the Equality Act 2010 should be anticipated – see Chapter 2.

---

[16] ERA 1996, s 57. For more detailed information, go to the employment tribunals website at http://www.justice.gov.uk/guidance/courts-and-tribunals/tribunals/employment/index.htm – use the menu options on the left of the screen. The menu across the top of the screen accesses the main Justice website.

[17] ERA 1996, s 57ZC.

[18] ERA 1996, s 57ZC(6).

## Agency workers

### *The qualifying period*

**3.26**   All agency workers have the right to equal treatment in relation to access to collective facilities and amenities provided by the hirer from the first day of any assignment. This includes equal access to collective facilities such as a workplace crèche or a mother and baby room.[19] Indeed, the Workplace (Health, Safety and Welfare) Regulations 1992, reg 25(4)[20] requires 'suitable facilities for any person at work who is a pregnant woman or nursing mother to rest.'

**3.27**   The qualifying period which triggers equal rights for agency workers is defined in the Agency Workers Regulations 2010, reg 7. A worker must have worked in the same role for the same hirer for 12 continuous calendar weeks. It makes no difference if she was placed in that role by two or more different agencies on different assignments. The default position is that the role is treated as the same one unless the agency or hirer prove that the work or duties that make up all or the main part of the new role are 'substantively different' from those that made up the previous role.[21] The hirer has to notify the agency in writing detailing the new job requirements. The agency in turn must give the worker written details about the new role. If it is a new role, it would be sensible for the agency to tell the worker that their qualifying period has re-started.

**3.28**   Time cannot start to run before 1 October 2011. Time starts on or after 1 October 2011, or from the first day of the assignment if that is later. If she starts work on a Monday, the first calendar week ends on the next Sunday. So long as she does some work for a particular hirer in a week, that week will always count towards satisfying or continuing to satisfy the qualifying period in relation to that hirer. A worker may have more than one qualifying period on the go or building up: each for a different role or hirer.

**3.29**   If she misses a week or more of work, or has a break between assignments, that does not necessarily mean that she must start the qualifying period all over again.

### *Treated as present*

**3.30**   Some breaks are treated as if she had been present throughout the period of absence. These are:

(a)   Where she had begun work on an assignment and is then unable to continue, if the reason for her absence is related to pregnancy, childbirth or maternity, including taking any type of maternity leave. It must also be at a time during the protected period. This means that she does not lose

---

[19]   AWR 2010, reg 12.
[20]   SI 1992/3004.
[21]   AWR 2010, reg 7(3). Note that promotion to a role higher in the management hierarchy may well require re-serving the qualifying period.

her protected status as an agency worker if she is off work for a pregnancy or maternity related reason at any time from conception to 26 weeks after the birth, or to when she returns to work if that is earlier. This protection lasts for as long as the original intended duration of the assignment. Where the assignment was not fixed, the protection lasts for its likely duration, if that is longer.[22]

(b) Where she had begun work but for health and safety reasons is not allowed to continue working in that role.[23] She is treated as being present in the original role for as long as the assignment was intended or is likely to last, if that is longer. This means she will also be paid at the original rate, whether or not the agency have found suitable alternative work for her with the same or with a different hirer. This also means that she can keep two qualifying periods going: the first with the original hirer and a second with the hirer for the suitable alternative job.

*Linking different spells at work*

**3.31** Other types of absence are ignored when considering whether a worker has worked in the same role for the same hirer for 12 continuous weeks. Unlike absences related to pregnancy, childbirth or maternity, these breaks do not count towards satisfying, or continuing to satisfy, the qualifying period. Instead, they are treated as interruptions that are overlooked and so do not require the worker having to start the 12 weeks, qualifying period all over again. These are:

(a) a break of six calendar weeks or less for any reason at all;[24]

(b) a break of no more than 28 weeks off sick. If the sickness is during the protected period and is related to pregnancy, childbirth or maternity, the Agency Workers Regulations 2010, (AWR 2010) reg 7(6) applies, or continues to apply, instead;[25]

(c) a break of no more than 28 weeks on jury service;[26]

(d) a break of any length to take contractual or statutory leave to which the worker is entitled (for example, annual leave);[27]

(e) a break caused by a regular and planned shutdown of the workplace by the hirer (for example, a Summer or Christmas break);[28]

---

[22]  AWR 2010, reg 7(6). Note a worker is also treated as present if he or she is taking any type of adoption leave or paternity leave.
[23]  AWR 2010, reg 7(7). See **3.45–3.49**.
[24]  AWR 2010, reg 7(8)(a).
[25]  AWR 2010, reg 7(8)(b) and (9). The worker must produce written medical evidence that is reasonably required if the agency requests.
[26]  AWR 2010, reg 7(8)(e).
[27]  AWR 2010, reg 7(8)(d).
[28]  AWR 2010, reg 7(8)(f).

(f)    a break caused by a strike, lock out or other industrial action at the hirer's undertaking.[29]

**3.32**  These breaks may themselves be linked together in whatever combination is most helpful to the worker. They may also be linked to breaks in which she is treated as present. For example, after the birth a worker could have 26 weeks on maternity leave, followed by taking two weeks accrued annual leave, followed by six weeks off for any reason at all. She could then go on jury service for 28 weeks. On her return to the same role for the same hirer she does not have to re-serve the qualifying period. There is no rule linking different spells of sickness: each break is treated separately.

**3.33**  If separate spells of work in the same role for the same hirer are not linked as outlined above, the worker must re-serve the 12 week qualifying period in relation to that role. For example, if she has 28 weeks and one day of continuous sickness, that breaks the continuity of her qualifying period. She has to re-serve it. However, continuity is not broken where each break is covered by the linking rules, for example, if she has three separate spells of 28 weeks of sickness during work in the same role for the same hirer.

*Anti-avoidance*

**3.34**  Anti-avoidance provisions are intended to catch arrangements that have been designed to avoid workers gaining the protection from having served the qualifying period. In addition, there is the anti-discrimination protection found in the Equality Act 2010. For example, it would be pregnancy and maternity discrimination to refuse to place or to accept a worker in a particular role because she is pregnant. Other refusals could amount to disability discrimination. See Chapters 2 and 9.

**3.35**  The anti-avoidance provisions are found in the Agency Workers Regulations 2010, reg 9. If they apply, a worker is treated as continuing to satisfy the qualifying period, or to have served the 12 weeks from the date she would have qualified but for the artificial structuring of the assignments. Additionally, an employment tribunal may also award up to £5,000 compensation.[30]

**3.36**  The way the assignments have been arranged must make it seem that the 'most likely explanation' for the structure is that it is 'intended' to prevent the worker gaining the protection of the Agency Worker Regulations.[31]

**3.37**  The core condition for triggering anti-avoidance provisions is that the worker has completed at least two assignments with the same hirer or with hirers connected to the original one (for example, rotating between companies in the same group).

---

[29]    AWR 2010, reg 7(8)(g).
[30]    AWR 2010, reg 18(14).
[31]    AWR 2010, reg 9(4).

**3.38** The anti-avoidance provisions are also triggered where a worker has stayed in the same assignment but has been shifted at least twice between roles that are substantively different.

**3.39** BIS guidance[32] to hirers and agencies suggests that the following factors might indicate that a pattern of assignments was deliberately structured so as to deprive the worker of rights to equal treatment:

(a)   the number of assignments;

(b)   the length of assignments;

(c)   the number of role changes;

(d)   whether the role changes were substantively different;

(e)   the length of break periods.

**3.40** Other relevant factors to take into account would be the effect of knowledge of the pregnancy or disability or of any other status that would be protected under the Regulations. Having a good reason for the structure is unlikely to be sufficient. Whatever the reason for the particular structure, it must be good enough to show that it really is the 'most likely explanation' for the arrangements. What is the 'most likely explanation' can change over time. If the structure was in fact deliberately intended to avoid the Regulations, avoidance would always be the 'most likely explanation', however reasonable the arrangements might otherwise seem.

## Risk assessments

**3.41** Fleshing out the general duty to protect the health and safety of all workers 'so far as is reasonably practicable'[33], the Management of Health and Safety at Work Regulations 1999 (MHSWR) include a duty to carry out risk assessments and take preventive action.

The standard duty is found in MHSWR, reg 3(1). Every employer must make a 'suitable and sufficient assessment' of:

(a)   the risks to the health and safety of his employees to which they are exposed whilst they are at work; and

(b)   the risks to the health and safety of persons not in his employment arising out of or in connection with the conduct by him of his undertaking,

---

[32]   Agency Workers Regulations: Guidance May 2011, available from http://www.bis.gov.uk.
[33]   Health and Safety at Work Act 1974, s 2(1).

for the purpose of identifying the measures he needs to take to comply with the requirements and prohibitions imposed upon him by or under the relevant statutory provisions.

**3.42**  Preventive and protective measures to address the risks identified must be in accordance with the general principles found in MHSWR, Sch 1. These include:

(a)  avoiding risks;

(b)  evaluating the risks that cannot be avoided;

(c)  combating the risks at source;

(d)  adapting the work to the individual;

(e)  adapting to technical progress;

(f)  replacing the dangerous by the non-dangerous or the less dangerous;

(g)  developing a coherent overall prevention policy which covers technology, organisation of work, working conditions, social relationships and the influence of factors relating to the working environment;

(h)  giving appropriate instructions to employees.

**3.43**  As part of this standard assessment, the presence of a single woman of childbearing age is sufficient to trigger a focused assessment of the general risks to which any pregnant woman, or a new or breastfeeding mother, would be exposed to by the work environment.[34] Until a risk materialises, or until a woman is pregnant, there is no requirement to prevent the risk or to remove a woman from the risk. Indeed, it would be sex discrimination to prevent a woman from doing particular work just because she might be at risk if she got pregnant. In all cases there is a need to balance the nature and incidence of the risk with the steps taken to remove or reduce the risk to its lowest possible level. If the action taken is disproportionate to the risk, it is likely to be less favourable treatment on grounds of sex or of pregnancy.[35]

**3.44**  For pregnant women, new and breastfeeding mothers, it is only once they have told their employer in writing of their status that additional specific duties are triggered.

**3.45**  Where a specific risk is identified, the employer or hirer must alter the working conditions or hours of work if it is 'reasonable to do so' and the

---

[34]  MHSWR 1999, reg 16.
[35]  See, eg, *New Southern Railway v Quinn* [2006] IRLR 266, EAT.

change would avoid that risk.[36] If the change means that she does not perform the work she 'normally performed' beforehand, that counts as a suspension on maternity grounds.[37] She is entitled to her normal remuneration.[38]

**3.46** If the change is not reasonable, or would not avoid the risk, then the employer must offer her any available suitable alternative work on the same terms and conditions, including the same pay.

**3.47** If that is not possible, or the woman refuses the alternative work, the employer must suspend the woman from work. If no suitable alternative work is available, the suspension must be on full pay for as long as it is necessary to avoid the risk.[39] If there is suitable alternative work and the employer shows that her refusal to perform it is unreasonable, she is not entitled to pay during the suspension.

**3.48** Unlike the position with an ordinary medical suspension, there is no minimum period of employment required before a woman becomes entitled to remuneration during suspension on maternity grounds. However, although the supply of an agency worker to a hirer may end on maternity grounds, the right to remuneration and to the offer of suitable alternative work depends on having served the qualifying period – see **3.26–3.40**.

**3.49** If the woman is an agency worker who has served the qualifying period, the provisions are in substance equivalent to an employee's rights.

## Health and Safety Executive

**3.50** The Health and Safety Executive (HSE) has issued guidance on the known risks associated with pregnancy or maternity and how employers can comply with their legal obligations. The HSE may prosecute an employer for failure to carry out its obligations. Such failures, including failure to carry out an individual risk assessment where the duty has been triggered, may be sex discrimination (see Chapter 2).[40]

## General assessment

**3.51** The presence of one woman of child-bearing age working in a work place is sufficient to trigger the duty to carry out a general assessment of the risks to women who are pregnant, breastfeeding or are new mothers. All workers should be provided with comprehensible and relevant information about the risks identified by that assessment.[41]

---

[36]  MHSWR 1999, regs 16, 16A.
[37]  ERA 1996, s 66(3)(b).
[38]  ERA 1996, s 68.
[39]  MHSWR 1999, reg 16(3), ERA 1996, ss 67, 68.
[40]  *Hardman v Mallon* [2002] IRLR 516, EAT; *O'Neill v Buckinghamshire County Council* [2010] IRLR 384, EAT.
[41]  MHSWR 1999, regs 10(1), 12.

**3.52**   There are two key conditions for triggering the general duty. First, is the nature of the risk being guarded against. This is the risk to the health and safety of any new or expectant mother because of her condition, or the risk to the health and safety of any unborn or breast feeding baby. Secondly, the work itself must be of a kind that could involve such risks whether they arise from any work processes or working conditions or from physical, biological or chemical agents.[42] If the work could involve that kind of risk, an assessment of it must be included within the standard risk assessment under MHSWR, reg 3(1). In *O'Neill v Buckinghamshire County Council*,[43] the EAT held that on the evidence before the tribunal there was no requirement under MHSWR, reg 16 to risk-assess disciplinary proceedings as these 'could not' amount to a work process or working conditions falling within the scope of reg 16. However, that approach is not obviously consistent with the approach taken in disability cases to making reasonable adjustments, where adjustments to disciplinary procedures are common. It would accordingly be sensible for an employer to take a broad view.

## *Specific assessment*

**3.53**   If an employee or agency worker notifies the employer or hirer and agency in writing that she is pregnant, has given birth within the previous six months, or is breastfeeding, the assessment must also assess any health and safety risk to that specific individual. However, an employer is entitled to request, in writing, confirmation of her status. It is only once that notification is received that this specific duty can be triggered.

**3.54**   In the case of pregnancy, an employer or hirer is entitled to inspect a certificate from a doctor or midwife confirming the pregnancy. Health professionals are advised to record their advice in the remarks section on the Med 3 fit note about any work adjustments required during pregnancy.[44]

**3.55**   The duty ends if the employer or hirer knows that the worker is no longer a new or expectant mother. Sometimes this will be straightforward, for example, if it has been six months since the birth and there was no notification of breast feeding. If, however, the employer or hirer cannot establish that the worker still counts as a 'new or expectant mother', the duty may be avoided. A simple letter confirming that breast feeding continues should be sufficient proof.

**3.56**   Once triggered, this specific duty is an on-going one and the situation should be regularly monitored and reviewed. Once the duty is triggered, a failure to carry out a risk assessment constitutes sex discrimination.[45]

---

[42]   MHSWR 1999, reg 16(1)(b). A non-exhaustive list of examples of such agents is specified in annexes to the Pregnant Workers Directive 92/85/EEC.

[43]   [2010] IRLR 384.

[44]   MHSWR 1999, regs 18, 18A.

[45]   *Hardman v Mallon* [2002] IRLR 516, EAT.

*Steps in the process*

**3.57**  If it is possible to remove the risk, it should be removed.

**3.58**  If it is not possible to remove the risk, the next step is to consider whether it would be avoided by a change in working conditions or hours of work. If so, and it is reasonable to change the working conditions or hours, the employer or hirer should do so. Remuneration should stay the same.[46]

**3.59**  If the risk cannot be avoided by changing working conditions or hours, the position is different depending on whether the woman is an employee or agency worker.

**3.60**  For employees, the employer must consider whether or not there is any suitable alternative work available. If such work is available it must be offered to the woman before she is suspended on maternity grounds.

**3.61**  For an agency worker in this situation, her supply to the hirer would end on maternity grounds.[47] However, if the agency has suitable alternative work available, the worker has a right to be proposed for that alternative work. Her remuneration must stay the same.[48] This applies for as long as the previous assignment was intended or is likely to last. It can end sooner but only if she confirms in writing that she no longer requires the work-finding services of the temporary work agency.[49]

**3.62**  In both cases, to count as 'suitable', the work must be of a kind which is both suitable in relation to her and appropriate for her to do in the circumstances. The terms and conditions must not be 'substantially' less favourable than her normal terms and conditions. Minor or trivial differences do not count.

**3.63**  If suitable work is available and offered as an alternative to a suspension on maternity grounds (for employees) or after her supply as an agency worker has been ended on maternity grounds, but the worker refuses the alternative offered, she remains entitled to pay unless the employer or agency can show that her refusal was 'unreasonable'.

## *Complaining to an employment tribunal*

**3.64**  An employee has the right to complain to an employment tribunal that her employer has:

(a)  failed to pay her any part or all of the remuneration she is entitled to under section 64 or section 68 of the ERA 1996;

---

[46]  ERA 1996, s 66(3)(b). There is no equivalent provision for agency workers.
[47]  MHSWR 1999, regs 16A(2), 17A.
[48]  ERA 1996, ss 68B, 68C, 69A(4).
[49]  ERA 1996, s 68B(3)(a).

(b)  failed to offer to provide her with work, contrary to section 67 of the ERA 1996.[50]

**3.65**  An agency worker has the right to complain to an employment tribunal that the temporary work agency has:

(a)  failed to pay her any part or all of the remuneration she is entitled to under section 68C of the ERA 1996;

(b)  failed to propose her to a hirer that has suitable work availably, contrary to section 68B of the ERA 1996.[51]

**3.66**  A claim must reach the tribunal within three months. The time limit starts on the date on which the employer failed to pay her remuneration or on the first day of the suspension. In agency cases, time starts on the day on which the worker's supply to the hirer was ended on maternity grounds.

**3.67**  If a claim is late, a tribunal may consider it if satisfied that it was not reasonably practicable for it to have been presented within the first three months and that it has been presented within a reasonable period thereafter. For example, missing the time limit because of ignorance could make it 'not reasonably practicable' to claim in time if, say she had not realised that a change in the work she 'normally performed' counts as a suspension on maternity grounds.

**3.68**  Where a tribunal finds in favour of a worker, it will award any shortfall in remuneration but has greater flexibility in awarding compensation for a failure to offer suitable work. The amount must be 'just and equitable' looking at both any loss sustained because of that failure and the nature of the infringement.

## Night work

**3.69**  If a new or expectant mother works at night and a health professional certifies that it is necessary for her health and safety that she should avoid night work, or avoid particular hours during the night, the employer must suspend her from that work for as long as is necessary for her health and safety.[52] In practice, an employer must offer any suitable alternative work that is available before a woman can be suspended on maternity grounds. If no such work is available, or a woman's refusal of an offer is not unreasonable, she will be entitled to remuneration on the basis of the night work position.

The position for an agency worker who has served the qualifying period is in substance equivalent to that of an employee – see **3.45–3.49**.

---

[50]  ERA 1996, s 70(1), (4).
[51]  ERA 1996, s 70A(1), (4).
[52]  MHSWR 1999, reg 17.

## *Birth and compulsory leave*

**3.70**  Section 205 of the Public Health Act 1936 makes it a criminal offence to permit a woman who is entitled to ordinary maternity leave to work during the compulsory maternity leave period. For a standard workplace, this is the two weeks starting from the date of birth. For a workplace that is a factory within the meaning of the Factories Act 1961, the exclusion is for the four weeks starting from the date of birth. Section 175 of the Factories Act defines 'factory' broadly. It includes, for example abattoirs and dry docks. The fine upon conviction is currently only a maximum of £200.

## Abbreviations

**3.71**  ERA – Employment Rights Act 1996

AWR – Agency Workers Regulations 2010, SI 2010/93

MHSWR – Management of Health and Safety at Work Regulations 1999, SI 1999/3242

MPLR – Maternity and Parental Leave etc Regulations 1999, SI 1999/3312

# Chapter 4

# MATERNITY LEAVE

*Sally Cowen*

## INTRODUCTION

**4.1**    The current law on maternity leave is more generous to employees and more straightforward than it was when maternity leave was first introduced in 1975. However, many of the provisions have, over the intervening years, been complex, onerous and difficult for both employer and employee to follow. The main provisions on the right to take maternity leave are found in sections 71–75 of the Employment Rights Act 1996 (ERA) (as amended). These have been supplemented by various regulations over the years, to add detail to the way in which these rights and obligations should be performed.

**4.2**    In 1999 the Maternity and Parental Leave Regulations ('the MAPLE Regulations')[1] came into force, setting out the rights and obligations of employees in connection with maternity and parental leave. These were amended in 2008 by the MPL Amendment Regulations,[2] which tended in particular to reduce the differences between Ordinary Maternity Leave (OML) and Additional Maternity Leave (AML). In 2002, the rights available to parents were extended by the Paternity and Adoption Leave (Amendment) Regulations.[3] The most recent changes in the Work and Families Act 2006 and the Maternity and Paternity Leave (Amendment) Regulations 2008 ('the 2008 Amendment Regulations') have simplified the system for everyone.

**4.3**    The UK government takes the view that all UK legislation on maternity leave now conforms to the EU Pregnant Workers Directive (92/85/EEC), although in the authors' view, there are areas in which this view may be inaccurate.

**4.4**    There is currently some debate within Europe as to whether the rights of pregnant women should be enhanced further. In March 2010, the Women's Rights and Gender Equality Committee of the European Parliament put forward a proposal to amend the Pregnant Workers' Directive. The proposed amendments would provide greater rights to leave and pay during maternity. Although they were passed by the European Parliament in October 2010, the revised Directive was blocked by the Council of Ministers and has been

---

[1]    SI 1999/3312.
[2]    SI 2008/1966.
[3]    SI 2002/2788.

returned to the European Commission for further consideration. The UK Government is not supportive of the improvements and has said that it considers that many employers would find it difficult to manage 20 weeks of fully paid maternity leave (amongst other proposals). It should be noted that SMP is paid by the State and not by the individual employer.

## WHO HAS THE RIGHT TO MATERNITY LEAVE?

### Qualification

**4.5**    Any employee who gives birth has the right to 26 weeks of Ordinary Maternity Leave ('OML') followed by 26 weeks of Additional Maternity Leave ('AML'): a total of 52 weeks of leave from her job.[4]

**4.6**    The reason that it is referred to as two separate periods of 26 weeks, is that despite reforms in the 2008 Amendment Regulations, there are still some differences in entitlement to pay, pensions and return to work depending on whether OML or AML is taken.

**4.7**    There is no requirement to have worked a qualifying period before being entitled to this leave. Thus, an employee who starts new employment when pregnant will be entitled to take the full 52 weeks of leave. This applies to both temporary and permanent employees. Furthermore, there is no obligation on the employee to remain in the job for a set period of time after her return from maternity leave.

**4.8**    Surrogate mothers are entitled to maternity leave, even if the child is handed over immediately after birth. Similarly mothers who give up their child for adoption are entitled to maternity leave, as the birth mother.

**4.9**    The recipient mother in a surrogate birth will not be entitled to maternity leave or adoption leave, but may be entitled to parental leave (if she has sufficient qualifying continuity of employment). It is possible that if no leave is granted, there may be scope for a disability discrimination claim, but such a claim will not necessarily succeed.

*Case Example*

The claimant, who was employed in a school, suffered from a congenital heart disorder, meaning that pregnancy would endanger her life. As a result, she had a child by a surrogate mother. Her employers refused to grant her paid post-natal leave because the school budget was in deficit. She was granted unpaid leave. She brought a claim of disability-related discrimination and failure to make reasonable adjustments under the Disability Discrimination Act 1995. These claims were dismissed by the ET and EAT on the basis that the refusal to grant paid leave was justified, because it would have had a serious effect on the school's precarious financial position. The Court of Appeal upheld this decision.

---

[4]    MAPLE, reg 7.

*Murphy v Slough Borough Council and another*[5]

**4.10** Mothers of multiple births are entitled to the same maternity leave provisions as those with single births. There is some prospect of change in this regard, as the Pregnant Workers Directive indicates that leave should be increased for each additional child. However, this Directive has not been approved by the European Parliament and therefore it is unknown whether this will happen in the future or not.

**4.11** If an employee takes another form of leave (parental leave, annual leave etc) and wishes to halt that leave and commence maternity leave, the employer should allow her to do so. *Kiiski v Tampereen Kaupunki*[6] is a Finnish case where the employer would not allow an employee to stop her parental leave to start maternity leave. This was held to be a breach of Articles 8 and 11 of the Pregnant Workers Directive and discriminatory under the Equal Treatment Directive.

**4.12** Under UK law, OML and AML are not available to workers (rather than employees) and the self-employed. The definition of 'employee' is that found in section 230 of the Employment Rights Act 1996.

**4.13** In the recent case of *Danosa v LKB Lizings SIA*,[7] the Court of Justice of the European Union (CJEU) held that a member of a capital company's Board of Directors, who provided services to that company and was an integral part of it, had to be regarded as having the status of worker under the Pregnant Workers Directive if she carried out that activity, for some time, under the direction or supervision of another body of that company, and received remuneration for her services.

**4.14** The claimant in *Danosa* itself would probably be classified, on the facts in the judgment, as an employee in UK law, and would thus qualify for these benefits in the UK. However, the general definition of 'worker' in EU law, which covers any person who performs services for and under the direction of another person, in return for which he or she receives remuneration, appears to be broader than the definition of 'employee' in UK law. It is therefore arguable that the limitation of entitlement to maternity leave to 'employees' as defined in the ERA 1996, is in breach of European law (see further Chapter 2, above).

**4.15** This issue may fall to be considered in the light of the new EU Directive on equal treatment for self-employed workers (Dir 2010/41/EU). Its terms must be transposed into domestic law by 5 August 2012. It sets a minimum of 14 weeks' maternity leave for the self-employed and demands a state-funded maternity allowance. The UK Government have not yet announced how they

---

[5]  [2005] EWCA Civ 122; [2005] ICR 721.
[6]  [2008] CMLR 67, ECJ.
[7]  Case no. C-232/09, [2011] 2 CMLR 45.

propose to ensure that these provisions are included in our law. It is possible
that no alteration will be required to cover the pay provisions (see Chapter 6,
below).

**4.16**  Although not covered by section 230 of the ERA or by the MAPLE
Regulations, Crown employees and Parliamentary staff have equal maternity
rights under sections 191(2)(c), 194(2)(e) and 195(2)(e) of the ERA 1996.
Women in the armed forces and police, have similar provisions in their
statutory conditions, but are not covered by the MAPLE Regulations. Share
fisherwomen are excluded, but those who work on ships registered in a port in
Great Britain, whose contract of employment states that they do not work
wholly outside Great Britain and whom are normally resident in Great Britain,
will be included.[8]

**4.17**  Members of the clergy of the Church of England became entitled to
paid maternity, paternity, parental and adoption leave from 1 January 2011.[9]
There are some additional obligations on the woman in these circumstances,
such as endeavouring to find a replacement for the duties of the office during
the period of maternity leave.[10] Clergy of other denominations and faiths are
not covered by the 2010 Directions. They will be reliant on the evolving
case-law on the employment status of the clergy, which has in recent years
moved towards the position that (at least some) clergy of varying
denominations may be employees.[11] As it has also been held that the clergy may
fall within the wider definition of employee in the Sex Discrimination Act[12] it is
also possible that non-Church of England clergy may be able to bring a claim
of race or religious discrimination if they are not afforded maternity rights.

## Notification

**4.18**  All employees may be entitled to OML and AML, but they must follow
the correct procedure in order to be allowed the time off work and to accrue
the statutory rights which accompany the time off. A failure to do so may mean
that they do not receive the time off as OML and AML. The requirements
under MAPLE, regulation 4(1) are far less stringent than previous maternity
leave provisions.

**4.19**  In order to obtain time off as OML and AML, the employee must notify
the employer as follows:

(a)  By no later than the end of the 15th week before Expected Week of
      Childbirth ('EWC'), or as soon as reasonably practicable.

---

[8]   ERA 1996, s 191.
[9]   Para 2 of the Ecclesiastical Offices (Terms of Service) Directions 2010, SI 2010/1923.
[10]  Para 2(2) of the 2010 Directions.
[11]  See e g *New Testament Church of God v Stewart* [2007] EWCA Civ 1004; [2008] ICR 282 and
      *Moore v President of the Methodist Conference* [2011] ICR 819.
[12]  *Percy v Church of Scotland Board of National Mission* [2005] UKHL 73; [2006] 2 AC 28.

(b)   The employee must tell her employer:

    (i)    that she is pregnant;
    (ii)   the date of her EWC;
    (iii)  the date she intends to start OML.[13]

(c)   The start of OML cannot be earlier than the 11th week before the EWC.[14]

**4.20**   The EWC starts at midnight on the Saturday night of the week in which the date of confinement is predicted.[15] The calculation of the date required for notification is best counted backwards from the Saturday immediately before the expected date of confinement.

**4.21**   The employer may ask for details of these points in writing.[16] The best advice to women giving notice would be to ensure that it is given in writing, so that they can prove when the notification was given. A MATB1 form can be obtained from a medical professional to prove the pregnancy and the EWC date, if there is any uncertainty. The MAPLE Regulations do not state the form of the written confirmation, so it may be possible that something less than a MATB1 certificate would suffice (eg a card from a midwife[17]), although this is the certificate required for the purposes of statutory maternity pay and therefore is the usual format.

**4.22**   There is no time limit stipulated for complying with the employer's request for written confirmation of these details. It may be possible to give the written confirmation at any time before, or even possibly after, starting the maternity leave.

**4.23**   If the employee fails to give notice, she may not be entitled to start her OML on the day that she intended. If notice cannot be given at the appropriate time, it must be given as soon as reasonably practicable. If the employee is undecided when to start OML she is best advised to notify a date, with the possibility of changing her mind later, as employees may vary the date up to 28 days before the original or new date (whichever is the earlier), or even later, if this is not reasonably practicable.[18] Uncertainty does not stop it being reasonably practicable to notify.[19]

**4.24**   A failure to give notice may lead to an 'unauthorised absence', although this is not a phrase which was included in the regulations and indeed there is no definition of what type of leave the employee will be deemed to have taken if no proper notice is given.

---

[13]   MAPLE, reg 4(1)(a).
[14]   MAPLE, reg 4(2)(b).
[15]   MAPLE, reg 2.
[16]   MAPLE, reg 4(2)(a).
[17]   *Eagles v Cadman t/a Baby Days* ET Case No 20154/82.
[18]   MAPLE, reg 4(1A).
[19]   *Nu-Swift International Ltd v Mallinson* [1978] IRLR 537, ICR 157, EAT.

**4.25**   The employment contract does not end due to such a lack of notice, unless the employee has resigned or is dismissed. However, it is highly likely that if an employee were to be dismissed for taking maternity leave without proper notice, this would be automatically unfair under section 99 of the ERA and reg 20(3), as the principal reason would be pregnancy, childbirth, or the fact that she sought to take maternity leave. It may also give rise to an action for discrimination under the Equality Act 2010.

**4.26**   An employer in that situation is best advised to overlook this procedural irregularity and allow the maternity leave in any event. To do otherwise is to leave himself open to criticism and claims.

## *Exceptions to the rules on notification*

### *If the child is born early*

**4.27**   If the child is born before notice is given, then there is no need to notify the employer of the intention to take leave.[20] The OML will automatically start on the day of the birth of the child.[21] The same will apply if the child is stillborn after 24 weeks of pregnancy (there is no right to leave if the child is stillborn or terminated before 24 weeks). The employee must notify the employer of the birth as soon as reasonably practicable after the birth. If she does not comply with this, she may lose the right to OML.[22]

**4.28**   The loss of the right to leave if notification is not given appears to be somewhat draconian and is left over from the early maternity leave provisions, which were very strict on the giving of notice and the timing of it. It is difficult to see how an employer would not be sympathetic in such a situation. Any employer who took a strict view on unauthorised absence in such a situation could face a discrimination claim from the employee.

### *Childbirth before OML*

**4.29**   Where the employee gives birth after notice of the intention to take leave has been given, but before OML has started, then OML automatically starts on the day after the child is born.[23] The employee must notify the employer as soon as reasonably practical that her absence from work was due to childbirth.[24]

**4.30**   Take as an example Emma, a secretary who intends to work until two weeks before her EWC. She goes into labour at 6pm on Wednesday evening three weeks before the EWC, and the baby is born at 11.55pm that night. She must contact her employer as soon as possible to explain her absence and her

---

[20]   MAPLE, reg 4(4)(a).
[21]   MAPLE, reg 6(2).
[22]   MAPLE, reg 4(4)(b).
[23]   MAPLE, reg 6(2).
[24]   MAPLE, reg 4(4)(b).

OML will commence. If she does not do this, then she may lose the right to OML, which may mean that she is not paid, or has to take the days as holiday until the date of her notified OML.

*In the last four weeks before the EWC*

**4.31** If the employee is absent during the last four weeks before the date she has notified as the start of her OML, for a reason which is wholly or partly due to pregnancy or childbirth (ie told to rest at home due to high blood pressure), then OML automatically begins on the day after her first day of absence.[25] As soon as is reasonably practicable, the employee must tell the employer that the reason for her absence is pregnancy-related. If she fails to do this, it can result in the loss of the OML right.[26] In practical terms a medical certificate, or even self-certification (if within a week of starting OML), will be sufficient to satisfy the notification requirement. If there is any question over whether the absence is 'wholly or partly because of pregnancy' then a medical certificate would provide a reliable answer.

**4.32** This would cover the situation where Emma goes into labour on a Wednesday at 6pm, but does not actually give birth until Thursday at 10am. She must tell her employer that she is absent because she is in labour (obviously pregnancy/childbirth related) as soon as reasonably practicable. This may not be until after the baby is born.

**4.33** This is one of the provisions that would be affected by the proposed new Pregnant Workers Directive. It seeks to ensure that any time taken off sick in the four weeks immediately prior to confinement should not be deducted from the overall maternity leave period. However, the proposed Directive has not yet become law and it is not clear whether it ever will.

**4.34** The reason for this provision was to stop employees taking extended periods of sick-leave prior to childbirth, in order to stave-off starting OML. However, where the employee has a short illness within the four weeks prior to the start date of OML and wishes to return to work, she may find that her OML and her statutory maternity pay ('SMP') have commenced. If she then continues to work up to the date she originally notified as her starting date, she may lose that period of time as OML and that SMP.

**4.35** In a situation where Emma suffers a urinary infection three weeks prior to the date she had chosen as the start of her OML, the MAPLE Regulations state that this would trigger her OML and SMP. If Emma returns to work after three days off and her employer does not tell her that her OML and SMP have started, then it may be possible to argue on behalf of Emma that the employer has waived the triggering provisions, although regulation 6(1)(b) appears to be in mandatory terms.

---

[25] MAPLE, reg 6(1)(b).
[26] MAPLE, reg 4(3)(b).

**4.36** An alternative view of that situation is that as the OML has commenced, Emma must give eight weeks' notice of her wish to return to work. This would effectively take her beyond her EWC and therefore there is nothing she can do to return to work before her OML starts.

**4.37** If Emma has contractual rights with regard to maternity leave then she can take advantage of whichever of the contractual or statutory right is of greater advantage to her. MAPLE regulation 21 refers to this as a 'composite right'. Emma's employer can offer not to allow the automatic trigger of the statutory right to apply and hence she would not lose any maternity leave or SMP. Neither the employer, nor Emma, can insist on this as it must be a contractual agreement, even if only proposed and agreed as the situation arises.

**4.38** It must be borne in mind that the same 'composite rights' do not apply to the rules on SMP and so the parties cannot agree to delay the starting of SMP. It too will automatically start if there is pregnancy-related illness absence in the four weeks leading up to the OML. If Emma returns to work, even for one day, she may lose a whole week of SMP. See Chapter 6 for further details.

**4.39** Another view is that the MAPLE Regulations and section 71 of the ERA provide for OML (as well as AML under section 73) as a protected period during which the employee has the right not to attend work. Therefore the employee can choose whether to attend work or not during OML (and AML).

**4.40** If the employee resigns or is dismissed prior to the start of the notified OML, or prior to giving the notification, then she loses the right to maternity leave. Employees should be careful to give notice of pregnancy and OML in order to keep their options open. The right to SMP is separate and considered in detail in Chapter 6.

## Notification requirements of the employer

**4.41** The employer is obliged to tell the employee within 28 days of her notice being given of the date on which he calculates that she will return to work (ie the end of AML).[27] If the employer fails to do this, he loses the right to complain if the employee chooses to return early or late. Employers would be advised to give this notice in writing, although there is no requirement to do so.

**4.42** Each time the employee changes the date notified as the start of her OML, the employer must respond with a change to the end date. This notification need not be provided until 28 days after the employee's OML commences.[28] Thus, in the above example, if Emma notifies him of the early birth of her child and OML starts automatically, the employer must still respond to her with the recalculated date for return. If he fails to do so, Emma could return on the original (later) date and the employer would not be able to

---

[27] MAPLE, reg 7(6) and 7(7).
[28] MAPLE, reg 7(7)(b).

take action against her. Any detriment she suffers if she returns too late would be unlawful[29] and any dismissal would be automatically unfair.[30]

**4.43** In *Sethi v Greentech International Ltd*[31] the employer was late in notifying the employee of the expected date of return. No breach of the MAPLE Regulations was found, but it was held that the assumption by the employer that it would not be 'appropriate' for the employee to return amounted to a breach of trust and confidence which justified constructive dismissal.

## WHAT LEAVE CAN BE TAKEN?

**4.44** OML (Ordinary Maternity Leave) is 26 weeks long. The employee can nominate a date to commence OML any time after the 11th week before EWC, subject to the notification provisions outlined above. Compulsory maternity leave is the first two weeks following childbirth and is part of the ordinary maternity leave period.[32] This starts on the day the child is born (and therefore will not tie in with OML if it is triggered by the birth of the child, as this starts the day after childbirth).

**4.45** AML (Additional Maternity Leave) is also up to 26 weeks long and starts on the day following the last day of OML.[33] The employee need not take the whole 26 weeks if she does not wish to do so, but must comply with the notification provisions in order to return 'early'. Thus, if Emma wishes to take nine months of maternity leave, she must notify her employer of the day on which she intends to start her maternity leave. The employer will then notify her of the date he expects her to return (which will be 52 weeks later). Emma will then notify her employer that she intends to return after 39 weeks. This notification must be given more than eight weeks before the date on which she intends to return.[34]

**4.46** Emma may subsequently vary the date of her return, as long as she provides at least eight weeks' notice of the new date (if it is earlier than the original date), or, if the proposed date is later than the original date, as long as she provides at least eight weeks' notice ending with the original date.[35]

**4.47** If no such notice is given, an employer does not have to allow the employee to return, either until the eight weeks have passed, or the AML has finished (whichever is the sooner).[36] Alongside this, the employee has no right to be paid until the date specified by the employer as her return date.

---

[29]  MAPLE, reg 19.
[30]  MAPLE, reg 20.
[31]  ET Case 1900752/07.
[32]  ERA 1996, s 72; MAPLE, reg 8.
[33]  MAPLE, reg 6(3).
[34]  MAPLE, reg 11(1).
[35]  MAPLE, reg 11(2A).
[36]  MAPLE, reg 11(2)(3).

**4.48**   The same provisions on returning early to work will apply if the reason for the early return is in order to allow her partner to take additional paternity leave. This new provision is addressed separately under the Chapter on parental rights.

**4.49**   A further reason why an employee may wish to return to work early is because she is pregnant again. If so, she must apply in the way outlined above. There is no obligation on the employee to disclose the fact that she is pregnant, in order to avoid any discrimination. If the employee returns to work, even for one day between two periods of maternity leave, she will be entitled to return to her own job after her second period of OML.

**4.50**   There would appear to be nothing to stop Emma from notifiying her employer of her intention to return after 39 weeks of leave at the point where she notifies the start date. However, the procedure appears to adopt the more piecemeal approach to notification by both sides.

**4.51**   There is no official requirement for either party to specify to the other when OML ends and when AML starts.

**4.52**   Women who hold more than one job are entitled to take maternity leave from all their employment. They do not have to return to each job at the same time. So Emma could return to one job earlier than the other.

## THE CONTRACT OF EMPLOYMENT DURING MATERNITY LEAVE

### Continuing employment

**4.53**   During maternity leave the employee's contract of employment continues to run.[37] She continues to accrue continuous employment and is entitled to the benefit of her terms and conditions with the exception of those in respect of remuneration.[38] This may include matters which are not express terms of her contract. Equally, she remains bound by all the obligations (privacy, copyright, goodwill etc) of her contract, except those which contradict the taking of maternity leave (ie obligation to attend and work). There is a large body of case-law with regard to the different aspects of the employee's contract which may be protected during maternity leave.

**4.54**   Details of the effect of maternity leave on pay and other benefits are set out in Chapter 6.

---

[37]   ERA 1996, ss 71(4) and 73(4).
[38]   ERA 1996, ss 71(5) and 73(5).

**4.55** Continuous employment accrues during maternity leave[39] and any benefit which is calculated on the basis of length of service should also count the period of maternity leave as valid and eligible (as though the employee were not absent from work).

## Annual leave

**4.56** Annual leave which accrues over the course of the year will continue to accrue throughout the period of maternity leave.[40] This commonly leads to employees adding their accrued and untaken holiday to their maternity leave (either at the beginning or end of the leave). If paid holiday is taken during maternity leave, an employee would have to comply with the notice provisions to end her maternity leave and would then be expected to return to work after the end of the holiday. It makes little sense to do this, unless the employee chooses to shorten her maternity leave and take holiday instead, in order to receive full pay for a greater period of time.

**4.57** UK law states that leave must be taken in the year in which it accrues. However, ECJ decisions in cases such as *Federatie Nederlandse Vakbeweging v Netherlands State*[41] state that there is nothing to preclude the holiday being carried over and that it should not be 'lost'. Employers may be best advised to allow an employee who is on maternity leave for the whole 52 weeks of a leave year, to carry her accrued holiday into the next holiday year, or possibly even take it prior to her maternity leave.

## Bonus and commission

**4.58** Bonuses and commissions which are contractual are likely to be considered as part of 'remuneration' and therefore not payable during OML or AML. However, such payments which are referable to periods prior to or post-maternity leave, or to times when the woman is on compulsory maternity leave, are payable, as to fail to do so would be to act in breach of the equal pay provisions in the Equality Act.[42]

**4.59** The entitlement to a discretionary bonus which accrues when on a period of maternity leave, is not as clear cut. It was considered in *GUS Home Shopping v Green and McLaughlin*,[43] where a bonus was not paid due to non-attendance at work. In that case the non-attendance was related to pregnancy and so a successful claim was brought as discrimination. This decision applies the principles in *Webb v EMO Cargo*, which were subsequently considered in

---

[39] ERA 1996, s 212(1).
[40] *Merino Gómez v Continental Industrias del Caucho SA* [2005] ICR 1040 (ECJ).
[41] [2006] ICR 962 (ECJ).
[42] Equality Act 2010, s 74(6) and (7).
[43] [2001] IRLR 75, EAT.

*Lewen v Denda*[44] where it was held that these principles do not extend to pay and bonus terms. Therefore it is unlikely that *GUS Home Shopping* would now be followed.

**4.60**   The issue is also addressed in paragraph 17 of Schedule 9 of the Equality Act which provides at (1) that there is no protection from discrimination in respect of pay. This is clarified in (2) and (5) as not including maternity pay, pay when not on maternity leave, or bonus paid during CML, which would therefore be protected.

**4.61**   It is likely therefore that claims under section 18 of the Equality Act will be possible where a discretionary bonus has been pro-rated to take into account periods that have been worked, or periods of CML. Further, a bonus which is of a goodwill nature and not related to contract and not forming part of wages/salary would be similarly actionable, if not paid.

**4.62**   It is also arguable that the same principle as set out in *Gillespie v Northern Health and Social Services Board*[45] and *Alabaster v Woolwich plc and Secretary of State for Social Security*[46] (cases on pay rise and calculation of pay during maternity leave) ought to be applied to the issue of discretionary bonus.

## Appraisals and pay reviews

**4.63**   If the employee is due to have a pay review or appraisal (which will affect her pay) during OML or AML, this must be carried out. A failure to do so may be discrimination and/or breach of contract; see *CNAVTS v Thibault*,[47] where the employee was refused a performance assessment due to maternity leave and sick leave. The ECJ held that depriving the employee an assessment which may lead to a promotion, was discrimination.

**4.64**   Employers should be advised to carry out appraisals either before the employee goes on maternity leave, or when she returns, but that any pay review should be backdated, so that she does not suffer any detriment. If productivity is a criterion, then an average should be taken during a period which did not include maternity leave. If there is Trade Union representation in the workplace, it may be in the interests of all parties if an agreed procedure can be followed in such circumstances.

## Notice period/pay

**4.65**   An employee's right to contractual notice remains during her maternity leave. If either the employer or the employee decides to end the employment, the usual terms will apply. The amount that she is entitled to receive in pay during this period is not protected, as the rights to terms and conditions during

[44]   [2000] IRLR 67, ECJ.
[45]   [1996] IRLR 214, ECJ.
[46]   [2004] IRLR 486.
[47]   [1999] 1 CMLR 692; [1998] IRLR 399 (EC).

maternity leave do not cover remuneration. Therefore her entitlement to pay may be less than if she were attending work.

**4.66** The entitlement to statutory notice pay remains during maternity leave. An employee who is given (or gives) notice whilst on maternity leave will be entitled to her full salary during that notice period, where the period of contractual notice due by the employer is no more than one week more than the statutory notice period.[48] This applies regardless of whether it is the employee or employer who gives the notice. Where the contractual notice is more than a week more than statutory notice, then only SMP or contractual maternity pay will be paid for the full period of notice.[49] On that basis a senior executive with a long period of notice, will be paid less for a longer period of time than the more junior employee who is entitled only to statutory notice, but who will receive their full pay during that period.

## Keeping in touch

**4.67** The amended MAPLE Regulations make it clear that 'reasonable contact' between the employer and employee is allowed, without bringing the maternity leave to an end.[50]

**4.68** The employee is also allowed to work for up to ten days during the maternity leave, without brining it to an end. These are known as Keeping In Touch (KIT) days.[51] Even a part-day's work counts as a whole number.[52] Training or away days count as work days.[53] Neither side is obliged to offer or to work during maternity leave.[54] These days are not to be added to the maternity leave period.[55] There is no obligation to pay for these days, but likewise it is not precluded. HMRC have given guidance on the payment of pension contributions to those on unpaid AML who are paid for KIT days. No employee is allowed to work during the first two weeks after childbirth – this is the compulsory maternity leave period.[56]

# RIGHT TO RETURN

**4.69** The right to return to work after maternity leave is set out in regulations 18 and 18A of the MAPLE Regulations.

---

[48]  ERA 1996, s 87(4).
[49]  *Scotts Company (UK) Ltd v Budd* [2003] IRLR 145.
[50]  MAPLE, reg 12A(4).
[51]  MAPLE, reg 12A(1).
[52]  MAPLE, reg 12A(2).
[53]  MAPLE, reg 12A(3).
[54]  MAPLE, reg 12A(6).
[55]  MAPLE, reg 12A(7).
[56]  MAPLE, reg 12A(5).

**4.70** After OML or AML is complete, the employee has the right to return to work. The rights with regard to return are slightly different depending on whether the return is from OML or AML.

**4.71** If an employee is not allowed to return to work, she is treated as dismissed. If the principal reason is pregnancy-related or due to maternity leave having been taken, then the dismissal is automatically unfair under section 99 of the ERA and MAPLE, regulation 20. It is also likely to be unlawful direct discrimination under sections 18 and 39(2) of the Equality Act 2010. No justification defence is open to the employer in those circumstances.

**4.72** If the employer did not notify the employee of the end date of her maternity leave, and the employee has therefore stayed off too long, any attempts to dismiss would also be regarded as an unfair dismissal.[57]

**4.73** If the employee is allowed to return to work, but not in the manner protected by statute, then she may be able to resign and claim unfair constructive dismissal. In some circumstances, she may be able to stay in the new post and still make a claim.

**4.74** After OML, the regulations stipulate that the employee must be allowed to return to the job that she had prior to her maternity leave.[58] 'Job' is defined in MAPLE, regulation 2(1) as 'the nature of the work which she is employed to do in accordance with her contract and the capacity and place in which she is so employed'.

*Case Example*

The claimant was a primary school teacher. Prior to her maternity leave, she taught the 'reception yellow' class. On her return, she was asked either to operate as a floating teacher, or to teach a year two class. She accepted the latter offer, but complained that this did not amount to a return to the same job. The EAT held that the contract alone was not definitive on this question, and further that the word 'capacity' in the interpretation section in MAPLE, regulation 2(1) referred to more than 'status', although it might encompass this. In considering the meaning of the term 'the same job', regard had to be had to the purpose of the legislation, which, the EAT held, was to ensure that there is as little dislocation as reasonably possible in a new mother's working life, so as to avoid adding to the burdens which will be imposed upon her in her private/family life by the demands of a young infant. It held that 'job' could be quite specifically defined. In the claimant's case, however, her job should be defined as a 'teacher', not a teacher of reception yellow, because the practice was to move teachers around after two years in a particular role, and the claimant could be asked to teach any class. The post offered was not outside the range of variability which the claimant could normally have expected.

*Blundell v Governing Body of St Andrews Roman Catholic Primary School*[59]

---

57   MAPLE, reg 20(3).
58   MAPLE, reg 18(1).
59   [2007] ICR 1451 (EAT).

**4.75** The right to return after OML is the right to return to the same rate of pay, seniority, pension rights, and on terms and conditions as though she had not been absent.[60]

**4.76** The 'OML' right to return also applies in circumstances where an employee returns from the last of two or more consecutive periods of statutory leave which did not include any period of AML, or additional adoption leave, or a period of parental leave of more than four weeks.

**4.77** If the employee indicates prior to starting maternity leave that they do not want to return to their existing job (eg location) and therefore their job is filled permanently, they cannot claim unfair dismissal/discrimination if they refuse a comparable job, but instead choose a secondment which comes to an end and no other position is available. This is akin to the employee who unreasonably rejects suitable alternative employment in a redundancy situation.

**4.78** After AML the rules are not quite as strict. The employee must be allowed to return to her previous job, or, if that is not reasonably practicable, then another job which is 'both suitable for her and appropriate for her to do in the circumstances'. The terms and conditions of any new position must not be less favourable than if she had not been absent.[61] This may be subject to change by the proposed new Pregnant Workers Directive in order to improve the rights of the employee, but this remains uncertain at the time of writing. The only terms and conditions to which this does not apply are pension rights, which do not accrue during AML.[62]

**4.79** If the employee has taken consecutive periods of statutory leave which do not fall within MAPLE, regulation 18(1)(b) (eg OML, followed by parental leave of more than four weeks) and it is not reasonably practicable for the employee to return to her previous job, for a reason which is not redundancy (in relation to which see **4.82–4.89** below), then she should be treated in the same way as someone returning from AML.[63]

**4.80** To continue with the example given above: Jane is employed to cover Emma's maternity leave. Towards the end of the period, the employer decides that Jane is better at the job, asks her to stay on and tells Emma that she cannot return to her previous job. This would be automatically unfair dismissal and would also be discriminatory on the grounds of maternity.[64]

**4.81** The employee returning from AML will also be entitled to receive the same level of pay, status and other terms and conditions. If terms have been altered for others in the same department or level as the employee, then she

---

[60]  MAPLE, reg 18A(1).
[61]  MAPLE, reg 18A(1).
[62]  Equality Act 2010, s 75(9).
[63]  MAPLE, reg 18(2).
[64]  See *Rees v Apollo Watch Repairs Plc* [1996] ICR 466.

should have been consulted about those changes in the same way as her colleagues were. To fail to do so may be discriminatory.

## REDUNDANCY DURING MATERNITY LEAVE

**4.82** Protection against redundancy is given to employees during their OML and AML under MAPLE, regulation 10(1). Where a redundancy situation arises and their job ceases to exist during the period that they are away from work, an employee will be entitled to be offered a 'suitable alternative vacancy'.[65]

**4.83** This is an important right, as it is not merely an opportunity to apply for the job, or an opportunity to be interviewed; the regulations impose an obligation on an employer to 'offer' a job which is considered a 'suitable alternative' if there is a 'vacancy'.[66] The employee on maternity leave who is made redundant will therefore have a right which surpasses that of other redundant employees to be placed into alternative work.

**4.84** A redundancy situation will arise at the point where the job ceases to exist. This may be whilst the employee is absent on OML or AML. The obligation on the employer to look for and offer a 'suitable alternative vacancy' arises at that point. This is despite the fact that the employee may still be on maternity leave and would not therefore be able to start work in an alternative position immediately. The employer cannot await the end of the maternity leave period, before commencing the search for, or offer of, alternative work.

**4.85** Although the redundancy situation may arise during the maternity leave, it may be that the employee is not in fact dismissed until her 'return to work' date. Negotiations as to the location of work and a change as a result of a mobility clause, do not release an employer from the obligation to offer 'suitable alternative vacancy'. If no such offer is made, the employer will be in breach of the regulations and an automatically unfair dismissal arises under MAPLE, regulation 20.[67]

**4.86** The work must be suitable in both content and equivalence in terms and conditions (including place of work, hours of work and level of pay).[68] The decision as to whether the work is a suitable alternative lies with the employer, not the employee. It is for the ET to scrutinise whether the employer was acting reasonably in making a decision on suitability.[69] *Simpson* is an example of a tribunal finding that the employer was correct to suggest that the job was not suitable, as it involved a relocation and working seven days rather than the previous five days per week.

---

[65]   MAPLE, reg 10(2).
[66]   MAPLE, reg 10(2).
[67]   See *Secretary of State v Slee* UKEAT/0349/06.
[68]   MAPLE, reg 10(3).
[69]   See *Simpson v Endsleigh Insurance Sevices Ltd* [2011] ICR 75, EAT.

**4.87** The search for suitable alternative employment may extend beyond the employer to other associated employers (ie those within groups of companies).[70]

**4.88** If the provisions of MAPLE, regulation 10 have not been complied with, the employee will be regarded as automatically unfairly dismissed under MAPLE, regulation 20 and also section 99 of the ERA. The burden on the employee is only to show some evidence (*prima facie*) that the dismissal was for an inadmissible reason. It is then for the employer to prove the real reason for dismissal as one of the section 98(1) or (2) reasons.

**4.89** An employee who refuses to accept a suitable alternative role may forfeit their right to redundancy pay (in a similar manner to the rights under ERA).

## EXTENDING TIME OFF WORK

**4.90** If an employee is not well at the end of her maternity leave period and cannot return to work, she must notify her employer in the normal way and will be entitled to sick pay/SSP in accordance with the normal rules.

**4.91** Likewise, if the employee wants to use some of the annual leave she has accrued during the period of maternity leave, she can do so, by notifying her employer in the normal manner of the request for holiday. The employee would be best advised to do so in writing to avoid any confusion about pay entitlement or date of return.

**4.92** If the employee finds that she cannot return to work on the appointed date for some other reason (eg related to her childcare arrangements) she can take parental leave, but must comply with the appropriate notification for taking such leave.

**4.93** If the employee wishes to alter her hours of work, she must make an application for flexible working prior to her return. An employee should not remain off work due to the fact that her flexible working application has not been resolved. An agreement should be reached between employer and employee as to what hours are to be worked until such time as a resolution can be reached between them.

**4.94** If an employee does not want to return to work, she must resign, giving the appropriate contractual or statutory notice. She will be entitled to be paid her SMP for the full period of time and to be paid any accrued holiday pay.

---

[70] See *Community Task Force v Rimmer* [1986] ICR 491 EAT.

# Chapter 5

# STATUTORY ADOPTION LEAVE AND PAY

*David Massarella*

## INTRODUCTION

### Statutory framework

**5.1**  Sections 75A and 75B of the Employment Rights Act 1996 (ERA 1996) confer the rights to ordinary and additional adoption leave. These are analogous to the right to ordinary and additional maternity leave contained in sections 71 and 73 of the ERA 1996.

**5.2**  The right to take 'paternity leave: adoption' (the equivalent of ordinary paternity leave) is conferred by section 80AA of the ERA 1996. The Paternity and Adoption Leave Regulations 2002[1] ('PAL Regs 2002'), as amended, contain the detailed provisions concerning the right to take adoption leave and 'paternity leave: adoption'.

**5.3**  Provision for a new right to 'Additional Paternity Leave: Adoption' was made by section 80BB of the ERA 1996. It was introduced by way of the Additional Paternity Leave Regulations 2010[2] ('APL Regs 2010') and came into force on 6 April 2010, although it only applies where the child was placed on or after 3 April 2011.[3]

**5.4**  The right to statutory adoption pay was conferred by the Social Security Contributions and Benefits Act 1992 ('SSCBA 1992'), sections 171ZL to 171ZT. The right to Statutory Paternity Pay (Adoption) was conferred by sections 171ZB to 171ZE. The Statutory Paternity Pay and Statutory Adoption Pay (General) Regulations 2002[4] ('SPP and SAP Regs 2002'), as amended, contain the detailed provisions. The right to Additional Statutory Paternity Pay was conferred by section 171ZEB of the SSCBA 1992 and was introduced on 6 April 2010 by means of the Additional Statutory Paternity Pay (General)

---

[1]  SI 2002/2788 as amended by the Maternity and Parental Leave etc and the Paternity and Adoption Leave (Amendment) Regulations 2006, SI 2006/2014; and the Maternity and Parental Leave etc and the Paternity and Adoption Leave (Amendment) Regulations 2008, SI 2008/1996.

[2]  SI 2010/1055.

[3]  APL Regs 2010, reg 3(2).

[4]  SI 2002/2822 as amended by the Statutory Paternity Pay and Statutory Adoption Pay (General) and the Statutory Paternity Pay and Statutory Adoption Pay (Weekly Rates) (Amendment) Regulations 2006, SI 2006/2236.

Regulations 2010[5] ('ASPP Regs 2010'). This too applies where the child was placed for adoption on or after 3 April 2011.[6]

**5.5**    The general regulations are modified to provide for specific rights and requirements in respect of those adopting children from overseas by: the Paternity and Adoption Leave (Adoptions from Overseas) Regulations 2003[7] ('PAL (Overseas) Regs 2003'); the Statutory Paternity Pay (Adoption) and Statutory Adoption Pay (Adoption from Overseas) (No 2) Regulations 2003[8] ('SPP and SAP (Overseas) Regs 2003'); the Additional Paternity Leave (Adoptions from Overseas) Regulations 2010[9] ('APL (Overseas) Regs 2010'); and the Additional Statutory Paternity Pay (Adoptions from Overseas) Regulations 2010[10] ('ASPP (Overseas) Regs 2010'). The differences will be highlighted in the course of this chapter.

## The rights

**5.6**    In brief, the rights to take leave are as follows.

(a)    Adoption leave of up to one year may be taken by a person of either sex who has been matched for adoption of a child under 18.

(b)    Where two people are jointly adopting the child, either partner (but not both) may elect to take adoption leave.

(c)    The partner of the person taking adoption leave (whether or not he or she is jointly adopting the child) may take 'paternity leave: adoption' of up to two weeks.

(d)    A partner of either sex who is jointly adopting the child may, in prescribed circumstances, take additional paternity leave for up to 26 weeks.

## ADOPTION LEAVE

### Who is entitled to take adoption leave?

**5.7**    A person of either sex who has been matched with the child may take statutory adoption leave. Where two people have been matched jointly, only one may elect to take adoption leave. In both cases, that person is referred to in all the regulations as 'the adopter' and this term will be used throughout the chapter.[11]

---

5    SI 2010/1056.
6    Regulation 3(a). ASPP Regs 2010, reg 3(a).
7    SI 2003/921.
8    SI 2003/1194.
9    SI 2010/1059.
10    SI 2010/1057.
11    For example, PAL Regs 2002, reg 2(1).

**5.8**   The adopter's married, civil or unmarried partner (of either sex and whether the same or opposite sex) is entitled to take 'paternity leave: adoption', provided he or she lives with the adopter in an 'enduring family relationship'.[12] That person will be referred to in this chapter as 'the partner'.

**5.9**   Blood relatives of the adopter are excluded from being partners for the purposes of the legislation.[13]

**5.10**   For simplicity's sake, the adopter will be referred to as 'she', the partner as 'he' and 'paternity leave: adoption' will be referred to as 'paternity leave'.

## Qualifying requirements

**5.11**   Adoption leave applies only to employees, not to workers or the self-employed. The police and share fishermen are excluded from the statutory right to take adoption leave. Seafarers are entitled to leave, provided they meet specific requirements.[14] Members of the armed forces are excluded from the statutory right because they are not employees. However, equivalent internal rights have been introduced by the armed forces and the relevant internal regulations (as updated from time to time by the MOD) should be consulted.[15] Similar provision is made for police officers.[16] These provisions largely mirror the civilian rights and were introduced at the same time.

**5.12**   In order to qualify for the right, the adopter must have 26 weeks' continuous employment before the beginning of the week when she is notified of having been matched with a child by a UK adoption agency. She must have notified the agency that she agrees to the placement of the child and the date of placement.[17] The date of placement is the date on which the child starts living permanently with the adopter.

**5.13**   In the case of overseas adoption, the adopter must have received official notification from the relevant UK authority[18] of her eligibility to adopt a child from abroad. She can take leave if she has 26 weeks' continuous employment by

---

[12]   PAL Regs 2002, reg 2.
[13]   PAL Regs 2002, reg 2(2).
[14]   These are: (1) that the ship is registered in accordance with section 8 of the Merchant Shipping Act 1995; (2) that it is registered as belonging to a port in Great Britain; (3) that the adopter does not work wholly outside Great Britain and is ordinarily resident in Great Britain (see ERA 1996, s 199(7) and (8)).
[15]   Adoption leave was introduced in the armed forces in April 2003 and announced in Defence Council Instruction (Joint Service) 40/2003. Joint Service Publication 760 (Tri-Service Regulations on Leave and Other Types of Absence) Chapter 21 gives the guidance for adoption leave. Defence Instructions and Notices 201101-037 details the introduction of Additional Paternity/Adoption Leave and Pay with effect from 3 April 2011.
[16]   See Police Regulations 2003, reg 33, and Home Office circular 033/2003.
[17]   PAL Regs 2002, reg 9.
[18]   For the definition of these terms see PAL (Overseas) Regs 2003, reg 4.

the time she receives that notification. Alternatively, she will become eligible once she has accrued 26 weeks' continuous employment.[19]

**5.14**  The right applies only where a child is newly matched with the adopter. Consequently, it would appear that, where a foster parent goes on to adopt a child, she will only be entitled to adoption leave if she is matched with the child for adoption by a UK adoption agency and the child goes on to be placed with her. Adoption via a court order will not entitle her to leave. Adoption leave is not available to special guardians.

**5.15**  The right to adoption leave is not dependent on the number of hours the adopter works or how much she is paid.

## Notice requirements and proof of the adoption

### *UK adoptions*

**5.16**  The adopter must give the employer notice of her intention to take adoption leave no more than seven days after receiving notification from the agency that she has been matched with the child. A person is 'matched' with a child for adoption when an adoption agency decides that the person would be a suitable adoptive parent for the child.[20] If it is not reasonably practicable to give notice within the seven-day period, she should do so as soon as reasonably practicable.[21]

**5.17**  The adopter must specify the expected date of placement and the date on which she has chosen to begin her period of leave.[22] Reg 16 sets limits as to when the adopter can choose to start leave: she may begin it either on the date of placement or on a date no more than 14 days before the expected date of placement.[23] The adopter can vary the start date, provided she gives the employer notice of the variation 28 days before the original date or 28 days before the new date, whichever is the sooner.[24] The new date must still comply with the requirements of reg 16. If it is not reasonably practicable to give 28 days' notice, the adopter must give notice as soon as she can.[25] The start date may be varied more than once.[26]

> 'EXAMPLE 1: Sally has given notice to her employer that she will start her leave on 30 April. The agency informs her on 1 March that the placement will be delayed until 30 May. Sally must notify her employer no later than 2 April that she needs to vary the start date of the leave. She may specify the 30 May as the new start date or choose a date within the permitted 14-day period before it.

[19]  PAL (Overseas) Regs 2003, reg 15(2).
[20]  PAL Regs 2002, reg 2(4).
[21]  PAL Regs 2002, reg 17(2).
[22]  PAL Regs 2002, reg 17(1).
[23]  PAL Regs 2002, reg 16.
[24]  PAL Regs 2002, reg 17(4).
[25]  PAL Regs 2002, reg 17(4).
[26]  PAL Regs 2002, reg 18(2).

EXAMPLE 2: Peter originally chose to start his adoption leave on 30 April when the child was due to be placed with him. On 6 April he is informed that the placement date has been brought forward to 20 April. He cannot comply with the notice requirements so he should inform his employer as soon as reasonably practicable that he needs to change the date, either to the new placement date or to a specific date within the permitted 14-day period before it.'

**5.18**  The employer may ask for notice of adoption, or variation of notice, to be provided in writing.[27] If the employer requests it, the adopter must provide evidence in the form of one or more documents from the adoption agency of the name and address of the adoption agency, the date on which the adopter was informed that she had been matched with the child and the date on which the child is expected to be placed with the adopter.[28] This is usually a matching certificate from the adoption agency.

**5.19**  The employer must write to the adopter within 28 days of receiving notice (or of the date on which adoption leave has begun, whichever is the sooner) telling her the date on which her statutory adoption leave will end.[29] This will be 52 weeks after it starts, the assumption being that she will take both Ordinary and Additional Adoption Leave. If he fails to do so, he forfeits the right to prevent the adopter from returning early from leave in circumstances where she has not given him adequate notice (see below at **5.42**). Furthermore he may be acting unlawfully if he dismisses the adopter, or treats her detrimentally, for failing to return at the end of her leave (see below at **5.45**).[30]

## Overseas adoption

**5.20**  In the case of overseas adoptions the same rules apply with the following variations.[31]

**5.21**  The adopter must give the employer notice of the date on which she received official notification and the date on which the child is expected to enter Great Britain within 28 days of receiving official notification or within 28 days of completing 26 weeks' continuous employment, whichever is later. Within 28 days of the child entering Great Britain she must inform her employer of the fact. She must give at least 28 days' notice of her chosen start date for adoption leave.[32]

---

[27]  PAL Regs 2002, reg 17(6).
[28]  PAL Regs 2002, reg 17(3).
[29]  PAL Regs 2002, reg 17(7) and (8).
[30]  PAL Regs 2002, regs 28(1)(c) and 29(3)(c).
[31]  By reg 9 of the PAL (Overseas) Regs 2003, different versions of regs 15 to 17 of the PAL Regs 2002 are substituted.
[32]  PAL (Overseas) Regs 2003, substituted reg 17(1) and (2) within reg 9.

**5.22**    The employer can request a copy of the official notification and proof of the date the child entered Great Britain.[33] The adopter must notify the employer as soon as reasonably practicable where it becomes known that the child will not enter Great Britain.[34]

**5.23**    The adopter can choose to start leave either on the date on which the child enters Great Britain or on a predetermined date no later than 28 days after the date of entry.[35]

**5.24**    The rules relating to the variation of the start date are the same as for a UK adoption with the 'date of entry into Great Britain' substituted for the 'date of placement'.[36]

## Length of adoption leave

### *Ordinary adoption leave ('OAL')*

**5.25**    Ordinary adoption leave ('OAL') may be taken for a period of up to 26 weeks.[37] The adopter is not entitled to a longer period of leave if she adopts more than one child.[38]

### *Additional adoption leave ('AAL')*

**5.26**    An adopter who has completed a period of OAL is eligible to take a further period of up to 26 weeks' additional adoption leave ('AAL'), provided her OAL period did not end prematurely either because she was dismissed during OAL or because the placement was disrupted (see below).[39] The adopter can also take up to four weeks' Parental Leave at the end of OAL and AAL without affecting her right to return.[40]

**5.27**    The entitlement to Statutory Adoption Pay continues only for the first 13 weeks of AAL (see below).

## Terms and conditions during OAL and AAL

**5.28**    During adoption leave the adopter's terms and conditions of employment continue to apply. This is now the case during both OAL and AAL.[41] These provisions mirror those for women taking Ordinary and Additional Maternity Leave. A summary of the position is provided here. Please see Chapter 4 for more details.

---

[33]    PAL (Overseas) Regs 2003, substituted reg 17(3) within reg 9.
[34]    PAL (Overseas) Regs 2003, substituted reg 17(9) within reg 9.
[35]    PAL (Overseas) Regs 2003, substituted reg 16 within reg 9.
[36]    PAL (Overseas) Regs 2003, substituted reg 17(4) to (6) within reg 9.
[37]    PAL Regs 2002, reg 18(1).
[38]    PAL Regs 2002, reg 15(4).
[39]    PAL Regs 2002, reg 20.
[40]    PAL Regs 2002, reg 26(1)(b).
[41]    This is the position for adopters of children placed for adoption on or after 5 October 2008.

**5.29** As with maternity leave, terms and conditions relating to remuneration are specifically excluded and do not continue to apply. However, remuneration is expressly defined as an employee's normal salary or wages[42] so the employee may continue to have access to other benefits under her contract such as a company car, gym membership or mobile phone. However, if the benefit is provided exclusively for business use the employer may be able to suspend it.

**5.30** The adopter's seniority, pension and other service-related rights continue to accrue as if she were not absent.[43] The adopter is entitled to her employer's usual pension contributions during Ordinary Adoption Leave or any time she is receiving any Statutory Adoption Pay or contractual adoption pay. She herself is only required to pay contributions based on the remunerations she actually receives.[44] There is no requirement that pension contributions be paid during the unpaid part of leave.[45]

**5.31** The adopter continues to accrue entitlement to paid holiday during adoption leave. She may add holiday to the beginning and end of her leave but may not be able to carry over untaken holiday entitlement if her adoption leave goes over two holiday years and it may be advisable to take this at the beginning of the leave period.

**5.32** During the leave period the adopter continues to be bound by her own obligations under the contract, except insofar as they are inconsistent with her entitlement to be absent on adoption leave.[46] Thus, she would continue to be bound by the implied term of trust and confidence and any terms relating to, for example, disclosure of confidential information, non-competition and notice requirements.

## Keeping in touch and working during the leave period

**5.33** The employer and the adopter are entitled to make reasonable contact with each other without bringing the leave period to an end. This would usually be for the purposes of providing information about any significant changes in the workplace or making arrangements for the return to work.[47]

**5.34** The adopter is permitted to do up to ten days' work during the leave period without losing adoption pay or bringing her leave to an end.[48] These are called 'keeping in touch days' and may only be worked if both employer and

---

Previously, there was a distinction in this respect between OAL and AAL, which was removed by the Maternity and Parental Leave etc and the Paternity and Adoption Leave (Amendment) Regulations 2008, SI 2008/1966.

[42] PAL Regs 2002, reg 19.
[43] PAL Regs 2002, reg 27(1)(a).
[44] Social Security Act 1989, Schedule 5, para 5B.
[45] PAL Regs 2002, reg 27(2).
[46] PAL Regs 2002, reg 19(1)(b), read together with ERA 1996, ss 75A(3)(b) and 75B(4)(b).
[47] PAL Regs 2002, reg 21A(4).
[48] PAL Regs 2002, reg 21A(1).

employee agree.[49] For these purposes a part-day's work will be treated as a full day.[50] They may be used for any form of work, although most commonly they are used for training or team events. It is for the employer and employee to agree what work is to be done and how much pay will be received.[51] There are specific provisions which protect the adopter from being subjected to detriment for refusing to work during her leave period (see below at **5.45**).

## Disrupted placement

**5.35**  The PAL Regs 2002 make provision for the possibility of an adoption placement ending in circumstances which might make it difficult for the adopter to return to work immediately. The adopter is allowed eight weeks' further leave from the end of the week in question before she must return to work if:[52]

(a)  the child dies;

(b)  the child is returned to the adoption agency (or, in the case of overseas adoptions, ceases to live with the adopter);

(c)  she has already begun her period of OAL and she is notified that the placement will not be made (not applicable to overseas adoptions).

**5.36**  If the eight weeks takes the adopter beyond the 26 weeks allowed for as OAL, she is entitled to take AAL until the end of the eight-week period.[53] However, if she is already taking AAL, her entitlement is cut short as it can continue for no more than eight weeks.[54] Indeed, if the adoption is disrupted, as above, in the last eight weeks of AAL, that leave nevertheless ends at the end of the 26 week AAL period, with no further extension.[55] It is left to contractual or other compassionate leave to assist if, say, the child dies in the last week of AAL.

## Right to return to the same job

**5.37**  Subject to the provisions concerning redundancy during the leave period (see below), the adopter has the right to return from OAL to her original job.[56] She is entitled to return on no less favourable terms and conditions and with her seniority, pension and other rights as they would have been had she not been away.[57]

---

[49]  PAL Regs 2002, reg 21A(5).
[50]  PAL Regs 2002, reg 21A(2).
[51]  PAL Regs 2002, reg 21A.
[52]  PAL Regs 2002, reg 22(1) and (3). For overseas adoptions see the variations in PAL (Overseas) Regs 2003, reg 12.
[53]  PAL Regs 2002, reg 22(2)(b).
[54]  PAL Regs 2002, reg 22(2)(a).
[55]  PAL Regs 2002, reg 22(2)(c).
[56]  PAL Regs 2002, reg 26(1).
[57]  PAL Regs 2002, reg 27.

**5.38**  The same applies if she is returning from a combination of OAL and other periods of statutory leave (for example, Ordinary Maternity Leave) provided it does not include any periods of Additional Maternity or Adoption Leave or a period of Parental Leave lasting more than four weeks.[58]

**5.39**  The position is different if she is returning from AAL. If the employer can show that it is not reasonably practicable to allow the adopter to return to her original job, for example if there has been a restructuring of the business, she must be offered an alternative position which is both suitable for her and appropriate for her to do in the circumstances.[59] This mirrors the equivalent maternity leave provisions. Reference should be made to the commentary on those provisions above at Chapter 4 for further details.

> 'EXAMPLE 1: Sally has taken OAL and a three-week period of Parental Leave. She is entitled to return to exactly the same job as before her leave.
>
> EXAMPLE 2: Sally has taken OAL followed by a period of AAL and has then taken a period of Ordinary Maternity Leave (she became pregnant during OAL). Because one of the periods of leave is AAL, she will not have the right to return to her old job, if it is not reasonably practicable.'

## Notice of intention to return

**5.40**  The presumption is that the full 52 weeks' of combined OAL and AAL leave will be taken. If that is so, no further notice of the return date is required. If the adopter wishes to return early, for example because she does not wish to take AAL or her partner is taking Additional Paternity Leave, she must give eight weeks' notice of her intention to return early, specifying the date of return.[60] She must also give eight weeks' notice if she is returning early because of a disrupted placement.

**5.41**  There is no obligation on the employer to agree to a return with less than eight weeks' notice and he is entitled to require her to postpone it until the eight weeks has elapsed[61] but he may not postpone it beyond the end of the AAL period.[62] It is worth noting that the employer has no entitlement to postpone the return in this way if, before the period of adoption leave started, he failed to comply with his own requirement formally to notify the adopter of the end date of the leave.[63]

**5.42**  The adopter may change her return date more than once. However, she must give notice eight weeks before the original return date or eight weeks

---

[58]   PAL Regs 2002, reg 26(1)(b).
[59]   Or from any combination of OAL and AAL.
[60]   PAL Regs 2002, reg 25(1).
[61]   PAL Regs 2002, reg 25(2).
[62]   PAL Regs 2002, reg 25(3).
[63]   PAL Regs 2002, reg 25(5).

before the new return date, whichever is the earlier.[64] If the adopter decides not to return to work at all, notice should be given in the usual way.

## Redundancy during adoption leave

**5.43**   The employer may make the adopter redundant during her adoption leave, subject to the usual rules as to fairness. However, as with maternity leave, the adopter has special rights. She has the right to be offered a suitable alternative vacancy,[65] even if this is in preference to other employees who may be equally qualified for the role. The alternative vacancy must be both suitable to the employee and appropriate for her to do in the circumstances. Its terms and conditions must be not substantially less favourable than those which applied under her old contract of employment.[66] If the employer dismisses in breach of these requirements, that dismissal will be automatically unfair.[67]

**5.44**   If there is no suitable alternative vacancy and the adopter is properly dismissed, her adoption leave ends on the date of dismissal. She is entitled to paid statutory notice during OAL and AAL and any contractual notice/notice pay to which she is entitled.

## Protection from detriment and dismissal

**5.45**   The adopter is protected against detriment[68] or dismissal[69] attributable to the fact that:

(a)   she took or sought to take adoption leave;

(b)   the employer believed she was likely to take leave;

(c)   she undertook, considered undertaking or refused to undertake work during the leave period under the 'keeping in touch days' provisions;

(d)   she failed to return from leave in circumstances where the employer had not complied with his obligation[70] formally to notify her of the end date of the leave period, gave her less than 28 days' notice of that end date and it was not reasonably practicable for her to return then.[71]

If she can show that the reason (or principal reason) for the dismissal was one of these prohibited grounds, the dismissal will be automatically unfair.[72] A

---

[64]   PAL Regs 2002, reg 25(2A).
[65]   PAL Regs 2002, reg 23(2).
[66]   PAL Regs 2002, reg 23(3).
[67]   PAL Regs 2002, reg 29(1)(b).
[68]   PAL Regs 2002, reg 28.
[69]   PAL Regs 2002, reg 29.
[70]   Under PAL Regs 2002, reg 17(7).
[71]   PAL Regs 2002, reg 28(1) and reg 29(3).
[72]   PAL Regs 2002, reg 29(1).

dismissal for redundancy will also be automatically unfair if she can show that the redundancy situation applied equally to another employee doing a similar job to her, that other person was not dismissed and her selection was for one of the prohibited grounds.[73]

**5.46** If it is not reasonably practicable for the employer to permit the adopter to return to a suitable job (for a reason other than redundancy), an associated employer offers her a suitable job, and she accepts or unreasonably refuses it, her right to claim unfair dismissal is lost.[74]

# STATUTORY ADOPTION PAY

## Period of pay

**5.47** Statutory adoption pay (SAP) is payable for 39 weeks. It is usually taken to cover the first 39 weeks of an employee's adoption leave.

## Eligibility criteria

**5.48** Where a child is jointly adopted, only one partner may elect to receive SAP.[75] The other partner may receive Statutory Paternity Pay ('SPP') and Additional Statutory Paternity Pay ('ASPP'). The adopter will not receive more SAP if she is adopting more than one child.[76]

**5.49** The adopter may be entitled to SAP, even if she is not entitled to statutory adoption leave. She must be an employee but, for these purposes, the definition of employee is wider. It covers anyone for whom the employer pays Class 1 National Insurance ('NI') contributions, or for whom he would pay them if their earnings were sufficiently high.[77] Consequently, office holders (members of the armed forces, police and MPs etc) will be eligible for SAP, as will apprentices and many agency and casual workers.

**5.50** The adopter qualifies for SAP provided she meets the following criteria.[78] She must have:

(a)   26 weeks' continuous employment before the beginning of the week when she is notified of having been matched with a child (UK adoptions)/when the child enters Great Britain (overseas adoptions);

---

[73]   PAL Regs 2002, reg 29(2).
[74]   PAL Regs 2002, reg 29(5).
[75]   SSCBA 1992, s 171ZL(4) and (4A).
[76]   SSCBA 1992, s 171ZL(5).
[77]   The Statutory Paternity Pay and Statutory Adoption Pay (General) Regulations 2002, as amended ('SPP and SAP Regs 2002'), reg 32(1).
[78]   Social Security Contributions and Benefits Act 1992 ('SSCBA 1992'), s 171ZL.

(b)    average earnings at least equal to the lower earnings limit for NI contributions;[79] and

(c)    she must have stopped working.

**5.51**    The provisions which specify what constitutes continuous employment[80] are the same as for SMP: see Chapter 6.

## Amount of SAP, payment and recovery

**5.52**    The amount payable is the lower of:

(a)    the standard weekly rate (which, from 9 April 2012, is £135.45); or

(b)    90 per cent of the adopter's average weekly pay.[81]

Rates change in April of each year by way of amendment of the Statutory Paternity Pay and Statutory Adoption Pay (Weekly Rates) Regulations 2002 ('Weekly Rates Regs 2002').

**5.53**    The parties cannot contract out of SAP.[82] SAP should be paid on the normal pay day or, if none exists, on the last day of the month.[83] SAP is subject to tax and NI and can be paid in a lump sum, if both parties agree.

**5.54**    HMRC provides a free software programme,[84] which can be downloaded from its website, and which will assist employers in deciding whether the employee is entitled to be paid SAP (and SPP and ASPP), how much is due and how much the employer can recover. The proportion of SAP which is recoverable from HMRC depends on the size of the employer's annual NI liability but will be at least 92 per cent.

## Notice requirements and evidence

**5.55**    The adopter must give at least 28 days' notice (or as soon as reasonably practicable) stating when she wants her SAP to begin and the expected date of placement. The notice must be in writing, if required by the employer.[85] She must also provide a declaration that she has elected to take SAP, rather than Statutory Paternity Pay ('SPP').[86]

---

[79]    £102 per week or £442 a month for the year 2011–2012.
[80]    SPP and SAP Regs 2002, regs 33 to 36.
[81]    Statutory Paternity Pay and Statutory Adoption Pay (Weekly Rates) Regulations 2002 ('Weekly Rates Regs 2002'), reg 3.
[82]    SSCBA 1992, s 171ZO.
[83]    SPP and SAP Regs 2002, reg 42(1).
[84]    'Basic PAYE Tools.'
[85]    SSCBA 1992, s 171ZL(6) and (7), SPP and SAP Regs 2002, reg 23(1).
[86]    SPP and SAP Regs 2002, reg 24(1)(b).

**5.56** In the case of a UK adoption, she must also provide documentary evidence from the adoption agency (usually a matching certificate) of the name and address of the adoption agency, her own name and address, the date on which the adopter was informed that she had been matched with the child and the date on which the child is expected to be placed (or was placed) with the adopter.[87]

**5.57** In the case of an overseas adoption, she must also provide her own name and address, a copy of the Official Notification from the relevant UK authority that they have agreed that she is suitable to adopt a child from overseas and the date on which the child is expected to enter (or already has entered) the UK. The adopter must also provide evidence of the child's actual date of entry into the UK (within 28 days of that date), such as a plane ticket or copies of entry clearance documents.[88]

## Start date

**5.58** In the case of a UK adoption, the adopter can choose to begin receiving SAP either on the day the child is placed with her or on a specified, earlier date, up to 14 days before the expected date of placement.[89]

**5.59** In the case of an overseas adopter, the adopter can elect to start receiving SAP on the date on which the child enters Great Britain or on a date of her choice no more than 28 days later.[90]

**5.60** The adopter may vary the start date of SAP, provided she gives notice 28 days before the new start date (or as soon as reasonably practicable).[91] At the same time she must give notice of the expected date of placement and then go on to inform the employer of the date on which the child has, in fact, been placed as soon as reasonably practicable after the placement.[92]

## Keeping in touch days

**5.61** As set out above at **5.34**, the adopter can do up to ten Keeping in Touch days without losing her entitlement to SAP. If she exceeds that limit, she is not entitled to SAP for the week, or weeks, in which the additional work is done.[93] As with SMP, the employer can offset payment for Keeping in Touch days against SAP.[94]

---

[87] SPP and SAP Regs 2002, reg 24(1) and (2).
[88] The Statutory Paternity Pay (Adoption) and Statutory Adoption Pay (Adoptions from Overseas)(No.2) Regulations 2003 ('the SPP and SAP (Overseas) Regs 2003'), regs 14 and 15.
[89] SPP and SAP Regs 2002, reg 21(1).
[90] SPP and SAP (Overseas) Regs 2003, reg 12.
[91] SPP and SAP Regs 2002, reg 21(6) and SSCBA 1992, s 171ZL(6).
[92] SPP and SAP Regs 2002, reg 23.
[93] SPP and SAP Regs 2002, reg 27A.
[94] SPP and SAP Regs 2002, reg 28 and SSCBA 1992, s 171ZP(5).

## Stopping payment of SAP

**5.62**  Entitlement to SAP ends after 39 weeks. Payment will stop earlier if any of the following applies:

(a)   the adopter returns to work (unless she is doing Keeping in Touch days). If she stops work again, however, payments should be resumed;

(b)   the adopter works for another employer, who is not liable to pay her SAP, and for whom she did not work during the week in which she was matched with the child (the adopter is obliged to notify the employer if she begins such employment);[95]

(c)   the adopter is imprisoned or dies.[96]

**5.63**  Entitlement to SAP will also cease eight weeks after:

(a)   the adopter is notified that the placement will not now take place;

(b)   the week in which the child is returned to the adoption agency (or, in the case of an adoption from overseas,[97] the week during which the child ceases to live with the adopter); or

(c)   the end of the week in which the child dies.[98]

## Termination of employment

**5.64**  If the adopter's employment ends after she has been notified of being matched with the child (and she satisfies the other qualifying criteria), the employer is still obliged to pay SAP[99] unless she starts work for another employer who is liable to pay her SAP.[100]

**5.65**  If the employment of an adopter who is entitled to SAP is terminated for whatever reason (including dismissal) before the employer has started to pay SAP, the employer must still pay it. Payments should begin on the day following the adopter's last day at work or 14 days before the date of placement, whichever is the later.[101] In the case of overseas adoptions, payments should begin on a date chosen by the adopter which is at least 28 days after she has given notice and within 28 days of the child's entry into Great Britain.[102] The adopted child must enter the UK within 26 weeks of the

---

[95]   SPP and SAP Regs 2002, reg 26 and SPP and SAP (Overseas) Regs 2003, reg 16.
[96]   SPP and SAP Regs 2002, reg 27. Note that entitlement resumes if the adopter is released subsequently without charge or is acquitted.
[97]   SPP and SAP (Overseas) Regs 2003, reg 13.
[98]   SPP and SAP Regs 2002, reg 22.
[99]   SSCBA 1992, s 171ZL(2) and (3) and s 171ZM.
[100]  SPP and SAP Regs 2002, reg 25; and SPP and SAP (Overseas) Regs 2003, reg 16.
[101]  SPP and SAP Regs 2002, reg 29.
[102]  SPP and SAP (Overseas) Regs 2003, reg 17.

termination of employment. After that time, liability to pay SAP passes to HMRC until such point as she qualifies for SAP with a new employer.[103]

**5.66** If the employment is terminated solely or mainly in order to avoid liability for SAP, the employer will still be liable to pay it, provided the adopter has eight weeks' continuous employment. The adopter will be deemed to have continuity ending with the week in which she was notified of having been matched with the child.[104] The adopter may also have a claim for automatic unfair dismissal (see below).

**5.67** As with SMP, if the employer is insolvent, HMRC will make SAP payments from the week of insolvency until the end of the adoption pay period.[105]

## Forms and records

**5.68** If the adopter does not qualify for SAP the employer must give her form SAP1: 'Why I Cannot Pay You SAP.' Form SC6 should be used to tell employees who are adopting jointly with their partner the conditions for SAP. It includes a declaration which the adopter must sign, stating that she does not wish to take paternity leave or receive paternity pay.

**5.69** The employer must keep a record of SAP: form SAP2 may be used for this. He must record any weeks in the 39-week period when SAP was not paid and the reason why. The employer must also keep a copy of the evidence from the adoption agency which the adopter gave him.

**5.70** The employer must also complete Forms P11 (payroll record), P14 (end of year summary) and P35 (employer annual return). Forms P12 and P37 should be used by employers using the Simplified Deduction Scheme.

**5.71** All these forms can be found on the HMRC website. Further information about record-keeping in relation to SAP can be found in the HMRC's publication E16, 'Employer Helpbook for Statutory Adoption Pay', which can be downloaded from the HMRC website.[106] All records must be kept for at least three years after the end of the tax year to which they relate.

## Challenging the SAP decision

**5.72** If the employer decides that the adopter is not eligible for SAP, he will explain his reasons in Form SAP1. He should set down:

(a)   the days, if any, for which he thinks he should pay SAP;

---

[103]   SPP and SAP (Overseas) Regs 2003, reg 17(2).
[104]   SPP and SAP Regs 2002, reg 30 and SPP and SAP (Overseas) Regs 2003, reg 18.
[105]   SPP and SAP Regs 2002, reg 43(2).
[106]   http://www.hmrc.gov.uk/index.htm.

(b)   how much SAP he thinks the adopter is entitled to; and

(c)   why he does not think he should pay SAP for the rest of the period in question.

**5.73**   If the adopter disagrees, she can ask her local HMRC Officer for a formal decision. If the decision is in her favour, the employer can be fined for then refusing to pay SAP.

## Enhanced adoption pay

**5.74**   If he wishes, the employer can offer enhanced adoption pay arrangements to attract and retain employees. By way of example only, he could:

(a)   pay full pay for the first six weeks, half pay for the next ten weeks, SAP for the remaining 23 weeks; or

(b)   make a bonus payment on the employee's return to work; or

(c)   change the qualification criteria for these additional contractual entitlements, eg by requiring the employee to have a year's continuous service.

The employer is still able to recover from HMRC the SAP portion of any enhanced adoption pay.

## 'PATERNITY LEAVE: ADOPTION' FOR THE PARTNER

### Introduction

**5.75**   The adopter's partner may take either one or two weeks' consecutive[107] paternity leave and pay, provided he satisfies the qualifying requirements.[108]

**5.76**   The partner may be of either sex but will be referred to in this section as 'he'. Unlike Additional Paternity Leave, the partner need not himself be matched for adoption with the child.

### Qualifying requirements

**5.77**   The partner must have 26 weeks' continuous employment, ending with the week in which the adopter is notified of having been matched with the

---

[107]   PAL Regs 2002, reg 9(1).
[108]   PAL Regs 2002, reg 8.

child.[109] In the case of overseas adoptions, he must have 26 weeks ending with the week official notification was received or 26 weeks from the start of his employment.[110]

**5.78** He must be the married, civil or unmarried partner of the adopter[111] and be living with the adopter in 'an enduring family relationship'.[112] Relatives of the adopter may not be partners for these purposes.[113] He must have, or expect to have, the main responsibility for the upbringing of the child, apart from that of the adopter.[114]

## Notice requirements and evidence

### *UK adoptions*

**5.79** The partner must give his employer notice of his intention to take leave within seven days of the adopter being notified that she has been matched with the child, or as soon as reasonably practicable thereafter.[115]

**5.80** The notice must be given in writing if the employer so requests.[116] It must state:

(a)  the date on which the adopter was notified of having been matched with the child;

(b)  the date on which the child is expected to be placed with the adopter;

(c)  whether the partner intends to take one or two weeks' leave;

(d)  the date on which he has chosen to start the leave (see next section for the options).

He must give his employer a further notice, as soon as reasonably practicable after the child's placement, of the date on which the child was placed.[117]

**5.81** If the employer requires it, the partner must also provide a signed declaration stating:

(a)  that the purpose of his absence is to care for the child or to support the adopter;

---

[109]  PAL Regs 2002, reg 8(2)(a).
[110]  PAL (Overseas) Regs 2003, reg 7, substituting regs 8 to 10 of the PAL Regs 2002.
[111]  PAL Regs 2002, reg 8(2)(b).
[112]  PAL Regs 2002, reg 2(1).
[113]  PAL Regs 2002, reg 2(1) and (2).
[114]  PAL Regs 2002, reg 8(2)(c).
[115]  PAL Regs 2002, reg 10(2).
[116]  PAL Regs 2002, reg 10(8).
[117]  PAL Regs 2002, reg 10(7).

(b)   that he is the married, civil or unmarried partner of the adopter; and

(c)   that he expects to have the main responsibility (apart from that of the adopter) for the upbringing of the child.[118]

## *Overseas adoptions*

**5.82**   In the case of overseas adoptions the same rules apply with the following variations.[119]

**5.83**   The partner must give the employer notice of the date on which he received official notification and the date on which the child is expected to enter Great Britain within 28 days of receiving official notification or within 28 days of completing 26 weeks' continuous employment, whichever is later. Within 28 days of the child entering Great Britain he must inform his employer of the fact. He must give at least 28 days' notice of his chosen start date for adoption leave, stating whether he wishes to take one or two weeks.

**5.84**   If the employer requests it, he must provide a written declaration that the adopter has received official notification, that he is her married, civil or unmarried partner and that he expects to have responsibility for the child's upbringing.

**5.85**   The rules relating to the variation of the start date are the same as for a UK adoption with the 'date of entry into Great Britain' substituted for the 'date of placement'.

## Date on which leave may begin

**5.86**   The partner may begin the leave on the date the child is placed with the adopter or on a later date, which the partner must identify in the employee notice. A specific start date may be given or the notice may simply state, for example, 'the date of the placement' or '14 days after the placement date'.[120] Leave must be taken within 56 days of the placement date[121] or, in the case of overseas adoption, within 56 days of the date on which the child enters Great Britain.[122]

**5.87**   In the case of overseas adoptions, the partner can choose to start his leave on the date the child enters Great Britain or on a predetermined date within 56 days of the date of entry.[123]

---

[118]   PAL Regs 2002, reg 10(3).
[119]   PAL (Overseas) Regs 2003, reg 7, substituting regs 8 to 10 of the PAL Regs 2002.
[120]   PAL Regs 2002, reg 9(3).
[121]   PAL Regs 2002, reg 9(2).
[122]   PAL (Overseas) Regs 2003, reg 7, substituting regs 8 to 10 of the PAL Regs 2002.
[123]   PAL (Overseas) Regs 2003, reg 7, substituting regs 8 to 10 of the PAL Regs 2002.

## Varying the start date

**5.88** The partner can change the date on which he starts paternity leave, provided he gives the employer notice 28 days before the original date or as soon as reasonably practicable thereafter.[124] If the partner had originally nominated a specific start date but the placement did not, in fact, go ahead on or before that date, he may vary the date by giving the employer notice as soon as reasonably practicable.[125] If he has chosen to start his leave on the day the child is placed with the adopter and he is at work when the placement occurs, his leave will start on the following day.[126]

# ORDINARY STATUTORY PATERNITY PAY: ADOPTION ('OSPP') FOR THE PARTNER

## Period of pay

**5.89** Ordinary Statutory Paternity Pay (OSPP) is payable to the adopter's married, civil or unmarried partner (of either sex) for one or two weeks.[127] If a child is being jointly adopted, the parents may choose which partner will receive SAP and which OSPP.

## Eligibility criteria

**5.90** The partner may be entitled to OSPP, even if he is not entitled to statutory paternity leave, as the wider definition of employee applies[128] (see above at **5.49**).

**5.91** The partner qualifies for OSPP provided he meets the following criteria:[129]

(a) He must have responsibility for the adopted child's upbringing.

(b) He must have 26 weeks' continuous employment before the beginning of the week when the adopter is notified of having been matched with a child by a UK adoption agency or the time he wants payment of OSPP to begin, whichever is later.

(c) He must continue to be employed by the employer up to the date of the child's placement, and have average earnings at least equal to the lower earnings limit for NI contributions.[130]

---

[124] PAL Regs 2002.
[125] PAL Regs 2002, reg 10(6).
[126] PAL Regs 2002, reg 11(2).
[127] SSCBA 1992, s 171ZE(2).
[128] SSCBA 1992, s 171ZB(2).
[129] SSCBA 1992, s 171ZB, SPP and SAP Regs 2002, reg 11.
[130] £102 per week or £442 a month for the year 2011–2012.

(d)   He must have declared his eligibility for OSPP by giving his employer Form SC4 at least 28 days before he wants his OSPP to start.

## Amount of OSPP, payment and recovery

**5.92**   The amount payable is the lower of:

(a)   the standard weekly rate (which, from 9 April 2012, is £135.45); or

(b)   90 per cent of the partner's average weekly pay.[131]

**5.93**   Rates change in April of each year by way of amendment of the Statutory Paternity Pay and Statutory Adoption Pay (Weekly Rates) Regulations 2002 ('Weekly Rates Regs 2002').

**5.94**   The parties cannot contract out of OSPP.[132] OSPP should be paid on the normal pay day or, if none exists, on the last day of the month.[133] OSPP is subject to tax and NI and can be paid in a lump sum, if both parties agree.

**5.95**   The HMRC software programme referred to above at **5.54** and **5.68** onwards will also assist employers with OSPP. The same principles of recovery apply.

## Notice requirements and evidence

### *UK adoption*

**5.96**   The partner must give at least 28 days' notice (or as soon as reasonably practicable) stating his name, when he wants his OSPP to begin, whether he is taking one or two weeks' leave and the expected (or actual) date of placement. The notice must be in writing.[134]

**5.97**   At the same time he must provide a written declaration that:[135]

(a)   he is the married, civil or unmarried partner of the adopter and he expects to have the main responsibility (apart from that of the adopter) for the upbringing of the child;

(b)   it is his purpose during the period of leave to care for the child and support the adopter; and

(c)   he has elected to take OSPP, rather than Statutory Adoption Pay ('SAP').

---

[131]   Statutory Paternity Pay and Statutory Adoption Pay (Weekly Rates) Regulations 2002 ('Weekly Rates Regs 2002'), reg 3.
[132]   SSCBA 1992, s 171ZF.
[133]   SPP and SAP Regs 2002, reg 42(1).
[134]   SPP and SAP Regs 2002, reg 15(2).
[135]   SPP and SAP Regs 2002, reg 15(1).

## *Overseas adoption*

**5.98** The partner must notify his employer of the date on which official notification was received within 28 days of receipt (or 28 days of his completion of 26 weeks' continuous employment, whichever is later) and must give notice of the date of the child's entry into Great Britain within 28 days.[136]

**5.99** Twenty-eight days before he wishes to start receiving OSPP (or as soon as reasonably practicable) he must provide a written notice containing the same elements as set out above for UK adoptions, with the expected (or actual) date of entry into Great Britain substituted for the date of placement.[137] The declaration must also contain the same elements but must state additionally that official notification has been received.[138]

## Start date

**5.100** In the case of a UK adoption, the partner can choose to begin receiving OSPP either on the date of placement or on a specified, later date,[139] which must be no more than 56 days after the date of placement.[140] The partner may vary the start date of OSPP, provided he gives notice 28 days before the new start date (or as soon as reasonably practicable).[141]

**5.101** In the case of an overseas adoption, the partner can elect to start receiving OSPP on the date on which the child enters Great Britain or on a predetermined date thereafter,[142] which must be no more than 56 days after the date of entry.[143] The same rules for variation apply.[144] If the child has not entered Great Britain on the expected date, or will not enter Great Britain at all, he must notify the employer as soon as reasonably practicable.[145]

## Stopping payment of OSPP

**5.102** The employer is not required to pay OSPP for any week during which the partner does any work for him.[146] The employer must stop paying OSPP altogether if: the employee works for another employer who did not employ them during the matching week; if he is arrested or imprisoned; or if he dies.[147]

---

[136] SPP and SAP (Overseas) Regs 2003, reg 7(1).
[137] SPP and SAP (Overseas) Regs 2003, reg 9(1).
[138] SPP and SAP (Overseas) Regs 2003, reg 9(2).
[139] SPP and SAP Regs 2002, reg 12(1).
[140] SPP and SAP Regs 2002, reg 14.
[141] SPP and SAP Regs 2002, reg 12(4) and SSCBA 1992, s 171ZC(1).
[142] SPP and SAP (Overseas) Regs 2003, reg 6.
[143] SPP and SAP (Overseas) Regs 2003, reg 8.
[144] SPP and SAP (Overseas) Regs 2003, reg 9(4) and SSCBA 1992, s 171ZC(1).
[145] SPP and SAP (Overseas) Regs 2003, reg 7(2) and (4).
[146] SPP and SAP Regs 2002, reg 17.
[147] SPP and SAP Regs 2002, reg 18.

## Forms and records

**5.103**  If the adopter does not qualify for OSPP the employer should give him form OSPP1, explaining the reasons for his decision. Other forms which can be used to discharge the various notice requirements can be found on the HMRC website.[148]

**5.104**  The employer must keep a record of OSPP and any changes in dates: form OSPP2 may be used for this. Otherwise, the requirements for forms and record-keeping are the same as for SAP (see **5.69** above). There is the same right to challenge a decision on OSPP with which the partner is not satisfied and, if necessary, to refer the matter to HMRC for guidance and/or a decision.

# ADDITIONAL PATERNITY LEAVE ('APL') FOR THE PARTNER

## Introduction

**5.105**  The Additional Paternity Leave Regulations 2010[149] ('APL Regs 2010'), which came into force on 6 April 2010,[150] allow partners who have been matched for adoption to take up to 26 weeks' Additional Paternity Leave ('APL') in addition to the two weeks' Statutory Paternity Leave, if the adopter returns to work. As above, 'partner' in this context includes married, civil and unmarried partners of either sex and whether the same or opposite sex.[151]

**5.106**  The Additional Paternity Leave (Adoption from Overseas) Regulations 2010[152] ('APL (Overseas) Regs 2010') set out the position for overseas adoptions.

**5.107**  Although some provisions (eg relating to protection from detriment) have applied since April 2010, the main rights relating to the entitlement to leave apply only where the child was placed on or after 3 April 2011.[153]

## Qualifying requirements

**5.108**  In the case of overseas adoptions, it is enough if the partner shares (or expects to share) responsibility for the upbringing of the child with the adopter.[154] However, in the case of UK adoptions, the requirement that the

---

[148]  Form SC3: Becoming a parent. Form SC4: Becoming an adoptive parent. Form SC5: Ordinary Statutory Paternity Pay and ordinary paternity leave when adopting from abroad.
[149]  SI 2010/1055.
[150]  APL Regs 2010, reg 1.
[151]  APL Regs 2010, reg 14(2)(c); APL (Overseas) Regs 2010, reg 4(2)(c).
[152]  SI 2010/1059.
[153]  APL Regs 2010, reg 3(2) and APL (Overseas) Regs 2010, reg 3(1).
[154]  APL (Overseas) Regs 2010, reg 4(2)(d).

partner must have been 'matched for adoption with the child'[155] means that only partners who are also co-adopters may take APL.

**5.109** The partner then qualifies for APL if:

(a) he and the adopter receive notification that they have been matched with a child for adoption on or after 3 April 2011;[156]

(b) in the case of overseas adoptions, the child enters Great Britain on or after 3 April 2011;[157]

(c) the adopter is entitled either to adoption leave or Statutory Adoption Pay;[158] but

(d) the adopter has returned to work.[159] The adopter is deemed to have returned to work when her adoption leave period has ended and any Statutory Adoption Pay is no longer payable.[160]

**5.110** He must be an employee with 26 weeks' employment by the qualifying week, which is:

(a) the end of the week he is notified that he is matched with the child (adopting within the UK);[161] or

(b) the date the child enters Great Britain (adopting from overseas).[162]

**5.111** He must then remain in employment from the qualifying week until the week (which runs Sunday to Saturday) before he wants to start the period of APL.[163]

**5.112** Agency workers, office holders and subcontractors do not normally have the right to take APL. However, they may be eligible for Additional Statutory Paternity Pay if they meet the other qualifying requirements and they have stopped working in order to care for the child (see below).

## Timing and length of leave

**5.113** APL can be taken at any time within the period which begins 20 weeks after the placement date (UK adoptions) or the date of the child's entry in

---

[155] APL Regs 2010, reg 14(2)(d).
[156] APL Regs 2010, reg 3(2).
[157] APL (Overseas) Regs 2010, reg 3(1).
[158] APL Regs 2010, reg 14(4)(a); APL (Overseas) Regs 2010, reg 4(4)(a).
[159] APL Regs 2010, reg 14(4)(b); APL (Overseas) Regs 2010, reg 4(4)(b). For the definition of 'returned to work' see reg 25.
[160] APL Regs 2010, reg 25; APL (Overseas) Regs 2010, reg 15.
[161] APL Regs 2010, reg 14(2)(a) and (3).
[162] APL (Overseas) Regs 2010, reg 4(2)(a) and (3).
[163] APL Regs 2010, reg 14(2)(b) and 14(3); APL (Overseas) Regs 2010, reg 4(2)(b) and (3).

Great Britain (overseas adoptions) and ends 12 months after that date. The minimum period of leave is two weeks, the maximum 26 and it must be taken in complete weeks and as one continuous period.[164]

## Notice and evidential requirements

**5.114**   The partner must give eight weeks' notice of his intention to take APL and provide his employer with a 'leave notice' and an 'employee declaration'. The adopter must provide an 'adopter declaration'.[165]

## UK adoptions

**5.115**   The information which must be contained in each of these documents is specified in the APL 2010 Regs and is illustrated in the following example.[166]

> 'EXAMPLE: Sally and Rob have co-adopted a child, Tom. Sally has elected to be the adopter for the purposes of leave and has taken OAL and a short period of AAL. She has now decided to return to work. Rob has already taken his two weeks of Ordinary Paternity Leave and wants to take APL to care for Tom.
>
> Eight weeks before he wants to start his APL, Rob must give his employer a written "leave notice", stating the date on which he was notified of having been matched with Tom; the date on which Tom was placed with him; and the dates which he has chosen to start and end his APL.
>
> At the same time he must provide a signed "employee declaration" document, stating that the purpose of the period of leave will be to care for Tom; that he has been matched with Tom for adoption; and that he satisfies the conditions in APL Regs 2010, reg14(2)(c) and (d), ie that he is either Sally's husband or partner.
>
> Sally must provide Rob's employer with a written declaration stating: Sally's name and address, the date she intends to return to work and her National Insurance number; that Rob satisfies the conditions in APL Regs 2010, reg14(2)(c), ie Rob is either her husband or partner; and stating that she consents to Rob's employer processing the information about Sally contained in the declaration.'

## Overseas adoptions

**5.116**   The information which must be contained in each of these documents is specified in the APL (Overseas) 2010 Regs and is illustrated in the following example.[167]

---

[164]   APL Regs 2010, reg 15; APL (Overseas) Regs 2010, reg 5.
[165]   APL Regs 2010, reg 16(1); APL (Overseas) Regs 2010, reg 6(1).
[166]   APL Regs 2010, reg 16(2).
[167]   APL (Overseas) Regs 2010, reg 6(2).

'EXAMPLE: Sally is adopting a child, Maria, from overseas and Rob is her partner. Sally has taken OAL and a short period of AAL. She has now decided to return to work. Rob has already taken his two weeks of Ordinary Paternity Leave and wants to take APL to care for Tom.

Eight weeks before he wants to start his APL, Rob must give his employer a written "leave notice", stating the date on which Sally received official notification; the date on which Maria entered Great Britain; and the dates which he has chosen to start and end his APL.

At the same time he must provide a signed "employee declaration" document, stating that the purpose of the period of leave will be to care for Maria; and that he satisfies the conditions in APL (Overseas) Regs 2010, reg4(2)(c) and (d), ie that he is either Sally's husband or partner.

Sally must provide Rob's employer with a written declaration stating: Sally's name and address, the date she intends to return to work and her National Insurance number; that Rob satisfies the conditions in APL Regs 2010, reg 4(2)(c), ie Rob is either her husband or partner; and stating that she consents to Rob's employer processing the information about Sally contained in the declaration.'

## Both types of adoption

**5.117** The employer must write to the partner within 28 days of receiving notice of APL, confirming the start and end dates of the APL. If the partner varies the dates, the employer must send fresh confirmation.[168] If he fails to do so, he forfeits the right to prevent the partner from returning early from leave in circumstances where he has not given him adequate notice. Furthermore he may be acting unlawfully if he dismisses the partner, or treats him detrimentally, for failing to return at the end of his leave (see below at **5.141**).[169]

**5.118** Within the same period, the employer can ask for proof of the information provided by the partner. The following example illustrates the information he may request for a UK adoption.[170]

'EXAMPLE: Just under 28 days after receiving the leave notice from him, Rob's employer writes to him confirming the dates of his APL and, at the same time, asking for proof (in the form of documents issued by the adoption agency) of: the name and address of the agency; the date on which Rob was notified that he had been matched with Tom; the date on which the agency expects to place Tom for adoption with Rob and Sally; and the name and address of Sally's employer. Rob provides the documents well within the 28-day period allowed for him to reply.'

**5.119** The following example illustrates the information he may request for an overseas adoption.[171]

---

[168] APL Regs 2010, reg 18; APL (Overseas) Regs, reg 8.
[169] APL Regs 2010, regs 33(1)(c) and 34(3)(c); APL (Overseas ) Regs, reg 23(1)(c) and 24(3)(c).
[170] APL Regs 2010, reg 16(3).
[171] APL (Overseas) Regs 2010, reg 6(3).

'EXAMPLE: Just under 28 days after receiving the leave notice from him, Rob's employer writes to him confirming the dates of his APL and, at the same time, asking for: a copy of the official notification; evidence of the date on which Maria entered Great Britain; and the name and address of Sally's employer. Rob provides the documents well within the 28-day period allowed for him to reply.'

## Varying the dates of APL

### *Variation or cancellation of APL by choice*

**5.120**   The leave can be cancelled, or the start or end date varied, provided the partner gives his employer written notice six weeks before the original date or six weeks before the new date, whichever is the earlier. Notice may be given 'as soon as is reasonably practicable' if the six-week notice requirement cannot be complied with.[172]

**5.121**   However, if less than six weeks' notice is given, and the new arrangement cannot be accommodated by the employer, the employer can require the partner to take a period of APL starting on the date previously agreed. The partner must be allowed to return to work no more than six weeks after he gave notice of cancellation or variation and, in any event, he cannot be required to remain on leave beyond the previously agreed end date.[173]

'EXAMPLE: Rob has previously agreed with his employer that his APL would end on 30 April. On 1 April Sally and Rob learn that a nursery place has become available for Tom at very short notice which reduces the need for Rob to care for him at home. On 2 April ("as soon as reasonably practicable") Rob tells his employer that he wants to bring the end date of his APL forward to 10 April. This is inconvenient for the employer as it has engaged cover for Rob on a fixed-term contract until the end of April. Because Rob has not given six weeks' notice, the employer is entitled to tell him to remain on leave for the rest of the month but it cannot extend his leave beyond the original end date of 30 April. The employer must confirm the requirement to remain on leave to Rob in writing as soon as reasonably practicable after Rob tells him of his wish to return to work.

If Rob had been able to give notice on 1 March, the employer could only have required him to remain on leave until 5 April, a maximum of 6 weeks.'

**5.122**   If the employer exercises this right to require the partner to take a period of APL against his wishes, the employer must confirm the dates of required APL to him in writing within 28 days of receipt of the partner's notice of variation or cancellation, or as soon as is reasonably practicable, and in any event before the beginning of the period of required leave.[174]

---

[172]   APL Regs 2010, reg 17(1); APL (Overseas) Regs 2010, reg 7(1).
[173]   APL Regs 2010, reg 17(2) and (3); APL (Overseas) Regs 2010, reg 7(2) and (3).
[174]   APL Regs 2010, reg 18; APL (Overseas) Regs 2010, reg 8.

## *Withdrawal from APL because of changed circumstances*

**5.123** APL cannot continue if the adopter is no longer at work, the partners split up or divorce or the child is no longer matched with the partner for adoption. In those circumstances, the partner must give his employer written 'withdrawal notice' of his intention to take APL as soon as reasonably practicable.[175]

**5.124** If that notice is given less than six weeks before the APL was due to begin, and it is not practical for the employer to accommodate the change of arrangement, the employer can require the partner to take a period of APL starting on the date previously agreed but he must be allowed to return to work no more than six weeks after he gave his 'withdrawal notice'.[176] That limit of six weeks applies equally if the 'withdrawal notice' is given after APL has already begun[177] but the partner cannot be required to remain on leave beyond the previously agreed end date.[178]

**5.125** The employer has the same obligation to notify the partner in writing and within a specific period of the dates of required leave as described in the previous section:

> 'EXAMPLE: Rob was due to start APL on 30 March. His partner, Sally, suddenly loses her job on 15 March. Because Sally will not be at work, Rob is no longer entitled to take APL and on 16 March ('as soon as reasonably practicable') gives his "withdrawal notice" to his employer. Because he has not given six weeks' notice, the employer is entitled to require him to take leave between 30 March (his original start date) and 3 May (six weeks after the withdrawal notice). The employer must confirm these dates to Rob in writing as soon as reasonably practicable after receiving the withdrawal notice and, in any event, before 30 March.'

## APL in the event of the death of the adopter

**5.126** There are specific provisions dealing with the partner's entitlement to take APL in the event of the death of the adopter. Unless the partner already taken and returned from a period of APL,[179] he may take it from the date of the adopter's death until 52 weeks after the date of placement (UK adoptions) or date of entry into Great Britain (overseas adoptions).[180] The leave may be taken immediately, provided he informs the employer of the adopter's death as soon as is reasonably practicable and then goes on to comply with the formal requirements set out below.[181]

---

[175] APL Regs 2010, reg 16(4); APL (Overseas) Regs 2010, reg 6(4).
[176] APL Regs 2010, reg 16(5); APL (Overseas) Regs 2010, reg 6(5).
[177] APL Regs 2010, reg 16(7); APL (Overseas) Regs 2010, reg 6(7).
[178] APL Regs 2010, reg 16(8); APL (Overseas) Regs 2010, reg 6(8).
[179] APL Regs 2010, reg 21(4); APL (Overseas) Regs 2010, reg 11(4).
[180] APL Regs 2010, reg 21(1); APL (Overseas) Regs 2010, reg 11(1).
[181] APL Regs 2010, reg 22(4); APL (Overseas) Regs 2010, reg 12(4).

**5.127**  If he is already on leave when the adopter dies, he may extend his APL within the overall limit of 52 weeks from the date of placement/date of entry.[182] As soon as reasonably practicable after the adopter's death, and in any event no later than eight weeks after the adopter's death, the partner must give his employer a 'leave notice' and an 'employee declaration'.[183] The leave notice must contain the same elements as it would in ordinary circumstances (see the above example at **5.115** and **5.116**). The requirements of the employee declaration are illustrated in the following example.

> 'EXAMPLE: Sally and Rob co-adopted a child, Tom but Sally was the elected adopter. Sally has died. As soon as reasonably practicable, Rob must give his employer a written "leave notice". At the same time he must provide a signed "employee declaration" document, stating that the purpose of the period of leave will be to care for Tom; that he satisfies the conditions in APL Regs 2010, reg14(2)(c) and (d), ie that he was either Sally's husband or partner; giving Sally's name and last address, the date of her death and her National Insurance number.'

**5.128**  If the partner does not want to take the leave immediately, he must provide the leave notice and employee declaration at least six weeks before the proposed start date of the APL.[184]

**5.129**  The employer may require the partner to produce the same evidence as in ordinary circumstances (see above at **5.118** and **5.119**), with the obvious variation that the placement date/date of entry will now be in the past and the relevant name and address will be that of the late adopter's last employer.[185]

**5.130**  The minimum period of leave is two weeks, the maximum 52 weeks.[186]

**5.131**  There is specific provision in both sets of 2010 Regulations for the variation or cancellation of leave which has been taken in these circumstances[187] which to a great extent mirrors the rules which apply in ordinary circumstances (see above at **5.120** onwards). The principal difference is that the partner may vary or cancel any start or end date simply by notifying the employer in writing on or before the date that is varied or cancelled, if he does so within eight weeks of the death of the adopter.[188] Once those eight weeks have passed, however, the usual requirement to give six weeks' notice applies as, does the employer's right to postpone the return to work if it is not reasonably practicable to accommodate the change.[189]

**5.132**  There is a continuing obligation on the partner to terminate the leave if the qualifying requirements for APL are no longer met, for example if the

---

[182]  APL Regs 2010, reg 21(5); APL (Overseas) Regs 2010, reg 11(5).
[183]  APL Regs 2010, reg 22(1); APL (Overseas) Regs 2010, reg 11(1).
[184]  APL Regs 2010, reg 22(5); APL (Overseas) Regs 2010, reg 12(5).
[185]  APL Regs 2010, reg 22(3); APL (Overseas) Regs 2010, reg 12(3).
[186]  APL Regs 2010, reg 21(2); APL (Overseas) Regs 2010, reg 11(2).
[187]  APL Regs 2010, reg 23; APL (Overseas) Regs 2010, reg 13.
[188]  APL Regs 2010, reg 23(1); APL (Overseas) Regs 2010, reg 13(1).
[189]  APL Regs 2010, reg 23(2) to (5); APL (Overseas) Regs 2010, reg 13(2) to (5).

adoption placement is terminated. The same rules apply as to the provision of a 'withdrawal notice'[190] and the employer's ability to postpone the return to week if insufficient notice is given[191] (see above at **5.123** onwards).

## Disrupted placement or death of a child in the course of APL

**5.133** If the child dies or is returned to the adoption agency within the APL leave notice period or during APL, the partner is entitled to remain on leave for a further eight weeks from the end of the week in question or until the notified end date of the APL, whichever is the sooner.[192]

## Right to return after APL

**5.134** The partner has the right to return to the same job, provided he is returning from:

(a) an isolated period of APL lasting no longer than 26 weeks;

(b) a period of APL lasting no more than 26 weeks, which was the last of two or more consecutive periods of statutory leave, provided the periods of leave did not include any AML, AAL or a period of parental leave lasting more than four weeks.[193]

**5.135** If he is returning from leave but he does not meet these requirements, he is entitled to return to the same job unless his employer can show that it is not reasonable practicable for him to permit it. In that case, the partner is entitled to return to a job which is both suitable for him and appropriate for him to do in the circumstances.[194]

**5.136** In either case he is entitled to return on terms and conditions no less favourable than those which applied before his period of leave.[195]

## APL provisions which mirror adoption leave

**5.137** Many of the provisions in the 2010 Regs which apply to APL mirror those which apply to OAL and AAL. They are summarised below.

---

[190] APL Regs 2010, reg 22(6); APL (Overseas) Regs 2010, reg 12(6).
[191] APL Regs 2010, reg 22(7) to (10); APL (Overseas) Regs 2010, reg 12(7) to (10).
[192] APL Regs 2010, reg 24; APL Regs (Overseas) Regs 2010, reg 14.
[193] APL Regs 2010, reg 31(1); APL (Overseas) Regs 2010, reg 21(1).
[194] APL Regs 2010, reg 31(2); APL (Overseas) Regs 2010, reg 21(2).
[195] APL Regs 2010, reg 32; APL (Overseas) Regs 2010, reg 22.

## *Keeping in touch and working during APL*

**5.138** The partner and employer are entitled to maintain reasonable contact and to work up to ten 'keeping in touch days' during the APL period[196] (see above at **5.33**).

## *Application of terms and conditions during APL*

**5.139** During APL the partner's terms and conditions of employment continue to apply. Terms and conditions relating to remuneration are excluded. Only wages and salary are deemed to be remuneration. There is no requirement that pension contributions be paid during the unpaid part of leave[197] (see above at **5.28** onwards).

## *Redundancy during APL*

**5.140** If by reason of redundancy it is not practicable for the employer to continue to employ the partner under his existing contract, he has the right to be offered a suitable alternative vacancy. The alternative vacancy must both suitable to the employee and appropriate for her to do in the circumstances. Its terms and conditions must be not substantially less favourable than those which applied under her old contract of employment.[198] If the employer dismisses in breach of these requirements, that dismissal will be automatically unfair.[199]

## *Protection from detriment and dismissal*

**5.141** The partner is entitled not to be subjected to detriment[200] or dismissed[201] on the same prohibited grounds as apply to Adoption Leave (see above at **5.45** onwards). A dismissal in breach of these provisions will be automatically unfair.

**5.142** The protection from detriment and unfair dismissal provisions apply where the detriment or dismissal occurred on or after 6 April 2010 (UK adoptions)[202] or on or after 9 April 2010 (overseas adoptions).[203] Where an act extends over a period, the last day of that period is the material date.[204] A failure to act is treated as done on the date when it is decided upon.[205]

---

196   APL Regs 2010, reg 26; APL (Overseas) Regs 2010, reg 16.
197   APL Regs 2010, reg 27; APL (Overseas) Regs 2010, reg 17.
198   APL Regs 2010, reg 28; APL (Overseas) Regs 2010, reg 18.
199   APL Regs 2010, reg 34(1)(b); APL (Overseas) Regs 2010, reg 24(1)(b).
200   APL Regs 2010, reg 33; APL (Overseas) Regs 2010, reg 23.
201   APL Regs 2010, reg 34; APL (Overseas) Regs 2010, reg 33.
202   APL Regs 2010, reg 3(3) and 3(6); APL (Overseas) Regs 2010.
203   APL (Overseas) Regs 2010, reg 3(2) and 3(5).
204   APL Regs 2010, reg 3(4)(a); APL (Overseas) Regs 2010, reg 3(3)(a).
205   APL Regs 2010, reg 3(4)(b); APL (Overseas) Regs 2010, reg 3(3)(b). Absent evidence as to when that date is, see Reg 3(5)/Reg 3(4) for the applicable deeming provisions.

# ADDITIONAL STATUTORY PATERNITY PAY ('ASPP')

## Introduction

**5.143** Additional Statutory Paternity Pay ('ASPP') is payable if the partner intends to care for the child during the period of the adopter's 39 week' Statutory Adoption Pay period.

**5.144** The relevant provisions are in the Additional Statutory Paternity Pay Regulations 2010[206] ('ASPP Regs 2010') and the Additional Statutory Paternity Pay (Adoption from Overseas) Regulations 2010[207] ('ASPP (Overseas) Regs 2010'), which came into force on 9 April 2010. The right applies to children placed for adoption (UK adoptions) or who entered Great Britain (overseas adoptions) on or after 3 April 2011.[208]

**5.145** Many of the provisions mirror those which apply to Additional Paternity Leave ('APL'). Reference will be made back to the relevant paragraphs in that section of the chapter.

## Qualifying for ASPP

**5.146** In the case of overseas adoptions, in order to be entitled to ASPP it is enough if the partner shares (or expects) to share responsibility for the upbringing of the child with the adopter.[209] However, in the case of UK adoptions, the partner is only entitled to ASPP if he is co-adopting the child.[210] This mirrors the position with APL.

**5.147** The partner may be entitled to ASPP, even if he is not entitled to APL. He must be an employee but, for these purposes, the definition of employee is wider. It covers anyone for whom the employer pays Class 1 National Insurance ('NI') contributions, or for whom he would pay them if their earnings were sufficiently high.[211] Consequently, office holders (members of the armed forces, police and MPs etc) will be eligible for SAP, as will apprentices and many agency and casual workers.

**5.148** ASPP is payable to a partner who:

(a)  intends to care for the child during the 39-week period covered by the adopter's statutory adoption pay;[212] and

---

[206]  SI 2010/1056.
[207]  SI 2010/1057.
[208]  ASPP Regs 2010 reg 3(a); ASPP (Overseas) Regs 2010, reg 4.
[209]  ASPP (Overseas) Regs 2010, reg 5(2)(b).
[210]  ASPP Regs 2010, reg 12(2)(b).
[211]  ASPP Regs 2010, reg 24; ASPP (Overseas) Regs 2010, reg 5(3)(a).
[212]  ASPP Regs 2010, reg 12(1); ASPP (Overseas) Regs 2010, reg 5(1).

(b)  has returned to work not less than two weeks after the child was placed for adoption (UK adoptions)/entered Great Britain (overseas adoptions); and

(c)  has at least two weeks of her statutory adoption pay remaining.[213]

**5.149**  The partner must meet all the eligibility criteria for taking APL.

(a)  He must have been continuously employed for the required period and remain employed when the pay period begins (see above at **5.110** onwards).[214] The ASPP Regs expressly adopt the definition of continuous employment contained in sections 210–218 of the ERA 1996.[215]

(b)  He must be in an appropriate relationship with the adopter (see above at **5.105**).[216]

(c)  He must complete the relevant notification formalities (see above at **5.114** onwards).[217]

**5.150**  In addition there is an earnings requirement. The partner must have had normal weekly earnings during the eight weeks ending with the relevant week not less than the National Insurance Lower Earnings Limit, £102 per week in the 2011–2012 tax year.[218]

**5.151**  The 'relevant week' in the case of UK adoptions is the week in which he is matched with the child for adoption. In the case of an overseas adoption it is the week in which official notification was received or in which the partner completes 26 weeks' continuous employment, whichever is the later.

**5.152**  The maximum length of the ASPP period is 26 weeks.[219]

**5.153**  The current rate of ASPP is the lower of either:

(a)  the standard weekly rate, which from 9 April 2012 is £135.45; or

(b)  90 per cent of the partner's average weekly earnings.[220]

**5.154**  As with other forms of statutory leave pay, the employer can recover some or all of its ASPP payments from HMRC.

---

[213] ASPP Regs 2010, reg 13; ASPP (Overseas) Regs 2010, reg 6. The definition of 'return to work' is contained in ASPP Regs 2010, reg 19 and ASPP (Overseas) Regs 2010, reg 12.

[214] ASPP Regs 2010, reg 12(3)(a); ASPP (Overseas) Regs 2010, reg 5(3)(a).

[215] ASPP Regs 2010, regs 26–30.

[216] ASPP Regs 2010, reg 12(2); ASPP (Overseas) Regs 2010, reg 5(2).

[217] ASPP Regs 2010, reg 12(1)(d); ASPP (Overseas) Regs 2010, reg 5(1)(d).

[218] The definitions of 'earnings' and 'normal weekly earnings' are set out in ASPP Regs 2010, regs 31 and 32.

[219] ASPP Regs 2010, reg 14(3); ASPP (Overseas) Regs 2010, reg 7(3).

[220] Additional Statutory Paternity Pay (Weekly Rates) Regulations 2010 (SI 2010/1060), reg 2.

## Notice and evidential requirements

**5.155**   The partner must give eight weeks' notice of his intention to take ASPP and provide his employer with a written 'application and declaration'. The adopter must provide an 'adopter declaration'.[221]

**5.156**   The information which must be contained in the partner's declaration is specified in the Regulations[222] and is the same as the information required in the partner's application for APL, as illustrated in the examples above at **5.115** and **5.116**, simply substituting the start and end dates for ASPP.

**5.157**   The 'adopter's declaration', however, is slightly different.[223] To adapt the example:

> 'Sally must provide Rob's employer with a written declaration stating: her name, address and National Insurance number; the start date of her period of Statutory Adoption Pay; that she has given notice to her employer that she is returning to work and the date on which she intends to return to work; she must confirm that Rob is the sole applicant for ASPP; and stating that she consents to Rob's employer processing the information about Sally contained in the declaration.'

**5.158**   As with APL, the employer can ask for proof of the information provided by the partner within 28 days.[224] The examples above at **5.118** and **5.119** illustrate the information he may request.

**5.159**   The employer must write to the partner within 28 days of receiving notice of intention to receive ASPP, confirming the start and end dates of the pay period.[225]

## Start date

**5.160**   The partner can choose to begin receiving ASPP on a date specified by him no earlier than the date the adopter returns to work and, in any event, no earlier than 20 weeks after the expected date of placement (UK adoptions)/after the date of entry into Great Britain (overseas adoptions).[226]

**5.161**   In the event of the adopter's death, the period of ASPP may start immediately, provided the partner notifies the employer as soon as reasonably practicable.[227]

---

[221]   ASPP Regs 2010, reg 15; ASPP (Overseas) Regs 2010, reg 8.
[222]   ASPP Regs 2010, reg 15; ASPP (Overseas) Regs 2010, reg 8.
[223]   ASPP Regs 2010, reg 15(1)(c); ASPP (Overseas) Regs 2010, reg 8(1)(c).
[224]   ASPP Regs 2010, reg 15(3); ASPP (Overseas) Regs 2010, reg 8(3).
[225]   ASPP Regs 2010, reg 15(8); ASPP (Overseas) Regs 2010, reg 8(8).
[226]   ASPP Regs 2010, reg 14(1); ASPP (Overseas) Regs 2010, reg 7(1).
[227]   ASPP Regs 2010, reg 14(4); ASPP (Overseas) Regs 2010, reg 7(4).

## Varying the dates of ASPP

### *Variation or cancellation of ASPP by choice*

**5.162** The application for ASPP can be cancelled, or the start or end date varied, provided the partner gives his employer written notice six weeks before the original date or six weeks before the new date, whichever is the earlier. Notice may be given 'as soon as is reasonably practicable' if the six-week notice requirement cannot be complied with.[228]

### *Withdrawal from ASPP because of changed circumstances*

**5.163** The entitlement to ASPP ceases if the adopter is no longer at work, the partners split up or divorce or the child is no longer matched with the partner for adoption. In those circumstances, the partner must inform his employer of the changed circumstances as soon as reasonably practicable.[229]

## ASPP in the event of the death of the adopter

**5.164** There are specific provisions dealing with the partner's entitlement to receive ASPP in the event of the death of the adopter.[230]

**5.165** The application should be made in writing in the usual form by providing a written application and declaration (see above at **5.155–5.159**) as soon as reasonably practicable. In addition the date of the adopter's death must be provided.[231] The start date may be backdated provided it falls within the period of entitlement.[232]

**5.166** The application must be made as soon as reasonably practicable after the adopter's death, and in any event no later than eight weeks after the adopter's death.[233]

**5.167** If the application is made more than eight weeks after the adopter's death, the partner must provide the application and declaration at least six weeks before the proposed start date of the ASPP.[234]

**5.168** There is specific provision in both sets of 2010 Regulations for the variation or cancellation of the ASPP pay period in the event of the adopter's death[235] which to a great extent mirrors the rules which apply in ordinary circumstances (see above at **5.162** onwards). The principal difference is that the partner may vary or cancel any start or end date simply by notifying the

---

[228] ASPP Regs 2010, reg15(6); ASPP (Overseas) Regs 2010, reg 8(6).
[229] ASPP Regs 2010, reg 15(7); ASPP (Overseas) Regs 2010, reg 8(7).
[230] ASPP Regs 2010, regs 16 and 17; ASPP (Overseas) Regs 2010, regs 9 and 10.
[231] ASPP Regs 2010, regs 17(1) to (3); ASPP (Overseas) Regs 2010, regs 10(1) to (3).
[232] ASPP Regs 2010, reg 17(1)(a); ASPP (Overseas) Regs 2010, reg 10(1)(a).
[233] ASPP Regs 2010, reg 17(4); ASPP (Overseas) Regs 2010, reg 10(4).
[234] ASPP Regs 2010, reg 17(5); ASPP (Overseas) Regs 2010, reg 10(5).
[235] ASPP Regs 2010, reg 17(7) and (8); ASPP (Overseas) Regs 2010, reg 10(7) and (8).

employer in writing on or before the date that is varied or cancelled, if he does so within eight weeks of the death of the adopter. Once those eight weeks have passed, however, the requirement to give six weeks' notice applies.

**5.169** When ASPP is claimed in these circumstances, there is the usual obligation on the employer formally to notify the employee of the start and end dates of the pay period within 28 days of receipt of the application.[236]

## Work during the ASPP period

**5.170** Entitlement to ASPP ceases if the partner works for another employer who is not liable to pay ASPP during the pay period, unless the partner worked for that other employer in the week preceding the 14th week before the expected week of placement. The partner must notify the employer who has been paying ASPP within seven days, in writing if so required. If the other work is for an employer who is liable to pay ASPP, the original employer remains liable to pay ASPP if no more than ten days are worked.[237]

## Other provisions

**5.171** There are parallel provisions in the ASPP Regulations 2010, which mirror the equivalent SMP or APL provisions.

(a) Reg 21 provides that there is no entitlement to ASPP following the partner's death, or for any week during which he is entitled to Statutory Sick Pay, or he is detained in custody (unless he is subsequently released without charge, acquitted or given a non-custodial sentence, in which case the entitlement is revived).

(b) Reg 22 provides for the mutual setting-off of contractual and statutory pay.

(c) Reg 23 provides for liability to pay where the employer dismissed the partner to avoid paying ASPP.

## Forms and records

**5.172** The employer has the same obligation as with SAP to notify the employee formally if he considers that the partner does not qualify for ASPP (see above at **5.72** onwards). These and other forms which can be used to discharge the various notice requirements can be found on the HMRC website.[238] The employer must keep a record of ASPP and any changes in dates. Otherwise, the requirements for forms and record-keeping are the same as for SAP (see **5.68** onwards above). There is the same right to challenge a decision

---

[236] ASPP Regs 2010, reg 17(9); ASPP (Overseas) Regs 2010, reg 10(9).

[237] ASPP Regs 2010, reg 20.

[238] Form SC3: Becoming a parent. Form SC4: Becoming an adoptive parent. Form SC5: Ordinary Statutory Paternity Pay and ordinary paternity leave when adopting from abroad.

on ASPP with which the partner is not satisfied and, if necessary, to refer the matter to HMRC for guidance and/or a decision.

# Chapter 6

# STATUTORY MATERNITY PAY AND ALLOWANCES

*Sally Robertson*

## MATERNITY BENEFITS

### Introduction

**6.1**  It is important to remember that maternity pay and maternity leave are different things. All employed women are legally entitled to 52 weeks of maternity leave – see Chapter 4.[1] This is the case even if they do not qualify for statutory maternity pay or state maternity allowance. Although there is no legal link between maternity leave and statutory maternity pay, the symmetry between the two regimes suggests that you can expect them to work in harmony.[2]

### *Statutory maternity pay*

**6.2**  Statutory maternity pay (SMP) was first introduced in 1986. It is paid for up to 39 weeks by the employer in the same way as salary or wages to female employees who meet the qualifying conditions. If a woman has more than one employer, she can get SMP from each employment where she meets the qualifying conditions.

**6.3**  The core conditions are first, that the woman's average weekly earnings in the eight weeks up to the end of the 15th week before the week in which the baby is due are at least equal to the lower earnings limit for national insurance contributions (£102 in the 2011–2012 tax year).[3]

**6.4**  Secondly, that she has been (or if the baby is born early, would have been) employed by the same employer for at least 26 weeks continuously by the last day of the 15th week before the week in which the baby is due.

---

[1]  See Maternity & Parental Leave etc Regulations 1999, SI1999/3312 (MPL Regs), reg 4. Note that if a woman was unable to give the notice required by reg 4(1)(a) by the end of the 15th week before her due date because she was not employed until later, it would usually only be 'reasonably practicable' to give that notice once she was able to accept a later offer of employment.

[2]  See *Wade v North Yorkshire Police Authority & HMRC* [2011] IRLR 393 for implicit support for that proposition from the Upper Tribunal.

[3]  This is lower than the level at which she would start paying NI contributions on her earnings. That point is known as the 'primary threshold' and is £139 pw in 2011–2012.

**6.5**    For the first six weeks SMP is paid at 90% of the woman's average weekly earnings. For the remaining 33 weeks, it is paid at either the standard weekly rate (£135.45 in 2012–2013[4]) or, where her average earnings are lower, SMP continues at the 90% rate.

**6.6**    If an employer dismisses a woman 'solely or mainly for the purpose of avoiding liability for SMP', that employer remains liable to pay SMP to her if she had been employed by him for at least eight weeks continuously. Her average earnings are based on the eight weeks before the last day in respect of which she was paid.[5]

**6.7**    Employers with an annual liability to Class 1 (employer and employee) national insurance contributions of £45,000 or less are entitled to recover all of their SMP payments, with an additional 3% to compensate for the employer national insurance contributions due on the SMP itself. Employers may also apply to HMRC for advance payment.

**6.8**    Employers with a higher annual liability to national insurance contributions can recover only 92% of their SMP payments.

**6.9**    SMP now comes under the Social Security Contributions and Benefits Act 1992 (SSCBA 1992), with most of the detail found in the Statutory Maternity Pay (General) Regulations 1986. The administration of SMP is overseen by HM Revenue & Customs (HMRC). Employers can get guidance from HMRC but do not have the right to a formal decision. Only an employee has the right to ask HMRC for a formal decision. Both employer and employee then have the right to appeal against that decision to the Tax Chamber of the First Tier Tribunal.

## State maternity allowance

**6.10**    If an employee does not qualify for SMP she may qualify for state maternity allowance instead. The employer must provide her with form SMP1 explaining why she does not qualify for SMP and, if requested, a more detailed written explanation. State maternity allowance is not means-tested and does not depend on national insurance contributions. Instead, there is a work test and an average earnings test. By the last day of the 15th week before her baby is due, she must have been an employee or self-employed in any part of any of the 26 weeks out of the previous 66 weeks. Taking her best 13 weeks of earnings in that period, the average should be not less than £30 a week.

**6.11**    The amount of state maternity allowance payable is the lower of the standard weekly rate (£135.45 in 2012–2013) or 90% of her average weekly earnings (worked out on her best 13 weeks). As state maternity allowance

---

[4]    The standard rate of SMP is uprated in the first week of April. The date varies but is always given in the Social Security Benefits Uprating Order each year. In 2011, SMP standard rate increased on 3 April.

[5]    Statutory Maternity Pay (General) Regulations 1986, SI 1986/1960 (SMPG Regs), reg 3.

works out average earnings on the best 13 weeks rather than on the last eight weeks used for SMP, the 90% rate is unlikely to be less than it would have been for SMP.

**6.12** State maternity allowance also comes under the Social Security Contributions and Benefits Act 1992, with most of the detail found in the Social Security (Maternity Allowance) Regulations 1987. Maternity allowance is administered by the jobcentre plus division of the Department for Work and Pensions, with a right of appeal to the Social Entitlement Chamber of the First Tier Tribunal.

## Key terms

**6.13** Qualifying week – this is the 15th week (Sunday to Saturday) before the week in which the baby is due. It is the key week for establishing entitlement and working out average earnings for SMP purposes.

**6.14** Relevant period – this is the eight-week period used to establish a woman's average earnings. It covers the period between two dates. The first date is the last normal payday on or before the last day (a Saturday) of the qualifying week. The second date is the day after the last normal pay day falling at least eight weeks earlier. A 'week' for this purpose runs from Sunday to Saturday.

**6.15** Maternity pay period – this is the period during which SMP can be paid, a maximum of 39 weeks. Unless the baby is born earlier, the maternity pay period cannot start before the start of the 11th week before the week in which the baby is due. As a benchmark date which defines the earliest start to the maternity pay period, the start of the 11th week before always falls on a Sunday. The start of the maternity pay period can only fall on another day of the week where a woman chooses to begin her SMP from a date later than the start of the 11th week before her due date. The weeks coming within the maternity pay period in that case start with the day of the week chosen by the woman as her first day of payment.

## Information

**6.16** HMRC produce an annual Employer Helpbook for SMP,[6] with detailed checklists and a table showing the key dates for each employee's entitlement to SMP and maternity leave. Forms and information assist with the mandatory record-keeping. If the payroll software used by the employer does not work out the SMP payments and the amounts recoverable, then on-line tools, such as the SMP calculator, are available. Invitations to access free training workshops or call an employer helpline offer help to more challenged employers. The range of provision does put in context the inclusion in the Helpbook of a list of civil financial penalties for failure to comply with the SMP rules. Even the

---

[6]   E15(2011).

downloadable forms give straightforward and helpful information. The help available to employers is such that a failure to access that help and a failure to deliver the right amount of SMP are arguably factors that could support an inference of sex or pregnancy and maternity discrimination.

## WHO QUALIFIES FOR SMP?

**6.17**  To qualify, a woman must be pregnant and, unless the baby was born earlier, have reached the 11th week before the week in which the baby is due.[7] She must also have given her employer the required notice,[8] stopped working[9] and meet the following conditions:

### Employee status

**6.18**  First, the woman must be an employee.[10] In essence, for SMP purposes, an employee is any woman who is (or would be but for her age or if she earned enough) liable to pay Class 1 national insurance contributions on her earnings. Switching viewpoints, if the 'employer' is liable (or would be liable but for her age or if the woman earned enough) to pay secondary (employer) Class 1 national insurance contributions on the woman's earnings, then the woman counts as an employee.

**6.19**  Apprentices and paid office holders count as employees. So too do Crown employees[11] and those treated as employees by the Social Security (Categorisation of Earners) Regulations 1978.[12] The rule of thumb is that the woman counts as an employee if she comes within scope of the liability to pay Class 1 contributions even where no contributions are required to be made. If in doubt, contact HMRC.

### Continuous employment

**6.20**  Secondly, she must have been employed continuously by the same employer for at least 26 weeks by the end of the 15th week before the week (Sunday to Saturday) in which the baby is due.[13]

---

[7]  SSCBA 1992, s 164(2)(c).
[8]  SSCBA 1992, s 164(4), (5).
[9]  SSCBA 1992, s 165(4), (5), (6).
[10]  SSCBA 1992, s 171(1).
[11]  SSCBA 1992, s 169.
[12]  SI 1978/1689 and SMPG Regs, reg 17.
[13]  SSCBA 1992, s164(2)(a), s 171(1A) and note that entitlement and payability are treated separately. There is a different definition of 'week' for purposes of the 'maternity pay period' and making SMP payments. Instead of starting with a Sunday, it starts with the day of the week from which the woman wishes her SMP to commence – see s 165(8) and s 166(1A).

**6.21**  Where a baby is born in the 15th week before the due date, or earlier, the continuous employment test is adjusted. She will pass this test if she would have been employed for 26 weeks by the end of the 15th week before the week in which the baby is due.

## Earnings

**6.22**  Thirdly, her average weekly earnings must not be less then the lower earnings limit for national insurance contributions (£102 in the 2011–2012 tax year). This is lower than the level at which she would have NI contributions deducted from her earnings. That limit is called the 'primary threshold' which is £139 a week in the 2011–2012 tax year.

**6.23**  The average is worked out over her weekly earnings in the eight weeks up to the end of the 15th week before the week in which the baby is due.[14] If the baby is born in the 15th week before the due date, or earlier, the average is worked out over the eight weeks before the week in which the baby is born. HMRC call this eight weeks the 'relevant period'. See **6.94–6.99**.

## Maternity pay period

**6.24**  Fourthly, she must have begun her maternity pay period. If the baby is born more than 11 weeks before her due date, the maternity pay period starts the day after the baby was born. In all other cases, the earliest the maternity pay period can start is the Sunday, the first day of the 11th week before the start of the week in which the baby is expected.

## Confinement

**6.25**  This is defined in SSCBA 1992, s 171(1). In all cases where the baby is born alive, even if he or she lives for a moment only, entitlement to SMP follows no matter how early in the pregnancy the birth occurs. If, however, the baby is still born, entitlement to SMP follows only if the stillbirth occurred after 24 weeks of pregnancy.

**6.26**  The date of birth is the date the baby (or if more than one, the last of the babies) is delivered.

## EVIDENCE OF PREGNANCY

**6.27**  Although medical evidence is not essential for the right to maternity leave, it is essential for the right to get SMP.[15] Any document giving the date the baby is due with the required information and signed by a doctor or registered midwife is sufficient. Usually, the medical evidence will be on form MATB1,

---

[14]  SSCBA 1992, s 164(2)(b).
[15]  Social Security Administration Act 1992 (SSAA 1992), s 15(1).

the maternity certificate. This can be issued no earlier than 20 weeks before the week the baby is due. It can also be issued after the birth.

**6.28**    Only one MATB1 with the same due date can be issued. If the certificate has been lost, a duplicate can be issued.[16]

**6.29**    To get SMP, the employee should produce medical evidence of her pregnancy within 21 days of the start of her maternity pay period. If she produces the evidence late and has a good reason for doing so, SMP should be paid so long as she produces that evidence no later than the end of thirteenth week from the start of her maternity pay period.[17]

**6.30**    To avoid doubt, if the employee can show that the medical evidence was sent by prepaid post in a properly addressed envelope, that evidence is treated as having been submitted on the day on which it was posted.[18]

**6.31**    If the woman has more than one employer, she can ask the first employer to take a copy of the MATB1 so that she can show the original to the next employer and so on. HMRC recommend that the employer annotate the photocopy saying that the original has been seen and that the copy is a true copy of the original.

**6.32**    If no medical evidence is produced, the employer cannot pay SMP. In this situation, HMRC suggest that the employer cannot issue form SMP1 (the form explaining why SMP cannot be paid, or cannot continue to be paid). However, so long as the woman has complied with the notice condition the SMPG Regs, reg 25A requires the employer to provide her with the equivalent of the SMP1 information.

## EMPLOYEE STATUS

**6.33**    First, the woman must be an employee.[19] This is defined more broadly than in the Employment Rights Act 1996. An 'employee' is defined as a woman who is 'gainfully employed in Great Britain either under a contract of service or in an office (including elective office) with general earnings (as defined by section 7 of the Income Tax (Earnings and Pensions) Act 2003'.[20] There is power to make regulations to treat a woman as if she was or was not such an employee.

**6.34**    In essence, for SMP purposes, an employee is any woman who is (or would be but for her age or if she earned enough) liable to pay Class 1 national insurance contributions on her earnings. Switching viewpoints, if the

---

[16]    Statutory Maternity Pay (Medical Evidence) Regulations 1987, SI 1987/235, Sch 1, para 5.
[17]    SMPG Regs, reg 22.
[18]    SMPG Regs, reg 22(4).
[19]    SSCBA 1992, s 171(1).
[20]    SSCBA 1992, s 171(1).

'employer' is liable (or would be liable but for her age or if the woman earned enough) to pay secondary (employer) Class 1 national insurance contributions on the woman's earnings, then the woman counts as an employee.

**6.35** The test covers agency workers as the temporary work agency is liable to pay secondary Class 1 national insurance contributions. Apprentices and paid office holders count as employees. So too do Crown employees[21] and those treated as employees by the Social Security (Categorisation of Earners) Regulations 1978.[22] The rule of thumb is that the woman counts as an employee if she and her employer come within scope of the liability to pay Class 1 contributions even where no contributions are required to be made. If in doubt, contact HMRC.

## In Great Britain

**6.36** Once a woman has qualified for SMP, she may go abroad without that affecting her continued entitlement to payment.

**6.37** While she is qualifying, part of the conditions for liability to pay national insurance contributions are residence and presence tests.[23] The norm is that an employee is liable to pay Class 1 national insurance contributions on her earnings if at the time of that employment she is either resident or present in Great Britain (or would be present but for her temporary absence) or that she is ordinarily resident in Great Britain.[24]

**6.38** However, if a woman is working in Britain for a foreign embassy she will nevertheless be excluded from SMP if her employer is not liable to pay secondary Class 1 contributions. This is the case even though she may pay voluntary Class 1 contributions.[25]

**6.39** A mariner who is employed on a home-trade ship by an employer with a place of business within the UK counts as an employee for SMP purposes even though she may not be employed in Great Britain. Conversely, even if she is in Britain, any employment on a foreign-going ship will exclude her from SMP, as will employment on a home-trade ship if the employer does not have a place of business in the UK.[26]

---

21  SSCBA 1992, s 169.
22  SI 1978/1689 and SMPG Regs, reg 17.
23  SMPG Regs, reg 17(3)(a) refers to the residence and presence conditions for liability for secondary (employer) Class 1 contributions found in the now revoked Social Security (Contributions) Regulations 1979, SI 1979/591, reg 119(1)(b). The equivalent provision is now found in the Social Security (Contributions) Regulations 2001 (SSC Regs) SI 2001/1004, reg 145(1)(b).
24  SSC Regs, reg 145(1)(a).
25  SMPG Regs, reg 17(3)(b).
26  Statutory Maternity Pay (Persons Abroad and Mariners) Regulations 1987 (SMPAM Regs), SI 1987/418, reg 7.

**6.40**   Women in certain employment on the continental shelf are treated as employees even though they are not employed in Great Britain.[27]

**6.41**   In general, if the woman is paying Class 1 national insurance contributions (or would do so if her earnings were high enough) while working abroad she is likely to qualify for SMP. If she is working for an employer with a place of business in Great Britain and that employer is liable to pay Class 1 contributions on her earnings (or would have been liable had her earnings been high enough), she can get SMP.[28]

**6.42**   If the employer is not liable to pay secondary Class 1 national insurance contributions on a woman's earnings, then the woman is treated as if she was not an employee for SMP purposes.[29]

**6.43**   If the woman is working in another member state of the European Union, her position is also affected by the Council Regulation providing a system for co-ordination of the different social security schemes so that those moving within the European Economic Area (EEA) are not disadvantaged as a result of exercising their right of free movement. Since 1 May 2010, new regulations co-ordinate all the social security schemes in the European Union (the free movement regulations).[30] In general an employee is liable to pay contributions to and get benefits from the social security scheme of the Member State in which they work.

**6.44**   Time spent in another state within the EEA by a woman who is an employee counts towards the continuous employment test where:

(a)   she was employed in the UK on any day during the qualifying week, with her employer liable to pay secondary Class 1 contributions on her earnings (or who would be liable if she earned enough); and

(b)   in any week within the previous 26 weeks she was employed in the EEA by the same employer.[31]

**6.45**   Only weeks in which she was in fact so employed in the EEA count towards the continuous employment test. See **6.48** for more about continuous employment.

---

[27]   SMPAM Regs, reg 8.
[28]   SMPAM Regs, reg 2A.
[29]   SMPG Regs, reg 17(3)(a).
[30]   See Council Regulation 883/2004/EC. This replaced Council Regulation (EEC) No 1408/71 which remains in force for some purposes. For an outline of the old and new rules, with links to the regulations go to: http://www.hmrc.gov.uk/nic/work/new-rules.htm.
[31]   SMPAM Regs, reg 2, reg 5(1).

## More than one job

**6.46** If a woman has more than one job with the same employer, whether or not she may be entitled to one or two series of SMP payments depends on the national insurance position. If her contracts are aggregated for national insurance purposes, resulting in only one set of NI deductions, she would be entitled to only one series of SMP payments.[32]

**6.47** Since the establishment of National Health Service Trusts, some NHS employees have contracts that are split between NHS Trusts and Strategic Health Authorities. Women in this position can choose whether or not to have the earnings from both jobs added together for SMP purposes.[33]

## CONTINUOUS EMPLOYMENT

**6.48** At the end of the HMRC Employer Helpbook is a complete set of tables giving the important dates for SMP and maternity leave. For each due date the tables give the latest date for a woman to have started employment if she is to satisfy the continuous employment test. In general, if she started work for an employer before getting pregnant, she will almost certainly have passed this test.

**6.49** The MATB1 maternity certificate gives the date the baby is due. As a 'week' for purposes of the continuous employment test always runs from Sunday to Saturday, in borderline cases entitlement could rest on whether the due date is on a Saturday or a Sunday. If it is on a Sunday, the qualifying week will be one week later than if the due date is the day before on the Saturday.

**6.50** This test requires a woman to have been employed continuously by the same employer for at least 26 weeks by the end of the qualifying week, ie by the end of the 15th week before the week in which the baby is due. She will also qualify if she would have been employed for that period if the baby had been born at the time expected.[34] For who counts as an employee, see **6.18–6.19**. The rule of thumb is that the employer liable for SMP is whoever is liable to pay employer Class 1 national insurance contributions and to deduct Class 1 contributions from a woman's pay. Part weeks of employment count as full weeks. If the contract of employment continues during any breaks from work, say during a suspension for health and safety reasons, the employment counts as continuous.

---

[32] SMPG Regs, reg 5.
[33] Statutory Maternity Pay (National Health Service Employees) Regulations 1991, SI 1991/590.
[34] SMPG Regs, reg 4(2)(a).

## Breaks in a contract

**6.51**  If there is no contract of employment during a break from work then so long as the woman was working before and after the break for the same employer, certain breaks count towards passing the test. These are where:

(a)   she is absent from work because of sickness or injury (unless the incapacity lasts for more than 26 consecutive weeks);[35]

(b)   there is a temporary cessation of work (this includes casual and agency workers where there was no work to offer);[36]

(c)   she is absent from work in circumstances that are such that by arrangement or custom she is seen as continuing in that employment for any purpose;[37]

(d)   she is absent from work wholly or partly because of pregnancy or having given birth (unless the period between contracts is more than 26 weeks);[38]

(e)   she is absent because of taking paternity, parental or adoption leave.

**6.52**  These provisions are similar to the continuity of employment provisions found in the Employment Rights Act 1996. They particularly help supply teachers, seasonal workers, other casual or bank workers and agency workers. If at least a day's work is done in each of the 26 weeks, the woman passes the test.

**6.53**  If she did not work for the employer in all of the 26 weeks, whether she passes the test depends on why she did not work in the weeks off. If the answer is as simple as the employer not having work to offer to the woman in that week, she passes the test.[39] Otherwise, any week in which she is on paid leave or is absent for one of the reasons listed above counts towards passing the test. For example, if a bank or agency worker had to turn down a shift because she had to attend an antenatal appointment, that absence would count as being partly because of pregnancy.

## Seasonal and regular temporary workers

**6.54**  The continuity rules are further adjusted to assist preserving continuity for seasonal workers and regular temporary workers.

**6.55**  If a seasonal worker has been absent from work because of pregnancy or incapacity, she can be treated as having been present during the qualifying week

---

[35]   SMPG Regs, reg 11(1)(a), (2).
[36]   SMPG Regs, reg 11(1)(b).
[37]   SMPG Regs, reg 11(1)(c).
[38]   SMPG Regs, reg 11(1)(d), (3).
[39]   HMRC Employer Helpbook E15(2011), p 16.

and there is no requirement that at the end of that break she returns to work for that employer.[40] This avoids the problem that if, for example, the end of the spell of sickness, or the qualifying week falls in the off-season, there is unlikely to be work available to return to.

**6.56** Seasonal or regular temporary work is defined as employment in which the custom is for the employer:

(a)   to offer work for a fixed period of not more than 26 weeks;

(b)   to offer that work on two or more occasions a year for periods which do not overlap; and

(c)   to offer that work to people who had worked for him in the last or a recent period.

**6.57**   As there is no lower limit for the length of the fixed period, nor an upper limit on the number of fixed periods of work offered, this definition will arguably include many staff bank workers. The key control is what the employer in practice has demonstrated to be a 'recent such period'. The fact that new employees are recruited from time to time is arguably irrelevant: otherwise no seasonal worker could ever qualify.[41]

## Trade disputes

**6.58**   If a woman was off work for part or all of any week because of a stoppage of work due to a trade dispute,[42] that week (Sunday to Saturday) does not interrupt her continuity of employment but it does not count when adding up the 26 weeks. If, say, looking back from the end of the qualifying week, there had been a one day stoppage in the previous 26 weeks, the week in which that stoppage took place cannot count and one must look back 27 weeks and so on.

**6.59**   If a woman is dismissed during a stoppage of work, her continuity of employment stops at the day she stopped work.

**6.60**   In each case the trade disputes provisions do not apply if a woman can prove that at no time did she have a 'direct interest' in the trade dispute in question. If the outcome of the dispute would be applied automatically across

---

[40]   SMPG Regs, reg 11(3A).
[41]   Note that SMPG Regs, reg 16 makes no difference to this argument. Reg 16 can no longer apply to anyone as its only area of applicability was repealed back in 1994.
[42]   By SMPG Regs, reg 13, this is as defined in Jobseekers Act 1995, s 14.

the board whether by a binding or non-binding collective agreement or by custom and practice and irrespective of union membership, she would have a 'direct interest'.[43]

**6.61**   If a woman is off work because of a different reason, say on holiday, or off sick, at the time of a stoppage of work due to a trade dispute, then her absence would not be 'because' of that dispute. In this case it is irrelevant if she has a direct interest in the outcome of the dispute.

## Change of employer

**6.62**   If the employer changes in circumstances in which the Transfer of Undertakings (Protection of Employment) Regulations 2006 (TUPE) applies, continuity of employment is not broken.

**6.63**   Even where TUPE does not apply, certain other changes are treated as not interrupting the continuity of employment. These are where:

(a)   one corporate body takes over as employer from another by or under an Act of Parliament;[44]

(b)   the employer dies and the deceased's personal representatives or trustees employ the woman;[45]

(c)   there is a change in the employing partners, personal representatives or trustees;[46]

(d)   where at the time of the change both the previous and the new employers are 'associated' in that:

    (i)   one employer is a company of which the other has direct or indirect control; or
    (ii)   both employers are companies of which a third person has direct or indirect control.;[47]

(e)   a teacher in a maintained school moves to another school maintained by the same local education authority. This includes cases where either or both of the employers are the governors of a maintained school.[48]

---

[43]   *Presho v Insurance Officer* [1984] ICR 463, HL and, in the context of unfair dismissal and a direct interest in a dispute at the time of a lock out, see *Campey & Sons v Bellwood* [1987] ICR 311, EAT.
[44]   SMPG Regs, reg 14(b).
[45]   SMPG Regs, reg 14(c). There is no requirement that the woman be 'kept on' and employed by the personal representatives or trustees in their capacity as personal representative or trustee of the deceased, although the HMRC Helpbook suggests so.
[46]   SMPG Regs, reg 14(d).
[47]   SMPG Regs, reg 14(e); ERA 1996, s 231.
[48]   SMPG Regs, reg 14(f).

**6.64**   If continuity is broken, liability for SMP depends on when the change of employer occurred:

(a)   If it was after the qualifying week, the new employer is liable.

(b)   If the change happened during the qualifying week, the previous employer remains liable for SMP (but the woman will be entitled to 52 weeks' maternity leave).

**6.65**   It is only if the change happened before the start of the qualifying week that she would not be entitled to SMP from either employer. HMRC advise that the new employer issue form SMP1 so that the woman can claim state maternity allowance.

## Reinstatement

**6.66**   If a woman has returned from service as a member of the reserve armed forces and goes back to her former employer no later than six months after the end of her service as a reservist, her previous period (or periods) of service with that employer counts. For example, she would qualify for SMP if she had returned to work in the qualifying week but had already worked for that employer for at least 25 weeks before working as a reservist.[49] Time spent as a reservist is ignored.

**6.67**   If a woman has been reinstated or re-engaged following an unfair dismissal claim, whether by a tribunal or through the help of ACAS, continuity of employment is maintained between the dates of dismissal and her reinstatement or re-engagement.[50] If she does not have sufficient service to claim unfair dismissal, the same effect may be achieved by individual arrangement using SMPG Regs, reg 11(1)(c).

## AVERAGE WEEKLY EARNINGS

**6.68**   If the woman always has Class 1 national insurance contributions deducted from her pay, she will satisfy this condition.

**6.69**   If a woman's earnings are variable, so that she pays national insurance in some weeks but not in others, and for maximising average earnings to increase the earnings-related rate of SMP, it is particularly important to calculate average weekly earnings accurately. To assist, the HMRC Helpbook includes checklists for working out average earnings for weekly paid, monthly paid and irregularly paid cases. If the case does not seem to be covered by the HMRC Helpbook, the employer should seek assistance from HMRC.

---

[49]   SMPG Regs, reg 15; Reserve Forces (Safeguard of Employment) Act 1985, s 1(4)(b).
[50]   SMPG Regs, reg 12.

**6.70**    To get SMP, the woman's average weekly earnings in the eight weeks up to the end of the qualifying week (the 15th week before the week in which the baby is due) must at least be equal to the lower earnings limit for national insurance contributions (£102 in the 2011–2012 tax year). This is lower than the 'primary threshold' of £139 pw in the 2011–2012 tax year at which she would actually start having national insurance contributions deducted.

**6.71**    The earnings of a company director count towards average earnings for SMP purposes if she is contractually paid a regular salary, or is paid by a formal vote or by a determination of the directors, or by a combination. However, money drawn from the business in anticipation of a formal vote does not count as earnings for SMP purposes – even if national insurance contributions were deducted.[51]

**6.72**    If a woman has more than one job, see **6.46–6.47**. Except for certain NHS employees, earnings from jobs for different employers will not be added together. If a woman has more than one job with the same employer, earnings from those jobs are added together only where there is just one set of national insurance deductions.

## Relevant period

**6.73**    The eight-week period used to establish a woman's average earnings is called the 'relevant period'. It covers the period between two dates. These are:

(a)    the first date is the last normal payday on or before the last day (a Saturday) of the qualifying week (this is the last day of the relevant period);

(b)    the second date looks back in time. It is the day after the last normal pay day falling at least eight weeks earlier (this is the first day of the relevant period).

**6.74**    A 'week' for this purpose runs from Sunday to Saturday.

**6.75**    A woman's normal payday is the day on which her contract requires her to be paid or on which in practice she is paid. If her normal payday is not identifiable, one looks instead at the days on which she was actually paid.

**6.76**    If the baby is born before the end of the qualifying week, the relevant period is adjusted. Instead of basing the relevant period on the qualifying week, it is based on the week immediately before the week in which the baby was born. The first date is the last normal payday immediately before the end of the week preceding the week of the birth. The second date is the day after the last normal pay day falling at least eight weeks earlier.[52]

---

[51]    HMRC Helpbook E15(2011), p 23.
[52]    SMPG Regs, reg 4(2)(b), (3).

## Earnings and pay rises

**6.77** Average pay is based on gross earnings. It includes any pay or remuneration, including the value of any contractual benefits that count as earnings for the purposes of Class 1 national insurance contributions.

**6.78** Any earnings actually paid during the eight weeks count, even if they relate to an earlier or a longer period, say a bonus, overtime or arrears of pay.

**6.79** Statutory payments paid by employers count as earnings, ie statutory sick pay, statutory maternity pay, statutory adoption pay and ordinary and additional statutory paternity pay. These statutory payments cannot be reduced under a salary sacrifice arrangement.

**6.80** If average earnings are not high enough to qualify but some of the woman's earnings have been included in a PAYE Settlement Agreement,[53] the employer should recalculate average earnings but this time including the amounts from the PAYE Settlement Agreement.

**6.81** If there is a salary sacrifice[54] arrangement in place, where an agreed change in the contract of employment means that the woman has given up part of her earnings to secure a benefit in kind, her average earnings for SMP purposes still depend on her actual earnings that are liable for Class 1 national insurance contributions. Childcare vouchers up to a certain level (£55 pw or £243 pcm in the 2011–2012 tax year) are exempt from tax and national insurance. Only the excess over the exempt amount is chargeable to tax and Class 1 contributions. Only that excess is included when working out average pay. Average pay is based on the reduced earnings after any amounts have been deducted under a salary sacrifice scheme. The other side of this coin is that, depending on the precise contractual agreement, childcare vouchers continue and no equivalent deductions can be made from SMP itself.

**6.82** If there is a later pay increase which comes into effect at any point from the start of the eight-week period right up to the end of additional maternity leave, the woman's average pay must be recalculated as if that pay increase had been in effect during the whole of the eight-week period.[55] In some cases a pay increase will mean a woman's earnings are high enough to get SMP. Arrears of SMP must be paid. Where a woman was paid state maternity allowance, she would be entitled only to any excess of SMP over state maternity allowance.

---

[53] See http://www.hmrc.gov.uk/paye/exb/schemes/PSA.htm for an explanation of PAYE Settlement Agreements.

[54] See http://www.hmrc.gov.uk/employers/sml-salary-sacrifice.pdf for an explanation of salary sacrifice schemes and the effect on SMP, other employer-paid statutory payments and on other aspects of remuneration.

[55] This has been the position since 5 April 2005 and is the result of *Alabaster v Barclays Bank plc* [2005] IRLR 576.

## Working out the average

**6.83**   In the standard case, the average is the total earnings paid between the first and last days of the relevant period divided by the number of whole weeks in the period. If there were not a whole number weeks in the period, simply divide the total earnings by the number of weeks' wages actually paid between the two dates. Do not round up or down to the nearest whole number.[56]

**6.84**   For monthly paid employees (including those paid in multiples of a month), the pay is converted to an average weekly amount. The dates are the same as in **6.73**. The first date is the last day on which she was paid that falls on or before the Saturday of the qualifying week. The second date is the day after the last normal pay day that falls at least eight weeks earlier. Divide her total earnings paid during the relevant period by the number of calendar months in the period. If there is not a whole number of calendar months in that period, round to the nearest whole number before dividing. Multiply the result by 12 and then divide by 52 to reach the weekly average pay.[57]

**6.85**   For women who don't have a regular payday nor a regular pay pattern, the first date is the last day on which she was paid that falls on or before the Saturday of the qualifying week. This is the last day of the relevant period. The second date looks back at least eight weeks. You take the day after the last day on which she was paid that falls on or earlier than the eight-week period. This is the first day of the relevant period. If there are an exact number of weeks during the period, divide the total earnings actually paid by that number. Otherwise, divide the total earnings by the number of days in the period and then multiply the result by seven.

**6.86**   Some employees, such as seasonal workers and those working and paid in term-time only, may have long gaps between paydays if the qualifying week falls during or close to the end of the off-season or vacation. To the extent that their average pay has to be based on weeks of no pay, they may well sink below SMP levels and would certainly have a lower earnings-related rate than if the relevant period had fallen entirely during the on-season or term time. This problem does not arise with state maternity allowance as that is based on the best 13 weeks earnings in the previous 66 weeks. Some of these women may as a result qualify for much less by way of SMP than they would have received had they been excluded from SMP and able to claim state maternity allowance.

## NOTICE

**6.87**   The employee, or someone on her behalf, must give the employer notice of the date from which she expects to be paid SMP. This is a precondition for

---

[56]   See HMRC Helpbook, p 20, although note that if there are not a whole number of weeks in the period, this is contrary to SMPG Regs, reg 21(6). If this is of concern, contact HMRC for specific advice.

[57]   SMPG Regs, reg 21(5).

entitlement. In each case, that notice does not have to be in writing unless the employer asks for written confirmation.[58] As SMP can be paid only during the maternity pay period, the notice should be for a date from the start of the 11th week before the due date up to the due date itself. Interaction with other provisions may prevent things working out as planned but the fundamental right is that the woman can choose from when to start her SMP.

**6.88**  Notice should be given at least 28 days before she expects SMP to begin. If that is not reasonably practicable, say the baby was born early, or the woman did not know she was pregnant early enough, then notice should be given as soon as is reasonably practicable. Ignorance of the notice requirement, if the ignorance is reasonable, would make it not reasonably practicable to give notice before becoming aware of the need.[59]

**6.89**  If the baby is born earlier than the start of the 14th week before the due date, the woman should give notice within 28 days of the birth, or 'if in the particular circumstances that is not practicable, as soon as is reasonably practicable thereafter'.[60]

**6.90**  If the woman has already given notice of the date she expects SMP to start, but the baby is born earlier, then she needs to give the employer a further notice. That notice should be within 28 days of the birth, or 'if in the particular circumstances that is not practicable, as soon as is reasonably practicable thereafter.'[61]

**6.91**  If the baby is born earlier than expected so that notice, or a fresh notice, can only be given after the birth, then if the woman can show that she sent the notice in a properly addressed envelope by prepaid post, the notice is treated as having been given on the date it was posted.[62]

**6.92**  If an employee is concerned that her employer or HMRC might consider she did not have a good reason for delaying giving notice, there is no reason why she cannot give notice to say she expects SMP to start from 28 days later. The possible scenarios are as follows:

(a)  If she is absent from work before her notified date, she may be able to fill any gap in pay with holiday pay or time off in lieu.

---

[58]  SSCBA 1992, s164(4), (5).
[59]  See *Nu-Swift International Ltd v Mallinson* [1979] ICR 157, EAT, in the context of the former requirement of giving notice of the intention to return at the end of statutory maternity leave. For the general principle, see *Wall's Meat Co. Ltd v Khan* [1979] ICR 52, CA, and for a review of the authorities on reasonable practicability, see *John Lewis Partnership v Charman* EAT/79/11, Underhill J (P).
[60]  SMPG Regs, reg 23(1).
[61]  SMPG Regs reg 23(2).
[62]  SMPG Regs reg 23(3).

(b)    If, however, she becomes unable to work before her notified date, and she has not yet reached the start of the 4th week before the week in which the baby is due, she can claim statutory sick pay.

(c)    If she goes off work because of her pregnancy within four weeks of the due date, that triggers the start of the maternity pay period. In this case her unexpected illness or inability to work would mean that it would not have been reasonably practicable to have given earlier notice.

(d)    If the baby is born earlier then her notified date, she just has to give a fresh notice within 28 days of the birth.

In all cases, whatever the date it starts from, SMP is paid for 39 weeks.

**6.93**    Employers should be wary of taking too robust a view of what is 'reasonably practicable' in the context of maternity, as doing so may well invite a discrimination claim. HMRC suggest that having a 'good reason' for giving notice late is sufficient.

## MATERNITY PAY PERIOD

**6.94**    The maternity pay period is the period during which SMP can be paid. Although section 165(1) of SSCBA 1992 limits its duration to a maximum of 52 weeks, the SMPG Regs limit the period to 39 consecutive weeks.[63]

**6.95**    If it has not already begun, the maternity pay period is always triggered by birth. If a baby is born earlier than expected, including earlier than the 11th week before the due date, the maternity pay period starts the day after the birth.

**6.96**    In all other cases, a woman has the right to choose the date on which her maternity pay period is to start. This is itself subject to two factors. First, that date cannot be earlier than the Sunday start to the 11th week before the week in which the baby is due.[64] Secondly, that during the last four weeks before the week in which the baby is due, she is not absent from work because of pregnancy.

**6.97**    In the normal case a woman can decide to start her maternity pay period on any day of the week. She must give her employer notice that she expects SMP to start from that day. If she stops work 'in conformity with that notice' at any point from the start of the 11th week before the due date, her maternity pay period starts from her notified date.[65] Unless she is in the last four weeks before

---

[63]    SMPG Regs, reg 2(2).
[64]    SSCBA 1992, s 165(2).
[65]    SMPG Regs, reg 2(1).

her due date, it makes no difference if she is already off work for another reason before reaching her notified date.[66] She is then entitled to 39 weeks SMP starting from that day.

**6.98** If she gives birth earlier than the start of the 11th week before the due date or earlier than her notified date, then the maternity pay period starts the day after the birth.[67]

**6.99** Once she reaches the start of the 4th week before the week in which the baby is due, a single day off work because of or partly because of her pregnancy is enough to trigger the start of the maternity pay period from the following day.[68] If she is already off work at that point for another reason, say because of sickness, holiday, or using up time off in lieu, the maternity pay period would commence. Once the maternity pay period has been triggered, a return to work will result in the loss of some SMP, unless she uses up some KIT days (see **6.110**). If the woman leaves her employment after the start of the 11th week before the due date but before her maternity pay period has begun, it will in any event begin the day after the day she left.[69] Despite her departure, which can be for any reason, the employer remains liable to pay SMP if she meets the qualifying conditions.

## PAYING SMP

**6.100** So long as the employee meets all the qualifying conditions SMP will be paid at:

(a) the earnings-related rate of 90% of her average weekly earnings for the first six weeks; and

(b) for the remaining 33 weeks, the 90% rate continues if it is lower than the weekly standard rate of £135.45 (in the year from 9 April 2012), otherwise payment will be at the standard rate.

**6.101** If the woman has more than one employer, she can get SMP from each employer so long as she meets all the qualifying conditions in respect of each employment. She also has the right to choose a different start date for SMP for each qualifying employment.

**6.102** SMP is usually paid in the same way and at the same time as contractual pay.[70] Like ordinary pay, SMP is liable to tax and national insurance contributions. So, although SMP can be paid as a single lump sum, doing so may cause difficulty if entitlement to SMP is later lost. Paying a lump

---

[66] *Wade v North Yorkshire Police Authority & HMRC* [2011] IRLR 393.
[67] SMPG Regs, reg 2(3).
[68] SMPG Regs, reg 2(4).
[69] SMPG Regs, reg 2(5).
[70] SMPG Regs, reg 27.

sum will also trigger paying more in national insurance contributions. This is because the woman will lose the benefit of not having to pay contributions on earnings up to the 'primary threshold' (currently £139 pw), while the employer will lose the benefit of not having to pay secondary Class 1 contributions on earnings up to the 'secondary threshold' (currently a bit lower at £136 pw) for each individual payment.

**6.103**  SMP cannot be paid in kind or by way of providing board or lodgings or of services or other facilities. The value of salary-sacrifice and non-cash benefits cannot be deducted from SMP. Attachment of earnings and child maintenance enforcement orders cannot be deducted from SMP, only from contractual pay.

**6.104**  SMP must be paid in full for each week the woman is entitled to it during the maternity pay period. If she is also entitled to a contractual maternity payment and has not paid any contribution towards it, that payment can be offset against the liability to pay SMP for the same week. If she has contributed any amount towards a contractual maternity payment, the proportion reflecting that amount cannot be offset against SMP.[71]

**6.105**  If SMP is higher than contractual maternity pay, the employer must pay the balance of SMP due.

**6.106**  Even where SMP is fully or partially off-set against an employee's contractual maternity pay, the employer is still entitled to recover an amount from HMRC based on full SMP liability.

**6.107**  An employee has the absolute right to state, in writing, the date from which she would like payment of her SMP to begin. The employer must comply with that wish unless:

(a)  The specified date is more than 11 weeks before the week in which the baby is due.

(b)  The specified date is later than four weeks before the week in which the baby is due and during that four week period the woman has a day or more off work because of her pregnancy. In this case, SMP starts the next day.

(c)  The baby is born earlier than the specified date, even if that is more than 11 weeks before the week in which the baby is due. In this case SMP starts the day after the birth.

**6.108**  If choice or the vagaries of chance mean that SMP must start with a day that does not line up easily with the normal pay period, SMP can be paid

---

[71]  HMRC Helpbook E15(2011), p 11.

as part weeks to help align payments. In this case, the weekly rate is divided by seven and the resulting daily rate paid as appropriate so as to achieve alignment with the normal pay period.[72]

## WHAT AFFECTS THE RIGHT TO GET SMP?

**6.109**  SMP comes to an end in any event at the end of 39 weeks. However, certain events may affect or interrupt the continued payment of SMP. These are:

(a)  Working.

(b)  Dismissal or leaving the job.

(c)  Employer's insolvency.

(d)  Legal custody.

(e)  Death.

### Working

**6.110**  KIT days – during the maternity pay period, a woman can work for up to ten days for her SMP-paying employer without that affecting her continued right to SMP.[73] These are known as 'keep in touch' or KIT days. The idea is to help ease a woman's eventual return to work but they can be used, by agreement, for any purpose. The KIT days may be used consecutively or spread out or not used at all. A woman has no obligation to use any KIT days; nor can an employer demand that she do so. Both employer and employee must agree all the arrangements, including pay and the type of work to be done, for each KIT day used. Any agreement on the amount of pay must deliver the SMP the woman is entitled to subject to that being at least at the level of the national minimum wage for the hours worked.

**6.111**  Once a woman has used up her ten KIT days, SMP is not payable for any week during which she does any day of work for that employer. Although SMP resumes if she does no work in a week, she will have lost one of her 39 weeks of SMP for each week in which she does some work after using up her KIT days.

**6.112**  If the woman is entitled to SMP from more than one employer, she will be entitled to use ten KIT days for each employer.

---

[72]  HMRC Helpbook E15(2011), p 11.
[73]  SMPG Regs, reg 9A.

**6.113**  If a woman is getting SMP from one employer and works for another employer during the maternity pay period but before the birth, this makes no difference to her continued right to get SMP from the first employer.

**6.114**  It is only where she works for another employer after the birth that this might affect her right to continue to get SMP from the first employer. She must tell the first employer if she starts or goes back to work for another employer after the baby is born.[74] If she was also employed by the other employer during the qualifying week, that does not affect her continued right to get SMP from the first employer.[75]

**6.115**  It is only if she had not been employed by the other employer during the qualifying week that she loses her right to SMP from the first employer. The first employer's liability to pay SMP ends on the last day of the week before the week in which she worked for the other employer. The first employer has to issue form SMP1 and, if he holds an original MATB1 maternity certificate, must return that to her.

**6.116**  If a woman returns to work for her employer before using up all 39 weeks of SMP, her partner may be entitled to additional statutory paternity pay (ASSP). However, if the woman then goes on sick leave at any point during the remainder of the maternity pay period, she cannot get statutory sick pay. HMRC suggest that an employer consider paying her SMP in this situation.[76]

## Dismissal or leaving the job

**6.117**  If the woman is dismissed at any stage solely or mainly to avoid liability to pay SMP, then so long as she has been employed for a continuous period of at least eight weeks, the employer is still liable to pay SMP. The woman is treated as having been employed from the date her employment ended up to the end of the qualifying week. Average weekly earnings are based on the eight weeks ending with the last day in respect of which she was paid.[77]

**6.118**  Where a woman leaves or is dismissed from employment, the key question is whether she had been employed on any day during the qualifying week, ie the 15th week before the week in which the baby is due.

**6.119**  If she leaves before the qualifying week, she will not be entitled to SMP from that employer and should claim state maternity allowance instead.

**6.120**  Once an employee has qualified for SMP from an employer, that employer remains liable to pay SMP. Leaving employment or being dismissed,

---

[74]    SMPG Regs, reg 24.
[75]    SSCBA 1992, s 165(6), SMPG Regs, reg 8.
[76]    HMRC Helpbook E15(2011), p 5.
[77]    SMPG Regs, reg 3.

no matter what the reason, makes no difference. If she leaves after the start of the qualifying week, that employer remains liable to pay SMP in the normal way.

**6.121** If the employee leaves her employment at any time after the start of the 11th week before the week in which the baby is due but before the baby is born, then her maternity pay period starts the day after she leaves.[78]

## Insolvency

**6.122** Liability to pay SMP continues even though the employer ceases to trade. HMRC only takes over SMP payments from the date of insolvency.[79]

## Legal custody

**6.123** If a woman is detained in legal custody or sentenced to imprisonment, SMP is not payable in respect of the week in which she is first detained. SMP does not resume once she is released from custody. A suspended sentence of imprisonment does not count.[80]

## Death

**6.124** If the woman dies, her employer will not be liable to pay SMP for any week after the week in which she died. If the baby is born alive, even if she or he dies within minutes, the woman will be entitled to SMP and maternity leave in the normal way. If the baby is stillborn after 24 weeks, the woman is similarly entitled to SMP and maternity leave in the normal way.[81]

# DECISION MAKING AND APPEALS

**6.125** The employer is responsible for making initial decisions on an employee's right to SMP. HMRC provides a range of written and on-line guides and tools to assist. If in any doubt, an employer can ask HMRC for advice, but cannot ask for a formal decision.

**6.126** Form SMP1 is used to notify an employee that she is not entitled to SMP or that the employer cannot continue to pay her SMP. Part D of the form lists all the possible reasons why an employer might decide he cannot pay SMP. The employer has to select the reason that applies.

**6.127** An employer must complete form SMP1 and give it to the employee along with her original MatB1 maternity certificate. She will then be able to

---

[78] SMPG Regs, reg 2(5).
[79] SMPG Regs, reg 7(3), (4).
[80] SMPG Regs, reg 9.
[81] SSCBA 1992, s 171(1).

claim maternity allowance from Jobcentre Plus. It is possible to put in a claim for maternity allowance and at the same time pursue entitlement to SMP.

**6.128**  An award of SMP ends entitlement to maternity allowance. It is not possible to be paid the full amount of maternity allowance and SMP in respect of the same period. If, for example, a backdated pay rise brings an employee's average earnings above the SMP level, she would then be entitled to be paid the balance of her entitlement as SMP.[82]

**6.129**  The employee has the right to ask the employer for a more detailed written explanation[83] about:

(a)    which weeks, if any, the employer considers that SMP is payable for and the amount of SMP;

(b)    why the employer does not see itself as liable to pay SMP for any of the other weeks in the maternity pay period.

**6.130**  HMRC suggest that if the request is reasonable, the employer should supply the statement within seven days of the request.[84]

**6.131**  The employee can then ask HMRC for a formal decision on her entitlement to SMP. Both employer and employee will be given the opportunity to make any further observations in writing and provide supporting documentary evidence. There is no oral hearing.

**6.132**  Although there is no set time limit for asking an employer for a written explanation, an employee has only six months to ask HMRC for a formal decision.[85] That time limit starts to run from the first day in respect of which payment of SMP is in dispute. Time cannot be extended. So if an employee asks for a written explanation after more than six months, supplying it would be pointless. Arguably, the request would not be a reasonable one unless, perhaps, the answer could affect other employees.

**6.133**  A copy of the HMRC decision is sent to her and to the employer. This letter will always explain appeal rights and the time limit for paying SMP.

**6.134**  If dissatisfied, both employee and employer have 30 days from the date of the decision in which to appeal within to the independent First Tier Tribunal.

**6.135**  If there is an appeal, the employer and employee will be sent copies of the other's evidence. If the employer appeals, HMRC will usually attempt to

---

[82]    SMPG Regs, reg 21B.
[83]    Social Security Administration Act 1992 (SSAA), s 15(2).
[84]    E15(2011), p 27.
[85]    Statutory Sick Pay and Statutory Maternity Pay (Decisions) Regulations 1999, SI 1999/776.

discuss the case with the employer to try and broker an agreement that is compliant with the law. However, the employer is entitled to proceed with the appeal.

## Payment

**6.136** If an HMRC decision is in the woman's favour, the employer must pay her the SMP due by her next pay day or, where that is not possible, by the second pay day after the time for appeal has run out.

**6.137** If the employer appeals, there is no requirement to pay SMP until the pay day after the day the employer is notified that the appeal has been finally disposed of, or that leave to appeal has been refused.[86]

**6.138** If, nevertheless, the employer does not make the SMP payments found to be due by the First-tier Tribunal or by the Upper Tribunal and the time for any further appeal has expired, HMRC will take over paying SMP.[87]

# ADMINISTRATION OF SMP

## Record keeping

**6.139** An employer must keep:[88]

(a) a copy of the MATB1 maternity certificate;

(b) a record of the date the maternity pay period began and of all relevant payment dates and amounts;

(c) a record of any decision to refuse to pay SMP, with dates and reasons.

**6.140** Forms and detailed practical information to help with this task are available from HMRC. At the end of each tax year an employer must record the amount of SMP paid and recovered on the P35 employer annual return form and on the P14 form.

**6.141** These records about SMP must be kept for three years after the end of the tax year in which the particular maternity pay period ended. As the maternity pay period ends with the woman's return to work, the whole period could well approach five years. The penalty for failing to keep the records required is up to £3,000, but there is more than one type of offence (and in all cases, a right of appeal).

---

[86] SMPG Regs, reg 20.
[87] SMPG Regs, reg 7(1), (2).
[88] SMPG Regs, reg 26.

**6.142**   The records kept may also be relevant to an employment tribunal claim. If not disclosed, or disclosure demonstrates they have not been kept properly, or at all, then as well as risking penalties from HMRC, the employer risks adverse inferences. Such negative behaviour would arguably help establish a prima facie case of discrimination.

## Recovery of SMP

**6.143**   An employer whose annual Class 1 contributions (employer and employee) amount to £45,000 or less is entitled to recover 100% of all SMP payments as well as an additional 3% of that SMP.[89] The test is applied to each individual employee who is paid SMP.

**6.144**   The contributions limit is based on the last complete tax year before the woman's qualifying week. However, recovery of SMP is on a monthly basis. It is recovered by deducting the amount of SMP from the money that would otherwise have been paid over that month or quarter to HMRC for PAYE, national insurance contributions, student loan deductions and any deductions under the Construction Industry Scheme.[90]

**6.145**   If an employer's SMP payments would exceed the amount of PAYE and other deductions, it is possible to apply for advance funding to bridge the gap.[91] If recovery of SMP relates to the current tax year, it can be applied for online. Otherwise there must be a written application.

**6.146**   If annual Class 1 contributions (employer and employee) are over £45,000, the employer is entitled to recover 92% of SMP payments.[92]

---

[89]   Statutory Maternity Pay and Miscellaneous Amendment Regulations 1994 (SMA Regs), SI 1994/1882, regs 2, 3 and see HMRC Helpbook E15(2011), pp 13, 14. The 3% rate is for the 2011–2012 tax year. It was formerly 4.5%.

[90]   SMA Regs, reg 5, 6.

[91]   SMA Regs, reg 5, 6A.

[92]   SMA Regs, reg 4.

# Chapter 7

# PART-TIME AND FLEXIBLE WORKING

*Christopher Milsom*

## FLEXIBLE WORKING IN CONTEXT

### The rise and rise of flexible working

**7.1**　For a number of years the issue of flexible working has gained increasing importance. This can be measured both in terms of the number of workers making use of flexible working patterns and the amount of attention the issue has received from the government. As at August 2010, the number of people in part-time employment had increased to 7.84 million, constituting 27% of the workforce.[1] Similarly, 56% of employees in a recent study said they had taken up at least one flexible working practice in the last 12 months with their current employer.[2] On the national scale government focus on the issue culminated in 2002 with the creation of a statutory right to request flexible working, a right which originated without the prompt or encouragement of an EU Directive.[3]

**7.2**　Before considering what this means for the workplace in practice it is worth considering why flexi-working is likely to remain significant in the future:

(a) there has been a change in society's understanding of parental responsibility. According to a recent survey[4], 62% of fathers thought that fathers in general should spend more time caring for their children. This has led employees to bestow greater importance on the availability of flexible working: 54% of employees who thought that flexible working would be available when they applied or were offered a position regarded such a policy as a "very important" or "quite important" factor in their acceptance;[5]

---

[1]　Labour Market Survey, Office for National Statistics/'ONS'.

[2]　Hooker, H, Neathey, F, Casebourne, J, and Munro, M (2007), The Third Work Life Balance Employee Survey, Department for Business, Innovation and Skills Research series No 58.

[3]　Sections 80F, 80G, 80H and 80I of the Employment Rights Act 1996; Flexible Working (Eligibility, Complaints and Remedies) Regulations 2002, SI 2002/3236 (see below).

[4]　Equality and Human Rights Commission (2009) 'Working Better: Fathers, family and work – contemporary perspectives'.

[5]　Department for Work and Pensions in house analysis of the British Market Research Bueau Omnibus module 'Caring and Flexible Working' (June 2008).

(b)     there has been a net increase of 1.5 million women in the labour market since the early 1990s recession,[6] many of whom have for reasons associated with childcare responsibilities opted for part-time work;

(c)     in light of straitened economic circumstances, flexibility has been used to achieve significant cost-savings and the avoidance of redundancies. Conversely, those who have been dismissed are more willing to return to a part-time (and often less well paid) position: 2010 figures suggest that 3,000,000 more people have returned to employment in a part-time position than at the start of the recession;[7]

(d)     with the end of compulsory retirement, a workplace with a strong emphasis on flexible working will undoubtedly prove more successful in retaining older workers and avoiding the pitfalls of age discrimination.

## The limits of flexibility and gender equality

**7.3**     Regrettably, however, the use of flexible working – and part-time arrangements in particular – often remains both divided along gender lines and a 'race to the bottom' in the pay and quality of work:

(a)     Part-time working is available to 52% of women as compared to 25% of men.[8]

(b)     42% of working women as compared to 12% of working men are currently in part-time employment.[9]

(c)     As at 2010, the gender pay gap as assessed on hourly pay between women and men working full-time had narrowed somewhat to 15.5%. By contrast, the gap between women working part-time and men working full-time was over double the same at 34.5%.[10]

(d)     Part-time work that is available is far too often at the low-skilled end: of every ten part-time workers, five have previously held jobs requiring a higher level of skills or qualifications or more managerial or supervisory responsibility and an additional three say that they could easily work at a higher level[11] ('Hours to Suit: the Hidden Brain Drain' (2005) Equal Opportunities Commission investigation).

---

6     'Working towards Equality: A Framework for Action', Government Equalities Office, February 2010.
7     'ONS', 2010.
8     Working Better (Equality and Human Rights Commission).
9     Labour Force Survey, 2009.
10    2010 Annual Survey for Hours and Earnings (ONS), 'Gender Pay Gaps' (Equality and Human Rights Commission, March 2011).
11    'Hours to Suit: the Hidden Brain Drain' (2005, Equal Opportunities Commission investigation). Among women who work full-time the proportion employed in high level occupations has risen threefold in over 20 years whilst for part-time workers the increase has

## The benefits of flexibility for an employer

**7.4**    Aside from the arguments based on the grounds of human rights and dignity at work there is a powerful business case for extending flexibility to higher status employment. Indeed, the concerns of many employers as to suspected disadvantages such as cost, cohesion of the workforce and a diminution in an employee's commitment to work as a consequence of flexible working have frequently proven ill-founded. At a state level, the estimated cost of under-utilising women in the workplace is between £15 and £23 billion or up to 2% of GDP.[12] The benefits of a strong policy of flexible working are both wider-ranging and more keenly felt by the individual employer:[13]

(a)    in economically straitened times innovative use of flexible working has led to a reduction in costs;[14]

(b)    studies suggest that flexibility is likely to improve productivity rather than hinder it;[15]

(c)    the talent pool of job applicants is considerably broadened and an employer enjoys access to a wider workforce;[16]

(d)    bestowing employees with the trust and confidence of a flexible working pattern is likely to encourage loyalty and commitment.[17]

**7.5**    The experience of BT plc is particularly telling. Of its 86,000 employees, 75,000 work flexibly in some way across all levels of seniority. Following an investigation as to the consequences of this the company found that absenteeism was down among home-workers by 20%, an estimated 12 million litres of fuel and 18 years of commuting time were avoided, and there was a reduction of approximately £500 million in office costs. Clearly the size and nature of the corporation makes a significant difference but even small employers are likely to experience positive results from a properly managed policy of flexible working.

**7.6**    It is within this factual matrix that the legal rights and obligations which surround flexible working should be viewed. Rather than viewing flexibility as a problem imposed by legislation, innovative negotiations between employer and employee are capable of achieving the aims of both parties. It remains the case, however, that all stages of the flexible working process are protected – to a

---

been negligible. (Connolly, M and Gregory M (2008a) pp 1–22, 'The Part time pay penalty: earnings trajectories of British Women', Oxford Economic Papers.)

12    'Shaping a Better Future', Women and Work Commission (February 2006).
13    'Flexible Working: working for families, working for business (a report by the Family Friendly Working Hours Taskforce)' 15 March 2010.
14    Ibid.
15    Ibid.
16    Ibid.
17    Ibid.

greater or lesser extent – by national and European law. The central limbs of protection considered in this chapter can be categorised as follows:

(a)   the right to request flexible working;

(b)   the protection of workers from less favourable treatment on the grounds of their part-time status;

(c)   the protection of those working flexibly from indirect sex discrimination.

**7.7**    In addition, differences in pay and other benefits between part-time and full-time workers can give rise to a cause of action under the Equality Act 2010. A detailed analysis of equal pay claims, however, is beyond the scope of this chapter. Crucially, whilst these elements of protection are considered in turn they frequently overlap. Accordingly and by way of example, the absence of any discrimination claim on the grounds of part-time work does not preclude a sex discrimination claim from succeeding. Seamless thinking therefore becomes essential for an employer.

## THE RIGHT TO REQUEST FLEXIBLE WORKING

### The source and scope of the right

**7.8**    In 2002 Parliament inserted section 80F into the Employment Rights Act 1996 (ERA). In so doing it created the right to request flexible working for the purposes of caring responsibilities. The scope and effect of the right was provided by two additional sets of Regulations:

(a)   Flexible Working (Procedural Requirements) Regulations 2002[18] (the Procedural Regulations); and

(b)   Flexible   Working   (Eligibility,   Complaints   and   Remedies) Regulations 2002[19] (The Eligibility Regulations).

**7.9**    The scope of the right is somewhat limited: rather than a substantive right to flexible working it is a procedural right to make the request. It can be refused by the employer on a number of specified grounds. Nevertheless, it was a significant step not least since, unusually, it was a 'home grown' creation rather than a product of a European Directive.[20] Further, even if the right as provided in section 80F of the ERA 1996 does not give rise to a distinct cause

---

[18]   Flexible Working (Procedural Requirements) Regulations 2002, SI 2002/3207.
[19]   Flexible Working (Eligibility, Complaints and Remedies) Regulations 2002, SI 2002/3236.
[20]   Subsequently, however, the Pregnant Workers Directive (92/85), approved in Parliament in October 2010, contains a right to request flexible working arrangements for workers returning from maternity leave (Article 11). This may lead to a more purposive approach taken to the scope of the right and an increase in the level of damages awarded so as to allow for an 'effective remedy' to enforce an EU right but at this stage one can do little more than speculate. Similarly the Framework Directive on Parental Leave was adopted in March 2010 which, at

of action for refusal of the request, such a refusal may in certain circumstances trigger a claim of sex discrimination or, following resignation, constructive dismissal.[21]

## Who can apply?

### A 'qualifying employee'

**7.10** The right to request applies to all 'qualifying employees'. This term is defined as including those who have entered into a contract of employment, service or apprenticeship whether express or implied, oral or in writing.[22] Agency workers – defined as those who are 'supplied by a person ("the agent") to do work for another ("the principal") under a contract or other arrangement made between the agent and the principal' – are excluded.[23] The rationale for this exclusion as stated in the Guidance Notes to the Employment Act 2002[24] is that an agency worker will have commenced work with a view to providing a specific service without expectation of any adjustment to his or her working pattern. Respectfully, this rationale serves only to perpetuate the vulnerability of agency workers in the labour market.

**7.11** There are a number of other specific provisions addressing the category of protected persons: armed forces[25] and share fishermen or women are excluded[26] whilst seafarers employed on ships registered under section 8 of the Merchant Shipping Act 1995 are covered if the ship is registered to a British port, the seafarer does not work wholly outside the UK and he or she is ordinarily resident in the UK[27] (199(7) and (8)). Crown employees and Parliamentary staff are entitled to make a request.[28]

**7.12** In addition, a 'qualifying employee' must have been employed for a continuous period of not less than 26 weeks.[29]

### A 'qualifying carer'

**7.13** It must be emphasised that the purpose behind the Regulations is to allow a qualifying employee to provide some form of care to another. Although

---

Article 6, requires member states to take such measures which ensure that workers returning from parental leave can request 'changes to their working patterns or hours for a set period of time'.

[21] *British Airways v Starmer* [2005] IRLR 862, EAT; *Clarke v Telewest Communications plc* [2004] ET 1301034/2004; *Shaw v CCL Ltd* [2008] IRLR 284, EAT (for further discussion see below).

[22] Section 80F(1) of the Employment Rights Act 1996; Regs 3, 3A and 3B of the Flexible Working (Eligibility, Complaints and Remedies) Regulations 2002, SI 2002/3236.

[23] Section 80F(8)(a) and (b) of the Employment Rights Act 1996.

[24] At para 128.

[25] Section 191 of the Employment Rights Act 1996.

[26] Section 192(2) of the Employment Rights Act 1996.

[27] Section 199(7) and (8) of the Employment Rights Act 1996.

[28] Sections 191, 194 and 195 of the Employment Rights Act 1996.

[29] Regulation 3(1)(a) of the Flexible Working (Eligibility, Complaints and Remedies) Regulations 2002, SI 2002/3236.

no definition of care is provided in the Regulations, a broad approach is likely to be taken since there is no requirement on a qualifying individual to state or justify the standard and extent of care provided.

**7.14**  Whilst the right was originally restricted to parents of children under six and parents of disabled children under 18, the understanding of caring responsibilities has now extended to the following categories:

(a)    adult dependants;[30]

(b)    children aged under 17;[31]

(c)    disabled children aged under 18.[32]

**7.15**  The extension of the right to encompass requests for more flexible parental leave which would in part allow the extension of the right to request to all parents of children under 18 was envisaged in the Flexible Working (Eligibility, Complaints and Remedies) (Amendment) Regulations 2010.[33] The Amendment Regulations have since been repealed.

**7.16**  The category of persons said to care for a child include that child's mother, father, adopter, special guardian, foster parent or private foster carer of child or a person in whose favour a residence order is in force in respect of the child.[34] It does not extend to relatives such as grandparents, aunts or uncles who may live in the same house as the child unless that relative has a specific order of parental responsibility.[35] However, the employee making the request may be married or related to – or a civil partner of – that carer or reside at the same address. The category of 'relatives' covered is wide and includes a carer's mother, father, adopter, guardian, special guardian, parent-in-law, step-parent, son, step-son, daughter, step-daughter, daughter-in-law, brother, step-brother, brother-in-law, sister, step-sister, sister-in-law, uncle, aunt or grandparent. It also includes equivalent adoptive relationships.

**7.17**  Again, whilst there are some threshold criteria for the purposes of the Eligibility Regulations, serious consideration should be given to any request for flexible working given that refusal without proper consideration could give rise to a claim of indirect discrimination.

---

[30]   Reg 3B of the Eligibility Regulations (inserted by the Work and Families Act 2006).
[31]   Flexible Working (Eligibility, Complaints and Remedies) (Amendment) Regulations 2009, SI 2009/595.
[32]   A disabled person for the purposes of this entitlement is defined as someone entitled to a disability allowance within the meaning of s 71 of the Social Security Contributions and Benefits Act 1992.
[33]   SI 2010/2991.
[34]   Reg 3(1)(b)(i) of the Eligibility Regulations.
[35]   Para 122 of the Explanatory Notes to the Employment Act 2002.

## Making a request

### *The nature of a request*

**7.18** A qualifying employee can apply to his or her employer for a change in terms and conditions where that claim relates to:

(a)   the hours of work;

(b)   the times that an employee is required to work (eg start or end time);

(c)   the location of that work;[36]

(d)   such other aspects of employee's terms and conditions as may be specified in the regulations.[37]

**7.19** The Regulations do not provide an exhaustive list of forms of flexible working. The Explanatory Notes of the Employment Act 2002 are of more assistance and give the following examples. These may be used in isolation or combined to accommodate an employee's request:

(1)   **Part-time working:** this can include a reduction in the number of days or hours worked and include an amendment to start or end times of the working day.

(2)   **Flexi-time:** this enables a qualifying worker to choose when to begin and end work within the agreed working day. It may specify core working hours within that day.

(3)   **Staggered hours:** allowing amendments to start, finish and/or break times.

(4)   **Compressed working hours:** the same number of hours over fewer working days (eg squeezing a five day week into four days).

(5)   **Job-sharing.**

(6)   **Shift-working.**

(7)   **Informal shift-swapping and self-rostering.**

(8)   **Time off in lieu/banked hours.**

(9)   **Term-time working.**

(10) **Annual hours** whereby an employer pools all hours a qualifying employee is due to work in a year and 'calls' them at short notice.

---

[36]   This does not extend to travelling requirements.

[37]   No additional grounds since May 2011 been added.

(11) **Home-working**.

(12) **Career breaks**.

## *The required form of a request*

**7.20**  Pursuant to section 80F(2) of the ERA 1996, a request must:

(a) state that the request is an application made under section 80F of the ERA 1996;[38]

(b) specify the change applied for and when it is proposed that the change should become effective;[39]

(c) explain the possible effect of the proposed change on the employer and suggest means of dealing with those effects;[40]

(d) explain how the employee meets the definition of a 'qualified carer' within the meaning of the Regulations;

(e) be in writing;[41]

(f) be dated;[42]

(g) state whether a previous application has been made and, if so, when.[43]

**7.21**  There is no requirement to state the reasons for the request or provide any detail as to the level of care provided. If, however, an employer discovers that the employee has lied in claiming that he or she had caring responsibilities and never intended to use flexible working to provide such care an employer is not precluded from taking disciplinary action.[44]

**7.22**  The Tribunal is likely to expect an employer to adopt a co-operative approach: where it is aware that an application is invalid, the employee should be notified at the earliest opportunity. Conversely, an employer has the right to

---

[38]  Section 80F(2)(d) of the ERA 1996.

[39]  Failure to provide this information may invalidate the request; see *Hussain v Consumer Credit Counselling* ET 1804305/04 by way of example.

[40]  'That does not mean that the employee is expected to know every factor that might influence the employer's decision. It simply means that they should show that they have considered the factors that they are aware of that are likely to influence the employer's decision. Evidence shows that applications for flexible working patterns succeed where they are soundly based on the business needs of the employer' (DTI Guidance, www.businesslink.gov.uk; www.direct.gov.uk).

[41]  Email form constitutes a written request for this purpose (reg 2(1) of the Eligibility Regulations).

[42]  Reg 4(c) of the Procedural Regulations.

[43]  Reg 4(b) of the Procedural Regulations.

[44]  Para 123 of the Explanatory Notes to the Employment Act 2002.

request further information: this request does not have to be in written form. If an employee unreasonably fails to provide this information his or her request may be treated as withdrawn provided the employer has notified the employee accordingly.[45]

## Timing of a request

**7.23** For the purposes of care provided to an adult there is no time limit for an application. With respect to childcare, a request must be made after the birth of a child but before the day on which the child concerned reaches the relevant age limit, e g 17 in the case of a non-disabled child and 18 if that child is disabled.

**7.24** Once a <u>valid</u> request is made, a further request cannot be made for twelve months beginning with the date on which that application was received. Where a request is made by email, that date is deemed to be the date of email transmission;[46] for applications submitted by post, the deemed date is the date on which an application would be delivered had a postal service operated normally.[47] There is no authoritative assistance on the implications of a TUPE on the bar for reiterating a request and so the presumption of continuous service should apply.

**7.25** This time bar does not apply to requests which failed to comply with the procedural requirements: in those circumstances a request can be resubmitted without having to wait for a further 12 months.

## Effect of granting a request

**7.26** If a request for a change in working patterns is granted, the effect is a consensual variation of contract. Save where otherwise agreed, the effect of this is permanent and indefinite. From a business perspective, it is likely that accommodating the request will have repercussions for the remainder of the workforce, leaving an employer with little appetite to revisit the issue at a later stage. Consequently, the employee making a request is left in a position of uncertainty: should he or she wish to return to a full-time position at a later stage there is no guarantee that such a request would: (a) be granted; or (b) be covered by the Regulations since it would have to be established that an increase in hours was for the purposes of providing care. This is a further example of the way in which flexible working can lead to a failure to maximise the potential of those with caring responsibilities.

---

[45]  Reg 17(2) of the Procedural Regulations.
[46]  Reg 5(2)(a) of the Procedural Regulations.
[47]  Reg 5(2)(b) of the Procedural Regulations.

# The duties of an employer

## *The duty to consider*

**7.27**   An employer may only refuse a request for flexible working on one or more of the following grounds:[48]

(1)   a burden of additional costs;

(2)   a detrimental effect on the ability to meet customer demand;

(3)   an inability to reorganise work among existing staff;

(4)   an inability to recruit additional staff;

(5)   a detrimental impact on quality;

(6)   a detrimental impact on performance;

(7)   an insufficiency of work in the periods an employee proposes to work;

(8)   planned structural changes;

(9)   any other ground the Secretary of State may specify.[49]

**7.28**   On a literal reading of the Regulations it seems that an employer does not have to substantiate its conclusion that one of the specified grounds is engaged for the purposes of the Regulations. It is not for the tribunal to substitute its opinion for that of the employer by departing from those conclusions.

**7.29**   Nevertheless, an employer must seriously consider a flexible working request and ensure that its response to a request is not predetermined.[50] Moreover, there are signs of the Tribunal applying a more stringent standard than the Regulations suggest.

> *Case Example*
>
> R wished to work a three-day week in order to care for her grandchild. This request was refused on the ostensible basis that it would constitute 'a strain on resources' and hinder the promotion of 'team spirit'. The employer failed to carry out any meaningful investigations as to the repercussions of the request and

---

[48]   Section 80G of the ERA 1996.

[49]   As at May 2011 no such additional ground has been specified.

[50]   *Mehaffy v Dunnes Stores (UK) Ltd* ET 1308076/03, *Clarke v Telewest Communications plc* ET 1301034/2004 (IDS Brief 790). In *Mehaffy* where the respondent adopted an attitude that all managers were compelled to work full-time and had failed to formulate a written policy on flexible working the Tribunal considered that 'reluctantly paying lip-service to working through the flexible work provisions … without any genuine commitment to considering the company's proposals' was not sufficient for the purposes of the Regulations.

whether these could be accommodated. Mrs Rutty successfully challenged the refusal and, in upholding the claim, the EAT concurred that in order for an employer to show that there must be a proper factual basis for a refusal

*Commotion Ltd v Rutty*[51]

As the EAT added:

> 'In order for the tribunal to establish whether or not the decision by the employer to reject the application was based on incorrect facts, the tribunal must examine the evidence as to the circumstances surrounding the situation to which the application gave rise. In doing so, the tribunal are entitled to enquire into what would have been the effect of granting the application. Could they have coped without disruption? What did other staff feel about it? Could they make up the time? And matters of that type. We do not propose to go exhaustively through the matters at which a tribunal might wish to look, but if the tribunal were to look at such matters in order to test whether the assertion made by the employer was factually correct, that would not be any misuse of their powers and they would not be committing an error of law' (at para 38).

**7.30** Moreover, employers are advised to fully consider the request since refusal may give rise to a claim of discrimination. Pursuant to section 20 of the Equality Act 2010 this could also include a claim of associative disability discrimination.[52]

## The procedure

*Initial meeting*

**7.31** The qualifying employee should be invited to a meeting to discuss the application within 28 days of the date on which that application was made.[53] There does not, however, need to be a meeting where the variation requested by the employee is agreed by the employer and both the variation and date of commencement are confirmed in writing.[54] If the employer wishes to adopt an alternative flexible working pattern to that requested, however, a meeting must take place: a compromise of this nature cannot be unilaterally imposed.

**7.32** This 28-day time scale may be extended by a further 28 days where the individual who would typically consider such a request is on annual or sick leave.[55] Alternatively an extension may be agreed between the parties.[56] The timing of this meeting should be mutually convenient[57] and the employee has the right to be accompanied.[58] A telephone meeting may not constitute a

---

[51] [2006] IRLR 171, [2006] ICR 290 (EAT) (John Burke QC presiding).
[52] For a further discussion see *EBR Attridge Law LLP v Coleman* [2010] IRLR 10.
[53] Reg 3(1) of the Procedural Regulations.
[54] Reg 3(2) of the Procedural Regulations.
[55] Reg 13 of the Procedural Regulations.
[56] Reg 12 of the Procedural Regulations.
[57] Reg 11 of the Procedural Regulations.
[58] Reg 14 of the Procedural Regulations.

meeting for the purposes of the Regulations.[59] Whilst there is no statutory obligation for an employer to pay the employee for a meeting held in working hours, a withholding of pay may constitute an unlawful detriment.[60]

**7.33**  The meeting should provide an opportunity to explore the consequences of the desired work pattern and the extent to which they can be accommodated. Recommendations as to how the meeting should be conducted can be found in the government guidance paper 'Flexible Working: A Guide for Employers and Employees'.[61] Alternative compromise solutions should also be considered by both parties. Each party should be prepared to be flexible and expand on their position. The employer should have discussed the available options with personnel and be open to consulting external expertise. An application should not be refused on the basis of generalisations.

*Written outcome*

**7.34**  A written outcome should be dated and provided within 14 days of the meeting.[62] Where a variation to a working pattern is agreed the nature and commencement date of the variation should be specified.[63] Where it is refused the notice of outcome must:

(a)  State the ground for refusal[64] citing one or more of the specified grounds for refusal.

(b)  Contain sufficient explanation as to why those grounds apply which goes beyond mere box-ticking. 'The explanation should include the key facts about why the business ground applies. These should be accurate and clearly relevant to the business ground. To prevent any uncertainty, the explanation should avoid the use of unfamiliar jargon and should be written in plain English ... The aim is for the employer to explain to the employee, in terms that are relevant, why the requested working pattern cannot be accepted as a result of the business ground applying in the circumstances. If the argument does not look convincing to the employer it is unlikely to look convincing to the claimant.'[65]

(c)  Inform the applicant as to the appeal procedure.[66]

---

[59]  *Humphrey v Hardings Estate Agency Ltd* ET 2701793/03.
[60]  Section 47D of the ERA 1996.
[61]  Department for Employment and Learning http://www.delni.gov.uk/flexible_working_-_a_ guide_for_employers_and_employees_er_36.pdf.
[62]  Reg 5(a) and (c) of the Procedural Regulations.
[63]  Reg 5(b)(i) of the Procedural Regulations.
[64]  Section 80G(1)(b) of the ERA 1996.
[65]  See note 62 above.
[66]  Reg 5(b)(ii) of the Procedural Regulations.

*The appeal*

**7.35** The employee is entitled to appeal within 14 days of the date on which notice is given.[67] Whilst the 'Form FW(D): Flexible Working Appeal template letter'[68] is likely to prove instructive, an appeal is valid provided it is dated, in writing and some grounds are provided. An appeal may be pursued on any ground but the grounds include the following:[69]

(a)  failure to follow procedure;

(b)  a challenge to the explanation of the business case; or

(c)  a challenge to the accuracy of the business reasons cited.

**7.36** The appeal must be held within 14 days of lodging notice[70] at a mutually convenient time and location.[71] Once again the employee has the right to be accompanied.[72] The appeal should preferably be heard by a senior manager with no prior involvement in considering the request. Should the employer accede to the precise terms of the request there is no need for a meeting to take place provided the nature and commencement date of the variation are communicated in writing.[73]

**7.37** Where an appeal hearing does takes place, the outcome should be communicated within 14 days of the appeal[74] and notice must be dated[75] and in writing.[76] If the appeal is upheld, the nature and commencement date of the variation must be stated:[77] if it is dismissed, grounds must be provided.[78]

*Extension of time*

**7.38** The parties may agree to the extension of time in respect of the original meeting, notice of decision, grounds for appeal, appeal hearing and decision on appeal provided that the following steps are taken:[79]

(a)  the employer records the agreement in writing;

---

[67]  Reg 6 of the Procedural Regulations.
[68]  Available at http://www.direct.gov.uk/en/Employment/Employees/Flexibleworking/DG_171775.
[69]  Para 135 of the Explanatory Notes to the Employment Act 2002.
[70]  Reg 8(1) of the Procedural Regulations.
[71]  Reg 11 of the Procedural Regulations.
[72]  Reg 14 of the Procedural Regulations.
[73]  Reg 8(2) of the Procedural Regulations.
[74]  Reg 9 of the Procedural Regulations.
[75]  Reg 10(a) of the Procedural Regulations.
[76]  Reg 10(c) of the Procedural Regulations.
[77]  Reg 10(b)(i) of the Procedural Regulations.
[78]  Reg 10(b)(ii) of the Procedural Regulations.
[79]  Reg 12(1)–(3) of the Procedural Regulations, see also Form FW(F): Flexible Working Extension of Time Limit.

(b)   the employer records the time limit to which the extension relates;

(c)   the employer records the date on which the extension is to end;

(d)   the record is signed and dated;

(e)   the record is sent to the employee.

*The right to be accompanied*

**7.39**   The employee is entitled to be accompanied at both the initial meeting and the appeal hearing on his or her request.[80] The companion must be employed by the employer (thus excluding union representatives employed elsewhere) and of the employee's choosing: if that companion is not available for the proposed meeting the meeting must be postponed to a time proposed by the employee provided that proposed date is convenient to all other parties and within seven days of the day proposed by the employer.[81]

**7.40**   Where an employer fails or threatens to fail in compliance with the right not to be accompanied or postpone a meeting to the convenience of that companion an employee may issue a complaint within three months of the actual or threatened failure.[82] Should the claim be upheld the employee is entitled to a maximum of two weeks' pay capped at £400 per week from 1 February 2011.[83] Moreover, the employee has the right not to be subjected to any detriment by reason of seeking to be accompanied.[84]

**7.41**   An employee must be permitted to take time off for the purposes of accompaniment.[85] Further, the protection offered to trade union officials is applicable to companions[86] even where they are not in fact union officials.[87] A companion has the right not to be subjected to any detriment[88] and where a companion is dismissed on the basis that he or she accompanied or sought to accompany a worker such a dismissal is to be regarded as automatically unfair.[89]

*Withdrawal of a request for flexible working*

**7.42**   Where a request has been or is deemed to have been withdrawn an employer is no longer under a duty to consider it.[90] A request is to be regarded as withdrawn where:

---

[80]   Reg 14(1) and (2).
[81]   Reg 14(4) and 14(5) of the Procedural Regulations.
[82]   Reg 15(1) of the Procedural Regulations.
[83]   Reg 15(3)–(5) of the Procedural Regulations; s 227(1) of the Employment Rights Act 1996.
[84]   Reg 16(1)(a) of the Procedural Regulations.
[85]   Reg 14(6) of the Procedural Regulations.
[86]   Sections 171–173 of the Trade Union and Labour Relations (Consolidation) Act 1992.
[87]   Reg 14(7) of the Procedural Regulations.
[88]   Reg 16(1)(b) of the Procedural Regulations.
[89]   Reg 16(3)(b) of the Procedural Regulations.
[90]   Reg 17 of the Procedural Regulations.

(a) an employee has notified the employer that it has been withdrawn whether orally or in writing. For the avoidance of doubt, however, if the withdrawal is relayed orally employers are advised to request written confirmation;

(b) the employee, without reasonable cause, fails to attend two first instance or appeal meetings;

(c) the employee, without reasonable cause, refuses to give the employer the information required in consideration of the request. Again, however, some caution is advised since the reason for non-attendance may be related to the very caring responsibilities which gave rise to the request.

## Enforcement

### *Grounds for a claim*

**7.43** Should the consideration procedure prove unsuccessful an employee may issue a claim[91] on the following grounds:

(a) the employer failed to comply with the procedural requirements;

(b) the refusal was not made on one of the prescribed grounds;[92]

(c) the employer relied on a prescribed ground but the refusal of the request was based on incorrect facts;[93]

(d) the employer contravened the right to be accompanied;[94]

(e) the employee was subjected to a detriment by reason of having made the request.

**7.44** As to the latter, an employee has the right not to be subjected to any detriment by any act or deliberate failure to act on the ground that he or she:[95]

(a) made or proposed to make an application under section 80F of the ERA 1996;

(b) exercised or proposed to exercise a right conferred by section 80G;

(c) brought proceedings against an employment under section 80H;

---

[91] Section 80H of the Employment Rights Act 1996.
[92] Section 80(G)(1)(b) of the Employment Rights Act 1996.
[93] Section 80H of the Employment Rights Act 1996.
[94] See **7.40–7.41** above.
[95] Section 47E of the Employment Rights Act 1996.

(d)    alleged the existence of any circumstance which would constitute a ground for bringing proceedings.

**7.45**    Whilst dismissal cannot constitute an act of detriment,[96] a dismissal on the basis of one or more of these grounds would be an automatically unfair dismissal[97] and no qualifying period of service is required.

**7.46**    The claim may only be issued, however, if one or more of the following have taken place:

(a)    the employer has notified the employee of the refusal to grant the request on appeal;

(b)    the employer has failed to hold an initial and/or appeal meeting;

(c)    the employer has failed to give notice of a meeting or refusal to grant the request as required by the Procedural Regulations.[98]

**7.47**    A claim may not be issued in respect of a request which has either been disposed by way of agreement or withdrawn in the manner described at **7.42** above. It must be issued within three months of the notification or breach relied upon subject to a proviso that time may be extended where it was not reasonably practicable for the claimant to issue in time.[99]

## *Remedy*

**7.48**    Should the employment tribunal uphold a claim under the Regulations it can:

(a)    order an employer to reconsider the employee's application;[100] and/or

(b)    award such monetary remedy as is considered just and equitable.[101] This is capped at eight weeks' pay (and each week capped with effect of 1 February 2011 at £400),[102] giving a maximum compensatory award of £3,200.

**7.49**    A tribunal has a wide degree of discretion in assessing the award but it should 'take into account the behaviour of the employer (eg whether they have lied) and of the employee (eg their willingness to consider alternatives)'.[103]

---

[96]    Section 47E(2) of the Employment Rights Act 1996.
[97]    Section 107C of the Employment Rights Act 1996; *Horn v Quinn Walker Security Ltd* ET.2505740/03.
[98]    Section 80H(3) of the Employment Rights Act 1996.
[99]    Section 80H(5)(a) and (6) of the Employment Rights Act 1996.
[100]    Section 80I of the Employment Rights Act 1996.
[101]    Section 80I(2) of the Employment Rights Act 1996.
[102]    Reg 7 of the Eligibility Regulations.
[103]    Para 140 of the Explanatory Notes of the Employment Act 2002.

Thus in *British Airways v Starmer*[104] an employer who promptly rectified its failure to provide a business ground for behaviour in such a manner not to prejudice S was obliged to pay one week only. By contrast, in *Coxon v Landesbank Baden-Wurttemberg*[105] an employer had 'patently failed' to observe the procedure contained in the Regulations; conversely had serious consideration been given to the request a reasonable employer would most likely have refused it. Accordingly C's remedy was capped at six weeks' pay.

## Where next for flexible working?

**7.50** The right to request procedure has in a general sense proved successful: according to a 2007 study some 80% of requests are made and addressed informally rather than through the statutory procedure. 60% of requests made are granted in full and a further 17% in part.[106] The number of claims issued dealing solely with the refusal to grant a flexible working request are negligible.

**7.51** It is perhaps the success of negotiation without recourse to the Tribunal which prompted the Coalition Government to launch a fresh consultation on 16 May 2011.[107] Among the proposals in the 'Modern Workplace' consultation are significant recommendations regarding equal pay audits and the creation of a more flexible parental leave regime. It is perhaps the changes to flexible working, however, which would, if implemented, have the greatest impact. In summary the proposals include:

(a) Extending the right to request flexible working from those with caring responsibilities to all workers with 26 weeks of service.

(b) Replacing the statutory process with a duty to act 'reasonably', to be construed in light of a prospective Code of Practice.

(c) Allowing but not requiring employers to consider individual circumstances and their priorities when dealing with competing requests.

(d) Facilitating temporary changes to working patterns by permitting employees to make an additional request within the 12-month period if they state in their original request that they expect the variation to be temporary only.

**7.52** Given the announcement in the 2011 Budget that there would be a moratorium on all 'red tape' for small businesses it is possible that the extension will be subject to a 'micro-business exemption' for a transitional period. Nevertheless, the intent is bold:

---

[104] [2005] IRLR 862.
[105] ET 2203702/04.
[106] Third Work-Life Balance Survey 2007.
[107] This consultation is ongoing at the time of writing.

'the full potential of flexible working in achieving (its) aims will only be realised if it becomes far more widespread, with decisive action being taken to tackle the misconception that non-traditional practices are only useful or justified for parents and carers, and women in particular. It is in fact possible that the existing legislation may inadvertently have reinforced this misconception by restricting the right to request to those groups.'[108]

**7.53** There is a context to this consultation. With the removal of the default retirement age it is likely that employers will be expected to permit more nuanced working practices for older workers. Moreover, there is a perceived need in light of fiscal constraints to maximise the full potential of those parts of the prospective workforce hitherto ignored. In any event, the scope of flexible working is only likely to expand with zeal: it is anticipated that the measures contained in the consultation paper will be adopted in some form by 2012.

## PROTECTION OF PART-TIME WORKERS

**7.54** On 1 July 2000 the Part-time Workers (Prevention of Less Favourable Treatment) Regulations 2000[109] (The Part-Time Regulations) came into force as a means of implementing the European framework agreement.[110] Consequently, unless such treatment is objectively justified, part-time workers are specifically protected from detrimental treatment in regard to:

(a)   pay;

(b)   pensions and overtime;

(c)   training;

(d)   holidays;

(e)   maternity and paternity leave;

(f)   career breaks; and

(g)   redundancy.

Effectively, a part-time working pattern has become in itself a protected characteristic.

**7.55** In 2002 the Fixed-Term Employees (Prevention etc) Regulations (the Fixed-Term Regulations)[111] followed. In removing the distinction between

---

[108]   Para 8 of 'Consultation on Modern Workplaces: Flexible Working' May 2011.
[109]   SI 2000/1551 as amended by the Part-time Workers (Prevention of Less Favourable Treatment) Regulations 2000 (Amendment) Regulations 2002, SI 2002/2035.
[110]   97/81/EC, 15 December 1997.
[111]   SI 2002/2034.

fixed-term and permanent contracts, the cumulative effect is – at least in theory – establishing a basic floor of equality amongst workers whether permanent or temporary and irrespective of hours of work, length of service or age. There are two central legal tools used to enshrine this floor of equality:

(1)   the availability of conventional discrimination claims;

(2)   the 'pro-rata' principle (ie any benefits enjoyed by full-time workers are, with certain exceptions, available to part-time workers on a pro-rata basis).

**7.56**   There are certain limits, however, to discrimination claims on the basis of part-time work. Firstly, no award for injury to feelings is available. Secondly, an actual rather than hypothetical comparator must be identified. Accordingly inasmuch as the claim may constitute a freestanding basis of complaint it should also be considered concurrently with other causes of action such as indirect discrimination and equal pay.

## Who is protected?

### *'A worker'*

**7.57**   The Part-Time Regulations apply to any 'worker', that is to say someone who has entered into or works under:[112]

(a)   a contract of employment;

(b)   some other contract 'whether express or implied and (if express) whether oral or in writing whereby the individual undertakes to do or perform personally any work or services for another party to the contract whose status is not by virtue of the contract that of a client or customer of any profession or business undertaking carried on by the individual'; or

(c)   trainees and apprentices.

**7.58**   The Regulations also cover crown employees and workers,[113] members of the armed forces save for those in the reserves and providing training,[114] and the police[115] including those holding the office of constable or an appointment as a police cadet (Reg 16). As such the Regulations have a similar ambit of protection to other areas of discrimination but are not as extensive as, for example, the Equal Pay Act.[116]

---

[112]   Reg 1(2) of the Part-Time Regulations.
[113]   Reg 12 of the Part-Time Regulations.
[114]   Reg 13(2) of the Part-Time Regulations.
[115]   This includes those holding the office of constable or an appointment as a police cadet, Reg 16 of the Part-Time Regulations.
[116]   Section 1(6) of the Equal Pay Act 1970.

**7.59**   One recent controversy, however, is the specific exclusion of any 'holder of a judicial office if he is remunerated on a daily fee basis'.[117] This has been subject to review by the Supreme Court in *O'Brien v Ministry of Justice*.[118]

> *Case Example*
>
> Mr O'Brien was a recorder (a part-time judge in full-time legal practice), paid for each day that he sat. In pursuing a claim under the Part-Time Regulations, he argued that recorders should be regarded as 'workers' both as a matter of EU law and under national law and the exclusion under Regulation 17 was therefore invalid. Whilst his claim was successful at first instance, the EAT and Court of Appeal rejected it on an appeal by the MoJ. The Supreme Court held, however, that the employment status of recorders as officeholders remained an open issue since all judges were expected to work during defined times and periods and were not free agents to work as and when they chose. Moreover, the expression 'worker' had to be applied in a manner that was sensitive to the purpose of the Regulations, namely the protection of individuals against discrimination. The Supreme Court referred the matter to the ECJ whose judgment which raised the question as to whether national law can discriminate between part-time and full-time (and indeed between different types of part-time) judges in the provision of pensions as permitted under Regulation 17. At the time of writing the ECJ decision is still pending.

## *'Part-time'*

**7.60**   'Part-time' status is, within the meaning of the Regulations, highly context-specific. A worker is part-time if:

> 'He is paid wholly or in part by reference to the time he works and, having regard to the custom and practice of the employer in relation to workers employed by the worker's employer under the same type of contract, is not identifiable as a full-time worker'.[119]

Conversely, a full-time worker is someone:

> 'Paid wholly or in part by reference to the time he works and having regard to the custom and practice of the employer in relation to workers employed by the worker's employer under the same type of contract is identifiable as a full-time worker'.[120]

**7.61**   Consequently, the definition of working status becomes relational: if an employer operates a specific contract at a full-time level of 45 hours per week a person working 43 hours could be regarded as a part-time worker.

---

[117]   Reg 17 of the Part-Time Regulations.
[118]   [2010] UKSC 34, [2010] 4 All ER 62, [2011] 1 CMLR 1172.
[119]   Reg 2(2) of the Part-Time Regulations.
[120]   Reg 2(1) of the Part-Time Regulations.

**7.62** A worker who undertakes a full-time working week may nevertheless be regarded as a part-timer where they are engaged on more than one part-time contract.

*Case Example*

H successfully appealed the strike out of his claim under the Regulations where he worked under two 50% contracts. Whilst collectively the contracts combined to form one single full-time job this did not preclude him from being a part-time worker under two contracts simultaneously.

*Hudson v University of Oxford*[121]

## Identifying a comparator

**7.63** In order to establish less favourable treatment the part-timer must identify an actual rather than hypothetical comparator.[122] A full-time worker can only be regarded as a comparable full-time worker in relation to a part-time worker if at the time of the less favourable treatment both workers are:[123]

(a)  employed by the same employer;

(b)  employed under the same or a similar type of contract;

(c)  engaged in the same or broadly similar work having regard to the level of qualifications, skills and experience; and

(d)  engaged at the same establishment, or – if there is no full-time worker with a similar contract doing similar work at the same establishment – at a different establishment but satisfying the above requirements.

The most contentious aspects have proved to be comparing the contract and work performed between full-time and part-time workers.

### *The same type of contract*

**7.64** For the purposes of establishing whether a part-time worker and the alleged comparator are engaged on the same or similar type of contract, the Part-Time Regulations provide the following categories:[124]

(a)  employees employed under a contract of employment;

(b)  employees employed under a contract of apprenticeship;

---

[121]  [2007] EWCA Civ 336, [2007] All ER (D) 356 (Feb) (CA).
[122]  *Carl v University of Sheffield* [2009] IRLR 616, [2009] 3 CMLR 846, [2009] ICR 1286 (EAT).
[123]  Reg 2(4) of the Part-Time Regulations.
[124]  Reg 2(3) of the Part-Time Regulations.

(c)   workers who are neither employees nor employed under a contract for a fixed term;

(d)   workers engaged under a fixed-term contract;

(e)   'any other description of a worker that it is reasonable for the employer to treat differently from other workers on the ground that workers of that description have a different type of contract'.[125]

**7.65**   The requirement to be engaged on the 'same type of contract' presents a significant hurdle for those with atypical working arrangements.

*Case Example*

W worked 'on demand', was not guaranteed any income, was paid for each hour worked and could refuse work at will. The maximum hours which she could have been asked to work per week was capped at the same level of 40 hours for all employees. On conclusion of her employment, W issued proceedings and contended that she should have been paid according to the 40 hours that could have been demanded of her. On referral from the Austrian Supreme Court the ECJ determined that whilst the Framework Agreement on part-time work was engaged, W's claim was ill-founded. A contract of employment according to need which did made no provisions for the length of weekly working time was entirely distinct from both part-time and full-time contracts which provided for fixed working weeks. As she did not have the same type of contract as the full-timers she could not identify a comparator.

*Wippel v Peek & Cloppenburg GbmH && Co KG*[126]

**7.66**   A more flexible approach was taken in *Matthews v Kent and Medway Fire Authority*[127] in which it fell to part-time retained workers to establish that they had the same type of contract as their full-time colleagues. Whilst their duties were broadly similar there were significant differences in the hours arrangement (in that part-timers were on call whilst full-timers had a regular 42-hour week with paid overtime) and the pay packages offered (in that part-timers received a lower hourly rate for additional duties and less favourable sick pay). The first instance Tribunal, EAT and Court of Appeal each determined that as there were 'measurable additional functions' carried out by full-time fire-fighters – including educative, preventative and administrative tasks – that were not undertaken by the part-timers the differences in both contracts and work undertaken meant that no comparator could be identified.

**7.67**   The House of Lords, however, upheld the appeal by the part-timers and concluded that there had been excessive focus on the differences between part-time and full-time fire-fighters rather than the core similarities in, inter alia, disciplinary rules, ranking structure and job description. Each category of

---

[125]   Reg 2(3)(f) of the Part-Time Regulations.
[126]   C-313/02; [2004] ECR I-9483; [2005] IRLR 211 (ECJ).
[127]   [2006] UKHL 8, [2006] 2 All ER 171, [2006] ICR 365, [2006] IRLR 367 (HL).

contract, it held, is defined broadly and can accommodate a wide range of contractual terms. Regulation 2(3) was a threshold provision only which, if set too high, would frustrate the aim of the Regulation, namely the achievement of some level of equality between full-time and part-time workers. The residual category contained in the Regulations should not allow employers to single out particular kinds of part-time working arrangements and thwart the ambit of the protection otherwise offered. *Wippel* was distinguishable on the basis that the part-time fire-fighters were contractually obliged to perform all work when requested.

**7.68** Accordingly, the House of Lords remitted the claim to the Tribunal. On remission the claims were upheld on the basis that they carried out the same/broadly similar work but treated less favourably regarding pension and sick-pay provision and differences not justified.

## *Broadly similar work*

**7.69** When it comes to comparing the work performed by a part-time worker and the prospective comparator, the guidance in *Matthews* is once again of assistance. As the House of Lords held, where the core work is actually performed by part-timers and full-timers the essential question becomes whether the differences are important enough to prevent the work being regarded as the same or broadly similar overall. Since it is likely that a full-timer will assume additional duties the focus should be on considering whether there are core similarities rather than identifying differences. The House of Lords continued to add that where a full-time comparator has a higher degree of skills or experience this only becomes relevant where it affects the work done.

## Workers changing from full-time to part-time status

**7.70** Where a full-time worker returns as a part-timer, there is no need to identify a comparator since the comparison is with his or her previous terms and conditions. He or she must, however:[128]

(a) have been a full-time worker immediately before the absence (it does not matter whether the previous contract has been terminated);

(b) return to the same employer within a period of less than 12 months from the start of any period of absence;

(c) return to either the same job or a job at the same level; and

(d) work fewer weekly hours than during the period prior to his or her absence (the reduction need only be an hour).

---

[128] Reg 3 of the Part-Time Regulations.

**7.71**  On satisfaction of these conditions, the 'pro-rata' principle applies, ie the worker is entitled to the same rate of pay and benefits previously enjoyed on a pro-rata basis. In addition, a move from full-time to part-time work cannot reduce the right to annual leave already accumulated during the period of full-time employment.[129]

## Less favourable treatment 'on the ground of' part-time status

**7.72**  As confusing as the 'threshold issues' identified above may appear, the core principle is a simple one: a part-time worker has the right not to be treated less favourably than a full-time comparator on the ground that s/he is a part-time worker unless the less favourable treatment is objectively justified.[130] The principle applies equally to any change in the terms of the contract and any deliberate act or failure to act on the part of the employer.[131]

**7.73**  In order for any claim to succeed, however, a part-timer must establish not only that there has been less favourable treatment but that this difference in treatment was 'on the ground that the worker is a part-time worker'.[132] There is not, therefore, a concept of indirect discrimination in the Regulations.

**7.74**  The judicial approach towards identifying the reason for treatment was somewhat restrictive at first. The Scottish EAT in *Gibson v Scottish Ambulance Service*,[133] determined that in order for a claim to succeed reason for treatment must be solely due to part-time status. This approach was confirmed in *McMenemy v Capita Business Services Ltd*.[134] M worked three days a week, excluding Mondays. Due to the structure of her working week she did not receive time off in lieu when public holidays fell on a Monday: she asserted that this amounted to less favourable treatment on the grounds of part-time work. The Court of Session, upholding the Tribunal decision, held that whilst there was less favourable treatment this was on the grounds of not working Mondays rather than her being a part-time worker. As there was no concept of indirect discrimination in the Regulations the claim was dismissed. The decision entirely overlooked the fact that since the business was open seven days a week there were full-timers who did not work on Mondays and nevertheless received additional leave or payment in lieu for bank holidays on a Monday.

**7.75**  Since then, however, a more flexible approach has been adopted. In *Sharma and ors v Manchester City Council*,[135] the EAT held that part-time status did not need to be the only reason for discriminatory treatment for a claim to succeed. The EAT cited the example of a policy discriminating all

---

[129]  *Zentralbetriebsrat der Landeskrankenhauser Tirols v Land Tirol* Case C-486/08, [2010] IRLR 631, [2010] All ER (D) 172 (Apr) (ECJ).
[130]  Reg 5(2)(b) of the Part-Time Regulations.
[131]  Reg 5(1) of the Part-Time Regulations.
[132]  Reg 5(2)(a) of the Part-Time Regulations.
[133]  [2004] EATS 0052/04 (unreported, EAT (Scotland)).
[134]  [2007] CSIH 25, [2007] IRLR 400, 2007 SC 492 (Court of Session).
[135]  [2008] ICR 623, [2008] IRLR 336, [2008] All ER (D) 37 (Mar) (EAT).

part-timers over 30: whilst true in such an instance that there would be two reasons for less favourable treatment (namely, age and part-time status) it would be peculiar if only because certain part-timers were affected the Regulations were inapplicable:

> 'In our judgment it is inconceivable that the Directive was not intended to outlaw such treatment (subject to justification) and we have no doubt whatsoever that it would inevitable be construed by the European Court of Justice to do so. Any other conclusion would wholly undermine the very purpose of the Directive. The fact that not all part-timers are treated adversely does not mean that those that are cannot take proceedings for discrimination if being part-time is a reason for adverse treatment.'

**7.76** In any event, as the EAT emphasised, even if such an interpretation was not required on a strict reading of the Directive, it remained open to a member state to give more favourable protection than that offered by Directive. Following the more recent decision of *Carl v University of Sheffield*[136] it is now established that a claimant need only establish that part-time work was the effective and predominant cause for less favourable treatment.

## Examples of less favourable treatment

**7.77** Examples of less favourable treatment might include the following:

(a) dismissal;[137]

(b) barring or restricting access to and funding of training to part-time workers;

(c) offering a new or promoted position subject to conditions which would not be applied to full-time workers;[138]

(d) restricting access to occupational pensions;[139]

(e) applying pressure on a part-time worker to increase his or her hours;

(f) requiring a part-time worker to do a disproportionate number of standby hours;

(g) discounting the length of service of a worker (for such purposes as promotion, redundancy exercises and calculating pension entitlements) on the basis of part-time status eg by calculating length of service for

---

[136] [2009] 3 CMLR 846, [2009] ICR 1286, [2009] IRLR 616, [2009] All ER (D) 86 (Jun) (EAT).
[137] Reg 7 of the Part-Time Regulations.
[138] *Royal Mail Group plc v Lynch* EAT/0426/03 2 September 2003.
[139] 'Employers must not discriminate between full-time and part-timers over access to pension schemes unless different treatment is justified on objective grounds' ('Part-time workers. The law and best practice – a detailed guide for employers and part-timers', Department of Business, Innovation and Skills/'BIS').

part-time workers on the basis of hours worked rather than giving full allowance for the length of the contract;[140]

(h)    allocating less interesting or fulfilling responsibilities to part-time workers;

(i)    failing to provide equal access to career break schemes.

**7.78**  It must be emphasised that claims under the Part-Time Regulations are very likely to be combined with some other cause of action. Given that in many employment sectors the majority of part-time workers are women, a difference in pay on the basis of working hours may give rise to an equal pay claim. Although analysis of the law regarding equal pay is beyond the scope of this book employers are advised to stay alive to the wider risks of differential treatment on the basis of contractual hours.

## The pro-rata principle

### The principle

**7.79**  'Where a comparable full-time worker receives or is entitled to receive pay or any other benefit, a part-time worker is to receive or be entitled to receive not less than the proportion of that pay or other benefit so that the number of his weekly hours bears to the number of weekly hours of the comparable full-time worker'.[141]

**7.80**  Essentially, benefits and entitlements for part-time workers should be calculated on a ratio of hours to those of a comparable full-timer. By way of example:

(a)    a full-time worker (five days per week) is entitled to 25 days' paid holiday. A part-timer working three days per week should therefore be entitled to 15 days' holiday;

(b)    a part-time worker works 50% of the hours of a full-timer. Full-timers receive 200 hours' holiday entitlement. The part-timer should therefore receive 100 hours' entitlement.

### 'Inappropriate' benefits

**7.81**  The Regulations expressly acknowledge, however, that it is 'inappropriate' to apply the pro-rata principle to certain benefits. It would be difficult, for example, to provide a ratio of a company car. Those benefits which are regarded as 'inappropriate' for apportionment are exempt from the principle. However:

---

[140]  *INPS v Bruno and anor* C-395/08 and C-396-08 [2010] IRLR 890, ECJ.
[141]  Reg 1(2) of the Part-Time Regulations.

'Where a benefit, such as health insurance or company cars, cannot be applied pro-rata, this is not of itself an objective justification for denying it to part-time workers. The less favourable treatment of part-time workers will still need to be justified on objective grounds. These might include the disproportionate cost to the organisation of providing such a benefit, or the imperative to meet a real need of the organisation.'[142]

It follows that serious thought should be given to means of reflecting a ratio of that entitlement, e g payment of travel expenses or a monthly car allowance.

**7.82** Furthermore, the benefits which fit into this excluded category are likely to be limited: contractual sick pay and maternity pay, holiday entitlement, share option schemes and rates of pay for all bonuses, weekend payments and unsocial hours are all subject to the pro-rata rule. Similarly, part-time workers should be provided with a pro-rata entitlement for all public holidays.[143]

## *Overtime*

**7.83** The second significant exception to the pro-rata principle is in the field of overtime. A part-timer is not subject to less favourable treatment simply because he or she is denied overtime rates until a stipulated number of hours have been worked.[144]

**7.84** Much depends, however, on whether the payment in question constitutes 'overtime'.

*Case Example*

J alleged that a difference in supposed overtime should be subject to the pro-rata principle. Under the terms of the GNR contracts, full-timers were contracted to work 40 hours per week, the first 35 of which were paid at the basic rate and the remaining 5 paid at 1.25 times basic salary. By contrast, the part-time workers did not receive any additional hours rate unless they worked over 35 hours. The EAT held that the additional hours allowance did not constitute 'overtime' since it was covered by ordinary contractual hours. Accordingly full-time workers received on average a higher hourly rate than part-time workers which amounted to less favourable treatment on the grounds of part-time status. As such, the issue of objective justification was remitted to the tribunal.

*James v Great Northeastern Railways*[145]

**7.85** Nor does the overtime exception apply where the burden imposed on a part-time worker in order to qualify for overtime pay amounts to less favourable treatment.

---

[142] BIS Guidance, see note 139.
[143] BIS Guidance, see note 139.
[144] Reg 5(4) of the Part-Time Regulations. This accords with the approach taken by the ECJ to equal pay (*Stadt Lengerich v Helmig* [1995] IRLR 216, ECJ).
[145] EAT/0496/04, [2005] All ER (D) 15, 1 March 2005, EAT (unreported).

*Case Example*

Part-time employees were required to work more than 5 hours per month in overtime in order to qualify for any overtime pay at all. V was a teacher working 23 hours a week whilst a full-time teacher worked 26.5 hours. It followed that if V worked 26.5 hours a week she would not earn as much as a full-timer working the same number of hours. Even though the threshold was the same for both full-time and part-time workers the ECJ concluded that the burden of part-time workers was greater when considered as a fraction of normal hours. Accordingly, the overtime scheme was less favourable to part-time workers who should have been paid for any overtime in full until they reached the normal working hours of a full-time worker.

*Voss v Land Berline*[146]

## Objective justification and written reasons

**7.86**   The right not to be subjected to less favourable treatment on the grounds of part-time work 'applies only if ... the treatment is not justified on objective grounds'.[147] The phrase is not defined at all in the Regulations and it should therefore be treated as having the same meaning as in other areas of discrimination law and is considered below in the context of indirect discrimination.

**7.87**   With a view to clarifying the justification relied upon, a worker has the right to request a written explanation giving reasons for less favourable treatment.[148] That explanation constitutes admissible evidence in proceedings. An employer must provide this statement within 21 days of the request.[149] If the tribunal concludes that the employer has deliberately and without reasonable excuse failed to provide a written statement or that statement is evasive or equivocal, it is entitled to draw such inferences as are just and equitable including the inference that the employer has infringed the right in question.[150] There is no qualifying period for the right to request this explanation. Nor does this displace the right for written reasons on dismissal conferred by section 92 of the Employment Rights Act 1996.[151] Where a part-time worker is dismissed they are entitled to written reasons under section 92 of the Employment Rights Act 1996.

## Detriment and dismissal under the Regulations

**7.88**   A part-time worker is entitled not to be subject to any detriment by any deliberate act or failure to act done by his employer on the ground that the worker has:[152]

---

[146]   C-300/06, [2007] ECR I-10573, [2008] 1 CMLR 1313, [2007] All ER (D) 87 (Dec) (ECJ).
[147]   Reg 5(2)(b) of the Part-Time Regulations.
[148]   Reg 6 of the Part-Time Regulations.
[149]   Reg 6(1) of the Part-Time Regulations.
[150]   Reg 6(3) of the Part-Time Regulations.
[151]   Reg 6(4) of the Part-Time Regulations.
[152]   Reg 7(3) of the Part-Time Regulations.

(a)    brought proceedings under the Part-Time Regulations;

(b)    requested written reasons for less favourable treatment;

(c)    given evidence in any proceedings under the Regulations;

(d)    otherwise done anything under the Regulations in relation to the employer or other person;

(e)    alleged that the employer has infringed the Regulations where that allegation is made in good faith;

(f)    refused to forego any right under the Regulations.

**7.89**  The protection from detriment applies equally where the employer believes the worker has done or intends to do one or more of the above.[153] Any dismissal on the ground of one of the above is unfair.[154] There is no qualifying period for this right.

## Enforcement and remedies

**7.90**  A part-time worker may issue a complaint to the Tribunal in respect of any right under the Regulations within three months of the treatment or detriment (or the last in a series of acts) taking place.[155] This time limit may be extended where in all the circumstances it is just and equitable to do so.[156] For the purposes of limitation, where a contractual detriment is the basis of complaint the less favourable treatment continues for the duration of the contract.[157] The one exception to this is claims based on a worker's change from full-time to part-time employment: in those circumstances time starts to run from the first day on which the worker commenced work under the new or varied contract.[158]

**7.91**  Should a claim prove successful, a Tribunal may:[159]

(a)    make a declaration as to the rights of the parties;

(b)    award such compensation as is just and equitable having regard to the infringement in question and the loss arising from that infringement

---

[153]  Reg 7(3)(b) of the Part-Time Regulations.
[154]  Reg 7(1) of the Part-Time Regulations.
[155]  Reg 8(2) of the Part-Time Regulations.
[156]  Reg 8(3) of the Part-Time Regulations.
[157]  Reg 8(4)(a) of the Part-Time Regulations.
[158]  Reg 8(4)(b) of the Part-Time Regulations.
[159]  Reg 8(7) of the Part-Time Regulations.

(eg expenses and anticipated benefits) *excluding* any award for injury to feelings.[160] The Tribunal is expected to consider any failure to mitigate[161] and contributory fault;[162]

(c)  make a recommendation that an employer takes reasonable steps to eliminate or reduce adverse effects of any matter covered by the complaint.[163] Employers' failure without reasonable justification may lead a tribunal to award compensation (if none originally awarded) or increase an earlier award.[164]

**7.92**  The scope of protection offered by the Part-Time Regulations represents a significant advance, offering a basic floor of equality irrespective of any other protected characteristics of a worker. Nevertheless, when compared to claims of indirect discrimination and equal pay there are a number of limitations:

(a)  there must be an actual rather than a hypothetical comparator (a higher hurdle than that for indirect discrimination claims);

(b)  the Equality Act is triggered at the selection and recruitment stage and can therefore be used as a means to challenge a refusal to offer a position on a part-time basis. By contrast, the Part-Time Regulations can only assist an individual who is already a part-timer; and

(c)  there is no award for injury to feelings for part-time workers' claims.

It is in this context that we move to consider indirect discrimination in the arena of flexible working.

## INDIRECT DISCRIMINATION

### Introduction

**7.93**  Statistically, more women than men work part-time.[165] It follows that less favourable treatment of part-time workers may often amount to less favourable treatment on the grounds of sex unless that difference in treatment can be objectively justified. As the Work and Parents Taskforce concluded:

'Where parents think they can demonstrate that a request from a person of the opposite sex would have been granted in the same circumstances or, where a mother can show that working in a non-flexible way is more likely to be detrimental to mothers than to fathers and is detrimental to her, they can also bring a case jointly under sex discrimination law. If the man proves direct

---

[160]  Reg 8(11) of the Part-Time Regulations.
[161]  Reg 8(12) of the Part-Time Regulations.
[162]  Reg 8(13) of the Part-Time Regulations.
[163]  Reg 8(7)(c) of the Part-Time Regulations.
[164]  Reg 8(14) of the Part-Time Regulations.
[165]  See **7.3–7.4** above.

discrimination there is no defence. For a woman brining a case of indirect discrimination the tribunal would apply the test of objective justification to the business evidence.'[166]

**7.94** The basic building-blocks of establishing indirect discrimination have been set out in Chapter 1. The remainder of this chapter will focus on the application of the four key questions in the area of flexible working, namely:

(1)   Is there a provision, criterion or practice (PCP)?

(2)   Does that PCP put women as compared with men to a particular disadvantage?

(3)   Has the complainant been put to that disadvantage?

(4)   Was the PCP a proportionate means of achieving a legitimate aim?

## Provision, criterion or practice

**7.95** The appropriate identification of a PCP is central to the basis of claim and it is for the complainant to identify it. For the purposes of the claim there may be more than one PCP e g a request to work part-time and partially from home. Moreover, there is considerable latitude in the definition of a PCP. A PCP can be oral or written, a long-standing practice or an isolated instruction or decision.

> *Case Example*
>
> An airline refused to allow a female pilot to work 50% of her full-time hours following a return from maternity leave but did offer a reduction to 75% of shifts. The airline sought to argue that this was not a PCP as it was a one-off decision. On appeal, the EAT upheld the Tribunal's decision that this one-off decision could constitute a 'provision'.
>
> *British Airways plc v Starmer*[167]

**7.96** Further examples of PCP's in the context of flexible working include:

(a)   the requirement to work full-time;[168]

(b)   the requirement to work particular hours if working part-time;[169]

(c)   the requirement to work inflexible hours or be fully 'flexible' and work on demand;[170]

---

[166] 'About Time: Flexible Working' (Work and Parents Taskforce).
[167] 2005 IRLR 862.
[168] *Michell v David Evans Agricultural Ltd* EAT 0083/06.
[169] *British Airways plc v Starmer* 2005 IRLR 862.
[170] *Commotion Ltd v Rutty* [2006] IRLR 171; *Oddbins v Robinson* EAT/96 (unreported).

(d)    the requirement to work full-time during core hours which may overlap with 'school runs';[171]

(e)    the requirement to work weekends;[172]

(f)    the requirement to work full-time or at least 25 hours a week in the office;[173]

(g)    the practice of counting childcare absences when assessing attendance records for dismissal purposes;[174]

(h)    the selection of part-timers before full-time workers in a redundancy situation;[175]

(i)    the adoption of redundancy selection criteria which are more difficult for part-time workers to comply with e g the need to work core office hours;[176]

(j)    the requirement that an employee work in any place within the UK pursuant to a mobility clause;[177]

(k)    the adoption of an informal policy to refuse any part-time or job-sharing requests;[178]

(l)    a demand that teaching staff in a school take on extra-curricular activities;[179]

(m)   a refusal to allow women returning from maternity leave to work part-time;[180]

(n)    refusing a female job applicant a position on the basis that she wished to undertake the post part-time;[181]

(o)    a requirement to work full-time in order to be eligible for management positions;[182]

---

[171]   *Glass v Newsquest (North East) Ltd* ET Case No 2508468/04.
[172]   *Sourbutts (nee Lowe) v Shackleton Garden Centre Ltd* ET Case No 2400502/09; *Sweeney v Chief Commissioner of Sussex Police* ET Case No 3103129/04.
[173]   *Gioles v Cornelia Care Homes* ET Case No 3100720/05, *Castleton v Dept for Work and Pensions* EAT 0715/02 30 October 2002, unreported.
[174]   *Ceesat v Deepdene Hostel Ltd and ors* ET Case No.2302853/02.
[175]   *Clarke v Eley (IMI) Kynoch Ltd* [1982] IRLR 482,(EAT).
[176]   *Bhudi v IMI Refiners Ltd* [1994] IRLR 204 (EAT).
[177]   *Meade-Hill and anor v British Council* 1995 ICR 847, (CA).
[178]   *Cast v Croydon College* 1998 ICR 500.
[179]   *Briggs v North Eastern Education and Library Board* 1990 IRLR 181, NICA.
[180]   *Home Office v Holmes* [1984] IRLR 299.
[181]   Section 39 of the Equality Act 2010.
[182]   *O'Donnell and anor v Legal and General Resources Ltd* ET Case No 3102905-06/03; *Kording v Senator fur Finanzen* [1997] IRLR 710; *Gerster v Freistaat Bayern* [1997] IRLR 699.

(p)   a requirement that part-time workers must accrue, proportionately, more years of service than full-time colleagues prior to obtaining promotion/ management positions;

(q)   consequential aspects of part-time status, e g female part-time cleaners working outside normal office hours made redundant in preference to male full-time colleagues. The employer may have applied a condition that employees should work office hours to avoid selection for redundancy;

(r)   a requirement to work particular shifts.[183]

*Case Example*

London Underground adopted a new shift system which precluded an employee from being at home with her children in afternoons and at weekends. The appropriate pool for comparison was not single-parent train operators but all train operators. On that basis the shift pattern had a disproportionate impact on women. Women were, so held the Court of Appeal, usually put at particular disadvantage if required to work longer hours given that they are often less able to work longer and inflexible hours by reason of childcare commitments.

*London Underground v Edwards (No 2)*[184]

**7.97**   A PCP must, however, have been applied to the complainant. If it is still being considered or its imposition remains speculative the complainant will be unable to establish that he or she was put to a particular disadvantage.

## Particular disadvantage and common knowledge

**7.98**   Whilst workplace or national statistics are no longer required, a mere assertion of disadvantage is rarely enough. Moreover, where statistics are readily available they should be provided; particularly where the effect of the PCP relied on is not well-documented.[185]

**7.99**   Until recently, however, the Tribunal appeared relatively willing to apply its human experience to the facts with which they are faced in order to take a more general picture into account.[186] In particular, the Tribunal has been willing to accept the following propositions as a matter of common sense in the past:

(a)   part-time work is overwhelmingly done by women;[187]

---

[183]   *London Underground Ltd v Edwards (No 2)* [1999] ICR, 494, [1998] IRLR 364, (1998) 142 SJLB 182.
[184]   [199] IRLR 364.
[185]   *Secretary of State for Trade and Industry v Rutherford* [2006] UKHL 19.
[186]   *British Airways v Starmer* [2005] IRLR 862.
[187]   *Allonby v Accrington and Rossendale College* [2001] IRLR 364.

(b)    a far greater proportion of sole parents undertaking childcare are women;[188]

(c)    a considerably larger proportion of women than men have to take time off to care for a sick child when ill;[189]

(d)    the majority of those who work part-time do so for childcare reasons which disproportionately fall on women;[190]

(e)    it is more difficult for women to work full-time when they have childcare responsibilities;[191]

(f)    a higher proportion of women than men are secondary earners;[192]

(g)    insisting on a particular rotational shift pattern is likely to have a disproportionate impact on women with childcare responsibilities.[193]

**7.100**  The 'common knowledge' approach, however, has faced a direct challenge in the form of *Hacking & Paterson and anor v Wilson*.[194]

> *Case Example*
>
> H&P were in the practice of refusing all flexible working requests from property managers. W as a property manager made a flexible working request which was duly refused. She claimed that this was an indirectly discriminatory practice and that the appropriate pool for comparison should be all property managers. On the basis of that pool women were put at a particular disadvantage by reason of the difficulties faced in working full-time. H&P argued that the pool should be limited to those property managers who made flexible working requests: since all requests would be refused there was little disadvantage suffered. On that basis they sought, unsuccessfully, to strike W's claim out for lack of prospects. H&P appealed the refusal to strike out. Whilst the appeal was unsuccessful the Scottish EAT agreed with H&P as to the appropriate pool. Nor could it be presumed that women suffered particular disadvantage in working full-time: in light of a more mobilised workforce, part-time working for mothers should be regarded more as a matter of choice than necessity. Refusal of the flexible working request, therefore, should not be of itself taken as evidence of particular disadvantage.
>
> *Hacking & Paterson and anor v Wilson*[195]

---

[188]   *London Underground Ltd v Edwards (No 2)* [1999] ICR, 494, [1998] IRLR 364, (1998) 142 SJLB 182.

[189]   *McCrimmon v Quality Fare* ET S/103350/02, 21 March 2003, reported EOR 121 (Scottish EAT).

[190]   *Chief Constable of Avon and Somerset Constabulary v Chew* EAT/503/00, 28.

[191]   *Mitchell v David Evans Agricultural Ltd* EAT/0083/06, 15 March 2006.

[192]   *Meade-Hill v British Council*.

[193]   *Aviance UK v Garcia-Bello*, UKEAT/0044/07/DA, EAT 20 December 2007.

[194]   EATS/0954/09 (unreported, EAT Scotland).

[195]   EATS/0954/09.

**7.101**   The decision is surprising to say the least. Given that the latest surveys of part-time working continue to show that men make up less than one-quarter of part-time workers in the UK it cannot be presumed that the labour market has developed to the extent implied by the Scottish EAT. Moreover, the EAT did not direct itself to the large volume of authorities emphasising the importance of the Tribunal being able to rely on common knowledge. To that extent the decision should perhaps be contextualised: *Hacking* did not, and could not, overrule the line of decisions following *London Underground*. Nevertheless, guidance from the Court of Appeal would be of considerable assistance, if only to reinstate the pre-*Hacking* approach.

## Put to that particular disadvantage?

**7.102**   Once established that a PCP puts one sex as compared to another to a particular disadvantage, a complainant must then establish that he or she was put to that disadvantage. The disadvantage cannot be a matter of personal choice or a self-imposed problem: 'It is axiomatic that detriment cannot be self-inflicted'.[196]

> *Case Example*
>
> A female naval officer lived 60 miles away from her base and submitted a part-time working request. Royal Navy policy dictates that all personnel work full-time: the officer was offered a home for her family on the base but this was refused due to her husband's work commitments. On appeal, the Scottish EAT concluded that the reason for the disadvantage was the claimant's personal decision to remain in a home which involved a 120 mile round trip from her place of work rather than her gender. Accordingly the sex discrimination claim failed.
>
> *MoD (Royal Navy) v MacMillan*[197]

**7.103**   Nevertheless, whilst a deprivation of choice by itself is unlikely to give rise to a particular disadvantage, where a further factor is present this is likely to be sufficient.[198] Regard should be paid to such features as the affordability of childcare, the need to attend a particular nursery or the effect of a particular working pattern on the claimant's 'time and energy'.[199]

**7.104**   The Tribunal is also entitled to consider the effect of combined provisions on an individual. In *Ministry of Defence v Debique*[200] a female soldier and citizen of St Vincent was required to be available for deployment on a 24/7 basis whilst at the same time prohibited from inviting a member of her family who was not of British origin to stay on the base and assist with childcare. The EAT held that as 'discrimination is often a multi-faceted

---

[196]   Para 33 *Ministry of Defence v MacMillan* (EATS/0003/04); *Shackleton Garden Centre v Lowe* UKEAT/0161/10, [2010] EqLR 138.

[197]   EATS/0003/04.

[198]   *Gill v El Vino* [1983] IRLR 206 (CA).

[199]   *Home Office v Holmes* [1984] IRLR 299 (EAT).

[200]   [2010] IRLR 471; [2009] All ER (D) 258 (Nov) (EAT).

experience' the dual effect of the provisions should be considered. Accordingly her sex and race discrimination claim was upheld.

## Objective justification

**7.105**

*Example*

'A woman is forced to leave her job because her employer operates a practice that staff must work in a shift pattern which she is unable to comply with because she needs to look after her children at particular times of the day, and no allowances are to be made because of those needs. This would put women (who are shown to be more likely to be responsible for childcare) at a disadvantage, and the employer will have indirectly discriminated against the woman unless the process can be justified.'

Paragraph 81 of the Explanatory Notes to the Equality Act 2010.

**7.106** Once established that there has been an indirectly discriminatory PCP which has caused the claimant to suffer detriment, there follows a balancing exercise between the discriminatory effects and the legitimate needs of the employer. As the EAT made clear in *Craddock v Cornwall County Council*,[201] however, a robust approach is taken:

'To say that employing part-time employees can be inconvenient in that it requires an employer to make adjustments is a glimpse of the obvious. Yet the failure to make such adjustments to enable posts to be part-time has a public as well as a private consequence in that it denies society the services of a wider pool of potential employees and in the context of school teaching reduces the number of parents; normally mothers, who can bring to their work the insight and experiences which parenting can confer.'

**7.107** The burden on the employer is not to demonstrate 'indispensability but proof of a real need'.[202] To that end, the tribunal is entitled to consider whether there is an alternative and less discriminatory means of achieving the same aim. The responsibility for identifying such an alternative rests with the employer: one aspect of the EAT's criticism towards the employer in *Craddock* was 'the general tenor of the decision ... that it was up to the employee to put forward proposals'. Similarly in *Hardy's & Hanson plc v Lax*[203] the Court of Appeal observed that the job-sharing proposal submitted by the claimant was 'insufficiently explored and objections overstated'. 'Obvious possibilities' which lessen the discriminatory impact on an individual should be considered once the employer becomes aware of the detrimental impact of a PCP.[204] In light of

---

[201]  EAT/0367/05; [2005] All ER (D) 278 (Dec).
[202]  *Allonby v Accrington and Rossendale College* [2001] EWCA Civ 529, [2001] 2 CMLR 559, [2001] ICR 1189, [2001] IRLR 364 (CA).
[203]  [2005] EWCA Civ 846, [2005] IRLR 726, (2005) *Times*, 26 July, [2005] All ER (D) 83 (Jul) (CA).
[204]  *Hokenjos v Secretary of State for Security* [2001] EWCA Civ 624, [2001] ICR 966 (CA).

increasing awareness as to flexible working practices, amendments to hours and location of work are more likely to be regarded as 'obvious'.

**7.108** An employee's position in refuting justification can be bolstered by evidence that he or she has been willing to consider and propose alternatives to their preferred position and evidence of previous employees working satisfactorily with flexible hours in the past at the same or a similar organisation. Conversely, the employer will be expected to:

(a) establish that there is a real business need for the PCP;

(b) explain why it is necessary to apply the PCP in a form or manner which disadvantaged the worker in question;

(c) explain why the need for the PCP outweighs the discriminatory effect.

**7.109** In particular, an employer should avoid the following pitfalls:

(a) reliance upon a discriminatory aim;[205]

(b) failing to follow its own flexible working policies: a departure from standard policy without a cogent explanation is unlikely to be justified;

(c) failing to consider the rationale behind a PCP at the time of its imposition. Whilst an employer can rely when defending proceedings on reasons not in its mind at the time a decision is made, the persuasiveness of such a reason is considerably diminished. 'Afterthoughts are allowed but they are seldom convincing';[206]

(d) failing to revisit PCPs where there has been a change in circumstances. Whilst a PCP may have been justified at one stage, eg for reasons relating to financial constraints, it does not continue to be so when those constraints are removed;[207]

(e) in the cases of flexible working requests, failing to hold[208] or properly assess[209] a trial period to consider the workability of a request;

(f) relying upon generalised statements and blanket assertions such as 'job-sharers have less experience than full-timers';

---

[205] *Allonby v Accrington and Rossendale College* [2001] EWCA Civ 529, [2001] 2 CMLR 559, [2001] ICR 1189, [2001] IRLR 364 (CA).

[206] *Hokenjos v Sec State for Social Security* [2001] EWCA Civ 624, [2001] ICR 966 (CA).

[207] *Benveniste v University of Southampton* [1989] IRLR 213 (CA).

[208] In *Dillon v Rentokil Initial UK Ltd* ET 2700899/01 the refusal to allow a long-serving and highly-regarded employee a trial period in respect of her flexible working request rendered the refusal of that application unjustified.

[209] In *Terry v ICM Computer Solutions plc* ET 2409119/03 the decision to bring a trial period to an end before appropriately assessing the assumption that the requested working pattern would impair the running of the business was not justified.

*Case Examples*

On the assumption that job sharers did not acquire the same level of experience as full-time employees, an employer treated a job-sharer's length of service as half that of a full-timer when calculating benefits. The ECJ concluded that this assumption without any evidence in its support could not justify the difference in treatment.

*Hill and Stapleton v Revenue Commissioners*[210]

And by contrast:

Where there was evidence to support the proposition that trainee doctors would be exposed to greater experience in the various scenarios that arise in general practice it was justified to compel that training to be undertaken on a full-time basis.

*Rinke v Artzekammer Hamburg*[211]

## Examples of objective justification

**7.110** Whilst each case is very much determined on its facts, a number of themes emerge in those instances where a discriminatory PCP has been justified.

### *The intrinsic requirements of the role*

**7.111** The strongest argument to support a PCP is the contention that the role simply cannot be performed any other way having regard to the nature of the role, the rhythm of the work and the size of the workforce. In *Norris v Chesterfield Law Centre*,[212] imposing the requirement to work full-time on commencement of the post was justified where close collaboration with an existing casework was essential and there was evidence to suggest that this would have been frustrated by job-sharing. A minimal office presence is likely to be reasonable in order to fulfill management responsibilities[213] and obligations to regularly attend conferences.[214] Similarly, where there are genuine security concerns at stake, for example the requirement for security of an internet network, this may support a requirement for office-based working.[215]

**7.112** Again, however, something more than a mere assertion is required: a failure on the employer's part to assess whether duties can be undertaken remotely is likely to undermine the justification defence.[216] This is particularly

---

[210]   Case C-243/95; [1998] IRLR 466.
[211]   Case C-25/02; [2003] ECR I-8349.
[212]   EAT 1359/95.
[213]   *Clymo v Wandsworth London Borough Council* [1989] IRLR 241 in which the managerial responsibilities at stake would, if a job-share had been adopted, have required lengthy and excessive weekly handover meetings.
[214]   *Castleton v Department of Work and Pensions* EAT/0715/02, unreported.
[215]   *Legall v Governing Body of Lewisham College* ET Case No 2306039/04.
[216]   *Given v Scottish Power plc* ET S/3172/94; *Hardy & Hansons v Lax* [2005] EWCA Civ 846.

so where there is evidence to suggest that the requirement for, by way of example, office working, has not been consistently applied.

## *Exhaustion of alternatives*

**7.113** Where an employer has attempted without success to mitigate the discriminatory effects of a PCP through use of flexible working, this is likely to support a defence of justification.

> *Case Example*
>
> A head nurse wished to change from full-time to part-time hours. The employer explored all reasonable options including part-time working without success: due to the nurse's absence in afternoons the surgery frequently found itself with clinical problems awaiting the next morning. In the circumstances the refusal to allow O to continue on a part-time basis was justified: the position of head nurse which, in light of the needs and resources of the business, required a full-time employee.
>
> *Ogilvie v Ross and anor t/a Braid Veterinary Hospital* (EAT)[217]

**7.114** Similarly, where an employer has exhausted reasonable steps to find a job-share partner unsuccessfully, a refusal of a job-share request is likely to be justified.[218]

## *Customer preference and client need*

**7.115** A discriminatory PCP may be justified in order to meet the needs of clients who, due to the nature of the particular business, expect prompt responses and one-on-one relationships.[219]

> *Case Example*
>
> S was appointed as a full-time employee at a shipping agency but soon after commencing the post she announced that she could only work part-time. She was allocated to a contract responsible for 75% of the agency's revenue and could not work from home as she was still being trained. In light of the needs of the client, her level of experience and the requirements of the role her dismissal for refusal to remain on a full-time contract was entirely justified in the eyes of the Tribunal.
>
> *Sullivan v John S Braid and Co Ltd*[220]

---

[217] EAT 1115/99 (unreported) (EAT).

[218] *Brown v McAlpine and Co Ltd* EATS/0009/05 (unreported) (EAT Scotland).

[219] *Coleman Coyle v Georgiou* EAT/535/00 (unreported); *Pryce v Blair Travel* EAT/443/01 (unreported); *Edgley v Oliver and Graimes Design Associates* ET 310172/05; *Eley v Huntleigh Diagnostics Ltd* [1996] EAT 1441/96 (unreported).

[220] ET 2302098/03.

## *Setting a precedent*

**7.116**   In certain circumstances a flexible working practice may be refused where this would set a dangerous precedent for the remainder of the workforce which could not be accommodated if writ large.

> *Case Example*
>
> Where the profits of a garden centre were heavily reliant on weekend trading and a large proportion of staff were working mothers who worked weekends, the refusal to excuse S from working any weekend days was objectively justified. The burden on other women with children having to work additional weekend shifts was one they may well resent and, conversely, it was not practicable to allow all female staff with children to be excused from working on a rota.
>
> *Sourbutts (nee Lowe) v Shackletons Garden Centre Ltd*[221]

**7.117**   The situation may be somewhat different where the mother in question does not have the support of a father to assist with caring responsibilities, even where there are a large number of working mothers within the business.[222]

## Miscellaneous claims

**7.118**   There are a number of additional claims which may be triggered in the context of flexible working. In addition to more obvious causes of action such as harassment and direct discrimination (discussed in Chapter 1) a new concept of 'associative discrimination' has developed protecting those who are in some way associated with someone who has a protected characteristic.

> *Case Example*
>
> Mrs. Coleman was the primary carer of her disabled son. She accepted voluntary redundancy and issued a claim for disability discrimination on the basis that the reason for her treatment was her son's disability. On referral, the ECJ stated that associative discrimination fell within the protection of the Equal Treatment Directive. So as to foster a 'robust conception of equality', a person need not possess the characteristic which forms the basis of a discrimination claim provided that the treatment is on the grounds of that protected characteristic (eg disability or age).
>
> *Coleman v Attridge Law*[223]

**7.119**   As the formulation of associative discrimination and the potential expansion of the right to request flexible working clearly demonstrate, developments in the law relating to flexi-working practices show no sign of slowing down.

---

[221]   ET Case No 2400502/09 (28 January 2011).
[222]   *McCroy v Royal Mail Group Ltd* [2010] EqLR 399, Newcastle Employment Tribunal, 21 September 2010.
[223]   C-303/06, [2008] IRLR 722, [2008] ICR 1128 (ECJ).

# FURTHER READING

**7.120** 'Working towards Equality: A Framework for Action' (Government Equalities Office, February 2010)

'Flexible working and work-life balance'/'Flexible working: making an application', 'Flexible working: the outcome of your application' (DTI)

'Flexible working – the law and best practice' (DTI)

'Flexible working and work-life balance' (ACAS): www.acas.org

'Working Better: A Manager's Guide to Flexible Working' (Equality and Human Rights Commission) www.equalityhumanrights.com/workingbetter

'Lifecycles: building business access through effective employment practice' www.workingfamilies.org.uk

'Wisework, consultants in flexible working' www.wisework.co.uk

'Flexible Working: working for families, working for business' (Family Friendly Working Hours Taskforce)

# Chapter 8

# PARENTAL LEAVE

*Tom Brown*

## HISTORY OF THE LEGAL FRAMEWORK GOVERNING PARENTAL LEAVE RIGHTS

**8.1**   Parental leave has been subject to European Community law since the adoption of Council Directive 96/34/EC of 3 June 1996 on the framework agreement on parental leave concluded by UNIE, CEEP and the ETUC. Council Directive 96/34/EC gave effect to a framework agreement between the Union of Industrial and Employers' Confederations of Europe, the European Centre of Enterprises with Public Participation and the European Trade Union Confederation.

**8.2**   However, as a result of the UK's opt out from the social chapter of the Maastricht Treaty, Council Directive 96/34/EC did not bind the UK on implementation. It became binding by virtue of Council Directive 97/75/EC when the social chapter was subsequently adopted by the UK.

**8.3**   Its provisions were implemented into UK law by additions to the Employment Rights Act 1996 (ERA)[1] and by the Maternity and Parental Leave Regulations 1999, SI 1999/3312, as amended (MPL Regulations).

**8.4**   Sections 76–79 of the ERA provide the power for the Secretary of State to make regulations entitling an employee to take parental leave. The relevant regulations are the MPL regulations.

### Domestic rights to paternity leave

**8.5**   Sections 80A and 80AA of the ERA empower the Secretary of State to make regulations providing for ordinary and additional paternity leave respectively. The relevant regulations are the Paternity and Adoption Leave Regulations 2002, SI 2002/2788 and the Additional Paternity Leave Regulations 2010, SI 2010/1055.

**8.6**   Council Directive 96/34/EC will be repealed and replaced by Council Directive 2010/18/EU from 8 March 2012.

---

[1]   ERA, ss 57A–B, 76–80A, 80C–E.

## THE SCOPE OF THE CURRENT DIRECTIVE

**8.7**   It is important to understand the scope of the Directive since domestic implementation of EU rights may be subject to different considerations from purely domestic rights.

**8.8**   Clause 2.1 of the Framework Agreement (which the Directive implements) provides that men and women workers are granted an individual right to parental leave on the grounds of the birth or adoption of a child to enable them to take care of that child for at least three months until a given age up to eight years, to be defined by member states and/or management and labour.

**8.9**   In *Chatzi v Ipourgos Ikonomikon*,[2] the ECJ held that clause 2.1 does not require member states to confer an entitlement to a separate period of parental leave for each child born where there are multiple births from one pregnancy. But it does require member states to take due account of the particular needs of the parents of twins when establishing their parental leave regime. In fact, the wording of the domestic implementation of clause 2.1 (see below) probably allows, theoretically at least, for a full separate allowance for each of two twins.

**8.10**   Member states and/or management and labour are to take necessary measures to protect workers against dismissal on the grounds of an application for, or the taking of, parental leave in accordance with national law, collective agreements or practices.[3]

**8.11**   At the end of parental leave, workers shall have the right to return to the same job or, if that is not possible, to an equivalent or similar job consistent with their employment contract or employment relationship.[4]

**8.12**   Rights acquired or in the process of being acquired by the worker on the date on which parental leave starts shall be maintained as they stand until the end of parental leave. At the end of parental leave, these rights, including any changes arising from national law, collective agreements or practice, shall apply.[5]

**8.13**   Clause 3.1 of the Framework Agreement provides that member states shall take the necessary measures to entitle workers to time off from work in accordance with national legislation, collective agreements and/or practice on the grounds of *force majeur* for urgent family reasons in cases of sickness or accident making the immediate presence of the worker indispensable.

---

[2]   [2010] EqLR 336.
[3]   Clause 2.4.
[4]   Clause 2.5.
[5]   Clause 2.6.

## Directive 2010/18/EU

**8.14** The new Directive will confirm that the entitlement to parental leave extends to part-time and limited-term workers and those with an employment relationship with a temporary agency.[6] The minimum period of leave will be four months and 'to encourage a more equal take-up of leave by both parents, at least one of the four months shall be provided on a non-transferable basis'.[7]

## LEAVE UNDER SECTION 57A OF THE EMPLOYMENT RIGHTS ACT 1996

**8.15** An employee is entitled to be permitted by his employer to take a reasonable amount of time off during the employee's working hours in order to take action which is necessary (amongst other things, and as relevant to this chapter):

(a) to provide assistance on an occasion when a child falls ill, gives birth or is injured or assaulted;

(b) to make arrangements for the provision of care for a child who is ill or injured;

(c) because of the unexpected disruption or termination of arrangements for the care of a child; or

(d) to deal with an incident which involves a child of the employee and which occurs unexpectedly in a period during which an educational establishment which the child attends is responsible for him.

**8.16** An employment tribunal determining whether the reason for an employee's dismissal was that she had taken, or had sought to take, time off under section 57A should ask itself the following questions:

(1) Did the applicant take time off or seek to take time off from work during his or her working hours? If so, on how many occasions and when?

(2) If so, on each of those occasions did the applicant: (a) as soon as reasonably practicable inform his or her employer of the reason for her absence; and (b) inform him how long s/he expected to be absent; (c) if not, were the circumstances such that s/he could not inform him of the reason until after s/he had returned to work?

    If the tribunal finds that the applicant had not complied with the requirements of section 57A(2), then the right to take time off work under subsection (1) does not apply. The absences would be unauthorised and dismissal would not be automatically unfair.

---

6   Clause 1.3.
7   Clause 1.2.

(3)   If the applicant had complied with these requirements then the following questions arise:

    (a)   Did s/he take or seek to take time off work in order to take action which was necessary to deal with one or more of the five situations listed at paragraphs (a) to (e) of subsection (1)?

    (b)   If so, was the amount of time off taken or sought to be taken reasonable in the circumstances?

(4)   If the applicant satisfied questions (3)(a) and (b), was the reason or principal reason for his or her dismissal that she had taken/sought to take that time off work?

**8.17**   If the tribunal answers that final question in the affirmative, then the applicant is entitled to a finding of automatic unfair dismissal.

**8.18**   The right is to a reasonable amount of time off to take action that is necessary. In considering whether action was necessary, factors to be taken into account will include the nature of the incident which has occurred, and the extent to which there was anyone else available to help out. It is not possible to specify maximum periods of leave: it will always depend on the circumstances and be a question of fact for an employment tribunal: see *Qua v Ford Morrison Solicitors*.[8]

**8.19**   Time off to make arrangements for the provision of care does not encompass time off to *provide* care.[9] The legislation contemplates a reasonable period of time off to enable an employee to deal with a child who has fallen ill unexpectedly. In other words, the section is dealing with something unforeseen. Once the employee knows that the child is suffering from an underlying medical condition, which is likely to cause the child to suffer regular relapses, the situation no longer falls within the scope of subsection (1)(a) or within section 57A at all. An employee would, in such circumstances, be permitted reasonable time off work in order to make longer-term arrangements for care, as is provided by subsection (1)(b). The issue is foreseeability and it will inevitably be a question of fact and degree in each situation. The right is, essentially, a right to time off to deal with the unexpected.

**8.20**   The unexpected disruption or termination of care arrangements need not take place on the day that the leave is taken, although the longer the time between the employee learning of the risk of disruption and the time when that risk becomes fact, the greater the time in which the employee can explore alternative arrangements.[10]

---

8   [2003] ICR 482; [2003] IRLR 184.
9   *Qua v Ford Morrison Solicitors* [2003] ICR 482; [2003] IRLR 184.
10  *Royal Bank of Scotland plc v Harrison* [2009] ICR 116; [2009] IRLR 28.

**8.21** The employee must tell his employer the reason for his absence as soon as reasonably practicable and except where he cannot tell his employer until after he has returned to work, he must tell his employer how long he expects to be absent.[11]

**8.22** The notice requirement is not onerous. The communication need only show the employer that something has happened to cause a breakdown in the employee's care arrangements.[12]

**8.23** Where, in employment tribunal proceedings, an employer argues that there is no entitlement to dependency leave because the employee has failed to give notice, an employment tribunal must determine this contention for each instance of leave and not take a broad brush approach.[13]

**8.24** An employee may present a complaint to an employment tribunal under section 57B that his employer has unreasonably refused to permit him to take time off as required by section 57A of the ERA. The ordinary time limit for presenting a complaint is three months. If an employment tribunal finds a complaint well-founded, it shall make a declaration to that effect and may make an award of compensation of such amount as it thinks just and equitable.

## PARENTAL LEAVE UNDER THE MPL REGULATIONS

### Contractual rights

**8.25** Employees may have contractual rights to parental leave which are equivalent to or more generous than the rights conferred by the MPL Regulations. The Regulations provide *minimum* rights. Parental leave under the Regulations is unpaid leave.

**8.26** Where an employee has a contractual, as well as the statutory, right to unpaid leave, he may not exercise both rights, but in taking leave for which the contractual and statutory rights provide, he may take advantage of whichever right is, in any particular respect, the more favourable, so as to create a 'composite' right to parental leave. The regulations are deemed to apply subject to any necessary modification, to give effect to any more favourable contractual terms.[14]

### Who is entitled to parental leave?

**8.27** Two conditions must be met: a **parental responsibility** condition and a **continuous employment** condition.

---

[11]   ERA, s. 57A(2).
[12]   *Truelove v Safeway Stores plc* [2005] ICR 589.
[13]   *Qua v Ford Morrison Solicitors* [2003] ICR 482; [2003] IRLR 184.
[14]   MPL Regs, reg 21.

## *Parental responsibility*

**8.28**  The employee must have, or expect to have, 'responsibility for a child': reg 13(1)(b).

**8.29**  'Responsibility for a child' means:[15]

(a)  parental responsibility within the meaning of section 3 of the Children Act 1989; or

(b)  parental responsibilities within the meaning of section 1(3) of the Children (Scotland) Act 1995; or

(c)  that the employee has been registered as the child's father under any provision of:

   (i)  section 10(1) or 10A(1) of the Births and Deaths Registration Act 1953; or
   (ii)  section 18(1) or 18(2) of the Registration of Births, Deaths and Marriages (Scotland) Act 1965.

## *Continuous employment*

**8.30**  The employee must have been continuously employed[16] for a period of not less than a year.[17]

**8.31**  Employees with less than a year's continuous employment also have an entitlement to take parental leave if each of the following conditions are met (in addition to the parental responsibility requirement):[18]

(a)  the case must concern a child who is entitled to disability living allowance;[19]

(b)  the entitlement to parental leave may not be exercised on or after the child's eighteenth birthday;

(c)  the employee must have been employed between 15 December 1999 and 9 January 2002 by someone other than his current employer;

---

15  MPL Regs, regs 2, 13(2).
16  'Continuous employment' is a concept imported from Chapter I of Part XIV of the Employment Rights Act 1996. A comprehensive treatment of it is beyond the scope of this work.
17  MPL Regs, reg 13(1).
18  MPL Regs, reg 13(1), (1A). A further exception to the one-year continuous employment concerned reg 15(2), but this governed entitlement to parental leave up until 31 March 2005 in respect of adopted children and so is now obsolete.
19  MPL Regs, reg 15(3).

(d)  the employee must have worked for that other employer (or, if employed by more than one employer during that period, any such employer) for a period of not less than one year.

## What is the entitlement?

**8.32**  An employee has an entitlement to thirteen weeks' unpaid leave in respect of any individual child, or eighteen weeks in respect of a child who is entitled to disability living allowance.[20]

## What does thirteen weeks' leave mean in practice?

**8.33**  Where an employee's contracted working time does not vary from week-to-week, a week's leave is a period of absence which is equal in duration to the period for which he is normally required to work in a week.[21]

**8.34**  Where an employee has an irregular working pattern week to week, a week's leave is reckoned by dividing the total periods for which the employee is normally required to work in a year by 52.

**8.35**  Where an employee takes parental leave in periods shorter than his working week as reckoned under reg 14(2) or (3), he completes a week's leave when the aggregate of the periods of leave he has taken equals the period constituting a week's leave for him under reg 14(2) or (3).

## When may parental leave be taken?

**8.36**  An entitlement to take parental leave may not be exercised after the date of the child's fifth birthday (see the chapter on adoption leave for details in relation to adopted children),[22] except where:

(a)  the child is in receipt of disability living allowance, in which case it may not be exercised after the date of the child's eighteenth birthday;[23] or

(b)  the employer has postponed the employee's entitlement to take leave in certain prescribed circumstances.[24]

## How does an employee exercise the right to take parental leave?

**8.37**  Schedule 2 to the MPL Regulations contains default provisions governing the entitlement to parental leave. If an employee's contract contains provision for taking parental leave, that process may be used. If there are no

---

[20]  MPL Regs, reg 14.
[21]  MPL Regs, reg 14(2).
[22]  MPL Regs, reg 15(1).
[23]  MPL Regs, reg 15(3).
[24]  MPL Regs, reg 15(4).

contractual provisions, or any contractual provision is less favourable than the default statutory provision, then that may be used.

## Schedule 2

### *Evidence of entitlement*

**8.38**   An employee may not exercise any entitlement to parental leave unless he has complied with any request made by his employer to produce for the employer's inspection evidence of his entitlement, namely of:

(a)   the employee's responsibility or expected responsibility for the child in respect of whom the employee proposes to take leave;

(b)   the child's date of birth; and

(c)   where an extended entitlement is sought because the child is in receipt of disability living allowance, proof of the child's entitlement to that allowance.[25]

**8.39**   Where an employee relies on regulation 13A to establish a year's continuous employment, then the employee may not exercise an entitlement to parental leave unless he has given his employer notice of that period of employment and such evidence of it as the employer may reasonably require.[26]

### *Notice*

**8.40**   An employee must give an employer notice of the period of leave he proposes to take.

**8.41**   Where the employee is the father of the child in respect of whom leave is to be taken and the period of leave is to begin on the date on which the child is born, the notice required must specify the expected week of childbirth and the duration of the period of leave and be given to the employer at least 21 days before the beginning of the expected week of childbirth.[27]

**8.42**   In all other cases, the notice required must specify the date on which the period of leave is to begin and end and must be given to the employer at least 21 days before the date on which that period is to begin.[28]

**8.43**   An employer may postpone a period of parental leave where all of the following conditions are met:

(a)   the leave is not a period of leave beginning with the birth of the child;

---

[25]   MPL Regs, Sch 2, paras 1–2.
[26]   MPL Regs, Sch 2, para 2A.
[27]   MPL Regs, Sch 2, para 4.
[28]   MPL Regs, Sch 2, para 3.

(b)  the employer considers that the operation of its business would be unduly disrupted if the employee took leave during that period;

(c)  the employer agrees to permit the employee to take a period of leave of the same duration as the period in the employee's notice beginning on a date determined by the employer which is no later than six months after the beginning of the original period sought and ends before the child's eighteenth birthday;

(d)  the employer gives the employee written notice of the postponement, stating the reasons for it and specifying the dates on which the employee may take leave and gives the employee that notice not more than seven days after the employee gave written notice.[29]

**8.44**  An employee may not take leave in periods (or multiples) of less than a week except where the child is entitled to disability living allowance (MPL Regulations, Sch 2, para 7).[30]

**8.45**  An employee may not take more than four weeks' leave in respect of any individual child during a particular year (MPL Regulations, Sch 2, para 8). A year runs from the date on which the employee first became entitled to take parental leave in respect of the child in question except where an employee's entitlement to take parental leave has been interrupted,[31] in which case time runs from the date on which the employee most recently became entitled to take parental leave in respect of that child. Following years begin on the anniversary that the entitlement was acquired.

## Application of terms and conditions during periods of leave

**8.46**  An employee taking parental leave is entitled during the period of leave to the benefit of the employer's implied obligation to him of trust and confidence and any terms and conditions relating to notice of termination, compensation in the event of redundancy and disciplinary and grievance procedures.

**8.47**  Correspondingly, the employee is bound by contractual terms and conditions relating to notice of termination, disclosure of confidential information, acceptance of gifts and benefits and participation by the employee in any other business.[32]

---

[29]  MPL Regs, Sch 2, para 6.
[30]  *New Southern Railway Ltd (Formerly South Central Trains Ltd) v Rodway* [2005] ICR 1162.
[31]  Eg, Employee A has an entitlement to parental leave with Employer X. A leaves to work for employer Y. He will not be entitled to take parental leave with his new employer until he has a year's continuous employment. Parental leave years will thereafter run from the date he reacquires the entitlement to parental leave in relation to a child.
[32]  MPL Regs, reg 17.

## Right to return after parental leave

**8.48**  An employee who returns to work after a period of parental leave which was an isolated period of leave of four weeks or less or the last of two or more periods of parental leave (none of which exceeded four weeks) is entitled to return to the job in which he worked before his absence.[33]

**8.49**  Where an employee returns after a period of parental leave of four weeks or more, he is entitled to return from leave to the job in which he was employed before his absence or, if it is not reasonably practicable for the employer to permit him to return to that job, to another job which is both suitable for him and appropriate for him to do in the circumstances.[34]

**8.50**  Where there have been consecutive periods of parental leave, the right is to return to the job in which the employer was employed before the first of the periods of leave.[35]

**8.51**  The right to return is a right to return on terms and conditions no less favourable than those which would have applied had the employee not been absent (since the beginning of the first period of parental leave) and with seniority, pension rights and similar rights as they would have been if the employee had not been absent.[36]

## Detrimental treatment for taking or seeking to take parental leave

**8.52**  An employee is entitled under section 47C of the ERA, not to be subjected to any detriment by any act, or any deliberate failure to act, by his employer for the reason that the employee took or sought to take parental leave or time off under section 57A of the 1996 Act.

**8.53**  An affected employee may bring proceedings in an employment tribunal under section 48 of the ERA within three months of the act complained about or within such further period as an employment tribunal considers reasonable in a case where it is satisfied that it was not reasonably practicable for the complaint to be presented before the end of the three-month period. Where an employment tribunal finds such a complaint well-founded, it shall make a declaration to that effect and may make an award of compensation.[37]

## Dismissal for taking or seeking to take parental leave

**8.54**  An employee who is dismissed is entitled to be regarded as automatically unfairly dismissed under section 99 of the ERA if the reason or principal

---

[33]  MPL Regs, reg 18(1).
[34]  MPL Regs, reg 18(2).
[35]  MPL Regs, reg 18(3).
[36]  MPL Regs, reg 18A(1).
[37]  ERA, s 49.

reason for dismissal is the fact that the employee took or sought to take parental leave or time off under section 57A of the ERA.[38]

**8.55** An employee is also entitled to be regarded as unfairly dismissed if:[39]

(a)   the reason for the dismissal was redundancy;

(b)   one or more other employees in the same undertaking held positions similar to the dismissed employee;

(c)   the redundancy situation applied equally to them;

(d)   that employee or those employees were not dismissed; and

(e)   it is shown that the reason or principal reason for which the employee was selected for dismissal was that she took or sought to take parental leave or time off under section 57A.

## HUMAN RIGHTS CONSIDERATIONS

**8.56**   In *Markin v Russia*,[40] the European Court of Human Rights found a violation of Article 8 (the right to respect for family life) and Article 14 (the prohibition against discrimination in securing convention rights). M was a soldier in the Russian army. He had principal sole care of three children. He applied for three years' parental leave. It was refused on the basis that leave was permitted only to female military personnel. M was subsequently disciplined for being absent from his place of work.

**8.57**   The Court said:[41]

'[...] by enabling one of the parents to stay at home to look after the children, parental leave and related allowances promote family life and necessarily affect the way in which it is organised. Parental leave and parental allowances therefore come within the scope of Article 8 of the Convention. It follows that Article 14, taken together with Article 8, is applicable. Accordingly, although Article 8 does not include a right to parental leave or impose any positive obligation on States to provide parental leave allowances, if a State does decide to create a parental leave scheme, it must do so in a manner which is compatible with Article 14 of the Convention.'

**8.58**   The Court was:[42]

---

[38]   MPL Regs, reg 20(1)–(3).
[39]   MPL Regs, reg 20(2)–(3).
[40]   [2010] EqLR 40.
[41]   Para 45.
[42]   Para 48.

'[...] not convinced by the Constitutional Court's argument that, as far as parental leave is concerned, the different treatment of male and female military personnel is justified by the special social role of mothers in the upbringing of children [...]. It observes that in contrast to maternity leave and associated allowances, which are primarily intended to enable the mother to recover from the fatigue of childbirth and to breastfeed her baby if she so wishes, parental leave and the parental leave allowances relate to the subsequent period and are intended to enable the parent to stay at home to look after the infant personally. Whilst being aware of the differences which may exist between mother and father in their relationship with the child, the Court considers that, as far as the role of taking care of the child during this period is concerned, both parents are "similarly placed".'

**8.59**  Rejecting an argument that restrictions on male military personnel were legitimate, the Court said:[43]

'By enabling the parent to stay at home, parental leave provides an opportunity for that parent to take care of the child in the earliest period of its life and to spend adequate time with it. The Court considers that, in their relations with their children, servicemen and servicewomen are in an analogous situation [...]. The Court considers that very weighty reasons are required to justify a difference in treatment between servicemen and servicewomen in this particularly important sphere of family life, which concerns parents' relations with their new-born children.'

# PATERNITY LEAVE

**8.60**  An employee who satisfies eligibility and notice requirements is entitled to take paternity leave.[44] Paternity leave is a misnomer, since it may be taken by people who are not a child's father, including women.

## Contractual and composite rights

**8.61**  Employees may have contractual rights to paternity leave which are equivalent to or more generous than the rights conferred by the PAL regulations. The regulations provide minimum rights.

**8.62**  Where an employee has a contractual, as well as the statutory, right to paternity leave, s/he may not exercise both rights, but, in taking leave for which the contractual and statutory rights provide, s/he may take advantage of whichever right is, in any particular respect, the more favourable, so as to create a 'composite' right to paternity leave. The regulations are deemed to apply subject to any necessary modification, to give effect to any more favourable contractual terms.[45]

---

[43]  Para 54.
[44]  Paternity and Adoption Leave Regulations 2002 (PAL), regs 4–7.
[45]  PAL Regs, reg 30.

## Paternity leave options

**8.63**  An employee may take one or two consecutive weeks' leave.[46]

**8.64**  The leave must be taken within the first 56 days after the child is born unless the child is born before the first day of the expected week of its birth, in which case, the leave must be taken within 56 days of the first day of the expected week of its birth.[47]

**8.65**  Subject to the 56-day time window, an employee may choose to begin a period of paternity leave on:

(a)  the date on which the child is born;

(b)  the date falling such number of days after the date of birth as the employer indicates in a written notice in accordance with regulation 6 (see below) (in other words, a date that is contingent until the date of birth is known); or

(c)  a predetermined date, specified in a notice under regulation 6, which is later than the first day of the expected week of the child's birth.

## Who is eligible?

**8.66**  Paternity leave is available to employees (in the narrow sense of those working under a contract of service).

### *Relationship and responsibility criteria*

**8.67**  The employee must be either:

(a)  the father of the child;[48] or

(b)  not the father, but:[49]

    (i)  the spouse of the child's mother;
    (ii)  the mother's civil partner; or
    (iii)  the mother's partner; and

(c)  must have or expect to have, responsibility (if the father) or (if not the child's father) the main responsibility (apart from any responsibility of the mother) for the upbringing of the child.[50]

---

[46]  PAL Regs, reg 5(1).
[47]  PAL Regs, reg 5(2).
[48]  PAL Regs, reg 4(2)(b)(i).
[49]  PAL Regs, reg 4(2)(b)(ii).
[50]  PAL Regs, reg 4(2)(c).

**8.68** 'Partner' means a person (whether of the same or a different sex) who lives with the mother and the child in an enduring family relationship but is not the mother's parent, grandparent, sibling, aunt or uncle.

**8.69** An employee shall be treated as being the spouse, civil partner or partner of the mother if s/he would have been if the mother had not died.[51]

**8.70** An employee shall be treated as having or expecting to have responsibility for bringing up the child if s/he would have had that responsibility (or expectation of it) if the child had not been stillborn after 24 weeks of pregnancy or died.[52]

**8.71** An employee's entitlement to leave is not affected by the birth or expected birth of more than one child as a result of the same pregnancy.[53]

## Continuous employment

**8.72** An employee is eligible for paternity leave if s/he has been continuously employed for not less than 26 weeks ending with the week immediately preceding the fourteenth week before the expected week of the child's birth or, where the child is born on a date earlier than the fourteenth week before the week in which its birth is expected (ie, it is very premature), if the employee would have been continuously employed for 26 weeks if his employment had continued until the fourteenth week.[54]

## Notice

**8.73** An employee must give his employer notice of his intention to take paternity leave.[55] The notice must be given in writing if the employer so requests.[56] The employee must give a further notice – also in writing if so requested – as soon as reasonably practicable after the child's birth of the date on which the child was born.[57]

**8.74** The employee's notice must specify:[58]

(a)  the expected week of the child's birth;[59]

(b)  the length of leave that s/he has chosen (ie, one week or two consecutive weeks);[60] and

---

51  PAL Regs, reg 4(4).
52  PAL Regs, reg 4(5).
53  PAL Regs, reg 4(6).
54  PAL Regs, reg 4(2)(a), (3).
55  PAL Regs, reg 6(1).
56  PAL Regs, reg 6(8).
57  PAL Regs, reg 6(7), 6(8).
58  PAL Regs, reg 6(1).
59  PAL Regs, reg 6(1)(a).
60  PAL Regs, reg 6(1)(b).

(c)   the date on which the employee has chosen to begin leave.[61]

**8.75**   The notice must be given to the employer in or before the fifteenth week before the expected week of the child's birth or, where it was not reasonably practicable for the employee to give that notice, as soon as is reasonably practicable.[62]

**8.76**   Where the employer requests it, an employee must also give his employer a declaration, signed by the employee, to the effect that the purpose of his absence is to care for a child or support the child's mother and that he satisfies the relationship and responsibility criteria in reg 4(2)(b) and (c).

**8.77**   An employee who has given notice may vary the date he has chosen as the date on which his paternity leave will begin provided he gives notice of the variation.[63]

**8.78**   The notice of variation must be given at least 28 days before:

(a)   the first day of the expected week of the child's birth where the variation is to provide for paternity leave to begin on the date on which the child is born;[64]

(b)   before a predetermined date, where the leave is to begin on a predetermined date;[65]

(c)   and, where leave is to begin on a date that is a specified number of days after the date on which the child is born, at least 28 days before the date falling the same number of days after the first day of the expected week of the child's birth.[66]

**8.79**   Where it is not reasonably practicable to give notice at least 28 days before the relevant date, notice of variation must be given as soon as is reasonably practicable.[67]

## Starting leave

**8.80**   Paternity leave starts on the date specified in a valid notice under reg 6.

---

[61]   PAL Regs, reg 6(1)(c).
[62]   PAL Regs, reg 6(2).
[63]   PAL Regs, reg 6(4).
[64]   PAL Regs, reg 6(4)(a).
[65]   PAL Regs, reg 6(4)(b).
[66]   PAL Regs, reg 6(4)(c).
[67]   PAL Regs, reg 6(4).

**8.81**   Where the employee has chosen to begin paternity leave on the date on which the child is born and the employee is at work on that date, the employee's period of leave begins on the day after that date.[68]

**8.82**   During paternity leave, an employee is entitled to the benefit of all of the terms and conditions of employment which would have applied if he had not been absent,[69] and is bound by any obligations arising under those terms and conditions, except insofar as they are inconsistent with absence from work on paternity leave.[70] Most obviously this means that the employee is not under a contractual obligation to work.

**8.83**   However, terms and conditions of employment does not include terms and conditions about remuneration insofar as those sums are wages or salary.[71]

**8.84**   An employee has the right to return after a period of paternity leave (or a period of paternity leave followed by a period of parental leave of no more than four weeks) to the job in which he was employed before his absence.[72] Where an employee takes paternity leave and then more than four weeks' parental leave, s/he has a right to return to the job in which s/he was employed before his or her absence, or, if it is not reasonably practicable for the employer to permit the employee to return to that job, another job which is both suitable for the employee and appropriate for the employee to do in the circumstances.

**8.85**   The employee's right is a right to return with his or her seniority, pension rights and similar rights as they would have been if s/he had not been absent (unless part of the absence is additional adoption leave or additional maternity leave) and on terms and conditions no less favourable than those which would have applied had s/he not been absent.[73]

## Protection from detriment and dismissal for taking parental or paternity leave

**8.86**   An employee is entitled under section 47C of the ERA 1996 not to be subjected to any detriment or any deliberate failure to act by his employer because the employee took or sought to take paternity leave.[74]

**8.87**   An employee who is dismissed is entitled under section 99 of the ERA to be regarded as unfairly dismissed if the reason for dismissal is that the employee took, or sought to take, paternity leave.[75]

---

68   PAL Regs, reg 7(2).
69   PAL Regs, reg 12(1)(a).
70   PAL Regs, reg 12(1)(b); ERA 1996, s 80C(1)(b).
71   PAL Regs, reg 12(2), (3).
72   PAL Regs, reg 13(1).
73   PAL Regs, reg 14.
74   PAL Regs, reg 28(1)(a).
75   PAL Regs, reg 29(1).

**8.88**   An employee is also entitled to be regarded as unfairly dismissed if:[76]

(a)   the reason for the dismissal was redundancy;

(b)   one or more other employees in the same undertaking held positions similar to the dismissed employee;

(c)   the redundancy situation applied equally to them;

(d)   that employee or those employees were not dismissed; and

(e)   it is shown that the reason or principal reason for which the employee was selected for dismissal was that s/he took or sought to take paternity leave.

**8.89**   But a dismissal is not unfair where the employer shows that:[77]

(a)   it was not reasonably practicable for a reason other than redundancy for the employer to permit the employee to return to a job which was both suitable for the employee and appropriate for him to do in the circumstances;

(b)   an associated employer offered the employee a job of that kind; and

(c)   the employee accepted or unreasonably refused that offer.

## ADDITIONAL PATERNITY LEAVE: THE ADDITIONAL PATERNITY LEAVE REGULATIONS 2010

**8.90**   APL is available in relation to children whose expected week of birth begins on or after 3 April 2011.[78]

### Contractual and composite rights

**8.91**   Employees may have contractual rights equivalent to additional paternity leave which are as or more generous than the rights conferred by the APL regulations. The regulations provide minimum rights.

**8.92**   Where an employee has a contractual, as well as the statutory, right equivalent to additional paternity leave, s/he may take not exercise both rights, but, in taking leave for which the contractual and statutory rights provide, s/he may take advantage of whichever right is, in any particular respect, the more

---

[76]   PAL Regs, reg 29(2).
[77]   PAL Regs, reg 29(5).
[78]   APL Regs, reg 3(1).

favourable, so as to create a 'composite' right to paternity leave. The regulations are deemed to apply subject to any necessary modification, to give effect to any more favourable contractual terms.[79]

## Entitlement

**8.93**   An employee ('P') is entitled to be absent from work to care for a child ('C') if:[80]

(a)   P has been continuously employed with an employer ('E') for 26 weeks or more ending with the week immediately preceding the fourteenth week before C's expected week of birth;

(b)   P remains in continuous employment with that employer until the week before the first week of P's additional paternity leave;

(c)   P is either C's father, or not C's father but the spouse, partner or civil partner of the child's mother ('M');

(d)   P has or expects to have the main responsibility (apart from M) for the upbringing of C;

(e)   M is entitled by becoming pregnant with C to maternity leave, statutory maternity pay or maternity allowance and has or is treated as having returned to work under regulation 25.

**8.94**   P shall be treated as having continuous employment of at least 26 weeks where the date on which C is born is earlier than the relevant week and P would have been continuously employed for such a period if P's employment had continued until the relevant week.[81]

**8.95**   P's entitlement to leave shall not be affected by the birth or expected birth of more than one child as a result of the same pregnancy.[82]

**8.96**   P may take APL at any time within the period beginning 20 weeks after C's birth and ending 12 months after that date.[83] The minimum period of leave which may be taken is two weeks and the maximum period is 26 weeks.[84]

**8.97**   The leave must be taken in multiples of weeks and must be taken as a continuous period.[85]

---

[79]   APL Regs, reg 35.
[80]   APL Regs, reg 4.
[81]   APL Regs, reg 4(4).
[82]   APL Regs, reg 4(6).
[83]   APL Regs, reg 5(1).
[84]   APL Regs, reg 5(2).
[85]   APL Regs, reg 5(3).

**8.98** Leave may not be taken until eight weeks after P gave a leave notice in accordance with regulation 6(1),[86] except where C dies during the leave notice period or P's additional paternity leave period, in which case, other provisions apply (see below).

## Leave notice

**8.99** Not less than eight weeks before the date P chooses to start paternity leave, P must give the employer:[87]

(a)   a leave notice;

(b)   an employee declaration; and

(c)   a mother's declaration.

**8.100**   A leave notice is a written notice specifying:[88]

(a)   the week which was C's expected week of birth;

(b)   C's date of birth; and

(c)   the dates P has chosen for additional paternity leave.

**8.101**   An employee declaration is a written declaration by P stating:[89]

(a)   that the purposes of the period of leave will be to care for C; and

(b)   that C satisfies the relationship and responsibility criteria in regulation 4.

**8.102**   A mother's declaration is a written declaration by M, stating:[90]

(a)   M's name and address;

(b)   the date of M's intended return to work;

(c)   M's national insurance number;

(d)   that P satisfies the relationship and responsibility criteria;

(e)   that P is, to M's knowledge, the only person exercising entitlement to additional paternity leave in respect of C; and

---

[86]   APL Regs, reg 5(4).
[87]   APL Regs, reg 6(1).
[88]   APL Regs, reg 6(2)(a).
[89]   APL Regs, reg 6(2)(b).
[90]   APL Regs, reg 6(2)(c).

(f)    that M consents to the employer processing such of M's information as is contained in the declaration.

**8.103**   Where the employer requests, within 28 days of receiving P's leave notice, P must within 28 days of E's request, give E such of:

(a)    a copy of C's birth certificate; and/or

(b)    the name and address of M's employer (or, if M is self-employed, M's business address),

as E requests.[91]

**8.104**   After giving leave notice, P must give E a written 'withdrawal notice' as soon as reasonably practicable if P:

(a)    is found not to be C's father; or

(b)    ceases to be M's spouse, partner or civil partner; or

(c)    no longer expects to have the main responsibility (apart from M) for C's upbringing;

or M:

(a)    ceases to be entitled, by becoming pregnant with C, to maternity leave, statutory maternity pay or maternity allowance; or

(b)    does not return, or is not treated as having returned, to work.[92]

**8.105**   E may require P to take a period of leave where P has given E withdrawal notice less than six weeks before the original (or varied) leave notice start date and it is not reasonably practicable for E to accommodate the change in P's arrangements.[93] Such leave shall be treated as APL for the purposes of the APL Regulations, shall start on the date in P's leave notice and shall end no later than six weeks after the date P gave E withdrawal notice or the end date of P's leave notice, whichever is earlier.[94]

**8.106**   E may require P to remain on leave where P has given E a withdrawal notice after the start of P's paternity leave and it is not reasonably practicable for E to accommodate the change in P's arrangements.[95] Such leave shall be

---

[91]   APL Regs, reg 6(3).
[92]   APL Regs, reg 6(4).
[93]   APL Regs, reg 6(5).
[94]   APL Regs, reg 6(6).
[95]   APL Regs, reg 6(7).

treated as APL for the purposes of the APL Regulations, and shall end no later than six weeks after the date P gave E withdrawal notice or the end date of P's leave notice, whichever is earlier.[96]

## Varying the dates of APL

### *Variation or cancellation of APL by choice*

**8.107**  P may cancel his leave notice, or vary the dates of leave, if he gives E 'subsequent [written] notice' six weeks before the date cancelled or varied, or six weeks before the new date, whichever is the earlier. If it is not reasonably practicable to give six weeks' notice, P must give notice as soon as is reasonably practicable.[97]

**8.108**  However, if fewer than six weeks' notice are given, and it is not reasonably practicable for E to accommodate the change in P's arrangements, E may require P to take a period of APL to start on the start date in P's leave notice.[98] E's paternity leave shall then end six weeks after P gave 'subsequent notice' or on the end date in P's leave notice, whichever is earlier.[99]

## Confirmation of P's leave period

**8.109**  Within 28 days of receiving P's leave notice (and within 28 days of receiving any 'subsequent notice' of variation), E shall confirm the relevant dates to P in writing.[100]

**8.110**  Where E requires P to take leave, notwithstanding P's desire to vary or cancel his leave, E shall notify P of the dates when E requires P to take leave as soon as reasonably practicable and at any event before the start of the leave that E requires P to take.[101]

## Entitlement to APL where a mother dies

**8.111**  If M dies, within the period of 12 months beginning with C's birth,[102] unless P has already taken a period of APL which has ended,[103] he is eligible to take a period of APL during the period from the date of M's death until 12 months after the date of C's birth.[104]

---

[96]  APL Regs, reg 6(8).
[97]  APL Regs, reg 7(1).
[98]  APL Regs, reg 7(2).
[99]  APL Regs, reg 7(3).
[100]  APL Regs, reg 8(1).
[101]  APL Regs, reg 8(2).
[102]  APL Regs, reg 10(1).
[103]  APL Regs, reg 11(4).
[104]  APL Regs, reg 11(1).

**8.112**    P may take between 2 and 52 weeks' leave.[105] It must be taken as one continuous period and must be taken in multiples of complete weeks.[106]

**8.113**    If P is already on APL at the date of M's death, he may extend his leave to include a further period of APL, provided that:

(a)    P satisfies the eligibility requirements that would have applied to APL if M had been alive (ie, the relationship and responsibility requirements);

(b)    the second period of APL immediately follows the first, so as to form a continuous period of leave; and

(c)    the total period of leave does not exceed 52 weeks and the entire period of APL is taken within 12 months of C's birth.[107]

**8.114**    APL may be taken immediately, provided that P informs the employer of M's death as soon as is reasonably practicable and complies with the formal requirements set out below.[108]

**8.115**    As soon as reasonably practicable after M's death, and in any event within eight weeks of it, P must give E a 'leave notice' and an 'employee declaration'. The leave notice must contain the same elements as it would in ordinary circumstances (see above). The employee declaration must state:

(a)    that the purpose of the leave is to care for C;

(b)    that P satisfies the relationship and responsibility criteria in reg 4(2)(c) and (d);

(c)    M's name and last address, date of death and national insurance number.[109]

**8.116**    If P does not take the leave immediately, he may still take APL, provided that he gives E a leave notice and employee declaration at least six weeks before the proposed start date of the APL.[110]

**8.117**    If E asks for a copy of C's birth certificate and/or the name and address of M's last employer within 28 days of receiving P's leave notice, P must provide what is requested within 28 days of E's request.[111]

---

[105]    APL Regs, reg 11(2).
[106]    APL Regs, reg 11(3).
[107]    APL Regs, reg 11(5).
[108]    APL Regs, reg 12(4).
[109]    APL Regs, reg 12(2)(b).
[110]    APL Regs, reg 12(5).
[111]    APL Regs, reg 12(3).

**8.118** P may vary or cancel his leave. If P wishes to cancel or vary his leave within eight weeks of M's death, he needs only to give E written notice on or before the date that is varied or cancelled.[112] After this time, P may vary or cancel his leave by giving written notice before the earliest of six weeks before the date cancelled or varied or six weeks before the new date, or, where it is not reasonably practicable to give six weeks' notice, as soon as is reasonably practicable.[113] Where P gives less than six weeks' notice of variation or cancellation and it is not reasonably practicable for E to accommodate him, E may require P to take APL of up to six weeks.[114]

## Death of a child in the course of APL

**8.119** If C dies within the APL leave notice period or during APL, the partner is entitled to remain on leave for a further eight weeks from the end of the week (reckoned Sunday to Saturday) in which C dies or until the end date of P's APL, whichever is sooner.[115]

## Working during APL

**8.120** P may carry out up to ten days' work for E during APL without bringing APL to an end.[116] 'Work' means any work done under P's contract of employment and can include training and/or keeping in touch.[117] Any day on which work is done counts as a day's work.[118] E cannot require P to work during APL and P cannot insist on doing work.[119] In addition, reasonable contact from time to time does not bring APL to an end.[120] Working during APL does not extend the duration of APL.[121]

**8.121** During P's APL, s/he is entitled to the benefit of all terms and conditions of employment which would have applied if P had not been absent,[122] and bound by any contractual obligations,[123] except that E is not required to pay P wages or salary[124] and P is not required to work. P may therefore be entitled to other benefits or remuneration not amounting to wages or salary.

---

[112] APL Regs, reg 13(1).
[113] APL Regs, reg 13(2).
[114] APL Regs, reg 13(3).
[115] APL Regs, reg 24.
[116] APL Regs, reg 26(1).
[117] APL Regs, reg 26(3).
[118] APL Regs, reg 26(2).
[119] APL Regs, reg 26(5).
[120] APL Regs, reg 26(4).
[121] APL Regs, reg 26(6).
[122] APL Regs, reg 27(1)(a).
[123] APL Regs, reg 27(1)(b).
[124] APL Regs, reg 27(2).

## Right to return after APL

**8.122**   P has the right to return to his job,[125] provided he is returning from:

(a)   an isolated period of APL lasting no longer that than 26 weeks;[126]

(b)   a period of APL lasting no more than 26 weeks, which was the last of two or consecutive periods of leave, provided the periods of leave did not include any additional maternity leave, additional adoption leave or a period of parental leave of more than four weeks.[127]

**8.123**   If P is returning from a period of APL of more than 26 weeks, he is entitled to return to the same job unless his employer can show that it is not reasonably practicable for him to permit it. In that case, P is entitled to return to a job which is both suitable and appropriate for him.[128]

**8.124**   In either case P is entitled to return with the same seniority and rights as,[129] and on terms and conditions no less favourable than,[130] those which applied before his period of leave.[131]

## Early return from APL

**8.125**   If P wishes to return to work early from APL, he must give his employer six weeks' notice. If he does not, E may postpone P's return date so that E has six weeks' notice.[132]

## Right to suitable alternative employment in the event of redundancy

**8.126**   Where, during P's APL, P faces dismissal by reason of redundancy, but there is a suitable vacancy, P is entitled to be offered alternative employment, to take effect immediately on the termination of P's contract. The work under the new contract must be suitable and appropriate for P and its provisions as to capacity and place, and other terms and conditions, must not be substantially less favorable than P's original contract.[133]

---

[125]   APL Regs, reg 31(1).
[126]   APL Regs, reg 31(1)(a).
[127]   APL Regs, reg 31(1)(b).
[128]   APL Regs, reg 31(2).
[129]   APL Regs, reg 32(1)(a).
[130]   APL Regs, reg 32(1)(b).
[131]   APL Regs, reg 32.
[132]   APL Regs, reg 30.
[133]   APL Regs, reg 28.

## Protection from detriment and dismissal for taking additional paternity leave

**8.127**  E is entitled under section 47C of the ERA not to be subjected to any detriment or any deliberate failure to act by his employer because E took or sought to take or made use of the benefits of APL, because E believed P was likely to take APL, because P failed to return to work after APL in certain circumstances or where P undertook, considered undertaking or refused to undertake work during APL.[134]

**8.128**  An employee who is dismissed is entitled under section 99 of the ERA to be regarded as unfairly dismissed if the reason for dismissal is that E took or sought to take or made use of the benefits of APL, because E believed P was likely to take APL, because P failed to return to work after APL in certain circumstances or where P undertook, considered undertaking or refused to undertake work during APL.[135]

**8.129**  An employee is also entitled to be regarded as unfairly dismissed if:[136]

(a)  the reason or principal reason for the dismissal was redundancy;

(b)  one or more other employees in the same undertaking held positions similar to the dismissed employee;

(c)  the redundancy situation applied equally to them;

(d)  that employee or those employees were not dismissed; and

(e)  it is shown that the reason or principal reason for which the employee was selected for dismissal was that s/he took or sought to take or made use of the benefits of APL, because E believed P was likely to take APL, because P failed to return to work after APL in certain circumstances or where P undertook, considered undertaking or refused to undertake work during APL.

**8.130**  But a dismissal is not unfair where the employer shows that:[137]

(a)  it was not reasonably practicable for a reason other than redundancy for the employer to permit the employee to return to a job which was both suitable for the employee and appropriate for him to do in the circumstances;

(b)  an associated employer offered the employee a job of that kind; and

---

[134]  APL Regs, reg. 33(1).
[135]  APL Regs, reg 34(1), (3).
[136]  APL Regs, reg 34(2).
[137]  APL Regs, reg 34(5), (6).

(c)    the employee accepted or unreasonably refused that offer.

## STATUTORY PATERNITY PAY AND ADDITIONAL STATUTORY PATERNITY PAY

**8.131**   'Employee' and 'employer' have special meanings under the 1992 Act in relation to payment of ordinary and additional paternity pay.

**8.132**   An 'employee' is a person who is gainfully employed in Great Britain either under a contract of service or in an office (including elective office) with general earnings and defined by section 7 of the Income Tax (Earnings and Pensions) Act 2003.

**8.133**   'Employer' in relation to an employee means a person who is liable under section 6 of the 1992 Act to pay secondary Class 1 contributions in relation to any of the earnings of the person who is an employee or would be liable to pay such contributions but for the employee being under 16 or not meeting the earnings threshold enough.

**8.134**   In addition, under the regulations, apprentices are treated as employees.[138] There are further restrictions and inclusions relating to the definition of 'employment' in the Regulations.

## STATUTORY PATERNITY PAY

**8.135**   The governing legislation is sections 171ZA and 171ZC–171ZE of the Social Security Contributions and Benefits Act 1992 ('SSCBA'). The Regulations made under that section are the Statutory Paternity Pay and Statutory Adoption Pay (General) Regulations 2002.[139]

**8.136**   SPP became payable in respect of children born (or expected to be born in a week beginning) on or after 6 April 2003.[140]

**8.137**   SPP is payable for two consecutive weeks, unless P chooses just one week's leave.[141]

**8.138**   A person is eligible to receive SPP if:

(a)    he satisfies the relationship and responsibility criteria applicable to eligibility for paternity leave;[142]

---

[138]   SPP Regs, reg 32(2).
[139]   SI 2002/2822.
[140]   SPP Regs, reg 3(1)(a).
[141]   SSCBA 1992, s 171ZE(2).
[142]   SSCBA 1992, s 171ZA(2)(a); SPP Regs, reg 4.

(b)   he has been continuously employed for at least 26 weeks ending with the week immediately preceding the 14th week before the expected week of C's birth (this week is called the 'relevant week'),[143] and continuous employment from the relevant week until the day that C is born;[144]

(c)   his normal weekly earnings in the eight weeks before the relevant week must not be lower than the lower earnings limit under section 5(1)(a) of the 1992 Act.[145]

**8.139**   As with the date of which OPL starts, P's SPP period may start on the day of C's birth, a date chosen by reference to C's birthdate (eg, seven days after C's birth) or a fixed date which is later than the first day of the expected week of C's birth (eg 27 October 2009).[146]

**8.140**   P may choose for SPP to be paid in respect of a period of one week, rather than two.[147]

**8.141**   P's choice about when he takes SPP is not irrevocable, but where he later makes a different choice, he must give his employer 28 days notice, or if that is not reasonably practicable, as much notice as is reasonably practicable.[148]

**8.142**   Where P chooses an uncertain date, relative to C's birthdate, he must notify his employer of its liability to pay P SPP as soon as is reasonably practicable after C's birthdate.[149]

**8.143**   Where P chooses a certain date, but C is born after that date, P must, if he wishes to claim SPP, give notice to the person liable to pay SPP (ie, his employer) that the period in respect of which SPP is payable shall begin on a different date.[150]

**8.144**   The SPP period must occur between the period starting with C's birth and ending 56 days later, or, where C is born before the first day of the expected week of C's birth, 56 days after that day.[151]

**8.145**   P must provide the following evidence of his entitlement to SPP at least 28 days before the date from which it is expected that liability to pay SPP will begin:[152]

(a)   his name;

---

[143]   SSCBA 1992, s 171ZA(2)(b).
[144]   SSCBA 1992, s 171ZA(2)(d).
[145]   SSCBA 1992, ss 171AZ(2), 171ZA(2)(c).
[146]   SPP Regs, reg 6(1).
[147]   SPP Regs, reg 6(3).
[148]   SPP regs, reg 6(4).
[149]   SPP Regs, reg 7(1).
[150]   SPP Regs, reg 7(2).
[151]   SPP Regs, reg 8.
[152]   SPP Regs, reg 9.

(b)  the expected week of C's birth and, where the birth has already occurred, C's birthdate;

(c)  the date from which it is expected liability to pay SPP will begin; and

(d)  whether the period chosen is a week.

**8.146**  Where the person liable to pay SPP so requests, P must provide the date of C's birth within 28 days or as soon as is reasonably practicable thereafter.[153]

## Other work during SPP period

**8.147**  Where P has more than one employer, SPP is payable in respect of any SPP week during any part of which P only works for an employer who is not liable to pay him SPP and whom he worked for in the week immediately preceding the 14th week before the expected week of C's birth.[154] But if P works for an employer for whom he had not worked in the week immediately preceding the 14th week before the expected week of C's birth, there is no liability on an employer to pay SPP in respect of any remaining part of the SPP period.[155] If P works for such a 'new' employer, he must notify the person liable to pay SPP within seven days of the first day during which he works during the SPP period.[156] That notification must be in writing if the person who has been liable to pay SPP so requests.[157]

**8.148**  There is no liability to pay SPP in respect of any week during which P is entitled to Statutory Sick Pay, or detained in custody or sentenced to a term of imprisonment, or following a week in which P dies.[158]

**8.149**  An entitlement to SPP does not affect any contractual rights to remuneration, sick pay or payments in connection with the birth of a child, but any contractual payment goes towards discharging E's liability to pay SPP.[159]

**8.150**  A former employer shall be liable to pay SPP where P has been employed for a continuous period of at least eight weeks and his contract of service was brought to an end by the former employer solely, or mainly, for the purpose of avoiding liability for SPP.[160] This does not seem to encompass 'constructive' dismissal. In such cases, the employee shall be treated as if employed for a continuous period ending with C's birth and his normal weekly

---

[153]  SPP Regs, reg 9(4).
[154]  SPP Regs, reg 10.
[155]  SPP Regs, reg 17(1).
[156]  SPP Regs, reg 17(2).
[157]  SPP Regs, reg 17(3).
[158]  SPP Regs, reg 18.
[159]  SSCBA 1992, s 171ZG; SPP Regs, reg 19.
[160]  SPP Regs, reg 20(1).

earnings shall be calculated by reference to his normal weekly earnings for the period of eight weeks ending with the last day in respect of which he was paid under his former contract.[161]

**8.151** The provisions governing continuous employment are materially identical to those for Statutory Maternity Pay: see Chapter 6.[162]

**8.152** The weekly rate of payment of SPP is the smaller of £135.45[163] or 90% of P's normal weekly earnings, as determined in accordance with regulations 39 and 40 of the SPP Regulations.[164]

# ADDITIONAL STATUTORY PATERNITY PAY

**8.153** Payment of Additional Statutory Paternity Pay (Birth) ('ASPP') is governed by SSCBA 1992, s 171ZEA and ss 171ZEC to s 171ZEE. Those provisions provide the regulation-making power under which the Additional Statutory Paternity Pay (General) Regulations 2010 ('ASPP Regs 2010') were made. The Regulations came into force on 6 April 2010.

**8.154** ASPP is payable where P intends to care for C during the additional statutory paternity pay period (of between 2 and 26 weeks).[165]

**8.155** There is entitlement to ASPP in respect of children whose expected week of birth began on or after 3 April 2011.[166]

## Qualifying for ASPP

**8.156** The eligibility requirements for ASPP reflect those for APL (above).

**8.157** P may be entitled to ASPP, even if he is not entitled to APL. He must be 'in employed earner's employment with an employee' but, for these purposes, the definition of employee is wider. It covers anyone for whom the employer pays Class 1 National Insurance ('NI') contributions, or for whom he would pay them if their earnings were sufficiently high. Consequently, office holders (eg, members of the armed forces, police and holders of elected office) will be eligible for SAP, as will apprentices and many agency and casual workers.

---

[161] SPP Regs, reg 20(2).
[162] SPP Regs, regs 33–36.
[163] As from 3 April 2011, pursuant to the Social Security Benefits Up-rating Order 2011, SI 2011/821, art 11(1)(a). The amount has been up-rated annually, each April.
[164] Statutory Paternity Pay and Statutory Adoption Pay (Weekly rates) Regulations 2002, SI 2002/2818, reg 2.
[165] ASPP Regs, reg 4(1)(c).
[166] ASPP Regs, reg 3(a).

**8.158**   ASPP is payable to a partner ('P') who:

(a)   is either C's father or is not C's father but is married to, or the civil partner or partner of, the mother;[167]

(b)   has or expects to have the main responsibility (apart from the mother's responsibility) for the upbringing of C;[168]

(c)   intends to care for C during the ASPP pay period;[169]

(d)   has complied with the requirements for applying for ASPP and evidencing entitlement.[170]

**8.159**   Those requirements are that P provides to his employer in writing:

(a)   his name;[171]

(b)   C's expected week of birth;[172]

(c)   C's date of birth;[173]

(d)   the date on which P expects E's liability to pay ASPP will begin;[174] and

(e)   the date on which P expects E's liability to pay ASPP will end;[175]

(f)   a written declaration that:

    (i)    the information provided is correct;[176]
    (ii)   P intends to care for C during the ASPP period in respect of C;[177] and
    (iii)  P meets the relationship and responsibility criteria in reg 4(2).[178]

**8.160**   If E so requests within 28 days of receiving P's written information and declaration, P shall provide, within 28 days of the request, a copy of C's birth certificate and the name and address of M's employer (or if M is self-employed, her business address).[179]

---

[167]   ASPP Regs, reg 4(1)(a)(i).
[168]   ASPP Regs, reg 4(2)(b).
[169]   ASPP Regs, reg 4(1)(c).
[170]   ASPP Regs, reg 4(1)(e).
[171]   ASPP Regs, reg 8(2)(a).
[172]   ASPP Regs, reg 8(2)(b).
[173]   ASPP Regs, reg 8(2)(c).
[174]   ASPP Regs, reg 8(2)(d).
[175]   ASPP Regs, reg 8(2)(e).
[176]   ASPP Regs, reg 8(1)(b)(i).
[177]   ASPP Regs, reg 8(1)(b)(ii).
[178]   ASPP Regs, reg 8(1)(b)(iii).
[179]   ASPP Regs, reg 8(3).

**8.161**  P must have been in employed earner's employment with an employer for a continuous period of at least 26 weeks ending with the week immediately preceding the 14th week before C's expected week of birth (know as 'the relevant week') and, then, from the relevant week until the week before the ASPP pay period in respect of C begins.[180]

**8.162**  The provisions governing the concept of continuous employment are the same as for statutory maternity pay: see Chapter 6.[181]

**8.163**  P's normal weekly earnings for the eight weeks ending with the relevant week must not be less than the lower earnings limit in force under section 5(1)(a) of the SSCBA 1992 at the end of the relevant week.[182]

**8.164**  In addition, in order for P to be eligible, the mother must have become entitled by becoming pregnant with C to a maternity allowance or statutory maternity pay, have taken action constituting a return to work not less than two weeks after C's birth and have at least two weeks of her maternity allowance period or maternity pay period which remain unexpired.[183]

**8.165**  Additionally, the mother must sign a declaration,[184] with the following information:

(a)   her name, address and National Insurance number;[185]

(b)   that she became entitled, by reference to becoming pregnant with C to a maternity allowance or statutory maternity pay;[186]

(c)   the start date of her maternity allowance period or maternity pay period in respect of C;[187]

(d)   the date on which she intends to return to work;[188]

(e)   that she has given notice to her employer that she is returning to work;[189]

(f)   that, in relation to C, P is, to M's knowledge, the only person seeking SPP;[190]

---

[180]   ASPP Regs, reg 4(3).
[181]   ASPP Regs, regs 25–28.
[182]   ASPP Regs, reg 4(3)(c).
[183]   ASPP Regs, reg 6.
[184]   ASPP Regs, reg 4(1)(d).
[185]   ASPP Regs, reg 8(1)(c)(iii).
[186]   ASPP Regs, reg 8(1)(c)(ii).
[187]   ASPP Regs, reg. 8(1)(c)(iv).
[188]   ASPP Regs, reg 8(1)(c)(v).
[189]   ASPP Regs, reg 8(1)(c)(1).
[190]   ASPP Regs, reg 8(1)(c)(6).

(g)   consent for E to process the information that M provides.[191]

**8.166**   E must confirm P's start and ends dates for ASPP in writing to P within 28 days of receiving the above information and declarations from P.[192]

## Cancelling or varying ASPP

**8.167**   P may withdraw an application for ASPP or vary the dates on which ASPP will begin and end by giving written notice to E at least six weeks before the cancelled date or, in the case of variation, at least six weeks before the earlier of the original or varied date. Where it is not reasonably practicable for P to give six weeks notice, he must give notice as soon as reasonably practicable.[193]

**8.168**   Where P has applied for ASPP and later fails to fulfill the relationship or responsibility criteria and/or M no longer intends to return to work, P must give E written notice.[194]

## Where the child's mother dies

**8.169**   If C's mother dies before the end of her maternity allowance or maternity pay period but before the ASPP period has begun, the ASPP period in respect of C begins on the date of M's death or a later date that P informs E of.[195] The ASPP period can last up to 39 weeks in these circumstances.[196]

**8.170**   P must apply for ASPP in these circumstances by applying to E, informing E of the date P wishes ASPP to begin or (if the date is in the past) the date on which P wishes such period to have begun,[197] and providing E with:[198]

(a)   P's name;

(b)   C's expected week of birth;

(c)   C's date of birth;

(d)   the date on which P expects E's liability to pay ASPP will end;

(e)   M's name, address and National Insurance number;

---

[191]   ASPP Regs, reg 8(1)(c)(vii).
[192]   ASPP Regs, reg 8(8).
[193]   ASPP Regs, reg 8(6).
[194]   ASPP Regs, reg 8(7).
[195]   ASPP Regs, reg 9(1)(c).
[196]   ASPP Regs, reg 9(1)(e).
[197]   ASPP Regs, reg 10(1)(a).
[198]   ASPP Regs, reg 10(2).

(f) the start date of maternity pay or maternity pay period (or the date the period would have started but for her death); and

(g) the date of M's death.

**8.171** P must also provide a written declaration that the information provided is correct, that P intends to care for C during the ASPP period and that P meets the relationship and responsibility criteria.[199]

**8.172** P shall also provide, if E so requests within 28 days of receiving the information and declaration from P, a copy of C's birth certificate and the name and business address of M's employer (or if M was self-employed, her business address).[200] P must provide the information within 28 days of the request.[201]

**8.173** P must provide the information as soon as reasonably practicable after, and in any event within eight weeks of, the date of M's death.[202] However, P may provide the information after this date, as long as it is at least six weeks before the date P wishes his ASPP to begin.[203]

**8.174** E must confirm in writing P's ASPP start and end dates within 28 days of receiving all of the information which P is required to provide.[204]

**8.175** P may withdraw an application for ASPP or vary the dates. If within eight weeks of M's death, he may do so with immediate effect;[205] if more than eight weeks after M's death, P must give six weeks' notice of the date P wishes to vary.[206] If it is not reasonably practicable for P to give six weeks' notice, he must give notice as soon as reasonably practicable.[207]

**8.176** If C's mother dies after the beginning but before the end of P's ASPP period and as soon as reasonably practicable after M's death, P gives his employer notice in writing of M's death, the date on which the ASPP period in respect of C ends is the date on which M's maternity allowance or maternity pay period would have ended or, if earlier, such earlier day as P chooses when notifying E of M's death.[208]

---

[199] ASPP Regs, reg 10(1)(c).
[200] ASPP Regs, reg 10(3).
[201] ASPP Regs, reg 10(6).
[202] ASPP Regs, reg 10(4).
[203] ASPP Regs, reg 10(5).
[204] ASPP Regs, reg 10(9).
[205] ASPP Regs, reg 10(7).
[206] ASPP Regs, reg 10(8).
[207] ASPP Regs, reg 10(8)(d).
[208] ASPP Regs, reg 7(4)–(5).

## Working for more than one employer

**8.177**   Where P has more than one employer, SPP is payable in respect of any SPP week during any part of which P only works for an employer who is not liable to pay him SPP and whom he worked for in the week immediately preceding the 14th week before the expected week of C's birth.[209]

**8.177**   The current rate of ASPP is the lower of either:[210]

(a)   the standard weekly rate, which from 9 April 2012 is £135.45; or

(b)   90 per cent of the partner's average weekly earnings.

**8.178**   As with other forms of statutory leave pay, the employer can recover some or all of its ASPP payments from HMRC.

**8.179**   Mirroring the APL provisions, P may work for up to ten days for E during the ASPP period without affecting P's entitlement to receive ASPP.[211]

**8.180**   Regulation 22 provides for the mutual setting-off of contractual and statutory pay.

**8.181**   Regulation 23 provides for liability to pay where the employer dismissed the partner to avoid paying ASPP.

**8.182**   These two provisions mirror those applicable to SPP.

---

[209]   ASPP Regs, reg 11.
[210]   Additional Statutory Paternity Pay (Weekly Rate) Regulations 2010, as amended by the Social Security Benefits Up-Rating Order 2011, reg 2.
[211]   ASPP Regs, reg 20(4).

# Chapter 9

# OTHER KINDS OF DISCRIMINATION

*Sarah Fraser Butlin*

## INTRODUCTION

**9.1**    This chapter will consider potential discrimination claims in the context of family-friendly rights. Sex and pregnancy discrimination have already been fully addressed (see Chapter 2). However, the scope for claims of discrimination when dealing with family rights is much broader than that.

**9.2**    The structure of this chapter will be to explore the potential for and boundaries of discrimination claims in relation to:

(a)    associative and perceptive discrimination;

(b)    race discrimination;

(c)    sexual orientation discrimination;

(d)    issues of sexual orientation and religion in adoption and fostering;

(e)    religious discrimination;

(f)    age discrimination; and

(g)    disability discrimination.

**9.3**    Nevertheless, the scope of discrimination claims in the realm of family-friendly rights is multifarious and the basic principles of discrimination claims should not be forgotten. The claims posited in this chapter are suggestions and possibilities but are by no means intended to be exhaustive.

## ASSOCIATIVE AND PERCEPTIVE DISCRIMINATION

### Position prior to the Equality Act 2010

**9.4**    Before the Equality Act, and particularly prior to the decision of the ECJ in *Coleman v Attridge Law*,[1] protection against discrimination based on

---

[1]    Case C-303/06, [2008] ECR I-5603; [2008] IRLR 722.

association with someone with a protected characteristic was only partial. Provisions prohibiting race discrimination have been interpreted as including associative discrimination since at least 1975.[2] This was on the basis that the legislation provided protection against discrimination 'on racial grounds'. The legislation was similarly interpreted to provide protection in relation to sex, religion or belief and sexual orientation.

**9.5**     Similarly this extended to protection against discrimination because the person was wrongly believed to have a protected characteristic (perceptive discrimination). Indeed in *English v Thomas Sanderson Blinds*[3] the Court of Appeal held that 'on the ground of' could extend to harassment using homophobic abuse, despite knowing that the person was not in fact gay.

**9.6**     However, age, disability and pregnancy were not protected. This was because the legislation referred to 'a person discriminates against a disabled person' (section 3A(1) of the Disability Discrimination Act 1995 (DDA 1995)), to 'a person discriminates against another person (B) if (a) on grounds of B's age...' (Reg 3(1)(a) of the Employment Equality (Age) Regulations 2006) and to 'on the ground of the woman's pregnancy' (section 3A of the Sex Discrimination Act 1975 (SDA 1975)).

**9.7**     This position changed following the decision of the ECJ in *Coleman*. The ECJ considered the appropriate interpretation of the language of the Framework Directive, namely the phrase 'on grounds of disability'. The ECJ held that the Directive:

> 'must be interpreted as meaning that the prohibition of direct discrimination ... is not limited only to people who are themselves disabled. Where an employer treats an employee who is not himself disabled less favourably than another employee is, has been or would be treated in a comparable situation, and it is established that the less favourable treatment of that employee is based on the disability of his child, whose care is provided primarily by that employee, such treatment is contrary to the prohibition of direct discrimination' (at para 56).

**9.8**     The ECJ reached the same conclusion with regard to harassment (see para 63).

**9.9**     When the case returned to the EAT, it was held that words were to be interpolated into the DDA 1995 to provide that protection. It was widely considered that this wider reading of 'on grounds of' would also encapsulate perceptive discrimination.

**9.10**     Nevertheless the Scottish EAT in *Kulikaoskas v Macduff Shellfish*[4] rejected a claim of associative pregnancy discrimination. The EAT held that the phrase 'related to pregnancy' in article 2(2) of Directive 2006/54 might well be

---

[2]     See *Race Relations Board v Applin* [1975] AC 259.
[3]     [2008] EWCA Civ 1421; [2009] IRLR 206; [2009] ICR 543.
[4]     [2011] ICR 48.

broader than 'on the ground of the woman's pregnancy'. Despite this, they considered that the approach of EU law was to identify pregnancy as a feature unique to women and as requiring special protection. Consequently it was intended to provide a means of achieving equal treatment because of the unequal biological conditions of men and women, rather than promoting a wider objective of securing the autonomy of women or respect for their gender.

**9.11** Thus it can be seen that even after the ground-breaking decision of *Coleman,* protection from associative and perceptive discrimination remained less than clear.

## *Provisions of the Equality Act 2010*

**9.12** Section 13(1) of the Equality Act 2010 provides that there is direct discrimination where 'because of a protected characteristic, A treats B less favourably than A treats or would treat others'. The use of the phrase 'because of a protected characteristic' means that this new definition of direct discrimination is broad enough to cover associative discrimination and discrimination based on mistaken perception.

**9.13** It is worth noting that the protection against associative and perceptive discrimination within the Equality Act is not express and this has been criticised, notably by the JCHR and the EHRC.

**9.14** More importantly, protection is not provided to all the protected characteristics. In the context of employment, section 13(4) provides that there is only direct discrimination where it is B who is married or in a civil partnership. The sub-section thereby expressly removes protection for associative and perceptive discrimination where the protected characteristic is marriage or civil partnership. The Employment Code of Practice makes this clear in paras 3.18 and 3.21. There is no equivalent exclusion in the context of services, public functions and associations.

**9.15** Within the Employment Code at paras 3.18 and 3.21 and the Services Code at paras 4.19 and 4.20, it is stated that pregnancy and maternity are also removed from the protection of associative and perceptive discrimination. However, the legislation itself is less clear on this point.

**9.16** Section 4 of the Equality Act provides a list of 'protected characteristics'. That list includes pregnancy and maternity as a protected characteristic. Section 13 then defines direct discrimination by reference to 'because of a protected discrimination'. This is echoed by the Explanatory Notes to the Equality Act at para 59. The natural reading of the two sections would be that pregnancy and maternity were covered by the definition of direct discrimination in section 13. That reading would mean that there was protection for associative and perceptive discrimination in relation to pregnancy and maternity.

**9.17** The Code says that associative discrimination 'does not apply to marriage and civil partnership or pregnancy and maternity'. No explanation is given for this assertion. However, reading the legislation itself makes it plain that associative discrimination is excluded with regard to pregnancy and maternity. Section 17(2) of the Equality Act provides, for non-work cases, that:

'A person (A) discriminates against a woman if A treats her unfavourably <u>because of a pregnancy of hers.</u>' (my emphasis added)

**9.18** Similarly, section 18(2) of the Equality Act, in relation to work, provides:

'A person (A) discriminates <u>against a woman</u> if, in the protected period in relation to a <u>pregnancy of hers,</u> A treats her unfavourably ....' (my emphasis added)

**9.19** It is plain from these sections that associative discrimination is excluded with regard to pregnancy and maternity. Similarly because the reference is to an actual pregnancy, rather than a mistaken perception of pregnancy, perceptive discrimination is also excluded.

**9.20** Importantly, section 25(5) provides that:

'Pregnancy and Maternity Discrimination is discrimination within section 17 or 18.'

**9.21** This suggests that section 13 does not apply to pregnancy at all and section 18 limits protection to the pregnant woman herself. Therefore while it may be argued that sections 4 and 13 should be read together to provide protection for associative and perceptive pregnancy and maternity discrimination, sections 17 and 18 render this unlikely. Section 25(5) emphasises this further. Nevertheless, there may still be scope for a claim of associative or perceptive sex discrimination.

**9.22** Finally, it is worth noting that protection is not provided to carers generally. Although there was considerable campaigning for such protection, this was rejected by the Government. Protection is only provided as associative, or perceptive, to certain protected characteristics.

## RACE DISCRIMINATION

**9.23** There may be occasions where family-friendly rights are applied in a discriminatory fashion. For example, where parental leave is not given to a black woman but is given to a white woman. That is straightforwardly direct race discrimination.

**9.24** A more challenging perspective on race discrimination in the sphere of family-friendly policies relates to cross-racial adoptions. This has been given a much higher profile following the new guidance for adoptions. Central

Government guidance, revised in February 2011, has put a greater emphasis on successful adoptions with race and ethnicity no longer being a 'dealbreaker'.

**9.25** The new guidance expressly states that 'Any practice that classifies couples/single people in a way that effectively rules out the adoption because of their status, age or because they and the child do not share the same racial or cultural background is not child-centred and is unacceptable' (Chapter 4, para 5).

**9.26** Public authorities are required to provide their services in a non-discriminatory manner (section 29 of the Equality Act 2010). More importantly, section 149 of the Equality Act provides that:

> (1) A public authority must, in the exercise of its functions, have due regard to the need to—
>    (a) eliminate discrimination, harassment, victimisation and any other conduct that is prohibited by or under this Act;
>    (b) advance equality of opportunity between persons who share a relevant protected characteristic and persons who do not share it;
>    (c) foster good relations between persons who share a relevant protected characteristic and persons who do not share it.'

**9.27** These provisions of the Equality Act together with the new guidance on adoption form a potent combination in challenging adoption matching decisions which appear to be discriminatory on the basis of race. It opens the door to a potential legal challenge where a match is not made because too much emphasis is placed on the different racial, ethnic or cultural backgrounds of the child and the prospective adopter. Such a challenge is likely to be by way of judicial review.

## SEXUAL ORIENTATION DISCRIMINATION

**9.28** There are several strands that need to be considered in the context of sexual orientation discrimination. This chapter will deal with the following:

(a) Application of the provision of maternity, paternity and adoption leave and benefits for to same sex couples.

(b) Application of parental leave and flexible working provisions to same sex couples.

(c) Parental orders and surrogacy.

### Maternity, paternity and adoption leave and benefits

**9.29** The wording of the Paternity and Adoption Leave Regulations 2002 makes it clear that paternity leave is available to a partner in a same sex couple. Specifically in regulation 2(1) 'partner' is defined as:

'in relation to a child's mother or adopter, means a person (whether of a different sex or the same sex) who lives with the mother or adopter and the child in an enduring family relationship ...'

**9.30**    Consequently where one partner either gives birth to a child or adopts a child, then the other partner may take paternity leave whether they themselves are male or female.

**9.31**    The payment of statutory benefits operates in the same way (for further detail see Chapters 5 and 6).

**9.32**    The situation is rather more complicated where surrogacy is involved. The birth mother is the only person who qualifies for maternity leave. With surrogacy, only the legal parent would be able to obtain paternity leave. Therefore if a gay couple has a child via surrogacy, and neither of them is considered the legal parent, then they will not be entitled to paternity leave. Obviously as this is also not an adoption, then adoption leave would also be unavailable.

**9.33**    Where leave would usually be given to heterosexual couples entitled to it under the Regulations but is withheld from a same sex couple who were also entitled to the leave under the Regulations, then there is likely to be a claim for sexual orientation discrimination. Similarly if there is a general practice of giving leave to heterosexual couples, even where they are not strictly entitled to it for some reason, but it is declined to homosexual couples, then again there is likely to be a potential discrimination claim. However, it will be much more difficult to argue that there has been discrimination if the reason leave is declined is because leave is only given within the parameters of the statutory provisions.

## Parental leave and flexible working

**9.34**    The right to request flexible working and to time off for dependants works in the same way as for heterosexual couples (on which see Chapter 7).

**9.35**    With regard to parental leave, same sex couples will qualify for it. The entitlement to parental leave depends on them having 'responsibility for a child' (regulation 13(1)(b)).

**9.36**    'Responsibility for a child' is defined as being 'parental responsibility' as per section 3 of the Children Act 1989 (see regulations 13(2) and 2(1)). Broadly this means that the birth or adoptive parents of a child, 'commissioning' parents in a surrogacy arrangement when there has been a parental order and those who are parents under sections 42 and 43 of the Human Fertilisation and Embryology Act 2008.

## Parental orders and surrogacy

**9.37** Historically there were concerns as to the discriminatory nature of surrogacy arrangements. This was because prior to April 2009, there were no automatic rules as to what was put on the child's birth certificate. There was a difficult legal process to go through to enable the intended parents to be put on a child's birth certificate and to assume legal responsibility for them.

**9.38** However, where conception occurred after 6 April 2009 the Human Embryology and Fertilisation Act 2008 applies. Broadly this means that the birth mother and her female partner can be named as parents (see section 42). Alternatively, as of 6 April 2010, where a surrogate was used and one of the same sex couple (whether male or female) provided gametes used to bring about the creation of the embryo, then a parental order can be sought (see section 54).

## ISSUE OF SEXUAL ORIENTATION AND RELIGION IN ADOPTION AND FOSTERING

**9.39** Schedule 3, paragraph 15 of the Equality Act 2010 provides:

'Care within the family

A person (A) does not contravene section 29 only by participating in arrangements under which (whether or not for reward) A takes into A's home, and treats as members of A's family, persons requiring particular care and attention.'

**9.40** Section 29 deals with non-discriminatory provision of services. Para 15 of Schedule 3 is an express exclusion but appears to only relate to the people taking the relevant person into their home and the participation of the service provider in such an arrangement. The Explanatory Note to the Act states at para 704:

'Similar provisions existed in previous legislation for race, religion or belief and sexual orientation. This provision extends the exception to all of the protected characteristics.

Examples

* A Muslim family could choose to foster only a Muslim child. This would not constitute discrimination against a non-Muslim child. ....'

**9.41** Therefore, it would appear that fostering/adoption-matching decisions must be non-discriminatory from the perspective of the agency (see similarly regarding race above at **9.24–9.27**). In addition, a religious family may request only to foster a child of a particular religion.

**9.42**  The real difficulty arises where there is a 'clash' of rights. This has arisen particularly in the context of where religious rights meet sexual orientation rights.

**9.43**  Firstly, with regard to religious adoption agencies. It is unlawful for adoption agencies to decline to offer adoption services to same sex couples. To do so would breach section 29 of the Equality Act 2010. The exception in Schedule 3 does not appear to apply on its face. It reads in a way that seems to only apply to the adopter or fosterer themselves rather than allowing the service provider to only provide services to certain groups.

**9.44**  Secondly the 'clash' has arisen in relation to individual adopters and fosterers. This is exemplified by the case of *R (Johns) v Derby City Council (Equality and Human Rights Commission intervening)*.[5]

**9.45**  In this case a Christian couple sought a declaration as to their suitability to act as foster carers where the local authority had expressed concern, but not made a decision, about the impact of their views on homosexuality. The couple's position was that they held orthodox religious views and this should not automatically exclude them from being foster carers. The local authority's position was that they may be acting lawfully if it decides not to approve a prospective foster carer who evinces 'antipathy, objection to or disapproval of homosexuality'. Ultimately the court declined permission for judicial review but they dealt with many of the difficulties in this arena.

**9.46**  The Court held that while the common law required respect for religious principles and 'benevolent tolerance' of cultural and religious diversity, the invocation of religion was not necessarily a defence to an otherwise valid claim of discrimination (at paras 41 and 43). They considered that a local authority was entitled to explore the extent that beliefs might impact a carer's behaviour and therefore the treatment of a child (at para 97). Importantly they held that if approval was declined because of an expressed antipathy, objection to or disapproval of homosexuality then that is not because of religious belief and cannot thereby be less favourable treatment (at para 99).

**9.47**  There has been considerable debate about this decision and the rights and wrongs of it. Legally it does appear difficult to reconcile the case with the exclusion in Schedule 3, para 15 of the Equality Act 2010. The claim of the couple was that their views on homosexuality were inextricably intertwined with their religious beliefs. Therefore it seems difficult to distinguish such a position from an exclusion whereby they would be permitted to only take children of a particular religion.

**9.48**  The issue is the same as in many different strands and contexts of equality law: namely, what happens where two rights collide. Legally it can be fairly simply stated: one protected characteristic is no defence to discrimination

---

5    [2011] EWHC 375 (Admin).

on grounds of another protected characteristic. Exceptions to discriminatory treatment are limited to those provided by the legislation.

**9.49** Many campaign groups believe that is too simplistic and the result is that sexual orientation rights will always 'trump' religious rights. However, while much debate and lobbying is likely, the position in the legislation is reasonably clear.

## RELIGIOUS DISCRIMINATION

**9.50** The issue of religion in adoption and fostering has been the most high profile issue in recent times. That is dealt with above in **9.39–9.49**. The other aspect of religious discrimination to consider is whether a request for time off for religious rituals associated with childbirth are required to be treated differently to other requests for time off for family reasons. Those rituals will not necessarily take place when the parent would be on leave in any event. For example, the Hindu ritual of Annaprasana does not take place until the child is precisely six months old.

**9.51** If a request for leave is refused, direct discrimination should firstly be considered. The question for a tribunal will be the 'reason why' the request was refused. If it is found to be because of the religious belief itself then that will be straightforward discrimination. The appropriate comparator would be someone who had also asked for time off on a particular day but for a non-religious reason.

**9.52** However, it is more likely that any request would be refused because of a business reason. In those circumstances, the employee will need to establish that the refusal constituted indirect discrimination within section 19 of the Equality Act 2010.

**9.53** The first point to note is that the refusal is likely to constitute a provision, criterion or practice. This was affirmed in *Starmer v British Airways*[6] which upheld a female pilot's claim for indirect discrimination for a single refusal of flexible working. Where a business reason is said to be the reason for the refusal of leave then it is assumed that it will be applied neutrally to others in the workforce. Consequently the issue will be whether it puts the employee at a particular disadvantage because of their protected characteristic.

**9.54** It is likely, provided there is good evidence as to the religious ritual, that particular disadvantage would be established. This is particularly so where the ritual must take place on a particular day and where it cannot take place outside of work time. There would be obvious disadvantage to an employee who is required by the religion to undertake a certain religious ritual on a specific day and they were unable to do so because of the refusal of a day's

---

[6]   [2005] IRLR 862.

leave. Nevertheless, careful evidence would need to be gathered as to the requirements of the religion regarding the ritual and the timing of it.

**9.55** Clearly an employer can seek to justify the discrimination. However, where the request is limited to a particular day's leave, this is likely to be difficult. Therefore, claims of indirect discrimination in this context should be given serious consideration.

## AGE DISCRIMINATION

**9.56** Age discrimination may be justified under section 13(2) of the Equality Act 2010 where A can show the treatment is a proportionate means of achieving a legitimate aim. Therefore, where there is discrimination in the context of family-friendly policies, on the basis of the person's age it may be justified.

**9.57** However, more importantly, the Equality Act provides for a specific exception to the principle of discrimination in relation to the provision of childcare and assistance with childcare.

**9.58** Schedule 9, paragraph 15 provides:

'(1) A person does not contravene a relevant provision, so far as relating to age, only by providing or making arrangements for or facilitating the provision of, care for children of a particular age group'.

**9.59** This includes paying for some or all of the cost of childcare provision, helping a parent find someone suitable to care for the child, enabling a parent to spend more time providing care for the child or otherwise assisting them with respect to that care (para 15(3)). The child must be less than 17 years old.

**9.60** The Employment Code notes that this covers all who have parental responsibility for a child (at para 14.31).

## DISABILITY DISCRIMINATION

**9.61** In the context of disability discrimination, there are a number of considerations in the context of family-friendly policies. Associative discrimination is dealt with above at **9.4–9.22**. In addition to the rights of carers of disabled people, it is important to consider whether public authorities can be required to provide any particular assistance, or care of a particular standard, to disabled people, particularly disabled people as they care for their children or for disabled children.

**9.62** There is important primary and secondary legislation setting out how local authorities will determine and provide the care needs of disabled people (for example, the National Assistance Act 1948 and onwards). This legislation is fiendishly complex and beyond the scope of this chapter. However, it is relevant to consider the applicability and scope for challenge using disability discrimination provisions.

**9.63** Firstly, it should be noted that the provisions at the core of the Equality Act do not require a specific level of care to be provided to disabled persons. They only require that public authorities do not treat people with disabilities or those associated with those with disabilities less favourably and that reasonable adjustments are made to mitigate disadvantage.

**9.64** Under section 158 of the Equality Act 2010 there is scope for a body to take positive action to enable or encourage particular groups of people to overcome or minimise disadvantage arising from a protected characteristic, to meet their needs or to enable or encourage that group to participate in activities. However, this is a permissive provision, not a requirement. Consequently local authorities cannot be criticised for taking appropriate positive action but equally they cannot be required to do so.

**9.65** Another alternative is to consider the public sector equality duties under section 149 of the Equality Act. This provides:

'(1) A public authority must, in the exercise of its functions, have due regard to the need to:
   (a) eliminate discrimination, harassment, victimisation and any other conduct that is prohibited by or under this Act;
   (b) advance equality of opportunity between persons who share a relevant protected characteristic and persons who do not share it;
   (c) foster good relations between persons who share a relevant protected characteristic and persons who do not share it.'

**9.66** The public sector equality duty has been considered by several cases. In *R (Brown) v Secretary of State for Work and Pensions*,[7] Scott Baker and Aikens LJJ sitting in the Divisional court considered the duty in respect of proposed Post Office closures. They set out six key factors about the duty (paras 89–96):

1.1.1 The decision-making body within the public authority must be made aware of the duty in order to have due regard to it.

1.1.2 The duty must be fulfilled before and at the time that the particular policy will or might affect disabled people. There must be a 'conscious approach and state of mind'.

1.1.3 The duty must be exercised in substance, with rigour and with an open mind.

1.1.4 It is non-delegable.

---

[7]   [2008] EWHC 3158 (Admin).

1.1.5 The duty is a continuing one.

1.1.6 It is good practice to keep adequate record showing they've considered duties and pondered relevant questions.

**9.67**   The duties have been considered in relation to a decision by a local authority to restrict the provision of adult care services to people with critical needs only (*R (Chavda and others) v London Borough of Harrow*[8]) and a decision to introduce charges for adult community care services (*R (Domb & Ors) v London Borough of Hammersmith & Fulham & Anor*[9]).

**9.68**   The key question in this chapter is whether these duties can be used to require a particular level of care and assistance to be provided to disabled parents or parents caring for a disabled child. However as can be seen in **9.66** above the duties are predominantly procedural and relate to how a decision is made. While they can be a useful subsidiary tool, where a complex set of factors must be balanced, the duties do not take matters much further forward in terms of the substantive level of care required.

**9.69**   A much more interesting argument arises out of the UK's ratification of the UN Convention on the Rights of Persons with Disabilities. Article 7 of the CRPD provides:

> 'Children with disabilities:
>
> 1.   States Parties shall take all necessary measures to ensure the full enjoyment by children with disabilities of all human rights and fundamental freedoms on an equal basis with other children.
> 2.   In all actions concerning children with disabilities, the best interests of the child shall be a primary consideration.
> 3.   States Parties shall ensure that children with disabilities have the right to express their views freely on all matters affecting them, their views being given due weight in accordance with their age and maturity, on an equal basis with other children, and to be provided with disability and age-appropriate assistance to realise that right.'

**9.70**   In relation to the provision of care and assistance for children with disabilities, there appears to be real scope for the argument that there is a level of assistance that is required in order to fulfill the duties in Article 7. This is most likely to arise in a challenge to a decision about care and funding under the primary and secondary legislation mentioned in **9.62** above. However, taking this legislation together with the procedural requirements of the public sector equality duties and the substantive duties in the CRPD, it may be feasible to argue for a particular level assistance for a disabled child.

---

[8]   [2007] EWHC 3064 (Admin).
[9]   [2009] EWCA Civ 941.

# Chapter 10

# POSITIVE ACTION AND FAMILY RIGHTS IN EMPLOYMENT

*Rachel Crasnow*

## INTRODUCTION

**10.1**   Some argue that UK legislation in relation to family rights at work does not go far enough in eliminating workplace inequality. It has been long recognised that simple equal treatment, without consideration of the context in which the treatment takes place, can easily perpetuate disadvantage since not everyone starts from the same position. Owing to past disadvantages protected groups such as women, mothers and parents may need special assistance to either compete for work, or access training or employment advancement, all of which aim to create a level playing field. This chapter will consider the ways in which current legislation permits positive action in order to eradicate existing inequalities in the context of family-friendly rights.

**10.2**   The Equality Act 2010 provides new powers for employers to implement positive action in the workplace. These permit **more favourable** treatment of those with protected characteristics in specific circumstances.

**10.3**   There are two sections which permit positive action. Neither overrides other statutory provisions.[1] Section 158 covers positive action generally but does not apply when section 159, which covers positive action at work, applies.[2] These provisions, especially section 159 with its emphasis on recruitment and promotion, will give rise to a number of questions of interpretation, which may undermine their utility. Since both provisions are permissive rather than obligatory, employers could be deterred from putting them to use. This would be unfortunate and a wasted opportunity. If the provisions are utilised with care and understanding, employers should retain confidence in their ability to use positive action measures effectively.

**10.4**   The kind of action which section 159 of the Equality Act contemplates is preferential appointment on specified grounds. This is a new and radical development from the previous provisions under repealed legislation such as the Sex Discrimination Act. The limits and context in which appointments will be permissible are developed further below.

---

[1]   See sections 158(6) and 159(3).
[2]   See section 158(4).

**10.5**   Accordingly, the structure of this chapter is to explore the potential for, and boundaries of, positive action in relation to:

(a)   The legal background to positive action measures.

(b)   The distinction with genuine occupational qualifications.

(c)   The temporary nature of positive action.

(d)   Section 159.

(e)   Section 158.

(f)   Examples of proportionality in practice.

(g)   Moving from equality of opportunity to equality of results: targets and quotas.

(h)   Guidelines for positive action in the context of the modern workplace and its interaction with the family.

## THE LEGAL BACKGROUND TO POSITIVE ACTION MEASURES

**10.6**   Specific provisions across domestic law enable limited positive action to be taken which is concerned with 'full equality in practice'. This is an explicit aim of European equality law. It was introduced first in relation to gender as an amendment to the equal pay provisions of the EC Treaty by the Treaty of Amsterdam, as Article 141(4) TEC (which is now Article 157(4) TFEU); it is now found more widely in anti-discrimination Union law.

**10.7**   The aim of full equality in practice closely relates to the principle of equal treatment. In European law the principle of equal treatment prohibits different situations from being treated in the same way just as much as it prohibits the same situations from being treated differently. The difficulty lies in determining when situations are not the same and to what extent different treatment is justified. The question is essentially: Are special measures necessary to remedy past disadvantage?

**10.8**   Prior to the new Equality Act, UK domestic law was much more limited and only permitted training and encouragement to be offered on a limited and targeted basis to under-represented groups.[3] This kind of action enhanced

---

[3]   See, for example, ss 35–38 of the Race Relations Act 1976 and s 47 of the Sex Discrimination Act 1975.

access to job and services opportunities, but the law did not permit selection for substantive benefits such as recruitment or promotion to take place, merely because of under-representation.

## THE DISTINCTION WITH GENUINE OCCUPATIONAL QUALIFICATIONS

**10.9** The law on positive action must be contrasted with that relating to genuine occupational requirements, where if the sex or race, religion or age of an employee or applicant is deemed genuinely essential for the post in question, there is a defence to a claim.

**10.10** In such circumstances what would otherwise be unlawful discrimination is lawful. The contrast is in the objective: these provisions do not seek to enhance opportunities for disadvantaged groups, as positive action measures do, but rather allow a defence to discriminatory acts where the essential nature of the job calls for a specific characteristic such as age, race, religion or sex for reasons including physiology, authenticity, privacy or decency.

**10.11** The key difference between an occupational requirement and positive action is that the latter does not imply that only those with a particular protected characteristic can do a particular job, but that the job can be done by anyone with the appropriate skill set, whereas when the former applies there are specific reasons to seek out applicants with particular protected characteristics.

**10.12** This chapter will not describe the law relating to genuine occupational requirements further, but it is important to emphasise that they are strictly defined in the legislation and carefully scrutinised by tribunals and courts to avoid stereotypes in the workplace (such as 'only women are suitable to working with babies in nurseries') being erroneously legitimated under these provisions.

## THE TEMPORARY NATURE OF POSITIVE ACTION

**10.13** In any case in which positive action is taken there is always a question as to how long the action can be maintained. The jurisprudence of the European Court of Human Rights (ECHR) recognises that positive action may be necessary but also establishes that it ought to be time limited. The ECHR permits the treatment of groups differently to ameliorate the inequalities between them. This will be essentially a political assessment although there are obvious limits. It should be noted that both the International Convention on the Elimination of All Forms of Racial Discrimination (ICERD) and the Convention on the Elimination of All Forms of Discrimination Against Women (CEDAW) indicate that positive action should not be continued after the objectives for which they were taken have been achieved.

**10.14** Accordingly, in *Hooper v Secretary of State for Work and Pensions* [2005] UKHL 29, [2005] 1 WLR 1681 the House of Lords debated the question of the duration of special treatment for a particular group and said at [32]:

> 'Once it is accepted that older widows were historically an economically disadvantaged class which merited special treatment but were gradually becoming less disadvantaged, the question of the precise moment at which such special treatment is no longer justified becomes a social and political question within the competence of Parliament.'

**10.15** Under Article 14 of the European Convention on Human Rights the question of phasing out positive action measures is a key element of the concept of proportionality. Member States are given a broad margin of appreciation as to the moment when such measures are no longer justified. Yet if the aim of positive action is a move towards greater equality, the suspension of temporary measures before the action in question is operating effectively would be inappropriate, just as their suspension when real change has been effected will be necessary.

## THE EQUALITY ACT 2010 SECTION 159 – POSITIVE ACTION IN PROMOTION AND RECRUITMENT

**10.16** Section 159 is concerned solely with the substantive benefits of recruitment or promotion and does not extend more widely than that, though these concepts are widely defined. It can be seen below that section 159(1) defines the basis on which positive action can be taken and in section 159(4) sets out the limits to that action:

> '159 Positive action: recruitment and promotion
>
> (1) This section applies if a person (P) reasonably thinks that—
>   (a) persons who share a protected characteristic suffer a disadvantage connected to the characteristic, or
>   (b) participation in an activity by persons who share a protected characteristic is disproportionately low.
> (2) Part 5 (work) does not prohibit P from taking action within subsection (3) with the aim of enabling or encouraging persons who share the protected characteristic to—
>   (a) overcome or minimise that disadvantage, or
>   (b) participate in that activity.
> (3) That action is treating a person (A) more favourably in connection with recruitment or promotion than another person (B) because A has the protected characteristic but B does not.
> (4) But subsection (2) applies only if—
>   (a) A is as qualified as B to be recruited or promoted,
>   (b) P does not have a policy of treating persons who share the protected characteristic more favourably in connection with recruitment or promotion than persons who do not share it, and

(c)   taking the action in question is a proportionate means of achieving the aim referred to in subsection (2).'

**10.17**   The explanatory notes to the Equality Act compare two different scenarios:

(a)   A police service which employs disproportionately low numbers of people from an ethnic minority background identifies a number of candidates who are as qualified as each other for recruitment to a post, including a candidate from an under-represented ethnic minority background. It would not be unlawful to give preferential treatment to that candidate, provided the comparative merits of other candidates were also taken into consideration.

(b)   An employer offers a job to a woman on the basis that women are under-represented in the company's workforce when there was a male candidate who was more qualified. This would be unlawful direct discrimination.[4]

## What do disadvantage and disproportionately low mean?

**10.18**   The section does not specifically require a statistical analysis, provided there is a reasonable basis to conclude that there is a connection between a protected characteristic and disadvantage, or the fact of disproportionately low participation.

**10.19**   In those circumstances it enables positive action, with the aim of enabling or encouraging persons who share the protected characteristic, to overcome or minimise that disadvantage, or participate in the relevant activity. Subject to limitations, this can include more favourable treatment of those who have a specific protected characteristic.

**10.20**   Two questions arise. The first is: is it necessary to prove that the disadvantage is generally recognised? The second is a causation issue: how does an employer go about proving that a disadvantage is connected to a characteristic? In the public sector, equality auditing under the Equality Duties is likely to provide an answer. However, it is clear that the legislation expects other employers, as well, to be aware of the diversity of their workforce and to wish to address any apparent deficiencies.

**10.21**   In the second part of section 159(1) it is necessary to consider how to determine whether participation is disproportionately low. For instance, it might be that the proportion of older people working in the fashion industry are disproportionately low compared to those in the population at large, but would such a generalised comparison be sufficient for the positive action (in the form of the proposed selection) to be legitimate? Unfortunately the

---

4    http://www.legislation.gov.uk/ukpga/2010/15/notes/division/2/11/2/2/3.

Explanatory Memorandum to the Act does not seek to answer these questions. Clearly some evidence is vital – without it the measure cannot be shown to be adequate or proportionate to the aim pursued.

**10.22**  Some answers to these questions can be obtained by reference to the case-law of the Court of Justice of the European Union (CJEU). For instance in Germany the 1990 Bremen Act on Equal Treatment for Men and Women in the Public Service provided that women who are 'under-represented' could be given priority over men for public sector appointments if they had the same qualifications. The legislation stated that there was under-representation if women did not make up at least half of the staff in the individual pay, remuneration and salary brackets in the relevant personnel group within a department.

**10.23**  Since the Bremen scheme had given unconditional preference to the under-represented candidate, the CJEU decided it was unlawful on grounds of lack of proportionality. However, the Court did not criticise the German legislation's approach to under-representation.[5]

**10.24**  Nevertheless, it is not always certain whether merely rough inequality between the proportions would be sufficient. Such statistics might be unreliable by reason of the numbers, or the time frame within which they are collected. They may simply show random events and not disadvantage. The better view is that the level of participation needs to be shown to be low when compared with other groups or with the expected level of participation. Practitioners should also note that section 159 of the Equality Act 2010 makes the test more subjective than the requirement under the German legislation by providing: 'if a person P (who is the person who will take the positive action) **reasonably** thinks that ...'. Whether in practice the UK courts will demand hard statistical data seems doubtful, but if so that requirement will no doubt be tested for the reasons given above.

**10.25**  An example given by the Government Equalities Office 'quick start guide to positive action in recruitment and promotion'[6] states that a DIY chain begins planning a new recruitment programme. In considering how to create a more diverse workforce the company realises that it does not keep detailed records on the personal details of its employees. However, the Area Manager is able to demonstrate that it is reasonable for him to think that there are a disproportionately low number of women in the workforce from his knowledge of who works for him and by consulting with his local branch managers. The employer could decide to use positive action in aiming to address the number of women in the workforce. Taking positive action based on that information would usually be lawful.

---

[5]  Case C-450/93 *Kalanke v Freie Hansestadt Bremen* [1995] ECR I-3051.
[6]  http://www.homeoffice.gov.uk/publications/equalities/equality-act-publications/equality-act-guidance/positive-action-recruitment?view=Binary.

**10.26** A further question is whether the under-representation must be specific to the workforce and community, locally or nationally? Again a proportionate consideration of the context will be necessary. Under-representation in a certain employment market is unlikely to justify positive action measures in a different area. On the other hand, the geographical spread of a labour market for some work may be quite large, and it may be wrong to look at it on too narrow a basis.

## There must not be a policy to discriminate

**10.27** It might seem that the Act expects section 159 to be used relatively rarely and that it is concerned essentially with a tie-break context. This is because there cannot be a policy of treating persons who share the protected characteristic more favourably in connection with recruitment or promotion than persons who do not share it. However, the prohibition on having a policy to prefer persons having a particular protected characteristic does not have quite that effect. The purpose of this prohibition is to ensure that whenever the section is applied there is a *specific* consideration of the candidates for recruitment and promotion and their competitors.[7] Thus an unthinking purported application of section 159 is likely to be unlawful.

**10.28** The Government Equalities Office gives a relevant example of unlawful action in its quick start guide to positive action in recruitment and promotion, as follows: a department store employs nine senior managers but only two of them are women. When a vacancy arises it seeks to address this under-representation by only interviewing women applicants, regardless of whether they meet the criteria for the post. This would be positive discrimination so would be unlawful.

## 'As qualified as'

**10.29** Secondly, candidates in respect of whom employers can take positive action must be equally suitable for the job. It is quite clear, for instance that a woman cannot be given an automatic preference over a man simply by reason of her gender: see Case C-158/97 *Badeck v Landesanwalt beim Staatsgerichtshof des Landes Hessen* [2000] IRLR 432 CJEU.

**10.30** The consequence of this is that there must be an objective selection process that assesses specific skills, qualifications and abilities, but does this mean that candidates have to be qualified or suitable in *exactly* the same way before a choice based on under-representation is legitimate? The present view is, probably not.

**10.31** The Act uses the phrase 'as qualified as' and it has been suggested by the Government in 2009 that whilst this does not authorise in any way the use

---

[7] The Explanatory Memorandum to the Act says at paragraph [526] 'each case must be considered on its merits'.

of quotas, it will cover situations where candidates meet the minimum qualifications or the particular requirements for the post, in contrast to a scenario where the applications in question are *identical* in their qualifications, skills and abilities.

**10.32**  Thus, even if a candidate from a protected group had some weaknesses in areas where her competitor was strong, if those related to desirable rather than essential aspects of the job specification, she may be considered as qualified for the post. Not all recruitment exercises divide the desired characteristics of the post into necessary and preferred. So the answer to this question may require a more specific examination as to how important the skills in question are for the job.

**10.33**  If a woman is applying for a new job after a career break when raising her children, it may be that her lack of very recent experience in the workplace does not count against her if she meets essential criteria and the prospective employer is seeking to boost the number of female workers in that field from a current under-represented percentage of the whole.

**10.34**  There are no fixed rules as to how such an assessment must operate. The Explanatory Memorandum to the Act says at paragraph [528] the section allows 'the maximum flexibility to address disadvantage and under-representation where candidates are as good as each other...'. While it seems inevitable that some litigation will arise from the use of positive action measures in recruitment exercises, it is also certain that the more demonstrably objective an assessment of the candidates has been, the less open to challenge the ultimate selection will be.

**10.35**  For instance, it would normally be straightforward to assess the qualifications required for the post of a legal secretary; by contrast, there would be a high degree of subjectivity in the value judgment involved in determining who is qualified to be a senior partner or even to perform a management role. So the meaning of the word 'qualified' will surely be the subject of future debate, and will require to be developed by commentary such as that in Codes of Practice, or judicial determination.

**10.36**  The draft Equality Act Code of Practice on Employment issued by the Equality and Human Rights Commission[8] suggested that the word 'qualified' should be given a broad meaning and comments that:

> '7.21 Candidates do not have to be identical in all ways before a preference can be shown. For example, candidates may have different strengths and weaknesses in different areas but both can be deemed to be "as qualified" for the post.'[9]

---

[8]  The final version excludes guidance on section 159 as it was not in force when the Codes were presented to Parliament.

[9]  http://www.equalityhumanrights.com/uploaded_files/Equality%20Bill/employment_code1. doc.

**10.37**   An example given by the Government Equalities Office 'quick start guide to positive action in recruitment and promotion'[10] provides that a health and fitness club is faced with making a choice between two applicants for a job as the manager of a leisure facility. One, a woman, has recently completed a Leisure Management Foundation Degree course but has little practical experience. The other candidate is a man who has no formal qualifications but has several years experience of working in leisure centres. Having interviewed both candidates, the employer decides that both could do the job to the same standard but in different ways as each would bring a different set of skills and experiences to the job. Therefore, because the candidates are of equal merit the manager could voluntarily use the positive action provisions when choosing between the candidates and opt to employ the man because all of the other senior positions at the leisure complex were held by women.

**10.38**   It is certain that automatic preferences or quotas will be unlawful under the Equality Act as they do not include the requisite exercise in proportionality by prioritising under-represented groups in an unconditional fashion. Hence the Swedish Equality Act 1991 which permitted employers to appoint a member of one sex over the other (even though the appointee was the worse candidate) where the appointment served to promise equality between men and women in the workplace, was held to be held unlawful by the CJEU in Case C-407/98 *Abrahamsson v Fogelqvist* [2000] IRLR 732.

**10.39**   However, the CJEU has not made this condition for positive action impossibly difficult to meet. In *Abrahamsson* the CJEU ruled that Article 2 of the Equal Treatment Directive did not preclude granting a preference to a candidate belonging to the under-represented group (here women), over a competitor of the opposite sex, provided that the candidates possessed equivalent or *substantially equivalent* merits and the candidatures were subjected to an objective assessment which took account of all their specific personal situations.

**10.40**   Thus as long as there is a substantive degree of objective assessment, EU law does not demand that candidates be *identically* qualified, as a condition for a tie-break to be permitted.

**10.41**   The House of Lords added an amendment to sections 158 and 159 to make it explicit that any positive action measure taken had to be a proportionate means of helping people overcome a disadvantage or participate in an activity: see sections 158(2) and 159(4)(c). A proportionality requirement is also added to section 104 of the Equality Act, which allows a political party to have a women-only shortlist of potential candidates to represent a particular constituency in Parliament, provided women remain under-represented in the party's Members of Parliament (see Explanatory Notes to the Equality Act at http://www.legislation.gov.uk/ukpga/2010/15/notes/division/2/7/5).

---

[10]   http://www.homeoffice.gov.uk/publications/equalities/equality-act-publications/equality-act-guidance/positive-action-recruitment?view=Binary.

**10.42**   Fortunately, further guidance to interpretation of these sections exists. The ECHR draft Equality Act Code of Practice on Employment provides practical assistance in relation to these issues where it states at paragraph 7.21:

> '**Example:** a local police force starts its annual recruitment drive in April. Its monitoring data shows that women are currently under-represented and it takes positive action measures to encourage women to apply for the posts. All candidates have to undertake various assessment exercises and an interview. A number of candidates of both sexes are assessed as equally suitable for the posts on the basis of their test results, performance at interview, qualifications and experience. The force could decide to appoint the women candidates who are as qualified as the men to address under-representation.'[11]

**10.43**   Possible models as to how the assessment process for positive action should take place are also available from other jurisdictions. For example in *Badeck*, the German state of Hesse utilised an innovative means of assessing skills and abilities of candidates in under-represented fields. The national legislation included the provision that:

> 'When qualifications are assessed, capabilities and experience which have been acquired by looking after children or persons requiring care in the domestic sector (family work) are to be taken into account, in so far as they are of importance for the suitability, performance and capability of applicants ... Part-time work, leave and delays in completing training as a result of looking after children ... must not have a negative effect on official assessment and not adversely affect progress in employment ... Seniority, age and the date of last promotion may be taken into account only in so far as they are of importance for the suitability, performance and capability of applicants.'

**10.44**   This approach was also considered by the European Free Trade Association Court in *EFTA Surveillance Authority v Kingdom of Norway* [2003] IRLR 318 where the Court stated at [57] that 'giving weight to the possibility that in numerous academic disciplines female life experience may be relevant to the determination of the suitability and capability for, and performance in, higher academic positions, could enhance the equality of men and women'.

**10.45**   Such an approach to the objective assessment of candidates could have a significant impact on the under-representation of women in management posts in the UK in the future, should employers embrace these voluntary measures.

**10.46**   This approach could also prove useful for carers applying for part-time work, job shares or flexible working. Candidates who can demonstrate their organisational skills in managing a household whilst holding down a job or show their effective use of electronic communication systems to stay in touch when out of the office may be able to show an impressive determination which would appeal to a recruiting employer in a novel way, despite the candidate not

---

[11]   See http://www.equalityhumanrights.com/uploaded_files/Equality%20Bill/employment_code1. doc.

being able to demonstrate identical experience to other full-time applicants. A useful stance was provided in the recent publication 'Judicial Appointments: Balancing Independence, Accountability and Legitimacy' (http://jac.judiciary. gov.uk/static/documents/JA_web.pdf) where Shami Chakrabarti Director of Liberty wrote in her chapter entitled: The Judiciary: Why Diversity and Merit Matter:

> 'Then there are the skills and qualities that more obviously and directly benefit from broader life experience and association. Empathy, life (as opposed to legal) experience and communication can all be vital assets on the bench. The same is true of knowledge of areas of the justice system not always associated with the intellectual and financial elites of either the Bar or Solicitors' profession. Legal aid and police station practice are obvious cases in point, but there is a whole wealth of extra-legal life and work experience that could benefit the holders of judicial office in addition to the litigation and advocacy achievements traditionally valued. Diversity in the composition of the bench should not be limited to obvious and vital issues of gender, race, sexuality, physical ability and degrees of privilege.'

**10.47** These comments also apply to working practices generally, not just to judicial appointments.

## THE EQUALITY ACT 2010, SECTION 158

**10.48** Section 158 says:

> '158 Positive action: general
>
> (1) This section applies if a person (P) reasonably thinks that—
>     (a) persons who share a protected characteristic suffer a disadvantage connected to the characteristic;
>     (b) persons who share a protected characteristic have needs that are different from the needs of persons who do not share it; or
>     (c) participation in an activity by persons who share a protected characteristic is disproportionately low.
> (2) This Act does not prohibit P from taking any action which is a proportionate means of achieving the aim of—
>     (a) enabling or encouraging persons who share the protected characteristic to overcome or minimise that disadvantage;
>     (b) meeting those needs; or
>     (c) enabling or encouraging persons who share the protected characteristic to participate in that activity.
> (3) Regulations may specify action, or descriptions of action, to which subsection (2) does not apply...'

**10.49** These provisions are very similar to those in section 159 and it is to be assumed that they will be interpreted in a very similar way. Whilst this section largely examines their use in the non-employment context, it is important to note they will be relevant in relation to aspects of employment such as training.

**10.50**   Section 158 extends the scope for positive action in all areas covered by the Equality Act. The pre-requisites are that the body applying the measure must reasonably think one of three factors:

(a)   that those who share a protected characteristic suffer a disadvantage connected to the characteristic;

(b)   that those who share a protected characteristic have needs that are different from the needs of persons who do not share it; or

(c)   that participation in an activity by persons who share a protected characteristic is disproportionately low.

**10.51**   The width of scope permitted can be seen from the broad spectrum of permitted aims set out in section 158(2):

(a)   enabling or encouraging persons who share the protected characteristic to overcome or minimise that disadvantage;

(b)   meeting those needs; or

(c)   enabling or encouraging persons who share the protected characteristic to participate in that activity.

**10.52**   These measures will only be legitimate if it is a proportionate means of achieving the aims set out above. Proportionality under section 158 will be applied in the same way as it will for recruitment questions under section 159: see the discussion above. The Government's Explanatory Notes in connection with proportionality under section 158 provide:

> '520. The extent to which it is proportionate to take positive action measures which may result in people not having the relevant characteristic being treated less favourably will depend, among other things, on the seriousness of the relevant disadvantage, the extremity of need or under-representation and the availability of other means of countering them. This provision will need to be interpreted in accordance with European law which limits the extent to which the kind of action it permits will be allowed.'[12]

**10.53**   The breadth of possible measures permitted under section 158 could be extremely wide, as can be seen by the disparate examples given in the ECHR Equality Act Code of Practice on Employment

> 'Para 12.24: The Act permits action to be taken to enable or encourage people who share the protected characteristic to participate in that activity. Provided that the action is a proportionate means of achieving the aim of enabling or encouraging participation, the Act does not limit what action could be taken. It could include:

---

[12]   See http://www.opsi.gov.uk/acts/acts2010.

- setting targets for increasing participation of the targeted group;
- providing bursaries to obtain qualifications in a profession such as journalism for members of the group whose participation in that profession might be disproportionately low;
- outreach work such as raising awareness of public appointments within the community;
- reserving places on training courses for people with the protected characteristic, for example, in management;
- targeted networking opportunities, for example, in banking;
- working with local schools and FE colleges, inviting students from groups whose participation in the workplace is disproportionately low to spend a day at the company;
- providing mentoring.'

**10.54** The ECHR Equality Act Code of Practice on Employment gives an example of action which goes too far where it states at para 12.8:

'**Example:** An LLP seeks to address the low participation of women partners by interviewing all women regardless of whether they meet the criteria for partnership. This would be positive discrimination and is unlawful.'

**10.55** However, if the LLP organised workshops for women interested in partnership progression at lunchtimes rather than in evenings when many of them were unable to attend, such extra assistance would be legitimate.

**10.56** The difficult scenarios arise when the action in question amounts to more than 'soft measures' such as mentoring or encouragement in the form of words in job adverts, and instead to more substantial forms of positive action such as exclusive training courses. The ECHR in its Code of Practice on Employment gives an example of action to remedy disadvantage at para 12.17 which is relevant to the issue of family rights in employment law:

'**Example:** Research shows that women in Britain experience significant disadvantage in pursuing careers in engineering, as reflected in their low participation in the profession and their low status within it. Some of the key contributing factors are gender stereotyping in careers guidance and a lack of visible role models. A leading equalities organisation, in partnership with employers in the engineering sector, offers opportunities exclusively to girls and women to learn more about the career choices through a careers fair attended by women working in the profession.'

**10.57** The question of how far can positive action measures extend and still be lawful is considered further in the practical section which follows concerning proportionality.

## EXAMPLES OF PROPORTIONALITY IN PRACTICE – THE CROSSOVER WITH SECTION 13(6) OF THE EQUALITY ACT AND SPECIAL TREATMENT

**10.58** Whether positive action is proportionate or not depends upon the factors relevant to the balancing test which is necessary to avoid exceeding the limitations set out in the Equality Act. From the context of family rights in the workplace, the challenges to employers taking positive action measures frequently arise when those who are **not** within the disadvantaged group perceive themselves as suffering a detriment which is not justified.

**10.59** Section 13(6)(b) provides another very important kind of positive action. Women who require special treatment as a result of pregnancy or childbirth will find that section 13(6) of the Equality Act is just as effective a source of legal assistance as section 158. Section 13(6) provides that:

'13(6) If the protected characteristic is sex—

(a)    less favourable treatment of a woman includes less favourable treatment of her because she is breastfeeding;
(b)    in a case where B is a man, no account is to be taken of special treatment afforded to a woman in connection with pregnancy or childbirth.'

**10.60** The prohibition on discrimination linked to breastfeeding in section 13(6)(a) is not linked to the age of the baby and would presumably cover requests for breaks to express milk during the working day, as well as needing to leave work by a certain time to breastfeed a baby. Note that this does not apply to rights at work (section 13(7)), but a refusal to allow a woman to express milk or to adjust her working conditions so she can continue to breastfeed may amount to unlawful sex discrimination.

**10.61** These points are raised in this chapter in the context of positive action, as working mothers may, for example, have requirements for special treatment connected with breastfeeding. Section 17(4) of the Equality Act expressly provides that treating a woman unfavourably because she has given birth 'includes, in particular, a reference to treating her unfavourably because she is breastfeeding'. If a link can be made between birth and breastfeeding in section 17(4) as set out above, it is surely relevant for section 13(6)(b) purposes.

**10.62** This second sub-section at section 13(6)(b) prevents men from claiming privileges for women connected with pregnancy or childbirth. Unlike section 158, there is no threshold to establish such as establishing low participation prior to an entitlement to positive action arising.

**10.63** The treatment which is potentially covered by pregnancy or childbirth is very wide. On a simple level, it means that male employees cannot complain that a female colleague received cards and flowers on the birth of her child but they did not when they broke a limb skiing. (It is not yet clear whether associative pregnancy claims may be brought under the Equality Act; they were not permitted under the Sex Discrimination Act 1975 (SDA): see *Kulikaoskas v MacDuff Shellfish*, EAT 0062/09.) Section 13(6)(b) entitles a pregnant employee to more frequent toilet breaks than would be allowed to a non-pregnant colleague. Yet what are the limits of the phrase 'in connection with pregnancy or childbirth'?

**10.64** Whilst it would probably cover health issues caused by pregnancy or childbirth which continue after these events, could it include special treatment needed in attempts to become pregnant? See Case C-506/06 *Mayr v Bäckerei* [2008] ECR I-01017.[13]

**10.65** Section 13(6) does cover special treatment of those on maternity leave (see discussion in *Eversheds Legal Services Ltd v De Belin* [2011] IRLR 448 below), as this is clearly 'in connection with' childbirth and pregnancy. Pregnancy in section 13(6) is not defined by reference to a protected period as is pregnancy and maternity discrimination in section 18 of the Equality Act. (The restrictions in sections 17(6) and 18(7) do not appear to bind section 13(6)(b) as it covers special treatment, not sex discrimination: see section 13(8).) Moreover, that the special treatment took place during a maternity leave period was not the reason for the employer failing in its application of section 13(6) (previously section 2(2) of the SDA 1975) in the case of *Eversheds Legal Services Ltd v De Belin* discussed below.

**10.66** Does the special treatment continue after a woman has returned to work at the end of her maternity leave? Would an employer be able to justify the provision of vouchers or subsidies for nursery or childcare facilities as falling within this section as well as within the exclusion given by section 6(1)(b) of the Equal Pay Act 1970 which removes from the scope of the equality clause terms that afford 'special treatment to women in connection with pregnancy or childbirth'?

**10.67** Whilst the prudent course would be for employers to offer such benefits to all parents with young children, irrespective of their sex, an employer who sought to make such payments only to working mothers might attempt to show that the impact of the pregnancy and childbirth was a loss in salary and therefore special treatment as regarding pay and benefits retained the necessary link to the earlier events. Such action would risk falling foul of the proportionality requirements although in C-476/99 *Lommers* [2002] ECR

---

[13] Although this CJEU does not go so far to say any unfavourable treatment related to IVF treatment is sex discrimination, it confirms that to dismiss someone on the grounds that she is likely to become pregnant is sex discrimination. See also *Sahota v Home Office* [2009] UKEAT/342/09 which explains just what is the protected period in IVF cases.

I-2891 the CJEU ruled that the Equal Treatment Directive 76/207 permitted a nursery scheme set up to tackle extensive under-representation of women within a workplace.[14]

**10.68** Both section 158 and section 13(6) seek to address a wide variety of scenarios where absence from the workplace for ante- and post-natal reasons may well cause detriment. A difficult balance exists between equal treatment and the permitted derogation from the principle of positive action, be it special treatment to be afforded a woman under the maternity legislation or positive action measures. Such a challenge is demonstrated by the following example.

**10.69** The interface between these competing interests provisions arose in the recent case of *De Belin v Eversheds Legal Services* [2011] IRLR 448, where an Employment Tribunal held that artificially increasing the scores of a woman solicitor on maternity leave during a redundancy scoring procedure was sex discrimination against a male solicitor, where the female employee would have been selected for redundancy save for the enhancement process. Eversheds appealed against the finding and argued that the employers were positively obliged to treat female employees more favourably on account of their maternity absence.

**10.70** However, the Employment Appeal Tribunal (EAT) upheld the first instance decision on the basis that:

(a)    The obligation to protect employees who are pregnant or on maternity leave cannot extend to favouring them beyond what is 'reasonably necessary to compensate them for the disadvantages occasioned by their condition'.

(b)    'The only justification for treating the woman more favourably is the need to see that she is not disadvantaged by her condition, and where the treatment in question goes beyond what is reasonably necessary for that purpose a real injustice may be done to a colleague'.

(c)    The measures adopted by the respondent 'went beyond what was reasonably necessary' and 'there were alternative ways of removing the maternity-related disadvantage without unfairly disadvantaging the claimant'.

**10.71** The appeal court found that such an approach accords a wide margin of discretion to employers to determine what *special treatment* to afford to employees who are pregnant or on maternity leave, particularly where any advantages or special treatment are not at the expense of their colleagues.

---

[14]    See also *Thibault v Caisse Nationale d'Assurance Vieillesse des Travailleurs Salariés* Case C-136/95 [1998] ECR I-2011; and *Abdoulaye v Régie Nationale des Usines Renault SA* C-218/98 [1999] ECR I-5723.

**10.72** The EAT acknowledged that the protection of the special position of employees who are pregnant or on maternity leave may sometimes require them to be accorded treatment which is more favourable than that accorded to their colleagues (other women as well as men) – this principle derives from Article 2.3 (subsequently Article 2.7) of the 1976 Directive. Importantly it acknowledged that maternity absence is an aspect of pregnancy or childbirth (para [13]).

**10.73** It is not automatically lawful to give those on maternity leave the benefit of the doubt when such scoring processes are undertaken in their absence. Although proportionality allows a wide margin of discretion to employers as to the appropriate special treatment to be accorded to pregnant employees and those on maternity leave, the degree of disadvantage and prejudice caused to colleagues will be particularly under scrutiny. The test here was what was 'reasonably necessary'. The EAT found that by giving the absent female solicitor the maximum score (rather than, for example, an average based on her last 12 months when at work), Eversheds had gone beyond what was reasonably necessary. There were alternative means of removing the disadvantages to their female employee without unfairly disadvantaging the Appellant Mr de Belin.

**10.74** The term 'reasonably necessary' requires the application of the proportionality principle (see summary in paragraphs 23–24 of the judgment of Sedley LJ in *Allonby v Accrington and Rossendale College* [2001] IRLR 364, at p 369).

**10.75** To what extent do the provisions of section 158 of the Equality Act have to be taken into account when considering 'special treatment' in connection with pregnancy and childbirth under section 13(6) of the Equality Act (previously section 2(2) of the SDA)? The defence under section 13(6) was said by the EAT only to apply to 'treatment accorded to a woman so far as it constitutes a proportionate means of achieving the legitimate aim of compensating her for the disadvantages occasioned by her pregnancy or her maternity leave'.

**10.76** What amounts to 'disadvantage' is not defined by the Act. There is no reason why it could not be a barrier to participating in redundancy scoring exercises – that is maternity-related absence. There is no domestic case-law on this issue as yet and it is likely that more cases on *de Belin v Eversheds* type facts will arise, particularly in an economic climate where jobs are scarce and those made redundant are increasingly willing to challenge the substance of their dismissal decisions. Permissible positive action is no longer limited to measures such as training and encouragement on a limited and targeted basis to under-represented groups as it was in section 47 of the Sex Discrimination Act 1975.

**10.77** Yet the current interpretation of the special treatment provision in section 13(6)(b) of the Equality Act could potentially be limiting for women in the context of employers who fear complaints of overreaching 'special treatment' afforded to women. It is important that pertinent evidence is utilised in order to ensure the proportionality arguments are correctly applied in both special treatment and section 158/159 cases.

**10.78**   It is difficult to ascertain whether section 158 of the Equality Act would have allowed the employer in the *de Belin* case to have defended its position any more robustly had the Act been in force at the relevant time.

**10.79**   Under section 158 the condition of experiencing a disadvantage because of maternity-related absence would apply and hence proportionate positive action could be taken to overcome that disadvantage.

**10.80**   In this situation the woman on maternity leave would certainly qualify under section 158 – her maternity-related absence means she is disadvantaged with regard to the application of the redundancy criterion in question.

**10.81**   Therefore, whilst the proportionality principle might have been applied in the same way, there could legitimately have been more emphasis on the need to remedy the disadvantage connected to the female employee and a failure to mark her more favourably than Mr Belin would not have removed that disadvantage.

**10.82**   One of the factors relevant to the requisite balancing exercise is whether it would be possible to achieve the proposed aim by another action less likely to result in less favourable treatment of others. This does not mean that any action detrimental to others is unlawful, just that alternatives must be considered first.

**10.83**   Therefore, suppose a female solicitor returning from a year's maternity leave is concerned to receive the same number of case referrals from the firm's partners, despite her not having worked with them for that year. Could it be reasonably be thought that her absence on maternity grounds had led her to suffer a disadvantage or have a different need from other groups in that she needs to be promoted over other colleagues for case referrals for a period of time? The Government Equalities Office states in its 2010 Guidance on section 158 that there is no need to show detailed statistical evidence that there is a disadvantage, low level of participation or different needs.

**10.84**   Paragraph 12.4 of the Employment Code states that 'In order to take positive action, an employer must reasonably think that one of the above conditions applies; that is, disadvantage, different needs or disproportionately low participation. This means that some indication or evidence will be required to show that one of these statutory conditions applies. It does not, however, need to be sophisticated statistical data or research. It may simply involve an employer looking at the profiles of their workforce and/or making enquiries of other comparable employers in the area or sector. Additionally, it could involve looking at national data such as labour force surveys for a national or local picture of the work situation for particular groups who share a protected characteristic. A decision could be based on qualitative evidence, such as consultation with workers and trade unions.'

**10.85** However, there will need to be a basis for holding such a 'reasonable belief'. It is relatively straightforward to argue that the intended action (in the above example directing a specific number of referrals to the solicitor in question in preference to her colleagues) is intended to meet her needs which are different from the rest of those colleagues, or that such action is aimed at enabling her to overcome the disadvantage caused by her absence.

**10.86** Disadvantage is not defined in order that it remains a flexible concept. It can mean lack of choice as well as barriers to securing opportunities. In the context of family rights in the workplace it relates to legal, social or economic barriers or obstacles which make it difficult for a carer or parent to enter into, or progress within a workplace. Working full-time may act as a barrier for parents to apply for a job where they require flexible working to allow for childcare responsibilities. In such a context the flexible working policy is one means of implementing positive action – which could encourage more parents (traditionally women) to apply for full-time jobs.

**10.87** The harder question is testing the proportionality of the intended action.

**10.88** The following questions should be applied to attempt to make the action in question challenge-proof:

(a)  Is the action appropriate to the aim? What is the evidence that the current system is the main barrier causing the disadvantage?

(b)  Is there other action which would be as effective in achieving this aim or would cause less disadvantage to other groups?

(c)  What is the currency of the suggested action and can its effectiveness be tested during the period of its existence?

**10.89** This is echoed in the Explanatory Notes to the Equality Act 2010 which state in relation to section 158:

'The extent to which it is proportionate to take positive action measures which may result in people not having the relevant characteristic being treated less favourably will depend, among other things, on the seriousness of the relevant disadvantage, the extremity of need or under-representation and the availability of other means of countering them.'

**10.90** The emphasis on appropriateness and necessity will mean that a cost benefit analysis as well as a report of the effectiveness of the measure will play an important role in any balancing test.

## MOVING FROM EQUALITY OF OPPORTUNITY TO EQUALITY OF RESULTS: TARGETS AND QUOTAS

**10.91**   The restrictive approach of the European model to positive action as interpreted by the CJEU thus far, clearly rejects any concept of generalised positive action, which does not require an individualised objective testing on a case by case basis. Quotas or targets are deemed contrary to both current interpretation of Article 157(4) of the TFEU and Article 3 of the Recast Directive 2006/54/EC. However, there is a growing awareness that such an approach is not having the impact upon the change to the workplace across the EU for which it was intended. Many in the business and legal community have reached the view that the 'soft' and voluntary options will not catalyse the necessary change which is needed to reform gender roles in the modern industrial relations field as well as assisting in closing the equal pay gap.

**10.92**   In a recent case decided by the CJEU to address positive action steps: Case C-319/2003 *Serge Briheche v Ministre de l'Intérieur, Ministre de l'Éducation Nationale and Ministre de la Justice*,[15] the court reviews prior case-law as well as the present thinking of the CJEU. In his Opinion AG Maduro considers how Article 141(4) of the TEC (now Article 157(4) of the TFEU) permits a broader, more expansive approach to authorised positive action.

**10.93**   In this case the CJEU had to consider whether a French law, which prohibited recruitment to employment in the Civil Service for anyone aged over 45, unless the applicant was a widow or an unmarried man with childcare responsibilities, was unlawful positive action. As the recast Sex Equality Directive had not yet been enacted the CJEU firstly reviewed the weaker provisions of Article 2(4) of the Equal Treatment Directive.[16] However, it then considered the nature of the obligation of 'full equality in practice' in Article 141(4) of the EC and held that whilst this provision and Article 2(4) looked beyond formal equality to substantive equality, it was not possible to say how far this goal could be achieved where positive action for a woman might create a claim of unlawful discrimination by a man.

**10.94**   The CJEU went on to hold that the French provision in question was *not* consistent with the limits to permissible positive action as the *automatic and unconditional disapplication* of the relevant conditions to certain women was insufficient on the facts to justify the step taken (see paras 27–28 of the judgment).

**10.95**   In his Opinion in the case, Advocate General Maduro considered whether positive action measures under European law could be extended by

---

[15]   [2004] ECR I-8807.
[16]   See Council Directive 76/207/EEC of 9 February 1976 on the implementation of the principle of equal treatment for men and women as regards access to employment, vocational training and promotion, and working conditions which was replaced with strengthened positive action provisions by Directive 2006/54/EC.

looking at compensatory forms of positive discrimination on 'equality of opportunities', rather than on 'equality of results' (which in the form of quotas and set targets has been deemed disproportionate to date), see paras 48–51. Practitioners should make use of this case as an excellent guide to an understanding of what constitutes legitimate positive action under Community law.

**10.96**   Recently the need to look beyond 'equality of opportunity' to 'equality of results' has been considered at a high level. In July 2011 the draft EU Capital Requirements Directive sort to impose mandatory quotas to increase the number of women of sitting on bank boards. These proposals would force major changes to be made to the composition of the boards of the major European banks, in order to comply with the requirement that 'representation of each gender shall not fall below one-third of membership of the management board'. It is not yet known whether the Directive would be passed by the European Parliament or thereafter implemented properly by Member States but the very fact of its being presented to the European Parliament demonstrates that hard measures are being seriously considered to bring a real difference to the question of gender diversity in the City. Despite the positive impact of the law in countries like Norway where 40% of firms' directors must be women, it seems that the Commission will be wary of accusations of 'back-door' gender rules and the UK will opt for the soft option of requiring companies to publish diversity policies.

**10.97**   The need for quotas has been considered on an informal basis with regard to the legal profession, in terms of whether quotas are necessary to make a meaningful shift to the make-up of the judiciary.[17] It may be that Advocate General Maduro's considerations of full equality in practice will translate to more permissive positive action measures in the future.

## GUIDELINES FOR POSITIVE ACTION IN THE CONTEXT OF THE MODERN WORKPLACE AND ITS INTERACTION WITH THE FAMILY

**10.98**   Of course, the difficulty in putting positive treatment into action comes not from 'soft' options which do disadvantage those who do **not** share the protected characteristic in question – such as additional training, mentoring or shadowing – but from preferential treatment which could result in additional work or extra work opportunities as well as impacting upon salary in the short or long-term. Accordingly it is not possible to give failsafe guidelines in the abstract. Examples are necessarily fact-specific. It is those difficult cases which will be the really important ones, and it is the instances where other colleagues or even clients are not provided with such opportunities and possibly adversely affected by the measures where the balancing test is pivotal, be it telephone

---

[17]   See http://ukscblog.com/women-in-law-getting-through-the-glass-ceiling.

conferencing or moving meetings from 6 pm to 12 pm, or giving the mothers in the office the meetings with clients which involve the least travelling.

**10.99**   There may be employers who point to the provision in the general positive action duty which states that it may not apply to recruitment or promotion cases (section 158(4)(a)), and argue that this renders section 158 meaningless since all such measures are concerned with the positive progress of employees within the workplace which is akin to promotion. Does 'promotion' include training aimed at those who are under-represented in senior positions? It is not obvious that such a training course is clearly being arranged in connection with recruitment or promotion. The definition of recruitment in section 159 includes a 'process for deciding whether to offer employment to a person'. Presumably this would extend the 'process' definition to promotion decisions as well although promotions are not specifically defined in section 159. What the definition does not cover are steps ancillary to such a process, including training, advertising to encourage participation or steps such as reducing membership fees to encourage interest in applications prior to promotion or recruitment processes commencing.

## Parents versus mothers and positive action

**10.100**   Parenthood is not a protected characteristic. Hence it is difficult for employers to take steps under sections 158 or 159 of the Equality Act 2010 which advantage working parents as opposed to purely mothers. Using sex as a protected characteristic in such circumstances only works as long as childcare remains predominantly women's responsibility. If mothers cannot establish that they are disadvantaged by workplace practices, then the preconditions for action are not met. Does the existence of gender as a protected characteristic rather than 'family responsibility' (some of Australia's anti-discrimination statutes prohibit discrimination on the grounds of parental status, see http://www.humanrights.gov.au/info_for_employers/law/index.html) mean that fathers have no rights in the workplace vis-à-vis the new positive action measures?

**10.101**   Ensuring that male employees with primary caring responsibilities had access to equivalent working conditions to colleagues who were mothers was of pivotal significance to the question of proportionality in the CJEU case of *Lommers v Minister van Landbouw, Natuurbeheer en Visserij* [2002] IRLR 430 CJEU.

**10.102**   There, provision of a limited number of subsidised nursery places to female staff only, in a context where the scheme had been set up by the employer to tackle extensive under-representation of women in a workplace characterised by a proven insufficiency of proper, affordable childcare facilities, was found by the Court to be permissible under the Equal Treatment Directive *so long as* male single parents had identical access to the scheme.

**10.103**   So proportionality was not breached by the policy failing to guarantee access to nursery places to employees of both sexes on an equal footing.

**10.104**   How would this case be decided today in the UK? The Dutch Ministry of Agriculture provided nursery places 'only to female employees … save in the case of an emergency.'

**10.105**   This scheme would infringe the Equality Act if implemented in the UK. It is also significant that even where nursery places are limited and it remains a current social and economic fact that far fewer men than women leave the workforce for childcare reasons, such a policy reinforces a stereotype that that childcare remains a woman's responsibility.

**10.106**   Proportionality would be achieved by a gender-neutral policy which conferred the nursery place upon on employees of either sex who could demonstrate they as parents were or had been the primary caregiver. Whilst in practice this might mean that the bulk of those who benefitted from such a scheme were female employees, the scheme would remain lawful under section 158.

# Chapter 11

# KEY PROCEDURES AND GETTING HELP

*Yvette Budé and Sarah Fraser Butlin*

## INTRODUCTION

**11.1** This chapter will consider key procedures in the tribunal and where specialist help can be obtained.

**11.2** It is impossible to deal with all the possible content and detail of the procedural mechanisms of the tribunal. Therefore this chapter is very limited in scope and only seeks to set out the basic principles. Further advice and/or information should be sought. The majority of procedural matters within the Tribunal are set out within Schedule 1 of the Employment Tribunals (Constitution and Rules of Procedure) Regulations 2004 (the Rules).

**11.3** The structure of this chapter will be:

(a)   time limits;

(b)   claim and response forms;

(c)   witnesses and documents;

(d)   questionnaires;

(e)   pre-hearing reviews;

(f)   procedure at the hearing;

(g)   costs; and

(h)   getting help.

**11.4** The final section of this chapter sets out a number of websites where further information can be obtained and a number of organisations who provide free legal advice.

## TIME LIMITS

### Non-discrimination claims

**11.5** With most family-friendly rights issues that are not concerned with discrimination, the time limit is three months from the act complained of. This includes:

(a) breach of contract claim in the tribunal, from the effective date of termination;

(b) unauthorised deductions from wages, from the date of payment of wages from which deduction was made (Employment Rights Act 1996 (ERA), s 23(2), (4));

(c) detriment relating to leave for family or domestic reasons or flexible working, from the date of the act or failure (ERA, s 48(3));

(d) time off for ante-natal, from the date of the appointment (ERA, s 57(2));

(e) time off for dependants, from the date beginning with the date when the failure occurred (ERA, s 57B(2));

(f) suspension from work on medical or maternity grounds, from the first day of suspension (ERA, s 70(2));

(g) parental leave, beginning with the date of the matters complained of (ERA, s 80(2));

(h) flexible working, from the relevant date (ERA, s 80H(5));

(i) unfair dismissal, from the effective date of termination (ERA, s 111(2));

(j) failure or threat to fail to comply with the right to be accompanied at a meeting to discuss flexible working, from the date of the failure or threat (Regulation 15(2) of the Flexible Working Regulations).

**11.6** An extension of time may be allowed for the claims above where the tribunal is satisfied that it was not reasonably practicable for the complaint to be presented before the end of the period of three months. This is a very strict test and the burden of proof rests on the claimant.[1] Where the claimant successfully establishes that it was not reasonably practicable to present the claim in time, they must also satisfy the tribunal that the time it was in fact presented in was reasonable.

**11.7** Where the complaint is under the Part-time Workers (Prevention of Less Favourable Treatment) Regulations 2000 or the Fixed-term Employees

---

[1]    See further *Palmer and Saunders v Southend-on-Sea Borough Council* [1984] ICR 372.

(Prevention of Less Favourable Treatment) Regulations 2002 then the time limit is also three months from the last date of less favourable treatment or detriment. This may be extended where it is just and equitable to do so, see below.

## Discrimination claims

**11.8** Discrimination claims must not be brought 'after the end of the period of three months starting with the date of the act to which the complaint relates' (Equality Act 2010 (EA), s 123(1)(a)). Therefore the act complained of starts the time limit running. The claim must be brought before the end of the three months. This is further extended by section 123(3)(a) and (b) of the EA 2010 which provides that:

(a)   conduct extending over a period is to be treated as done at the end of the period; and

(b)   failure to do something is to be treated as occurring when the person in question decided on it.

**11.9**   In *Hendricks v Metropolitan Police Comr*[2] the Court of Appeal held that the test to determine whether there is a continuing act is whether there was an ongoing situation or continuing state of affairs. One relevant factor is whether the same individuals or different individuals were involved in those incidents.[3]

**11.10**   If an employer applies a discriminatory policy, the act is deemed to continue for as long as the policy applies against the claimant. Consequently, a claimant can bring a claim for a series of failures as a consequence of a discriminatory policy, provided the last failure was within three months of the date the claim was brought.[4] Moreover, a reconsideration of a previous decision may be a further act which causes time to run from the final reconsideration.[5]

**11.11**   Time may be extended where it is just and equitable to do so. This is a very broad discretion, and certainly much broader than the Tribunal has in relation to a 'not reasonably practicable' extension, see above.

**11.12**   The key factors in determining whether to grant an extension include:

(a)   the length of and reasons for the delay;

(b)   the extent to which the cogency of the evidence is likely to be affected by the delay;

---

[2]   [2003] IRLR 96.
[3]   *Aziz v FDA* [2010] EWCA Civ 304.
[4]   *Owusu v London Fire and Civil Defence Authority* [1995] IRLR 574.
[5]   *Cast v Croydon College* [1998] IRLR 318.

(c)   the extent to which the party sued had co-operated with any requests for information;

(d)   the promptness with which the claimant acted once he or she knew of the facts giving rise to the cause of action; and

(e)   the steps taken by the claimant to obtain appropriate professional advice once he or she knew of the possibility of taking action.[6]

## CLAIM AND RESPONSE FORMS

**11.13**   A claim must be brought by using the prescribed form ET1. This is widely available and is online at the Employment Tribunal Service website. The form must contain:

(a)   each claimant's name;

(b)   each claimant's address;

(c)   the name of each person against whom the claim is made (the 'respondent');

(d)   the address of each respondent; and

(e)   details of the claim (rule 1(4)).

**11.14**   A claim may be made either by post, by electronic communication or by personal delivery. The claim should be sent to the appropriate office according to the postcode of the place where the claimant worked: details of the offices are in the booklet accompanying the ET1 form. Where a claim is made online, then the ET1 is automatically forwarded to the correct office.

**11.15**   It is critical that the ET1 contains clear details of the claim to be made. It is particularly important to ensure that all the factual matters that are to be relied on are included. If there is a need to amend the form, it is much easier to persuade a tribunal to exercise their discretion to allow this where the amendment is to 're-label' the facts that have already been pleaded into the correct legal complaint. The process and detail of seeking an amendment to a claim are beyond the scope of the chapter but are dealt with in rules 10(1), 2(q) and 60(1).[7]

**11.16**   The ET1 is sent to the respondent(s) and they must present a response within 28 days of the date when the ET1 was sent to the tribunal. The form

---

6   *British Coal Corpn v Keeble* [1997] IRLR 336, at para 8.
7   See also *Selkent Bus Co Ltd v Moore* [1996] IRLR 661 and *Cocking v Sandhurst (Stationers) Ltd* [1974] ICR 650.

ET3 must be used. It must include the respondent's full name and address, whether or not he/she intends to resist the claim in whole or in part and if so, on what grounds (rule 4(1), (3)).

**11.17** Where the respondent also wishes to present a counterclaim within Article 4 of the Employment Tribunals Extension of Jurisdiction (England and Wales) Order 1994, then this should be made in writing to the tribunal office.

**11.18** A respondent may apply for an extension of time for presenting his response (rule 11). This application must be presented within 28 days of when the ET1 was sent to the respondent and must explain why the extension is required. The extension will only be granted where it is just and equitable to do so (rule 4(4)).

## WITNESSES AND DOCUMENTS

**11.19** Evidence is admissible in a case if it is relevant. Where it is irrelevant, then it is inadmissible. When considering issues of disclosure, documents and witnesses a key consideration is the overriding objective and particularly the questions of saving expense and proportionality. The overarching concern is to ensure that a case is dealt with justly.

**11.20** Generally, once the issues of a case have been clarified, often at a case management discussion, it should be clear whether certain evidence is relevant to those issues or not. The tribunal must then balance the need for sufficient disclosure and discovery to enable the issues in the case to be dealt with fairly and ensuring that any orders for disclosure are not oppressive. This will be a particularly difficult balance to strike where there is a claim relating to a large number of individuals or relating to events over a very long period of time.

**11.21** A tribunal will order standard disclosure of documents. This means that parties must disclose to the other side a list of documents that is in their possession or control which relate to the proceedings. Those documents must include documents on which they rely and which adversely affect their case or support the other side's case. Once the list is sent to the other side, either party may request 'inspection' of any of the documents unless they are marked as privileged. A party may also inspect any document referred to in a statement of case, witness statement or expert report.

**11.22** The duty of disclosure continues throughout the proceedings. Therefore if a document comes to a party's attention during proceedings, they must disclose it to the other side.

**11.23** Where a party considers that the other side has failed to disclose certain documents, or challenges their assertion of privilege, then an application for specific disclosure may be made to the tribunal. This should be made at the case management stage, rather than at the start of a substantive hearing.

**11.24**   Certain documents are excluded from the duty of disclosure. This includes where documents are subject to public interest immunity and where they are legally privileged. Confidentiality alone is not a good ground for refusing disclosure or inspection although certain matters, such as names of individuals, may be redacted where appropriate.

**11.25**   Witnesses are usually required to produce a witness statement prior to the substantive hearing. These should be exchanged according to the orders of the tribunal. The usual practice is to exchange witness statements simultaneously. However, this may be varied according to the particular circumstances of the case.

**11.26**   Where a witness refuses to attend, an order for their attendance may be made. A judge has the power to order attendance of a person, or for them to produce documents or information (rule 10(2)(c) and (d)). They may do this on their own initiative or upon application from a party. The power to issue a witness order is discretionary. The key questions for the tribunal in determining whether to make such an order will be the relevance of the evidence to be given and whether it is necessary to issue an order.[8]

**11.27**   Where a person declines to attend following such an order then they may face criminal sanctions or a fine. Where a party fails to comply with such an order then they may be penalised by an order of costs or the whole or part of their claim or response may be struck out.

## QUESTIONNAIRES

**11.28**   In a discrimination claim, the use of questionnaires can be critical. A person may require a person to answer certain questions where they think they have been discriminated against. The questions should be used to ascertain whether they have been discriminated against and to enable them to formulate their claim properly (EA 2010, s 138).

**11.29**   Certain forms have been provided to enable this and can be found on the EHRC website at: http://www.equalityhumanrights.com/advice-and-guidance/new-equality-act-guidance/taking-a-discrimination-case/. This also provides very helpful practical guidance about using the questionnaire procedure.

**11.30**   A question and answer will be admissible in evidence, whether or not the correct form has been used, provided they are asked within the appropriate time limit. For a question to be admissible, it must be served either before proceedings are begun or before the end of the period of 28 days beginning with the day on which proceedings were begun, or such other period as the

---

[8]   *Dada v Metal Box Co Ltd* [1974] IRLR 251.

tribunal specifies. An answer must be served before the end of eight weeks from the day on which the questionnaire was served.

**11.31** Where an answer is not given, or it is evasive or equivocal, a tribunal may draw an adverse inference against the respondent (EA 2010, s 138(4)).

**11.32** A carefully drafted questionnaire can be of critical importance in establishing whether a claimant has a claim. Similarly, a response must be produced that is accurate and carefully thought through to avoid the risk of adverse inferences being drawn.

## PRE-HEARING REVIEWS

**11.33** A pre-hearing review (PHR) is an interim hearing that is used for a variety of situations (rule 18(2) and (7)). A judge may convene a hearing on his own initiative or a party may request one. Unless the parties agree otherwise, they should be given 14 days' notice of the hearing. A PHR is usually heard by a judge sitting alone, unless a party requests that a full tribunal hears the case or a judge considers that issues of fact are likely to be determined and it would be desirable for a full tribunal to sit (rule 18(3)).

**11.34** PHRs are used to deal with preliminary issues between the parties. This means that they can be used in a large variety of matters. Preliminary issues may include whether a claim has been brought in time, whether a claimant is disabled within the Equality Act 2010, whether parts of a claim should be struck out because they are misconceived and whether a restricted reporting order should be made.

**11.35** A PHR may also determine whether a deposit order should be made. Such an order requires a party to pay a deposit up to £500 as a condition of continuing to participate (rule 20(1)). This may be ordered where the Tribunal considers that the party's arguments have little reasonable prospect of success (rule 20(1)).

## PROCEDURE AT THE HEARING

**11.36** Prior to a full hearing of a claim, there may be a case management discussion. This is conducted by a judge alone. The purpose of the hearing is to define what the issues are between the parties and to set a timetable of what must be done when so that the case is ready for a full hearing (rule 17). On smaller, simpler cases directions may be issued by the tribunal without there being a case management discussion. These will set out dates by which certain matters must be completed, such as documents being disclosed and witness statements being exchanged. If a party fails to comply with the orders, the whole or part of the claim or response may be struck out. There are also potential costs consequences (rule 13).

**11.37** Claims are usually heard by a judge sitting with two lay members. A judge may hear certain claims sitting alone, including pre-hearing reviews and case management discussions. Other cases that may be heard by a judge alone are set out in section 4(2) of the Employment Tribunals Act 1996. In relation to family-friendly rights, the relevant matters might include complaints under section 23 of the ERA 1996, relating to unauthorised deductions from wages, and section 64 regarding remuneration on suspension on medical grounds. However, the majority of claims will be heard by a full tribunal.

**11.38** The judge is legally qualified and sits in the middle of the panel. The judge usually sits with two lay members. One of them will come from a panel of representatives of employers and the other of employees. This is to bring industrial experience to bear on the issues that the Tribunal is determining. Although they come from a particular industrial relations perspective, the lay members must not be partisan and must determine the issues independently and impartially.

**11.39** The lay members have an equal vote to the judge. Therefore, the judge can be outvoted by the lay members.

**11.40** The tribunal is addressed as 'Sir' or 'Madam', as appropriate.

**11.41** At the outset of a hearing, time may be taken to clarify the issues or to deal with the process that will be applied. Generally it is the party on whom the burden of proof lies that will give their evidence first.[9] Therefore, in discrimination cases it is usually the claimant who will start first.

**11.42** The usual format is for the opening party to call his evidence. This means that each witness will give their evidence. This is usually via a prepared witness statement which the witness reads out loud, or the tribunal reads to themselves. Some supplementary questions may be asked of them by the party. They will then be cross-examined by the opposing party or his representative. It is important in cross-examination to put to the witness the matters with which the party disagrees as well as the opposing party's own case. The tribunal will then often ask questions of the witness and at the end, the opening party may ask questions that are arising from any of the earlier questions. This process is repeated for each witness.

**11.43** Once the opening party has completed their evidence, then the opposing party may do the same with their witness. At the end of the case, the parties have the right to make final submissions. The purpose of these submissions is to persuade the tribunal that the party's case is the correct one, highlighting important points of evidence and any matters of law. In England and Wales the opening party will make the final closing submission whereas in Scotland, the opening party usually makes their closing submission first.

---

[9]   *Gill v Harold Andrews Sheepbridge Ltd* [1974] IRLR 109.

**11.44** Generally, witnesses are present in the tribunal room throughout the hearing. However, where a tribunal considers it to be in the interests of justice, they may exclude witnesses from the room before they give evidence (rule 27(4)).

**11.45** The members of a tribunal may intervene in a hearing to a significant extent or very little. It is a matter for them. They may seek to clarify issues or the evidence being given and the judge will generally seek to control the proceedings to ensure that they are conducted appropriately (rule 14(3)). Importantly, where a matter arises that the tribunal considers to be relevant to their decision, they should raise this with the parties. The parties should be given the opportunity to be heard on any such issue, as well as on those issues being raised by the other party.

## Without prejudice communications

**11.46** Parties may not refer to 'without prejudice' communications during proceedings before the tribunal. Such communications are inadmissible and are privileged from disclosure. The rationale behind the rule is to encourage parties to seek to resolve their disputes by agreement and thus to avoid going to court. Therefore, by preventing the communications from being seen by the tribunal, it should allow parties to be freer in what they say.

**11.47** Very often, documents are headed 'without prejudice'. However, this is not decisive. There must be an existing dispute between the parties at the time of the communication, and there must be a genuine attempt to settle that dispute. Where neither of these requirements is fulfilled then the communications will not be privileged.

## Failure to attend

**11.48** Where a party fails to attend or be represented at a hearing, the tribunal may dismiss the proceedings or deal with them in their absence. Alternatively they may adjourn the case (rule 27(5)). Before deciding which route to take, the tribunal must consider the information they have, particularly if they know of any reason why the party has failed to attend. Where a tribunal knows that a party intends to attend but is unable to do so, then they would be wrong to refuse to adjourn. Where a party is unwell, and has informed the tribunal of this fact, the tribunal should advise them that they could apply for an adjournment. Medical evidence is usually required to prove the illness. Costs of the adjournment may follow (see rule 40(1)).

## Judgments, orders and giving reasons

**11.49** When a tribunal has made a decision, they produce either a 'judgment' or an 'order'. A 'judgment' is defined as 'a final determination of the proceedings or of a particular issue in those proceedings, and may include an award of compensation, a declaration or recommendation, and orders for costs, preparation time or wasted costs' (rule 28(1)(a)). An 'order' is defined as requiring 'a person to do or not to do something' (rule 28(1)(b)). An order is generally used for interim decisions such as those at a case management discussion.

**11.50**   Where a judgment is made, reasons must be given. However, reasons are only required to be given in relation to an order if a request is made before or at the hearing at which the order is made (rule 30(1)). Reasons may be oral or in writing.

**11.51**   In relation to a judgment, where oral reasons have been given, a party may request in writing for written reasons to be provided. This request can be made orally at the hearing or in writing within 14 days of the date of the judgment (rule 30(5)). A judge may extend this time limit where it is just and equitable to do so. The EAT may also request them at any time. Written reasons for an order will only be provided when requested by the EAT.

## Power to review judgments and decisions

**11.52**   Certain judgments and decisions may be reviewed by the same judge or tribunal who considered the matter originally. This may be the tribunal or judge acting on their own initiative or upon application by a party. Where a judge undertakes a review on their own motion, they must give notice to the parties of their intention, summarising the grounds on which it is proposed to review the decision and giving them an opportunity to make submissions as to whether a review is an appropriate course of action.

**11.53**   A party may seek a review orally at the hearing or in writing to the tribunal within 14 days of the decision being sent to the parties. This time limit may be extended where it is just and equitable to do so (rule 35(1) and (2)). The application should identify the grounds for the review.

**11.54**   A review may be sought of the following:

(a)   a decision not to accept a claim, response or counterclaim;

(b)   a judgment, other than a default judgment; or

(d)   a decision under rule 6(3), Schedule 4 of the Rules, namely in relation to health and safety prohibition notices (rule 34(1)),

there is a separate review procedure for default judgments, which is dealt with in rule 33.

**11.55**   A decision may be reviewed where:

(a)   the decision was wrongly made as a result of an administrative error;

(b)   a party did not receive notice of the proceedings leading to the decision;

(c)   the decision was made in the absence of a party;

(d)   new evidence has become available since the conclusion of the hearing to which the decision relates and that evidence could not reasonably have been known of or foreseen at the time;

(e)   the interests of justice require such a review (rule 34(3)).

**11.56**   Where the decision to be reviewed relates to the decision not to accept a claim or response, then it can only be reviewed on grounds of an administrative error and the interests of justice.

## Appeals to the EAT

**11.57**   Matters relating to the EAT are not straightforward and advice should be sought before pursuing an appeal. Different procedural rules apply: see EAT Rules 1993 and EAT Practice Direction 2008.

**11.58**   An appeal may only be made about a point of law. This means that there must be an error of law in the tribunal's decision or the decision must be perverse. A decision is perverse where it is one that no reasonable tribunal could reasonably have reached on the evidence before them.

**11.59**   Any appeal must be lodged within 42 days of the date on which the tribunal judgment was sent to the parties. Further information may be obtained from:        http://www.justice.gov.uk/guidance/courts-and-tribunals/tribunals/ employment-appeals/appeals.htm.

## COSTS

**11.60**   Where a case is heard in a Tribunal, each party must usually pay their own legal costs. This means that irrespective of who wins the case, the losing party will not pay the winning party's legal costs.

**11.61**   However, there are certain circumstances where a Tribunal may order one party to pay another's legal costs. Where a party is not legally represented then an order to pay for the preparation time up to, but not including any time at the hearing itself, may be made. That time is costed at £25 per hour (rules 42–45). Orders for wasted costs may also be awarded against representatives but this is not addressed in this section (rule 48).

**11.62**   An order may be made where:

(a)   the paying party has in bringing the proceedings, or he or his representative has in conducting the proceedings, acted vexatiously, abusively, disruptively or otherwise unreasonably; or

(b)   the bringing or conducting of the proceedings by the paying party has been misconceived (rule 40).

**11.63**   As can be seen, this covers a very broad range of conduct and covers the entirety of proceedings, not just the hearing itself. It can include bringing a claim with no discernible basis in law or obviously lacking merit, acting in a way which is costly to the party defending the claim with no real gain for the claimant, excessive time wasting at the hearing and unnecessarily lengthy cross examination of witnesses.

**11.64**   Costs may also be awarded where a party has applied for a postponement or adjournment of the hearing and that has been granted but the other party has incurred costs. Costs in those circumstances are discretionary and may only relate to the costs of the postponement/ adjournment, rather than the whole of proceedings (rule 40(1)). Where an adjournment is caused by the employer not having evidence in relation to a claim in unfair dismissal proceedings to reinstate or re-engage, the Tribunal must make an order for costs unless the employer can evince a reason for their failure (rule 39).

**11.65**   Where a deposit order has previously been made (see **11.35** above), and a Tribunal subsequently dismisses the claim, then they must consider whether to make a costs order. A key consideration is whether their decision to dismiss the claim is on the same grounds as the deposit order was made. If so, then an award is ordinarily made (rule 47).

**11.66**   Similarly, where a party has failed to comply with case management orders then costs may be awarded in relation to those failures.

**11.67**   Nevertheless. the power to award costs is discretionary and the paying party's ability to pay may also be taken into account (rule 41(2)). Where a party threatens the other side with making a costs application, then advice should be sought as to whether that is a real risk or whether it is a tactical point from the other side.

## GETTING HELP

**11.68**   The government has two websites with information on employment:

http://www.direct.gov.uk/en/Employment/index.htm

http://www.bis.gov.uk/employment

**11.69** ACAS and the Equality and Human Rights Commission have information to assist both employees and employers know their legal rights and responsibilities. The following websites provide a lot of information which is easily accessible:

http://www.acas.org.uk

http://www.equalityhumanrights.com/advice-and-guidance/

**11.70** Both ACAS and the Equality and Human Rights Commission also have telephone helplines. These are staffed by people who can provide a limited amount of free advice. The contact details are on the websites above.

**11.71** You may also consider seeking further free advice from the organisations below.

## Citizens Advice Bureaux

**11.72** There are numerous CABs across England and Wales. They provide free advice and information through face to face consultations, telephone advice and via their website. They may also be able to assist in writing letters and making phone calls for clients. Some CAB advisers are specialist employment advisers who can assist with taking cases to Tribunal. However, there are strict criteria for this provision and not every CAB is able to offer this service. A CAB will be able to provide advice or refer a client on to someone who is better able to assist. Their website is www.citizensadvice.org.uk. This website provides a link to their advice website: www.adviceguide.org.uk.

## Law Centres

**11.73** There are a large number of Law Centres around the country which provide free legal advice. They have an advice website which may assist clients with initial enquiries: http://www.advicenow.org.uk/. They also have centres in particular areas with specialist advisors who can meet face to face and discuss the particular issues. The list of Law Centres can be found at: http://www.lawcentres.org.uk/lawcentres/.

## Free Representation Unit

**11.74** The FRU provides assistance with representation at Tribunal hearings. However, they can only provide that assistance where a case has been referred to them by one of their referral agencies. These agencies will be able to provide initial assistance and the list of them is at: http://www.thefru.org.uk/get-advice/list-of-agencies.

## Bar Pro Bono Unit

**11.75**  The BPBU provides assistance from barristers at Tribunal hearings. However, this is only provided where the case has been referred to them by a CAB, local Law Centre or a local MP. Their website is at: http://www.barprobono.org.uk.

**11.76**  As can be seen, some of the agencies above only take referrals from particular sources. Therefore, the telephone helplines at ACAS and EHRC, or visiting the CAB or Law Centre are often the best first step. If one has home contents insurance, then this should also be checked carefully as sometimes this has provision for legal expenses. The CAB or Law Centre will also be able to assist on this.

# APPENDIX A

# EMPLOYMENT RIGHTS ACT 1996

\*\*\*\*

### 3 Note about disciplinary procedures and pensions

(1) A statement under section 1 shall include a note –

   (a)   specifying any disciplinary rules applicable to the employee or referring the employee to the provisions of a document specifying such rules which is reasonably accessible to the employee,

   (aa)  specifying any procedure applicable to the taking of disciplinary decisions relating to the employee, or to a decision to dismiss the employee, or referring the employee to the provisions of a document specifying such a procedure which is reasonably accessible to the employee,

   (b)   specifying (by description or otherwise) –

       (i)   a person to whom the employee can apply if dissatisfied with any disciplinary decision relating to him or any decision to dismiss him, and

       (ii)  a person to whom the employee can apply for the purpose of seeking redress of any grievance relating to his employment,

and the manner in which any such application should be made, and

   (c)   where there are further steps consequent on any such application, explaining those steps or referring to the provisions of a document explaining them which is reasonably accessible to the employee.

(2) Subsection (1) does not apply to rules, disciplinary decisions, decisions to dismiss, grievances or procedures relating to health or safety at work.

(3) (*repealed*)

(4) (*repealed*)

(5) The note shall also state whether there is in force a contracting-out certificate (issued in accordance with Chapter 1 of Part III of the Pension Schemes Act 1993) stating that the employment is contracted-out employment (for the purposes of that Part of that Act).

**Amendments**—Employment Act 2002, s 35(1), (2).

### 4 Statement of changes

(1) If, after the material date, there is a change in any of the matters particulars of which are required by sections 1 to 3 to be included or referred to in a statement under section 1, the employer shall give to the employee a written statement containing particulars of the change.

(2) For the purposes of subsection (1) –

    (a)    in relation to a matter particulars of which are included or referred to in a statement given under section 1 otherwise than in instalments, the material date is the date to which the statement relates,

    (b)    in relation to a matter particulars of which –

        (i)    are included or referred to in an instalment of a statement given under section 1, or

        (ii)    are required by section 2(4) to be included in a single document but are not included in an instalment of a statement given under section 1 which does include other particulars to which that provision applies,

the material date is the date to which the instalment relates, and

    (c)    in relation to any other matter, the material date is the date by which a statement under section 1 is required to be given.

(3) A statement under subsection (1) shall be given at the earliest opportunity and, in any event, not later than –

    (a)    one month after the change in question, or

    (b)    where that change results from the employee being required to work outside the United Kingdom for a period of more than one month, the time when he leaves the United Kingdom in order to begin so to work, if that is earlier.

(4) A statement under subsection (1) may refer the employee to the provisions of some other document which is reasonably accessible to the employee for a change in any of the matters specified in sections 1(4)(d)(ii) and (iii) and 3(1)(a) and (c).

(5) A statement under subsection (1) may refer the employee for a change in either of the matters specified in section 1(4)(e) to the law or to the provisions of any collective agreement directly affecting the terms and conditions of the employment which is reasonably accessible to the employee.

(6) Where, after an employer has given to an employee a statement under section 1, either –

    (a)    the name of the employer (whether an individual or a body corporate or partnership) is changed without any change in the identity of the employer, or

    (b)    the identity of the employer is changed in circumstances in which the continuity of the employee's period of employment is not broken,

and subsection (7) applies in relation to the change, the person who is the employer immediately after the change is not required to give to the employee a statement under section 1; but the change shall be treated as a change falling within subsection (1) of this section.

(7) This subsection applies in relation to a change if it does not involve any change in any of the matters (other than the names of the parties) particulars of which are required by sections 1 to 3 to be included or referred to in the statement under section 1.

(8) A statement under subsection (1) which informs an employee of a change such as is referred to in subsection (6)(b) shall specify the date on which the employee's period of continuous employment began.

\*\*\*\*

# PART II
# PROTECTION OF WAGES

*Deductions by employer*

### 13 Right not to suffer unauthorised deductions

(1) An employer shall not make a deduction from wages of a worker employed by him unless –

    (a)  the deduction is required or authorised to be made by virtue of a statutory provision or a relevant provision of the worker's contract, or

    (b)  the worker has previously signified in writing his agreement or consent to the making of the deduction.

(2) In this section "relevant provision", in relation to a worker's contract, means a provision of the contract comprised –

    (a)  in one or more written terms of the contract of which the employer has given the worker a copy on an occasion prior to the employer making the deduction in question, or

    (b)  in one or more terms of the contract (whether express or implied and, if express, whether oral or in writing) the existence and effect, or combined effect, of which in relation to the worker the employer has notified to the worker in writing on such an occasion.

(3) Where the total amount of wages paid on any occasion by an employer to a worker employed by him is less than the total amount of the wages properly payable by him to the worker on that occasion (after deductions), the amount of the deficiency shall be treated for the purposes of this Part as a deduction made by the employer from the worker's wages on that occasion.

(4) Subsection (3) does not apply in so far as the deficiency is attributable to an error of any description on the part of the employer affecting the computation by him of the gross amount of the wages properly payable by him to the worker on that occasion.

(5) For the purposes of this section a relevant provision of a worker's contract having effect by virtue of a variation of the contract does not operate to authorise the making of a deduction on account of any conduct of the worker, or any other event occurring, before the variation took effect.

(6) For the purposes of this section an agreement or consent signified by a worker does not operate to authorise the making of a deduction on account of any conduct of the worker, or any other event occurring, before the agreement or consent was signified.

(7) This section does not affect any other statutory provision by virtue of which a sum payable to a worker by his employer but not constituting "wages" within the meaning of this Part is not to be subject to a deduction at the instance of the employer.

\*\*\*\*

*Cash shortages and stock deficiencies in retail employment*

**17 Introductory**

(1) In the following provisions of this Part –

"cash shortage" means a deficit arising in relation to amounts received in connection with retail transactions, and
"stock deficiency" means a stock deficiency arising in the course of retail transactions.

(2) In the following provisions of this Part "retail employment", in relation to a worker, means employment involving (whether or not on a regular basis) –

(a)    the carrying out by the worker of retail transactions directly with members of the public or with fellow workers or other individuals in their personal capacities, or
(b)    the collection by the worker of amounts payable in connection with retail transactions carried out by other persons directly with members of the public or with fellow workers or other individuals in their personal capacities.

(3) References in this section to a "retail transaction" are to the sale or supply of goods or the supply of services (including financial services).

(4) References in the following provisions of this Part to a deduction made from wages of a worker in retail employment, or to a payment received from such a worker by his employer, on account of a cash shortage or stock deficiency include references to a deduction or payment so made or received on account of –

(a)    any dishonesty or other conduct on the part of the worker which resulted in any such shortage or deficiency, or
(b)    any other event in respect of which he (whether or not together with any other workers) has any contractual liability and which so resulted,
in each case whether or not the amount of the deduction or payment is designed to reflect the exact amount of the shortage or deficiency.

(5) References in the following provisions of this Part to the recovery from a worker of an amount in respect of a cash shortage or stock deficiency accordingly include references to the recovery from him of an amount in respect of any such conduct or event as is mentioned in subsection (4)(a) or (b).

(6) In the following provisions of this Part "pay day", in relation to a worker, means a day on which wages are payable to the worker.

## 18 Limits on amount and time of deductions

(1) Where (in accordance with section 13) the employer of a worker in retail employment makes, on account of one or more cash shortages or stock deficiencies, a deduction or deductions from wages payable to the worker on a pay day, the amount or aggregate amount of the deduction or deductions shall not exceed one-tenth of the gross amount of the wages payable to the worker on that day.

(2) Where the employer of a worker in retail employment makes a deduction from the worker's wages on account of a cash shortage or stock deficiency, the employer shall not be treated as making the deduction in accordance with section 13 unless (in addition to the requirements of that section being satisfied with respect to the deduction) –

(a) the deduction is made, or
(b) in the case of a deduction which is one of a series of deductions relating to the shortage or deficiency, the first deduction in the series was made,

not later than the end of the relevant period.

(3) In subsection (2) "the relevant-period" means the period of twelve months beginning with the date when the employer established the existence of the shortage or deficiency or (if earlier) the date when he ought reasonably to have done so.

\*\*\*\*

*Enforcement*

## 23 Complaints to employment tribunals

(1) A worker may present a complaint to an employment tribunal –

(a) that his employer has made a deduction from his wages in contravention of section 13 (including a deduction made in contravention of that section as it applies by virtue of section 18(2)),
(b) that his employer has received from him a payment in contravention of section 15 (including a payment received in contravention of that section as it applies by virtue of section 20(1)),
(c) that his employer has recovered from his wages by means of one or more deductions falling within section 18(1) an amount or aggregate amount exceeding the limit applying to the deduction or deductions under that provision, or
(d) that his employer has received from him in pursuance of one or more demands for payment made (in accordance with section 20) on a particular pay day, a payment or payments of an amount or aggregate amount exceeding the limit applying to the demand or demands under section 21(1).

(2) Subject to subsection (4), an employment tribunal shall not consider a complaint under this section unless it is presented before the end of the period of three months beginning with –

  (a)   in the case of a complaint relating to a deduction by the employer, the date of payment of the wages from which the deduction was made, or

  (b)   in the case of a complaint relating to a payment received by the employer, the date when the payment was received.

(3) Where a complaint is brought under this section in respect of –

  (a)   a series of deductions or payments, or

  (b)   a number of payments falling within subsection (1)(d) and made in pursuance of demands for payment subject to the same limit under section 21(1) but received by the employer on different dates,

the references in subsection (2) to the deduction or payment are to the last deduction or payment in the series or to the last of the payments so received.

(3A) Section 207A(3) (extension because of mediation in certain European cross-border disputes) applies for the purposes of subsection (2).

(4) Where the employment tribunal is satisfied that it was not reasonably practicable for a complaint under this section to be presented before the end of the relevant period of three months, the tribunal may consider the complaint if it is presented within such further period as the tribunal considers reasonable.

(5) No complaint shall be presented under this section in respect of any deduction made in contravention of section 86 of the Trade Union and Labour Relations (Consolidation) Act 1992 (deduction of political fund contribution where certificate of exemption or objection has been given).

**Amendments**—Employment Rights (Dispute Resolution) Act 1998, s 1(2)(a); SI 1998/1658, art 2(1), Sch 1; SI 2011/1133, regs 30, 32.

\*\*\*\*

### 25  Determinations: supplementary

(1) Where, in the case of any complaint under section 23(1)(a), a tribunal finds that, although neither of the conditions set out in section 13(1)(a) and (b) was satisfied with respect to the whole amount of the deduction, one of those conditions was satisfied with respect to any lesser amount, the amount of the deduction shall for the purposes of section 24(a) be treated as reduced by the amount with respect to which that condition was satisfied.

(2) Where, in the case of any complaint under section 23(1)(b), a tribunal finds that, although neither of the conditions set out in section 15(1)(a) and (b) was satisfied with respect to the whole amount of the payment, one of those conditions was satisfied with respect to any lesser amount, the amount of the payment shall for the purposes of section 24(b) be treated as reduced by the amount with respect to which that condition was satisfied.

(3) An employer shall not under section 24 be ordered by a tribunal to pay or repay to a worker any amount in respect of a deduction or payment, or in respect of any combination of deductions or payments, in so far as it appears to the tribunal that he has already paid or repaid any such amount to the worker.

(4) Where a tribunal has under section 24 ordered an employer to pay or repay to a worker any amount in respect of a particular deduction or payment falling within section 23(1)(a) to (d), the amount which the employer is entitled to recover (by whatever means) in respect of the matter in relation to which the deduction or payment was originally made or received shall be treated as reduced by that amount.

(5) Where a tribunal has under section 24 ordered an employer to pay or repay to a worker any amount in respect of any combination of deductions or payments falling within section 23(1)(c) or (d), the aggregate amount which the employer is entitled to recover (by whatever means) in respect of the cash shortages or stock deficiencies in relation to which the deductions or payments were originally made or required to be made shall be treated as reduced by that amount.

\*\*\*\*

# PART IV
## SUNDAY WORKING FOR SHOP AND BETTING WORKERS

\*\*\*\*

### 39 Reduction of pay etc

(1) This section applies where –

   (a)   under the contract of employment under which a shop worker or betting worker who satisfies section 36(2)(a) was employed on the day before the relevant commencement date, the shop worker or betting worker was, or might have been, required to work on Sunday before the relevant commencement date,

   (b)   the shop worker has done shop work, or the betting worker has done betting work, on Sunday in that employment (whether or not before that date) but has, on or after that date, ceased to do so, and

   (c)   it is not apparent from the contract what part of the remuneration payable, or of any other benefit accruing, to the shop worker or betting worker was intended to be attributable to shop work, or betting work, on Sunday.

(2) So long as the shop worker remains a protected shop worker, or the betting worker remains a protected betting worker, the contract shall be regarded as enabling the employer to reduce the amount of remuneration paid, or the extent of the other benefit provided, to the shop worker or betting worker in respect of any period by the relevant proportion.

(3)  In subsection (2) "the relevant proportion" means the proportion which the hours of shop work, or betting work, which (apart from this Part) the shop worker, or betting worker, could have been required to do on Sunday in the period ("the contractual Sunday hours") bears to the aggregate of those hours and the hours of work actually done by the shop worker, or betting worker, in the period.

(4)  Where, under the contract of employment, the hours of work actually done on weekdays in any period would be taken into account determining the contractual Sunday hours, they shall be taken into account in determining the contractual Sunday hours for the purposes of subsection (3).

(5)  For the purposes of section 36(2)(b), the appropriate date in relation to this section is the end of the period in respect of which the remuneration is paid or the benefit accrues.

\*\*\*\*

### 41  Opted-out shop workers and betting workers

(1)  Subject to subsection (2), a shop worker or betting worker is regarded as "opted-out" for the purposes of any provision of this (and only if) –

> (a)   he has given his employer an opting-out notice,
> (b)   he has been continuously employed during the period beginning with the day on which the notice was given and ending with the day which, in relation to the provision concerned, is the appropriate date, and
> (c)   throughout that period, or throughout every part of it during which his relations with his employer were governed by a contract of employment, he was a shop worker or a betting worker.

(2)  A shop worker is not an opted-out shop worker, and a betting worker is not an opted out betting worker, if –

> (a)   after giving the opting-out notice concerned, he has given his employer an opting-in notice, and
> (b)   after giving the opting-in notice, he has expressly agreed with his employer to do shop work, or betting work, on Sunday or on a particular Sunday.

(3)  In this Act "notice period", in relation to an opted-out shop worker or an opted-out betting worker, means, subject to section 42(2), the period of three months beginning with the day on which the opting-out notice concerned was given.

\*\*\*\*

### 47E  Flexible working

(1)  An employee has the right not to be subjected to any detriment by any act, or any deliberate failure to act, by his employer done on the ground that the employee –

> (a)   made (or proposed to make) an application under section 80F,

(b)     exercised (or proposed to exercise) a right conferred on him under section 80G,

(c)     brought proceedings against the employer under section 80H, or

(d)     alleged the existence of any circumstance which would constitute a ground for bringing such proceedings.

(2) This section does not apply where the detriment in question amounts to dismissal within the meaning of Part 10.

**Amendments**—Inserted by the Employment Act 2002, s 47(1), (3).

\*\*\*\*

## Enforcement

### 48  Complaints to employment tribunals

(1) An employee may present a complaint to an employment tribunal that he has been subjected to a detriment in contravention of section 43M, 44, 45, 46, 47, 47A, 47C or 47E, 47E or 47F.

(1ZA) A worker may present a complaint to an employment tribunal that he has been subjected to a detriment in contravention of section 45A.

(1A) A worker may present a complaint to an employment tribunal that he has been subjected to a detriment in contravention of section 47B.

(1B) A person may present a complaint to an employment tribunal that he has been subjected to a detriment in contravention of section 47D.

(2) On such a complaint it is for the employer to show the ground on which any act, or deliberate failure to act, was done.

(3) An employment tribunal shall not consider a complaint under this section unless it is presented –

(a)     before the end of the period of three months beginning with the date of the act or failure to act to which the complaint relates or, where that act or failure is part of a series of similar acts or failures, the last of them, or

(b)     within such further period as the tribunal considers reasonable in a case where it is satisfied that it was not reasonably practicable for the complaint to be presented before the end of that period of three months.

(4) For the purposes of subsection (3) –

(a)     where an act extends over a period, the "date of the act" means the last day of that period, and

(b)     a deliberate failure to act shall be treated as done when it was decided on;

and, in the absence of evidence establishing the contrary, an employer shall be taken to decide on a failure to act when he does an act inconsistent with doing the failed act or, if he has done no such inconsistent act, when the period expires within which he might reasonably have been expected do the failed act if it was to be done.

(4A) Section 207A(3) (extension because of mediation in certain European cross-border disputes) applies for the purposes of subsection (3)(a).

(5) In this section and section 49 any reference to the employer includes, where a person complains that he has been subjected to a detriment in contravention of section 47A, the principal (within the meaning of section 63A(3)).

**Amendments**—Employment Rights (Dispute Resolution) Act 1998, s 1(2)(b); Employment Relations Act 2004, s 40(2); Teaching and Higher Education Act 1998, s 44(1), Sch 3, para 11(a); Employment Relations Act 1999, s 9, Sch 4, Pt III, paras 5, 9; Employment Act 2002, s 53, Sch 7, paras 24, 27; Apprenticeships, Skills, Children and Learning Act 2009, s 40(5), Sch 1, paras 1, 2; Employment Relations Act 2004, s 41(3); SI 1998/1833, reg 31(2); Public Interest Disclosure Act 1998, s 3; , art 2; Tax Credits Act 2002, s 27, Sch 1, para 1(1), (3); SI 1999/1547; SI 2011/1133.

\*\*\*\*

*Ante-natal care*

## 55 Right to time off for ante-natal care

(1) An employee who –

    (a)    is pregnant, and

    (b)    has, on the advice of a registered medical practitioner, registered midwife or registered nurse, made an appointment to attend at any place for the purpose of receiving ante-natal care,

is entitled to be permitted by her employer to take time off during the employee's working hours in order to enable her to keep the appointment.

(2) An employee is not entitled to take time off under this section to keep an appointment unless, if her employer requests her to do so, she produces for his inspection –

    (a)    a certificate from a registered medical practitioner, registered midwife or registered nurse stating that the employee is pregnant, and

    (b)    an appointment card or some other document showing that the appointment has been made.

(3) Subsection (2) does not apply where the employee's appointment is the first appointment during her pregnancy for which she seek permission to take time off in accordance with subsection (1).

(4) For the purposes of this section the working hours of an employee shall be taken to be any time when, in accordance with her contract of employment, the employee is required to be at work.

(5) References in this section to a registered nurse are to such a nurse –

    (a)    who is also registered in the Specialist Community Public Health Nurses' Part of the register maintained under article 5 of the Nursing and Midwifery Order 2001, and

(b)  whose entry in that Part of the register is annotated to show that he holds a qualification in health visiting.

**Amendments**—SI 2002/253; SI 2004/1771.

## 56  Right to remuneration for time off under section 55

(1) An employee who is permitted to take time off under section 55 is entitled to be paid remuneration by her employer for the period of absence at the appropriate hourly rate.

(2) The appropriate hourly rate, in relation to an employee, is the amount of one week's pay divided by the number of normal working hours in a week for that employee when employed under the contract of employment in force on the day when the time off is taken.

(3) But where the number of normal working hours differs from week to week or over a longer period, the amount of one week's pay shall be divided instead by –

(a)  the average number of normal working hours calculated by dividing by twelve the total number of the employee's normal working hours during the period of twelve weeks ending with the last complete week before the day on which the time off taken, or

(b)  where the employee has not been employed for a sufficient period to enable the calculation to be made under paragraph (a), a number which fairly represents the number of normal working hours in a week having regard to such of the considerations specified in subsection (4) as are appropriate in the circumstances.

(4) The considerations referred to in subsection (3)(b) are –

(a)  the average number of normal working hours in a week which the employee could expect in accordance with the terms of her contract, and

(b)  the average number of normal working hours of other employees engaged in relevant comparable employment with the same employer.

(5) A right to any amount under subsection (1) does not affect any right of an employee in relation to remuneration under her contract of employment ("contractual remuneration").

(6) Any contractual remuneration paid to an employee in respect of a period of time off under section 55 goes towards discharging any liability of the employer to pay remuneration under subsection (1) in respect of that period; and, conversely, any payment of remuneration under subsection (1) in respect of a period goes towards discharging any liability of the employer to pay contractual remuneration in respect of that period.

## 57  Complaints to employment tribunals

(1) An employee may present a complaint to an employment tribunal that her employer –

(a)    has unreasonably refused to permit her to take time off as required by section 55, or

(b)    has failed to pay the whole or any part of any amount to which the employee is entitled under section 56.

(2) An employment tribunal shall not consider a complaint under this action unless it is presented –

(a)    before the end of the period of three months beginning with the date of the appointment concerned, or

(b)    within such further period as the tribunal considers reasonable in a case where it is satisfied that it was not reasonably practicable for the complaint to be presented before the end of that period of three months.

(2A) Section 207A(3) (extension because of mediation in certain European cross-border disputes) applies for the purposes of subsection (3)(a).

(3) Where an employment tribunal finds a complaint under this section well-founded, the tribunal shall make a declaration to that effect.

(4) If the complaint is that the employer has unreasonably refused to permit the employee to take time off, the tribunal shall also order the employer to pay to the employee an amount equal to the remuneration to which she would have been entitled under section 56 if the employer had not refused.

(5) If the complaint is that the employer has failed to pay the employee the whole or part of any amount to which she is entitled under section 56, the tribunal shall also order the employer to pay to the employee the amount which it finds due to her.

**Amendments**—Employment Rights (Dispute Resolution) Act 1998, s 1(2)(b); SI 2011/1133.

*Ante-natal care: agency workers*

**57ZA  Right to time off for ante-natal care (agency workers)**

(1) An agency worker who –

(a)    is pregnant, and

(b)    has, on the advice of a registered medical practitioner, registered midwife or registered nurse, made an appointment to attend at any place for the purpose of receiving ante-natal care,

is entitled to be permitted, by the temporary work agency and the hirer, to take time off during the agency worker's working hours in order to enable her to keep the appointment.

(2) An agency worker is not entitled to be permitted by either of those persons to take time off under this section to keep an appointment unless, if that person requests her to do so, she produces for that person's inspection –

(a)    a certificate from a registered medical practitioner, registered midwife or registered nurse stating that the agency worker is pregnant, and

(b) an appointment card or some other document showing that the appointment has been made.

(3) Subsection (2) does not apply where the agency worker's appointment is the first appointment during her pregnancy for which she seeks permission to take time off in accordance with subsection (1).

(4) For the purposes of this section the working hours of an agency worker shall be taken to be any time when, in accordance with the terms under which the agency worker works temporarily for and under the supervision and direction of the hirer, the agency worker is required to be at work.

(5) In this section references to a registered nurse have the same meaning as in section 55.

**Amendments**—Inserted by SI 2010/93

*Ante-natal care: agency workers*

**57ZB Right to remuneration for time off under section 57ZA**

(1) An agency worker who is permitted to take time off under section 57ZA is entitled to be paid remuneration by the temporary work agency for the period of absence at the appropriate hourly rate.

(2) The appropriate hourly rate, in relation to an agency worker, is the amount of one week's pay divided by the number of normal working hours in a week for that agency worker in accordance with the terms under which the agency worker works temporarily for and under the supervision and direction of the hirer that are in force on the day when the time off is taken.

(3) But where the number of normal working hours during the assignment differs from week to week or over a longer period, the amount of one week's pay shall be divided instead by the average number of normal working hours calculated by dividing by twelve the total number of the agency worker's normal working hours during the period of twelve weeks ending with the last complete week before the day on which the time off is taken.

(4) A right to any amount under subsection (1) does not affect any right of an agency worker in relation to remuneration under her contract with the temporary work agency ("contractual remuneration").

(5) Any contractual remuneration paid to an agency worker in respect of a period of time off under section 57ZA goes towards discharging any liability of the temporary work agency to pay remuneration under subsection (1) in respect of that period; and, conversely, any payment of remuneration under subsection (1) in respect of a period goes towards discharging any liability of the temporary work agency to pay contractual remuneration in respect of that period.

**Amendments**—Inserted by SI 2010/93.

**57ZC  Complaint to employment tribunal: agency workers**

(1) An agency worker may present a complaint to an employment tribunal that the temporary work agency –

    (a)    has unreasonably refused to permit her to take time off as required by section 57ZA, or

    (b)    has failed to pay the whole or any part of any amount to which she is entitled under section 57ZB.

(2) An agency worker may present a complaint to an employment tribunal that the hirer has unreasonably refused to permit her to take time off as required by section 57ZA.

(3) An employment tribunal shall not consider a complaint under subsection (1) or (2) unless it is presented –

    (a)    before the end of the period of three months beginning with the date of the appointment concerned, or

    (b)    within such further period as the tribunal considers reasonable in a case where it is satisfied that it was not reasonably practicable for the complaint to be presented before the end of that period of three months.

(4) Where an employment tribunal finds a complaint under this section well-founded, the tribunal shall make a declaration to that effect.

(5) If the complaint is that the temporary work agency or hirer has unreasonably refused to permit the agency worker to take time off, the tribunal shall also order payment to the agency worker of an amount equal to the remuneration to which she would have been entitled under section 57ZB if she had not been refused the time off.

(6) Where the tribunal orders payment under subsection (5), the amount payable by each party shall be such as may be found by the tribunal to be just and equitable having regard to the extent of each respondent's responsibility for the infringement to which the complaint relates.

(7) If the complaint is that the temporary work agency has failed to pay the agency worker the whole or part of any amount to which she is entitled under section 57ZB, the tribunal shall also order the temporary work agency to pay to the agency worker the amount which it finds due to her.

**Amendments**—Inserted by SI 2010/93.

**57ZD  Agency workers: supplementary**

(1) Without prejudice to any other duties of the hirer or temporary work agency under any enactment or rule of law sections 57ZA to 57ZC do not apply where the agency worker –

    (a)    has not completed the qualifying period, or

(b)   is no longer entitled to the rights conferred by regulation 5 of the Agency Workers Regulations 2010 pursuant to regulation 8(a) or (b) of those Regulations.

(2) Nothing in those sections imposes a duty on the hirer or temporary work agency beyond the original intended duration, or likely duration of the assignment, whichever is the longer.

(3) Those sections do not apply where sections 55 to 57 apply.

(4) In this section and sections 57ZA to 57ZC the following have the same meaning as in the Agency Workers Regulations 2010 –

"agency worker";
"assignment";
"hirer";
"qualifying period";
"temporary work agency".

**Amendments**—Inserted by SI 2010/93.

*Dependants*

### 57A   Time off for dependants

(1) An employee is entitled to be permitted by his employer to take a reasonable amount of time off during the employee's working hours in order to take action which is necessary –

(a)   to provide assistance on an occasion when a dependant falls ill, gives birth or is injured or assaulted,

(b)   to make arrangements for the provision of care for a dependant who is ill or injured,

(c)   in consequence of the death of a dependant,

(d)   because of the unexpected disruption or termination of arrangements for the care of a dependant, or

(e)   to deal with an incident which involves a child of the employee and which occurs unexpectedly in a period during which an educational establishment which the child attends is responsible for him.

(2) Subsection (1) does not apply unless the employee –

(a)   tells his employer the reason for his absence as soon as reasonably practicable, and

(b)   except where paragraph (a) cannot be complied with until after the employee has returned to work, tells his employer for how long he expects to be absent.

(3) Subject to subsections (4) and (5), for the purposes of this section "dependant" means, in relation to an employee –

(a)   a spouse or civil partner,

(b)   a child,

(c)   a parent,

(d)    a person who lives in the same household as the employee, otherwise than by reason of being his employee, tenant, lodger or boarder.

(4) For the purposes of subsection (1)(a) or (b) "dependant" includes, in addition to the persons mentioned in subsection (3), any person who reasonably relies on the employee –

(a)    for assistance on an occasion when the person falls ill or is injured or assaulted, or
(b)    to make arrangements for the provision of care in the event of illness or injury.

(5) For the purposes of subsection (1)(d) "dependant" includes, in addition to the persons mentioned in subsection (3), any person who reasonably relies on the employee to make arrangements for the provision of care.

(6) A reference in this section to illness or injury includes a reference to mental illness or injury.

**Amendments**—Employment Relations Act 1999, s 8, Sch 4, Pt II; Civil Partnership Act 2004, s 261(1), Sch 27, para 151.

## 57B  Complaint to employment tribunal

(1) An employee may present a complaint to an employment tribunal that his employer has unreasonably refused to permit him to take time off as required by section 57A.

(2) An employment tribunal shall not consider a complaint under this section unless it is presented –

(a)    before the end of the period of three months beginning with the date when the refusal occurred, or
(b)    within such further period as the tribunal considers reasonable in a case where it is satisfied that it was not reasonably practicable for the complaint to be presented before the end of that period of three months.

(2A) Section 207A(3) (extension because of mediation in certain European cross-border disputes) applies for the purposes of subsection (2)(a).

(3) Where an employment tribunal finds a complaint under subsection (1) well-founded, it –

(a)    shall make a declaration to that effect, and
(b)    may make an award of compensation to be paid by the employer to the employee.

(4) The amount of compensation shall be such as the tribunal considers just and equitable in all the circumstances having regard to –

(a)    the employer's default in refusing to permit time off to be taken by the employee, and
(b)    any loss sustained by the employee which is attributable to the matters complained of.

**Amendments**—Inserted by the Employment Relations Act 1999, s 8, Sch 4, Pt II; SI 2011/1133.

\*\*\*\*

*Suspension on maternity grounds*

## 66 Meaning of suspension on maternity grounds

(1) For the purposes of this Part an employee is suspended from work on maternity grounds if, in consequence of any relevant requirement or relevant recommendation, she is suspended from work by her employer on the ground that she is pregnant, has recently given birth or is breastfeeding a child.

(2) In subsection (1) –

"relevant requirement" means a requirement imposed by or under a specified provision of an enactment or of an instrument made under an enactment, and

"relevant recommendation" means a recommendation in a specified provision of a code of practice issued or approved under section 16 of the Health and Safety at Work etc Act 1974;

and in this subsection "specified provision" means a provision for the time being specified in an order made by the Secretary of State under this subsection.

(3) For the purposes of this Part an employee shall be regarded as suspended from work on maternity grounds only if and for so long as she –

(a)  continues to be employed by her employer, but

(b)  is not provided with work or (disregarding alternative work for the purposes of section 67) does not perform the work she normally performed before the suspension.

## 67 Right to offer of alternative work

(1) Where an employer has available suitable alternative work for an employee, the employee has a right to be offered to be provided with the alternative work before being suspended from work on maternity grounds.

(2) For alternative work to be suitable for an employee for the purposes of this section –

(a)  the work must be of a kind which is both suitable in relation to her and appropriate for her to do in the circumstances, and

(b)  the terms and conditions applicable to her for performing the work, if they differ from the corresponding terms and conditions applicable to her for performing the work she normally performs under her contract of employment, must not be substantially less favourable to her than those corresponding terms and conditions.

## 68  Right to remuneration

(1) An employee who is suspended from work on maternity grounds is entitled to be paid remuneration by her employer while she is so suspended.

(2) An employee is not entitled to remuneration under this section in respect of any period if –

    (a)    her employer has offered to provide her during the period with work which is suitable alternative work for her for the purposes of section 67, and

    (b)    the employee has unreasonably refused to perform that work.

*Ending the supply of an agency worker on maternity grounds*

## 68A  Meaning of ending the supply of an agency worker on maternity grounds

(1) For the purposes of this Part the supply of an agency worker to a hirer is ended on maternity grounds if, in consequence of action taken pursuant to a provision listed in subsection (2), the supply of the agency worker to the hirer is ended on the ground that she is pregnant, has recently given birth or is breastfeeding a child.

(2) The provisions are –

    (a)    regulations 8(3) or 9(2) of the Merchant Shipping and Fishing Vessels (Health and Safety at Work) Regulations 1997;

    (b)    regulation 16A(2) or 17A of the Management of Health and Safety at Work Regulations 1999; or

    (c)    regulation 20 of the Conduct of Employment Agencies and Employment Businesses Regulations 2003.

**Amendments**—Inserted by SI 2010/93.

## 68B  Right to offer of alternative work

(1) Where the supply of an agency worker to a hirer is ended on maternity grounds and the temporary work agency has available suitable alternative work, the agency worker has a right to be offered to be proposed for such alternative work.

(2) For alternative work to be suitable for an agency worker for the purposes of this section –

    (a)    the work must be of a kind which is both suitable in relation to her and appropriate for her to do in the circumstances, and

    (b)    the terms and conditions applicable to her whilst performing the work, if they differ from the corresponding terms and conditions which would have applied to her but for the fact that the supply of the agency worker to the hirer was ended on maternity grounds, must not be substantially less favourable to her than those corresponding terms and conditions.

(3) Subsection (1) does not apply –

(a) where the agency worker has confirmed in writing that she no longer requires the work-finding services of the temporary work agency, or

(b) beyond the original intended duration, or likely duration, whichever is the longer, of the assignment which ended when the supply of the agency worker to the hirer was ended on maternity grounds.

**Amendments**—Inserted by SI 2010/93.

### 68C Right to remuneration

(1) Where the supply of an agency worker to a hirer is ended on maternity grounds, that agency worker is entitled to be paid remuneration by the temporary work agency.

(2) An agency worker is not entitled to remuneration under this section in respect of any period if –

(a) the temporary work agency has –
   (i) offered to propose the agency worker to a hirer that has alternative work available which is suitable alternative work for her for the purposes of section 68B, or
   (ii) proposed the agency worker to a hirer that has such suitable alternative work available, and that hirer has agreed to the supply of that agency worker, and

(b) the agency worker has unreasonably refused that offer or to perform that work.

(3) Nothing in this section imposes a duty on the temporary work agency to pay remuneration beyond the original intended duration, or likely duration, whichever is the longer, of the assignment which ended when the supply of the agency worker to the hirer was ended on maternity grounds.

**Amendments**—Inserted by SI 2010/93.

\*\*\*\*

### 69A Calculation of remuneration (agency workers)

(1) The amount of remuneration payable by a temporary work agency to an agency worker under section 68C is a week's pay in respect of each week for which remuneration is payable in accordance with section 68C; and if in any week remuneration is payable in respect of only part of that week the amount of a week's pay shall be reduced proportionately.

(2) A right to remuneration under section 68C does not affect any right of the agency worker in relation to remuneration under the contract with the temporary work agency ("contractual remuneration").

(3) Any contractual remuneration paid by the temporary work agency to an agency worker in respect of any period goes towards discharging the temporary work agency's liability under section 68C in respect of that period; and, conversely, any payment of remuneration in discharge of a temporary work

agency's liability under section 68C in respect of any period goes towards discharging any obligation of the temporary work agency to pay contractual remuneration in respect of that period.

(4) For the purposes of subsection (1), a week's pay is the weekly amount that would have been payable to the agency worker for performing the work, according to the terms of the contract with the temporary work agency, but for the fact that the supply of the agency worker to the hirer was ended on maternity grounds.

(5) Expressions used in this section and sections 68A to 68C have the same meaning as in those sections (see section 68D).

**Amendments**—Inserted by SI 2010/93.

### 70 Complaints to employment tribunals

(1) An employee may present a complaint to an employment tribunal that his or her employer has failed to pay the whole or any part of remuneration to which the employee is entitled under section 64 or 68.

(2) An employment tribunal shall not consider a complaint under subsection (1) relating to remuneration in respect of any day unless it is presented –

    (a)    before the end of the period of three months beginning with that day, or

    (b)    within such further period as the tribunal considers reasonable in a case where it is satisfied that it was not reasonably practicable for the complaint to be presented within that period of three months.

(3) Where an employment tribunal finds a complaint under subsection (1) well-founded, the tribunal shall order the employer to pay the employee the amount of remuneration which it finds is due to him or her.

(4) An employee may present a complaint to an employment tribunal that in contravention of section 67 her employer has failed to offer to provide her with work.

(5) An employment tribunal shall not consider a complaint under subsection (4) unless it is presented –

    (a)    before the end of the period of three months beginning with the first day of the suspension, or

    (b)    within such further period as the tribunal considers reasonable in a case where it is satisfied that it was not reasonably practicable for the complaint to be presented within that period of three months.

(6) Where an employment tribunal finds a complaint under subsection (4) well-founded, the tribunal may make an award of compensation to be paid by the employer to the employee.

(7) The amount of the compensation shall be such as the tribunal considers just and equitable in all the circumstances having regard to –

(a)   the infringement of the employee's right under section 67 by the failure on the part of the employer to which the complaint relates, and

(b)   any loss sustained by the employee which is attributable to that failure.

(8) Section 207A(3) (extension because of mediation in certain European cross-border disputes) applies for the purposes of subsections (2)(a) and (5)(a).

**Amendments**—Employment Rights (Dispute Resolution) Act 1998, s 1(2)(b); SI 2011/1133.

### 70A  Complaints to employment tribunals: agency workers

(1) An agency worker may present a complaint to an employment tribunal that the temporary work agency has failed to pay the whole or any part of remuneration to which the agency worker is entitled under section 68C.

(2) An employment tribunal shall not consider a complaint under subsection (1) relating to remuneration in respect of any day unless it is presented –

(a)   before the end of the period of three months beginning with the day on which the supply of the agency worker to a hirer was ended on maternity grounds, or

(b)   within such further period as the tribunal considers reasonable in a case where it is satisfied that it was not reasonably practicable for the complaint to be presented within that period of three months.

(3) Where an employment tribunal finds a complaint under subsection (1) well-founded, the tribunal shall order the temporary work agency to pay the agency worker the amount of remuneration which it finds is due to her.

(4) An agency worker may present a complaint to an employment tribunal that in contravention of section 68B the temporary work agency has failed to offer to propose the agency worker to a hirer that has suitable alternative work available.

(5) An employment tribunal shall not consider a complaint under subsection (4) unless it is presented –

(a)   before the end of the period of three months beginning with the day on which the supply of the agency worker to a hirer was ended on maternity grounds, or

(b)   within such further period as the tribunal considers reasonable in a case where it is satisfied that it was not reasonably practicable for the complaint to be presented within that period of three months.

(6) Where an employment tribunal finds a complaint under subsection (4) well-founded, the tribunal shall order the temporary work agency to pay the agency worker the amount of compensation which it finds is due to her.

(7) The amount of the compensation shall be such as the tribunal considers just and equitable in all the circumstances having regard to –

(a)   the infringement of the agency worker's right under section 68B by the failure on the part of the temporary work agency to which the complaint relates, and

(b)    any loss sustained by the agency worker which is attributable to that failure.

(8) Expressions used in this section and sections 68A to 68C have the same meaning as in those sections (see section 68D).

**Amendments**—Inserted by SI 2010/93.

## PART VIII

*Chapter I*
*Maternity Leave*

### 71 Ordinary maternity leave

(1) An employee may, provided that she satisfies any conditions which may be prescribed, be absent from work at any time during an ordinary maternity leave period.

(2) An ordinary maternity leave period is a period calculated in accordance with regulations made by the Secretary of State.

(3) Regulations under subsection (2) –

(a)    shall secure that, where an employee has a right to leave under this section, she is entitled to an ordinary maternity leave period of at least 26 weeks;

(b)    may allow an employee to choose, subject to prescribed restrictions, the date on which an ordinary maternity leave period starts;

(c)    may specify circumstances in which an employee may work for her employer during an ordinary maternity leave period without bringing the period to an end.

(4) Subject to section 74, an employee who exercises her right under subsection (1) –

(a)    is entitled, for such purposes and to such extent as may be prescribed, to the benefit of the terms and conditions of employment which would have applied if she had not been absent,

(b)    is bound, for such purposes and to such extent as may be prescribed, by any obligations arising under those terms and conditions (except in so far as they are inconsistent with subsection (1)), and

(c)    is entitled to return from leave to a job of a prescribed kind.

(5) In subsection (4)(a) "terms and conditions of employment" –

(a)    includes matters connected with an employee's employment whether or not they arise under her contract of employment, but

(b)    does not include terms and conditions about remuneration.

(6) The Secretary of State may make regulations specifying matters which are, or are not, to be treated as remuneration for the purposes of this section.

(7) The Secretary of State may make regulations making provision, in relation to the right to return under subsection (4)(c) above, about –

(a)   seniority, pension rights and similar rights;

(b)   terms and conditions of employment on return.

**Amendments**—Employment Relations Act 1999, s 7, Sch 4, Pt I; Work and Families Act 2006, s 11(1), Sch 1, para 31; Employment Act 2002, s 17(1), (2)(a), (b).

\*\*\*\*

*Chapter IA*
*Adoption Leave*

### 75A   Ordinary adoption leave

(1) An employee who satisfies prescribed conditions may be absent from work at any time during an ordinary adoption leave period.

(2) An ordinary adoption leave period is a period calculated in accordance with regulations made by the Secretary of State.

(2A) Regulations under subsection (2) may specify circumstances in which an employee may work for his employer during an ordinary adoption leave period without bringing the period to an end.

(3) Subject to section 75C, an employee who exercises his right under subsection (1) –

(a)   is entitled, for such purposes and to such extent as may be prescribed, to the benefit of the terms and conditions of employment which would have applied if he had not been absent,

(b)   is bound, for such purposes and to such extent as may be prescribed, by any obligations arising under those terms and conditions (except in so far as they are inconsistent with subsection (1)), and

(c)   is entitled to return from leave to a job of a prescribed kind.

(4) In subsection (3)(a) "terms and conditions of employment" –

(a)   includes matters connected with an employee's employment whether or not they arise under his contract of employment, but

(b)   does not include terms and conditions about remuneration.

(5) In subsection (3)(c), the reference to return from leave includes, where appropriate, a reference to a continuous period of absence attributable partly to ordinary adoption leave and partly to maternity leave.

(6) The Secretary of State may make regulations specifying matters which are, or are not, to be treated as remuneration for the purposes of this section.

(7) The Secretary of State may make regulations making provision, in relation to the right to return under subsection (3)(c), about –

(a)   seniority, pension rights and similar rights;

(b)   terms and conditions of employment on return.

**Amendments**—Inserted by the Employment Act 2002, s 3; Work and Families Act 2006, s 11(1), Sch 1, para 33.

### 75B  Additional adoption leave

(1) An employee who satisfies prescribed conditions may be absent from work at any time during an additional adoption leave period.

(2) An additional adoption leave period is a period calculated in accordance with regulations made by the Secretary of State.

(3) Regulations under subsection (2) –

    (a)    may allow an employee to choose, subject to prescribed restrictions, the date on which an additional adoption leave period ends;

    (b)    may specify circumstances in which an employee may work for his employer during an additional adoption leave period without bringing the period to an end.

(4) Subject to section 75C, an employee who exercises his right under subsection (1) –

    (a)    is entitled, for such purposes and to such extent as may be prescribed, to the benefit of the terms and conditions of employment which would have applied if he had not been absent,

    (b)    is bound, for such purposes and to such extent as may be prescribed, by obligations arising under those terms and conditions (except in so far as they are inconsistent with subsection (1)), and

    (c)    is entitled to return from leave to a job of a prescribed kind.

(5) In subsection (4)(a) "terms and conditions of employment" –

    (a)    includes matters connected with an employee's employment whether or not they arise under his contract of employment, but

    (b)    does not include terms and conditions about remuneration.

(6) In subsection (4)(c), the reference to return from leave includes, where appropriate, a reference to a continuous period of absence attributable partly to additional adoption leave and partly to –

    (a)    maternity leave, or

    (b)    ordinary adoption leave,

or to both.

(7) The Secretary of State may make regulations specifying matters which are, or are not, to be treated as remuneration for the purposes of this section.

(8) The Secretary of State may make regulations making provision, in relation to the right to return under subsection (4)(c), about –

    (a)    seniority, pension rights and similar rights;

    (b)    terms and conditions of employment on return.

**Amendments**—Employment Act 2002, s 3; Work and Families Act 2006, s 11(1), Sch 1, para 34.

\*\*\*\*

## 80 Complaint to employment tribunal

(1) An employee may present a complaint to an employment tribunal that his employer –

    (a)    has unreasonably postponed a period of parental leave requested by the employee, or

    (b)    has prevented or attempted to prevent the employee from taking parental leave.

(2A) Section 207A(3) (extension because of mediation in certain European cross-border disputes) applies for the purposes of subsection (2)(a).

(2) An employment tribunal shall not consider a complaint under this section unless it is presented –

    (a)    before the end of the period of three months beginning with the date (or last date) of the matters complained of, or

    (b)    within such further period as the tribunal considers reasonable in a case where it is satisfied that it was not reasonably practicable for the complaint to be presented before the end of that period of three months.

(3) Where an employment tribunal finds a complaint under this section well-founded it –

    (a)    shall make a declaration to that effect, and

    (b)    may make an award of compensation to be paid by the employer to the employee.

(4) The amount of compensation shall be such as the tribunal considers just and equitable in all the circumstances having regard to –

    (a)    the employer's behaviour, and

    (b)    any loss sustained by the employee which is attributable to the matters complained of.

**Amendments**—SI 2011/1133.

\*\*\*\*

## 80AA Entitlement to additional paternity leave: birth

(1) The Secretary of State may make regulations entitling an employee who satisfies specified conditions –

    (a)    as to duration of employment,

    (b)    as to relationship with a child, and

    (c)    as to relationship with the child's mother,

to be absent from work on leave under this section for the purpose of caring for the child, at a time when the child's mother satisfies any conditions prescribed under subsection (2).

(2) The conditions that may be prescribed under this subsection are conditions relating to any one or more of the following –

(a)    any employment or self-employment of the child's mother;

(b)    her entitlement (or lack of entitlement) to leave under this Part or to statutory maternity pay or maternity allowance;

(c)    whether, and to what extent, she is exercising or has exercised any such entitlement.

(3)  Any regulations under this section shall include provision for determining –

(a)    the extent of an employee's entitlement to leave under this section in respect of a child;

(b)    when leave under this section may be taken.

(4) Provision under subsection (3)(a) shall secure that an employee is not entitled to more than 26 weeks' leave in respect of a child.

(5)  Provision under subsection (3)(b) shall secure that leave under this section –

(a)    may not be taken before the end of a specified period beginning with the date of the child's birth, but

(b)    must be taken before the end of the period of twelve months beginning with that date.

(6) Subsections (4) and (5)(a) do not limit the provision that may be made under subsection (3) in relation to cases where the child's mother has died before the end of the period mentioned in subsection (5)(b).

(7)  Regulations under subsection (1) may –

(a)    specify things which are, or are not, to be taken as done for the purpose of caring for a child;

(b)    make provision excluding the right to be absent on leave under this section in respect of a child where more than one child is born as a result of the same pregnancy;

(c)    specify a minimum period which may be taken as leave under this section;

(d)    make provision about how leave under this section may be taken;

(e)    specify circumstances in which an employee may work for his employer during a period of leave under this section without bringing the period of leave to an end.

(8)  Where more than one child is born as a result of the same pregnancy, the reference in subsection (5) to the date of the child's birth shall be read as a reference to the date of birth of the first child born as a result of the pregnancy.

(9)  In this section "week" means any period of seven days.

**Amendments**—Inserted by the Work and Families Act 2006, s 3.

\*\*\*\*

*Part 8A*
*Flexible Working*

**80F  Statutory right to request contract variation**

(1)  A qualifying employee may apply to his employer for a change in his terms and conditions of employment if –

  (a)  the change relates to –
    (i)   the hours he is required to work,
    (ii)  the times when he is required to work,
    (iii) where, as between his home and a place of business of his employer, he is required to work, or
    (iv)  such other aspect of his terms and conditions of employment as the Secretary of State may specify by regulations, and
  (b)  his purpose in applying for the change is to enable him to care for someone who, at the time of application, is –
    (i)   a child who has not reached the prescribed age or falls within a prescribed description and in respect of whom (in either case) the employee satisfies prescribed conditions as to relationship, or
    (ii)  a person aged 18 or over who falls within a prescribed description and in respect of whom the employee satisfies prescribed conditions as to relationship.

(2)  An application under this section must –

  (a)  state that it is such an application,
  (b)  specify the change applied for and the date on which it is proposed the change should become effective,
  (c)  explain what effect, if any, the employee thinks making the change applied for would have on his employer and how, in his opinion, any such effect might be dealt with, and
  (d)  explain how the employee meets, in respect of the child or other person to be cared for, the conditions as to relationship mentioned in subsection (1)(b)(i) or (ii).

(3)  (*repealed*)

(4)  If an employee has made an application under this section, he may not make a further application under this section to the same employer before the end of the period of twelve months beginning with the date on which the previous application was made.

(5)  The Secretary of State may by regulations make provision about –

  (a)  the form of applications under this section, and
  (b)  when such an application is to be taken as made.

(6)  (*repealed*)

(7)  (*repealed*)

(8)  For the purposes of this section, an employee is –

  (a)  a qualifying employee if he –

(i) satisfies such conditions as to duration of employment as the Secretary of State may specify by regulations, and

(ii) is not an agency worker;

(b) an agency worker if he is supplied by a person ("the agent") to do work for another ("the principal") under a contract or other arrangement made between the agent and the principal.

(9) Regulations under this section may make different provision for different cases.

(10) In this section –

"child" means a person aged under 18;
"prescribed" means prescribed by regulations made by the Secretary of State.

**Amendments**—Employment Act 2002, s 47(1), (2); Work and Families Act 2006, s 12(1), (2).

### 80G Employer's duties in relation to application under section 80F

(1) An employer to whom an application under section 80F is made –

(a) shall deal with the application in accordance with regulations made by the Secretary of State, and

(b) shall only refuse the application because he considers that one or more of the following grounds applies –

(i) the burden of additional costs,

(ii) detrimental effect on ability to meet customer demand,

(iii) inability to re-organise work among existing staff,

(iv) inability to recruit additional staff,

(v) detrimental impact on quality,

(vi) detrimental impact on performance,

(vii) insufficiency of work during the periods the employee proposes to work,

(viii) planned structural changes, and

(ix) such other grounds as the Secretary of State may specify by regulations.

(2) Regulations under subsection (1)(a) shall include –

(a) provision for the holding of a meeting between the employer and the employee to discuss an application under section 80F within twenty eight days after the date the application is made;

(b) provision for the giving by the employer to the employee of notice of his decision on the application within fourteen days after the date of the meeting under paragraph (a);

(c) provision for notice under paragraph (b) of a decision to refuse the application to state the grounds for the decision;

(d) provision for the employee to have a right, if he is dissatisfied with the employer's decision, to appeal against it within fourteen days after the date on which notice under paragraph (b) is given;

(e) provision about the procedure for exercising the right of appeal under paragraph (d), including provision requiring the employee to set out the grounds of appeal;

(f) provision for notice under paragraph (b) to include such information as the regulations may specify relating to the right of appeal under paragraph (d);

(g) provision for the holding, within fourteen days after the date on which notice of appeal is given by the employee, of a meeting between the employer and the employee to discuss the appeal;

(h) provision for the employer to give the employee notice of his decision on any appeal within fourteen days after the date of the meeting under paragraph (g);

(i) provision for notice under paragraph (h) of a decision to dismiss an appeal to state the grounds for the decision;

(j) provision for a statement under paragraph (c) or (i) to contain a sufficient explanation of the grounds for the decision;

(k) provision for the employee to have a right to be accompanied at meetings under paragraph (a) or (g) by a person of such description as the regulations may specify;

(l) provision for postponement in relation to any meeting under paragraph (a) or (g) which a companion under paragraph (k) is not available to attend;

(m) provision in relation to companions under paragraph (k) corresponding to section 10(6) and (7) of the Employment Relations Act 1999 (c 26) (right to paid time off to act as companion, etc);

(n) provision, in relation to the rights under paragraphs (k) and (l), for the application (with or without modification) of sections 11 to 13 of the Employment Relations Act 1999 (provisions ancillary to right to be accompanied under section 10 of that Act).

(3) Regulations under subsection (1)(a) may include –

(a) provision for any requirement of the regulations not to apply where an application is disposed of by agreement or withdrawn;

(b) provision for extension of a time limit where the employer and employee agree, or in such other circumstances as the regulations may specify;

(c) provision for applications to be treated as withdrawn in specified circumstances;

and may make different provision for different cases.

(4) The Secretary of State may by order amend subsection (2).

**Amendments**—Inserted by the Employment Act 2002, s 47(1), (2).

## 80H Complaints to employment tribunals

(1) An employee who makes an application under section 80F may present a complaint to an employment tribunal –

(a)    that his employer has failed in relation to the application to comply with section 80G(1), or

(b)    that a decision by his employer to reject the application was based on incorrect facts.

(2) No complaint under this section may be made in respect of an application which has been disposed of by agreement or withdrawn.

(3) In the case of an application which has not been disposed of by agreement or withdrawn, no complaint under this section may be made until the employer –

(a)    notifies the employee of a decision to reject the application on appeal, or

(b)    commits a breach of regulations under section 80G(1)(a) of such description as the Secretary of State may specify by regulations.

(4) No complaint under this section may be made in respect of failure to comply with provision included in regulations under subsection (1)(a) of section 80G because of subsection (2)(k), (l) or (m) of that section.

(5) An employment tribunal shall not consider a complaint under this section unless it is presented –

(a)    before the end of the period of three months beginning with the relevant date, or

(b)    within such further period as the tribunal considers reasonable in a case where it is satisfied that it was not reasonably practicable for the complaint to be presented before the end of that period of three months.

(6) In subsection (5)(a), the reference to the relevant date is –

(a)    in the case of a complaint permitted by subsection (3)(a), the date on which the employee is notified of the decision on the appeal, and

(b)    in the case of a complaint permitted by subsection (3)(b), the date on which the breach concerned was committed.

(7) Section 207A(3) (extension because of mediation in certain European cross-border disputes) applies for the purposes of subsection (5)(a).

**Amendments**—Inserted by the Employment Act 2002, s 47(1), (2); SI 2011/1133.

## 80I  Remedies

(1) Where an employment tribunal finds a complaint under section 80H well-founded it shall make a declaration to that effect and may –

(a)    make an order for reconsideration of the application, and

(b)    make an award of compensation to be paid by the employer to the employee.

(2) The amount of compensation shall be such amount, not exceeding the permitted maximum, as the tribunal considers just and equitable in all the circumstances.

(3) For the purposes of subsection (2), the permitted maximum is such number of weeks' pay as the Secretary of State may specify by regulations.

(4) Where an employment tribunal makes an order under subsection (1)(a), section 80G, and the regulations under that section, shall apply as if the application had been made on the date of the order.

**Amendments**—Inserted by the Employment Act 2002, s 47(1), (2).

\*\*\*\*

*Written statement of reasons for dismissal*

## 92 Right to written statement of reasons for dismissal

(1) An employee is entitled to be provided by his employer with a written statement giving particulars of the reasons for the employee's dismissal –

    (a)    if the employee is given by the employer notice of termination of his contract of employment,

    (b)    if the employee's contract of employment is terminated by the employer without notice, or

    *(c)    if the employee is employed under a contract for a fixed term and that term expires without being renewed under the same contract*

    (c)    if the employee is employed under a limited-term contract and the contract terminates by virtue of the limiting event without being renewed under the same contract.

(2) Subject to subsections (4) and (4A), an employee is entitled to a written statement under this section only if he makes a request for one; and a statement shall be provided within fourteen days of such a request.

(3) Subject to subsections (4) and (4A), an employee is not entitled to a written statement under this section unless on the effective date of termination he has been, or will have been, continuously employed for a period of not less than one year ending with that date.

(4) An employee is entitled to a written statement under this section without having to request it and irrespective of whether she has been continuously employed for any period if she is dismissed –

    (a)    at any time while she is pregnant, or

    (b)    after childbirth in circumstances in which her ordinary or additional maternity leave period ends by reason of the dismissal.

(4A) An employee who is dismissed while absent from work during an ordinary or additional adoption leave period is entitled to a written statement under this section without having to request it and irrespective of whether he has been continuously employed for any period if he is dismissed in circumstances in which that period ends by reason of the dismissal.

(5) A written statement under this section is admissible in evidence in any proceedings.

(6) Subject to subsection (7), in this section "the effective date of termination" –

    (a)    in relation to an employee whose contract of employment is terminated by notice, means the date on which the notice expires,

    (b)    in relation to an employee whose contract of employment is terminated without notice, means the date on which the termination takes effect, and

    (c)    in relation to an employee who is employed under a limited-term contract which terminates by virtue of the limiting event without being renewed under the same contract, means the date on which the termination takes effect.

(7) Where –

    (a)    the contract of employment is terminated by the employer, and

    (b)    the notice required by section 86 to be given by an employer would, if duly given on the material date, expire on a date later than the effective date of termination (as defined by subsection (6)),

the later date is the effective date of termination.

(8) In subsection (7)(b) "the material date" means –

    (a)    the date when notice of termination was given by the employer, or

    (b)    where no notice was given, the date when the contract of employment was terminated by the employer.

**Amendments**—SI 1999/1436; Sub-s (1): para (c) substituted, except in relation to Government training schemes, agency workers or apprentices, by SI 2002/2034, regs 11, 18–20, Sch 2, Pt 1, para 3(1), (5); Employment Act 2002, s 53, Sch 7, paras 24, 31; Employment Relations Act 2004, s 57(1), Sch 1, para 28.

\*\*\*\*

### 107 Pressure on employer to dismiss unfairly

(1) This section applies where there falls to be determined for the purposes of this Part a question –

    (a)    as to the reason, or principal reason, for which an employee was dismissed,

    (b)    whether the reason or principal reason for which an employee was dismissed was a reason fulfilling the requirement of section 98(1)(b), or

    (c)    whether an employer acted reasonably in treating the reason or principal reason for which an employee was dismissed as a sufficient reason for dismissing him.

(2) In determining the question no account shall be taken of any pressure which by calling, organising, procuring or financing a strike or other industrial action, or threatening to do so, was exercised on the employer to dismiss the employee; and the question shall be determined as if no such pressure had been exercised.

\*\*\*\*

*Chapter II*
*Remedies for Unfair Dismissal*

*Introductory*

## 111 Complaints to employment tribunal

(1) A complaint may be presented to an employment tribunal against an employer by any person that he was unfairly dismissed by the employer.

(2) Subject to the following provisions of this section, an employment tribunal shall not consider a complaint under this section unless it is presented to the tribunal –

    (a)  before the end of the period of three months beginning with the effective date of termination, or

    (b)  within such further period as the tribunal considers reasonable in a case where it is satisfied that it was not reasonably practicable for the complaint to be presented before the end of that period of three months.

(2A) Section 207A(3) (extension because of mediation in certain European cross-border disputes) applies for the purposes of subsection (2)(a).

(3) Where a dismissal is with notice, an employment tribunal shall consider a complaint under this section if it is presented after the notice is given but before the effective date of termination.

(4) In relation to a complaint which is presented as mentioned in subsection (3), the provisions of this Act, so far as they relate to unfair dismissal, have effect as if –

    (a)  references to a complaint by a person that he was unfairly dismissed by his employer included references to a complaint by a person that his employer has given him notice in such circumstances that he will be unfairly dismissed when the notice expires,

    (b)  references to reinstatement included references to the withdrawal of the notice by the employer,

    (c)  references to the effective date of termination included references to the date which would be the effective date of termination on the expiry of the notice, and

    (d)  references to an employee ceasing to be employed included references to an employee having been given notice of dismissal.

(5) Where the dismissal is alleged to be unfair by virtue of section 104F (blacklists),

    (a)  subsection (2)(b) does not apply, and

    (b)  an employment tribunal may consider a complaint that is otherwise out of time if, in all the circumstances of the case, it considers that it is just and equitable to do so.

**Amendments**—Employment Rights (Dispute Resolution) Act 1998, s 1(2)(a); SI 2010/493; SI 2011/1133.

\*\*\*\*

# PART XIII
# MISCELLANEOUS

*Chapter I*
*Particular Types of Employment*

*Crown employment etc*

### 191  Crown employment

(1) Subject to sections 192 and 193, the provisions of this Act to which this section applies have effect in relation to Crown employment and persons in Crown employment as they have effect in relation to other employment and other employees or workers.

(2) This section applies to –

- (a)  Parts I to III,
- (aa)  Part IVA,
- (b)  Part V, apart from section 45,
- (c)  Parts VI to VIIIA,
- (d)  in Part IX, sections 92 and 93,
- (e)  Part X, apart from section 101, and
- (f)  this Part and Parts XIV and XV.

(3) In this Act "Crown employment" means employment under or for the purposes of a government department or any officer or body exercising on behalf of the Crown functions conferred by a statutory provision.

(4) For the purposes of the application of provisions of this Act in relation to Crown employment in accordance with subsection (1) –

- (a)  references to an employee or a worker shall be construed as references to a person in Crown employment,
- (b)  references to a contract of employment, or a worker's contract, shall be construed as references to the terms of employment of a person in Crown employment,
- (c)  references to dismissal, or to the termination of a worker's contract, shall be construed as references to the termination of Crown employment,
- (d)  references to redundancy shall be construed as references to the existence of such circumstances as are treated, in accordance with any arrangements falling within section 177(3) for the time being in force, as equivalent to redundancy in relation to Crown employment,
- (da)  the reference in section 98B(2)(a) to the employer's undertaking shall be construed as a reference to the national interest, and
- (e)  any other reference to an undertaking shall be construed –

(i)    in relation to a Minister of the Crown, as references to his functions or (as the context may require) to the department of which he is in charge, and

(ii)   in relation to a government department, officer or body, as references to the functions of the department, officer or body or (as the context may require) to the department, officer or body.

(5) Where the terms of employment of a person in Crown employment restrict his right to take part in –

(a)    certain political activities, or

(b)    activities which may conflict with his official functions,

nothing in section 50 requires him to be allowed time off work for public duties connected with any such activities.

(6) Sections 159 and 160 are without prejudice to any exemption or immunity of the Crown.

**Amendments**—Public Interest Disclosure Act 1998, s 10; Employment Act 2002, s 53, Sch 7, paras 24, 41; Employment Relations Act 2004, s 57, Sch 1, para 34(1), (2), Sch 2.

\*\*\*\*

## 192  Armed forces

(1) Section 191 –

(a)    applies to service as a member of the naval, military or air forces of the Crown but subject to the following provisions of this section, and

(b)    applies to employment by an association established for the purposes of Part XI of the Reserve Forces Act 1996.

(2) The provisions of this Act which have effect by virtue of section 191 in relation to service as a member of the naval, military or air forces of the Crown are –

(a)    Part I,

(aa)   in Part V, sections 43M, 45A, 47C and 47D, and sections 48 and 49 so far as relating to those sections,

(ab)   section 47C,

(b)    in Part VI, sections 55 to 57B,

(c)    Parts VII and VIII,

(d)    in Part IX, sections 92 and 93,

(e)    Part X, apart from sections 98B(2) and (3), 100 to 103, 104C and 134, and

(f)    this Part and Parts XIV and XV.

(3) Her Majesty may by Order in Council –

(a)    amend subsection (2) by making additions to, or omissions from, the provisions for the time being specified in that subsection, and

(b)    make any provision for the time being so specified apply to service as a member of the naval, military or air forces of the Crown subject to such exceptions and modifications as may be specified in the Order in Council,

but no provision contained in Part II may be added to the provisions for the time being specified in subsection (2).

(4) Modifications made by an Order in Council under subsection (3) may include provision precluding the making of a complaint or reference to any employment tribunal unless –

(a)    the person aggrieved has made a service complaint; and
(b)    the Defence Council have made a determination with respect to the service complaint.

(5) Where modifications made by an Order in Council under subsection (3) include provision such as is mentioned in subsection (4), the Order in Council shall also include provision –

(a)    enabling a complaint or reference to be made to an employment tribunal in such circumstances as may be specified in the Order, notwithstanding that provision such as is mentioned in subsection (4) would otherwise preclude the making of the complaint or reference; and

(b)    where a complaint or reference is made to an employment tribunal by virtue of provision such as is mentioned in paragraph (a), enabling the service complaint procedures to continue after the complaint or reference is made.

(6A)  In subsections (4) and (5) –

"service complaint" means a complaint under section 334 of the Armed Forces Act 2006;
"the service complaint procedures" means the procedures prescribed by regulations under that section.

(7)  No provision shall be made by virtue of subsection (4) which has the effect of substituting a period longer than six months for any period specified as the normal period for a complaint or reference.

(8) In subsection (7) "the normal period for a complaint or reference", in relation to any matter within the jurisdiction of an employment tribunal, means the period specified in the relevant enactment as the period within which the complaint or reference must be made (disregarding any provision permitting an extension of that period at the discretion of the tribunal).

**Amendments**—Employment Rights (Dispute Resolution) Act 1998, s 1(2)(a); SI 1998/1833; Tax Credits Act 2002, s 27, Sch 1, para 1(1), (5)(a); Employment Relations Act 2004, s 57(1), Sch 1, para 35(a); Armed Forces Act 1996, s 26(3); Armed Forces Act 2006, s 378(1), Sch 16, para 136(b).

\*\*\*\*

**199 Mariners**

(1) Sections 1 to 7, Part II and sections 86 to 91 do not apply to a person employed as a seaman in a ship registered in the United Kingdom under a crew agreement the provisions and form of which are of a kind approved by the Secretary of State.

(2) Sections 8 to 10, Part III, sections 44, 45, 47, 47C, 47E, 47F, 50 to 57B and 61 to 63, Parts VIA, VII, VIII and VIIIA, sections 92 and 93 and Parts X to XII do not apply to employment as master, or as a member of the crew, of a fishing vessel where the employee is remunerated only by a share in the profits or gross earnings of the vessel.

(3) *(repealed)*

(4) Sections 8 to 10 and 50 to 54 and Part XII do not apply to employment as a merchant seaman.

(5) In subsection (4) "employment as a merchant seaman" –

    (a)    does not include employment in the fishing industry or employment on board a ship otherwise than by the owner, manager or charterer of that ship except employment as a radio officer, but

    (b)    subject to that, includes –

        (i)    employment as a master or a member of the crew of any ship,

        (ii)    employment as a trainee undergoing training for the sea service, and

        (iii)    employment in or about a ship in port by the owner, manager or charterer of the ship to do work of the kind ordinarily done by a merchant seaman on a ship while it is in port.

(6) Section 197(3) does not apply to a contract of employment, if the employee is –

    (a)    employed as a master or seaman in a British ship, and

    (b)    ordinarily resident in Great Britain.

(7) The provisions mentioned in subsection (8) apply to employment on board a ship registered in the register maintained under section 8 of the Merchant Shipping Act 1995 if and only if –

    (a)    the ship's entry in the register specifies a port in Great Britain as the port to which the vessel is to be treated as belonging,

    (b)    under his contract of employment the person employed does not work wholly outside Great Britain, and

    (c)    the person employed is ordinarily resident in Great Britain.

(8) The provisions are –

    (a)    sections 8 to 10,

    (b)    Parts II, III and V,

    (c)    Part VI, apart from sections 58 to 60,

    (d)    Parts VIA, VII, VIII and VIIIA,

    (e)    sections 92 and 93, and

(f)    Part X.

**Amendments**—Employment Relations Act 1999, s 9, Sch 4, Pt III, paras 5, 34(a); Employment Act 2002, s 53, sch 7, paras 24, 244(1), (2)(a)) by the Employment Relations Act 2004, s 41(8); Apprenticeships, Skills, Children and Learning Act 2009, s 40(5), Sch 1, paras 1, 7(a).

\*\*\*\*

*Maximum amount of week's pay*

## 227  Maximum amount

(1)  For the purpose of calculating –

(zza)  an award of compensation under section 63J(1)(b),

(za)   an award of compensation under section 80I(1)(b),

(a)    a basic award of compensation for unfair dismissal,

(b)    an additional award of compensation for unfair dismissal,

(ba)   an award under section 112(5), or

(c)    a redundancy payment,

the amount of a week's pay shall not exceed £400.

(2)  (*repealed*)

(3)  (*repealed*)

(4)  (*repealed*)

**Amendments**—Employment Relations Act 1999, s 9, Sch 4, Pt III, paras 5, 34(a); Employment Act 2002, s 53, sch 7, paras 24, 244(1), (2)(a)); SI 2010/2926; Apprenticeships, Skills, Children and Learning Act 2009, s 269(4).

\*\*\*\*

## 231  Associated employers

For the purposes of this Act any two employers shall be treated as associated if –

(a)    one is a company of which the other (directly or indirectly) has control, or

(b)    both are companies of which a third person (directly or indirectly) has control;

and "associated employer" shall be construed accordingly.

\*\*\*\*

# EQUALITY ACT 2010

Chapter 15

## 1 PART
## SOCIO-ECONOMIC INEQUALITIES

\*\*\*\*

## PART 2
## EQUALITY: KEY CONCEPTS

*Chapter 1*
*Protected characteristics*

### The 4 protected characteristics

The following characteristics are protected characteristics –

> age;
> disability;
> gender reassignment;
> marriage and civil partnership;
> pregnancy and maternity;
> race;
> religion or belief;
> sex;
> sexual orientation.

\*\*\*\*

### 8 Marriage and civil partnership

(1) A person has the protected characteristic of marriage and civil partnership if the person is married or is a civil partner.

(2) In relation to the protected characteristic of marriage and civil partnership –

(a) a reference to a person who has a particular protected characteristic is a reference to a person who is married or is a civil partner;

(b) a reference to persons who share a protected characteristic is a reference to persons who are married or are civil partners.

\*\*\*\*

*Chapter 2*
*Prohibited conduct*

*Discrimination*

## 13 Direct discrimination

(1) A person (A) discriminates against another (B) if, because of a protected characteristic, A treats B less favourably than A treats or would treat others.

(2) If the protected characteristic is age, A does not discriminate against B if A can show A's treatment of B to be a proportionate means of achieving a legitimate aim.

(3) If the protected characteristic is disability, and B is not a disabled person, A does not discriminate against B only because A treats or would treat disabled persons more favourably than A treats B.

(4) If the protected characteristic is marriage and civil partnership, this section applies to a contravention of Part 5 (work) only if the treatment is because it is B who is married or a civil partner.

(5) If the protected characteristic is race, less favourable treatment includes segregating B from others.

(6) If the protected characteristic is sex –

    (a)    less favourable treatment of a woman includes less favourable treatment of her because she is breast-feeding;

    (b)    in a case where B is a man, no account is to be taken of special treatment afforded to a woman in connection with pregnancy or childbirth.

(7) Subsection (6)(a) does not apply for the purposes of Part 5 (work).

(8) This section is subject to sections 17(6) and 18(7).

\*\*\*\*

## 18 Pregnancy and maternity discrimination: work cases

(1) This section has effect for the purposes of the application of Part 5 (work) to the protected characteristic of pregnancy and maternity.

(2) A person (A) discriminates against a woman if, in the protected period in relation to a pregnancy of hers, A treats her unfavourably –

    (a)    because of the pregnancy, or

    (b)    because of illness suffered by her as a result of it.

(3) A person (A) discriminates against a woman if A treats her unfavourably because she is on compulsory maternity leave.

(4) A person (A) discriminates against a woman if A treats her unfavourably because she is exercising or seeking to exercise, or has exercised or sought to exercise, the right to ordinary or additional maternity leave.

(5) For the purposes of subsection (2), if the treatment of a woman is in implementation of a decision taken in the protected period, the treatment is to be regarded as occurring in that period (even if the implementation is not until after the end of that period).

(6) The protected period, in relation to a woman's pregnancy, begins when the pregnancy begins, and ends –

(a) if she has the right to ordinary and additional maternity leave, at the end of the additional maternity leave period or (if earlier) when she returns to work after the pregnancy;

(b) if she does not have that right, at the end of the period of 2 weeks beginning with the end of the pregnancy.

(7) Section 13, so far as relating to sex discrimination, does not apply to treatment of a woman in so far as –

(a) it is in the protected period in relation to her and is for a reason mentioned in paragraph (a) or (b) of subsection (2), or

(b) it is for a reason mentioned in subsection (3) or (4).

\*\*\*\*

## 19 Indirect discrimination

(1) A person (A) discriminates against another (B) if A applies to B a provision, criterion or practice which is discriminatory in relation to a relevant protected characteristic of B's.

(2) For the purposes of subsection (1), a provision, criterion or practice is discriminatory in relation to a relevant protected characteristic of B's if –

(a) A applies, or would apply, it to persons with whom B does not share the characteristic,

(b) it puts, or would put, persons with whom B shares the characteristic at a particular disadvantage when compared with persons with whom B does not share it,

(c) it puts, or would put, B at that disadvantage, and

(d) A cannot show it to be a proportionate means of achieving a legitimate aim.

(3) The relevant protected characteristics are –

age;
disability;
gender reassignment;
marriage and civil partnership;
race;
religion or belief;
sex;
sexual orientation.

*Adjustments for disabled persons*

## 20 Duty to make adjustments

(1) Where this Act imposes a duty to make reasonable adjustments on a person, this section, sections 21 and 22 and the applicable Schedule apply; and for those purposes, a person on whom the duty is imposed is referred to as A.

(2) The duty comprises the following three requirements.

(3) The first requirement is a requirement, where a provision, criterion or practice of A's puts a disabled person at a substantial disadvantage in relation to a relevant matter in comparison with persons who are not disabled, to take such steps as it is reasonable to have to take to avoid the disadvantage.

(4) The second requirement is a requirement, where a physical feature puts a disabled person at a substantial disadvantage in relation to a relevant matter in comparison with persons who are not disabled, to take such steps as it is reasonable to have to take to avoid the disadvantage.

(5) The third requirement is a requirement, where a disabled person would, but for the provision of an auxiliary aid, be put at a substantial disadvantage in relation to a relevant matter in comparison with persons who are not disabled, to take such steps as it is reasonable to have to take to provide the auxiliary aid.

(6) Where the first or third requirement relates to the provision of information, the steps which it is reasonable for A to have to take include steps for ensuring that in the circumstances concerned the information is provided in an accessible format.

(7) A person (A) who is subject to a duty to make reasonable adjustments is not (subject to express provision to the contrary) entitled to require a disabled person, in relation to whom A is required to comply with the duty, to pay to any extent A's costs of complying with the duty.

(8) A reference in section 21 or 22 or an applicable Schedule to the first, second or third requirement is to be construed in accordance with this section.

(9) In relation to the second requirement, a reference in this section or an applicable Schedule to avoiding a substantial disadvantage includes a reference to –

    (a)   removing the physical feature in question,
    (b)   altering it, or
    (c)   providing a reasonable means of avoiding it.

(10) A reference in this section, section 21 or 22 or an applicable Schedule (apart from paragraphs 2 to 4 of Schedule 4) to a physical feature is a reference to –

    (a)   a feature arising from the design or construction of a building,
    (b)   a feature of an approach to, exit from or access to a building,
    (c)   a fixture or fitting, or furniture, furnishings, materials, equipment or other chattels, in or on premises, or
    (d)   any other physical element or quality.

(11) A reference in this section, section 21 or 22 or an applicable Schedule to an auxiliary aid includes a reference to an auxiliary service.

(12) A reference in this section or an applicable Schedule to chattels is to be read, in relation to Scotland, as a reference to moveable property.

(13) The applicable Schedule is, in relation to the Part of this Act specified in the first column of the Table, the Schedule specified in the second column.

| Part of this Act | Applicable Schedule |
|---|---|
| Part 3 (services and public functions) | Schedule 2 |
| Part 4 (premises) | Schedule 4 |
| Part 5 (work) | Schedule 8 |
| Part 6 (education) | Schedule 13 |
| Part 7 (associations) | Schedule 15 |
| Each of the Parts mentioned above | Schedule 21 |

\*\*\*\*

*Discrimination: supplementary*

**23 Comparison by reference to circumstances**

(1) On a comparison of cases for the purposes of section 13, 14, or 19 there must be no material difference between the circumstances relating to each case.

(2) The circumstances relating to a case include a person's abilities if –

    (a)    on a comparison for the purposes of section 13, the protected characteristic is disability;

    (b)    on a comparison for the purposes of section 14, one of the protected characteristics in the combination is disability.

(3) If the protected characteristic is sexual orientation, the fact that one person (whether or not the person referred to as B) is a civil partner while another is married is not a material difference between the circumstances relating to each case.

\*\*\*\*

**25 References to particular strands of discrimination**

(1) Age discrimination is –

    (a)    discrimination within section 13 because of age;

    (b)    discrimination within section 19 where the relevant protected characteristic is age.

(2) Disability discrimination is –

(a)    discrimination within section 13 because of disability;
(b)    discrimination within section 15;
(c)    discrimination within section 19 where the relevant protected characteristic is disability;
(d)    discrimination within section 21.

(3)  Gender reassignment discrimination is –

(a)    discrimination within section 13 because of gender reassignment;
(b)    discrimination within section 16;
(c)    discrimination within section 19 where the relevant protected characteristic is gender reassignment.

(4)  Marriage and civil partnership discrimination is –

(a)    discrimination within section 13 because of marriage and civil partnership;
(b)    discrimination within section 19 where the relevant protected characteristic is marriage and civil partnership.

(5)  Pregnancy and maternity discrimination is discrimination within section 17 or 18.

(6)  Race discrimination is –

(a)    discrimination within section 13 because of race;
(b)    discrimination within section 19 where the relevant protected characteristic is race.

(7)  Religious or belief-related discrimination is –

(a)    discrimination within section 13 because of religion or belief;
(b)    discrimination within section 19 where the relevant protected characteristic is religion or belief.

(8)  Sex discrimination is –

(a)    discrimination within section 13 because of sex;
(b)    discrimination within section 19 where the relevant protected characteristic is sex.

(9)  Sexual orientation discrimination is –

(a)    discrimination within section 13 because of sexual orientation;
(b)    discrimination within section 19 where the relevant protected characteristic is sexual orientation.

*Other prohibited conduct*

**26 Harassment**

(1)  A person (A) harasses another (B) if –

(a)    A engages in unwanted conduct related to a relevant protected characteristic, and
(b)    the conduct has the purpose or effect of –

    (i)     violating B's dignity, or

    (ii)    creating an intimidating, hostile, degrading, humiliating or offensive environment for B.

(2) A also harasses B if –

    (a)    A engages in unwanted conduct of a sexual nature, and

    (b)    the conduct has the purpose or effect referred to in subsection (1)(b).

(3) A also harasses B if –

    (a)    A or another person engages in unwanted conduct of a sexual nature or that is related to gender reassignment or sex,

    (b)    the conduct has the purpose or effect referred to in subsection (1)(b), and

    (c)    because of B's rejection of or submission to the conduct, A treats B less favourably than A would treat B if B had not rejected or submitted to the conduct.

(4) In deciding whether conduct has the effect referred to in subsection (1)(b), each of the following must be taken into account –

    (a)    the perception of B;

    (b)    the other circumstances of the case;

    (c)    whether it is reasonable for the conduct to have that effect.

(5) The relevant protected characteristics are –

age;
disability;
gender reassignment;
race;
religion or belief;
sex;
sexual orientation.

## 27 Victimisation

(1) A person (A) victimises another person (B) if A subjects B to a detriment because –

    (a)    B does a protected act, or

    (b)    A believes that B has done, or may do, a protected act.

(2) Each of the following is a protected act –

    (a)    bringing proceedings under this Act;

    (b)    giving evidence or information in connection with proceedings under this Act;

    (c)    doing any other thing for the purposes of or in connection with this Act;

    (d)    making an allegation (whether or not express) that A or another person has contravened this Act.

(3) Giving false evidence or information, or making a false allegation, is not a protected act if the evidence or information is given, or the allegation is made, in bad faith.

(4) This section applies only where the person subjected to a detriment is an individual.

(5) The reference to contravening this Act includes a reference to committing a breach of an equality clause or rule.

\*\*\*\*

*Provision of services, etc.*

## 29 Provision of services, etc.

(1) A person (a "service-provider") concerned with the provision of a service to the public or a section of the public (for payment or not) must not discriminate against a person requiring the service by not providing the person with the service.

(2) A service-provider (A) must not, in providing the service, discriminate against a person (B) –

    (a)    as to the terms on which A provides the service to B;

    (b)    by terminating the provision of the service to B;

    (c)    by subjecting B to any other detriment.

(3) A service-provider must not, in relation to the provision of the service, harass –

    (a)    a person requiring the service, or

    (b)    a person to whom the service-provider provides the service.

(4) A service-provider must not victimise a person requiring the service by not providing the person with the service.

(5) A service-provider (A) must not, in providing the service, victimise a person (B) –

    (a)    as to the terms on which A provides the service to B;

    (b)    by terminating the provision of the service to B;

    (c)    by subjecting B to any other detriment.

(6) A person must not, in the exercise of a public function that is not the provision of a service to the public or a section of the public, do anything that constitutes discrimination, harassment or victimisation.

(7) A duty to make reasonable adjustments applies to –

    (a)    a service-provider (and see also section 55(7));

    (b)    a person who exercises a public function that is not the provision of a service to the public or a section of the public.

(8) In the application of section 26 for the purposes of subsection (3), and subsection (6) as it relates to harassment, neither of the following is a relevant protected characteristic –

    (a)   religion or belief;

    (b)   sexual orientation.

(9) In the application of this section, so far as relating to race or religion or belief, to the granting of entry clearance (within the meaning of the Immigration Act 1971), it does not matter whether an act is done within or outside the United Kingdom.

(10) Subsection (9) does not affect the application of any other provision of this Act to conduct outside England and Wales or Scotland.

\*\*\*\*

## PART 5
## WORK

*Chapter 1*
*Employment, etc.*

*Employees*

### 39 Employees and applicants

(1) An employer (A) must not discriminate against a person (B) –

    (a)   in the arrangements A makes for deciding to whom to offer employment;

    (b)   as to the terms on which A offers B employment;

    (c)   by not offering B employment.

(2) An employer (A) must not discriminate against an employee of A's (B) –

    (a)   as to B's terms of employment;

    (b)   in the way A affords B access, or by not affording B access, to opportunities for promotion, transfer or training or for receiving any other benefit, facility or service;

    (c)   by dismissing B;

    (d)   by subjecting B to any other detriment.

(3) An employer (A) must not victimise a person (B) –

    (a)   in the arrangements A makes for deciding to whom to offer employment;

    (b)   as to the terms on which A offers B employment;

    (c)   by not offering B employment.

(4) An employer (A) must not victimise an employee of A's (B) –

    (a)   as to B's terms of employment;

(b)    in the way A affords B access, or by not affording B access, to opportunities for promotion, transfer or training or for any other benefit, facility or service;

(c)    by dismissing B;

(d)    by subjecting B to any other detriment.

(5) A duty to make reasonable adjustments applies to an employer.

(6) Subsection (1)(b), so far as relating to sex or pregnancy and maternity, does not apply to a term that relates to pay –

(a)    unless, were B to accept the offer, an equality clause or rule would have effect in relation to the term, or

(b)    if paragraph (a) does not apply, except in so far as making an offer on terms including that term amounts to a contravention of subsection (1)(b) by virtue of section 13, 14 or 18.

(7) In subsections (2)(c) and (4)(c), the reference to dismissing B includes a reference to the termination of B's employment –

(a)    by the expiry of a period (including a period expiring by reference to an event or circumstance);

(b)    by an act of B's (including giving notice) in circumstances such that B is entitled, because of A's conduct, to terminate the employment without notice.

(8) Subsection (7)(a) does not apply if, immediately after the termination, the employment is renewed on the same terms.

****

## 41  Contract workers

(1) A principal must not discriminate against a contract worker –

(a)    as to the terms on which the principal allows the worker to do the work;

(b)    by not allowing the worker to do, or to continue to do, the work;

(c)    in the way the principal affords the worker access, or by not affording the worker access, to opportunities for receiving a benefit, facility or service;

(d)    by subjecting the worker to any other detriment.

(2) A principal must not, in relation to contract work, harass a contract worker.

(3) A principal must not victimise a contract worker –

(a)    as to the terms on which the principal allows the worker to do the work;

(b)    by not allowing the worker to do, or to continue to do, the work;

(c)    in the way the principal affords the worker access, or by not affording the worker access, to opportunities for receiving a benefit, facility or service;

(d)    by subjecting the worker to any other detriment.

(4) A duty to make reasonable adjustments applies to a principal (as well as to the employer of a contract worker).

(5) A "principal" is a person who makes work available for an individual who is –

(a)    employed by another person, and
(b)    supplied by that other person in furtherance of a contract to which the principal is a party (whether or not that other person is a party to it).

(6) "Contract work" is work such as is mentioned in subsection (5).

(7) A "contract worker" is an individual supplied to a principal in furtherance of a contract such as is mentioned in subsection (5)(b).

*Police officers*

## 42 Identity of employer

(1) For the purposes of this Part, holding the office of constable is to be treated as employment –

(a)    by the chief officer, in respect of any act done by the chief officer in relation to a constable or appointment to the office of constable;
(b)    by the responsible authority, in respect of any act done by the authority in relation to a constable or appointment to the office of constable.

(2) For the purposes of this Part, holding an appointment as a police cadet is to be treated as employment –

(a)    by the chief officer, in respect of any act done by the chief officer in relation to a police cadet or appointment as one;
(b)    by the responsible authority, in respect of any act done by the authority in relation to a police cadet or appointment as one.

(3) Subsection (1) does not apply to service with the Civil Nuclear Constabulary (as to which, see section 55(2) of the Energy Act 2004).

(4) Subsection (1) does not apply to a constable at SOCA, SPSA or SCDEA.

(5) A constable at SOCA or SPSA is to be treated as employed by it, in respect of any act done by it in relation to the constable.

(6) A constable at SCDEA is to be treated as employed by the Director General of SCDEA, in respect of any act done by the Director General in relation to the constable.

\*\*\*\*

*Partners*

## 44 Partnerships

(1) A firm or proposed firm must not discriminate against a person –

    (a)    in the arrangements it makes for deciding to whom to offer a position as a partner;

    (b)    as to the terms on which it offers the person a position as a partner;

    (c)    by not offering the person a position as a partner.

(2) A firm (A) must not discriminate against a partner (B) –

    (a)    as to the terms on which B is a partner;

    (b)    in the way A affords B access, or by not affording B access, to opportunities for promotion, transfer or training or for receiving any other benefit, facility or service;

    (c)    by expelling B;

    (d)    by subjecting B to any other detriment.

(3) A firm must not, in relation to a position as a partner, harass –

    (a)    a partner;

    (b)    a person who has applied for the position.

(4) A proposed firm must not, in relation to a position as a partner, harass a person who has applied for the position.

(5) A firm or proposed firm must not victimise a person –

    (a)    in the arrangements it makes for deciding to whom to offer a position as a partner;

    (b)    as to the terms on which it offers the person a position as a partner;

    (c)    by not offering the person a position as a partner.

(6) A firm (A) must not victimise a partner (B) –

    (a)    as to the terms on which B is a partner;

    (b)    in the way A affords B access, or by not affording B access, to opportunities for promotion, transfer or training or for receiving any other benefit, facility or service;

    (c)    by expelling B;

    (d)    by subjecting to any other detriment.

(7) A duty to make reasonable adjustments applies to –

    (a)    a firm;

    (b)    a proposed firm.

(8) In the application of this section to a limited partnership within the meaning of the Limited Partnerships Act 1907, "partner" means a general partner within the meaning of that Act.

### 45  Limited liability partnerships

(1) An LLP or proposed LLP must not discriminate against a person –

    (a)    in the arrangements it makes for deciding to whom to offer a position as a member;

    (b)    as to the terms on which it offers the person a position as a member;

    (c)    by not offering the person a position as a member.

(2) An LLP (A) must not discriminate against a member (B) –

(a)   as to the terms on which B is a member;
(b)   in the way A affords B access, or by not affording B access, to opportunities for promotion, transfer or training or for receiving any other benefit, facility or service;
(c)   by expelling B;
(d)   by subjecting B to any other detriment.

(3) An LLP must not, in relation to a position as a member, harass –

(a)   a member;
(b)   a person who has applied for the position.

(4) A proposed LLP must not, in relation to a position as a member, harass a person who has applied for the position.

(5) An LLP or proposed LLP must not victimise a person –

(a)   in the arrangements it makes for deciding to whom to offer a position as a member;
(b)   as to the terms on which it offers the person a position as a member;
(c)   by not offering the person a position as a member.

(6) An LLP (A) must not victimise a member (B) –

(a)   as to the terms on which B is a member;
(b)   in the way A affords B access, or by not affording B access, to opportunities for promotion, transfer or training or for receiving any other benefit, facility or service;
(c)   by expelling B;
(d)   by subjecting B to any other detriment.

(7) A duty to make reasonable adjustments applies to –

(a)   an LLP;
(b)   a proposed LLP.

****

*The Bar*

**47 Barristers**

(1) A barrister (A) must not discriminate against a person (B) –

(a)   in the arrangements A makes for deciding to whom to offer a pupillage or tenancy;
(b)   as to the terms on which A offers B a pupillage or tenancy;
(c)   by not offering B a pupillage or tenancy.

(2) A barrister (A) must not discriminate against a person (B) who is a pupil or tenant –

(a)   as to the terms on which B is a pupil or tenant;

(b)    in the way A affords B access, or by not affording B access, to opportunities for training or gaining experience or for receiving any other benefit, facility or service;

(c)    by terminating the pupillage;

(d)    by subjecting B to pressure to leave chambers;

(e)    by subjecting B to any other detriment.

(3) A barrister must not, in relation to a pupillage or tenancy, harass –

(a)    the pupil or tenant;

(b)    a person who has applied for the pupillage or tenancy.

(4) A barrister (A) must not victimise a person (B) –

(a)    in the arrangements A makes for deciding to whom to offer a pupillage or tenancy;

(b)    as to the terms on which A offers B a pupillage or tenancy;

(c)    by not offering B a pupillage or tenancy.

(5) A barrister (A) must not victimise a person (B) who is a pupil or tenant –

(a)    as to the terms on which B is a pupil or tenant;

(b)    in the way A affords B access, or by not affording B access, to opportunities for training or gaining experience or for receiving any other benefit, facility or service;

(c)    by terminating the pupillage;

(d)    by subjecting B to pressure to leave chambers;

(e)    by subjecting B to any other detriment.

(6) A person must not, in relation to instructing a barrister –

(a)    discriminate against a barrister by subjecting the barrister to a detriment;

(b)    harass the barrister;

(c)    victimise the barrister.

(7) A duty to make reasonable adjustments applies to a barrister.

(8) The preceding provisions of this section (apart from subsection (6)) apply in relation to a barrister's clerk as they apply in relation to a barrister; and for that purpose the reference to a barrister's clerk includes a reference to a person who carries out the functions of a barrister's clerk.

(9) A reference to a tenant includes a reference to a barrister who is permitted to work in chambers (including as a squatter or door tenant); and a reference to a tenancy is to be construed accordingly.

### 48  Advocates

(1) An advocate (A) must not discriminate against a person (B) –

(a)    in the arrangements A makes for deciding who to take as A's devil or to whom to offer membership of a stable;

(b)    as to the terms on which A offers to take B as A's devil or offers B membership of a stable;

(c)    by not offering to take B as A's devil or not offering B membership of a stable.

(2) An advocate (A) must not discriminate against a person (B) who is a devil or a member of a stable –

(a)    as to the terms on which B is a devil or a member of the stable;
(b)    in the way A affords B access, or by not affording B access, to opportunities for training or gaining experience or for receiving any other benefit, facility or service;
(c)    by terminating A's relationship with B (where B is a devil);
(d)    by subjecting B to pressure to leave the stable;
(e)    by subjecting B to any other detriment.

(3) An advocate must not, in relation to a relationship with a devil or membership of a stable, harass –

(a)    a devil or member;
(b)    a person who has applied to be taken as the advocate's devil or to become a member of the stable.

(4) An advocate (A) must not victimise a person (B) –

(a)    in the arrangements A makes for deciding who to take as A's devil or to whom to offer membership of a stable;
(b)    as to the terms on which A offers to take B as A's devil or offers B membership of a stable;
(c)    by not offering to take B as A's devil or not offering B membership of a stable.

(5) An advocate (A) must not victimise a person (B) who is a devil or a member of a stable –

(a)    as to the terms on which B is a devil or a member of the stable;
(b)    in the way A affords B access, or by not affording B access, to opportunities for training or gaining experience or for receiving any other benefit, facility or service;
(c)    by terminating A's relationship with B (where B is a devil);
(d)    by subjecting B to pressure to leave the stable;
(e)    by subjecting B to any other detriment.

(6) A person must not, in relation to instructing an advocate –

(a)    discriminate against the advocate by subjecting the advocate to a detriment;
(b)    harass the advocate;
(c)    victimise the advocate.

(7) A duty to make reasonable adjustments applies to an advocate.

(8) This section (apart from subsection (6)) applies in relation to an advocate's clerk as it applies in relation to an advocate; and for that purpose the reference to an advocate's clerk includes a reference to a person who carries out the functions of an advocate's clerk.

(9) "Advocate" means a practising member of the Faculty of Advocates.

*Office-holders*

### 49 Personal offices: appointments, etc.

(1) This section applies in relation to personal offices.

(2) A personal office is an office or post –

    (a)    to which a person is appointed to discharge a function personally under the direction of another person, and

    (b)    in respect of which an appointed person is entitled to remuneration.

(3) A person (A) who has the power to make an appointment to a personal office must not discriminate against a person (B) –

    (a)    in the arrangements A makes for deciding to whom to offer the appointment;

    (b)    as to the terms on which A offers B the appointment;

    (c)    by not offering B the appointment.

(4) A person who has the power to make an appointment to a personal office must not, in relation to the office, harass a person seeking, or being considered for, the appointment.

(5) A person (A) who has the power to make an appointment to a personal office must not victimise a person (B) –

    (a)    in the arrangements A makes for deciding to whom to offer the appointment;

    (b)    as to the terms on which A offers B the appointment;

    (c)    by not offering B the appointment.

(6) A person (A) who is a relevant person in relation to a personal office must not discriminate against a person (B) appointed to the office –

    (a)    as to the terms of B's appointment;

    (b)    in the way A affords B access, or by not affording B access, to opportunities for promotion, transfer or training or for receiving any other benefit, facility or service;

    (c)    by terminating B's appointment;

    (d)    by subjecting B to any other detriment.

(7) A relevant person in relation to a personal office must not, in relation to that office, harass a person appointed to it.

(8) A person (A) who is a relevant person in relation to a personal office must not victimise a person (B) appointed to the office –

    (a)    as to the terms of B's appointment;

    (b)    in the way A affords B access, or by not affording B access, to opportunities for promotion, transfer or training or for receiving any other benefit, facility or service;

    (c)    by terminating B's appointment;

    (d)   by subjecting B to any other detriment.

(9) A duty to make reasonable adjustments applies to –

    (a)   a person who has the power to make an appointment to a personal office;

    (b)   a relevant person in relation to a personal office.

(10) For the purposes of subsection (2)(a), a person is to be regarded as discharging functions personally under the direction of another person if that other person is entitled to direct the person as to when and where to discharge the functions.

(11) For the purposes of subsection (2)(b), a person is not to be regarded as entitled to remuneration merely because the person is entitled to payments –

    (a)   in respect of expenses incurred by the person in discharging the functions of the office or post, or

    (b)   by way of compensation for the loss of income or benefits the person would or might have received had the person not been discharging the functions of the office or post.

(12) Subsection (3)(b), so far as relating to sex or pregnancy and maternity, does not apply to a term that relates to pay –

    (a)   unless, were B to accept the offer, an equality clause or rule would have effect in relation to the term, or

    (b)   if paragraph (a) does not apply, except in so far as making an offer on terms including that term amounts to a contravention of subsection (3)(b) by virtue of section 13, 14 or 18.

### 50 Public offices: appointments, etc.

(1) This section and section 51 apply in relation to public offices.

(2) A public office is –

    (a)   an office or post, appointment to which is made by a member of the executive;

    (b)   an office or post, appointment to which is made on the recommendation of, or subject to the approval of, a member of the executive;

    (c)   an office or post, appointment to which is made on the recommendation of, or subject to the approval of, the House of Commons, the House of Lords, the National Assembly for Wales or the Scottish Parliament.

(3) A person (A) who has the power to make an appointment to a public office within subsection (2)(a) or (b) must not discriminate against a person (B) –

    (a)   in the arrangements A makes for deciding to whom to offer the appointment;

    (b)   as to the terms on which A offers B the appointment;

    (c)   by not offering B the appointment.

(4) A person who has the power to make an appointment to a public office within subsection (2)(a) or (b) must not, in relation to the office, harass a person seeking, or being considered for, the appointment.

(5) A person (A) who has the power to make an appointment to a public office within subsection (2)(a) or (b) must not victimise a person (B) –

(a)    in the arrangements A makes for deciding to whom to offer the appointment;
(b)    as to the terms on which A offers B the appointment;
(c)    by not offering B the appointment.

(6) A person (A) who is a relevant person in relation to a public office within subsection (2)(a) or (b) must not discriminate against a person (B) appointed to the office –

(a)    as to B's terms of appointment;
(b)    in the way A affords B access, or by not affording B access, to opportunities for promotion, transfer or training or for receiving any other benefit, facility or service;
(c)    by terminating the appointment;
(d)    by subjecting B to any other detriment.

(7) A person (A) who is a relevant person in relation to a public office within subsection (2)(c) must not discriminate against a person (B) appointed to the office –

(a)    as to B's terms of appointment;
(b)    in the way A affords B access, or by not affording B access, to opportunities for promotion, transfer or training or for receiving any other benefit, facility or service;
(c)    by subjecting B to any other detriment (other than by terminating the appointment).

(8) A relevant person in relation to a public office must not, in relation to that office, harass a person appointed to it.

(9) A person (A) who is a relevant person in relation to a public office within subsection (2)(a) or (b) must not victimise a person (B) appointed to the office –

(a)    as to B's terms of appointment;
(b)    in the way A affords B access, or by not affording B access, to opportunities for promotion, transfer or training or for receiving any other benefit, facility or service;
(c)    by terminating the appointment;
(d)    by subjecting B to any other detriment.

(10) A person (A) who is a relevant person in relation to a public office within subsection (2)(c) must not victimise a person (B) appointed to the office –

(a)    as to B's terms of appointment;

(b)   in the way A affords B access, or by not affording B access, to opportunities for promotion, transfer or training or for receiving any other benefit, facility or service;

(c)   by subjecting B to any other detriment (other than by terminating the appointment).

(11) A duty to make reasonable adjustments applies to –

(a)   a relevant person in relation to a public office;

(b)   a person who has the power to make an appointment to a public office within subsection (2)(a) or (b).

(12) Subsection (3)(b), so far as relating to sex or pregnancy and maternity, does not apply to a term that relates to pay –

(a)   unless, were B to accept the offer, an equality clause or rule would have effect in relation to the term, or

(b)   if paragraph (a) does not apply, except in so far as making an offer on terms including that term amounts to a contravention of subsection (3)(b) by virtue of section 13, 14 or 18.

**51 Public offices: recommendations for appointments, etc.**

(1) A person (A) who has the power to make a recommendation for or give approval to an appointment to a public office within section 50(2)(a) or (b), must not discriminate against a person (B) –

(a)   in the arrangements A makes for deciding who to recommend for appointment or to whose appointment to give approval;

(b)   by not recommending B for appointment to the office;

(c)   by making a negative recommendation of B for appointment to the office;

(d)   by not giving approval to the appointment of B to the office.

(2) A person who has the power to make a recommendation for or give approval to an appointment to a public office within section 50(2)(a) or (b) must not, in relation to the office, harass a person seeking or being considered for the recommendation or approval.

(3) A person (A) who has the power to make a recommendation for or give approval to an appointment to a public office within section 50(2)(a) or (b), must not victimise a person (B) –

(a)   in the arrangements A makes for deciding who to recommend for appointment or to whose appointment to give approval;

(b)   by not recommending B for appointment to the office;

(c)   by making a negative recommendation of B for appointment to the office;

(d)   by not giving approval to the appointment of B to the office.

(4) A duty to make reasonable adjustments applies to a person who has the power to make a recommendation for or give approval to an appointment to a public office within section 50(2)(a) or (b).

(5) A reference in this section to a person who has the power to make a recommendation for or give approval to an appointment to a public office within section 50(2)(a) is a reference only to a relevant body which has that power; and for that purpose "relevant body" means a body established –

(a)    by or in pursuance of an enactment, or
(b)    by a member of the executive.

## 52 Interpretation and exceptions

(1) This section applies for the purposes of sections 49 to 51.

(2) "Personal office" has the meaning given in section 49.

(3) "Public office" has the meaning given in section 50.

(4) An office or post which is both a personal office and a public office is to be treated as being a public office only.

(5) Appointment to an office or post does not include election to it.

(6) "Relevant person", in relation to an office, means the person who, in relation to a matter specified in the first column of the table, is specified in the second column (but a reference to a relevant person does not in any case include the House of Commons, the House of Lords, the National Assembly for Wales or the Scottish Parliament).

| *Matter* | *Relevant person* |
| --- | --- |
| A term of appointment | The person who has the power to set the term. |
| Access to an opportunity | The person who has the power to afford access to the opportunity (or, if there is no such person, the person who has the power to make the appointment). |
| Terminating an appointment | The person who has the power to terminate the appointment. |
| Subjecting an appointee to any other detriment | The person who has the power in relation to the matter to which the conduct in question relates (or, if there is no such person, the person who has the power to make the appointment). |
| Harassing an appointee | The person who has the power in relation to the matter to which the conduct in question relates. |

(7) A reference to terminating a person's appointment includes a reference to termination of the appointment –

(a) by the expiry of a period (including a period expiring by reference to an event or circumstance);

(b) by an act of the person (including giving notice) in circumstances such that the person is entitled, because of the relevant person's conduct, to terminate the appointment without notice.

(8) Subsection (7)(a) does not apply if, immediately after the termination, the appointment is renewed on the same terms.

(9) Schedule 6 (excluded offices) has effect.

*Qualifications*

### 53 Qualifications bodies

(1) A qualifications body (A) must not discriminate against a person (B) –

(a) in the arrangements A makes for deciding upon whom to confer a relevant qualification;

(b) as to the terms on which it is prepared to confer a relevant qualification on B;

(c) by not conferring a relevant qualification on B.

(2) A qualifications body (A) must not discriminate against a person (B) upon whom A has conferred a relevant qualification –

(a) by withdrawing the qualification from B;

(b) by varying the terms on which B holds the qualification;

(c) by subjecting B to any other detriment.

(3) A qualifications body must not, in relation to conferment by it of a relevant qualification, harass –

(a) a person who holds the qualification, or

(b) a person who applies for it.

(4) A qualifications body (A) must not victimise a person (B) –

(a) in the arrangements A makes for deciding upon whom to confer a relevant qualification;

(b) as to the terms on which it is prepared to confer a relevant qualification on B;

(c) by not conferring a relevant qualification on B.

(5) A qualifications body (A) must not victimise a person (B) upon whom A has conferred a relevant qualification –

(a) by withdrawing the qualification from B;

(b) by varying the terms on which B holds the qualification;

(c) by subjecting B to any other detriment.

(6) A duty to make reasonable adjustments applies to a qualifications body.

(7) The application by a qualifications body of a competence standard to a disabled person is not disability discrimination unless it is discrimination by virtue of section 19.

**54 Interpretation**

(1) This section applies for the purposes of section 53.

(2) A qualifications body is an authority or body which can confer a relevant qualification.

(3) A relevant qualification is an authorisation, qualification, recognition, registration, enrolment, approval or certification which is needed for, or facilitates engagement in, a particular trade or profession.

(4) An authority or body is not a qualifications body in so far as –

    (a)    it can confer a qualification to which section 96 applies,
    (b)    it is the responsible body of a school to which section 85 applies,
    (c)    it is the governing body of an institution to which section 91 applies,
    (d)    it exercises functions under the Education Acts, or
    (e)    it exercises functions under the Education (Scotland) Act 1980.

(5) A reference to conferring a relevant qualification includes a reference to renewing or extending the conferment of a relevant qualification.

(6) A competence standard is an academic, medical or other standard applied for the purpose of determining whether or not a person has a particular level of competence or ability.

*Employment services*

**55 Employment service-providers**

(1) A person (an "employment service-provider") concerned with the provision of an employment service must not discriminate against a person –

    (a)    in the arrangements the service-provider makes for selecting persons to whom to provide, or to whom to offer to provide, the service;
    (b)    as to the terms on which the service-provider offers to provide the service to the person;
    (c)    by not offering to provide the service to the person.

(2) An employment service-provider (A) must not, in relation to the provision of an employment service, discriminate against a person (B) –

    (a)    as to the terms on which A provides the service to B;
    (b)    by not providing the service to B;
    (c)    by terminating the provision of the service to B;
    (d)    by subjecting B to any other detriment.

(3) An employment service-provider must not, in relation to the provision of an employment service, harass –

    (a)    a person who asks the service-provider to provide the service;
    (b)    a person for whom the service-provider provides the service.

(4) An employment service-provider (A) must not victimise a person (B) –

(a) in the arrangements A makes for selecting persons to whom to provide, or to whom to offer to provide, the service;

(b) as to the terms on which A offers to provide the service to B;

(c) by not offering to provide the service to B.

(5) An employment service-provider (A) must not, in relation to the provision of an employment service, victimise a person (B) –

(a) as to the terms on which A provides the service to B;

(b) by not providing the service to B;

(c) by terminating the provision of the service to B;

(d) by subjecting B to any other detriment.

(6) A duty to make reasonable adjustments applies to an employment service-provider, except in relation to the provision of a vocational service.

(7) The duty imposed by section 29(7)(a) applies to a person concerned with the provision of a vocational service; but a failure to comply with that duty in relation to the provision of a vocational service is a contravention of this Part for the purposes of Part 9 (enforcement).

****

*Trade organisations*

## 57 Trade organisations

(1) A trade organisation (A) must not discriminate against a person (B) –

(a) in the arrangements A makes for deciding to whom to offer membership of the organisation;

(b) as to the terms on which it is prepared to admit B as a member;

(c) by not accepting B's application for membership.

(2) A trade organisation (A) must not discriminate against a member (B) –

(a) in the way it affords B access, or by not affording B access, to opportunities for receiving a benefit, facility or service;

(b) by depriving B of membership;

(c) by varying the terms on which B is a member;

(d) by subjecting B to any other detriment.

(3) A trade organisation must not, in relation to membership of it, harass –

(a) a member, or

(b) an applicant for membership.

(4) A trade organisation (A) must not victimise a person (B) –

(a) in the arrangements A makes for deciding to whom to offer membership of the organisation;

(b) as to the terms on which it is prepared to admit B as a member;

(c) by not accepting B's application for membership.

(5) A trade organisation (A) must not victimise a member (B) –

(a) in the way it affords B access, or by not affording B access, to opportunities for receiving a benefit, facility or service;

(b) by depriving B of membership;

(c) by varying the terms on which B is a member;

(d) by subjecting B to any other detriment.

(6) A duty to make reasonable adjustments applies to a trade organisation.

(7) A trade organisation is –

(a) an organisation of workers,

(b) an organisation of employers, or

(c) any other organisation whose members carry on a particular trade or profession for the purposes of which the organisation exists.

*Local authority members*

## 58 Official business of members

(1) A local authority must not discriminate against a member of the authority in relation to the member's carrying out of official business –

(a) in the way the authority affords the member access, or by not affording the member access, to opportunities for training or for receiving any other facility;

(b) by subjecting the member to any other detriment.

(2) A local authority must not, in relation to a member's carrying out of official business, harass the member.

(3) A local authority must not victimise a member of the authority in relation to the member's carrying out of official business –

(a) in the way the authority affords the member access, or by not affording the member access, to opportunities for training or for receiving any other facility;

(b) by subjecting the member to any other detriment.

(4) A member of a local authority is not subjected to a detriment for the purposes of subsection (1)(b) or (3)(b) only because the member is –

(a) not appointed or elected to an office of the authority,

(b) not appointed or elected to, or to an office of, a committee or subcommittee of the authority, or

(c) not appointed or nominated in exercise of an appointment power of the authority.

(5) In subsection (4)(c), an appointment power of a local authority is a power of the authority, or of a group of bodies including the authority, to make –

(a) appointments to a body;

(b) nominations for appointment to a body.

(6) A duty to make reasonable adjustments applies to a local authority.

\*\*\*\*

*Chapter 3*
*Equality of terms*

*Sex equality*

## 64 Relevant types of work

(1) Sections 66 to 70 apply where –

  (a)  a person (A) is employed on work that is equal to the work that a comparator of the opposite sex (B) does;
  (b)  a person (A) holding a personal or public office does work that is equal to the work that a comparator of the opposite sex (B) does.

(2) The references in subsection (1) to the work that B does are not restricted to work done contemporaneously with the work done by A.

## 65 Equal work

(1) For the purposes of this Chapter, A's work is equal to that of B if it is –

  (a)  like B's work,
  (b)  rated as equivalent to B's work, or
  (c)  of equal value to B's work.

(2) A's work is like B's work if –

  (a)  A's work and B's work are the same or broadly similar, and
  (b)  such differences as there are between their work are not of practical importance in relation to the terms of their work.

(3) So on a comparison of one person's work with another's for the purposes of subsection (2), it is necessary to have regard to –

  (a)  the frequency with which differences between their work occur in practice, and
  (b)  the nature and extent of the differences.

(4) A's work is rated as equivalent to B's work if a job evaluation study –

  (a)  gives an equal value to A's job and B's job in terms of the demands made on a worker, or
  (b)  would give an equal value to A's job and B's job in those terms were the evaluation not made on a sex-specific system.

(5) A system is sex-specific if, for the purposes of one or more of the demands made on a worker, it sets values for men different from those it sets for women.

(6) A's work is of equal value to B's work if it is –

  (a)  neither like B's work nor rated as equivalent to B's work, but
  (b)  nevertheless equal to B's work in terms of the demands made on A by reference to factors such as effort, skill and decision-making.

## 66 Sex equality clause

(1) If the terms of A's work do not (by whatever means) include a sex equality clause, they are to be treated as including one.

(2) A sex equality clause is a provision that has the following effect –

    (a)   if a term of A's is less favourable to A than a corresponding term of B's is to B, A's term is modified so as not to be less favourable;

    (b)   if A does not have a term which corresponds to a term of B's that benefits B, A's terms are modified so as to include such a term.

(3) Subsection (2)(a) applies to a term of A's relating to membership of or rights under an occupational pension scheme only in so far as a sex equality rule would have effect in relation to the term.

(4) In the case of work within section 65(1)(b), a reference in subsection (2) above to a term includes a reference to such terms (if any) as have not been determined by the rating of the work (as well as those that have).

\*\*\*\*

## 73 Maternity equality clause

(1) If the terms of the woman's work do not (by whatever means) include a maternity equality clause, they are to be treated as including one.

(2) A maternity equality clause is a provision that, in relation to the terms of the woman's work, has the effect referred to in section 74(1), (6) and (8).

(3) In the case of a term relating to membership of or rights under an occupational pension scheme, a maternity equality clause has only such effect as a maternity equality rule would have.

## 74 Maternity equality clause: pay

(1) A term of the woman's work that provides for maternity-related pay to be calculated by reference to her pay at a particular time is, if each of the following three conditions is satisfied, modified as mentioned in subsection (5).

(2) The first condition is that, after the time referred to in subsection (1) but before the end of the protected period –

    (a)   her pay increases, or

    (b)   it would have increased had she not been on maternity leave.

(3) The second condition is that the maternity-related pay is not –

    (a)   what her pay would have been had she not been on maternity leave, or

    (b)   the difference between the amount of statutory maternity pay to which she is entitled and what her pay would have been had she not been on maternity leave.

(4) The third condition is that the terms of her work do not provide for the maternity-related pay to be subject to –

(a)    an increase as mentioned in subsection (2)(a), or

(b)    an increase that would have occurred as mentioned in subsection (2)(b).

(5) The modification referred to in subsection (1) is a modification to provide for the maternity-related pay to be subject to –

(a)    any increase as mentioned in subsection (2)(a), or

(b)    any increase that would have occurred as mentioned in subsection (2)(b).

(6) A term of her work that –

(a)    provides for pay within subsection (7), but

(b)    does not provide for her to be given the pay in circumstances in which she would have been given it had she not been on maternity leave,

is modified so as to provide for her to be given it in circumstances in which it would normally be given.

(7) Pay is within this subsection if it is –

(a)    pay (including pay by way of bonus) in respect of times before the woman is on maternity leave,

(b)    pay by way of bonus in respect of times when she is on compulsory maternity leave, or

(c)    pay by way of bonus in respect of times after the end of the protected period.

(8) A term of the woman's work that –

(a)    provides for pay after the end of the protected period, but

(b)    does not provide for it to be subject to an increase to which it would have been subject had she not been on maternity leave,

is modified so as to provide for it to be subject to the increase.

(9) Maternity-related pay is pay (other than statutory maternity pay) to which a woman is entitled –

(a)    as a result of being pregnant, or

(b)    in respect of times when she is on maternity leave.

(10) A reference to the protected period is to be construed in accordance with section 18.

## 75 Maternity equality rule

(1) If an occupational pension scheme does not include a maternity equality rule, it is to be treated as including one.

(2) A maternity equality rule is a provision that has the effect set out in subsections (3) and (4).

(3) If a relevant term does not treat time when the woman is on maternity leave as it treats time when she is not, the term is modified so as to treat time when she is on maternity leave as time when she is not.

(4) If a term confers a relevant discretion capable of being exercised so that time when she is on maternity leave is treated differently from time when she is not, the term is modified so as not to allow the discretion to be exercised in that way.

(5) A term is relevant if it is –

    (a)    a term relating to membership of the scheme,
    (b)    a term relating to the accrual of rights under the scheme, or
    (c)    a term providing for the determination of the amount of a benefit payable under the scheme.

(6) A discretion is relevant if its exercise is capable of affecting –

    (a)    membership of the scheme,
    (b)    the accrual of rights under the scheme, or
    (c)    the determination of the amount of a benefit payable under the scheme.

(7) This section does not require the woman's contributions to the scheme in respect of time when she is on maternity leave to be determined otherwise than by reference to the amount she is paid in respect of that time.

(8) This section, so far as relating to time when she is on ordinary maternity leave but is not being paid by her employer, applies only in a case where the expected week of childbirth began on or after 6 April 2003.

(9) This section, so far as relating to time when she is on additional maternity leave but is not being paid by her employer –

    (a)    does not apply to the accrual of rights under the scheme in any case;
    (b)    applies for other purposes only in a case where the expected week of childbirth began on or after 5 October 2008.

(10) In this section –

    (a)    a reference to being on maternity leave includes a reference to having been on maternity leave, and
    (b)    a reference to being paid by the employer includes a reference to receiving statutory maternity pay from the employer.

### 76 Exclusion of pregnancy and maternity discrimination provisions

(1) The relevant pregnancy and maternity discrimination provision has no effect in relation to a term of the woman's work that is modified by a maternity equality clause or rule.

[(1A) The relevant pregnancy and maternity discrimination provision has no effect in relation to a term of the woman's work –

    (a)    that relates to pay, but

(b)   in relation to which a maternity equality clause or rule has no effect.][1]

(2)  The inclusion in the woman's terms of a term that requires modification by virtue of section 73(2) or (3) is not pregnancy and maternity discrimination for the purposes of the relevant pregnancy and maternity discrimination provision.

(3)  The relevant pregnancy and maternity discrimination provision is, in relation to a description of work given in the first column of the table, the provision referred to in the second column so far as relating to pregnancy and maternity.

| *Description of work* | *Provision* |
| --- | --- |
| Employment | Section 39(2) |
| Appointment to a personal office | Section 49(6) |
| Appointment to a public office | Section 50(6) |

**Amendments**—SI 2010/2622.

\*\*\*\*

## 83 Interpretation and exceptions

(1)  This section applies for the purposes of this Part.

(2)  "Employment" means –

(a)   employment under a contract of employment, a contract of apprenticeship or a contract personally to do work;
(b)   Crown employment;
(c)   employment as a relevant member of the House of Commons staff;
(d)   employment as a relevant member of the House of Lords staff.

(3)  This Part applies to service in the armed forces as it applies to employment by a private person; and for that purpose –

(a)   references to terms of employment, or to a contract of employment, are to be read as including references to terms of service;
(b)   references to associated employers are to be ignored.

(4)  A reference to an employer or an employee, or to employing or being employed, is (subject to section 212(11)) to be read with subsections (2) and (3); and a reference to an employer also includes a reference to a person who has no employees but is seeking to employ one or more other persons.

(5)  "Relevant member of the House of Commons staff" has the meaning given in section 195 of the Employment Rights Act 1996; and such a member of staff is an employee of –

(a)   the person who is the employer of that member under subsection (6) of that section, or
(b)   if subsection (7) of that section applies in the case of that member, the person who is the employer of that member under that subsection.

---

[1]   Amendment: Subsection inserted: SI 2010/2622, art 2, with effect from 30 October 2010.

(6) "Relevant member of the House of Lords staff" has the meaning given in section 194 of that Act (which provides that such a member of staff is an employee of the Corporate Officer of the House of Lords).

(7) In the case of a person in Crown employment, or in employment as a relevant member of the House of Commons staff, a reference to the person's dismissal is a reference to the termination of the person's employment.

(8) A reference to a personal or public office, or to an appointment to a personal or public office, is to be construed in accordance with section 52.

(9) "Crown employment" has the meaning given in section 191 of the Employment Rights Act 1996.

(10) Schedule 8 (reasonable adjustments) has effect.

(11) Schedule 9 (exceptions) has effect.

\*\*\*\*

# PART 8
## PROHIBITED CONDUCT: ANCILLARY

### 108 Relationships that have ended

(1) A person (A) must not discriminate against another (B) if –

   (a)   the discrimination arises out of and is closely connected to a relationship which used to exist between them, and
   (b)   conduct of a description constituting the discrimination would, if it occurred during the relationship, contravene this Act.

(2) A person (A) must not harass another (B) if –

   (a)   the harassment arises out of and is closely connected to a relationship which used to exist between them, and
   (b)   conduct of a description constituting the harassment would, if it occurred during the relationship, contravene this Act.

(3) It does not matter whether the relationship ends before or after the commencement of this section.

(4) A duty to make reasonable adjustments applies to A [if B is]² placed at a substantial disadvantage as mentioned in section 20.

(5) For the purposes of subsection (4), sections 20, 21 and 22 and the applicable Schedules are to be construed as if the relationship had not ended.

(6) For the purposes of Part 9 (enforcement), a contravention of this section relates to the Part of this Act that would have been contravened if the relationship had not ended.

(7) But conduct is not a contravention of this section in so far as it also amounts to victimisation of B by A.

---

2    Amendment: Words substituted: SI 2010/2279, arts 2, 5, with effect from 1 October 2010.

**Amendments**—SI 2010/2279.

\*\*\*\*

*Chapter 3*
*Employment tribunals*

## 120 Jurisdiction

(1) An employment tribunal has, subject to section 121, jurisdiction to determine a complaint relating to –

    (a)    a contravention of Part 5 (work);
    (b)    a contravention of section 108, 111 or 112 that relates to Part 5.

(2) An employment tribunal has jurisdiction to determine an application by a responsible person (as defined by section 61) for a declaration as to the rights of that person and a worker in relation to a dispute about the effect of a non-discrimination rule.

(3) An employment tribunal also has jurisdiction to determine an application by the trustees or managers of an occupational pension scheme for a declaration as to their rights and those of a member in relation to a dispute about the effect of a non-discrimination rule.

(4) An employment tribunal also has jurisdiction to determine a question that –

    (a)    relates to a non-discrimination rule, and
    (b)    is referred to the tribunal by virtue of section 122.

(5) In proceedings before an employment tribunal on a complaint relating to a breach of a non-discrimination rule, the employer –

    (a)    is to be treated as a party, and
    (b)    is accordingly entitled to appear and be heard.

(6) Nothing in this section affects such jurisdiction as the High Court, a county court, the Court of Session or the sheriff has in relation to a non-discrimination rule.

(7) Subsection (1)(a) does not apply to a contravention of section 53 in so far as the act complained of may, by virtue of an enactment, be subject to an appeal or proceedings in the nature of an appeal.

(8) In subsection (1), the references to Part 5 do not include a reference to section 60(1).

## 121 Armed forces cases

(1) Section 120(1) does not apply to a complaint relating to an act done when the complainant was serving as a member of the armed forces unless –

    (a)    the complainant has made a service complaint about the matter, and
    (b)    the complaint has not been withdrawn.

(2) If the complaint is made under the service complaint procedures, it is to be treated for the purposes of subsection (1)(b) as withdrawn if –

    (a)    neither the officer to whom it is made nor a superior officer refers it to the Defence Council, and

    (b)    the complainant does not apply for it to be referred to the Defence Council.

(3) If the complaint is made under the old service redress procedures, it is to be treated for the purposes of subsection (1)(b) as withdrawn if the complainant does not submit it to the Defence Council under those procedures.

(4) The reference in subsection (3) to the old service redress procedures is a reference to the procedures (other than those relating to the making of a report on a complaint to Her Majesty) referred to in –

    (a)    section 180 of the Army Act 1955,

    (b)    section 180 of the Air Force Act 1955, or

    (c)    section 130 of the Naval Discipline Act 1957.

(5) The making of a complaint to an employment tribunal in reliance on subsection (1) does not affect the continuation of the service complaint procedures or (as the case may be) the old service redress procedures.

\*\*\*\*

### 123 Time limits

(1) [Subject to section 140A,][3] proceedings on a complaint within section 120 may not be brought after the end of –

    (a)    the period of 3 months starting with the date of the act to which the complaint relates, or

    (b)    such other period as the employment tribunal thinks just and equitable.

(2) Proceedings may not be brought in reliance on section 121(1) after the end of –

    (a)    the period of 6 months starting with the date of the act to which the proceedings relate, or

    (b)    such other period as the employment tribunal thinks just and equitable.

(3) For the purposes of this section –

    (a)    conduct extending over a period is to be treated as done at the end of the period;

    (b)    failure to do something is to be treated as occurring when the person in question decided on it.

(4) In the absence of evidence to the contrary, a person (P) is to be taken to decide on failure to do something –

---

3    Amendment: Words inserted: SI 2011/1133, regs 54, 56, with effect from 20 May 2011.

    (a)    when P does an act inconsistent with doing it, or

    (b)    if P does no inconsistent act, on the èxpiry of the period in which P might reasonably have been expected to do it.

**Amendments**—SI 2011/1133.

*Chapter 5*
*Miscellaneous*

### 136 Burden of proof

(1) This section applies to any proceedings relating to a contravention of this Act.

(2) If there are facts from which the court could decide, in the absence of any other explanation, that a person (A) contravened the provision concerned, the court must hold that the contravention occurred.

(3) But subsection (2) does not apply if A shows that A did not contravene the provision.

(4) The reference to a contravention of this Act includes a reference to a breach of an equality clause or rule.

(5) This section does not apply to proceedings for an offence under this Act.

(6) A reference to the court includes a reference to –

    (a)    an employment tribunal;

    (b)    the Asylum and Immigration Tribunal;

    (c)    the Special Immigration Appeals Commission;

    (d)    the First-tier Tribunal;

    (e)    the Special Educational Needs Tribunal for Wales;

    (f)    an Additional Support Needs Tribunal for Scotland.

\*\*\*\*

### 138 Obtaining information, etc.

(1) In this section –

    (a)    P is a person who thinks that a contravention of this Act has occurred in relation to P;

    (b)    R is a person who P thinks has contravened this Act.

(2) A Minister of the Crown must by order prescribe –

    (a)    forms by which P may question R on any matter which is or may be relevant;

    (b)    forms by which R may answer questions by P.

(3) A question by P or an answer by R is admissible as evidence in proceedings under this Act (whether or not the question or answer is contained in a prescribed form).

(4) A court or tribunal may draw an inference from –

    (a)    a failure by R to answer a question by P before the end of the period of 8 weeks beginning with the day on which the question is served;

    (b)    an evasive or equivocal answer.

(5) Subsection (4) does not apply if –

    (a)    R reasonably asserts that to have answered differently or at all might have prejudiced a criminal matter;

    (b)    R reasonably asserts that to have answered differently or at all would have revealed the reason for not commencing or not continuing criminal proceedings;

    (c)    R's answer is of a kind specified for the purposes of this paragraph by order of a Minister of the Crown;

    (d)    R's answer is given in circumstances specified for the purposes of this paragraph by order of a Minister of the Crown;

    (e)    R's failure to answer occurs in circumstances specified for the purposes of this paragraph by order of a Minister of the Crown.

(6) The reference to a contravention of this Act includes a reference to a breach of an equality clause or rule.

(7) A Minister of the Crown may by order –

    (a)    prescribe the period within which a question must be served to be admissible under subsection (3);

    (b)    prescribe the manner in which a question by P, or an answer by R, may be served.

(8) This section –

    (a)    does not affect any other enactment or rule of law relating to interim or preliminary matters in proceedings before a county court, the sheriff or an employment tribunal, and

    (b)    has effect subject to any enactment or rule of law regulating the admissibility of evidence in such proceedings.

\*\*\*\*

# PART 11
## ADVANCEMENT OF EQUALITY

*Chapter 1*
*Public sector equality duty*

### 149 Public sector equality duty

(1) A public authority must, in the exercise of its functions, have due regard to the need to –

    (a)    eliminate discrimination, harassment, victimisation and any other conduct that is prohibited by or under this Act;

    (b)    advance equality of opportunity between persons who share a relevant protected characteristic and persons who do not share it;

(c)    foster good relations between persons who share a relevant protected characteristic and persons who do not share it.

(2) A person who is not a public authority but who exercises public functions must, in the exercise of those functions, have due regard to the matters mentioned in subsection (1).

(3) Having due regard to the need to advance equality of opportunity between persons who share a relevant protected characteristic and persons who do not share it involves having due regard, in particular, to the need to –

(a)    remove or minimise disadvantages suffered by persons who share a relevant protected characteristic that are connected to that characteristic;

(b)    take steps to meet the needs of persons who share a relevant protected characteristic that are different from the needs of persons who do not share it;

(c)    encourage persons who share a relevant protected characteristic to participate in public life or in any other activity in which participation by such persons is disproportionately low.

(4) The steps involved in meeting the needs of disabled persons that are different from the needs of persons who are not disabled include, in particular, steps to take account of disabled persons' disabilities.

(5) Having due regard to the need to foster good relations between persons who share a relevant protected characteristic and persons who do not share it involves having due regard, in particular, to the need to –

(a)    tackle prejudice, and
(b)    promote understanding.

(6) Compliance with the duties in this section may involve treating some persons more favourably than others; but that is not to be taken as permitting conduct that would otherwise be prohibited by or under this Act.

(7) The relevant protected characteristics are –

age;
disability;
gender reassignment;
pregnancy and maternity;
race;
religion or belief;
sex;
sexual orientation.

(8) A reference to conduct that is prohibited by or under this Act includes a reference to –

(a)    a breach of an equality clause or rule;
(b)    a breach of a non-discrimination rule.

(9) Schedule 18 (exceptions) has effect.

\*\*\*\*

*Chapter 2*
*Positive action*

**158 Positive action: general**

(1) This section applies if a person (P) reasonably thinks that –

   (a)   persons who share a protected characteristic suffer a disadvantage connected to the characteristic,

   (b)   persons who share a protected characteristic have needs that are different from the needs of persons who do not share it, or

   (c)   participation in an activity by persons who share a protected characteristic is disproportionately low.

(2) This Act does not prohibit P from taking any action which is a proportionate means of achieving the aim of –

   (a)   enabling or encouraging persons who share the protected characteristic to overcome or minimise that disadvantage,

   (b)   meeting those needs, or

   (c)   enabling or encouraging persons who share the protected characteristic to participate in that activity.

(3) Regulations may specify action, or descriptions of action, to which subsection (2) does not apply.

(4) This section does not apply to –

   (a)   action within section 159(3), or

   (b)   anything that is permitted by virtue of section 104.

(5) If section 104(7) is repealed by virtue of section 105, this section will not apply to anything that would have been so permitted but for the repeal.

(6) This section does not enable P to do anything that is prohibited by or under an enactment other than this Act.

**159 Positive action: recruitment and promotion**

(1) This section applies if a person (P) reasonably thinks that –

   (a)   persons who share a protected characteristic suffer a disadvantage connected to the characteristic, or

   (b)   participation in an activity by persons who share a protected characteristic is disproportionately low.

(2) Part 5 (work) does not prohibit P from taking action within subsection (3) with the aim of enabling or encouraging persons who share the protected characteristic to –

   (a)   overcome or minimise that disadvantage, or

   (b)   participate in that activity.

(3) That action is treating a person (A) more favourably in connection with recruitment or promotion than another person (B) because A has the protected characteristic but B does not.

(4) But subsection (2) applies only if –

(a)　A is as qualified as B to be recruited or promoted,

(b)　P does not have a policy of treating persons who share the protected characteristic more favourably in connection with recruitment or promotion than persons who do not share it, and

(c)　taking the action in question is a proportionate means of achieving the aim referred to in subsection (2).

(5) "Recruitment" means a process for deciding whether to –

(a)　offer employment to a person,

(b)　make contract work available to a contract worker,

(c)　offer a person a position as a partner in a firm or proposed firm,

(d)　offer a person a position as a member of an LLP or proposed LLP,

(e)　offer a person a pupillage or tenancy in barristers' chambers,

(f)　take a person as an advocate's devil or offer a person membership of an advocate's stable,

(g)　offer a person an appointment to a personal office,

(h)　offer a person an appointment to a public office, recommend a person for such an appointment or approve a person's appointment to a public office, or

(i)　offer a person a service for finding employment.

(6) This section does not enable P to do anything that is prohibited by or under an enactment other than this Act.

\*\*\*\*

*Interpretation*

## 212 General interpretation

(1) In this Act –

"armed forces" means any of the naval, military or air forces of the Crown;

"the Commission" means the Commission for Equality and Human Rights;

"detriment" does not, subject to subsection (5), include conduct which amounts to harassment;

"the Education Acts" has the meaning given in section 578 of the Education Act 1996;

"employment" and related expressions are (subject to subsection (11)) to be read with section 83;

"enactment" means an enactment contained in –

(a)　an Act of Parliament,

(b)　an Act of the Scottish Parliament,

(c)　an Act or Measure of the National Assembly for Wales, or

(d)　subordinate legislation;

"equality clause" means a sex equality clause or maternity equality clause;
"equality rule" means a sex equality rule or maternity equality rule;
"man" means a male of any age;
"maternity equality clause" has the meaning given in section 73;
"maternity equality rule" has the meaning given in section 75;
"non-discrimination rule" has the meaning given in section 61;
"occupational pension scheme" has the meaning given in section 1 of the
    Pension Schemes Act 1993;
"parent" has the same meaning as in –
    (a)   the Education Act 1996 (in relation to England and Wales);
    (b)   the Education (Scotland) Act 1980 (in relation to Scotland);

"prescribed" means prescribed by regulations;
"profession" includes a vocation or occupation;
"sex equality clause" has the meaning given in section 66;
"sex equality rule" has the meaning given in section 67;
"subordinate legislation" means –
    (a)   subordinate legislation within the meaning of the Interpretation
        Act 1978, or
    (b)   an instrument made under an Act of the Scottish Parliament or
        an Act or Measure of the National Assembly for Wales;

"substantial" means more than minor or trivial;
"trade" includes any business;
"woman" means a female of any age.

(2) A reference (however expressed) to an act includes a reference to an omission.

(3) A reference (however expressed) to an omission includes (unless there is express provision to the contrary) a reference to –

(a)   a deliberate omission to do something;
(b)   a refusal to do it;
(c)   a failure to do it.

(4) A reference (however expressed) to providing or affording access to a benefit, facility or service includes a reference to facilitating access to the benefit, facility or service.

(5) Where this Act disapplies a prohibition on harassment in relation to a specified protected characteristic, the disapplication does not prevent conduct relating to that characteristic from amounting to a detriment for the purposes of discrimination within section 13 because of that characteristic.

(6) A reference to occupation, in relation to premises, is a reference to lawful occupation.

(7) The following are members of the executive –

(a)   a Minister of the Crown;
(b)   a government department;

(c)   the Welsh Ministers, the First Minister for Wales or the Counsel General to the Welsh Assembly Government;

(d)   any part of the Scottish Administration.

(8) A reference to a breach of an equality clause or rule is a reference to a breach of a term modified by, or included by virtue of, an equality clause or rule.

(9) A reference to a contravention of this Act does not include a reference to a breach of an equality clause or rule, unless there is express provision to the contrary.

(10) "Member", in relation to an occupational pension scheme, means an active member, a deferred member or a pensioner member (within the meaning, in each case, given by section 124 of the Pensions Act 1995).

(11) "Employer", "deferred member", "pension credit member", "pensionable service", "pensioner member" and "trustees or managers" each have, in relation to an occupational pension scheme, the meaning given by section 124 of the Pensions Act 1995.

(12) A reference to the accrual of rights under an occupational pension scheme is to be construed in accordance with that section.

(13) Nothing in section 28, 32, 84, 90, 95 or 100 is to be regarded as an express exception.

\*\*\*\*

## Schedule 6
## Office-holders: Excluded Offices

Section 52

\*\*\*\*

## 2 Political offices

(1) An office or post is not a personal or public office if it is a political office.

(2) A political office is an office or post set out in the second column of the following Table –

| Political setting | Office or post |
| --- | --- |
| Houses of Parliament | An office of the House of Commons held by a member of that House |
| | An office of the House of Lords held by a member of that House |
| | A Ministerial office within the meaning of section 2 of the House of Commons Disqualification Act 1975 |

| | The office of the Leader of the Opposition within the meaning of the Ministerial and other Salaries Act 1975 |
|---|---|
| | The office of the Chief Opposition Whip, or of an Assistant Opposition Whip, within the meaning of that Act |
| Scottish Parliament | An office of the Scottish Parliament held by a member of the Parliament |
| | The office of a member of the Scottish Executive |
| | The office of a junior Scottish Minister |
| National Assembly for Wales | An office of the National Assembly for Wales held by a member of the Assembly |
| | The office of a member of the Welsh Assembly Government |
| Local government in England (outside London) | An office of a county council, district council or parish council in England held by a member of the council |
| | An office of the Council of the Isles of Scilly held by a member of the Council |
| Local government in London | An office of the Greater London Authority held by the Mayor of London or a member of the London Assembly |
| | An office of a London borough council held by a member of the council |
| | An office of the Common Council of the City of London held by a member of the Council |
| Local government in Wales | An office of a county council, county borough council or community council in Wales held by a member of the council |
| Local government in Scotland | An office of a council constituted under section 2 of the Local Government etc. (Scotland) Act 1994 held by a member of the council |
| | An office of a council established under section 51 of the Local Government (Scotland) Act 1973 held by a member of the council |
| Political parties | An office of a registered political party |

(3) The reference to a registered political party is a reference to a party registered in the Great Britain register under Part 2 of the Political Parties, Elections and Referendums Act 2000.

# INCOME TAX (EARNINGS AND PENSIONS) ACT 2003

****

## 7 Meaning of "employment income", "general earnings" and "specific employment income"

(1) This section gives the meaning for the purposes of the Tax Acts of "employment income", "general earnings" and "specific employment income".

(2) "Employment income" means –

(a) earnings within Chapter 1 of Part 3,
(b) any amount treated as earnings (see subsection (5)), or
(c) any amount which counts as employment income (see subsection (6)).

(3) "General earnings" means –

(a) earnings within Chapter 1 of Part 3, or
(b) any amount treated as earnings (see subsection (5)),

excluding in each case any exempt income.

(4) "Specific employment income" means any amount which counts as employment income (see subsection (6)), excluding any exempt income.

(5) Subsection (2)(b) or (3)(b) refers to any amount treated as earnings under –

(a) Chapters 7 to 9 of this Part (agency workers, workers under arrangements made by intermediaries, and workers providing services through managed service companies),
(b) Chapters 2 to 11 of Part 3 (the benefits code),
(c) Chapter 12 of Part 3 (payments treated as earnings), or
(d) section 262 of CAA 2001 (balancing charges to be given effect by treating them as earnings).

(6) Subsection (2)(c) or (4) refers to any amount which counts as employment income by virtue of –

(a) Part 6 (income which is not earnings or share-related),
(b) Part 7 (income and exemptions relating to securities and securities options),
(ba) Part 7A (employment income provided through third parties), or
(c) any other enactment.

**Amendments**—Finance Act 2003, s 140, Sch 22, paras 1, 17(1), (2); Finance Act 2007, s 25(1), Sch 3, Pt 1, paras 1, 2; Finance Act 2011, s 26, Sch 2, paras 2, 5.

****

# JOBSEEKERS ACT 1995

\*\*\*\*

*Trade disputes*

## 14 Trade disputes

(1) [Except in prescribed circumstances,] where—

    (a)    there is a stoppage of work which causes a person not to be employed on any day, and

    (b)    the stoppage is due to a trade dispute at his place of work,

that person is not entitled to a jobseeker's allowance for the week which includes that day unless he proves that he is not directly interested in the dispute.

(2) [Except in prescribed circumstances,] a person who withdraws his labour on any day in furtherance of a trade dispute, but to whom subsection (1) does not apply, is not entitled to a jobseeker's allowance for the week which includes that day.

[(2A) Subsections (1) and (2) do not apply to a person who is a member of a couple unless the other member of the couple is a person to whom either of those subsections apply (but see instead the provision made by section 15).]

(3) If a person who is prevented by subsection (1) from being entitled to a jobseeker's allowance proves that during the stoppage—

    (a)    he became bona fide employed elsewhere;

    (b)    his employment was terminated by reason of redundancy within the meaning of [section 139(1) of the Employment Rights Act 1996], or

    (c)    he bona fide resumed employment with his employer but subsequently left for a reason other than the trade dispute,

subsection (1) shall be taken to have ceased to apply to him on the occurrence of the event referred to in paragraph (a) or (b) or (as the case may be) the first event referred to in paragraph (c).

(4) In this section "place of work", in relation to any person, means the premises or place at which he was employed.

(5) Where separate branches of work which are commonly carried on as separate businesses in separate premises or at separate places are in any case carried on in separate departments on the same premises or at the same place, each of those departments shall, for the purposes of subsection (4), be deemed to be separate premises or (as the case may be) a separate place.

**Amendments**—Employment Rights Act 1996, s 240, Sch 1, para 67(1), (2)(a).

**Prospective Amendments**—Words and subsection in brackets prospectively inserted by Welfare Reform Act 2009, s 4(4), Sch 1, Pt 1, paras 1, 15(1), (2).

\*\*\*\*

# NATIONAL MINIMUM WAGE ACT 1998

\*\*\*\*

## 35 Home workers who are not otherwise "workers"

(1) In determining for the purposes of this Act whether a home worker is or is not a worker, section 54(3)(b) below shall have effect as if for the word "personally" there were substituted "(whether personally or otherwise)".

(2) In this section "home worker" means an individual who contracts with a person, for the purposes of that person's business, for the execution of work to be done in a place not under the control or management of that person.

\*\*\*\*

## 54 Meaning of "worker", "employee" etc

(1) In this Act "employee" means an individual who has entered into or works under (or, where the employment has ceased, worked under) a contract of employment.

(2) In this Act "contract of employment" means a contract of service or apprenticeship, whether express or implied, and (if it is express) whether oral or in writing.

(3) In this Act "worker" (except in the phrases "agency worker" and "home worker") means an individual who has entered into or works under (or, where the employment has ceased, worked under)—

(a) a contract of employment; or
(b) any other contract, whether express or implied and (if it is express) whether oral or in writing, whereby the individual undertakes to do or perform personally any work or services for another party to the contract whose status is not by virtue of the contract that of a client or customer of any profession or business undertaking carried on by the individual;

and any reference to a worker's contract shall be construed accordingly.

(4) In this Act "employer", in relation to an employee or a worker, means the person by whom the employee or worker is (or, where the employment has ceased, was) employed.

(5) In this Act "employment"—

(a) in relation to an employee, means employment under a contract of employment; and
(b) in relation to a worker, means employment under his contract;
and "employed" shall be construed accordingly.

\*\*\*\*

# SOCIAL SECURITY CONTRIBUTIONS AND BENEFITS ACT 1992

\*\*\*\*

*Class 4 contributions*

**15 Class 4 contributions recoverable under the Income Tax Acts**

(1) Class 4 contributions shall be payable for any tax year in respect of all profits which –

   (a)   are immediately derived from the carrying on or exercise of one or more trades, professions or vocations,

   (b)   'are profits chargeable to income tax under Chapter 2 of Part 2 of the Income Tax (Trading and Other Income) Act 2005 for the year of assessment corresponding to that tax year, and

   (c)   are not profits of a trade, profession or vocation carried on wholly outside the United Kingdom.

(2) Class 4 contributions in respect of profits shall be payable –

   (a)   in the same manner as any income tax which is, or would be, chargeable in respect of those profits (whether or not income tax in fact falls to be paid), and

   (b)   by the person on whom the income tax is (or would be) charged,

in accordance with assessments made from time to time under the Income Tax Acts.

(3) The amount of a Class 4 contribution under this section for any tax year is equal to the aggregate of –

   (a)   the main Class 4 percentage of so much of the profits referred to in subsection (1) above (computed in accordance with Schedule 2 to this Act) as exceeds £7,225 but does not exceed £42,475; and

   (b)   the additional Class 4 percentage of so much of those profits as exceeds £42,475;

but the figures specified in this subsection are subject to alteration under section 141 of the Administration Act.

(3ZA) For the purposes of this Act –

   (a)   the main Class 4 percentage is 9 per cent; and

   (b)   the additional Class 4 percentage is 2 per cent;

but the main Class 4 percentage is subject to alteration under section 143 of the Administration Act.

(3A) Where income tax is (or would be) charged on a member of a limited liability partnership in respect of profits arising from the carrying on of a trade or profession by the limited liability partnership, Class 4 contributions shall be payable by him if they would be payable were the trade or profession carried on in partnership by the members.

(4) (*repealed*)

(5) For the purposes of this section the year of assessment which corresponds to a tax year is the year of assessment (within the meaning of the Tax Acts) which consists of the same period as that tax year.

**Amendments**—Limited Liability Partnerships Act 2000, s 13; Income Tax (Trading and Other Income) Act 2005, ss 882(1), 884, Sch 1, Pt 2, paras 419, 420(1), (4), Sch 3; National Insurance Contributions Act 2011, s 2(1)(b); SI 2011/938.

\*\*\*\*

### 39  Rate of widowed mother's allowance and widow's pension

(1) The weekly rate of –

    (a)   a widowed mother's allowance,
    (b)   a widow's pension,

shall be determined in accordance with the provisions of sections 44 to 45B below as they apply in the case of a Category A retirement pension, but subject, in particular, to the following provisions of this section and section 46(2) 46 below.

(2) In the application of sections 44 to 45B below by virtue of subsection (1) above –

    (a)   where the woman's husband was over pensionable age when he died, references in those sections to the pensioner shall be taken as references to the husband, and
    (b)   where the husband was under pensionable age when he died, references in those sections to the pensioner and the tax year in which he attained pensionable age shall be taken as references to the husband and the tax year in which he died.

(2A) In its application by virtue of subsection (1) above, section 44(4) below is to be read as if for the first amount specified in that provision there were substituted a reference to the amount prescribed for the purposes of this subsection.

(3) (*repealed*)

(4) Where a widow's pension is payable to a woman who was under the age of 55 at the time when the applicable qualifying condition was fulfilled, the weekly rate of the pension shall be reduced by 7 per cent. of what it would be apart from this subsection multiplied by the number of years by which her age at that time was less than 55 (any fraction of a year being counted as a year).

(5) For the purposes of subsection (4) above, the time when the applicable qualifying condition was fulfilled is the time when the woman's late husband died or, as the case may be, the time when she ceased to be entitled to a widowed mother's allowance.

(6) In the case of a widow whose late husband died before 11th April 1988 and who either –

    (a)   was over the age of 40 but under the age of 55 at the time of her husband's death; or

    (b)   is over the age of 40 but under the age of 55 at the time when she ceases to be entitled to a widowed mother's allowance,

subsection (4) above shall have effect as if for "55" there were substituted "50", in both places where it occurs.

**Amendments**—Tax Credits Act 2002, s 47, Sch 3, paras 24, 27; Welfare Reform and Pensions Act 1999, s 84(1), Sch 12, Pt I, paras 14, 17; Child Support, Pensions and Social Security Act 2000, s 35(1), (3); Pensions Act 2007, ss 11(5)(c), 27(2), Sch 2, Pt 3, para 3(a), Sch 7, Pt 5; Pensions Act 2008, s 104, Sch 4, paras 1, 3.

\*\*\*\*

*Disability living allowance*

### 71 Disability living allowance

(1) Disability living allowance shall consist of a care component and a mobility component.

(2) A person's entitlement to a disability living allowance may be an entitlement to either component or to both of them.

(3) A person may be awarded either component for a fixed period or for an indefinite period, but if his award of a disability living allowance consists of both components, he may not be awarded the components for different fixed periods.

(4) The weekly rate of a person's disability living allowance for a week for which he has only been awarded one component is the appropriate weekly rate for that component as determined in accordance with this Act or regulations under it.

(5) The weekly rate of a person's disability living allowance for a week for which he has been awarded both components is the aggregate of the appropriate weekly rates for the two components as so determined.

(6) A person shall not be entitled to a disability living allowance unless he satisfies prescribed conditions as to residence and presence in Great Britain.

**Amendments**—Welfare Reform and Pensions Act 1999, s 67(1).

\*\*\*\*

## PART XII
## STATUTORY MATERNITY PAY

### 164 Statutory maternity pay – entitlement and liability to pay

(1) Where a woman who is or has been an employee satisfies the conditions set out in this section, she shall be entitled, in accordance with the following provisions of this Part of this Act, to payments to be known as "statutory maternity pay".

(2) The conditions mentioned in subsection (1) above are –

   (a)   that she has been in employed earner's employment with an employer for a continuous period of at least 26 weeks ending with the week immediately preceding the 14th week before the expected week of confinement but has ceased to work for him.;

   (b)   that her normal weekly earnings for the period of 8 weeks ending with the week immediately preceding the 14th week before the expected week of confinement are not less than the lower earnings limit in force under section 5(1)(a) above immediately before the commencement of the 14th week before the expected week of confinement; and

   (c)   that she has become pregnant and has reached, or been confined before reaching, the commencement of the 11th week before the expected week of confinement.

(3) The liability to make payments of statutory maternity pay to a woman is a liability of any person of whom she has been an employee as mentioned in subsection (2)(a) above.

(4) A woman shall be entitled to payments of statutory maternity pay only if –

   (a)   she gives the person who will be liable to pay it notice of the date from which she expects his liability to pay her statutory maternity pay to begin; and

   (b)   the notice is given at least 28 days before that date or, if that is not reasonably practicable, as soon as is reasonably practicable.

(5) The notice shall be in writing if the person who is liable to pay the woman statutory maternity pay so requests.

(6) Any agreement shall be void to the extent that it purports –

   (a)   to exclude, limit or otherwise modify any provision of this Part of this Act; or

   (b)   to require an employee or former employee to contribute (whether directly or indirectly) towards any costs incurred by her employer or former employer under this Part of this Act.

(7) For the avoidance of doubt, any agreement between an employer and an employee authorising any deductions from statutory maternity pay which the employer is liable to pay to the employee in respect of any period shall not be void by virtue of subsection (6)(a) above if the employer –

(a)    is authorised by that or another agreement to make the same deductions from any contractual remuneration which he is liable to pay in respect of the same period, or

(b)    would be so authorised if he were liable to pay contractual remuneration in respect of that period.

(8) Regulations shall make provision as to a former employer's liability to pay statutory maternity pay to a woman in any case where the former employer's contract of service with her has been brought to an end by the former employer solely, or mainly, for the purpose of avoiding liability for statutory maternity pay.

(9) The Secretary of State may by regulations –

(a)    specify circumstances in which, notwithstanding subsections (1) to (8) above, there is to be no liability to pay statutory maternity pay in respect of a week;

(b)    specify circumstances in which, notwithstanding subsections (1) to (8) above, the liability to make payments of statutory maternity pay is to be a liability of the Commissioners of Inland Revenue;

(c)    specify in what circumstances employment is to be treated as continuous for the purposes of this Part of this Act;

(d)    provide that a woman is to be treated as being employed for a continuous period of at least 26 weeks where –

    (i)    she has been employed by the same employer for at least 26 weeks under two or more separate contracts of service; and

    (ii)    those contracts were not continuous;

(e)    provide that any of the provisions specified in subsection (10) below shall have effect subject to prescribed modifications in such cases as may be prescribed;

(ea)    provide that subsection (4) above shall not have effect, or shall have effect subject to prescribed modifications, in such cases as may be prescribed;

(f)    provide for amounts earned by a woman under separate contracts of service with the same employer to be aggregated for the purposes of this Part of this Act; and

(g)    provide that –

    (i)    the amount of a woman's earnings for any period, or

    (ii)    the amount of her earnings to be treated as comprised in any payment made to her or for her benefit,

shall be calculated or estimated in such manner and on such basis as may be prescribed and that for that purpose payments of a particular class or description made or falling to be made to or by a woman shall, to such extent as may be prescribed, be disregarded or, as the case may be, be deducted from the amount of her earnings.

(10) The provisions mentioned in subsection (9)(e) above are –

(a)    subsection (2)(a) and (b) above; and

(b)    section 166(1) and (2), below.

(11) Any regulations under subsection (9) above which are made by virtue of paragraph (b) of that subsection must be made with the concurrence of the Commissioners of Inland Revenue.

**Amendments**—Employment Act 2002, ss 20(a), 54, Sch 8; Social Security Contributions (Transfer of Functions, etc) Act 1999, s 1(1).

### 165 The maternity pay period

(1) Statutory maternity pay shall be payable, subject to the provisions of this Part of this Act, in respect of each week during a prescribed period ("the maternity pay period") of a duration not exceeding 52 weeks.

(2) Subject to subsections (3) and (7), the maternity pay period shall begin with the 11th week before the expected week of confinement.

(3) Cases may be prescribed in which the first day of the period is to be a prescribed day after the beginning of the 11th week before the expected week of confinement, but not later than the day immediately following the day on which she is confined.

(4) Except in such cases as may be prescribed, statutory maternity pay shall not be payable to a woman by a person in respect of any week during any part of which she works under a contract of service with him.

(5) It is immaterial for the purposes of subsection (4) above whether the work referred to in that subsection is work under a contract of service which existed immediately before the maternity pay period or a contract of service which did not so exist.

(6) Except in such cases as may be prescribed, statutory maternity pay shall not be payable to a woman in respect of any week after she has been confined and during any part of which she works for any employer who is not liable to pay her statutory maternity pay.

(7) Regulations may provide that this section shall have effect subject to prescribed modifications in relation –

- (a) to cases in which a woman has been confined before the 11th week before the expected week of confinement; and
- (b) to cases in which –
- (i) a woman is confined at any time after the end of the week immediately preceding the 11th week before the expected week of confinement; and
- (ii) the maternity pay period has not then commenced for her.

(8) In subsections (1), (4) and (6) "week" means a period of seven days beginning with the day of the week on which the maternity pay period begins.

**Amendments**—Work and Families Act 2006.

\*\*\*\*

### 166 Rate of statutory maternity pay

(1) Statutory maternity pay shall be payable to a woman –

(a) at the earnings-related rate, in respect of the first 6 weeks in respect of which it is payable; and

(b) at whichever is the lower of the earnings-related rate and such weekly rate as may be prescribed, in respect of the remaining portion of the maternity pay period.

(1A) In subsection (1) "week" means any period of seven days.

(2) The earnings-related rate is a weekly rate equivalent to 90 per cent of a woman's normal weekly earnings for the period of 8 weeks immediately preceding the 14th week before the expected week of confinement.

(3) The weekly rate prescribed under subsection (1)(b) above must not be less than the weekly rate of statutory sick pay for the time being specified in section 157(1) above or, if two or more such rates are for the time being so specified, the higher or highest of those rates.

(4) Where for any purpose of this Part of this Act or of regulations it is necessary to calculate the daily rate of statutory maternity pay, the amount payable by way of statutory maternity pay for any day shall be taken as one seventh of the weekly rate.

**Amendments**—Employment Act 2002; Work and Families Act 2006.

\*\*\*\*

### 169 Crown employment – Part XII

The provisions of this Part of this Act apply in relation to women employed by or under the Crown as they apply in relation to women employed otherwise than by or under the Crown.

\*\*\*\*

### 171 Interpretation of Part XII and supplementary provisions

(1) In this Part of this Act –

"confinement" means –
    (a) labour resulting in the issue of a living child, or
    (b) labour after 24 weeks of pregnancy resulting in the issue of a child whether alive or dead,

and "confined" shall be construed accordingly; and where a woman's labour begun on one day results in the issue of a child on another day she shall be taken to be confined on the day of the issue of the child or, if labour results in the issue of twins or a greater number of children, she shall be taken to be confined on the day of the issue of the last of them;

"dismissed" is to be construed in accordance with Part X of the Employment Rights Act 1996;

"employee" means a woman who is –

(a)    gainfully employed in Great Britain either under a contract of
service or in an office (including elective office) with general
earnings (as defined by section 7 of the Income Tax (Earnings
and Pensions) Act 2003);

(b)    *(repealed)*

but subject to regulations made with the concurrence of Her Majesty's Revenue
and Customs which may provide for cases where any such woman is not to be
treated as an employee for the purposes of this Part of this Act and for cases
where a woman who would not otherwise be an employee for those purposes is
to be treated as an employee for those purposes;

"employer", in relation to a woman who is an employee, means a person
who –

(a)    under section 6 above is liable to pay secondary Class 1
contributions in relation to any of her earnings; or

(b)    would be liable to pay such contributions but for –

(i)    the condition in section 6(1)(b), or

(ii)    the employee being under the age of 16;

"maternity pay period" has the meaning assigned to it by section 165(1)
above;

"modifications" includes additions, omissions and amendments, and related
expressions shall be construed accordingly;

"prescribed" means specified in or determined in accordance with
regulations;

(1A) In this Part, except section 165(1), (4) and (6), section 166(1) and
paragraph 3(2) of Schedule 13, "week" means a period of 7 days beginning
with Sunday or such other period as may be prescribed in relation to any
particular case or class of case.

(2) Without prejudice to any other power to make regulations under this Part
of this Act, regulations may specify cases in which, for the purposes of this Part
of this Act or of such provisions of this Part of this Act as may be prescribed –

(a)    two or more employers are to be treated as one;

(b)    two or more contracts of service in respect of which the same woman
is an employee are to be treated as one.

(3) Where, in consequence of the establishment of one or more National
Health Service trusts under the National Health Service Act 2006, the National
Health Service (Wales) Act 2006 or the National Health Service (Scotland)
Act 1978, a woman's contract of employment is treated by a scheme under any
of those Acts as divided so as to constitute two or more contracts, or where an
order under paragraph 26(1) of Schedule 3 to the National Health Service
Act 2006 provides that a woman's contract of employment is so divided,
regulations may make provision enabling her to elect for all of those contracts
to be treated as one contract for the purposes of this Part of this Act or of such
provisions of this Part of this Act as may be prescribed; and any such
regulations may prescribe –

(a)     the conditions that must be satisfied if a woman is to be entitled to make such an election;

(b)     the manner in which, and the time within which, such an election is to be made;

(c)     the persons to whom, and the manner in which, notice of such an election is to be given;

(d)     the information which a woman who makes such an election is to provide, and the persons to whom, and the time within which, she is to provide it;

(e)     the time for which such an election is to have effect;

(f)     which one of the woman's employers under the two or more contracts is to be regarded for the purposes of statutory maternity pay as her employer under the one contract;

and the powers conferred by this subsection are without prejudice to any other power to make regulations under this Part of this Act.

(4) For the purposes of this Part of this Act a woman's normal weekly earnings shall, subject to subsection (6) below, be taken to be the average weekly earnings which in the relevant period have been paid to her or paid for her benefit under the contract of service with the employer in question.

(5) For the purposes of subsection (4) above "earnings" and "relevant period" shall have the meanings given to them by regulations.

(6) In such cases as may be prescribed a woman's normal weekly earnings shall be calculated in accordance with regulations.

(7) Regulations under any of subsections (2) to (6) above must be made with the concurrence of the Commissioners of Inland Revenue.

**Amendments**—Still-Birth (Definition) Act 1992; Employment Rights Act 1996; Income Tax (Earnings and Pensions) Act 2003; SI 2006/1031; Social Security Contributions (Transfer of Functions, etc) Act 1999; Commissioners for Revenue and Customs Act 2005, s 50(6); Work and Families Act 2006; National Health Service (Consequential Provisions) Act 2006.

\*\*\*\*

## 171ZB Entitlement: adoption

(1) Where a person satisfies the conditions in subsection (2) below, he shall be entitled in accordance with the following provisions of this Part to payments to be known as "ordinary statutory paternity pay".

(2) The conditions are –

(a)     that he satisfies prescribed conditions –

(i)     as to relationship with a child who is placed for adoption under the law of any part of the United Kingdom, and

(ii)     as to relationship with a person with whom the child is so placed for adoption;

(b)     that he has been in employed earner's employment with an employer for a continuous period of at least 26 weeks ending with the relevant week;

(c)    that his normal weekly earnings for the period of 8 weeks ending with the relevant week are not less than the lower earnings limit in force under section 5(1)(a) at the end of the relevant week;

(d)    that he has been in employed earner's employment with the employer by reference to whom the condition in paragraph (b) above is satisfied for a continuous period beginning with the end of the relevant week and ending with the day on which the child is placed for adoption; and

(e)    where he is a person with whom the child is placed for adoption, that he has elected to receive statutory paternity pay.

(3) The references in subsection (2) to the relevant week are to the week in which the adopter is notified of being matched with the child for the purposes of adoption.

(4) A person may not elect to receive ordinary statutory paternity pay if he has elected in accordance with section 171ZL below to receive statutory adoption pay.

(5) Regulations may make provision about elections for the purposes of subsection (2)(e) above.

(6) A person's entitlement to ordinary statutory paternity pay under this section shall not be affected by the placement for adoption of more than one child as part of the same arrangement.

(7) In this section, "adopter", in relation to a person who satisfies the condition under subsection (2)(a)(ii) above, means the person by reference to whom he satisfies that condition.

**Amendments**—Work and Families Act 2006, s 11(1), Sch 1, para 13.

### 171ZE  Rate and period of pay

(1) Ordinary statutory paternity pay shall be payable at such fixed or earnings-related weekly rate as may be prescribed by regulations, which may prescribe different kinds of rate for different cases.

(2) Ordinary statutory paternity pay shall be payable in respect of –

(a)    a period of two consecutive weeks within the qualifying period beginning on such date within that period as the person entitled may choose in accordance with regulations, or

(b)    if regulations permit the person entitled to choose to receive ordinary statutory paternity pay in respect of –
(i)    a period of a week, or
(ii)    two non-consecutive periods of a week,

such week or weeks within the qualifying period as he may choose in accordance with regulations.

(3) For the purposes of subsection (2) above, the qualifying period shall be determined in accordance with regulations, which shall secure that it is a period of at least 56 days beginning –

(a) in the case of a person to whom the conditions in section 171ZA(2) above apply, with the date of the child's birth, and

(b) in the case of a person to whom the conditions in section 171ZB(2) above apply, with the date of the child's placement for adoption.

(4) Ordinary statutory paternity pay shall not be payable to a person in respect of a statutory pay week if it is not his purpose at the beginning of the week –

(a) to care for the child by reference to whom he satisfies the condition in sub-paragraph (i) of section 171ZA(2)(a) or 171ZB(2)(a) above, or

(b) to support the person by reference to whom he satisfies the condition in sub-paragraph (ii) of that provision.

(5) A person shall not be liable to pay ordinary statutory paternity pay to another in respect of a statutory pay week during any part of which the other works under a contract of service with him.

(6) It is immaterial for the purposes of subsection (5) above whether the work referred to in that subsection is work under a contract of service which existed immediately before the statutory pay week or a contract of service which did not so exist.

(7) Except in such cases as may be prescribed, ordinary statutory paternity pay shall not be payable to a person in respect of a statutory pay week during any part of which he works for any employer who is not liable to pay him ordinary statutory paternity pay.

(8) The Secretary of State may by regulations specify circumstances in which there is to be no liability to pay ordinary statutory paternity pay in respect of a statutory pay week.

(9) Where more than one child is born as a result of the same pregnancy, the reference in subsection (3)(a) to the date of the child's birth shall be read as a reference to the date of birth of the first child born as a result of the pregnancy.

(10) Where more than one child is placed for adoption as part of the same arrangement, the reference in subsection (3)(b) to the date of the child's placement shall be read as a reference to the date of placement of the first child to be placed as part of the arrangement.

(10A) Where for any purpose of this Part of this Act or of regulations it is necessary to calculate the daily rate of ordinary statutory paternity pay, the amount payable by way of ordinary statutory paternity pay for any day shall be taken as one seventh of the weekly rate.

(11) In this section –

"statutory pay week", in relation to a person entitled to ordinary statutory paternity pay, means a week chosen by him as a week in respect of which ordinary statutory paternity pay shall be payable;

"week" means any period of seven days.

**Amendments**—Work and Families Act 2006, s 11(1), Sch 1, para 13.

*Ordinary and additional statutory paternity pay: supplementary provisions*

### 171ZF  Restrictions on contracting out

(1) Any agreement shall be void to the extent that it purports –

    (a)    to exclude, limit or otherwise modify any provision of this Part of this Act, or

    (b)    to require an employee or former employee to contribute (whether directly or indirectly) towards any costs incurred by his employer or former employer under this Part of this Act.

(2) For the avoidance of doubt, any agreement between an employer and an employee authorising any deductions from ordinary statutory paternity pay or additional statutory paternity pay which the employer is liable to pay to the employee in respect of any period shall not be void by virtue of subsection (1)(a) above if the employer –

    (a)    is authorised by that or another agreement to make the same deductions from any contractual remuneration which he is liable to pay in respect of the same period, or

    (b)    would be so authorised if he were liable to pay contractual remuneration in respect of that period.

**Amendments**—Employment Act 2002, s 2; Work and Families Act 2006, s 11(1), Sch 1, para 13.

\*\*\*\*

### 171ZEB  Entitlement to additional statutory paternity pay: adoption

(1) The Secretary of State may by regulations provide that, where all the conditions in subsection (2) are satisfied in relation to a person ("the claimant"), the claimant shall be entitled in accordance with the following provisions of this Part to payments to be known as "additional statutory paternity pay".

(2) Those conditions are –

    (a)    that the claimant satisfies prescribed conditions –

    (i)    as to relationship with a child who has been placed for adoption under the law of any part of the United Kingdom, and

    (ii)    as to relationship with a person with whom the child is so placed for adoption ("the adopter");

    (b)    that the claimant has been in employed earner's employment with an employer for a continuous period of at least the prescribed length ending with a prescribed week;

    (c)    that the claimant's normal weekly earnings for a prescribed period ending with a prescribed week are not less than the lower earnings limit in force under section 5(1)(a) at the end of that week;

    (d)    if regulations so provide, that the claimant continues to work in employed earner's employment (whether or not with that employer) until a prescribed time;

(e) that the adopter became entitled to statutory adoption pay by reference to the placement of the child for adoption;

(f) that the adopter has, in relation to employment as an employed or self-employed earner, taken action that is treated by regulations as constituting for the purposes of this section the adopter's return to work;

(g) that the day on which the adopter is treated as returning to work falls –

(i) after the end of a prescribed period beginning with the placement of the child for adoption, but

(ii) at a time when at least a prescribed part of the adopter's adoption pay period remains unexpired;

(h) that it is the claimant's intention to care for the child during a period beginning not later than a prescribed time.

(3) The regulations may –

(a) exclude the application of the conditions mentioned in paragraphs (f) and (g) of subsection (2) in cases where the adopter has died, and

(b) provide that the condition mentioned in paragraph (e) of that subsection shall have effect with prescribed modifications in such cases.

(4) A person may not elect to receive additional statutory paternity pay if he has elected in accordance with section 171ZL to receive statutory adoption pay.

(5) A person's entitlement to additional statutory paternity pay under this section shall not be affected by the placement for adoption of more than one child as part of the same arrangement.

**Amendments**—Work and Families Act 2006, s 11(1), Sch 1, para 13.

\*\*\*\*

*Statutory Adoption Pay*

### 171ZL Entitlement

(1) Where a person who is, or has been, an employee satisfies the conditions in subsection (2) below, he shall be entitled in accordance with the following provisions of this Part to payments to be known as "statutory adoption pay".

(2) The conditions are –

(a) that he is a person with whom a child is, or is expected to be, placed for adoption under the law of any part of the United Kingdom;

(b) that he has been in employed earner's employment with an employer for a continuous period of at least 26 weeks ending with the relevant week;

(c) that he has ceased to work for the employer;

(d) that his normal weekly earnings for the period of 8 weeks ending with the relevant week are not less than the lower earnings limit in force under section 5(1)(a) at the end of the relevant week; and

(e) that he has elected to receive statutory adoption pay.

(3) The references in subsection (2)(b) and (d) above to the relevant week are to the week in which the person is notified that he has been matched with the child for the purposes of adoption.

(4) A person may not elect to receive statutory adoption pay if –

   (a)   he has elected in accordance with section 171ZB above to receive statutory paternity pay, or

   (b)   he falls within subsection (4A).

(4A) A person falls within this subsection if –

   (a)   the child is, or is expected to be, placed for adoption with him as a member of a couple;

   (b)   the other member of the couple is a person to whom the conditions in subsection (2) above apply; and

   (c)   the other member of the couple has elected to receive statutory adoption pay.

(4B) For the purposes of subsection (4A), a person is a member of a couple if –

   (a)   in the case of an adoption or expected adoption under the law of England and Wales, he is a member of a couple within the meaning of section 144(4) of the Adoption and Children Act 2002;

   (b)   in the case of an adoption or an expected adoption under the law ... of Northern Ireland, he is a member of a married couple;

   (c)   in the case of an adoption or expected adoption under the law of Scotland he is a member of a relevant couple within the meaning of section 29(3) of the Adoption and Children (Scotland) Act 2007.

(5) A person's entitlement to statutory adoption pay shall not be affected by the placement, or expected placement, for adoption of more than one child as part of the same arrangement.

(6) A person shall be entitled to payments of statutory adoption pay only if –

   (a)   he gives the person who will be liable to pay it notice of the date from which he expects the liability to pay him statutory adoption pay to begin; and

   (b)   the notice is given at least 28 days before that date or, if that is not reasonably practicable, as soon as is reasonably practicable.

(7) The notice shall be in writing if the person who is liable to pay the statutory adoption pay so requests.

(8) The Secretary of State may by regulations –

   (a)   provide that subsection (2)(b), (c) or (d) above shall have effect subject to prescribed modifications in such cases as may be prescribed;

   (b)   provide that subsection (6) above shall not have effect, or shall have effect subject to prescribed modifications, in such cases as may be prescribed;

   (c)   impose requirements about evidence of entitlement;

(d)   specify in what circumstances employment is to be treated as continuous for the purposes of this section;

(e)   provide that a person is to be treated for the purposes of this section as being employed for a continuous period of at least 26 weeks where –

    (i)    he has been employed by the same employer for at least 26 weeks under two or more separate contracts of service; and

    (ii)   those contracts were not continuous;

(f)   provide for amounts earned by a person under separate contracts of service with the same employer to be aggregated for the purposes of this section;

(g)   provide that –

    (i)    the amount of a person's earnings for any period, or

    (ii)   the amount of his earnings to be treated as comprised in any payment made to him or for his benefit,

shall be calculated or estimated for the purposes of this section in such manner and on such basis as may be prescribed and that for that purpose payments of a particular class or description made or falling to be made to or by a person shall, to such extent as may be prescribed, be disregarded or, as the case may be, be deducted from the amount of his earnings;

(h)   make provision about elections for statutory adoption pay.

**Amendments**—Employment Act 2002, s 4; SI 2006/2012; SI 2011/1740.

### 171ZM  Liability to make payments

(1) The liability to make payments of statutory adoption pay is a liability of any person of whom the person entitled to the payments has been an employee as mentioned in section 171ZL(2)(b) above.

(2) Regulations shall make provision as to a former employer's liability to pay statutory adoption pay to a person in any case where the former employee's contract of service with him has been brought to an end by the former employer solely, or mainly, for the purpose of avoiding liability for statutory adoption pay.

(3) The Secretary of State may, with the concurrence of the Board, by regulations specify circumstances in which, notwithstanding this section, liability to make payments of statutory adoption pay is to be a liability of the Board.

**Amendments**—Inserted by the Employment Act 2002.

### 171ZO  Restrictions on contracting out

(1) Any agreement shall be void to the extent that it purports –

(a)   to exclude, limit or otherwise modify any provision of this Part of this Act, or

(b)   to require an employee or former employee to contribute (whether directly or indirectly) towards any costs incurred by his employer or former employer under this Part of this Act.

(2) For the avoidance of doubt, any agreement between an employer and an employee authorising any deductions from statutory adoption pay which the employer is liable to pay to the employee in respect of any period shall not be void by virtue of subsection (1)(a) above if the employer –

(a) is authorised by that or another agreement to make the same deductions from any contractual remuneration which he is liable to pay in respect of the same period, or

(b) would be so authorised if he were liable to pay contractual remuneration in respect of that period.

**Amendments**—Inserted by the Employment Act 2002.

## PART XIIA
## INCAPACITY FOR WORK

### 171A  Test of incapacity for work

*(1)  For the purposes of this Act, save as otherwise expressly provided, whether a person is capable or incapable of work shall be determined in accordance with the provisions of this Part of this Act.*

*(2)  Regulations may make provision as to –*

*(a)  the information or evidence required for the purpose of determining whether a person is capable or incapable of work, and*

*(b)  the manner in which that information or evidence is to be provided,*

*and may provide that if a person without good cause fails to provide that information or evidence, or to do so in the manner required, he shall be treated as capable of work.*

*(2A)  In subsection (2)(a) above the reference to such information or evidence as is there mentioned includes information or evidence capable of being used for assisting or encouraging the person in question to obtain work or enhance his prospects of obtaining it.*

*(3)  Regulations may provide that in any case where it falls to be determined whether a person is capable of work –*

*(a)  he may be called to attend for such medical examination as may be required in accordance with regulations, and*

*(b)  if he fails without good cause to attend for or submit himself to such examination, he shall be treated as capable of work.*

*(4)  Regulations may prescribe for the purposes of this section –*

*(a)  matters which are or are not to be taken into account in determining whether a person does or does not have good cause for any act or omission, or*

*(b)  circumstances in which a person is or is not to be regarded as having or not having good cause for any act or omission.*

*(5) All information supplied in pursuance of this section shall be taken for all purposes to be information relating to social security.*

**Amendments**—Social Security (Incapacity for Work) Act 1994, s 5; Welfare Reform and Pensions Act 1999, s 70, Sch 8, Pt II, paras 20, 23(1), (2).

**Prospective Amendments**—Prospectively repealed by Welfare Reform Act 2007, ss 28(1), 67, Sch 3, para 9(1), (12), Sch 8 with effect from a date to be appointed.

### 171ZP  Relationship with benefits and other payments etc

*(1) Except as may be prescribed, a day which falls within the adoption pay period shall not be treated as a day of incapacity for work for the purposes of determining, for this Act, whether it forms part of a period of incapacity for work for the purposes of incapacity benefit.*

*(2) Regulations may provide that in prescribed circumstances a day which falls within the adoption pay period shall be treated as a day of incapacity for work for the purposes of determining entitlement to the higher rate of short-term incapacity benefit or to long-term incapacity benefit.*

*(3) Regulations may provide that an amount equal to a person's statutory adoption pay for a period shall be deducted from any such benefit in respect of the same period and a person shall be entitled to such benefit only if there is a balance after the deduction and, if there is such a balance, at a weekly rate equal to it.*

(4) Subject to subsections (5) and (6) below, any entitlement to statutory adoption pay shall not affect any right of a person in relation to remuneration under any contract of service ("contractual remuneration").

(5) Subject to subsection (6) below –

(a)  any contractual remuneration paid to a person by an employer of his in respect of a week in the adoption pay period shall go towards discharging any liability of that employer to pay statutory adoption pay to him in respect of that week; and

(b)  any statutory adoption pay paid by an employer to a person who is an employee of his in respect of a week in the adoption pay period shall go towards discharging any liability of that employer to pay contractual remuneration to him in respect of that week.

(6) Regulations may make provision as to payments which are, and those which are not, to be treated as contractual remuneration for the purposes of subsections (4) and (5) above.

(7) In subsection (5) above, "week" means a period of seven days beginning with the day of the week on which the adoption pay period begins.

**Amendments**—Employment Act 2002, s 4.

**Prospective Amendments**—Prospectively repealed by Welfare Reform Act 2007, ss 28(1), 67, Sch 3, para 9(1), (12), Sch 8 with effect from a date to be appointed.

\*\*\*\*

# TRADE UNION AND LABOUR RELATIONS (CONSOLIDATION) ACT 1992

\*\*\*\*

### 16  Remedy against trustees for unlawful use of union property

\*\*\*\*

(1) A member of a trade union who claims that the trustees of the union's property—

- (a)  have so carried out their functions, or are proposing so to carry out their functions, as to cause or permit an unlawful application of the union's property, or
- (b)  have complied, or are proposing to comply, with an unlawful direction which has been or may be given, or purportedly given, to them under the rules of the union,

may apply to the court for an order under this section.

(2)  In a case relating to property which has already been unlawfully applied, or to an unlawful direction that has already been complied with, an application under this section may be made only by a person who was a member of the union at the time when the property was applied or, as the case may be, the direction complied with.

(3) Where the court is satisfied that the claim is well-founded, it shall make such order as it considers appropriate.

The court may in particular—

- (a)  require the trustees (if necessary, on behalf of the union) to take all such steps as may be specified in the order for protecting or recovering the property of the union;
- (b)  appoint a receiver of, or in Scotland a judicial factor on, the property of the union;
- (c)  remove one or more of the trustees.

(4) Where the court makes an order under this section in a case in which—

- (a)  property of the union has been applied in contravention of an order of any court, or in compliance with a direction given in contravention of such an order, or
- (b)  the trustees were proposing to apply property in contravention of such an order or to comply with any such direction,

the court shall by its order remove all the trustees except any trustee who satisfies the court that there is a good reason for allowing him to remain a trustee.

(5) Without prejudice to any other power of the court, the court may on an application for an order under this section grant such interlocutory relief (in Scotland, such interim order) as it considers appropriate.

(6) This section does not affect any other remedy available in respect of a breach of trust by the trustees of a trade union's property.

(7) In this section "member", in relation to a trade union consisting wholly or partly of, or of representatives of, constituent or affiliated organisations, includes a member of any of the constituent or affiliated organisations.

\*\*\*\*

# APPENDIX B

# AGENCY WORKERS REGULATIONS 2010

## SI 2010/93

\*\*\*\*

### 7 Qualifying period

(1) Regulation 5 does not apply unless an agency worker has completed the qualifying period.

(2) To complete the qualifying period the agency worker must work in the same role with the same hirer for 12 continuous calendar weeks, during one or more assignments.

(3) For the purposes of this regulation and regulations 8 and 9, the agency worker works in "the same role" unless –

(a)  the agency worker has started a new role with the same hirer, whether supplied by the same or by a different temporary work agency;

(b)  the work or duties that make up the whole or the main part of that new role are substantively different from the work or duties that made up the whole or the main part of the previous role; and

(c)  the temporary work agency has informed the agency worker in writing of the type of work the agency worker will be required to do in the new role.

(4) For the purposes of this regulation and regulation 10, any week during the whole or part of which an agency worker works during an assignment is counted as a calendar week.

(5) For the purposes of this regulation and regulations 8 and 9, when calculating whether any weeks completed with a particular hirer are continuous, where –

(a)  the agency worker has started working during an assignment, and there is a break, either between assignments or during an assignment, when the agency worker is not working,

(b)  paragraph (8) applies to that break, and

(c)  the agency worker returns to work in the same role with the same hirer, any continuous weeks during which the agency worker worked for that hirer before the break shall be carried forward and treated as continuous with any weeks during which the agency worker works for that hirer after the break.

(6) For the purposes of this regulation and regulation 8, when calculating the number of weeks during which the agency worker has worked, where the agency worker has –

(a)  started working in a role during an assignment, and

   (b)   is unable to continue working for a reason described in paragraph (8)(c) or (8)(d)(i), (ii) or (iii),

for the period that is covered by one or more such reasons, that agency worker shall be deemed to be working in that role with the hirer, for the original intended duration, or likely duration of the assignment, whichever is the longer.

(7) Where –

   (a)   an assignment ends on grounds which are maternity grounds within the meaning of section 68A of the 1996 Act, and
   (b)   the agency worker is deemed to be working in that role in accordance with paragraph (6),

the fact that an agency worker is actually working in another role, whether for the same or a different hirer during the period mentioned in paragraph (6) or any part of that period, does not affect the operation of that paragraph.

(8) This paragraph applies where there is a break between assignments, or during an assignment, when the agency worker is not working, and the break is –

   (a)   for any reason and the break is not more than six calendar weeks;
   (b)   wholly due to the fact that the agency worker is incapable of working in consequence of sickness or injury, and the requirements of paragraph (9) are satisfied;
   (c)   related to pregnancy, childbirth or maternity and is at a time in a protected period;
   (d)   wholly for the purpose of taking time off or leave, whether statutory or contractual, to which the agency worker is otherwise entitled which is –
      (i)   ordinary, compulsory or additional maternity leave;
      (ii)   ordinary or additional adoption leave;
      (iii)   paternity leave;
      (iv)   time off or other leave not listed in sub-paragraph (d)(i), (ii) or (iii); or
      (v)   for more than one of the reasons listed in sub-paragraph (d)(i) to (iv);
   (e)   wholly due to the fact that the agency worker is required to attend at any place in pursuance of being summoned for service as a juror under the Juries Act 1974, the Coroners Act 1988, the Court of Session Act 1988 or the Criminal Procedure (Scotland) Act 1995, and the break is 28 calendar weeks or less;
   (f)   wholly due to a temporary cessation in the hirer's requirement for any worker to be present at the establishment and work in a particular role, for a pre-determined period of time according to the established custom and practices of the hirer; or
   (g)   wholly due to a strike, lock-out or other industrial action at the hirer's establishment; or
   (h)   wholly due to more than one of the reasons listed in sub-paragraphs (b), (c), (d), (e), (f) or (g).

(9) Paragraph (8)(b) only applies where –

(a)    the break is 28 calendar weeks or less;

(b)    paragraph (8)(c) does not apply; and

(c)    if required to do so by the temporary work agency, the agency worker has provided such written medical evidence as may reasonably be required.

(10) For the purposes of paragraph (8)(c), a protected period begins at the start of the pregnancy, and the protected period associated with any particular pregnancy ends at the end of the 26 weeks beginning with childbirth or, if earlier, when the agency worker returns to work.

(11) For the purposes of paragraph (10) "childbirth" means the birth of a living child or the birth of a child whether living or dead after 24 weeks of pregnancy.

(12) Time spent by an agency worker working during an assignment before 1st October 2011 does not count for the purposes of this regulation.

****

## 9 Structure of assignments

(1) Notwithstanding paragraphs (1) and (2) of regulation 7, and regulation 8, if paragraphs (3) and (4) apply an agency worker shall be treated as having completed the qualifying period from the time at which the agency worker would have completed the qualifying period but for the structure of the assignment or assignments mentioned in paragraph (3).

(2) Notwithstanding paragraphs (1) and (2) of regulation 7, and regulation 8, if paragraphs (3) and (4) apply an agency worker who has completed the qualifying period and –

(a)    is no longer entitled to the rights conferred by regulation 5, but

(b)    would be so entitled but for the structure of the assignment or assignments mentioned in paragraph (3),

shall be treated as continuing to be entitled to those rights from the time at which the agency worker completed that period.

(3) This paragraph applies when an agency worker has –

(a)    completed two or more assignments with a hirer (H),

(b)    completed at least one assignment with H and one or more earlier assignments with hirers connected to H, or

(c)    worked in more than two roles during an assignment with H, and on at least two occasions has worked in a role that was not the "same role" as the previous role within the meaning of regulation 7(3).

(4) This paragraph applies where –

(a)    the most likely explanation for the structure of the assignment, or assignments, mentioned in paragraph (3) is that H, or the temporary work agency supplying the agency worker to H, or, where applicable, H and one or more hirers connected to H, intended to prevent the agency worker from being entitled to, or from continuing to be entitled to, the rights conferred by regulation 5; and

(b)     the agency worker would be entitled to, or would continue to be entitled to, the rights conferred by regulation 5 in relation to H, but for that structure.

(5) The following matters in particular shall be taken into account in determining whether the structure of the assignment or assignments mentioned in paragraph (3) shows that the most likely explanation for it is that mentioned in paragraph (4)(a) –

(a)     the length of the assignments;

(b)     the number of assignments with H and, where applicable, hirers connected to H;

(c)     the number of times the agency worker has worked in a new role with H and, where applicable, hirers connected to H, and that new role is not the "same role" within the meaning of regulation 7(3);

(d)     the number of times the agency worker has returned to work in the same role within the meaning of regulation 7(3) with H and, where applicable, hirers connected to H;

(e)     the period of any break between assignments with H and, where applicable, hirers connected to H.

(6) For the purposes of this regulation hirers are connected to a hirer if one hirer (directly or indirectly) has control of the other hirer or a third person (directly or indirectly) has control of both hirers.

\*\*\*\*

### 18  Complaints to employment tribunals etc

(1) In this regulation "respondent" includes the hirer and any temporary work agency.

(2) Subject to regulation 17(5), an agency worker may present a complaint to an employment tribunal that a temporary work agency or the hirer has infringed a right conferred on the agency worker by regulation 5, 12, 13 or 17 (2).

(3) An agency worker may present a complaint to an employment tribunal that a temporary work agency has –

(a)     breached a term of the contract of employment described in regulation 10(1)(a); or

(b)     breached a duty under regulation 10(1)(b), (c) or (d).

(4) Subject to paragraph (5), an employment tribunal shall not consider a complaint under this regulation unless it is presented before the end of the period of three months beginning –

(a)     in the case of an alleged infringement of a right conferred by regulation 5, 12 or 17(2) or a breach of a term of the contract described in regulation 10(1)(a) or of a duty under regulation 10(1)(b),

(c) or (d), with the date of the infringement, detriment or breach to which the complaint relates or, where an act or failure to act is part of a series of similar acts or failures comprising the infringement, detriment or breach, the last of them;

(b) in the case of an alleged infringement of the right conferred by regulation 13, with the date, or if more than one the last date, on which other individuals, whether or not employed by the hirer, were informed of the vacancy.

(5) A tribunal may consider any such complaint which is out of time if, in all the circumstances of the case, it considers that it is just and equitable to do so.

(6) For the purposes of calculating the date of the infringement, detriment or breach, under paragraph (4)(a) –

(a) where a term in a contract infringes a right conferred by regulation 5, 12 or 17(2), or breaches regulation 10(1), that infringement or breach shall be treated, subject to sub-paragraph (b), as taking place on each day of the period during which the term infringes that right or breaches that duty;

(b) a deliberate failure to act that is contrary to regulation 5, 12 or 17(2) or 10(1) shall be treated as done when it was decided on.

(7) In the absence of evidence establishing the contrary, a person (P) shall be taken for the purposes of paragraph (6)(b) to decide not to act –

(a) when P does an act inconsistent with doing the failed act; or

(b) if P has done no such inconsistent act, when the period expires within which P might reasonably have been expected to have done the failed act if it was to be done.

(8) Where an employment tribunal finds that a complaint presented to it under this regulation is well founded, it shall take such of the following steps as it considers just and equitable –

(a) making a declaration as to the rights of the complainant in relation to the matters to which the complaint relates;

(b) ordering the respondent to pay compensation to the complainant;

(c) recommending that the respondent take, within a specified period, action appearing to the tribunal to be reasonable, in all the circumstances of the case, for the purpose of obviating or reducing the adverse effect on the complainant of any matter to which the complaint relates.

(9) Where a tribunal orders compensation under paragraph (8)(b), and there is more than one respondent, the amount of compensation payable by each or any respondent shall be such as may be found by the tribunal to be just and equitable having regard to the extent of each respondent's responsibility for the infringement to which the complaint relates.

(10) Subject to paragraphs (12) and (13), where a tribunal orders compensation under paragraph (8)(b), the amount of the compensation awarded shall be such as the tribunal considers just and equitable in all the circumstances having regard to –

    (a)    the infringement or breach to which the complaint relates; and

    (b)    any loss which is attributable to the infringement.

(11) The loss shall be taken to include –

    (a)    any expenses reasonably incurred by the complainant in consequence of the infringement or breach; and

    (b)    loss of any benefit which the complainant might reasonably be expected to have had but for the infringement or breach.

(12) Subject to paragraph (13), where a tribunal orders compensation under paragraph (8)(b), any compensation which relates to an infringement or breach of the rights –

    (a)    conferred by regulation 5 or 10; or

    (b)    conferred by regulation 17(2) to the extent that the infringement or breach relates to regulation 5 or 10,

shall not be less than two weeks' pay, calculated in accordance with regulation 19.

(13) Paragraph (12) does not apply where the tribunal considers that in all the circumstances of the case, taking into account the conduct of the claimant and respondent, two weeks' pay is not a just and equitable amount of compensation, and the amount shall be reduced as the tribunal consider appropriate.

(14) Where a tribunal finds that regulation 9(4) applies and orders compensation under paragraph (8)(b), the tribunal may make an additional award of compensation under paragraph 8(b), which shall not be more than £5,000, and where there is more than one respondent the proportion of any additional compensation awarded that is payable by each of them shall be such as the tribunal considers just and equitable having regard to the extent to which it considers each to have been responsible for the fact that regulation 9(4)(a) applies.

(15) Compensation in respect of treating an agency worker in a manner which infringes the right conferred by regulation 5, 12 or 13 or breaches regulation 10(1)(b), (c) or (d), or breaches a term of the contract described in regulation 10(1)(a), shall not include compensation for injury to feelings.

(16) In ascertaining the loss the tribunal shall apply the same rule concerning the duty of a person to mitigate loss as applies to damages recoverable under the common law of England and Wales or (as the case may be) the law of Scotland.

(17) Where the tribunal finds that the act, or failure to act, to which the complaint relates was to any extent caused or contributed to by action of the

complainant, it shall reduce the amount of the compensation by such proportion as it considers just and equitable having regard to that finding.

(18) If a temporary work agency or the hirer fails, without reasonable justification, to comply with a recommendation made by an employment tribunal under paragraph (8)(c) the tribunal may, if it thinks it just and equitable to do so –

    (a)    increase the amount of compensation required to be paid to the complainant in respect of the complaint, where an order was made under paragraph (8)(b); or

    (b)    make an order under paragraph (8)(b).

\*\*\*\*

# PATERNITY AND ADOPTION LEAVE REGULATIONS 2002

## SI 2002/2788

\*\*\*\*

### 2 Interpretation

(1) In these Regulations –

"the 1996 Act" means the Employment Rights Act 1996;

"additional adoption leave" means leave under section 75B of the 1996 Act;

"additional maternity leave" means leave under section 73 of the 1996 Act;

"adopter", in relation to a child, means a person who has been matched with the child for adoption, or, in a case where two people have been matched jointly, whichever of them has elected to be the child's adopter for the purposes of these Regulations;

"adoption agency" has the meaning given, in relation to England and Wales, by section 1(4) of the Adoption Act 1976 and, in relation to Scotland, by section 119(1) of the Adoption and Children (Scotland) Act 2007;

"adoption leave" means ordinary or additional adoption leave;

"child" means a person who is, or when placed with an adopter for adoption was, under the age of 18;

"contract of employment" means a contract of service or apprenticeship, whether express or implied, and (if it is express) whether oral or in writing;

"employee" means an individual who has entered into or works under (or, where the employment has ceased, worked under) a contract of employment;

"employer" means the person by whom an employee is (or, where the employment has ceased, was) employed;

"expected week", in relation to the birth of a child, means the week, beginning with midnight between Saturday and Sunday, in which it is expected that the child will be born;

"ordinary adoption leave" means leave under section 75A of the 1996 Act;

"parental leave" means leave under regulation 13(1) of the Maternity and Parental Leave etc Regulations 1999;

"partner", in relation to a child's mother or adopter, means a person (whether of a different sex or the same sex) who lives with the mother or adopter and the child in an enduring family relationship but is not a relative of the mother or adopter of a kind specified in paragraph (2);

"paternity leave" means leave under regulation 4 or regulation 8 of these Regulations;

"statutory adoption leave" means ordinary adoption leave and additional adoption leave;

"statutory adoption leave period" means the period during which the adopter is on statutory adoption leave;

"statutory leave" means leave provided for in Part 8 of the 1996 Act.

(2) The relatives of a child's mother or adopter referred to in the definition of "partner" in paragraph (1) are the mother's or adopter's parent, grandparent, sister, brother, aunt or uncle.

(3) References to relationships in paragraph (2) –

    (a)    are to relationships of the full blood or half blood or, in the case of an adopted person, such of those relationships as would exist but for the adoption, and

    (b)    include the relationship of a child with his adoptive, or former adoptive, parents,

but do not include any other adoptive relationships.

(4) For the purposes of these Regulations –

    (a)    a person is matched with a child for adoption when an adoption agency decides that that person would be a suitable adoptive parent for the child, either individually or jointly with another person, and

    (b)    a person is notified of having been matched with a child on the date on which he receives notification of the agency's decision, under regulation 11(2) of the Adoption Agencies Regulations 1983 or regulation 8(5) of the Adoption Agencies (Scotland) Regulations 2009;

    (c)    a person elects to be a child's adopter, in a case where the child is matched with him and another person jointly, if he and that person agree, at the time at which they are matched, that he and not the other person will be the adopter.

(5) A reference in any provision of these Regulations to a period of continuous employment is to a period computed in accordance with Chapter 1 of Part 14 of the 1996 Act, as if that provision were a provision of that Act.

(6) For the purposes of these Regulations, any two employers shall be treated as associated if –

    (a)    one is a company of which the other (directly or indirectly) has control; or

    (b)    both are companies of which a third person (directly or indirectly) has control;

    and "associated employer" shall be construed accordingly.

**Amendments**—SI 2011/1740.

\*\*\*\*

### 8 Entitlement to paternity leave: adoption

(1) An employee is entitled to be absent from work for the purpose of caring for a child or supporting the child's adopter if he –

    (a)    satisfies the conditions specified in paragraph (2), and

    (b)    has complied with the notice requirements in regulation 10 and, where applicable, the evidential requirements in that regulation.

(2) The conditions referred to in paragraph (1) are that the employee –

(a) has been continuously employed for a period of not less than 26 weeks ending with the week in which the child's adopter is notified of having been matched with the child;

(b) is either married to, the civil partner or the partner of the child's adopter, and

(c) has, or expects to have, the main responsibility (apart from the responsibility of the adopter) for the upbringing of the child.

(3) In paragraph (2)(a), "week" means the period of seven days beginning with Sunday.

(4) An employee shall be treated as having satisfied the condition in paragraph (2)(b) if he would have satisfied it but for the fact that the child's adopter died during the child's placement.

(5) An employee shall be treated as having satisfied the condition in paragraph (2)(c) if he would have satisfied it but for the fact that the child's placement with the adopter has ended.

(6) An employee's entitlement to leave under this regulation shall not be affected by the placement for adoption of more than one child as part of the same arrangement

**Amendments**—SI 2005/2114.

## 9 Options in respect of leave under regulation 8

(1) An employee may choose to take either one week's leave or two consecutive weeks' leave in respect of a child under regulation 8.

(2) The leave may only be taken during the period of 56 days beginning with the date on which the child is placed with the adopter.

(3) Subject to paragraph (2) and, where applicable, paragraph (4), an employee may choose to begin a period of leave under regulation 8 on –

(a) the date on which the child is placed with the adopter;

(b) the date falling such number of days after the date on which the child is placed with the adopter as the employee may specify in a notice under regulation 10, or

(c) a predetermined date, specified in a notice under that regulation, which is later than the date on which the child is expected to be placed with the adopter.

(4) In a case where the adopter was notified of having been matched with the child before 6th April 2003, the employee may choose to begin a period of leave only on a predetermined date, specified in a notice under regulation 10, which is at least 28 days after the date on which that notice is given.

**10 Notice and evidential requirements for leave under regulation 8**

(1) An employee must give his employer notice of his intention to take leave in respect of a child under regulation 8, specifying –

    (a)    the date on which the adopter was notified of having been matched with the child;

    (b)    the date on which the child is expected to be placed with the adopter;

    (c)    the length of the period of leave that, in accordance with regulation 9(1), the employee has chosen to take, and

    (d)    the date on which, in accordance with regulation 9(3) or (4), the employee has chosen that his period of leave should begin.

(2) The notice provided for in paragraph (1) must be given to the employer –

    (a)    no more than seven days after the date on which the adopter is notified of having been matched with the child, or

    (b)    in a case where it was not reasonably practicable for the employee to give notice in accordance with sub-paragraph (a), as soon as is reasonably practicable.

(3) Where the employer requests it, an employee must also give his employer a declaration, signed by the employee, to the effect that the purpose of his absence from work will be that specified in regulation 8(1) and that he satisfies the conditions of entitlement in regulation 8(2)(b) and (c).

(4) An employee who has given notice under paragraph (1) may vary the date he has chosen as the date on which his period of leave will begin, subject to paragraph (5) and provided that he gives his employer notice of the variation –

    (a)    where the variation is to provide for the employee's period of leave to begin on the date on which the child is placed with the adopter, at least 28 days before the date specified in the employee's notice under paragraph (1) as the date on which the child is expected to be placed with the adopter;

    (b)    where the variation is to provide for the employee's period of leave to begin on a date that is a specified number of days (or a different specified number of days) after the date on which the child is placed with the adopter, at least 28 days before the date falling that number of days after the date specified in the employee's notice under paragraph (1) as the date on which the child is expected to be placed with the adopter;

    (c)    where the variation is to provide for the employee's period of leave to begin on a predetermined date, at least 28 days before that date,

or, if it is not reasonably practicable to give the notice at least 28 days before whichever date is relevant, as soon as is reasonably practicable.

(5) In a case where regulation 9(4) applies, an employee may only vary the date which he has chosen as the date on which his period of leave will begin by substituting a different predetermined date.

(6) In a case where –

(a)  the employee has chosen to begin his period of leave on a particular predetermined date, and

(b)  the child is not placed with the adopter on or before that date,

the employee must vary his choice of date, by substituting a later predetermined date or (except in a case where regulation 9(4) applies) exercising an alternative option under regulation 9(3), and give his employer notice of the variation as soon as is reasonably practicable.

(7) An employee must give his employer a further notice, as soon as is reasonably practicable after the child's placement, of the date on which the child was placed.

(8) Notice under paragraph (1), (4), (6) or (7) shall be given in writing, if the employer so requests.

\*\*\*\*

**11  Commencement of leave under regulation 8**

(1) Except in the case referred to in paragraph (2), an employee's period of paternity leave under regulation 8 begins on the date specified in his notice under regulation 10(1), or, where he has varied his choice of date under regulation 10(4) or (6), on the date specified in his notice under that provision (or the last such date if he has varied his choice more than once).

(2) In a case where –

(a)  the employee has chosen to begin his period of leave on the date on which the child is placed with the adopter, and

(b)  he is at work on that date,

the employee's period of leave begins on the day after that date.

\*\*\*\*

## PART 3
## ADOPTION LEAVE

**15  Entitlement to ordinary adoption leave**

(1) An employee is entitled to ordinary adoption leave in respect of a child if he –

(a)  satisfies the conditions specified in paragraph (2), and

(b)  has complied with the notice requirements in regulation 17 and, where applicable, the evidential requirements in that regulation.

(2) The conditions referred to in paragraph (1) are that the employee –

(a)  is the child's adopter;

(b)  has been continuously employed for a period of not less than 26 weeks ending with the week in which he was notified of having been matched with the child, and

(c)     has notified the agency that he agrees that the child should be placed with him and on the date of placement.

(3) In paragraph (2)(b), "week" means the period of seven days beginning with Sunday.

(4) An employee's entitlement to leave under this regulation shall not be affected by the placement for adoption of more than one child as part of the same arrangement.

### 16 Options in respect of ordinary adoption leave

(1) Except in the case referred to in paragraph (2), an employee may choose to begin a period of ordinary adoption leave on –

(a)     the date on which the child is placed with him for adoption, or
(b)     a predetermined date, specified in a notice under regulation 17, which is no more than 14 days before the date on which the child is expected to be placed with the employee and no later than that date.

(2) In a case where the employee was notified of having been matched with the child before 6th April 2003, the employee may choose to begin a period of leave only on a predetermined date, specified in a notice under regulation 17, which is after 6th April 2003 and at least 28 days after the date on which that notice is given.

### 17 Notice and evidential requirements for ordinary adoption leave

(1) An employee must give his employer notice of his intention to take ordinary adoption leave in respect of a child, specifying –

(a)     the date on which the child is expected to be placed with him for adoption, and
(b)     the date on which, in accordance with regulation 16(1) or (2), the employee has chosen that his period of leave should begin.

(2) The notice provided for in paragraph (1) must be given to the employer –

(a)     no more than seven days after the date on which the employee is notified of having been matched with the child for the purposes of adoption, or
(b)     in a case where it was not reasonably practicable for the employee to give notice in accordance with sub-paragraph (a), as soon as is reasonably practicable.

(3) Where the employer requests it, an employee must also provide his employer with evidence, in the form of one or more documents issued by the adoption agency that matched the employee with the child, of –

(a)     the name and address of the agency;
(b)     (*revoked*)
(c)     the date on which the employee was notified that he had been matched with the child, and

(d)    the date on which the agency expects to place the child with the employee.

(4) An employee who has given notice under paragraph (1) may vary the date he has chosen as the date on which his period of leave will begin, subject to paragraph (5) and provided that he gives his employer notice of the variation –

(a)    where the variation is to provide for the employee's period of leave to begin on the date on which the child is placed with him for adoption, at least 28 days before the date specified in his notice under paragraph (1) as the date on which the child is expected to be placed with him;

(b)    where the variation is to provide for the employee's period of leave to begin on a predetermined date (or a different predetermined date), at least 28 days before that date,

or, if it is not reasonably practicable to give the notice 28 days before whichever date is relevant, as soon as is reasonably practicable.

(5) In a case where regulation 16(2) applies, an employee may only vary the date which he has chosen as the date on which his period of leave will begin by substituting a different predetermined date.

(6) Notice under paragraph (1) or (4) shall be given in writing, if the employer so requests.

(7) An employer who is given notice under paragraph (1) or (4) of the date on which an employee has chosen that his period of ordinary adoption leave should begin shall notify the employee, within 28 days of his receipt of the notice, of the date on which the period of additional adoption leave to which the employee will be entitled (if he satisfies the conditions in regulation 20(1)) after his period of ordinary adoption leave ends.

(8) The notification provided for in paragraph (7) shall be given to the employee –

(a)    where the employer is given notice under paragraph (1), within 28 days of the date on which he received that notice;

(b)    where the employer is given notice under paragraph (4), within 28 days of the date on which the employee's ordinary adoption leave period began.

Amendments—SI 2004/923

## 18 Duration and commencement of ordinary adoption leave

(1) Subject to regulations 22 and 24, an employee's ordinary adoption leave period is a period of 26 weeks.

(2) Except in the case referred to in paragraph (3), an employee's ordinary adoption leave period begins on the date specified in his notice under regulation 17(1), or, where he has varied his choice of date under regulation 17(4), on the date specified in his notice under that provision (or the last such date if he has varied his choice more than once).

(3) In a case where –

(a)    the employee has chosen to begin his period of leave on the date on which the child is placed with him, and

(b)    he is at work on that date,

the employee's period of leave begins on the day after that date.

### 19 Application of terms and conditions during ordinary adoption leave and additional adoption leave

(1) An employee who takes ordinary adoption leave or additional adoption leave –

(a)    is entitled, during the period of leave, to the benefit of all of the terms and conditions of employment which would have applied if he had not been absent, and

(b)    is bound, during that period, by any obligations arising under those terms and conditions, subject only to the exceptions in sections 75A(3)(b) and 75B(4)(b) of the 1996 Act.

(2) In paragraph (1)(a), "terms and conditions of employment" has the meaning given by sections 75A(4) and 75B(5) of the 1996 Act, and accordingly does not include terms and conditions about remuneration.

(3) For the purposes of sections 75A and 75B of the 1996 Act, only sums payable to an employee by way of wages or salary are to be treated as remuneration.

Amendments—SI 2008/1966.

### 20 Additional adoption leave: entitlement, duration and commencement

(1) An employee is entitled to additional adoption leave in respect of a child if –

(a)    the child was placed with him for adoption,

(b)    he took ordinary adoption leave in respect of the child, and

(c)    his ordinary adoption leave period did not end prematurely under regulation 22(2)(a) or 24.

(2) Subject to regulations 22 and 24, an employee's additional adoption leave period is a period of 26 weeks beginning on the day after the last day of his ordinary adoption leave period.

### 21 (revoked)

Amendments—Revoked by SI 2008/1966.

### 22 Disrupted placement in the course of adoption leave

(1) This regulation applies where –

(a) an employee has begun a period of adoption leave in respect of a child before the placement of the child with him, and the employee is subsequently notified that the placement will not be made, or

(b) during an employee's period of adoption leave in respect of a child placed with him –
   (i) the child dies, or
   (ii) the child is returned to the adoption agency under section 30(3) of the Adoption Act 1976 or in Scotland, the child is returned to the adoption agency, adoption society or nominated person in accordance with section 25(6) of the Adoption and Children (Scotland) Act 2007.

(2) Subject to regulation 24, in a case where this regulation applies –

(a) except in the circumstances referred to in sub-paragraphs (b) and (c), the employee's adoption leave period ends eight weeks after the end of the relevant week specified in paragraph (3);

(b) where the employee is taking ordinary adoption leave and the period of 26 weeks provided for in regulation 18 ends within eight weeks of the end of the relevant week –
   (i) the employee's ordinary adoption leave period ends on the expiry of the 26-week period;
   (ii) the employee is entitled to additional adoption leave, and
   (iii) the employee's additional adoption leave period ends eight weeks after the end of the relevant week;

(c) where the employee is taking additional adoption leave and the period of 26 weeks provided for in regulation 20 ends within eight weeks of the end of the relevant week, the employee's additional adoption leave period ends on the expiry of the 26-week period.

(3) The relevant week referred to in paragraph (2) is –

(a) in a case falling within paragraph (1)(a), the week during which the person with whom the child was to be placed for adoption is notified that the placement will not be made;

(b) in a case falling within paragraph (1)(b)(i), the week during which the child dies;

(c) in a case falling within paragraph (1)(b)(ii), the week during which the child is returned.

(4) In paragraph (3), "week" means the period of seven days beginning with Sunday.

**Amendments**—SI 2011/1740.

### 23 Redundancy during adoption leave

(1) This regulation applies where, during an employee's ordinary or additional adoption leave period, it is not practicable by reason of redundancy for his employer to continue to employ him under his existing contract of employment.

(2) Where there is a suitable available vacancy, the employee is entitled to be offered (before the end of his employment under his existing contract) alternative employment with his employer or his employer's successor, or an associated employer, under a new contract of employment which complies with paragraph (3) and takes effect immediately on the ending of his employment under the previous contract.

(3) The new contract of employment must be such that –

    (a)    the work to be done under it is of a kind which is both suitable in relation to the employee and appropriate for him to do in the circumstances, and

    (b)    its provisions as to the capacity and place in which he is to be employed, and as to the other terms and conditions of his employment, are not substantially less favourable to him than if he had continued to be employed under the previous contract.

\*\*\*\*

### 25  Requirement to notify intention to return during adoption leave period

(1) An employee who intends to return to work earlier than the end of his additional adoption leave period must give his employer at least 8 weeks' notice of the date on which he intends to return.

(2) If an employee attempts to return to work earlier than the end of his additional adoption leave period without complying with paragraph (1), his employer is entitled to postpone his return to a date such as will secure, subject to paragraph (3), that he has at least 8 weeks' notice of the employee's return.

(2A) An employee who complies with his obligations in paragraph (1) or whose employer has postponed his return in the circumstances described in paragraph (2), and who then decides to return to work –

    (a)    earlier than the original return date, must give his employer not less than 8 weeks' notice of the date on which he now intends to return;

    (b)    later than the original return date, must give his employer not less than 8 weeks' notice ending with the original return date.

(2B) In paragraph (2A) the "original return date" means the date which the employee notified to his employer as the date of his return to work under paragraph (1), or the date to which his return was postponed by his employer under paragraph (2).

(3) An employer is not entitled under paragraph (2) to postpone an employee's return to work to a date after the end of the employee's additional adoption leave period.

(4) If an employee whose return has been postponed under paragraph (2) has been notified that he is not to return to work before the date to which his return was postponed, the employer is under no contractual obligation to pay him remuneration until the date to which his return was postponed if he returns to work before that date.

(5) This regulation does not apply in a case where the employer did not notify the employee in accordance with regulation 17(7) and (8) of the date on which the employee's additional adoption leave period would end.

(6) In a case where an employee's adoption leave is curtailed because regulation 22 applies, the references in this regulation to the end of an employee's additional adoption leave period are references to the date on which that period would have ended had that regulation not applied, irrespective of whether it was the employee's ordinary adoption leave period or his additional adoption leave period that was curtailed.

**Amendments**—SI 2006/2014.

### 26 Right to return after adoption leave

(1) An employee who returns to work after a period of ordinary adoption leave which was –

   (a)   an isolated period of leave, or
   (b)   the last of two or more consecutive periods of statutory leave, which did not include any period of additional maternity leave or additional adoption leave or a period of parental leave of more than four weeks,

is entitled to return from leave to the job in which he was employed before his absence.

(2) An employee who returns to work after –

   (a)   a period of additional adoption leave, whether or not preceded by another period of statutory leave, or
   (b)   a period of ordinary adoption leave not falling within the description in paragraph (1)(a) or (b) above,

is entitled to return from leave to the job in which he was employed before his absence, or, if it is not reasonably practicable for the employer to permit him to return to that job, to another job which is both suitable for him and appropriate for him to do in the circumstances.

(3) The reference in paragraphs (1) and (2) to the job in which an employee was employed before his absence is a reference to the job in which he was employed –

   (a)   if his return is from an isolated period of adoption leave, immediately before that period began;
   (b)   if his return is from consecutive periods of statutory leave, immediately before the first such period.

(4) This regulation does not apply where regulation 23 applies.

### 27 Incidents of the right to return from adoption leave

(1) An employee's right to return una\der regulation 26 is to return –

   (a)   with his seniority, pension rights and similar rights as they would have been if he had not been absent, and

(b)     on terms and conditions not less favourable than those which would have been applied to him if he had not been absent.

(2) In the case of accrual of rights under an employment-related benefit scheme within the meaning given by Schedule 5 to the Social Security Act 1989, nothing in paragraph (1)(a) concerning the treatment of additional adoption leave shall be taken to impose a requirement which exceeds the requirements of paragraphs 5, 5B and 6 of that Schedule.

(3) The provisions in paragraph (1) for an employee to be treated as if he had not been absent refer to his absence –

(a)     if his return is from an isolated period of ordinary adoption leave, since the beginning of that period;

(b)     if his return is from consecutive periods of statutory leave, since the beginning of the first such period.

**Amendments**—SI 2008/1966; SI 2004/923.

## PART 4
## PROVISIONS APPLICABLE IN RELATION TO BOTH PATERNITY AND ADOPTION LEAVE

### 28 Protection from detriment

(1) An employee is entitled under section 47C of the 1996 Act not to be subjected to any detriment by any act, or any deliberate failure to act, by his employer because –

(a)     the employee took or sought to take paternity leave or ordinary or additional adoption leave;

(b)     the employer believed that the employee was likely to take ordinary or additional adoption leave,

(bb)    the employee undertook, considered undertaking or refused to undertake work in accordance with regulation 21A; or

(c)     the employee failed to return after a period of additional adoption leave in a case where –

(i)     the employer did not notify him, in accordance with regulation 17(7) and (8) or otherwise, of the date on which that period ended, and he reasonably believed that the period had not ended, or

(ii)    the employer gave him less than 28 days' notice of the date on which the period would end, and it was not reasonably practicable for him to return on that date.

(2) Paragraph (1) does not apply where the detriment in question amounts to dismissal within the meaning of Part 10 of the 1996 Act.

**Amendments**—SI 2006/2014.

**29 Unfair dismissal**

(1) An employee who is dismissed is entitled under section 99 of the 1996 Act to be regarded for the purpose of Part 10 of that Act as unfairly dismissed if –

    (a)    the reason or principal reason for the dismissal is of a kind specified in paragraph (3), or

    (b)    the reason or principal reason for the dismissal is that the employee is redundant, and regulation 23 has not been complied with.

(2) An employee who is dismissed shall also be regarded for the purposes of Part 10 of the 1996 Act as unfairly dismissed if –

    (a)    the reason (or, if more than one, the principal reason) for the dismissal is that the employee was redundant;

    (b)    it is shown that the circumstances constituting the redundancy applied equally to one or more employees in the same undertaking who had positions similar to that held by the employee and who have not been dismissed by the employer, and

    (c)    it is shown that the reason (or, if more than one, the principal reason) for which the employee was selected for dismissal was a reason of a kind specified in paragraph (3).

(3) The kinds of reason referred to in paragraph (1) and (2) are reasons connected with the fact that –

    (a)    the employee took, or sought to take, paternity or adoption leave;

    (b)    the employer believed that the employee was likely to take ordinary or additional adoption leave,

    (bb)    the employee undertook, considered undertaking or refused to undertake work in accordance with regulation 21A; or

    (c)    the employee failed to return after a period of additional adoption leave in a case where –

        (i)    the employer did not notify him, in accordance with regulation 17(7) and (8) or otherwise, of the date on which that period would end, and he reasonably believed that the period had not ended, or

        (ii)    the employer gave him less than 28 days' notice of the date on which the period would end, and it was not reasonably practicable for him to return on that date.

(4) (*revoked*)

(5) Paragraph (1) does not apply in relation to an employee if –

    (a)    it is not reasonably practicable for a reason other than redundancy for the employer (who may be the same employer or a successor of his) to permit the employee to return to a job which is both suitable for the employee and appropriate for him to do in the circumstances;

    (b)    an associated employer offers the employee a job of that kind, and

    (c)    the employee accepts or unreasonably refuses that offer.

(6) Where, on a complaint of unfair dismissal, any question arises as to whether the operation of paragraph (1) is excluded by the provisions of paragraph (5), it is for the employer to show that the provisions in question were satisfied in relation to the complainant.

**Amendments**—SI 2006/2014.

# ADDITIONAL PATERNITY LEAVE REGULATIONS 2010

## SI 2010/1055

\*\*\*\*

### 3  Application

\*\*\*\*

(2) The provisions relating to additional paternity leave under regulation 14 have effect only in relation to children matched with a person who is notified of having been matched on or after 3rd April 2011.

\*\*\*\*

# ADDITIONAL STATUTORY PATERNITY PAY (GENERAL) REGULATIONS 2010

## SI 2010/1056

### PART 1
### INTRODUCTION

### 1 Citation and commencement

These Regulations may be cited as the Additional Statutory Paternity Pay (General) Regulations 2010 and come into force on 6th April 2010.

\*\*\*\*

### 3 Application

Subject to the provisions of Part 12ZA of the Act and of these Regulations, there is entitlement to –

    (a)    additional statutory paternity pay (birth) in respect of children whose expected week of birth begins on or after 3rd April 2011;

    (b)    additional statutory paternity pay (adoption) in respect of children matched with a person who is notified of having been matched on or after 3rd April 2011.

\*\*\*\*

### PART 3
### ADDITIONAL STATUTORY PATERNITY PAY (ADOPTION)

### 12 Entitlement to additional statutory paternity pay (adoption)

(1) A person ("P") is entitled to additional statutory paternity pay (adoption) if –

    (a)    P satisfies the conditions –

        (i)    as to relationship with a child placed for adoption ("C") and the child's adopter ("A") specified in paragraph (2); and

        (ii)    as to continuity of employment and normal weekly earnings specified in paragraph (3);

    (b)    A satisfies the conditions specified in regulation 13;

    (c)    P intends to care for C during the additional statutory paternity pay period (adoption) in respect of C;

    (d)    A has signed the declaration referred to in regulation 15(1)(c); and

    (e)    P has complied with the requirements in regulation 15, including, where applicable, the requirements in regulation 15(3).

(2) The conditions referred to in paragraph (1)(a)(i) are that –

    (a)    P is married to, or is the civil partner or the partner of, A; and

(b)    P has been matched with C for adoption.

(3)  The conditions referred to in paragraph (1)(a)(ii) are that –

(a)    P has been in employed earner's employment with an employer for a continuous period of at least 26 weeks ending with the relevant week;

(b)    P's normal weekly earnings for the period of eight weeks ending with the relevant week are not less than the lower earnings limit in force under section 5(1)(a) of the Act at the end of the relevant week; and

(c)    P continues in employed earner's employment with the employer by reference to whom the condition in sub-paragraph (a) is satisfied for a continuous period beginning with the relevant week and ending with the week before the additional statutory paternity pay period (adoption) in respect of C begins.

(4) The references in paragraph (3) to the relevant week are to the week in which P was notified of having been matched with C.

### 13  Conditions to be satisfied by the child's adopter

The conditions referred to in regulation 12(1)(b) are that A –

(a)    became entitled, by reference to the adoption of C, to statutory adoption pay;

(b)    has taken action constituting a return to work within the meaning of regulation 19;

(c)    has taken the action referred to in paragraph (b) not less than two weeks after the date C was placed for adoption with A; and

(d)    has at least two weeks of their adoption pay period which remain unexpired.

### 14  Additional statutory paternity pay period (adoption)

(1)  For the purposes of section 171ZEE(2)(a) of the Act, the date on which the additional statutory paternity pay period (adoption) in respect of C begins is –

(a)    the date specified by P in accordance with regulation 15(2)(d) or last varied in accordance with regulation 15(6); or

(b)    if later, the date of A's taking action constituting a return to work within the meaning of regulation 19,

being, in either case, a date which falls no earlier than 20 weeks after the date on which C was placed for adoption.

(2)  For the purposes of section 171ZEE(2)(b)(ii) of the Act, the date on which the additional statutory paternity pay period (adoption) in respect of C ends is the date specified by P in accordance with regulation 15(2)(e) or last varied in accordance with regulation 15(6).

(3)  For the purposes of section 171ZEE(4)(a) of the Act, the additional statutory paternity pay period (adoption) in respect of C shall not last longer than 26 weeks.

(4)  This paragraph applies instead of paragraph (2) where –

(a)    A dies after the beginning but before the end of the additional statutory paternity pay period (adoption) in respect of C; and

(b)    as soon as reasonably practicable after A's death, P gives the person paying P additional statutory paternity pay (adoption) notice in writing of A's death.

(5) Where paragraph (4) applies, the date on which the additional statutory paternity pay period (adoption) in respect of C ends is the date –

(a)    on which the adoption pay period in respect of C, which would have applied but for A's death, would have ended; or

(b)    if earlier, such date which, for the purposes of section 171ZEE(2)(b)(ii) of the Act, P may specify in the notice given under paragraph (4)(b).

**Amendments**—SI 2011/678.

### 15 Application for, and evidence of entitlement to, additional statutory paternity pay (adoption)

(1) P shall apply for additional statutory paternity pay (adoption) to the person ("E") who will be liable to pay P such pay by providing to E –

(a)    the information, in writing, specified in paragraph (2);

(b)    a written declaration, signed by P –
   (i)    that that information is correct;
   (ii)    that P intends to care for C during the additional statutory paternity pay period (adoption) in respect of C; and
   (iii)    that P meets the conditions in regulation 12(2);

(c)    a written declaration, signed by A –
   (i)    that they have given notice to their employer that they are returning to work;
   (ii)    that they satisfy the condition in regulation 13(a);
   (iii)    specifying their name, address and National Insurance Number;
   (iv)    specifying the start date of their adoption pay period in respect of C;
   (v)    specifying the date on which they intend to return to work;
   (vi)    confirming that, in relation to C, P is, to A's knowledge, the sole applicant for additional statutory paternity pay; and
   (vii)    providing A's consent as regards the processing by E of the information provided pursuant to paragraphs (i) to (vi).

(2) The information referred to in paragraph (1)(a) is as follows –

(a)    P's name;

(b)    the date on which P was notified that they had been matched with C;

(c)    the date of C's placement for adoption;

(d)    the date on which P expects that E's liability to pay additional statutory paternity pay (adoption) will begin; and

(e)    the date on which P expects that E's liability to pay additional statutory paternity pay (adoption) will end.

(3) P shall also provide, if E so requests within 28 days of receiving the information and declarations referred to in paragraph (1) –

(a)  evidence, in the form of one or more documents issued by the adoption agency that matched P with C, of –
   (i)   the name and address of the agency;
   (ii)  the date on which P was notified that they had been matched with C; and
   (iii) the date on which the agency was expecting to place C with A and P; and
(b)  the name and business address of A's employer (or, if A is self-employed, A's business address).

(4) The information and declarations referred to in paragraph (1) must be provided to E at least eight weeks before the date specified by P pursuant to paragraph (2)(d).

(5) P must give E what is requested under paragraph (3) within 28 days of E requesting it.

(6) P may, after applying for additional statutory paternity pay (adoption) under paragraph (1), withdraw that application, vary the date on which it is expected that E's liability to pay additional statutory paternity pay (adoption) will begin, or (before the additional statutory paternity pay period (adoption) in respect of C has begun) vary the date on which it is expected that E's liability to pay additional statutory paternity pay (adoption) will end, by notice in writing to E given –

(a)  if withdrawing an application, at least six weeks before the date specified by P pursuant to paragraph (2)(d), or
(b)  if varying the date on which it is expected that E's liability to pay additional statutory paternity pay (adoption) will begin, at least six weeks before the earlier of the date varied or the new date, or
(c)  if varying the date on which it is expected that E's liability to pay additional statutory paternity pay (adoption) will end, at least six weeks before the earlier of the date varied or the new date, or
(d)  in a case where it was not reasonably practicable to give notice in accordance with sub-paragraph (a), (b) or (c), as soon as is reasonably practicable.

(7) When P has applied for additional statutory paternity pay (adoption) under paragraph (1), P must give E written notice as soon as reasonably practicable if at any time –

(a)  P no longer satisfies the conditions in regulation 12(2); or
(b)  A no longer intends to take action constituting a return to work within the meaning of regulation 19.

(8) When E has been provided with all of the information and the declarations referred to in paragraph (1) (together with, if applicable, what E has requested

under paragraph (3)), E must, within 28 days, confirm the start and end dates of E's liability to pay P additional statutory paternity pay (adoption), by notice in writing to P.

## 16 Entitlement to additional statutory paternity pay (adoption) in the event of the death of the adopter

(1) In a case where A dies before the end of their adoption pay period in respect of C (but before the additional statutory paternity pay period (adoption) in respect of C has begun) –

(a)   the provisions in regulations 12 and 13 shall apply, subject to the following modifications –
    (i)   regulation 12(1)(d) shall not apply;
    (ii)   regulation 12(1)(e) shall apply –
(aa)   as if the references to regulation 15 were references to regulation 17; and
(bb)   in a case where the date of which P informs E pursuant to regulation 17(1)(a) is earlier than the date by which P has complied with the other requirements of regulation 17, as if such other requirements had been complied with on such earlier date provided that they are complied with as soon as reasonably practicable thereafter;
    (i)   the condition in regulation 12(2)(a) shall be taken to be satisfied if it would have been satisfied but for the fact that A had died;
    (ii)   the condition in regulation 13(a) shall be taken to be satisfied if A would have satisfied it but for the fact that A had died; and.
    (iii)   regulation 13(b), (c) and (d) shall not apply;
(b)   regulation 14 shall not apply;
(c)   for the purposes of section 171ZEE(2)(a) of the Act, the date on which the additional statutory paternity pay period (adoption) in respect of C begins is such date, being the date of A's death or a later date, as P informs E of in accordance with regulation 17(1)(a) or as is last varied in accordance with regulation 17(7) or 17(8);
(d)   for the purposes of section 171ZEE(2)(b)(ii) of the Act, the date on which the additional statutory paternity pay period (adoption) in respect of C ends is, where earlier than the relevant date, the date specified by P in accordance with regulation 17(2)(d) or last varied in accordance with regulation 17(7) or 17(8);
(e)   for the purposes of section 171ZEE(4)(a) of the Act, the additional statutory paternity pay period (adoption) in respect of C shall not last longer than 39 weeks; and
(f)   regulation 15 shall be replaced by regulation 17.

(2) In paragraph (1)(d), "the relevant date" means the date on which the adoption pay period in respect of C which would have applied but for A's death, would have ended.

(3) References in this regulation to A's adoption pay period in respect of C include, where A's death occurred before A's adoption pay period in respect of C started, references to such period as would have existed but for the fact that A had died.

**17 Application for, and evidence of entitlement to, additional statutory paternity pay (adoption) in the event of the death of the adopter**

(1) P shall apply for additional statutory paternity pay (adoption) to the person ("E") who will be liable to pay P such pay by –

- (a) informing E of the date on which P wishes the additional statutory paternity pay period (adoption) in respect of C to begin or the date (if in the past) on which P wishes such period to have begun;
- (b) providing E with the information, in writing, specified in paragraph (2); and
- (c) providing E with a written declaration, signed by P –
  - (i) that the information referred to in sub-paragraph (b) is correct;
  - (ii) that P intends to care for C during the additional statutory paternity pay period (adoption) in respect of C; and
  - (iii) that P meets the conditions in regulation 12(2) (as modified by regulation 16(1)(a)(iii)).

(2) The information referred to in paragraph (1)(b) is as follows –

- (a) P's name;
- (b) the date on which P was notified that they had been matched with C;
- (c) the date of C's placement for adoption;
- (d) the date on which P expects that E's liability to pay additional statutory paternity pay (adoption) will end;
- (e) A's name, address, and National Insurance number;
- (f) the start date of A's adoption pay period in respect of C or, where A's death occurred before their adoption pay period in respect of C started, the date that that period would have started but for the fact that A had died; and
- (g) the date of A's death.

(3) P shall also provide, if E so requests within 28 days of receiving the information and declaration referred to in paragraph (1) –

- (a) evidence, in the form of one or more documents issued by the adoption agency that matched P with C, of
  - (i) the name and address of the agency;
  - (ii) the date on which P was notified that they had been matched with C; and
  - (iii) the date on which the agency was expecting to place C with A and P; and
- (b) the name and business address of A's employer (or, if A was self-employed, A's business address).

(4) Subject to paragraph (5), the information and declaration referred to in paragraph (1) must be provided to E as soon as reasonably practicable after, and in any event within eight weeks of, the date of A's death.

(5) If provided at least six weeks before the date of which P informs E pursuant to paragraph (1)(a), the information and evidence referred to in paragraph (1)(b) and (c) may be provided more than eight weeks after the date of A's death.

(6) P must give E what is requested under paragraph (3) within 28 days of E requesting it.

(7) Within eight weeks of the date of A's death, P may, after applying for additional statutory paternity pay (adoption) under paragraph (1) and by giving E notice in writing, withdraw that application, vary the date (if in the future) on which P wishes the additional statutory paternity pay period (adoption) in respect of C to begin, or (either before or after such period has begun) vary the date on which it is expected that E's liability to pay additional statutory paternity pay (adoption) will end, with immediate effect.

(8) More than eight weeks after the date of A's death, P may, after applying for additional statutory paternity pay (adoption) under paragraph (1), withdraw that application, vary the date (if in the future) on which P wishes the additional statutory paternity pay period (adoption) in respect of C to begin, or (before such period has begun), vary the date on which it is expected that E's liability to pay additional statutory paternity pay (adoption) will end, by notice in writing to E given –

(a)   if withdrawing an application, at least six weeks before the date of which P informs E pursuant to paragraph (1)(a), or

(b)   if varying the date on which P wishes the additional statutory paternity pay period (adoption) in respect of C to begin, at least six weeks before the earlier of the date varied or the new date, or

(c)   if varying the date on which it is expected that E's liability to pay additional statutory paternity pay (adoption) will end, at least six weeks before the earlier of the date varied or the new date, or

(d)   in a case where it was not reasonably practicable to give notice in accordance with sub-paragraph (a), (b) or (c), as soon as is reasonably practicable.

(9) When E has been provided with all of the information and the declaration referred to in paragraph (1) (together with, if applicable, what E has requested under paragraph (3)), E must, within 28 days, confirm the date on which the additional statutory paternity pay period (adoption) in respect of C begins or began and the date on which E's liability to pay P additional statutory paternity pay (adoption) ends, by notice in writing to P.

**18 Entitlement to additional statutory paternity pay (adoption) where there is more than one employer**

(1) Additional statutory paternity pay (adoption) shall be payable to a person in respect of a statutory pay week during any part of which that person works only for an employer –

    (a)    who is not liable to pay that person additional statutory paternity pay (adoption); and

    (b)    for whom that person worked in the week immediately preceding the 14th week before the expected week of the placement for adoption.

(2) In this regulation "statutory pay week" means a week that that person has chosen in respect of which additional statutory paternity pay (adoption) shall be payable.

\*\*\*\*

**20 Work during the additional statutory paternity pay period**

(1) In a case where additional statutory paternity pay is being paid to a person who works during the additional statutory paternity pay period for an employer who is not liable to pay that person additional statutory paternity pay and who does not fall within, as appropriate, regulation 11(1)(b) or regulation 18(1)(b), there shall be no liability to pay additional statutory paternity pay in respect of the week in which the person does that work.

(2) In a case falling within paragraph (1), the person shall notify the person liable to pay additional statutory paternity pay within seven days of the first day during which the former works during the additional statutory paternity pay period.

(3) The notification mentioned in paragraph (2) shall be in writing, if the person who has been liable to pay additional statutory paternity pay so requests.

(4) In a case where an employee does any work on any day, under a contract of service with an employer who is liable to pay that employee additional statutory paternity pay, for not more than ten such days during the employee's additional statutory paternity pay period, whether consecutive or not, additional statutory paternity pay shall continue to be payable to the employee by the employer.

**21 Cases where there is no liability to pay additional statutory paternity pay**

(1) There shall be no liability to pay additional statutory paternity pay in respect of any week –

    (a)    during any part of which the person entitled to it is entitled to statutory sick pay under Part 11 of the Act;

    (b)    following that in which the person claiming it has died; or

    (c)    subject to paragraph (2), during any part of which the person entitled to it is detained in legal custody or sentenced to a term of imprisonment (except where the sentence is suspended).

(2) There shall be liability to pay additional statutory paternity pay in respect of any week during any part of which the person entitled to it is detained in legal custody where that person –

(a)     is released subsequently without charge;
(b)     is subsequently found not guilty of any offence and is released; or
(c)     is convicted of an offence but does not receive a custodial sentence.

## 22 Additional statutory paternity pay and contractual remuneration

(1) For the purposes of section 171ZG(1) and (2) of the Act (as such provisions apply to additional statutory paternity pay), the payments which are to be treated as contractual remuneration are sums payable under a contract of service –

(a)     by way of remuneration;
(b)     for incapacity for work due to sickness or injury; and
(c)     by reason of birth or adoption of a child.

## 23 Avoidance of liability for additional statutory paternity pay

(1) A former employer shall be liable to make payments of additional statutory paternity pay to a former employee in any case where the employee had been employed for a continuous period of at least eight weeks and the employee's contract of service was brought to an end by the former employer solely, or mainly, for the purpose of avoiding liability for additional statutory paternity pay or ordinary statutory paternity pay, or both.

(2) In a case falling within paragraph (1) –

(a)     the employee shall be treated as if they had been employed for a continuous period ending with the earliest date that they could have been entitled to additional statutory paternity pay; and
(b)     their normal weekly earnings shall be calculated by reference to their normal weekly earnings for the period of eight weeks ending with the last day in respect of which they were paid under their former contract of service.

## 24 Treatment of persons as employees

(1) Subject to paragraph (2), in a case where, and in so far as, a person is treated as an employed earner by virtue of the Social Security (Categorisation of Earners) Regulations 1978 that person shall be treated as an employee for the purposes of Part 12ZA of the Act, and in a case where, and in so far as, such a person is treated otherwise than as an employed earner by virtue of those regulations, that person shall not be treated as an employee for the purposes of Part 12ZA of the Act.

(2) Paragraph (1) shall have effect in relation to a person who –

(a)     is under the age of 16; and

(b)     would or, as the case may be, would not have been treated as an employed earner by virtue of the Social Security (Categorisation of Earners) Regulations 1978 had they been over that age,

as it has effect in relation to a person who is or, as the case may be, is not so treated.

(3) A person who is in employed earner's employment under a contract of apprenticeship shall be treated as an employee for the purposes of Part 12ZA of the Act.

(4) A person who is in employed earner's employment but whose employer –

(a)     does not fulfil the conditions prescribed in regulation 145(1) of the Contributions Regulations in so far as that provision relates to residence or presence in Great Britain; or

(b)     is a person who, by reason of any international treaty to which the United Kingdom is a party or of any international convention binding the United Kingdom –

(i)     is exempt from the provisions of the Act; or

(ii)     is a person against whom the provisions of the Act are not enforceable,

shall not be treated as an employee for the purposes of Part 12ZA of the Act.

## 25 Continuous employment

(1) Subject to the following provisions of this regulation, where in any week a person is, for the whole or part of the week –

(a)     incapable of work in consequence of sickness or injury;

(b)     absent from work on account of a temporary cessation of work;

(c)     absent from work in circumstances such that, by arrangement or custom, that person is regarded as continuing in the employment of their employer for all or any purposes,

and returns to work for their employer after the incapacity for or absence from work, that week shall be treated for the purposes of sections 171ZEA and 171ZEB of the Act as part of a continuous period of employment with that employer, notwithstanding that no contract of service exists with that employer in respect of that week.

(2) Incapacity for work which lasts for more than 26 consecutive weeks shall not count for the purposes of paragraph (1)(a).

(3) Where a person –

(a)     is an employee in employed earner's employment in which the custom is for the employer –

(i)     to offer work for a fixed period of not more than 26 consecutive weeks;

(ii)     to offer work for such period on two or more occasions in a year for periods which do not overlap; and

> (iii)   to offer the work available to those persons who had worked for the employer during the last or a recent such period, but

(b)   is absent from work because of incapacity arising from some specific disease or bodily or mental disablement,

then in that case paragraph (1) shall apply as if the words "and returns to work for their employer after the incapacity for or absence from work," were omitted.

## 26  Continuous employment and unfair dismissal

(1) This regulation applies to a person in relation to whose dismissal an action is commenced which consists –

(a)   of the presentation by that person of a complaint under section 111(1) of the Employment Rights Act 1996;

(b)   of their making a claim in accordance with a dismissal procedures agreement designated by an order under section 110 of that Act; or

(c)   of any action taken by a conciliation officer under section 18 of the Employment Tribunals Act 1996.

(2) If, in consequence of an action of the kind specified in paragraph (1), a person is reinstated or re-engaged by their employer or by a successor or associated employer of that employer, the continuity of their employment shall be preserved for the purposes of Part 12ZA of the Act, and any week which falls within the interval beginning with the effective date of termination and ending with the date of reinstatement or re-engagement, as the case may be, shall count in the computation of their period of continuous employment.

(3) In this regulation –

"dismissal procedures agreement" and "successor" have the same meanings as in section 235 of the Employment Rights Act 1996; and

"associated employer" shall be construed in accordance with section 231 of the Employment Rights Act 1996.

## 27  Continuous employment and stoppages of work

(1) Where, for any week or part of a week a person does not work because there is a stoppage of work due to a trade dispute within the meaning of section 35(1) of the Jobseekers Act 1995 at their place of employment, that person's continuity of employment shall, subject to paragraph (2), be treated, for the purposes of Part 12ZA of the Act, as continuing throughout the stoppage but, subject to paragraph (3), no such week shall count in the computation of their period of employment.

(2) Subject to paragraph (3), where during the stoppage of work a person is dismissed from their employment, that person's continuity of employment shall not be treated in accordance with paragraph (1) as continuing beyond the commencement of the day they stopped work.

(3) The provisions of paragraph (1), to the extent that they provide that a week in which the stoppage of work occurred shall not count in the computation of

a period of employment, and paragraph (2) shall not apply to a person who proves that at no time did they have a direct interest in the trade dispute in question.

## 28  Change of employer

A person's employment shall, notwithstanding a change of employer, be treated, for the purposes of Part 12ZA of the Act, as continuous employment with the second employer where –

(a)    the employer's trade or business or an undertaking (whether or not it is an undertaking established by or under an Act of Parliament) is transferred from one person to another;

(b)    by or under an Act of Parliament, whether public or local and whenever passed, a contract of employment between any body corporate and the person is modified and some other body corporate is substituted as that person's employer;

(c)    on the death of their employer, the person is taken into the employment of the personal representatives or trustees of the deceased;

(d)    the person is employed by partners, personal representatives or trustees and there is a change in the partners, or, as the case may be, personal representatives or trustees;

(e)    the person is taken into the employment of an employer who is, at the time they entered that employer's employment, an associated employer of their previous employer, and for this purpose "associated employer" shall be construed in accordance with section 231 of the Employment Rights Act 1996; or

(f)    on the termination of the person's employment with an employer they are taken into the employment of another employer and those employers are governors of a school maintained by a local education authority.

## 29  Reinstatement after service with the armed forces etc

If a person who is entitled to apply to their employer under the Reserve Forces (Safeguard of Employment) Act 1985 enters the employment of that employer within the six month period mentioned in section 1(4)(b) of that Act, their previous period of employment with that employer (or if there was more than one such period, the last of those periods) and the period of employment beginning in that six-month period shall be treated as continuous.

## 30  Treatment of two or more employers or two or more contracts of service as one

(1) In a case where the earnings paid to a person in respect of two or more employments are aggregated and treated as a single payment of earnings under regulation 15(1) of the Contributions Regulations, the employers of that person in respect of those employments shall be treated as one for the purposes of Part 12ZA of the Act.

(2) Where two or more employers are treated as one under the provisions of paragraph (1), liability for additional statutory paternity pay shall be apportioned between them in such proportions as they may agree, or in default of agreement, in the proportions which the person's earnings from each employment bear to the amount of the aggregated earnings.

(3) Where two or more contracts of service exist concurrently between one employer and one employee, they shall be treated as one for the purposes of Part 12ZA of the Act, except where, by virtue of regulation 14 of the Contributions Regulations, the earnings from those contracts of service are not aggregated for the purposes of earnings-related contributions.

### 31 Meaning of "earnings"

(1) For the purposes of section 171ZJ(6) of the Act (as such provision applies to additional statutory paternity pay) (normal weekly earnings for the purposes of Part 12ZA of the Act), the expression "earnings" shall be construed in accordance with the following provisions of this regulation.

(2) The expression "earnings" refers to gross earnings and includes any remuneration or profit derived from a person's employment except any payment or amount which is –

   (a)   excluded from the computation of a person's earnings under regulation 25 of and Schedule 3 to, and regulation 123 of, the Contributions Regulations (payments to be disregarded) and regulation 27 of those Regulations (payments to directors to be disregarded) (or would have been so excluded had they not been under the age of 16);

   (b)   a chargeable emolument under section 10A of the Act except where, in consequence of such a chargeable emolument being excluded from earnings, a person would not be entitled to additional statutory paternity pay (or where such a payment or amount would have been so excluded and in consequence the person would not have been entitled to additional statutory paternity pay had they not been under the age of 16).

(3) For the avoidance of doubt, "earnings" includes –

   (a)   any amount retrospectively treated as earnings by regulations made by virtue of section 4B(2) of the Act;

   (b)   any sum payable in respect of arrears of pay in pursuance of an order for reinstatement or re-engagement under the Employment Rights Act 1996;

   (c)   any sum payable by way of pay in pursuance of an order made under the Employment Rights Act 1996 for the continuation of a contract of employment;

   (d)   any sum payable by way of remuneration in pursuance of a protective award under section 189 of the Trade Union and Labour Relations (Consolidation) Act 1992;

(e)     any sum payable by way of statutory sick pay, including sums payable in accordance with regulations made under section 151(6) of the Act;

(f)     any sum payable by way of statutory maternity pay;

(g)     any sum payable by way of ordinary statutory paternity pay;

(h)     any sum payable by way of additional statutory paternity pay; and

(i)     any sum payable by way of statutory adoption pay.

\*\*\*\*

### 33 Payment of additional statutory paternity pay

Payments of additional statutory paternity pay may be made in a like manner to payments of remuneration but shall not include payment in kind or by way of the provision of board or lodgings or of services or other facilities.

### 34 Time when additional statutory paternity pay is to be paid

(1) In this regulation, "pay day" means a day on which it has been agreed, or it is the normal practice between an employer or former employer and a person who is or was an employee of theirs, that payments by way of remuneration are to be made, or, where there is no such agreement or normal practice, the last day of a calendar month.

(2) In any case where –

(a)     a decision has been made by an officer of Revenue and Customs under section 8(1) of the Social Security Contributions (Transfer of Functions, etc) Act 1999 as a result of which a person is entitled to an amount of additional statutory paternity pay; and

(b)     the time for bringing an appeal against the decision has expired and either –

(i)     no such appeal has been brought; or

(ii)    such an appeal has been brought and has been finally disposed of,

that amount of additional statutory paternity pay shall be paid within the time specified in paragraph (3).

(3) Subject to paragraphs (4) and (5), the employer or former employer shall pay the amount not later than the first pay day after –

(a)     where an appeal has been brought, the day on which the employer or former employer receives notification that it has been finally disposed of;

(b)     where leave to appeal has been refused and there remains no further opportunity to apply for leave, the day on which the employer or former employer receives notification of the refusal; and

(c)     in any other case, the day on which the time for bringing an appeal expires.

(4) Subject to paragraph (5), where it is impracticable, in view of the employer's or former employer's methods of accounting for and paying

remuneration, for the requirement of payment referred to in paragraph (3) to be met by the pay day referred to in that paragraph, it shall be met not later than the next following pay day.

(5) Where the employer or former employer would not have remunerated the employee for their work in the week in question as early as the pay day specified in paragraph (3) or (if it applies) paragraph (4), the requirement of payment shall be met on the first day on which the employee would have been remunerated for his work in that week.

****

# PATERNITY AND ADOPTION LEAVE (ADOPTION FROM OVERSEAS) REGULATIONS 2003

## SI 2003/921

\*\*\*\*

### 3 Application of the Leave Regulations to adoptions from overseas

The provisions of the Leave Regulations shall apply to adoptions from overseas with the modifications set out in these Regulations.

### 4 Interpretation

(1) Regulation 2 of the Leave Regulations shall be modified in accordance with the following paragraphs of this regulation.

(2) In paragraph (1),

   (a)   for the definition of "adopter", substitute –

""adopter", in relation to a child, means a person by whom the child has been or is to be adopted or, in a case where the child has been or is to be adopted by two people jointly, whichever of them has elected to take adoption leave in respect of the child;" and

   (b)   in the appropriate places in alphabetical order insert –

""adoption from overseas" means the adoption of a child who enters Great Britain from outside the United Kingdom in connection with or for the purposes of adoption which does not involve the placement of the child for adoption under the law of any part of the United Kingdom;"

""enter Great Britain" means enter Great Britain from outside the United Kingdom in connection with or for the purposes of adoption, and cognate expressions shall be construed accordingly;"

""official notification" means written notification, issued by or on behalf of the relevant domestic authority, that it is prepared to issue a certificate to the overseas authority concerned with the adoption of the child, or has issued a certificate and sent it to that authority, confirming, in either case, that the adopter is eligible to adopt and has been assessed and approved as being a suitable adoptive parent;" and

""relevant domestic authority" means –

   (a)   in the case of an adopter to whom the Intercountry Adoption (Hague Convention) Regulations 2003 apply and who is habitually resident in Wales, the National Assembly for Wales;

   (b)   in the case of an adopter to whom the Adoptions with a Foreign Element (Scotland) Regulations 2009 apply and who is habitually resident in Scotland, the Scottish Ministers; and

   (c)   in any other case, the Secretary of State;".

(3) For paragraph (4) substitute –

"(4) For the purposes of these Regulations, in a case where a child is to be adopted by two people jointly, a person elects to be a child's adopter, if he and the other person agree, at the time when the official notification is received, that he and not the other person will be the adopter."

**Amendments**—SI 2011/1740

## 5 Application

(1)  Regulation 3 of the Leave Regulations shall be modified in accordance with the following paragraphs of this regulation.

(2)  For paragraphs (1) and (2), substitute –

"(1) The provisions relating to adoption leave under regulation 15 below have effect only where the adopter's child enters Great Britain on or after 6th April 2003.

(2) The provisions relating to paternity leave under regulation 8 below have effect only in relation to a person who is married to or the partner of an adopter whose child enters Great Britain on or after 6th April 2003.".

(3)  In paragraph (3), for "8th December 2002" substitute "6th April 2003".

(4)  In paragraph (6), for "8th December 2002" substitute "6th April 2003".

## 6 Entitlement to paternity leave: birth

Regulations 4 to 7 of the Leave Regulations shall be omitted.

## 7 Entitlement to paternity leave: adoption from overseas

For regulations 8 to 10 of the Leave Regulations substitute –

### 8 "Entitlement to paternity leave

(1)  An employee is entitled to be absent from work for the purpose of caring for a child adopted from overseas or supporting the child's adopter if he –

  (a)   satisfies the conditions in paragraph (2); and
  (b)   has complied with the notice requirements in regulation 10 and, where applicable, the evidential requirements in that regulation.

(2)  The conditions referred to in paragraph (1) are that –

  (a)   the child's adopter has received an official notification;
  (b)   the employee has been continuously employed for a period of not less than 26 weeks either –
     (i)    ending with the week in which the official notification was received, or
     (ii)   commencing with the week in which the employee's employment with the employer began;
  (c)   the employee is either married to, the civil partner or the partner of the child's adopter, and
  (d)   the employee has, or expects to have, the main responsibility (apart from the responsibility of the child's adopter) for the upbringing of the child.

(3) In paragraph (2)(b), "week" means the period of seven days beginning with Sunday.

(4) An employee shall be treated as having satisfied the condition in paragraph (2)(c) if he would have satisfied it but for the fact that the child's adopter died during the period of 56 days commencing with the date on which the child entered Great Britain.

(5) An employee shall be treated as having satisfied the condition in paragraph (2)(d) if he would have satisfied it but for the fact that the child has ceased to live with the adopter.

(6) An employee's entitlement to leave under this regulation shall not be affected by the fact that more than one child is the subject of adoption from overseas by the adopter as part of the same arrangement.

### 9 Options in respect of leave under regulation 8

(1) An employee may choose to take either one week's leave or two consecutive weeks' leave in respect of a child under regulation 8.

(2) The leave may only be taken during the period of 56 days beginning with the date on which the child enters Great Britain.

(3) Subject to paragraph (2) and, where applicable, paragraph (4), an employee may choose to begin the period of leave under regulation 8 on –

(a)   the date on which the child enters Great Britain; or
(b)   a predetermined date, specified in a notice under regulation 10, which is later than the date on which the child enters Great Britain.

(4) In a case where the adopter received an official notification before 6th April 2003 and the adopter's child enters Great Britain on or after that date, the employee may choose to begin a period of paternity leave only on a predetermined date, specified in a notice under regulation 10, which is later than the date of entry and, unless the employer agrees to an earlier commencement of the leave period, is at least twenty-eight days after the date on which that notice was given.

### 10 Notice and evidential requirements for leave under regulation 8

(1) An employee intending to take paternity leave in respect of a child must give his employer notice of each of the following matters –

(a)   the date on which the adopter of the child received an official notification;
(b)   the date on which the child is expected to enter Great Britain;
(c)   the date which the employee has chosen as the date on which his period of paternity leave should begin, and
(d)   the date on which the child enters Great Britain.

(2) Notice provided for in –

(a)   paragraph (1)(a) and (b) must be given to the employer no more than 28 days after the date on which the adopter of the child receives the official notification or the date on which he completes 26 weeks' continuous employment with the employer, whichever is later;

(b)     paragraph (1)(c) must be given to the employer at least 28 days prior to the date which the employee has chosen as the date on which his period of paternity leave should begin, and

(c)     paragraph (1)(d) must be given to the employer no more than 28 days after the date on which the child enters Great Britain.

(3) Where the employer requests it, an employee must give his employer, within 14 days of receipt of a request, a written declaration, signed by the employee, to the effect that his partner, spouse or civil partner has received an official notification and that he satisfies the conditions of entitlement in regulation 8(2)(c) and (d).

(4) A choice made under regulation 9(3) is not irrevocable but where an employee subsequently makes a different choice the notification requirements contained in paragraphs (1)(c) and (2)(b) shall apply to that choice.

(5) Any notice under paragraph (1) shall be given in writing, if the employer so requests.

(6) Where it becomes known to the employee that the child will not enter Great Britain, he shall notify the employer of the fact as soon as is reasonably practicable."

**Amendments**—SI 2005/2114.

## 8  Commencement of leave under regulation 8

In regulation 11(2)(a) of the Leave Regulations, for "is placed with the adopter" substitute "enters Great Britain".

## 9  Entitlement to ordinary adoption leave: adoption from overseas

For regulations 15 to 17 of the Leave Regulations substitute –

### 15 "Entitlement to ordinary adoption leave

(1)  An employee is entitled to ordinary adoption leave in respect of a child if he –

(a)     satisfies the conditions specified in paragraph (2); and

(b)     has complied with the notice requirements in regulation 17 and, where applicable, the evidential requirements in that regulation.

(2)  The conditions referred to in paragraph (1) are that the employee –

(a)     is the child's adopter; and

(b)     has been continuously employed for a period of not less than 26 weeks either –

(i)     ending with the week in which he received an official notification; or

(ii)    commencing with the week in which the employee's employment with the employer began.

(3)  In paragraph (2)(b), "week" means the period of seven days beginning with Sunday.

(4)  An employee's entitlement to leave under this regulation shall not be affected by the fact that more than one child is the subject of adoption from overseas by the adopter as part of the same arrangement.

**16 Options in respect of ordinary adoption leave**

(1) Subject to paragraph (2), an employee may choose to begin a period of ordinary adoption leave on –

(a)     the date on which the child enters Great Britain; or

(b)     a predetermined date, specified in a notice under regulation 17, which is no later than twenty-eight days after the date on which the child enters Great Britain.

(2) In a case where the employee receives an official notification before 6th April 2003 and the adopter's child enters Great Britain on or after that date, the employee may choose to begin a period of ordinary adoption leave only on a predetermined date, specified in a notice under regulation 17, which is later than the date of entry, and, unless the employer agrees to an earlier commencement of the leave period, is at least twenty-eight days after the date on which that notice was given.

**17 Notice and evidential requirements for ordinary adoption leave**

(1) An employee intending to take ordinary adoption leave in respect of a child must give his employer notice of each of the following matters –

(a)     the date on which he received an official notification;

(b)     the date on which the child is expected to enter Great Britain;

(c)     the date which he has chosen as the date on which his period of adoption leave should begin; and

(d)     the date on which the child enters Great Britain.

(2) Notice provided for –

(a)     in paragraph (1)(a) and (b) must be given to the employer no more than 28 days after the date on which the employee receives the official notification or the date on which he completes 26 weeks' continuous employment with the employer, whichever is later;

(b)     in paragraph (1)(c) must be given to the employer at least 28 days prior to the date which the employee has chosen as the date on which his period of adoption leave should begin, and

(c)     in paragraph (1)(d) must be given to the employer no more than 28 days after the date on which the child enters Great Britain.

(3) Where the employer requests it, an employee must also provide his employer with a copy of the official notification together with evidence of the date of the entry of the child into Great Britain.

(4) An employee who has given notice under paragraph (1)(c) may vary the date he has chosen as the date on which his leave will begin, subject to paragraph (5) and provided that he gives his employer notice of the variation –

(a)     where the variation is to provide for the employee's period of leave to begin on the date on which the child enters Great Britain, at least 28 days before the date specified in his notice under paragraph (1)(b) as the date on which the child is expected to enter Great Britain;

(b)     where the variation is to provide for the employee's period of leave to begin on a predetermined date (or a different predetermined date), at least 28 days before that date, or, if it is not reasonably practicable to give notice 28 days before whichever date is relevant, as soon as is reasonably practicable.

(5) In a case where regulation 16(2) applies, an employee may only vary the date which he has chosen as the date on which his period of leave should begin by substituting a different predetermined date.

(6) Notice under paragraph (1) or (4) shall be given in writing, if the employer so requests.

(7) An employer who is given notice under paragraph (1) or (4) of the date on which an employee has chosen that his period of ordinary adoption leave should begin shall notify the employee, within 28 days of his receipt of the notice, of the date on which the period of additional adoption leave to which the employee will be entitled (if he satisfies the conditions in regulation 20(1)) after his period of ordinary adoption leave ends.

(8) The notification provided for in paragraph (7) shall be given to the employee –

(a)   where the employer is given notice under paragraph (1)(c), within 28 days of the date on which he received that notice;
(b)   where the employer is given notice under paragraph (4), within 28 days of the date on which the employee's ordinary adoption leave period began.

(9) Where it becomes known to the employee that the child will not enter Great Britain, he shall notify the employer of the fact as soon as is reasonably practicable."

## 10 Duration and commencement of ordinary adoption leave

(1) Regulation 18 of the Leave Regulations shall be modified in accordance with the following paragraphs of this regulation.

(2) In regulation 18(2), for "regulation 17(1)" substitute "regulation 17(1)(c)".

(3) In regulation 18(3)(a), for "is placed with him" substitute "enters Great Britain".

## 11 Additional adoption leave: entitlement, duration and commencement

In regulation 20(1)(a) of the Leave Regulations, for "was placed with him for adoption" substitute "has entered Great Britain".

## 12 Disruption in the course of adoption leave

(1) Regulation 22 of the Leave Regulations shall be modified in accordance with the following paragraphs of this regulation.

(2) For paragraph (1), there shall be substituted –

"(1) This regulation applies where, during an employee's period of adoption leave in respect of a child, the child –

(a)   dies, or
(b)   ceases to live with the adopter."

(3) For paragraph (3), there shall be substituted –

"(3) The relevant week referred to in paragraph (2) is –

(a)    in a case falling within paragraph (1)(a), the week during which the child dies;

(b)    in a case falling within paragraph (1)(b), the week during which the child ceased to live with the adopter."

# MANAGEMENT OF HEALTH AND SAFETY AT WORK REGULATIONS 1999

## SI 1999/3242

### 1 Citation, commencement and interpretation

(1) These Regulations may be cited as the Management of Health and Safety at Work Regulations 1999 and shall come into force on 29th December 1999.

(2) In these Regulations –

"the 1996 Act" means the Employment Rights Act 1996;

"the assessment" means, in the case of an employer or self-employed person, the assessment made or changed by him in accordance with regulation 3;

"child" –

    (a)    as respects England and Wales, means a person who is not over compulsory school age, construed in accordance with section 8 of the Education Act 1996; and

    (b)    as respects Scotland, means a person who is not over school age, construed in accordance with section 31 of the Education (Scotland) Act 1980;

"employment business" means a business (whether or not carried on with a view to profit and whether or not carried on in conjunction with any other business) which supplies persons (other than seafarers) who are employed in it to work for and under the control of other persons in any capacity;

"fixed-term contract of employment" means a contract of employment for a specific term which is fixed in advance or which can be ascertained in advance by reference to some relevant circumstance;

"given birth" means delivered a living child or, after twenty-four weeks of pregnancy, a stillborn child;

"new or expectant mother" means an employee who is pregnant; who has given birth within the previous six months; or who is breastfeeding;

"the preventive and protective measures" means the measures which have been identified by the employer or by the self-employed person in consequence of the assessment as the measures he needs to take to comply with the requirements and prohibitions imposed upon him by or under the relevant statutory provisions . . .;

"young person" means any person who has not attained the age of eighteen.

(3) Any reference in these Regulations to –

    (a)    a numbered regulation or Schedule is a reference to the regulation or Schedule in these Regulations so numbered; or

    (b)    a numbered paragraph is a reference to the paragraph so numbered in the regulation in which the reference appears.

**Amendments**—SI 2005/1541.

\*\*\*\*

## 3  Risk assessment

(1) Every employer shall make a suitable and sufficient assessment of –

    (a)   the risks to the health and safety of his employees to which they are exposed whilst they are at work; and

    (b)   the risks to the health and safety of persons not in his employment arising out of or in connection with the conduct by him of his undertaking,

for the purpose of identifying the measures he needs to take to comply with the requirements and prohibitions imposed upon him by or under the relevant statutory provisions . . ..

(2) Every self-employed person shall make a suitable and sufficient assessment of –

    (a)   the risks to his own health and safety to which he is exposed whilst he is at work; and

    (b)   the risks to the health and safety of persons not in his employment arising out of or in connection with the conduct by him of his undertaking,

for the purpose of identifying the measures he needs to take to comply with the requirements and prohibitions imposed upon him by or under the relevant statutory provisions.

(3) Any assessment such as is referred to in paragraph (1) or (2) shall be reviewed by the employer or self-employed person who made it if –

    (a)   there is reason to suspect that it is no longer valid; or

    (b)   there has been a significant change in the matters to which it relates;

and where as a result of any such review changes to an assessment are required, the employer or self-employed person concerned shall make them.

(4) An employer shall not employ a young person unless he has, in relation to risks to the health and safety of young persons, made or reviewed an assessment in accordance with paragraphs (1) and (5).

(5) In making or reviewing the assessment, an employer who employs or is to employ a young person shall take particular account of –

    (a)   the inexperience, lack of awareness of risks and immaturity of young persons;

    (b)   the fitting-out and layout of the workplace and the workstation;

    (c)   the nature, degree and duration of exposure to physical, biological and chemical agents;

    (d)   the form, range, and use of work equipment and the way in which it is handled;

    (e)   the organisation of processes and activities;

(f)    the extent of the health and safety training provided or to be provided to young persons; and

(g)    risks from agents, processes and work listed in the Annex to Council Directive 94/33/EC on the protection of young people at work.

(6) Where the employer employs five or more employees, he shall record –

(a)    the significant findings of the assessment; and

(b)    any group of his employees identified by it as being especially at risk.

**Amendments**—SI 2005/1541.

****

## 6 Health surveillance

Every employer shall ensure that his employees are provided with such health surveillance as is appropriate having regard to the risks to their health and safety which are identified by the assessment.

****

## 10 Information for employees

(1) Every employer shall provide his employees with comprehensible and relevant information on –

(a)    the risks to their health and safety identified by the assessment;

(b)    the preventive and protective measures;

(c)    the procedures referred to in regulation 8(1)(a);

(d)    the identity of those persons nominated by him in accordance with regulation 8(1)(b); and

(e)    the risks notified to him in accordance with regulation 11(1)(c).

(2) Every employer shall, before employing a child, provide a parent of the child with comprehensible and relevant information on –

(a)    the risks to his health and safety identified by the assessment;

(b)    the preventive and protective measures; and

(c)    the risks notified to him in accordance with regulation 11(1)(c).

(3) The reference in paragraph (2) to a parent of the child includes –

(a)    in England and Wales, a person who has parental responsibility, within the meaning of section 3 of the Children Act 1989, for him; and

(b)    in Scotland, a person who has parental rights, within the meaning of section 8 of the Law Reform (Parent and Child) (Scotland) Act 1986 for him.

**Amendments**—SI 2005/1541.

****

## 12  Persons working in host employers' or self-employed persons' undertakings

(1) Every employer and every self-employed person shall ensure that the employer of any employees from an outside undertaking who are working in his undertaking is provided with comprehensible information on –

    (a)   the risks to those employees' health and safety arising out of or in connection with the conduct by that first-mentioned employer or by that self-employed person of his undertaking; and

    (b)   the measures taken by that first-mentioned employer or by that self-employed person in compliance with the requirements and prohibitions imposed upon him by or under the relevant statutory provisions ... in so far as the said requirements and prohibitions relate to those employees.

(2) Paragraph (1) shall apply to a self-employed person who is working in the undertaking of an employer or a self-employed person as it applies to employees from an outside undertaking who are working therein; and the reference in that paragraph to the employer of any employees from an outside undertaking who are working in the undertaking of an employer or a self-employed person and the references in the said paragraph to employees from an outside undertaking who are working in the undertaking of an employer or a self-employed person shall be construed accordingly.

(3) Every employer shall ensure that any person working in his undertaking who is not his employee and every self-employed person (not being an employer) shall ensure that any person working in his undertaking is provided with appropriate instructions and comprehensible information regarding any risks to that person's health and safety which arise out of the conduct by that employer or self-employed person of his undertaking.

(4) Every employer shall –

    (a)   ensure that the employer of any employees from an outside undertaking who are working in his undertaking is provided with sufficient information to enable that second-mentioned employer to identify any person nominated by that first mentioned employer in accordance with regulation 8(1)(b) to implement evacuation procedures as far as those employees are concerned; and

    (b)   take all reasonable steps to ensure that any employees from an outside undertaking who are working in his undertaking receive sufficient information to enable them to identify any person nominated by him in accordance with regulation 8(1)(b) to implement evacuation procedures as far as they are concerned.

(5) Paragraph (4) shall apply to a self-employed person who is working in an employer's undertaking as it applies to employees from an outside undertaking who are working therein; and the reference in that paragraph to the employer of any employees from an outside undertaking who are working in an employer's undertaking and the references in the said paragraph to employees from an outside undertaking who are working in an employer's undertaking shall be construed accordingly.

**Amendments**—SI 2005/1541.

\*\*\*\*

## 16 Risk assessment in respect of new or expectant mothers

(1) Where –

(a) the persons working in an undertaking include women of child-bearing age; and

(b) the work is of a kind which could involve risk, by reason of her condition, to the health and safety of a new or expectant mother, or to that of her baby, from any processes or working conditions, or physical, biological or chemical agents, including those specified in Annexes I and II of Council Directive 92/85/EEC on the introduction of measures to encourage improvements in the safety and health at work of pregnant workers and workers who have recently given birth or are breastfeeding,

the assessment required by regulation 3(1) shall also include an assessment of such risk.

(2) Where, in the case of an individual employee, the taking of any other action the employer is required to take under the relevant statutory provisions would not avoid the risk referred to in paragraph (1) the employer shall, if it is reasonable to do so, and would avoid such risks, alter her working conditions or hours of work.

(3) If it is not reasonable to alter the working conditions or hours of work, or if it would not avoid such risk, the employer shall, subject to section 67 of the 1996 Act suspend the employee from work for so long as is necessary to avoid such risk.

(4) In paragraphs (1) to (3) references to risk, in relation to risk from any infectious or contagious disease, are references to a level of risk at work which is in addition to the level to which a new or expectant mother may be expected to be exposed outside the workplace.

## 16A Alteration of working conditions in respect of new or expectant mothers (agency workers)

(1) Where, in the case of an individual agency worker, the taking of any other action the hirer is required to take under the relevant statutory provisions would not avoid the risk referred to in regulation 16(1) the hirer shall, if it is reasonable to do so, and would avoid such risks, alter her working conditions or hours of work.

(2) If it is not reasonable to alter the working conditions or hours of work, or if it would not avoid such risk, the hirer shall without delay inform the temporary work agency, who shall then end the supply of that agency worker to the hirer.

(3) In paragraphs (1) and (2) references to risk, in relation to risk from any infectious or contagious disease, are references to a level of risk at work which is in addition to the level to which a new or expectant mother may be expected to be exposed outside the workplace.

**Amendments**—Inserted by SI 2010/93.

### 17 Certificate from registered medical practitioner in respect of new or expectant mothers

Where –

(a)     a new or expectant mother works at night; and
(b)     a certificate from a registered medical practitioner or a registered midwife shows that it is necessary for her health or safety that she should not be at work for any period of such work identified in the certificate,

the employer shall, subject to section 67 of the 1996 Act, suspend her from work for so long as is necessary for her health or safety.

### 17A Certificate from registered medical practitioner in respect of new or expectant mothers (agency workers)

Where –

(a)     a new or expectant mother works at night; and
(b)     a certificate from a registered medical practitioner or a registered midwife shows that it is necessary for her health or safety that she should not be at work for any period of such work identified in the certificate,

the hirer shall without delay inform the temporary work agency, who shall then end the supply of that agency worker to the hirer.

**Amendments**—Inserted by SI 2010/93.

### 18 Notification by new or expectant mothers

(1) Nothing in paragraph (2) or (3) of regulation 16 shall require the employer to take any action in relation to an employee until she has notified the employer in writing that she is pregnant, has given birth within the previous six months, or is breastfeeding.

(2) Nothing in paragraph (2) or (3) of regulation 16 or in regulation 17 shall require the employer to maintain action taken in relation to an employee –

(a)     in a case –
(i)      to which regulation 16(2) or (3) relates; and
(ii)     where the employee has notified her employer that she is pregnant, where she has failed, within a reasonable time of being requested to do so in writing by her employer, to produce for the employer's inspection a certificate from a registered medical practitioner or a registered midwife showing that she is pregnant;

(b)  once the employer knows that she is no longer a new or expectant mother; or

(c)  if the employer cannot establish whether she remains a new or expectant mother.

### 18A  Notification by new or expectant mothers (agency workers)

(1) Nothing in regulation 16A(1) or (2) shall require the hirer to take any action in relation to an agency worker until she has notified the hirer in writing that she is pregnant, has given birth within the previous six months, or is breastfeeding.

(2) Nothing in regulation 16A(2) shall require the temporary work agency to end the supply of the agency worker until she has notified the temporary work agency in writing that she is pregnant, has given birth within the previous six months, or is breastfeeding.

(3) Nothing in regulation 16A(1) shall require the hirer to maintain action taken in relation to an agency worker –

(a)  in a case –
    (i)  to which regulation 16A(1) relates; and
    (ii)  where the agency worker has notified the hirer, that she is pregnant, where she has failed, within a reasonable time of being requested to do so in writing by the hirer, to produce for the hirer's inspection a certificate from a registered medical practitioner or a registered midwife showing that she is pregnant; or

(b)  once the hirer knows that she is no longer a new or expectant mother; or

(c)  if the hirer cannot establish whether she remains a new or expectant mother.

**Amendments**—Inserted by SI 2010/93.

### 18AB  Agency workers: general provisions

(1) Without prejudice to any other duties of the hirer or temporary work agency under any enactment or rule of law in relation to health and safety at work, regulation 16A, 17A and 18A shall not apply where the agency worker –

(a)  has not completed the qualifying period, or

(b)  is no longer entitled to the rights conferred by regulation 5 of the Agency Workers Regulations 2010 pursuant to regulation 8(a) or (b) of those Regulations.

(2) Nothing in regulations 16A or 17A imposes a duty on the hirer or temporary work agency beyond the original intended duration, or likely duration of the assignment, whichever is the longer.

(3) This regulation, and regulations 16A, 17A and 18A do not apply in circumstances where regulations 16, 17 and 18 apply.

(4) For the purposes of this regulation and regulations 16A, 17A or 18A the following have the same meaning as in the Agency Workers Regulations 2010 –

"agency worker";
"assignment";
"hirer";
"qualifying period";
"temporary work agency".

**Amendments**—Inserted by SI 2010/93.

\*\*\*\*

# MATERNITY AND PARENTAL LEAVE ETC REGULATIONS 1999

## SI 1999/3312

\*\*\*\*

### 6 Commencement of maternity leave periods

(1) Subject to paragraph (2), an employee's ordinary maternity leave period commences with the earlier of –

   (a)   the date which she notifies to her employer, in accordance with regulation 4, as the date on which she intends her ordinary maternity leave period to start, or, if by virtue of the provision for variation in that regulation she has notified more than one such date, the last date she notifies, and
   (b)   the day which follows the first day after the beginning of the fourth week before the expected week of childbirth on which she is absent from work wholly or partly because of pregnancy.

(2) Where the employee's ordinary maternity leave period has not commenced by virtue of paragraph (1) when childbirth occurs, her ordinary maternity leave period commences on the day which follows the day on which childbirth occurs.

(3) An employee's additional maternity leave period commences on the day after the last day of her ordinary maternity leave period.

**Amendments**—SI 2002/2789.

\*\*\*\*

### 7 Duration of maternity leave periods

(1) Subject to paragraphs (2) and (5), an employee's ordinary maternity leave period continues for the period of 26 weeks from its commencement, or until the end of the compulsory maternity leave period provided for in regulation 8 if later.

(2) Subject to paragraph (5), where any requirement imposed by or under any relevant statutory provision prohibits the employee from working for any period after the end of the period determined under paragraph (1) by reason of her having recently given birth, her ordinary maternity leave period continues until the end of that later period.

(3) In paragraph (2), "relevant statutory provision" means a provision of –

   (a)   an enactment, or
   (b)   an instrument under an enactment,

other than a provision for the time being specified in an order under section 66(2) of the 1996 Act.

(4) Subject to paragraph (5), where an employee is entitled to additional maternity leave her additional maternity leave period continues until the end of the period of 26 weeks from the day on which it commenced.

(5) Where the employee is dismissed after the commencement of an ordinary or additional maternity leave period but before the time when (apart from this paragraph) that period would end, the period ends at the time of the dismissal.

(6) An employer who is notified under any provision of regulation 4 of the date on which, by virtue of any provision of regulation 6, an employee's ordinary maternity leave period will commence or has commenced shall notify the employee of the date on which her additional maternity leave period shall end –

   (a)   *(revoked)*
   (b)   *(revoked)*

(7) The notification provided for in paragraph (6) shall be given to the employee –

   (a)   where the employer is notified under regulation 4(1)(a)(iii), (3)(b) or (4)(b), within 28 days of the date on which he received the notification;
   (b)   where the employer is notified under regulation 4(1A), within 28 days of the date on which the employee's ordinary maternity leave period commenced.

**Amendments**—SI 2002/2789; SI 2006/2014.

# PART-TIME WORKERS (PREVENTION OF LESS FAVOURABLE TREATMENT) REGULATIONS 2000

## SI 2000/1551

\*\*\*\*

### 2 Meaning of full-time worker, part-time worker and comparable full-time worker

(1) A worker is a full-time worker for the purpose of these Regulations if he is paid wholly or in part by reference to the time he works and, having regard to the custom and practice of the employer in relation to workers employed by the worker's employer under the same type of contract, is identifiable as a full-time worker.

(2) A worker is a part-time worker for the purpose of these Regulations if he is paid wholly or in part by reference to the time he works and, having regard to the custom and practice of the employer in relation to workers employed by the worker's employer under the same type of contract, is not identifiable as a full-time worker.

[(3) For the purposes of paragraphs (1), (2) and (4), the following shall be regarded as being employed under different types of contract –

    (a)    employees employed under a contract that is not a contract of apprenticeship;

    (b)    employees employed under a contract of apprenticeship;

    (c)    workers who are not employees;

    (d)    any other description of worker that it is reasonable for the employer to treat differently from other workers on the ground that workers of that description have a different type of contract.]

(4) A full-time worker is a comparable full-time worker in relation to a part-time worker if, at the time when the treatment that is alleged to be less favourable to the part-time worker takes place –

    (a)    both workers are –
        (i)    employed by the same employer under the same type of contract, and
        (ii)    engaged in the same or broadly similar work having regard, where relevant, to whether they have a similar level of qualification, skills and experience; and

    (b)    the full-time worker works or is based at the same establishment as the part-time worker or, where there is no full-time worker working or based at that establishment who satisfies the requirements of sub-paragraph (a), works or is based at a different establishment and satisfies those requirements.

**Amendments**—SI 2002/2035.

\*\*\*\*

### 3 Workers becoming part-time

(1) This regulation applies to a worker who –

(a)　was identifiable as a full-time worker in accordance with regulation 2(1); and

(b)　following a termination or variation of his contract, continues to work under a new or varied contract, whether of the same type or not, that requires him to work for a number of weekly hours that is lower than the number he was required to work immediately before the termination or variation.

(2) Notwithstanding regulation 2(4), regulation 5 shall apply to a worker to whom this regulation applies as if he were a part-time worker and as if there were a comparable full-time worker employed under the terms that applied to him immediately before the variation or termination.

(3) The fact that this regulation applies to a worker does not affect any right he may have under these Regulations by virtue of regulation 2(4).

### 4 Workers returning part-time after absence

(1) This regulation applies to a worker who –

(a)　was identifiable as a full-time worker in accordance with regulation 2(1) immediately before a period of absence (whether the absence followed a termination of the worker's contract or not);

(b)　returns to work for the same employer within a period of less than twelve months beginning with the day on which the period of absence started;

(c)　returns to the same job or to a job at the same level under a contract, whether it is a different contract or a varied contract and regardless of whether it is of the same type, under which he is required to work for a number of weekly hours that is lower than the number he was required to work immediately before the period of absence.

(2) Notwithstanding regulation 2(4), regulation 5 shall apply to a worker to whom this regulation applies ("the returning worker") as if he were a part-time worker and as if there were a comparable full-time worker employed under –

(a)　the contract under which the returning worker was employed immediately before the period of absence; or

(b)　where it is shown that, had the returning worker continued to work under the contract mentioned in sub-paragraph (a) a variation would have been made to its term during the period of absence, the contract mentioned in that sub-paragraph including that variation.

(3) The fact that this regulation applies to a worker does not affect any right he may have under these Regulations by virtue of regulation 2(4).

## PART II
## RIGHTS AND REMEDIES

### 5 Less favourable treatment of part-time workers

(1) A part-time worker has the right not to be treated by his employer less favourably than the employer treats a comparable full-time worker –

(a) as regards the terms of his contract; or
(b) by being subjected to any other detriment by any act, or deliberate failure to act, of his employer.

(2) The right conferred by paragraph (1) applies only if –

(a) the treatment is on the ground that the worker is a part-time worker, and
(b) the treatment is not justified on objective grounds.

(3) In determining whether a part-time worker has been treated less favourably than a comparable full-time worker the pro rata principle shall be applied unless it is inappropriate.

(4) A part-time worker paid at a lower rate for overtime worked by him in a period than a comparable full-time worker is or would be paid for overtime worked by him in the same period shall not, for that reason, be regarded as treated less favourably than the comparable full-time worker where, or to the extent that, the total number of hours worked by the part-time worker in the period, including overtime, does not exceed the number of hours the comparable full-time worker is required to work in the period, disregarding absences from work and overtime.

### 6 Right to receive a written statement of reasons for less favourable treatment

(1) If a worker who considers that his employer may have treated him in a manner which infringes a right conferred on him by regulation 5 requests in writing from his employer a written statement giving particulars of the reasons for the treatment, the worker is entitled to be provided with such a statement within twenty-one days of his request.

(2) A written statement under this regulation is admissable as evidence in any proceedings under these Regulations.

(3) If it appears to the tribunal in any proceedings under these Regulations –

(a) that the employer deliberately, and without reasonable excuse, omitted to provide a written statement, or
(b) that the written statement is evasive or equivocal,

it may draw any inference which it considers it just and equitable to draw, including an inference that the employer has infringed the right in question.

(4) This regulation does not apply where the treatment in question consists of the dismissal of an employee, and the employee is entitled to a written statement of reasons for his dismissal under section 92 of the 1996 Act.

## 7 Unfair dismissal and the right not to be subjected to detriment

(1) An employee who is dismissed shall be regarded as unfairly dismissed for the purposes of Part X of the 1996 Act if the reason (or, if more than one, the principal reason) for the dismissal is a reason specified in paragraph (3).

(2) A worker has the right not to be subjected to any detriment by any act, or any deliberate failure to act, by his employer done on a ground specified in paragraph (3).

(3) The reasons or, as the case may be, grounds are –

   (a)   that the worker has –
   - (i)   brought proceedings against the employer under these Regulations;
   - (ii)  requested from his employer a written statement of reasons under regulation 6;
   - (iii) given evidence or information in connection with such proceedings brought by any worker;
   - (iv)  otherwise done anything under these Regulations in relation to the employer or any other person;
   - (v)   alleged that the employer had infringed these Regulations; or
   - (vi)  refused (or proposed to refuse) to forgo a right conferred on him by these Regulations, or
   
   (b)   that the employer believes or suspects that the worker has done or intends to do any of the things mentioned in sub-paragraph (a).

(4) Where the reason or principal reason for dismissal or, as the case may be, ground for subjection to any act or deliberate failure to act, is that mentioned in paragraph (3)(a)(v), or (b) so far as it relates thereto, neither paragraph (1) nor paragraph (2) applies if the allegation made by the worker is false and not made in good faith.

(5) Paragraph (2) does not apply where the detriment in question amounts to the dismissal of an employee within the meaning of Part X of the 1996 Act.

## 8 Complaints to employment tribunals etc

(1) Subject to regulation 7(5), a worker may present a complaint to an employment tribunal that his employer has infringed a right conferred on him by regulation 5 or 7(2).

(2) Subject to paragraph (3), an employment tribunal shall not consider a complaint under this regulation unless it is presented before the end of the period of three months (or, in a case to which regulation 13 applies, six months) beginning with the date of the less favourable treatment or detriment to which the complaint relates or, where an act or failure to act is part of a series of similar acts or failures comprising the less favourable treatment or detriment, the last of them.

(3) A tribunal may consider any such complaint which is out of time if, in all the circumstances of the case, it considers that it is just and equitable to do so.

(4) For the purposes of calculating the date of the less favourable treatment or detriment under paragraph (2) –

(a)   where a term in a contract is less favourable, that treatment shall be treated, subject to paragraph (b), as taking place on each day of the period during which the term is less favourable;

(b)   where an application relies on regulation 3 or 4 the less favourable treatment shall be treated as occurring on, and only on, in the case of regulation 3, the first day on which the applicant worked under the new or varied contract and, in the case of regulation 4, the day on which the applicant returned; and

(c)   a deliberate failure to act contrary to regulation 5 or 7(2) shall be treated as done when it was decided on.

(5) In the absence of evidence establishing the contrary, a person shall be taken for the purposes of paragraph (4)(c) to decide not to act –

(a)   when he does an act inconsistent with doing the failed act; or

(b)   if he has done no such inconsistent act, when the period expires within which he might reasonably have been expected to have done the failed act if it was to be done.

(6) Where a worker presents a complaint under this regulation it is for the employer to identify the ground for the less favourable treatment or detriment.

(7) Where an employment tribunal finds that a complaint presented to it under this regulation is well founded, it shall take such of the following steps as it considers just and equitable –

(a)   making a declaration as to the rights of the complainant and the employer in relation to the matters to which the complaint relates;

(b)   ordering the employer to pay compensation to the complainant;

(c)   recommending that the employer take, within a specified period, action appearing to the tribunal to be reasonable, in all the circumstances of the case, for the purpose of obviating or reducing the adverse effect on the complainant of any matter to which the complaint relates.

(8) (*revoked*)

(9) Where a tribunal orders compensation under paragraph (7)(b), the amount of the compensation awarded shall be such as the tribunal considers just and equitable in all the circumstances having regard to –

(a)   the infringement to which the complaint relates, and

(b)   any loss which is attributable to the infringement having regard, in the case of an infringement of the right conferred by regulation 5, to the pro rata principle except where it is inappropriate to do so.

(10) The loss shall be taken to include –

(a)   any expenses reasonably incurred by the complainant in consequence of the infringement, and

    (b)    loss of any benefit which he might reasonably be expected to have had but for the infringement.

(11) Compensation in respect of treating a worker in a manner which infringes the right conferred on him by regulation 5 shall not include compensation for injury to feelings.

(12) In ascertaining the loss the tribunal shall apply the same rule concerning the duty of a person to mitigate his loss as applies to damages recoverable under the common law of England and Wales or (as the case may be) Scotland.

(13) Where the tribunal finds that the act, or failure to act, to which the complaint relates was to any extent caused or contributed to by action of the complainant, it shall reduce the amount of the compensation by such proportion as it considers just and equitable having regard to that finding.

(14) If the employer fails, without reasonable justification, to comply with a recommendation made by an employment tribunal under paragraph (7)(c) the tribunal may, if it thinks it just and equitable to do so –

    (a)    increase the amount of compensation required to be paid to the complainant in respect of the complaint, where an order was made under paragraph (7)(b); or

    (b)    make an order under paragraph (7)(b).

**17 Holders of judicial offices**

These Regulations do not apply to any individual in his capacity as the holder of a judicial office if he is remunerated on a daily fee-paid basis.

**Amendments**—SI 2002/2035.

# STATUTORY PATERNITY PAY AND STATUTORY ADOPTION PAY (GENERAL) REGULATIONS 2002

## SI 2002/2822

### PART 1
### INTRODUCTION

### 1 Citation and commencement

These Regulations may be cited as the Statutory Paternity Pay and Statutory Adoption Pay (General) Regulations 2002 and shall come into force on 8th December 2002.

### 2 Interpretation

(1) In these Regulations –

"the Act" means the Social Security Contributions and Benefits Act 1992;
"adopter", in relation to a child, means a person who has been matched with the child for adoption;
"adoption agency" has the meaning given, in relation to England and Wales, by section 1(4) of the Adoption Act 1976 and in relation to Scotland, by section 119(1) of the Adoption and Children (Scotland) Act 2007;
"the Board" means the Commissioners of Inland Revenue;
"the Contributions Regulations" means the Social Security (Contributions) Regulations 2001;
"expected week", in relation to the birth of a child, means the week, beginning with midnight between Saturday and Sunday, in which it is expected that the child will be born;
"statutory paternity pay (adoption)" means statutory paternity pay payable in accordance with the provisions of Part 12ZA of the Act where the conditions specified in section 171ZB(2) of the Act are satisfied;
"statutory paternity pay (birth)" means statutory paternity pay payable in accordance with the provisions of Part 12ZA of the Act where the conditions specified in section 171ZA(2) of the Act are satisfied.

(2) For the purposes of these Regulations –

(a) a person is matched with a child for adoption when an adoption agency decides that that person would be a suitable adoptive parent for the child, either individually or jointly with another person, and

(b) a person is notified of having been matched with a child on the date on which he receives notification of the agency's decision, under regulation 11(2) of the Adoption Agencies Regulations 1983 or regulation 8(5) of the Adoption Agencies (Scotland) Regulations 2009.

Amendments—SI 2011/1740.

**3 Application**

(1) Subject to the provisions of Part 12ZA of the Act (statutory paternity pay) and of these Regulations, there is entitlement to –

    (a)    statutory paternity pay (birth) in respect of children –
        (i)    born on or after 6th April 2003; or
        (ii)    whose expected week of birth begins on or after that date;
    (b)    statutory paternity pay (adoption) in respect of children –
        (i)    matched with a person who is notified of having been matched on or after 6th April 2003; or
        (ii)    placed for adoption on or after that date.

(2) Subject to the provisions of Part 12ZB of the Act (statutory adoption pay) and of these Regulations, there is entitlement to statutory adoption pay in respect of children –

    (a)    matched with a person who is notified of having been matched on or after 6th April 2003; or
    (b)    placed for adoption on or after that date.

**PART 2**
**STATUTORY PATERNITY PAY (BIRTH)**

**4 Conditions of entitlement to statutory paternity pay (birth): relationship with newborn child and child's mother**

The conditions prescribed under section 171ZA(2)(a) of the Act are those prescribed in regulation 4(2)(b) and (c) of the Paternity and Adoption Leave Regulations 2002

**5 Modification of entitlement conditions: early birth**

Where a person does not meet the conditions specified in section 171ZA(2)(b) to (d) of the Act because the child's birth occurred earlier than the 14th week before the expected week of the birth, it shall have effect as if, for the conditions there set out, there were substituted the conditions that –

    (a)    the person would, but for the date on which the birth occurred, have been in employed earner's employment with an employer for a continuous period of at least 26 weeks ending with the week immediately preceding the 14th week before the expected week of the child's birth;
    (b)    his normal weekly earnings for the period of 8 weeks ending with the week immediately preceding the week in which the child is born are not less than the lower earnings limit in force under section 5(1)(a) of the Act immediately before the commencement of the week in which the child is born.

## 6 Period of payment of statutory paternity pay (birth)

(1) Subject to paragraph (2) and regulation 8, a person entitled to statutory paternity pay (birth) may choose the statutory paternity pay period to begin on –

(a)  the date on which the child is born or, where he is at work on that day, the following day;

(b)  the date falling such number of days after the date on which the child is born as the person may specify;

(c)  a predetermined date, specified by the person, which is later than the first day of the expected week of the child's birth.

(2) In a case where statutory paternity pay (birth) is payable in respect of a child whose expected week of birth begins before 6th April 2003, the statutory paternity pay period shall begin on a predetermined date, specified by the person entitled to such pay in a notice under section 171ZC(1) of the Act, which is at least 28 days after the date on which that notice was given, unless the person liable to pay statutory paternity pay (birth) agrees to the period beginning earlier.

(3) A person may choose for statutory paternity pay (birth) to be paid in respect of a period of a week.

(4) A choice made in accordance with paragraph (1) or (2) is not irrevocable, but where a person subsequently makes a different choice in relation to the beginning of the statutory pay period, section 171ZC(1) of the Act shall apply to it.

## 7 Additional notice requirements for statutory paternity pay (birth)

(1) Where the choice made by a person in accordance with paragraph (1) of regulation 6 and notified in accordance with section 171ZC(1) of the Act is that mentioned in sub-paragraph (a) or (b) of that paragraph, the person shall give further notice to the person liable to pay him statutory paternity pay, as soon as is reasonably practicable after the child's birth, of the date the child was born;

(2) Where the choice made by a person in accordance with paragraph (1) of regulation 6 and notified in accordance with section 171ZC(1) of the Act is that specified in sub-paragraph (c) of that paragraph, and the date of the child's birth is later than the date so specified, the person shall, if he wishes to claim statutory paternity pay (birth), give notice to the person liable to pay it, as soon as is reasonably practicable, that the period in respect of which statutory paternity pay is to be paid shall begin on a date different from that originally chosen by him.

(3) That date may be any date chosen in accordance with paragraph (1) of regulation 6.

## 8  Qualifying period for statutory paternity pay (birth)

The qualifying period for the purposes of section 171ZE(2) of the Act (period within which the statutory paternity pay period must occur) is a period which begins on the date of the child's birth and ends –

    (a)    except in the case referred to in paragraph (b), 56 days after that date;

    (b)    in a case where the child is born before the first day of the expected week of its birth, 56 days after that day.

## 9  Evidence of entitlement to statutory paternity pay (birth)

(1) A person shall provide evidence of his entitlement to statutory paternity pay (birth) by providing in writing to the person who will be liable to pay him statutory paternity pay (birth) –

    (a)    the information specified in paragraph (2);

    (b)    a declaration that he meets the conditions prescribed under section 171ZA(2)(a) of the Act and that it is not the case that statutory paternity pay (birth) is not payable to him by virtue of the provisions of section 171ZE(4) of the Act.

    (2)The information referred to in paragraph (1)(a) is as follows –

    (a)    the name of the person claiming statutory paternity pay (birth);

    (b)    the expected week of the child's birth and, where the birth has already occurred, the date of birth;

    (c)    the date from which it is expected that the liability to pay statutory paternity pay (birth) will begin;

    (d)    whether the period chosen in respect of which statutory paternity pay (birth) is to be payable is a week.

(3) The information and declaration referred to in paragraph (1) shall be provided at least 28 days before the date mentioned in sub-paragraph (c) of paragraph (2) or, if that is not reasonably practicable, as soon as is reasonably practicable thereafter.

(4) Where the person who will be liable to pay statutory paternity pay (birth) so requests, the person entitled to it shall inform him of the date of the child's birth within 28 days, or as soon as is reasonably practicable thereafter.

## 10  Entitlement to statutory paternity pay (birth) where there is more than one employer

Statutory paternity pay (birth) shall be payable to a person in respect of a statutory pay week during any part of which he works only for an employer –

    (a)    who is not liable to pay him statutory paternity pay (birth); and

    (b)    for whom he has worked in the week immediately preceding the 14th week before the expected week of the child's birth.

## PART 3
## STATUTORY PATERNITY PAY (ADOPTION)

**11 Conditions of entitlement to statutory paternity pay (adoption): relationship with child and with person with whom the child is placed for adoption**

(1) The conditions prescribed under section 171ZB(2)(a) of the Act are that a person –

    (a)   is married to, the civil partner or the partner of a child's adopter (or in a case where there are two adopters, married to, the civil partner or the partner of the other adopter), and

    (b)   has, or expects to have, the main responsibility (apart from the responsibility of the child's adopter, or in a case where there two adopters, together with the other adopter) for the upbringing of the child.

(2) For the purposes of paragraph (1), "partner" means a person (whether of a different sex or the same sex) who lives with the adopter and the child in an enduring family relationship but is not a relative of the adopter of a kind specified in paragraph (2A).

(2A) The relatives of the adopter referred to in paragraph (2) are the adopter's parent, grandparent, sister, brother, aunt or uncle.

(3) References to relationships in paragraph (2A) –

    (a)   are to relationships of the full blood or half blood, or, in the case of an adopted person, such of those relationships as would exist but for the adoption, and

    (b)   include the relationship of a child with his adoptive, or former adoptive parents but do not include any other adoptive relationships.

**Amendments**—SI 2004/488; SI 2005/2114.

**12 Period of payment of statutory paternity pay (adoption)**

(1) Subject to paragraph (2) and regulation 14, a person entitled to statutory paternity pay (adoption) may choose the statutory paternity pay period to begin on –

    (a)   the date on which the child is placed with the adopter or, where the person is at work on that day, the following day;

    (b)   the date falling such number of days after the date on which the child is placed with the adopter as the person may specify;

    (c)   a predetermined date, specified by the person, which is later than the date on which the child is expected to be placed with the adopter.

(2) In a case where statutory paternity pay (adoption) is payable in respect of a child matched with an adopter who is notified of having been matched before 6th April 2003, the statutory paternity pay period shall begin on a predetermined date, specified by the person entitled to such pay in a notice under section 171ZC(1) of the Act, which is at least 28 days after the date on

which that notice was given, unless the person liable to pay statutory paternity pay (birth) agrees to the period beginning earlier.

(3) A person may choose for statutory paternity pay (adoption) to be paid in respect of a period of a week.

(4) A choice made in accordance with paragraph (1) is not irrevocable, but where a person subsequently makes a different choice in relation to the beginning of the statutory paternity pay period, section 171ZC(1) of the Act shall apply to it.

### 13 Additional notice requirements for statutory paternity pay (adoption)

(1) Where the choice made by a person in accordance with paragraph (1) of regulation 12 and notified in accordance with section 171ZC(1) of the Act is that mentioned in sub-paragraph (a) or (b) of that paragraph, the person shall give further notice to the person liable to pay him statutory paternity pay as soon as is reasonably practicable of the date on which the placement occurred.

(2) Where the choice made by a person in accordance with paragraph (1) of regulation 12 and notified in accordance with section 171ZC(1) of the Act is that mentioned in sub-paragraph (c) of that paragraph, or a date is specified under paragraph (2) of that regulation, and the child is placed for adoption later than the date so specified, the person shall, if he wishes to claim statutory paternity pay (adoption), give notice to the person liable to pay it, as soon as is reasonably practicable, that the period in respect of which statutory paternity pay is to be paid shall begin on a date different from that originally chosen by him.

(3) That date may be any date chosen in accordance with paragraph (1) of regulation 12.

### 14 Qualifying period for statutory paternity pay (adoption)

The qualifying period for the purposes of section 171ZE(2) of the Act (period within which the statutory pay period must occur) is a period of 56 days beginning with the date of the child's placement for adoption.

### 15 Evidence of entitlement for statutory paternity pay (adoption)

(1) A person shall provide evidence of his entitlement to statutory paternity pay (adoption) by providing in writing to the person who will be liable to pay him statutory paternity pay (adoption) –

  (a)  the information specified in paragraph (2);
  (b)  a declaration that he meets the conditions prescribed under section 171ZB(2)(a) of the Act and that it is not the case that statutory paternity pay (adoption) is not payable to him by virtue of the provisions of section 171ZE(4) of the Act;
  (c)  a declaration that he has elected to receive statutory paternity pay (adoption), and not statutory adoption pay under Part 12ZB of the Act.

(2) The information referred to in paragraph (1) is as follows –

(a)    the name of the person claiming statutory paternity pay (adoption);

(b)    the date on which the child is expected to be placed for adoption or, where the child has already been placed for adoption, the date of placement of the child;

(c)    the date from which it is expected that the liability to pay statutory paternity pay (adoption) will begin;

(d)    whether the period chosen in respect of which statutory paternity pay (adoption) is to be payable is a week;

(e)    the date the adopter was notified he had been matched with the child for the purposes of adoption.

(3) The information and declarations referred to in paragraph (1) shall be provided to the person liable to pay statutory paternity pay at least 28 days before the date mentioned in sub-paragraph (c) of paragraph (2) or, if that is not reasonably practicable, as soon as is reasonably practicable thereafter.

(4) Where the person who will be liable to pay statutory paternity pay (adoption) so requests, the person entitled to it shall inform him of the date of the child's placement within 28 days, or as soon as is reasonably practicable thereafter.

**16  Entitlement to statutory paternity pay (adoption) where there is more than one employer**

Statutory paternity pay (adoption) shall be payable to a person in respect of a statutory pay week during any part of which he works only for an employer –

(a)    who is not liable to pay him statutory paternity pay (adoption); and

(b)    for whom he has worked in the week in which the adopter is notified of being matched with the child.

## PART 4
## STATUTORY PATERNITY PAY: PROVISIONS APPLICABLE TO BOTH STATUTORY PATERNITY PAY (BIRTH) AND STATUTORY PATERNITY PAY (ADOPTION)

**17  Work during a statutory paternity pay period**

(1) Where, in a case where statutory paternity pay is being paid to a person who works during the statutory paternity pay period for an employer who is not liable to pay him statutory paternity pay and who does not fall within paragraph (b) of regulation 10 or, as the case may be, paragraph (b) of regulation 16, there shall be no liability to pay statutory paternity pay in respect of any remaining part of the statutory paternity pay period.

(2) In a case falling within paragraph (1), the person shall notify the person liable to pay statutory paternity pay within 7 days of the first day during which he works during the statutory pay period.

(3) The notification mentioned in paragraph (2) shall be in writing, if the person who has been liable to pay statutory paternity pay so requests.

### 18 Cases where there is no liability to pay statutory paternity pay

There shall be no liability to pay statutory paternity pay in respect of any week –

(a)     during any part of which the person entitled to it is entitled to statutory sick pay under Part 11 of the Act;

(b)     following that in which the person claiming it has died; or

(c)     during any part of which the person entitled to it is detained in legal custody or sentenced to a term of imprisonment (except where the sentence is suspended), or which is a subsequent week within the same statutory paternity pay period.

### 19 Statutory paternity pay and contractual remuneration

For the purposes of section 171ZG(1) and (2) of the Act, the payments which are to be treated as contractual remuneration are sums payable under a contract of service –

(a)     by way of remuneration;

(b)     for incapacity for work due to sickness or injury;

(c)     by reason of the birth or adoption of a child.

### 20 Avoidance of liability for statutory paternity pay

(1) A former employer shall be liable to make payments of statutory paternity pay to a former employee in any case where the employee had been employed for a continuous period of at least 8 weeks and his contract of service was brought to an end by the former employer solely, or mainly, for the purpose of avoiding liability for statutory paternity pay.

(2) In a case falling within paragraph (1) –

(a)     the employee shall be treated as if he had been employed for a continuous period ending with the child's birth or, as the case may be, the placement of the child for adoption;

(b)     his normal weekly earnings shall be calculated by reference to his normal weekly earnings for the period of 8 weeks ending with the last day in respect of which he was paid under his former contract of service.

**PART 5**
**STATUTORY ADOPTION PAY**

### 21 Adoption pay period

(1) Subject to paragraph (2), a person entitled to statutory adoption pay may choose the adoption pay period to begin –

   (a)   on the date on which the child is placed with him for adoption or, where he is at work on that day, on the following day;

   (b)   subject to paragraph (2), on a predetermined date, specified by him, which is no more than 14 days before the date on which the child is expected to be placed with him and no later than that date.

(2) In a case where statutory adoption pay is payable in respect of a child matched with an adopter who is notified of having been matched before 6th April 2003, the statutory adoption pay period shall begin on a predetermined date which is –

   (a)   on or after 6th April 2003, and

   (b)   no more than 14 days before the date on which the child is expected to be placed with the adopter.

(3) Subject to paragraph (4), where the choice made is that mentioned in sub-paragraph (b) of paragraph (1) or in a case where paragraph (2) applies, the adoption pay period shall, unless the employer agrees to the adoption pay period beginning earlier, begin no earlier than 28 days after notice under section 171ZL(6) of the Act has been given.

(4) Where the beginning of the adoption pay period determined in accordance with paragraph (3) is later than the date of placement, it shall be the date of placement.

(5) Subject to regulation 22, the duration of any adoption pay period shall be a continuous period of 39 weeks.

(6) A choice made under paragraph (1), or a date specified under paragraph (2), is not irrevocable, but where a person subsequently makes a different choice, section 171ZL(6) of the Act shall apply to it.

**Amendments**—SI 2006/2236.

## 22 Adoption pay period in cases where adoption is disrupted

(1) Where –

   (a)   after a child has been placed for adoption –

      (i)   the child dies;

      (ii)   the child is returned to the adoption agency under section 30(3) of the Adoption Act 1976 or in Scotland, the child is returned to the adoption agency, adoption society or nominated person in accordance with section 25(6) of the Adoption and Children (Scotland) Act 2007, or

   (b)   the adoption pay period has begun prior to the date the child has been placed for adoption, but the placement does not take place,

the adoption pay period shall terminate in accordance with the provisions of paragraph (2).

(2) The adoption pay period shall, in a case falling within paragraph (1), terminate 8 weeks after the end of the week specified in paragraph (3).

(3) The week referred to in paragraph (2) is –

 (a) in a case falling within paragraph (1)(a)(i), the week during which the child dies;

 (b) in a case falling within paragraph (1)(a)(ii), the week during which the child is returned;

 (c) in a case falling within paragraph (1)(b), the week during which the person with whom the child was to be placed for adoption is notified that the placement will not be made.

(4) For the purposes of paragraph (3), "week" means a period of seven days beginning with Sunday.

Amendments—SI 2011/1740

## 23 Additional notice requirements for statutory adoption pay

(1) Where a person gives notice under section 171ZL(6) of the Act he shall at the same time give notice of the date on which the child is expected to be placed for adoption.

(2) Where the choice made in accordance with paragraph (1) of regulation 21 and notified in accordance with section 171ZL(6) of the Act is that mentioned in sub-paragraph (a) of that paragraph, the person shall give further notice to the person liable to pay him statutory adoption pay as soon as is reasonably practicable of the date the child is placed for adoption.

## 24 Evidence of entitlement to statutory adoption pay

(1) A person shall provide evidence of his entitlement to statutory adoption pay by providing to the person who will be liable to pay it –

 (a) the information specified in paragraph (2), in the form of one or more documents provided to him by an adoption agency, containing that information;

 (b) a declaration that he has elected to receive statutory adoption pay, and not statutory paternity pay (adoption) under Part 12ZA of the Act.

(2) The information referred to in paragraph (1) is –

 (a) the name and address of the adoption agency and of the person claiming payment of statutory adoption pay;

 (b) the date on which the child is expected to be placed for adoption or, where the child has already been placed for adoption, the date of placement; and

 (c) the date on which the person claiming payment of statutory adoption pay was informed by the adoption agency that the child would be placed for adoption with him.

(3) The information and declaration referred to in paragraph (1) shall be provided to the person liable to pay statutory adoption pay at least 28 days before the date chosen as the beginning of the adoption pay period in

accordance with paragraph (1) of regulation 21, or, if that is not reasonably practicable, as soon as is reasonably practicable thereafter.

### 25 Entitlement to statutory adoption pay where there is more than one employer

Statutory adoption pay shall be payable to a person in respect of a week during any part of which he works only for an employer –

(a) who is not liable to pay him statutory adoption pay; and
(b) for whom he has worked in the week in which he is notified of being matched with the child.

### 26 Work during an adoption pay period

(1) Where, in a case where statutory adoption pay is being paid to a person who works during the adoption pay period for an employer who is not liable to pay him statutory adoption pay and who does not fall within paragraph (b) of regulation 25, there shall be no liability to pay statutory adoption pay in respect of any remaining part of the adoption pay period.

(2) In a case falling within paragraph (1), the person shall notify the person liable to pay statutory adoption pay within 7 days of the first day during which he works during the adoption pay period.

(3) The notification contained in paragraph (2) shall be in writing if the person who has been liable to pay statutory adoption pay so requests.

### 27 Cases where there is no liability to pay statutory adoption pay

(1) There shall be no liability to pay statutory adoption pay in respect of any week –

(a) during any part of which the person entitled to it is entitled to statutory sick pay under Part 11 of the Act;
(b) following that in which the person claiming it has died; or
(c) subject to paragraph (2), during any part of which the person entitled to it is detained in legal custody or sentenced to a term of imprisonment (except where the sentence is suspended).

(2) There shall be liability to pay statutory adoption pay in respect of any week during any part of which the person entitled to it is detained in legal custody where that person –

(a) is released subsequently without charge;
(b) is subsequently found not guilty of any offence and is released; or
(c) is convicted of an offence but does not receive a custodial sentence.

### 27A Working for not more than 10 days during an adoption pay period

In the case where an employee does any work under a contract of service with his employer on any day for not more than 10 such days during his adoption pay period, whether consecutive or not, statutory adoption pay shall continue to be payable to the employee by the employer.

Amendments—SI 2006/2236.

### 28 Statutory adoption pay and contractual remuneration

For the purposes of section 171ZP(4) and (5) of the Act, the payments which are to be treated as contractual remuneration are sums payable under a contract of service –

    (a)    by way of remuneration;
    (b)    for incapacity for work due to sickness or injury;
    (c)    by reason of the adoption of a child.

### 29 Termination of employment before start of adoption pay period

(1) Where the employment of a person who satisfies the conditions of entitlement to statutory adoption pay terminates for whatever reason (including dismissal) before the adoption pay period chosen in accordance with regulation 21 has begun, the period shall begin 14 days before the expected date of placement or, where the termination occurs on, or within 14 days before, the expected date of placement, on the day immediately following the last day of his employment.

(2) In a case falling within paragraph (1), the notice requirements set out in section 171ZL(6) of the Act and these Regulations shall not apply.

### 30 Avoidance of liability for statutory adoption pay

(1) A former employer shall be liable to make payments of statutory adoption pay to a former employee in any case where the employee had been employed for a continuous period of at least 8 weeks and his contract of service was brought to an end by the former employer solely, or mainly, for the purpose of avoiding liability for statutory adoption pay.

(2) In a case falling within paragraph (1) –

    (a)    the employee shall be treated as if he had been employed for a continuous period ending with the week in which he was notified of having been matched with the child for adoption; and
    (b)    his normal weekly earnings shall be calculated by reference to his normal weekly earnings for the period of 8 weeks ending with the last day in respect of which he was paid under his former contract of service.

## PART 6
## STATUTORY PATERNITY PAY AND STATUTORY ADOPTION PAY: PROVISIONS APPLICABLE TO BOTH STATUTORY PATERNITY PAY AND STATUTORY ADOPTION PAY

### 31 Introductory

(1) Subject to paragraph (2), the provisions of regulations 32 to 47 below apply to statutory paternity pay payable under Part 12ZA of the Act and to statutory adoption pay payable under 12ZB of the Act.

(2) The provisions of regulation 44 only apply to statutory adoption pay.

### 32 Treatment of persons as employees

(1) Subject to paragraph (1A), in a case where, and in so far as, a person is treated as an employed earner by virtue of the Social Security (Categorisation of Earners) Regulations 1978 he shall be treated as an employee for the purposes of Parts 12ZA and 12ZB of the Act, and in a case where, and in so far as, such a person is treated otherwise than as an employed earner by virtue of those regulations, he shall not be treated as an employee for the purposes of Parts 12ZA and 12ZB of the Act.

(1A) Paragraph (1) shall have effect in relation to a person who –

(a)    is under the age of 16; and
(b)    would or, as the case may be, would not have been treated as an employed earner by virtue of the Social Security (Categorisation of Earners) Regulations 1978 had he been over that age,

as it has effect in relation to a person who is or, as the case may be, is not so treated.

(2) A person who is in employed earner's employment within the meaning of the Act under a contract of apprenticeship shall be treated as an employee for the purposes of Parts 12ZA and 12ZB of the Act.

(3) A person who is in employed earner's employment within the meaning of the Act but whose employer –

(a)    does not fulfil the conditions prescribed in regulation 145(1) of the Contributions Regulations in so far as that provision relates to residence or presence in Great Britain; or
(b)    is a person who, by reason of any international treaty to which the United Kingdom is a party or of any international convention binding the United Kingdom –
(i)    is exempt from the provisions of the Act; or
(ii)    is a person against whom the provisions of the Act are not enforceable,

shall not be treated as an employee for the purposes of Parts 12ZA and 12ZB of the Act.

**Amendments**—SI 2006/1031; SI 2007/825.

### 33 Continuous employment

(1) Subject to the following provisions of this regulation, where in any week a person is, for the whole or part of the week –

(a)  incapable of work in consequence of sickness or injury;

(b)  absent from work on account of a temporary cessation of work;

(c)  absent from work in circumstances such that, by arrangement or custom, he is regarded as continuing in the employment of his employer for all or any purposes,

and returns to work for his employer after the incapacity for or absence from work, that week shall be treated for the purposes of sections 171ZA, 171ZB and 171ZL of the Act as part of a continuous period of employment with that employer, notwithstanding that no contract of service exists with that employer in respect of that week.

(2) Incapacity for work which lasts for more than 26 consecutive weeks shall not count for the purposes of paragraph (1)(a).

(3) Where a person –

(a)  is an employee in an employed earner's employment in which the custom is for the employer –

(i)   to offer work for a fixed period of not more than 26 consecutive weeks;

(ii)  to offer work for such period on two or more occasions in a year for periods which do not overlap; and

(iii) to offer the work available to those persons who had worked for him during the last or a recent such period, but

(b)  is absent from work because of incapacity arising from some specific disease or bodily or mental disablement,

then in that case paragraph (1) shall apply as if the words "and returns to work for his employer after the incapacity for or absence from work," were omitted and paragraph (4) shall not apply.

(4) Where a person is employed under a contract of service for part only of the relevant week within the meaning of subsection (3) of section 171ZL of the Act (entitlement to statutory adoption pay), the whole of that week shall count in computing a period of continuous employment for the purposes of that section.

### 34 Continuous employment and unfair dismissal

(1) This regulation applies to a person in relation to whose dismissal an action is commenced which consists –

(a)  of the presentation by him of a complaint under section 111(1) of the Employment Rights Act 1996;

(b)  of his making a claim in accordance with a dismissals procedure agreement designated by an order under section 110 of that Act;

(c)  of any action taken by a conciliation officer under section 18 of the Employment Tribunals Act 1996; or

(d)  of a decision arising out of the use of a statutory dispute resolution procedure contained in Schedule 2 to the Employment Act 2002 in a case where, in accordance with the Employment Act 2002 (Dispute Resolution) Regulations 2004, such a procedure applies.

(2) If, in consequence of an action of the kind specified in paragraph (1), a person is reinstated or re-engaged by his employer or by a successor or associated employer of that employer, the continuity of his employment shall be preserved for the purposes of Part 12ZA or, as the case may be, Part 12ZB of the Act, and any week which falls within the interval beginning with the effective date of termination and ending with the date of reinstatement or re-engagement, as the case may be, shall count in the computation of his period of continuous employment.

(3) In this regulation –

"successor" and "dismissal procedures agreement" have the same meanings as in section 235 of the Employment Rights Act 1996; and

"associated employer" shall be construed in accordance with section 231 of the Employment Rights Act 1996.

**Amendments**—SI 2005/358.

## 35 Continuous employment and stoppages of work

(1) Where, for any week or part of a week a person does not work because there is a stoppage of work due to a trade dispute within the meaning of section 35(1) of the Jobseekers Act 1995 at his place of employment, the continuity of his employment shall, subject to paragraph (2), be treated as continuing throughout the stoppage but, subject to paragraph (3), no such week shall count in the computation of his period of employment.

(2) Subject to paragraph (3), where during the stoppage of work a person is dismissed from his employment, the continuity of his employment shall not be treated in accordance with paragraph (1) as continuing beyond the commencement of the day he stopped work.

(3) The provisions of paragraph (1), to the extent that they provide that a week in which the stoppage of work occurred shall not count in the computation of a period of employment, and paragraph (2) shall not apply to a person who proves that at no time did he have a direct interest in the trade dispute in question.

## 36 Change of employer

A person's employment shall, notwithstanding a change of employer, be treated as continuous employment with the second employer where –

(a)  the employer's trade or business or an undertaking (whether or not it is an undertaking established by or under an Act of Parliament) is transferred from one person to another;

(b)    by or under an Act of Parliament, whether public or local and whenever passed, a contract of employment between any body corporate and the person is modified and some other body corporate is substituted as his employer;

(c)    on the death of his employer, the person is taken into employment of the personal representatives or trustees of the deceased;

(d)    the person is employed by partners, personal representatives or trustees and there is a change in the partners, or, as the case may be, personal representatives or trustees;

(e)    the person is taken into the employment of an employer who is, at the time he entered his employment, an associated employer of his previous employer, and for this purpose "associated employer" shall be construed in accordance with section 231 of the Employment Rights Act 1996;

(f)    on the termination of his employment with an employer he is taken into the employment of another employer and those employers are governors of a school maintained by a local authority and that authority.

**Amendments**—SI 2010/1172.

### 37 Reinstatement after service with the armed forces etc

If a person who is entitled to apply to his employer under the Reserve Forces (Safeguard of Employment) Act 1985 enters the employment of that employer within the 6-month period mentioned in section 1(4)(b) of that Act, his previous period of employment with that employer (or if there was more than one such period, the last of those periods) and the period of employment beginning in that 6-month period shall be treated as continuous.

### 38 Treatment of two or more employers or two or more contracts of service as one

(1) In a case where the earnings paid to a person in respect of two or more employments are aggregated and treated as a single payment of earnings under regulation 15(1) of the Contributions Regulations, the employers of that person in respect of those employments shall be treated as one for the purposes of Part 12ZA or, as the case may be, Part 12ZB of the Act.

(2) Where two or more employers are treated as one under the provisions of paragraph (1), liability for statutory paternity pay or, as the case may be, statutory adoption pay, shall be apportioned between them in such proportions as they may agree or, in default of agreement, in the proportions which the person's earnings from each employment bear to the amount of the aggregated earnings.

(3) Where two or more contracts of service exist concurrently between one employer and one employee, they shall be treated as one for the purposes of Part 12ZA or, as the case may be, Part 12ZB of the Act, except where, by virtue

of regulation 14 of the Contributions Regulations, the earnings from those contracts of service are not aggregated for the purposes of earnings-related contributions.

### 39 Meaning of "earnings"

(1) For the purposes of section 171ZJ(6) (normal weekly earnings for the purposes of Part 12ZA of the Act) and of section 171ZS(6) of the Act (normal weekly earnings for the purposes of Part 12ZB of the Act), the expression "earnings" shall be construed in accordance with the following provisions of this regulation.

(2) The expression "earnings" refers to gross earnings and includes any remuneration or profit derived from a person's employment except any payment or amount which is –

  (a)  excluded from the computation of a person's earnings under regulation 25 of and Schedule 3 to, and regulation 123 of, the Contributions Regulations (payments to be disregarded) and regulation 27 of those Regulations (payments to directors to be disregarded) (or would have been so excluded had he not been under the age of 16);

  (b)  a chargeable emolument under section 10A of the Act, except where, in consequence of such a chargeable emolument being excluded from earnings, a person would not be entitled to statutory paternity pay or, as the case may be, statutory adoption pay (or where such a payment or amount would have been so excluded and in consequence he would not have been entitled to statutory paternity pay or, as the case may be, statutory adoption pay had he not been under the age of 16).

(3) For the avoidance of doubt, "earnings" includes –

  (za)  any amount retrospectively treated as earnings by regulations made by virtue of section 4B(2) of the Act;

  (a)  any sum payable in respect of arrears of pay in pursuance of an order for reinstatement or re-engagement under the Employment Rights Act 1996;

  (b)  any sum payable by way of pay in pursuance of an order made under the Employment Rights Act 1996 for the continuation of a contract of employment;

  (c)  any sum payable by way of remuneration in pursuance of a protective award under section 189 of the Trade Union and Labour Relations (Consolidation) Act 1992;

  (d)  any sum payable by way of statutory sick pay, including sums payable in accordance with regulations made under section 151(6) of the Act;

  (e)  any sum payable by way of statutory maternity pay;

  (f)  any sum payable by way of statutory paternity pay;

  (g)  any sum payable by way of statutory adoption pay.

**Amendments**—SI 2006/1031; SI 2007/1154.

**40 Normal weekly earnings**

(1) For the purposes of Part 12ZA and Part 12ZB of the Act, a person's normal weekly earnings shall be calculated in accordance with the following provisions of this regulation.

(2) In this regulation –

"the appropriate date" means –

(a)    in relation to statutory paternity pay (birth), the first day of the 14th week before the expected week of the child's birth or the first day in the week in which the child is born, whichever is the earlier;

(b)    in relation to statutory paternity pay (adoption) and statutory adoption pay, the first day of the week after the week in which the adopter is notified of being matched with the child for the purposes of adoption;

"normal pay day" means a day on which the terms of a person's contract of service require him to be paid, or the practice in his employment is for him to be paid, if any payment is due to him; and

"day of payment" means a day on which the person was paid.

(3)Subject to paragraph (4), the relevant period for the purposes of section 171ZJ(6) and 171ZS(6) is the period between –

(a)    the last normal pay day to fall before the appropriate date; and

(b)    the last normal pay day to fall at least 8 weeks earlier than the normal pay day mentioned in sub-paragraph (a),

including the normal pay day mentioned in sub-paragraph (a) but excluding that first mentioned in sub-paragraph (b).

(4) In a case where a person has no identifiable normal pay day, paragraph (3) shall have effect as if the words "day of payment" were substituted for the words "normal pay day" in each place where they occur.

(5) In a case where a person has normal pay days at intervals of or approximating to one or more calendar months (including intervals of or approximating to a year) his normal weekly earnings shall be calculated by dividing his earnings in the relevant period by the number of calendar months in that period (or, if it is not a whole number, the nearest whole number), multiplying the result by 12 and dividing by 52.

(6) In a case to which paragraph (5) does not apply and the relevant period is not an exact number of weeks, the person's normal weekly earnings shall be calculated by dividing his earnings in the relevant period by the number of days in the relevant period and multiplying the result by 7.

(7) In any case where a person receives a back-dated pay increase which includes a sum in respect of a relevant period, normal weekly earnings shall be calculated as if such a sum was paid in that relevant period even though received after that period.

## 41  Payment of statutory paternity pay and statutory adoption pay

Payments of statutory paternity pay and statutory adoption pay may be made in a like manner to payments of remuneration but shall not include payment in kind or by way of the provision of board or lodgings or of services or other facilities.

## 42  Time when statutory paternity pay and statutory adoption pay are to be paid

(1) In this regulation, "pay day" means a day on which it has been agreed, or it is the normal practice between an employer or former employer and a person who is or was an employee of his, that payments by way of remuneration are to be made, or, where there is no such agreement or normal practice, the last day of a calendar month.

(2) In any case where –

    (a) a decision has been made by an officer of the Board under section 8(1) of the Social Security Contributions (Transfer of Functions, etc) Act 1999 as a result of which a person is entitled to an amount of statutory paternity pay or statutory adoption pay; and

    (b) the time for bringing an appeal against the decision has expired and either –

        (i) no such appeal has been brought; or

        (ii) such an appeal has been brought and has been finally disposed of,

that amount of statutory paternity pay or statutory adoption pay shall be paid within the time specified in paragraph (3).

(3) Subject to paragraphs (4) and (5), the employer or former employer shall pay the amount not later than the first pay day after –

    (a) where an appeal has been brought, the day on which the employer or former employer receives notification that it has been finally disposed of;

    (b) where leave to appeal has been refused and there remains no further opportunity to apply for leave, the day on which the employer or former employer receives notification of the refusal; and

    (c) in any other case, the day on which the time for bringing an appeal expires.

(4) Subject to paragraph (5), where it is impracticable, in view of the employer's or former employer's methods of accounting for and paying remuneration, for the requirement of payment referred to in paragraph (3) to be met by the pay day referred to in that paragraph, it shall be met not later than the next following pay day.

(5) Where the employer or former employer would not have remunerated the employee for his work in the week in question as early as the pay day specified

in paragraph (3) or (if it applies) paragraph (4), the requirement of payment shall be met on the first day on which the employee would have been remunerated for his work in that week.

## 43 Liability of the Board to pay statutory paternity pay or statutory adoption pay

(1) Where –

    (a)    an officer of the Board has decided that an employer is liable to make payments of statutory paternity pay or, as the case may be, statutory adoption pay to a person;

    (b)    the time for appealing against the decision has expired; and

    (c)    no appeal against the decision has been lodged or leave to appeal against the decision is required and has been refused,

then for any week in respect of which the employer was liable to make payments of statutory paternity pay or, as the case may be, statutory adoption pay but did not do so, and for any subsequent weeks in the paternity pay period or, as the case may be, adoption pay period, the liability to make those payments shall, notwithstanding sections 171ZD and 171ZM of the Act, be that of the Board and not the employer.

(2) Liability to make payments of statutory paternity pay or, as the case may be, statutory adoption pay shall, notwithstanding sections 171ZD and 171ZM of the Act, be a liability of the Board and not the employer as from the week in which the employer first becomes insolvent until the end of the paternity pay or adoption pay period.

(3) For the purposes of paragraph (2) an employer shall be taken to be insolvent if, and only if –

    (a)    in England and Wales –

        (i)    he has been adjudged bankrupt or has made a composition or arrangement with his creditors;

        (ii)    he has died and his estate falls to be administered in accordance with an order made under section 421 of the Insolvency Act 1986; or

        (iii)    where an employer is a company or a limited liability partnership, a winding-up order is made or a resolution for a voluntary winding-up is passed (or, in the case of a limited liability partnership, a determination for a voluntary winding-up has been made) with respect to it or it enters administration, or a receiver or a manager of its undertaking is duly appointed, or possession is taken, by or on behalf of the holders of any debentures secured by a floating charge, of any property of the company or limited liability partnership comprised in or subject to the charge, or a voluntary arrangement proposed for the purposes of Part 1 of the Insolvency Act 1986 is approved under that Part of that Act;

    (b)    in Scotland –

(i)      an award of sequestration is made on his estate or he executes a trust deed for his creditors or enters into a composition contract;

(ii)     he has died and a judicial factor appointed under section 11A of the Judicial Factors (Scotland) Act 1889 is required by that section to divide his insolvent estate among his creditors; or

(iii)    where the employer is a company or a limited liability partnership, a winding-up order is made or a resolution for voluntary winding-up is passed (or, in the case of a limited liability partnership, a determination for a voluntary winding-up is made) with respect to it or it enters administration, or a receiver of its undertaking is duly appointed, or a voluntary arrangement proposed for the purposes of Part 1 of the Insolvency Act 1986 is approved under that Part.

**Amendments**—SI 2003/2096.

## 44 Liability of the Board to pay statutory adoption pay in cases of legal custody or imprisonment

Where –

(a)      there is liability to pay statutory adoption pay in respect of a period which is subsequent to the last week falling within paragraph (1)(c) of regulation 27, or

(b)      there is liability to pay statutory adoption pay during a period of detention in legal custody by virtue of the provisions of paragraph (2) of that regulation,

that liability shall, notwithstanding section 171ZM of the Act, be that of the Board and not the employer.

## 45 Payments by the Board

Where the Board become liable in accordance with regulation 43 or 44 to make payments of statutory paternity pay or, as the case may be, statutory adoption pay to a person, the first payment shall be made as soon as reasonably practicable after they become so liable, and payments thereafter shall be made at weekly intervals, by means of an instrument of payment or by such other means as appears to the Board to be appropriate in the circumstance of any particular case.

## 46 Persons unable to act

(1) Where in the case of any person –

(a)      statutory paternity pay or, as the case may be, statutory adoption pay is payable to him or he is alleged to be entitled to it;

(b)      he is unable for the time being to act; and

(c)      either –

(i)      no receiver has been appointed by the Court of Protection with power to receive statutory paternity pay or, as the case may be, statutory adoption pay on his behalf, or

(ii)    in Scotland, his estate is not being administered by any tutor, curator or other guardian acting or appointed in terms of law,

the Board may, upon written application to them by a person who, if a natural person, is over the age of 18, appoint that person to exercise, on behalf of the person unable to act, any right to which he may be entitled under Part 12ZA or, as the case may be, Part 12ZB of the Act and to deal on his behalf with any sums payable to him.

(2)  Where the Board have made an appointment under paragraph (1) –

(a)    they may at any time in their absolute discretion revoke it;

(b)    the person appointed may resign his office after having given one month's notice in writing to the Board of his intention to do so; and

(c)    the appointment shall terminate when the Board are notified that a receiver or other person to whom paragraph (1)(c) applies has been appointed.

(3)  Anything required by Part 12ZA or 12ZB of the Act to be done by or to any person who is unable to act may be done by or to the person appointed under this regulation to act on his behalf, and the receipt of the person so appointed shall be a good discharge to the person's employer or former employer for any sum paid.

## 47  Service of notices by post

A notice given in accordance with the provisions of these Regulations in writing contained in an envelope which is properly addressed and sent by prepaid post shall be treated as having been given on the day on which it is posted.

# STATUTORY PATERNITY PAY AND STATUTORY ADOPTION PAY (WEEKLY RATES) REGULATIONS 2002

## SI 2002/2818

### 1 Citation and commencement

These Regulations may be cited as the Statutory Paternity Pay and Statutory Adoption Pay (Weekly Rates) Regulations and shall come into force on 8th December 2002.

### 2 Weekly rate of payment of statutory paternity pay

The weekly rate of payment of statutory paternity pay shall be the smaller of the following two amounts—

(a) £128.73;

(b) 90 per cent of the normal weekly earnings of the person claiming statutory paternity pay, determined in accordance with regulations 39 and 40 of the Statutory Paternity Pay and Statutory Adoption Pay (General) Regulations 2002.

**Amendments**—SI 2004/925; SI 2011/821.

### 3 Weekly rate of payment of statutory adoption pay

The weekly rate of payment of statutory adoption pay shall be the smaller of the following two amounts—

(a) £128.73;

(b) 90 per cent of the normal weekly earnings of the person claiming statutory adoption pay, determined in accordance with regulations 39 and 40 of the Statutory Paternity Pay and Statutory Adoption Pay (General) Regulations 2002.

**Amendments**—SI 2011/821.

### 4 Rounding of fractional amounts

Where any payment of—

(a) statutory paternity pay is made on the basis of a calculation at—
    (i) the weekly rate specified in regulation 2(b); or
    (ii) the daily rate of one-seventh of the weekly rate specified in regulation 2(a) or (b); or

(b) statutory adoption pay is made on the basis of a calculation at—
    (i) the weekly rate specified in regulation 3(b); or
    (ii) the daily rate of one-seventh of the weekly rate specified in regulation 3(a) or (b),

and that amount includes a fraction of a penny, the payment shall be rounded up to the next whole number of pence.

**Amendments**—SI 2006/2236.

# APPENDIX C

# COUNCIL DIRECTIVE NO 2006/54/EC

*of 5th July 2006*

*on the implementation of the principle of equal opportunities and equal treatment of men and women in matters of employment and occupation (recast)*

THE EUROPEAN PARLIAMENT AND THE COUNCIL OF THE EUROPEAN UNION,

Having regard to the Treaty establishing the European Community, and in particular Articles 141(3) thereof,

Having regard to the proposal from the Commission,

Having regard to the Opinion of the European Economic and Social Committee,

Acting in accordance with the procedure laid down in Article 251 of the Treaty,

Whereas:

(1) Council Directive 76/207/EEC of 9 February 1976 on the implementation of the principle of equal treatment for men and women as regards access to employment, vocational training and promotion, and working conditions (3) and Council Directive 86/378/EEC of 24 July 1986 on the implementation of the principle of equal treatment for men and women in occupational social security schemes (4) have been significantly amended (5). Council Directive 75/117/ EEC of 10 February 1975 on the approximation of the laws of the Member States relating to the application of the principle of equal pay for men and women (6) and Council Directive 97/80/EC of 15 December 1997 on the burden of proof in cases of discrimination based on sex (7) also contain provisions which have as their purpose the implementation of the principle of equal treatment between men and women. Now that new amendments are being made to the said Directives, it is desirable, for reasons of clarity, that the provisions in question should be recast by bringing together in a single text the main provisions existing in this field as well as certain developments arising out of the case-law of the Court of Justice of the European Communities (hereinafter referred to as the Court of Justice).

(2) Equality between men and women is a fundamental principle of Community law under Article 2 and Article 3 (2) of the Treaty and the case-law of the Court of Justice. Those Treaty provisions proclaim equality between men and women as a 'task' and an 'aim' of the Community and impose a positive obligation to promote it in all its activities.

(3) The Court of Justice has held that the scope of the principle of equal treatment for men and women cannot be confined to the prohibition of discrimination based on the fact that a person is of one or other sex. In view of

its purpose and the nature of the rights which it seeks to safeguard, it also applies to discrimination arising from the gender reassignment of a person.

(4) Article 141(3) of the Treaty now provides a specific legal basis for the adoption of Community measures to ensure the application of the principle of equal opportunities and equal treatment in matters of employment and occupation, including the principle of equal pay for equal work or work of equal value.

(5) Articles 21 and 23 of the Charter of Fundamental Rights of the European Union also prohibit any discrimination on grounds of sex and enshrine the right to equal treatment between men and women in all areas, including employment, work and pay.

(6) Harassment and sexual harassment are contrary to the principle of equal treatment between men and women and constitute discrimination on grounds of sex for the purposes of this Directive. These forms of discrimination occur not only in the workplace, but also in the context of access to employment, vocational training and promotion. They should therefore be prohibited and should be subject to effective, proportionate and dissuasive penalties.

(7) In this context, employers and those responsible for vocational training should be encouraged to take measures to combat all forms of discrimination on grounds of sex and, in particular, to take preventive measures against harassment and sexual harassment in the workplace and in access to employment, vocational training and promotion, in accordance with national law and practice.

(8) The principle of equal pay for equal work or work of equal value as laid down by Article 141 of the Treaty and consistently upheld in the case-law of the Court of Justice constitutes an important aspect of the principle of equal treatment between men and women and an essential and indispensable part of the acquis communautaire, including the case-law of the Court concerning sex discrimination. It is therefore appropriate to make further provision for its implementation.

(9) In accordance with settled case-law of the Court of Justice, in order to assess whether workers are performing the same work or work of equal value, it should be determined whether, having regard to a range of factors including the nature of the work and training and working conditions, those workers may be considered to be in a comparable situation.

(10) The Court of Justice has established that, in certain circumstances, the principle of equal pay is not limited to situations in which men and women work for the same employer.

(11) The Member States, in collaboration with the social partners, should continue to address the problem of the continuing gender-based wage differentials and marked gender segregation on the labour market by means such as flexible working time arrangements which enable both men and women to combine family and work commitments more successfully. This could also include appropriate parental leave arrangements which could be taken up by

either parent as well as the provision of accessible and affordable child-care facilities and care for dependent persons.

(12) Specific measures should be adopted to ensure the implementation of the principle of equal treatment in occupational social security schemes and to define its scope more clearly.

(13) In its judgment of 17 May 1990 in Case C-262/88 (1), the Court of Justice determined that all forms of occupational pension constitute an element of pay within the meaning of Article 141 of the Treaty.

(14) Although the concept of pay within the meaning of Article 141 of the Treaty does not encompass social security benefits, it is now clearly established that a pension scheme for public servants falls within the scope of the principle of equal pay if the benefits payable under the scheme are paid to the worker by reason of his/her employment relationship with the public employer, notwithstanding the fact that such scheme forms part of a general statutory scheme. According to the judgments of the Court of Justice in Cases C-7/93 (2) and C-351/00 (3), that condition will be satisfied if the pension scheme concerns a particular category of workers and its benefits are directly related to the period of service and calculated by reference to the public servant's final salary. For reasons of clarity, it is therefore appropriate to make specific provision to that effect.

(15) The Court of Justice has confirmed that whilst the contributions of male and female workers to a definedbenefit pension scheme are covered by Article 141 of the Treaty, any inequality in employers' contributions paid under funded defined-benefit schemes which is due to the use of actuarial factors differing according to sex is not to be assessed in the light of that same provision.

(16) By way of example, in the case of funded defined-benefit schemes, certain elements, such as conversion into a capital sum of part of a periodic pension, transfer of pension rights, a reversionary pension payable to a dependant in return for the surrender of part of a pension or a reduced pension where the worker opts to take earlier retirement, may be unequal where the inequality of the amounts results from the effects of the use of actuarial factors differing according to sex at the time when the scheme's funding is implemented.

(17) It is well established that benefits payable under occupational social security schemes are not to be considered as remuneration insofar as they are attributable to periods of employment prior to 17 May 1990, except in the case of workers or those claiming under them who initiated legal proceedings or brought an equivalent claim under the applicable national law before that date. It is therefore necessary to limit the implementation of the principle of equal treatment accordingly.

(18) The Court of Justice has consistently held that the Barber Protocol (4) does not affect the right to join an occupational pension scheme and that the limitation of the effects in time of the judgment in Case C-262/88 does not apply to the right to join an occupational pension scheme. The Court of Justice also ruled that the national rules relating to time limits for bringing actions

under national law may be relied on against workers who assert their right to join an occupational pension scheme, provided that they are not less favourable for that type of action than for similar actions of a domestic nature and that they do not render the exercise of rights conferred by Community law impossible in practice. The Court of Justice has also pointed out that the fact that a worker can claim retroactively to join an occupational pension scheme does not allow the worker to avoid paying the contributions relating to the period of membership concerned.

(19) Ensuring equal access to employment and the vocational training leading thereto is fundamental to the application of the principle of equal treatment of men and women in matters of employment and occupation. Any exception to this principle should therefore be limited to those occupational activities which necessitate the employment of a person of a particular sex by reason of their nature or the context in which they are carried out, provided that the objective sought is legitimate and complies with the principle of proportionality.

(20) This Directive does not prejudice freedom of association, including the right to establish unions with others and to join unions to defend one's interests. Measures within the meaning of Article 141(4) of the Treaty may include membership or the continuation of the activity of organisations or unions whose main objective is the promotion, in practice, of the principle of equal treatment between men and women.

(21) The prohibition of discrimination should be without prejudice to the maintenance or adoption of measures intended to prevent or compensate for disadvantages suffered by a group of persons of one sex. Such measures permit organisations of persons of one sex where their main object is the promotion of the special needs of those persons and the promotion of equality between men and women.

(22) In accordance with Article 141(4) of the Treaty, with a view to ensuring full equality in practice between men and women in working life, the principle of equal treatment does not prevent Member States from maintaining or adopting measures providing for specific advantages in order to make it easier for the under-represented sex to pursue a vocational activity or to prevent or compensate for disadvantages in professional careers. Given the current situation and bearing in mind Declaration No 28 to the Amsterdam Treaty, Member States should, in the first instance, aim at improving the situation of women in working life.

(23) It is clear from the case-law of the Court of Justice that unfavourable treatment of a woman related to pregnancy or maternity constitutes direct discrimination on grounds of sex. Such treatment should therefore be expressly covered by this Directive.

(24) The Court of Justice has consistently recognised the legitimacy, as regards the principle of equal treatment, of protecting a woman's biological condition during pregnancy and maternity and of introducing maternity protection measures as a means to achieve substantive equality. This Directive should therefore be without prejudice to Council Directive 92/85/EEC of 19

October1992 on the introduction of measures to encourage improvements in the safety and health at work of pregnant workers and workers who have recently given birth or are breastfeeding (1). This Directive should further be without prejudice to Council Directive 96/34/EC of 3 June 1996 on the framework agreement on parental leave concluded by UNICE, CEEP and the ETUC.

(25) For reasons of clarity, it is also appropriate to make express provision for the protection of the employment rights of women on maternity leave and in particular their right to return to the same or an equivalent post, to suffer no detriment in their terms and conditions as a result of taking such leave and to benefit from any improvement in working conditions to which they would have been entitled during their absence.

(26) In the Resolution of the Council and of the Ministers for Employment and Social Policy, meeting within the Council, of 29 June 2000 on the balanced participation of women and men in family and working life (3), Member States were encouraged to consider examining the scope for their respective legal systems to grant working men an individual and non-transferable right to paternity leave, while maintaining their rights relating to employment.

(27) Similar considerations apply to the granting by Member States to men and women of an individual and non-transferable right to leave subsequent to the adoption of a child. It is for the Member States to determine whether or not to grant such a right to paternity and/or adoption leave and also to determine any conditions, other than dismissal and return to work, which are outside the scope of this Directive.

(28) The effective implementation of the principle of equal treatment requires appropriate procedures to be put in place by the Member States.

(29) The provision of adequate judicial or administrative procedures for the enforcement of the obligations imposed by this Directive is essential to the effective implementation of the principle of equal treatment.

(30) The adoption of rules on the burden of proof plays a significant role in ensuring that the principle of equal treatment can be effectively enforced. As the Court of Justice has held, provision should therefore be made to ensure that the burden of proof shifts to the respondent when there is a prima facie case of discrimination, except in relation to proceedings in which it is for the court or other competent national body to investigate the facts. It is however necessary to clarify that the appreciation of the facts from which it may be presumed that there has been direct or indirect discrimination remains a matter for the relevant national body in accordance with national law or practice. Further, it is for the Member States to introduce, at any appropriate stage of the proceedings, rules of evidence which are more favourable to plaintiffs.

(31) With a view to further improving the level of protection offered by this Directive, associations, organisations and other legal entities should also be empowered to engage in proceedings, as the Member States so determine, either on behalf or in support of a complainant, without prejudice to national rules of procedure concerning representation and defence.

(32) Having regard to the fundamental nature of the right to effective legal protection, it is appropriate to ensure that workers continue to enjoy such protection even after the relationship giving rise to an alleged breach of the principle of equal treatment has ended. An employee defending or giving evidence on behalf of a person protected under this Directive should be entitled to the same protection.

(33) It has been clearly established by the Court of Justice that in order to be effective, the principle of equal treatment implies that the compensation awarded for any breach must be adequate in relation to the damage sustained. It is therefore appropriate to exclude the fixing of any prior upper limit for such compensation, except where the employer can prove that the only damage suffered by an applicant as a result of discrimination within the meaning of this Directive was the refusal to take his/her job application into consideration.

(34) In order to enhance the effective implementation of the principle of equal treatment, Member States should promote dialogue between the social partners and, within the framework of national practice, with non-governmental organisations.

(35) Member States should provide for effective, proportionate and dissuasive penalties for breaches of the obligations under this Directive.

(36) Since the objectives of this Directive cannot be sufficiently achieved by the Member States and can therefore be better achieved at Community level, the Community may adopt measures in accordance with the principle of subsidiarity as set out in Article 5 of the Treaty. In accordance with the principle of proportionality, as set out in that Article, this Directive does not go beyond what is necessary in order to achieve those objectives.

(37) For the sake of a better understanding of the different treatment of men and women in matters of employment and occupation, comparable statistics disaggregated by sex should continue to be developed, analysed and made available at the appropriate levels.

(38) Equal treatment of men and women in matters of employment and occupation cannot be restricted to legislative measures. Instead, the European Union and the Member States should continue to promote the raising of public awareness of wage discrimination and the changing of public attitudes, involving all parties concerned at public and private level to the greatest possible extent. The dialogue between the social partners could play an important role in this process.

(39) The obligation to transpose this Directive into national law should be confined to those provisions which represent a substantive change as compared with the earlier Directives.The obligation to transpose the provisions which are substantially unchanged arises under the earlier Directives.

(40) This Directive should be without prejudice to the obligations of the Member States relating to the time limits for transposition into national law and application of the Directives set out in Annex I, Part B.

**Title 1**
**General Provisions**

*Article 1*
*Purpose*

The purpose of this Directive is to ensure the implementation of the principle of equal opportunities and equal treatment of men and women in matters of employment and occupation. To that end, it contains provisions to implement the principle of equal treatment in relation to:

(a)  access to employment, including promotion, and to vocational training;
(b)  working conditions, including pay;
(c)  occupational social security schemes.

It also contains provisions to ensure that such implementation is made more effective by the establishment of appropriate procedures.

*Article 2*
*Definitions*

1  For the purposes of this Directive, the following definitions shall apply:

(a)  'direct discrimination': where one person is treated less favourably on grounds of sex than another is, has been or would be treated in a comparable situation;
(b)  'indirect discrimination': where an apparently neutral provision, criterion or practice would put persons of one sex at a particular disadvantage compared with persons of the other sex, unless that provision, criterion or practice is objectively justified by a legitimate aim, and the means of achieving that aim are appropriate and necessary;
(c)  'harassment': where unwanted conduct related to the sex of a person occurs with the purpose or effect of violating the dignity of a person, and of creating an intimidating, hostile, degrading, humiliating or offensive environment;
(d)  'sexual harassment': where any form of unwanted verbal, non-verbal or physical conduct of a sexual nature occurs, with the purpose or effect of violating the dignity of a person, in particular when creating an intimidating, hostile, degrading, humiliating or offensive environment;
(e)  'pay': the ordinary basic or minimum wage or salary and any other consideration, whether in cash or in kind, which the worker receives directly or indirectly, in respect of his/ her employment from his/her employer;
(f)  'occupational social security schemes': schemes not governed by Council Directive 79/7/EEC of 19 December 1978 on the progressive implementation of the principle of equal treatment for men and women in matters of social security (1) whose purpose is to provide workers, whether employees or self-employed, in an undertaking or group of undertakings, area of economic activity, occupational sector

or group of sectors with benefits intended to supplement the benefits provided by statutory social security schemes or to replace them, whether membership of such schemes is compulsory or optional.

2  For the purposes of this Directive, discrimination includes:

(a)  harassment and sexual harassment, as well as any less favourable treatment based on a person's rejection of or submission to such conduct;

(b)  nstruction to discriminate against persons on grounds of sex;

(c)  any less favourable treatment of a woman related to pregnancy or maternity leave within the meaning of Directive 92/85/EEC.

*Article 3*
*Positive action*

Member States may maintain or adopt measures within the meaning of Article 141(4) of the Treaty with a view to ensuring full equality in practice between men and women in working life.

*Title II*
*Specific Provisions*

**Chapter 1**
**Equal pay**

*Article 4*
*Prohibition of discrimination*

For the same work or for work to which equal value is attributed, direct and indirect discrimination on grounds of sex with regard to all aspects and conditions of remuneration shall be eliminated. In particular, where a job classification system is used for determining pay, it shall be based on the same criteria for both men and women and so drawn up as to exclude any discrimination on grounds of sex.

**Chapter II**
**Equal treatment in occupational social security schemes**

*Article 5*

*Prohibition of discrimination*

Without prejudice to Article 4, there shall be no direct or indirect discrimination on grounds of sex in occupational social security schemes, in particular as regards:

(a)  the scope of such schemes and the conditions of access to them;

(b)  the obligation to contribute and the calculation of contributions;

(c)  the calculation of benefits, including supplementary benefits due in respect of a spouse or dependants, and the conditions governing the duration and retention of entitlement to benefits.

*Article 6*
*Personal scope*

1 This Chapter shall apply to members of the working population, including self-employed persons, persons whose activity is interrupted by illness, maternity, accident or involuntary unemployment and persons seeking employment and to retired and disabled workers, and to those claiming under them, in accordance with national law and/or practice.

2 This Chapter does not preclude an employer granting to persons who have already reached the retirement age for the purposes of granting a pension by virtue of an occupational social security scheme, but who have not yet reached the retirement age for the purposes of granting a statutory retirement pension, a pension supplement, the aim of which is to make equal or more nearly equal the overall amount of benefit paid to these persons in relation to the amount paid to persons of the other sex in the same situation who have already reached the statutory retirement age, until the persons benefiting from the supplement reach the statutory retirement age.

*Article 7*
*Material scope*

1 This Chapter applies to:

   (a)   occupational social security schemes which provide protection against the following risks:
        (i)    sickness,
        (ii)   invalidity,
        (iii)  old age, including early retirement,
        (iv)   industrial accidents and occupational diseases,
        (v)    unemployment;
   (b)   occupational social security schemes which provide for other social benefits, in cash or in kind, and in particular survivors' benefits and family allowances, if such benefits constitute a consideration paid by the employer to the worker by reason of the latter's employment.

2 This Chapter also applies to pension schemes for a particular category of worker such as that of public servants if the benefits payable under the scheme are paid by reason of the employment relationship with the public employer. The fact that such a scheme forms part of a general statutory scheme shall be without prejudice in that respect.

*Article 8*
*Exclusions from the material scope*

1 This Chapter does not apply to:

   (a)   individual contracts for self-employed persons;
   (b)   single-member schemes for self-employed persons;
   (c)   insurance contracts to which the employer is not a party, in the case of workers;
   (d)   optional provisions of occupational social security schemes offered to participants individually to guarantee them:

  (i)    either additional benefits,
  (ii)   or a choice of date on which the normal benefits for
         self-employed persons will start, or a choice between several
         benefits;
(e)    occupational social security schemes in so far as benefits are financed
       by contributions paid by workers on a voluntary basis.

2 This Chapter does not preclude an employer granting to persons who have
already reached the retirement age for the purposes of granting a pension by
virtue of an occupational social security scheme, but who have not yet reached
the retirement age for the purposes of granting a statutory retirement pension,
a pension supplement, the aim of which is to make equal or more nearly equal
the overall amount of benefit paid to these persons in relation to the amount
paid to persons of the other sex in the same situation who have already reached
the statutory retirement age, until the persons benefiting from the supplement
reach the statutory retirement age.

*Article 9*
*Examples of Discrimination*

1 Provisions contrary to the principle of equal treatment shall include those
based on sex, either directly or indirectly, for:

(a)    determining the persons who may participate in an occupational social
       security scheme;
(b)    fixing the compulsory or optional nature of participation in an
       occupational social security scheme;
(c)    laying down different rules as regards the age of entry into the scheme
       or the minimum period of employment or membership of the scheme
       required to obtain the benefits thereof;
(d)    laying down different rules, except as provided for in points (h) and (j),
       for the reimbursement of contributions when a worker leaves a scheme
       without having fulfilled the conditions guaranteeing a deferred right to
       long-term benefits;
(e)    setting different conditions for the granting of benefits or restricting
       such benefits to workers of one or other of the sexes;
(f)    fixing different retirement ages;
(g)    suspending the retention or acquisition of rights during periods of
       maternity leave or leave for family reasons which are granted by law or
       agreement and are paid by the employer;
(h)    setting different levels of benefit, except in so far as may be necessary
       to take account of actuarial calculation factors which differ according
       to sex in the case of definedcontribution schemes; in the case of
       funded defined-benefit schemes, certain elements may be unequal
       where the inequality of the amounts results from the effects of the use
       of actuarial factors differing according to sex at the time when the
       scheme's funding is implemented;
(i)    setting different levels for workers' contributions;
(j)    setting different levels for employers' contributions, except:

(i) in the case of defined-contribution schemes if the aim is to equalise the amount of the final benefits or to make them more nearly equal for both sexes;

(ii) in the case of funded defined-benefit schemes where the employer's contributions are intended to ensure the adequacy of the funds necessary to cover the cost of the benefits defined;

(k) laying down different standards or standards applicable only to workers of a specified sex, except as provided for in points (h) and (j), as regards the guarantee or retention of entitlement to deferred benefits when a worker leaves a scheme.

2 Where the granting of benefits within the scope of this Chapter is left to the discretion of the scheme's management bodies, the latter shall comply with the principle of equal treatment.

*Article 10*
*Implementation as regards self-employed persons*

1 Member States shall take the necessary steps to ensure that the provisions of occupational social security schemes for self employed persons contrary to the principle of equal treatment are revised with effect from 1 January 1993 at the latest or for Member States whose accession took place after that date, at the date that Directive 86/378/EEC became applicable in their territory.

2 This Chapter shall not preclude rights and obligations relating to a period of membership of an occupational social security scheme for self-employed persons prior to revision of that scheme from remaining subject to the provisions of the scheme in force during that period.

*Article 11*
*Possibility of deferral as regards self-employed persons*

As regards occupational social security schemes for selfemployed persons, Member States may defer compulsory application of the principle of equal treatment with regard to:

(a) determination of pensionable age for the granting of oldage or retirement pensions, and the possible implications for other benefits:

(i) either until the date on which such equality is achieved in statutory schemes,

(ii) or, at the latest, until such equality is prescribed by a directive;

(b) survivors' pensions until Community law establishes the principle of equal treatment in statutory social security schemes in that regard;

(c) the application of Article 9(1)(i) in relation to the use of actuarial calculation factors, until 1 January 1999 or for Member States whose accession took place after that date until the date that Directive 86/378/EEC became applicable in their territory.

*Article 12*
*Retroactive effect*

1 Any measure implementing this Chapter, as regards workers, shall cover all benefits under occupational social security schemes derived from periods of

employment subsequent to 17 May 1990 and shall apply retroactively to that date, without prejudice to workers or those claiming under them who have, before that date, initiated legal proceedings or raised an equivalent claim under national law. In that event, the implementation measures shall apply retroactively to 8 April 1976 and shall cover all the benefits derived from periods of employment after that date. For Member States which acceded to the Community after 8 April 1976, and before 17 May 1990, that date shall be replaced by the date on which Article 141 of the Treaty became applicable in their territory.

2 The second sentence of paragraph 1 shall not prevent national rules relating to time limits for bringing actions under national law from being relied on against workers or those claiming under them who initiated legal proceedings or raised an equivalent claim under national law before 17 May 1990, provided that they are not less favourable for that type of action than for similar actions of a domestic nature and that they do not render the exercise of rights conferred by Community law impossible in practice.

3 For Member States whose accession took place after 17 May 1990 and which were on 1 January 1994 Contracting Parties to the Agreement on the European Economic Area, the date of 17 May 1990 in the first sentence of paragraph 1 shall be replaced by 1 January 1994.

4 For other Member States whose accession took place after 17 May 1990, the date of 17 May 1990 in paragraphs 1 and 2 shall be replaced by the date on which Article 141 of the Treaty became applicable in their territory.

*Article 13*
*Flexible pensionable age*

Where men and women may claim a flexible pensionable age under the same conditions, this shall not be deemed to be incompatible with this Chapter.

**Chapter 3**
**Equal treatment as regards access to employment, vocational training and promotion and working conditions**

*Article 14*
*Prohibition of discrimination*

1 There shall be no direct or indirect discrimination on grounds of sex in the public or private sectors, including public bodies, in relation to:

  (a)  conditions for access to employment, to self-employment or to occupation, including selection criteria and recruitment conditions, whatever the branch of activity and at all levels of the professional hierarchy, including promotion;
  (b)  access to all types and to all levels of vocational guidance, vocational training, advanced vocational training and retraining, including practical work experience;
  (c)  employment and working conditions, including dismissals, as well as pay as provided for in Article 141 of the Treaty;

(d) membership of, and involvement in, an organisation of workers or employers, or any organisation whose members carry on a particular profession, including the benefits provided for by such organisations.

2 Member States may provide, as regards access to employment including the training leading thereto, that a difference of treatment which is based on a characteristic related to sex shall not constitute discrimination where, by reason of the nature of the particular occupational activities concerned or of the context in which they are carried out, such a characteristic constitutes a genuine and determining occupational requirement, provided that its objective is legitimate and the requirement is proportionate.

*Article 15*
*Return from maternity leave*

A woman on maternity leave shall be entitled, after the end of her period of maternity leave, to return to her job or to an equivalent post on terms and conditions which are no less favourable to her and to benefit from any improvement in working conditions to which she would have been entitled during her absence.

*Article 16*
*Paternity and adoption leave*

This Directive is without prejudice to the right of Member States to recognise distinct rights to paternity and/or adoption leave. Those Member States which recognise such rights shall take the necessary measures to protect working men and women against dismissal due to exercising those rights and ensure that, at the end of such leave, they are entitled to return to their jobs or to equivalent posts on terms and conditions which are no less favourable to them, and to benefit from any improvement in working conditions to which they would have been entitled during their absence.

## TITLE III
## HORIZONTAL PROVISIONS

**Chapter I**
**Remedies and enforcement**

*Section 1*
*Remedies*

*Article 17*

*Defence of rights*

1 Member States shall ensure that, after possible recourse to other competent authorities including where they deem it appropriate conciliation procedures, judicial procedures for the enforcement of obligations under this Directive are available to all persons who consider themselves wronged by failure to apply the principle of equal treatment to them, even after the relationship in which the discrimination is alleged to have occurred has ended.

2 Member States shall ensure that associations, organisations or other legal entities which have, in accordance with the criteria laid down by their national law, a legitimate interest in ensuring that the provisions of this Directive are complied with, may engage, either on behalf or in support of the complainant, with his/her approval, in any judicial and/or administrative procedure provided for the enforcement of obligations under this Directive.

3 Paragraphs 1 and 2 are without prejudice to national rules relating to time limits for bringing actions as regards the principle of equal treatment.

*Article 18*
*Compensation or reparation*

Member States shall introduce into their national legal systems such measures as are necessary to ensure real and effective compensation or reparation as the Member States so determine for the loss and damage sustained by a person injured as a result of discrimination on grounds of sex, in a way which is dissuasive and proportionate to the damage suffered. Such compensation or reparation may not be restricted by the fixing of a prior upper limit, except in cases where the employer can prove that the only damage suffered by an applicant as a result of discrimination within the meaning of this Directive is the refusal to take his/her job application into consideration.

*Section 2*

*Article 19*
*Burden of proof*

Member States shall take such measures as are necessary, in accordance with their national judicial systems, to ensure that, when persons who consider themselves wronged because the principle of equal treatment has not been applied to them establish, before a court or other competent authority, facts from which it may be presumed that there has been direct or indirect discrimination, it shall be for the respondent to prove that there has been no breach of the principle of equal treatment.

2 Paragraph 1 shall not prevent Member States from introducing rules of evidence which are more favourable to plaintiffs.

3 Member States need not apply paragraph 1 to proceedings in which it is for the court or competent body to investigate the facts of the case.

4 Paragraphs 1, 2 and 3 shall also apply to:

    (a)    the situations covered by Article 141 of the Treaty and, insofar as discrimination based on sex is concerned, by Directives 92/85/EEC and 96/34/EC;

    (b)    any civil or administrative procedure concerning the public or private sector which provides for means of redress under national law pursuant to the measures referred to in (a) with the exception of out-of-court procedures of a voluntary nature or provided for in national law.

5 This Article shall not apply to criminal procedures, unless otherwise provided by the Member States.

## Chapter 2
## Promotion of equal treatment — dialogue

*Article 20*
*Equality bodies*

1 Member States shall designate and make the necessary arrangements for a body or bodies for the promotion, analysis, monitoring and support of equal treatment of all persons without discrimination on grounds of sex. These bodies may form part of agencies with responsibility at national level for the defence of human rights or the safeguard of individuals' rights.

2 Member States shall ensure that the competences of these bodies include:

(a) without prejudice to the right of victims and of associations, organisations or other legal entities referred to in Article 17(2), providing independent assistance to victims of discrimination in pursuing their complaints about discrimination;

(b) conducting independent surveys concerning discrimination;

(c) publishing independent reports and making recommendations on any issue relating to such discrimination;

(d) at the appropriate level exchanging available information with corresponding European bodies such as any future European Institute for Gender Equality.

*Article 21*
*Social dialouge*

1 Member States shall, in accordance with national traditions and practice, take adequate measures to promote social dialogue between the social partners with a view to fostering equal treatment, including, for example, through the monitoring of practices in the workplace, in access to employment, vocational training and promotion, as well as through the monitoring of collective agreements, codes of conduct, research or exchange of experience and good practice.

2 Where consistent with national traditions and practice, Member States shall encourage the social partners, without prejudice to their autonomy, to promote equality between men and women, and flexible working arrangements, with the aim of facilitating the reconciliation of work and private life, and to conclude, at the appropriate level, agreements laying down antidiscrimination rules in the fields referred to in Article 1 which fall within the scope of collective bargaining. These agreements shall respect the provisions of this Directive and the relevant national implementing measures.

3 Member States shall, in accordance with national law, collective agreements or practice, encourage employers to promote equal treatment for men and women in a planned and systematic way in the workplace, in access to employment, vocational training and promotion.

4 To this end, employers shall be encouraged to provide at appropriate regular intervals employees and/or their representatives with appropriate information on equal treatment for men and women in the undertaking.

Such information may include an overview of the proportions of men and women at different levels of the organisation; their pay and pay differentials; and possible measures to improve the situation in cooperation with employees' representatives.

*Article 22*
*Dialogue with non-governmental organisations*

Member States shall encourage dialogue with appropriate nongovernmental organisations which have, in accordance with their national law and practice, a legitimate interest in contributing to the fight against discrimination on grounds of sex with a view to promoting the principle of equal treatment.

**Chapter 3**

*General horizontal provisions*

*Article 23*
*compliance*

Member States shall take all necessary measures to ensure that:

(a)   any laws, regulations and administrative provisions contrary to the principle of equal treatment are abolished;
(b)   provisions contrary to the principle of equal treatment in individual or collective contracts or agreements, internal rules of undertakings or rules governing the independent occupations and professions and workers' and employers' organisations or any other arrangements shall be, or may be, declared null and void or are amended;
(c)   occupational social security schemes containing such provisions may not be approved or extended by administrative measures.

*Article 24*
*Victimisation*

Member States shall introduce into their national legal systems such measures as are necessary to protect employees, including those who are employees' representatives provided for by national laws and/or practices, against dismissal or other adverse treatment by the employer as a reaction to a complaint within the undertaking or to any legal proceedings aimed at enforcing compliance with the principle of equal treatment.

*Article 25*
*Penalties*

Member States shall lay down the rules on penalties applicable to infringements of the national provisions adopted pursuant to this Directive, and shall take all measures necessary to ensure that they are applied. The penalties, which may comprise the payment of compensation to the victim, must be effective, proportionate and dissuasive. The Member States shall notify those provisions to the Commission by 5 October 2005 at the latest and shall notify it without delay of any subsequent amendment affecting them.

*Article 26*

*Prevention of discrimination*

Member States shall encourage, in accordance with national law, collective agreements or practice, employers and those responsible for access to vocational training to take effective measures to prevent all forms of discrimination on grounds of sex, in particular harassment and sexual harassment in the workplace, in access to employment, vocational training and promotion.

*Article 27*
*Minimum requirements*

1 Member States may introduce or maintain provisions which are more favourable to the protection of the principle of equal treatment than those laid down in this Directive.

2 Implementation of this Directive shall under no circumstances be sufficient grounds for a reduction in the level of protection of workers in the areas to which it applies, without prejudice to the Member States' right to respond to changes in the situation by introducing laws, regulations and administrative provisions which differ from those in force on the notification of this Directive, provided that the provisions of this Directive are complied with.

*Article 28*
*Relationship to Community and national provisions*

1 This Directive shall be without prejudice to provisions concerning the protection of women, particularly as regards pregnancy and maternity.

2 This Directive shall be without prejudice to the provisions of Directive 96/34/EC and Directive 92/85/EEC.

*Article 29*
*Gender mainstreaming*

Member States shall actively take into account the objective of equality between men and women when formulating and implementing laws, regulations, administrative provisions, policies and activities in the areas referred to in this Directive.

*Article 30*
*Dissemination of information*

Member States shall ensure that measures taken pursuant to this Directive, together with the provisions already in force, are brought to the attention of all the persons concerned by all suitable means and, where appropriate, at the workplace.

*Title IV*
*Final Provisions*

*Article 31*
*Reports*

1 By 15 February 2011, the Member States shall communicate to the Commission all the information necessary for the Commission to draw up a report to the European Parliament and the Council on the application of this Directive.

2 Without prejudice to paragraph 1, Member States shall communicate to the Commission, every four years, the texts of any measures adopted pursuant to Article 141(4) of the Treaty, as well as reports on these measures and their implementation. On the basis of that information, the Commission will adopt and publish every four years a report establishing a comparative assessment of any measures in the light of Declaration No 28 annexed to the Final Act of the Treaty of Amsterdam.

3 Member States shall assess the occupational activities referred to in Article 14(2), in order to decide, in the light of social developments, whether there is justification for maintaining the exclusions concerned. They shall notify the Commission of the results of this assessment periodically, but at least every 8 years.

*Article 32*
*Review*

By 15 February 2011 at the latest, the Commission shall review the operation of this Directive and if appropriate, propose any amendments it deems necessary.

*Article 33*
*Implementation*

Member States shall bring into force the laws, regulations and administrative provisions necessary to comply with this Directive by 15 August 2008 at the latest or shall ensure, by that date, that management and labour introduce the requisite provisions by way of agreement. Member States may, if necessary to take account of particular difficulties, have up to one additional year to comply with this Directive. Member States shall take all necessary steps to be able to guarantee the results imposed by this Directive. They shall forthwith communicate to the Commission the texts of those measures. When Member States adopt these measures, they shall contain a reference to this Directive or be accompanied by such reference on the occasion of their official publication. They shall also include a statement that references in existing laws, regulations and administrative provisions to the Directives repealed by this Directive shall be construed as references to this Directive. Member States shall determine how such reference is to be made and how that statement is to be formulated. The obligation to transpose this Directive into national law shall be confined to those provisions which represent a substantive change as compared with the earlier Directives. The obligation to transpose the provisions which are substantially unchanged arises under the earlier Directives. Member States shall communicate to the Commission the text of the main provisions of national law which they adopt in the field covered by this Directive.

*Article 34*
*Repeal*

1 With effect from 15 August 2009 Directives 75/117/EEC, 76/207/EEC, 86/378/EEC and 97/80/EC shall be repealed without prejudice to the obligations of the Member States relating to the time-limits for transposition into national law and application of the Directives set out in Annex I, Part B.

2 References made to the repealed Directives shall be construed as being made to this Directive and should be read in accordance with the correlation table in Annex II.

*Article 34*
*Repeal*

1 With effect from 15 August 2009 Directives 75/117/EEC, 76/207/EEC, 86/378/EEC and 97/80/EC shall be repealed without prejudice to the obligations of the Member States relating to the time-limits for transposition into national law and application of the Directives set out in Annex I, Part B.

2 References made to the repealed Directives shall be construed as being made to this Directive and should be read in accordance with the correlation table in Annex II.

*Article 35*
*Entry into force*

This Directive shall enter into force on the 20th day following its publication in the Official Journal of the European Union.

*Article 36*
*Addressees*

Done at Strasbourg, 5 July 2006..

*For the European Parliament*

*The President*

J. BORRELL FONTELLES

*For the Council*

*The President*

P. LEHTOMÄKI

****

# COUNCIL DIRECTIVE NO 92/85/EEC

*of 19 October 1992*

*on the introduction of measures to encourage improvements in the safety and health at work of pregnant workers and workers who have recently given birth or are breastfeeding (tenth individual Directive within the meaning of Article 16 (1) of Directive 89/391/EEC)*

THE COUNCIL OF THE EUROPEAN COMMUNITIES,

Having regard to the Treaty establishing the European Economic Community, and in particular Article 118a thereof,

Having regard to the proposal from the Commission, drawn up after consultation with the Advisory Committee on Safety, Hygiene and Health Protection at work (1),

In cooperation with the European Parliament (2),

Having regard to the opinion of the Economic and Social Committee (3),

Whereas Article 118a of the Treaty provides that the Council shall adopt, by means of directives, minimum requirements for encouraging improvements, especially in the working environment, to protect the safety and health of workers;

Whereas this Directive does not justify any reduction in levels of protection already achieved in individual Member States, the Member States being committed, under the Treaty, to encouraging improvements in conditions in this area and to harmonizing conditions while maintaining the improvements made;

Whereas, under the terms of Article 118a of the Treaty, the said directives are to avoid imposing administrative, financial and legal constraints in a way which would hold back the creation and development of small and medium-sized undertakings;

Whereas, pursuant to Decision 74/325/EEC (4), as last amended by the 1985 Act of Accession, the Advisory Committee on Safety, Hygiene and Health protection at Work is drafting of proposals in this field;

Whereas the Community Charter of the fundamental social rights of workers, adopted at the Strasbourg European Council on 9 December 1989 by the Heads of State or Government of 11 Member States, lays down, in paragraph 19 in particular, that:

'Every worker must enjoy satisfactory health and safety conditions in his working environment. Appropriate measures must be taken in order to achieve further harmonization of conditions in this area while maintaining the improvements made';

Whereas the Commission, in its action programme for the implementation of the Community Charter of the fundamental social rights of workers, has included among its aims the adoption by the Council of a Directive on the protection of pregnant women at work;

Whereas Article 15 of Council Directive 89/391/EEC of 12 June 1989 on the introduction of measures to encourage improvements in the safety and health of workers at work (5) provides that particularly sensitive risk groups must be protected against the dangers which specifically affect them

Whereas pregnant workers, workers who have recently given birth or who are breastfeeding must be considered a specific risk group in many respects, and measures must be taken with regard to their safety and health;

Whereas the protection of the safety and health of pregnant workers, workers who have recently given birth or workers who are breastfeeding should not treat women on the labour market unfavourably nor work to the detriment of directives concerning equal treatment for men and women;

Whereas some types of activities may pose a specific risk, for pregnant workers, workers who have recently given birth or workers who are breastfeeding, of exposure to dangerous agents, processes or working conditions; whereas such risks must therefore be assessed and the result of such assessment communicated to female workers and/or their representatives;

Whereas, further, should the result of this assessment reveal the existence of a risk to the safety or health of the female worker, provision must be made for such worker to be protected;

Whereas pregnant workers and workers who are breastfeeding must not engage in activities which have been assessed as revealing a risk of exposure, jeopardizing safety and health, to certain particularly dangerous agents or working conditions;

Whereas provision should be made for pregnant workers, workers who have recently given birth or workers who are breastfeeding not to be required to work at night where such provision is necessary from the point of view of their safety and health;

Whereas the vulnerability of pregnant workers, workers who have recently given birth or who are breastfeeding makes it necessary for them to be granted the right to maternity leave of at least 14 continuous weeks, allocated before and/or after confinement, and renders necessary the compulsory nature of maternity leave of at least two weeks, allocated before and/or after confinement;

Whereas the risk of dismissal for reasons associated with their condition may have harmful effects on the physical and mental state of pregnant workers, workers who have recently given birth or who are breastfeeding; whereas provision should be made for such dismissal to be prohibited;

Whereas measures for the organization of work concerning the protection of the health of pregnant workers, workers who have recently given birth or workers who are breastfeeding would serve no purpose unless accompanied by the maintenance of rights linked to the employment contract, including maintenance of payment and/or entitlement to an adequate allowance;

Whereas, moreover, provision concerning maternity leave would also serve no purpose unless accompanied by the maintenance of rights linked to the employment contract and or entitlement to an adequate allowance;

Whereas the concept of an adequate allowance in the case of maternity leave must be regarded as a technical point of reference with a view to fixing the minimum level of protection and should in no circumstances be interpreted as suggesting an analogy between pregnancy and illness,

HAS ADOPTED THIS DIRECTIVE

## Section I
## Purpose and Definitions

*Article 1*
*Purpose*

1 The purpose of this Directive, which is the tenth individual Directive within the meaning of Article 16 (1) of Directive 89/391/EEC, is to implement measures to encourage improvements in the safety and health at work of pregnant workers and workers who have recently given birth or who are breastfeeding.

2 The provisions of Directive 89/391/EEC, except for Article 2 (2) thereof, shall apply in full to the whole area covered by paragraph 1, without prejudice to any more stringent and/or specific provisions contained in this Directive.

3 This Directive may not have the effect of reducing the level of protection afforded to pregnant workers, workers who have recently given birth or who are breastfeeding as compared with the situation which exists in each Member State on the date on which this Directive is adopted.

*Article 2*
*Definitions*

For the purposes of this Directive:

(a) pregnant worker shall mean a pregnant worker who informs her employer of her condition, in accordance with national legislation and/or national practice;

(b) worker who has recently given birth shall mean a worker who has recently given birth within the meaning of national legislation and/ or national practice and who informs her employer of her condition, in accordance with that legislation and/or practice;

(c) worker who is breastfeeding shall mean a worker who is breastfeeding within the meaning of national legislation and/or national practice and who informs her employer of her condition, in accordance with that legislation and/or practice.

*Section II*
*General Provisions*

*Article 3*
*Guidelines*

1 In consultation with the Member States and assisted by the Advisory Committee on Safety, Hygiene and Health Protection at Work, the Commission shall draw up guidelines on the assessment of the chemical, physical and biological agents and industrial processes considered hazardous for the safety or health of workers within the meaning of Article 2.

The guidelines referred to in the first subparagraph shall also cover movements and postures, mental and physical fatigue arid other types of physical and mental stress connected with the work done by workers within the meaning of Article 2.

2 The purpose of the guidelines referred to in paragraph 1 is to serve as a basis for the assessment referred to in Article 4 (1).

To this end, Member States shall bring these guidelines to the attention of all employers and all female workers and/or their representatives in the respective Member State.

*Article 4*
*Assessment and information*

1 For all activities liable to involve a specific risk of exposure to the agents, processes or working conditions of which a non-exhaustive list is given in Annex I, the employer shall assess the nature, degree and duration of exposure, in the undertaking and/or establishment concerned, of workers within the meaning of Article 2, either directly or by way of the protective and preventive services referred to in Article 7 of Directive 89/391/EEC, in order to:

   assess any risks to the safety or health and any possible effect on the pregnancys or breastfeeding of workers within the meaning of Article 2, decide what measures should be taken.

2 Without prejudice to Article 10 of Directive 89/391/EEC, workers within the meaning of Article 2 and workers likely to be in one of the situations referred to in Article 2 in the undertaking and/or establishment concerned and/or their representatives shall be informed of the results of the assessment referred to in paragraph 1 and of all measures to be taken concerning health and safety at work.

*Article 5*

*Action further to the results of the assessment*

1 Without prejudice to Article 6 of Directive 89/391/EEC, if the results of the assessment referred to in Article 4(1) reveal a risk to the safety or health or an effect on the pregnancy or breastfeeding of a worker within the meaning of Article 2, the employer shall take the necessary measures to ensure that, by

temporarily adjusting the working conditions and/or the working hours of the worker concerned, the exposure of that worker to such risks is avoided.

2 If the adjustment of her working conditions and/or working hours is not technically and/or objectively feasible, or cannot reasonably be required on duly substantiated grounds, the employer shall take the necessary measures to move the worker concerned to another job.

3 If moving her to another job is not technically and/or objectively feasible or cannot reasonably be required on duly substantiated grounds, the worker concerned shall be granted leave in accordance with national legislation and/or national practice for the whole of the period necessary to protect her safety or health.

4 The provisions of this Article shall apply mutatis mutandis to the case where a worker pursuing an activity which is forbidden pursuant to Article 6 becomes pregnant or starts breastfeeding and informs her employer thereof.

*Article 6*
*Cases in which exposure is prohibited*

In addition to the general provisions concerning the protection of workers, in particular those relating to the limit values for occupational exposure:

1 pregnant workers within the meaning of Article 2 (a) may under no circumstances be obliged to perform duties for which the assessment has revealed a risk of exposure, which would jeopardize safety or health, to the agents and working conditions listed in Annex II, Section A;

2 workers who are breastfeeding, within the meaning of Article 2 (c), may under no circumstances be obliged to perform duties for which the assessment has revealed a risk of exposure, which would jeopardize safety or health, to the agents and working conditions listed in Annex II, Section B.

*Article 7*
*Night work*

1 Member States shall take the necessary measures to ensure that workers referred to in Article 2 are not obliged to perform night work during their pregnancy and for a period following childbirth which shall be determined by the national authority competent for safety and health, subject to submission, in accordance with the procedures laid down by the Member States, of a medical certificate stating that this is necessary for the safety or health of the worker concerned.

2 The measures referred to in paragraph 1 must entail the possibility, in accordance with national legislation and/or national practice, of:

- (a)  transfer to daytime work; or
- (b)  leave from work or extension of maternity leave where such a transfer is not technically and/or objectively feasible or cannot reasonably by required on duly substantiated grounds.

*Article 8*
*Maternity leave*

1 Member States shall take the necessary measures to ensure that workers within the meaning of Article 2 are entitled to a continuous period of maternity leave of a least 14 weeks allocated before and/or after confinement in accordance with national legislation and/or practice.

2 The maternity leave stipulated in paragraph 1 must include compulsory maternity leave of at least two weeks allocated before and/or after confinement in accordance with national legislation and/or practice.

*Article 9*
*Time off for ante-natal examinations*

Member States shall take the necessary measures to ensure that pregnant workers within the meaning of Article 2 (a) are entitled to, in accordance with national legislation and/or practice, time off, without loss of pay, in order to attend ante-natal examinations, if such examinations have to take place during working hours.

*Article 10*
*Prohibition of dismissal*

In order to guarantee workers, within the meaning of Article 2, the exercise of their health and safety protection rights as recognized under this Article, it shall be provided that:

1 Member States shall take the necessary measures to prohibit the dismissal of workers, within the meaning of Article 2, during the period from the beginning of their pregnancy to the end of the maternity leave referred to in Article 8(1), save in exceptional cases not connected with their condition which are permitted under national legislation and/or practice and, where applicable, provided that the competent authority has given its consent;

2 if a worker, within the meaning of Article 2, is dismissed during the period referred to in point 1, the employer must cite duly substantiated grounds for her dismissal in writing;

3 Member States shall take the necessary measures to protect workers, within the meaning of Article 2, from consequences of dismissal which is unlawful by virtue of point 1.

*Article 11*
*Employment rights*

In order to guarantee workers within the meaning of Article 2 the exercise of their health and safety protection rights as recognized in this Article, it shall be provided that:

1 in the cases referred to in Articles 5, 6 and 7, the employment rights relating to the employment contract, including the maintenance of a payment to,

and/or entitlement to an adequate allowance for, workers within the meaning of Article 2, must be ensured in accordance with national legislation and/or national practice;

2 in the case referred to in Article 8, the following must be ensured:

(a) the rights connected with the employment contract of workers within the meaning of Article 2, other than those referred to in point (b) below;

(b) maintenance of a payment to, and/or entitlement to an adequate allowance for, workers within the meaning of Article 2;

3 he allowance referred to in point 2 (b) shall be deemed adequate if it guarantees income at least equivalent to that which the worker concerned would receive in the event of a break in her activities on grounds connected with her state of health, subject to any ceiling laid down under national legislation;

4 Member States may make entitlement to pay or the allowance referred to in points 1 and 2 (b) conditional upon the worker concerned fulfilling the conditions of eligibilty for such benefits laid down under national legislation.

These conditions may under no circumstances provide for periods of previous employment in excess of 12 months immediately prior to the presumed date of confinement

*Article 12*

Defence of rights Member States shall introduce into their national legal systems such measures as are necessary to enable all workers who should themselves wronged by failure to comply with the obligations arising from this Directive to pursue their claims by judicial process (and/or, in accordance with national laws and/or practices) by recourse to other competent authorities.

*Article 13*
*Amendments to the Annexes*

1 Strictly technical adjustments to Annex I as a result of technical progress, changes in international regulations or specifications and new findings in the area covered by this Directive shall be adopted in accordance with the procedure laid down in Article 17 of Directive 89/391/EEC.

2 Annex II may be amended only in accordance with the procedure laid down in Article 118a of the Treaty

**Chapter 3**
**Equal treatment as regards access to employment, vocational training and promotion and working conditions**

*Article 14*
*Final provisions*

1 Member States shall bring into force the laws, regulations and administrative provisions necessary to comply with this Directive not later than two years after the adoption thereof or ensure, at the latest two years after adoption of this

Directive, that the two sides of industry introduce the requisite provisions by means of collective agreements, with Member States being required to make all the necessary provisions to enable them at all times to guarantee the results laid down by this Directive. They shall forthwith inform the Commission thereof.

2 When Member States adopt the measures referred to in paragraph 1, they shall contain a reference of this Directive or shall be accompanied by such reference on the occasion of their official publication. The methods of making such a reference shall be laid down by the Member States.

3 Member States shall communicate to the Commission the texts of the essential provisions of national law which they have already adopted or adopt in the field governed by this Directive

## ANNEX I
**Non-Exhaustive List Of Agents, Processes And Working Conditions**

referred to in Article 4 (1)

*A Agents*

1 Physical agents where these are regarded as agents causing foetal lesions and/or likely to disrupt placental attachment, and in particular:

 (a) shocks, vibration or movement;
 (b) handling of loads entailing risks, particularly of a dorsolumbar nature;
 (c) noise;
 (d) ionizing radiation (*);
 (e) non-ionizing radiation;
 (f) extremes of cold or heat;
 (g) movements and postures, travelling either inside or outside the establishment, mental and physical fatigue and other physical burdens connected with the activity of the worker within the meaning of Article 2 of the Directive.

## 2 Biological agents

Biological agents of risk groups 2, 3 and 3 within the meaning of Article 2 (d) numbers 2, 3 and 4 of Directive 90/679/EEC (1), in so far as it is known that these agents or the therapeutic measures necessitated by such agents endanger the health of pregnant women and the unborn child and in so far as they do not yet appear in Annex II.

## 3 Chemical agents

The following chemical agents in so far as it is known that they endanger the health of pregnant women and the unborn child and in so far as they do not yet appear in Annex II:

 (a) substances labelled R 40, R 45, R 46, and R 47 under Directive 67/548/EEC (2) in so far as they do not yet appear in Annex II;
 (b) chemical agents in Annex I to Directive 90/394/EEC (3);
 (c) mercury and mercury derivatives;

(d)   antimitotic drugs;

(e)   carbon monoxide;

(f)   chemical agents of known and dangerous percutaneous absorption.

*B  Processes*

Industrial processes listed in AnneI to Directive 90/394/EEC.

*C  Working conditions*

Underground mining work.

*Non-Exhaustive List Of Agents And Working Conditions*

referred to in Article 6

*A  Pregnant workers within the meaning of Article 2 (a)*

## 1  Agents

(a)   Physical agents

Work in hyperbaric atmosphere, e.g. pressurized enclosures and underwater diving.

(b)   Biological agents

The following biological agents:

toxoplasma,
rubella virus,

unless the pregnant workers are proved to be adequately protected against such agents by immunization.

(c)   Chemicl agent

Lead and lead derivatives in so far as these agents are capable of being absorbed by the human organism.

## 2  Working conditions

Underground mining work.

*B  Workers who are breastfeeding within the meaning of Article 2 (c)*

## 1  Agents

(a)   Chemical agent s

Lead and lead derivatives in so far as these agents are capable of being absorbed by the human organism.

## 2  Working conditions

Underground mining work

Statement of the Council and the Commission concerning Article 11 (3) of Directive 92/85/EEC, entered in the minutes of the 1608th meeting of the Council (Luxembourg, 19 October 1992)

THE COUNCIL AND THE COMMISSION stated that:

'In determining the level of the allowances referred to in Article 11 (2) (b) and (3), reference shall be made, for purely technical reasons, to the allowance which a worker would receive in the event of a break in her activities on grounds connected with her state of health. Such a reference is not intended in any way to imply that pregnancy and childbirth be equated with sickness. The national social security legislation of all Member States provides for an allowance to be paid during an absence from work due to sickness. The link with such allowance in the chosen formulation is simply intended to serve as a concrete, fixed reference amount in all Member States for the determination of the minimum amount of maternity allowance payable. In so far as allowances are paid in individual Member States which exceed those provided for in the Directive, such allowances are, of course, retained. This is clear from Article 1 (3) of the Directive.'

# COUNCIL DIRECTIVE NO 76/207/EEC

*of 9 February 1976*

*on the implementation of the principle of equal treatment for men and women as regards access to employment, vocational training and promotion, and working conditions*

THE COUNCIL OF THE EUROPEAN COMMUNITIES,

particular Article 235 thereof,

Having regard to the proposal from the Commission,

Having regard to the opinion of the European Parliament (1),

Having regard to the opinion of the Economic and Social Committee (2),

Whereas the Council, in its resolution of 21 January 1974 concerning a social action programme (3), included among the priorities action for the purpose of achieving equality between men and women as regards access to employment and vocational training and promotion and as regards working conditions, including pay;

Whereas, with regard to pay, the Council adopted on 10 February 1975 Directive 75/117/EEC on the approximation of the laws of the Member States relating to the application of the principle of equal pay for men and women (4);

Whereas Community action to achieve the principle of equal treatment for men and women in respect of access to employment and vocational training and promotion and in respect of other working conditions also appears to be necessary; whereas, equal treatment for male and female workers constitutes one of the objectives of the Community, in so far as the harmonization of living and working conditions while maintaining their improvement are inter alia to be furthered; whereas the Treaty does not confer the necessary specific powers for this purpose;

Whereas the definition and progressive implementation of the principle of equal treatment in matters of social security should be ensured by means of subsequent instruments,

HAS ADOPTED THIS DIRECTIVE

*Article 1*
*Purpose*

1 The purpose of this Directive is to put into effect in the Member States the principle of equal treatment for men and women as regards access to employment, including promotion, and to vocational training and as regards working conditions and, on the conditions referred to in paragraph 2, social security. This principle is herinafter referred to as 'the principle of equal treatment'.

2 With a view to ensuring the progressive implementation of the principle of equal treatment in matters of social security, the Council, acting on a proposal

from the Commission, will adopt provisions defining its substance, its scope and the arrangements for its application.

*Article 2*

1 For the purposes of the following provisions, the principle of equal treatment shall mean that there shall be no discrimination whatsover on grounds of sex either directly or indirectly by reference in particular to marital or family status.

2 This Directive shall be without prejudice to the right of Member States to exclude from its field of application those occupational activities and, where appropriate, the training leading thereto, for which, by reason of their nature or the context in which they are carried out, the sex of the worker constitutes a determining factor.

3 This Directive shall be without prejudice to provisions concerning the protection of women, particularly as regards pregnancy and maternity.

4 This Directive shall be without prejudice to measures to promote equal opportunity for men and women, in particular by removing existing inequalities which affect women's opportunities in the areas referred to in Article 1 (1). (1) OJ No C 111, 20.5.1975, p. 14. (2) OJ No C 286, 15.12.1975, p. 8. (3) OJ No C 13, 12.2.1974, p. 1. (4) OJ No L 45, 19.2.1975, p. 19.

*Article 3*

1 Application of the principle of equal treatment means that there shall be no discrimination whatsover on grounds of sex in the conditions, including selection criteria, for access to all jobs or posts, whatever the sector or branch of activity, and to all levels of the occupational hierarchy.

2 To this end, Member States shall take the measures necessary to ensure that:

(a)    any laws, regulations and administrative provisions contrary to the principle of equal treatment shall be abolished;

(b)    any provisions contrary to the principle of equal treatment which are included in collective agreements, individual contracts of employment, internal rules of undertakings or in rules governing the independent occupations and professions shall be, or may be declared, null and void or may be amended;

(c)    those laws, regulations and administrative provisions contrary to the principle of equal treatment when the concern for protection which originally inspired them is no longer well founded shall be revised ; and that where similar provisions are included in collective agreements labour and management shall be requested to undertake the desired revision.

*Article 4*

Application of the principle of equal treatment with regard to access to all types and to all levels, of vocational guidance, vocational training, advanced vocational training and retraining, means that Member States shall take all necessary measures to ensure that:

(a)  any laws, regulations and administrative provisions contrary to the principle of equal treatment shall be abolished;

(b)  any provisions contrary to the principle of equal treatment which are included in collective agreements, individual contracts of employment, internal rules of undertakings or in rules governing the independent occupations and professions shall be, or may be declared, null and void or may be amended;

(c)  without prejudice to the freedom granted in certain Member States to certain private training establishments, vocational guidance, vocational training, advanced vocational training and retraining shall be accessible on the basis of the same criteria and at the same levels without any discrimination on grounds of sex.

*Article 5*

1 Application of the principle of equal treatment with regard to working conditions, including the conditions governing dismissal, means that men and women shall be guaranteed the same conditions without discrimination on grounds of sex.

2 To this end, Member States shall take the measures necessary to ensure that:

(a)  any laws, regulations and administrative provisions contrary to the principle of equal treatment shall be abolished;

(b)  any provisions contrary to the principle of equal treatment which are included in collective agreements, individual contracts of employment, internal rules of undertakings or in rules governing the independent occupations and professions shall be, or may be declared, null and void or may be amended;

(c)  those laws, regulations and administrative provisions contrary to the principle of equal treatment when the concern for protection which originally inspired them is no longer well founded shall be revised ; and that where similar provisions are included in collective agreements labour and management shall be requested to undertake the desired revision.

*Article 6*

Member States shall introduce into their national legal systems such measures as are necessary to enable all persons who consider themselves wronged by failure to apply to them the principle of equal treatment within the meaning of Articles 3, 4 and 5 to pursue their claims by judicial process after possible recourse to other competent authorities.

*Article 7*
*Material scope*

Member States shall take the necessary measures to protect employees against dismissal by the employer as a reaction to a complaint within the undertaking or to any legal proceedings aimed at enforcing compliance with the principle of equal treatment.

*Article 8*

Member States shall take care that the provisions adopted pursuant to this Directive, together with the relevant provisions already in force, are brought to the attention of employees by all appropriate means, for example at their place of employment.

*Article 9*

1 Member States shall put into force the laws, regulations and administrative provisions necessary in order to comply with this Directive within 30 months of its notification and shall immediately inform the Commission thereof.

However, as regards the first part of Article 3 (2) (c) and the first part of Article 5 (2) (c), Member States shall carry out a first examination and if necessary a first revision of the laws, regulations and administrative provisions referred to therein within four years of notification of this Directive.

2 Member States shall periodically assess the occupational activities referred to in Article 2 (2) in order to decide, in the light of social developments, whether there is justification for maintaining the exclusions concerned. They shall notify the Commission of the results of this assessment.

3 Member States shall also communicate to the Commission the texts of laws, regulations and administrative provisions which they adopt in the field covered by this Directive.

*Article 10*

Within two years following expiry of the 30-month period laid down in the first subparagraph of Article 9 (1), Member States shall forward all necessary information to the Commission to enable it to draw up a report on the application of this Directive for submission to the Council

*Article 11*

This Directive is addressed to the Member States

*Addressees*

Done at Brussels; 9 July 1976

*For the Council*

*The President*

G. THORN

# COUNCIL DIRECTIVE NO 2010/18/EU

*Of 8 March 2010*

*implementing the revised Framework Agreement on parental leave concluded by BUSINESSEUROPE, UEAPME, CEEP and ETUC and repealing Directive 96/34/EC*

THE COUNCIL OF THE EUROPEAN UNION,

Having regard to the Treaty on the Functioning of the European Union, and in particular Article 155(2) thereof,

Having regard to the proposal from the European Commission,

Whereas:

(1) Article 153 of the Treaty on the Functioning of the European Union (the 'TFEU') enables the Union to support and complement the activities of the Member States, inter alia in the field of equality between men and women with regard to labour market opportunities and treatment at work.

(2) Social dialogue at Union level may, in accordance with Article 155(1) of the TFEU, lead to contractual relations, including agreements, should management and labour (the 'social partners') so desire. The social partners may, in accordance with Article 155(2) of the TFEU, request jointly that agreements concluded by them at Union level in matters covered by Article 153 of the TFEU be implemented by a Council decision on a proposal from the Commission.

(3) A Framework Agreement on parental leave was concluded by the European cross-industry social partner organisations (ETUC, UNICE and CEEP) on 14 December 1995 and was given legal effect by Council Directive 96/34/EC of 3 June 1996 on the framework agreement on parental leave concluded by UNICE, CEEP and the ETUC [OJ L 145, 19.6.1996, p. 4.]. That Directive was amended and extended to the United Kingdom of Great Britain and Northern Ireland by Council Directive 97/75/EC [OJ L 10, 16.1.1998, p. 24]. Directive 96/34/EC contributed greatly to improving the opportunities available to working parents in the Member States to better reconcile their work and family responsibilities through leave arrangements.

(4) In accordance with Article 138(2) and (3) of the Treaty establishing the European Community (the 'EC Treaty') [Renumbered: Article 154(2) and (3) of the TFEU], the Commission consulted the European social partners in 2006 and 2007 on ways of further improving the reconciliation of work, private and family life and, in particular, the existing Community legislation on maternity protection and parental leave, and on the possibility of introducing new types of family-related leave, such as paternity leave, adoption leave and leave to care for family members.

(5) The three European general cross-industry social partner organisations (ETUC, CEEP and BUSINESSEUROPE, formerly named UNICE) and the European cross-industry social partner organisation representing a certain

category of undertakings (UEAPME) informed the Commission on 11 September 2008 of their wish to enter into negotiations, in accordance with Article 138(4) and Article 139 of the EC Treaty [Renumbered: Articles 154(4) and 155 of the TFEU], with a view to revising the Framework Agreement on parental leave concluded in 1995.

(6) On 18 June 2009, those organisations signed the revised Framework Agreement on parental leave (the 'revised Framework Agreement') and addressed a joint request to the Commission to submit a proposal for a Council decision implementing that revised Framework Agreement.

(7) In the course of their negotiations, the European social partners completely revised the 1995 Framework Agreement on parental leave. Therefore Directive 96/34/EC should be repealed and replaced by a new directive rather than being simply amended.

(8) Since the objectives of the Directive, namely to improve the reconciliation of work, private and family life for working parents and equality between men and women with regard to labour market opportunities and treatment at work across the Union, cannot be sufficiently achieved by the Member States and can therefore be better achieved at Union level, the Union may adopt measures, in accordance with the principle of subsidiarity as set out in Article 5 of the Treaty on European Union. In accordance with the principle of proportionality, as set out in that Article, this Directive does not go beyond what is necessary in order to achieve those objectives.

(9) When drafting its proposal for a Directive, the Commission took account of the representative status of the signatory parties to the revised Framework Agreement, their mandate and the legality of the clauses in that revised Framework Agreement and its compliance with the relevant provisions concerning small and medium-sized undertakings.

(10) The Commission informed the European Parliament and the European Economic and Social Committee of its proposal.

(11) Clause 1(1) of the revised Framework Agreement, in line with the general principles of Union law in the social policy area, states that the Agreement lays down minimum requirements.

(12) Clause 8(1) of the revised Framework Agreement states that the Member States may apply or introduce more favourable provisions than those set out in the Agreement.

(13) Clause 8(2) of the revised Framework Agreement states that the implementation of the provisions of the Agreement shall not constitute valid grounds for reducing the general level of protection afforded to workers in the field covered by the Agreement.

(14) Member States should provide for effective, proportionate and dissuasive penalties in the event of any breach of the obligations under this Directive.

(15) Member States may entrust the social partners, at their joint request, with the implementation of this Directive, as long as such Member States take all the steps necessary to ensure that they can at all times guarantee the results imposed by this Directive.

(16) In accordance with point 34 of the Interinstitutional agreement on better law-making [OJ C 321, 31.12.2003, p. 1], Member States are encouraged to draw up, for themselves and in the interests of the Union, their own tables which will, as far as possible, illustrate the correlation between this Directive and the transposition measures, and to make them public,

HAS ADOPTED THIS DIRECTIVE:

*Article 1*

This Directive puts into effect the revised Framework Agreement on parental leave concluded on 18 June 2009 by the European cross-industry social partner organisations (BUSINESSEUROPE, UEAPME, CEEP and ETUC), as set out in the Annex.

*Article 2*

Member States shall determine what penalties are applicable when national provisions enacted pursuant to this Directive are infringed. The penalties shall be effective, proportionate and dissuasive.

*Article 3*

1. Member States shall bring into force the laws, regulations and administrative provisions necessary to comply with this Directive or shall ensure that the social partners have introduced the necessary measures by agreement by 8 March 2012 at the latest. They shall forthwith inform the Commission thereof.

When those provisions are adopted by Member States, they shall contain a reference to this Directive or shall be accompanied by such reference on the occasion of their official publication. The methods of making such reference shall be laid down by Member States.

2. Member States may have a maximum additional period of one year to comply with this Directive, if this is necessary to take account of particular difficulties or implementation by collective agreement. They shall inform the Commission thereof by 8 March 2012 at the latest, stating the reasons for which an additional period is required.

3. Member States shall communicate to the Commission the text of the main provisions of national law which they adopt in the field covered by this Directive.

*Article 4*

Directive 96/34/EC shall be repealed with effect from 8 March 2012. References to Directive 96/34/EC shall be construed as references to this Directive.

*Article 5*

This Directive shall enter into force on the 20th day following its publication in the Official Journal of the European Union.

*Article 6*

This Directive is addressed to the Member States.

Done at Brussels, 8 March 2010.

### Annex
### Framework Agreement on Parental Leave (Revised)

*18 June 2009*

*Preamble*

This framework agreement between the European social partners, BUSINES-SEUROPE, UEAPME, CEEP and ETUC (and the liaison committee Eurocadres/CEC) revises the framework agreement on parental leave, concluded on 14 December 1995, setting out the minimum requirements on parental leave, as an important means of reconciling professional and family responsibilities and promoting equal opportunities and treatment between men and women.

The European social partners request the Commission to submit this framework agreement to the Council for a Council decision making these requirements binding in the Member States of the European Union.

## I. General considerations

1. Having regard to the EC Treaty and in particular Articles 138 and 139 thereof [Renumbered: Articles 154 and 155 of the TFEU];

2. Having regard to Articles 137(1)(c) and 141 of the EC Treaty [Renumbered: Articles 153(1)c and 157 of the TFEU] and the principle of equal treatment (Articles 2, 3 and 13 of the EC Treaty [Article 2 of the EC Treaty is repealed and replaced, in substance, by Article 3 of the Treaty on the European Union. Article 3(1) of the EC Treaty is repealed and replaced, in substance, by Articles 3 to 6 of the TFEU. Article 3(2) of the EC Treaty is renumbered as Article 8 of the TFEU. Article 13 of the EC Treaty is renumbered as Article 19 of the TFEU]) and the secondary legislation based on this, in particular Council Directive 75/117/EEC on the approximation of the laws of the Member States relating to the application of the principle of equal pay for men and women [OJ L 45, 19.2.1975, p. 19–20]; Council Directive 92/85/EEC on the introduction of measures to encourage improvements in the safety and health at work of pregnant workers and workers who have recently given birth or are breastfeeding [OJ L 348, 28.11.1992, p. 1–8]; Council Directive 96/97/EC amending Directive 86/378/EEC on the implementation of the principle of equal treatment for men and women in occupational social security schemes [OJ L 46, 17.2.1997, p. 20–24]; and Directive 2006/54/EC on the

implementation of the principle of equal opportunities and equal treatment of men and women in matters of employment and occupation (recast) [OJ L 204, 26.7.2006, p. 23–36];

3. Having regard to the Charter of Fundamental Rights of the European Union of 7 December 2000 and Articles 23 and 33 thereof relating to equality between men and women and reconciliation of professional, private and family life;

4. Having regard to the 2003 Report from the Commission on the Implementation of Council Directive 96/34/EC of 3 June 1996 on the framework agreement on parental leave concluded by UNICE, CEEP and the ETUC;

5. Having regard to the objective of the Lisbon strategy on growth and jobs of increasing overall employment rates to 70%, women's employment rates to 60% and the employment rates of older workers to 50%; to the Barcelona targets on the provision of childcare facilities; and to the contribution of policies to improve reconciliation of professional, private and family life in achieving these targets;

6. Having regard to the European social partners' Framework of Actions on Gender Equality of 22 March 2005 in which supporting work-life balance is addressed as a priority area for action, while recognising that, in order to continue to make progress on the issue of reconciliation, a balanced, integrated and coherent policy mix must be put in place, comprising of leave arrangements, working arrangements and care infrastructures;

7. Whereas measures to improve reconciliation are part of a broader policy agenda to address the needs of employers and workers and improve adaptability and employability, as part of a flexicurity approach;

8. Whereas family policies should contribute to the achievement of gender equality and be looked at in the context of demographic changes, the effects of an ageing population, closing the generation gap, promoting women's participation in the labour force and the sharing of care responsibilities between women and men;

9. Whereas the Commission has consulted the European social partners in 2006 and 2007 in a first and second stage consultation on reconciliation of professional, private and family life, and, among other things, has addressed the issue of updating the regulatory framework at Community level, and has encouraged the European social partners to assess the provisions of their framework agreement on parental leave with a view to its review;

10. Whereas the Framework agreement of the European social partners of 1995 on parental leave has been a catalyst for positive change, ensured common ground on work life balance in the Member States and played a significant role in helping working parents in Europe to achieve better reconciliation; however, on the basis of a joint evaluation, the European social partners consider that certain elements of the agreement need to be adapted or revised in order to better achieve its aims;

11. Whereas certain aspects need to be adapted, taking into account the growing diversity of the labour force and societal developments including the increasing diversity of family structures, while respecting national law, collective agreements and/or practice;

12. Whereas in many Member States encouraging men to assume an equal share of family responsibilities has not led to sufficient results; therefore, more effective measures should be taken to encourage a more equal sharing of family responsibilities between men and women;

13. Whereas many Member States already have a wide variety of policy measures and practices relating to leave facilities, childcare and flexible working arrangements, tailored to the needs of workers and employers and aiming to support parents in reconciling their professional, private and family life; these should be taken into account when implementing this agreement;

14. Whereas this framework agreement provides one element of European social partners' actions in the field of reconciliation;

15. Whereas this agreement is a framework agreement setting out minimum requirements and provisions for parental leave, distinct from maternity leave, and for time off from work on grounds of force majeure, and refers back to Member States and social partners for the establishment of conditions for access and modalities of application in order to take account of the situation in each Member State;

16. Whereas the right of parental leave in this agreement is an individual right and in principle non-transferable, and Member States are allowed to make it transferable. Experience shows that making the leave non-transferable can act as a positive incentive for the take up by fathers, the European social partners therefore agree to make a part of the leave non-transferable;

17. Whereas it is important to take into account the special needs of parents with children with disabilities or long term illness;

18. Whereas Member States should provide for the maintenance of entitlements to benefits in kind under sickness insurance during the minimum period of parental leave;

19. Whereas Member States should also, where appropriate under national conditions and taking into account the budgetary situation, consider the maintenance of entitlements to relevant social security benefits as they stand during the minimum period of parental leave as well as the role of income among other factors in the take-up of parental leave when implementing this agreement;

20. Whereas experiences in Member States have shown that the level of income during parental leave is one factor that influences the take up by parents, especially fathers;

21. Whereas the access to flexible working arrangements makes it easier for parents to combine work and parental responsibilities and facilitates the reintegration into work, especially after returning from parental leave;

22. Whereas parental leave arrangements are meant to support working parents during a specific period of time, aimed at maintaining and promoting their continued labour market participation; therefore, greater attention should be paid to keeping in contact with the employer during the leave or by making arrangements for return to work;

23. Whereas this agreement takes into consideration the need to improve social policy requirements, to enhance the competitiveness of the European Union economy and to avoid imposing administrative, financial and legal constraints in a way which would hold back the creation and development of small and medium sized undertakings;

24. Whereas the social partners are best placed to find solutions that correspond to the needs of both employers and workers and shall therefore play a special role in the implementation, application, monitoring and evaluation of this agreement, in the broader context of other measures to improve the reconciliation of professional and family responsibilities and to promote equal opportunities and treatment between men and women.

THE SIGNATORY PARTIES HAVE AGREED THE FOLLOWING:

## II. Content

*Clause 1*
*Purpose and scope*

1. This agreement lays down minimum requirements designed to facilitate the reconciliation of parental and professional responsibilities for working parents, taking into account the increasing diversity of family structures while respecting national law, collective agreements and/or practice.

2. This agreement applies to all workers, men and women, who have an employment contract or employment relationship as defined by the law, collective agreements and/or practice in force in each Member State.

3. Member States and/or social partners shall not exclude from the scope and application of this agreement workers, contracts of employment or employment relationships solely because they relate to part-time workers, fixed-term contract workers or persons with a contract of employment or employment relationship with a temporary agency.

*Clause 2*
*Parental leave*

1. This agreement entitles men and women workers to an individual right to parental leave on the grounds of the birth or adoption of a child to take care of that child until a given age up to eight years to be defined by Member Statbhes and/or social partners.

2. The leave shall be granted for at least a period of four months and, to promote equal opportunities and equal treatment between men and women, should, in principle, be provided on a non-transferable basis. To encourage a more equal take-up of leave by both parents, at least one of the four months shall be provided on a non-transferable basis. The modalities of application of

the non-transferable period shall be set down at national level through legislation and/or collective agreements taking into account existing leave arrangements in the Member States.

*Clause 3*
*Modalities of application*

1. The conditions of access and detailed rules for applying parental leave shall be defined by law and/or collective agreements in the Member States, as long as the minimum requirements of this agreement are respected. Member States and/or social partners may, in particular:

(a)   decide whether parental leave is granted on a full-time or part-time basis, in a piecemeal way or in the form of a time-credit system, taking into account the needs of both employers and workers;

(b)   make entitlement to parental leave subject to a period of work qualification and/or a length of service qualification which shall not exceed one year; Member States and/or social partners shall ensure, when making use of this provision, that in case of successive fixed term contracts, as defined in Council Directive 1999/70/EC on fixed-term work, with the same employer the sum of these contracts shall be taken into account for the purpose of calculating the qualifying period;

(c)   define the circumstances in which an employer, following consultation in accordance with national law, collective agreements and/or practice, is allowed to postpone the granting of parental leave for justifiable reasons related to the operation of the organisation. Any problem arising from the application of this provision should be dealt with in accordance with national law, collective agreements and/or practice;

(d)   in addition to (c), authorise special arrangements to meet the operational and organisational requirements of small undertakings.

2. Member States and/or social partners shall establish notice periods to be given by the worker to the employer when exercising the right to parental leave, specifying the beginning and the end of the period of leave. Member States and/or social partners shall have regard to the interests of workers and of employers in specifying the length of such notice periods.

3. Member States and/or social partners should assess the need to adjust the conditions for access and modalities of application of parental leave to the needs of parents of children with a disability or a long-term illness.

*Clause 4*
*Adoption*

1. Member States and/or social partners shall assess the need for additional measures to address the specific needs of adoptive parents.

*Clause 5*
*Employment rights and non-discrimination*

1. At the end of parental leave, workers shall have the right to return to the same job or, if that is not possible, to an equivalent or similar job consistent with their employment contract or employment relationship.

2. Rights acquired or in the process of being acquired by the worker on the date on which parental leave starts shall be maintained as they stand until the end of parental leave. At the end of parental leave, these rights, including any changes arising from national law, collective agreements and/or practice, shall apply.

3. Member States and/or social partners shall define the status of the employment contract or employment relationship for the period of parental leave.

4. In order to ensure that workers can exercise their right to parental leave, Member States and/or social partners shall take the necessary measures to protect workers against less favourable treatment or dismissal on the grounds of an application for, or the taking of, parental leave in accordance with national law, collective agreements and/or practice.

5. All matters regarding social security in relation to this agreement are for consideration and determination by Member States and/or social partners according to national law and/or collective agreements, taking into account the importance of the continuity of the entitlements to social security cover under the different schemes, in particular health care.

All matters regarding income in relation to this agreement are for consideration and determination by Member States and/or social partners according to national law, collective agreements and/or practice, taking into account the role of income – among other factors – in the take-up of parental leave.

*Clause 6*
*Return to work*

1. In order to promote better reconciliation, Member States and/or social partners shall take the necessary measures to ensure that workers, when returning from parental leave, may request changes to their working hours and/or patterns for a set period of time. Employers shall consider and respond to such requests, taking into account both employers' and workers' needs.

The modalities of this paragraph shall be determined in accordance with national law, collective agreements and/or practice.

2. In order to facilitate the return to work following parental leave, workers and employers are encouraged to maintain contact during the period of leave and may make arrangements for any appropriate reintegration measures, to be decided between the parties concerned, taking into account national law, collective agreements and/or practice.

*Clause 7*
*Time off from work on grounds of force majeure*

1. Member States and/or social partners shall take the necessary measures to entitle workers to time off from work, in accordance with national legislation, collective agreements and/or practice, on grounds of force majeure for urgent family reasons in cases of sickness or accident making the immediate presence of the worker indispensable.

2. Member States and/or social partners may specify the conditions of access and detailed rules for applying clause 7.1 and limit this entitlement to a certain amount of time per year and/or per case.

*Clause 8*
*Final provisions*

1. Member States may apply or introduce more favourable provisions than those set out in this agreement.

2. Implementation of the provisions of this agreement shall not constitute valid grounds for reducing the general level of protection afforded to workers in the field covered by this agreement. This shall not prejudice the right of Member States and/or social partners to develop different legislative, regulatory or contractual provisions, in the light of changing circumstances (including the introduction of non-transferability), as long as the minimum requirements provided for in the present agreement are complied with.

3. This agreement shall not prejudice the right of social partners to conclude, at the appropriate level including European level, agreements adapting and/or complementing the provisions of this agreement in order to take into account particular circumstances.

4. Member States shall adopt the laws, regulations and administrative provisions necessary to comply with the Council decision within a period of two years from its adoption or shall ensure that social partners introduce the necessary measures by way of agreement by the end of this period. Member States may, if necessary to take account of particular difficulties or implementation by collective agreements, have up to a maximum of one additional year to comply with this decision.

5. The prevention and settlement of disputes and grievances arising from the application of this agreement shall be dealt with in accordance with national law, collective agreements and/or practice.

6. Without prejudice to the respective role of the Commission, national courts and the European Court of Justice, any matter relating to the interpretation of this agreement at European level should, in the first instance, be referred by the Commission to the signatory parties who will give an opinion.

7. The signatory parties shall review the application of this agreement five years after the date of the Council decision if requested by one of the parties to this agreement.

Done at Brussels, 18 June 2009.

# INDEX

References are to paragraph numbers.